D1759581

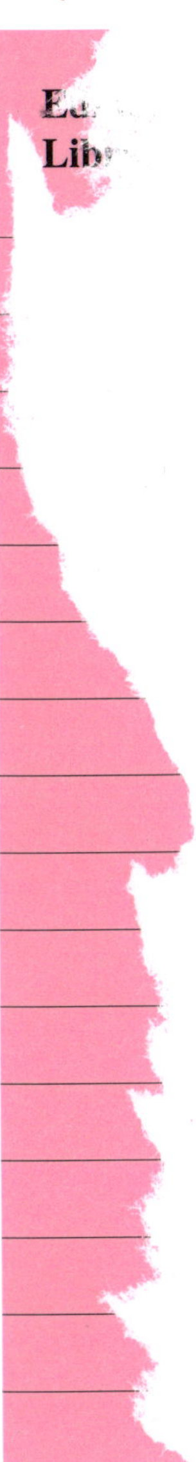
Ed
Lib

University of Edinburgh
30150 026951324

The Routledge Companion to Cost Management

Over the last two decades, cost management has been an area of dynamic change and development. This is evident in the extensive inventory of new, high-profile techniques that have emerged.

With cost management now firmly established as a distinct sub-discipline within management accounting, *The Routledge Companion to Cost Management* is a timely reference volume covering both practical developments and research in this area. Topics covered include:

- Cost control issues
- Cost analysis and decision-making
- Cost management systems
- Environmental cost management

With chapters from an international team of contributors, this prestigious companion will prove an indispensable addition to any library with aspirations of keeping up to date with the world of accounting.

Falconer Mitchell is Professor of Management Accounting at the University of Edinburgh, UK.

Hanne Nørreklit is Professor of Management Accounting at the Norwegian School of Economics, Bergen, Norway.

Morten Jakobsen is Associate Professor of Management Accounting at the University of Aarhus, Denmark.

Routledge Companions in Business, Management and Accounting

Routledge Companions in Business, Management and Accounting are similar to what some publishers call 'handbooks' i.e. prestige reference works providing an overview of a whole subject area or sub-discipline, and which survey the state of the discipline including emerging and cutting-edge areas. These books provide a comprehensive, up-to-date, definitive work of reference which can be cited as an authoritative source on the subject.

One of the key aspects of the Routledge Companions in Business, Management and Accounting series is their international scope and relevance. Edited by an array of well-regarded scholars, these volumes also benefit from teams of contributors which reflect an international range of perspectives.

Individually, Routledge Companions in Business, Management and Accounting provide an impactful one-stop-shop resource for each theme covered, whilst collectively they represent a comprehensive learning and research resource for researchers, postgraduates and practitioners.

Published titles in this series include:

The Routledge Companion to Fair Value and Financial Reporting
Edited by Peter Walton

The Routledge Companion to Nonprofit Marketing
Edited by Adrian Sargeant and Walter Wymer Jr

The Routledge Companion to Accounting History
Edited by John Richard Edwards and Stephen P. Walker

The Routledge Companion to Creativity
Edited by Tudor Rickards, Mark A. Runco and Susan Moger

The Routledge Companion to Strategic Human Resource Management
Edited by John Storey, Patrick M. Wright and David Ulrich

The Routledge Companion to International Business Coaching
Edited by Michel Moral and Geoffrey Abbott

The Routledge Companion to Organizational Change
Edited by David M. Boje, Bernard Burnes and John Hassard

The Routledge Companion to Cost Management
Edited by Falconer Mitchell, Hanne Nørreklit and Morten Jakobsen

The Routledge Companion to Cost Management

Edited by Falconer Mitchell, Hanne Nørreklit and Morten Jakobsen

LONDON AND NEW YORK

First published 2013
by Routledge
2 Park Square, Milton Park, Abingdon, Oxon OX14 4RN

Simultaneously published in the USA and Canada
by Routledge
711 Third Avenue, New York, NY 10017

Routledge is an imprint of the Taylor & Francis Group, an informa business

British Library Cataloguing in Publication Data
A catalogue record for this book is available from the British Library

Library of Congress Cataloging in Publication Data
The Routledge companion to cost management/edited by Falconer Mitchell, Hanne Nørreklit and Morten Jakobsen.
p. cm.—(Routledge companions in business, management and accounting)
Includes bibliographical references and index.
1. Cost accounting. 2. Managerial accounting. 3. Cost control.
I. Mitchell, Falconer. II. Nørreklit, Hanne. III. Jakobsen, Morten.
HF5686.C8R597 2012
658.15'52—dc23 2012007433

ISBN: 978-0-415-59247-5 (hbk)
ISBN: 978-0-203-10126-1 (ebk)

Typeset in Bembo
by RefineCatch Limited, Bungay, Suffolk

Printed and bound in Great Britain by
CPI Group (UK) Ltd, Croydon, CR0 4YY

Contents

Tables and figures

Tables

Figures

Contributors

The authors of the book chapters are all leading researchers, active in a range of the sub-areas of cost management. Each of the researchers has been selected to make their contribution in a topic in which they specialize.

Alnoor Bhimani is Professor of Management Accounting and Head of Department of Accounting, Department of Accounting, London School of Economics, UK.

Trond Bjørnenak is Professor of Management Accounting, Department of Accounting, Auditing and Law, Norwegian School of Economics, Norway.

Chris Carr is Professor of Corporate Strategy, University of Edinburgh Business School, University of Edinburgh, UK.

David Dugdale is Emeritus Professor of Management Accounting, Department of Accounting and Finance, University of Bristol, UK.

Lino Cinquini is Professor of Management Accounting and Business Administration, Institute of Management, Scuola Superiore Sant' Anna, Pisa, Italy.

Riccardo Giannetti is Associate Professor of Cost Management and Business Administration at the University of Pisa, Italy.

Øyvind Helgesen is Professor of Marketing, Department of International Marketing, Aalesund University College, Norway.

Ian Herbert is a Senior Lecturer in Accounting and Financial Management, School of Business and Economics, Loughborough University, UK.

Sophie Hoozée is Assistant Professor of Management Accounting at IESEG School of Management, Rille France.

Timo Hyvönen is a Professor of Management Accounting at the Turku School of Economics, University of Turku, Pori Unit, Finland.

John Innes is Professor Emeritus in Accounting and Finance, School of Business, University of Dundee, UK.

Poul Israelsen is Professor of Management Accounting, Center for Industrial Production, Department of Business and Management, Aalborg University, Denmark.

Morten Jakobsen is Associate Professor of Management Accounting, Department of Economics, Aarhus University, Denmark.

Katarina Kaarbøe is Professor of Management Control and Head of Department of Accounting. Auditing and Law, Norwegian School of Economics, Norway.

Peter Kajüter is Professor of Accounting, Chair of International Accounting, University of Münster, Germany.

Katja Kolehmainen is Assistant Professor of Accounting, Department of Accounting, School of Economics, Aalto University, Helsinki, Finland.

Reza Kouhy is Professor of Energy and Environmental Accounting, Dundee Business School, University of Abertay, Dundee, UK.

Thomas Borup Kristensen is Assistant Professor of Management Accounting, Department of Business and Managemt, Aalborg University, Denmark.

Rainer Lueg is Assistant Professor of Management Accounting, Department of Economics, Aarhus University, Denmark.

Alessandro Marelli is Associate Professor of Management Accounting at the University of Teramo, Italy.

David Marginson is Professor of Management Accounting, Cardiff Business School, Cardiff University, UK.

Falconer Mitchell is Professor of Management Accounting University at Edinburgh Business School, University of Edinburgh, UK.

Lars Bråd Nielsen. Ph.D. is a Management Consultant for Booz & Company, Copenhagen, Denmark.

Hanne Nørreklit is a Professor of Management Accounting, Department of Accounting, Auditing and Law, Norwegian School of Economics, Norway.

Samuel C. A. Pereira is Professor of Management Accounting and Control, Faculty of Economics, University of Porto, Portugal.

Will Seal is Professor of Accounting, School of Management, University of Southampton, UK.

Andrea Tenucci is Assistant Professor of Management Accounting and Business Administration, Institute of Management, Scuola Superiore Sant'Anna, Pisa, Italy.

Takeo Yoshikawa is Professor of Accounting, Graduate School, Hosei University, Tokyo, Japan.

1 Introduction

Morten Jakobsen, Falconer Mitchell and Hanne Nørreklit

Cost management

The pursuit of organizational goals requires the acquisition and use of resources and this generates costs. Creating profit, increasing market share or enhancing sustainability are all commercial goals involving resource consumption and so they have a direct link to cost while in a not-for-profit setting the need to adhere to budgetary constraints ensures that cost also plays an important part in organizational functioning. Understanding the nature of costs, how they behave and their links to value creation therefore constitutes an important aspect of organizational management. This information represents much of the knowledge that facilitates sound cost management, i.e. the use of cost-related information as a lens through which the organization is represented to and viewed by management as they strive to gain improvements in economy, efficiency and effectiveness. Costs have a direct impact on profit but they are also linked to the other key financial elements of revenue generation, investment and funding. Thus, rather than being viewed and managed in isolation these links have to be kept under consideration. Consequently, a strong managerial demand exists for a wide variety of information to enable successful cost management to occur.

In response to this demand, the generation of information to support cost management activity has become a popular and dynamic area in recent decades (see, for example, Simmonds, 1981; Shank and Govandarajan, 1993; Brinker, 1991; Bromwich and Bhimani, 1994). This text is designed to describe and explore the main contemporary developments in the topic. It also examines research activity undertaken on the various aspects of cost management and assesses the possibilities for future developments. Cost is a multi-faceted concept addressed in both the disciplines of accounting and economics. How cost is conceived and quantified is fundamental to its management. Thus, this introduction examines the notion of cost and its measurement as a foundation for the wide variety of chapters that follow. It then explains the significance and interrelationships of these chapters to provide a cohesive basis for various components of cost management that are covered.

An accounting perspective on cost

Costs are a representation of sacrifices made. Conventionally, from an accounting perspective, these sacrifices are based on the monetary outflows associated with the acquisition and/or use of a resource. Consequently, the traditional accounting measurement of costs is achieved through their quantification in terms of the resource's acquisition price, i.e. its historic cost. In this way, resource costs are readily identifiable and easy to record. The accounting perspective on costs can therefore make them susceptible to systematization. For example, book-keeping systems and the costing systems that support them routinely gather information on costs incurred and report on them regularly for management.

However, even within the accounting perspective, the cost information produced can be analyzed and presented in a multitude of ways. When contained within an income statement format, costs are normally categorized by the type of input they represent, e.g. materials, labour and overhead type. Alternatively they can be divided on the basis of how they behave, e.g. traditionally in terms of whether they are fixed or variable in nature or, more contemporarily, in terms of the cost hierarchy of unit, batch, process and facility advocated by proponents of activity-based costing (ABC). ABC itself provides yet another perspective on cost by showing how inputs have been used to undertake the variety of activities that constitute so much of organizational work. Costs can also be made informative and useful by attaching them to a great variety of cost objects, e.g. divisions, departments, market segments, products or customers. Additionally, cost information can be designed for specific purposes, e.g. relevant costs for decisions such as avoidable costs, irrelevant costs for decisions such as sunk costs, committed costs for life-cycle cost analysis, budgeted, standard and target costs for cost control, product attribute costs and cost driver rates for cost-effective design and benchmarked costs for performance appraisal.

Thus, accountants have at their disposal a very broad range of possible types of cost information that can be used to support cost management. However, it should always be borne in mind that they are typically based on outlay costs and, as the economic perspective reveals, these may not always be the most appropriate measurement of cost.

An economic perspective on cost

From an economic perspective, the sacrifice underlying cost is represented by the highest benefits foregone as a result of committing resources to a particular course of action. This, of course, can produce measurements of cost that differ from those produced by the accountant. It does, however, mean that the cost information provided is in the nature of opportunity cost and, as such, is appropriate as a basis for economically rational decision-making.

The opportunity cost of a resource can be conveniently identified using Bonbright's (1937) notion of deprival value (see also Baxter, 2003 for a summary of the application of Bonbright's concept to some areas of accounting), i.e. what is the value the resource possessor loses if the resource is lost to them (through use)? Any of three different values may represent the sacrifice in terms of opportunity foregone or lost. They are replacement cost (RC), net realizable value (NRV) and economic value (EV). The first two are market-based values drawn respectively from the current (not the historic) acquisition cost or the disposal proceeds of the resource. The third represents the best value that can be derived from using the resource within the organization (other than in the commitment being assessed). It is, thus, its value in use, i.e. the net present value of the future cash flows generated from the resource.

Table 1.1 shows the six possible permutations for these measures in terms of their relative monetary magnitudes. From this comparison the deprival value or opportunity cost of the resource can be identified on the basis described.

Where replacement of the resource is merited (i.e. where either NRV or EV exceed RC), then the commitment (or loss) of the resource will have a cost of RC. This is because that is the outlay incurred when the committed resource is replaced. This measure occurs in all but two of

Table 1.1 Resource deprival value (or opportunity cost)

Permutations	*Opportunity cost*	*Comment*
NRV>RC>EV	RC	Resource worth replacing
NRV>EV>RC	RC	Resource worth replacing
EV>RC>NRV	RC	Resource worth replacing
EV>NRV>RC	RC	Resource worth replacing
RC>NRV>EV	NRV	Resource not worth replacing
RC>EV>NRV	EV	Resource not worth replacing

the permutations. When replacement of the resource is not merited, then deprival (i.e. resource consumption through use) represents a loss that is the higher of NRV or EV.

This view of the sacrifice that leads to cost identification is not readily susceptible to use as a basis for routine systems of costs information for management. The notion of opportunity costs is too fluid for that to be possible. Not only does each resource have three potential alternative values but the determined value can change over time as the values change and create different permutations of the three possible values. However, when managing issues like the special order decision (e.g. Arnold, 1973; Drury, 2008) this type of cost measurement and analysis can be undertaken on an ad hoc basis.

Content review

Although these different conceptions of cost exist they may be, to some extent, reconcilable. The accountant can adopt the economist's opportunity cost measurements for some specific decision analyses. Moreover, the prominence of RC as the appropriate cost in the economic analysis may also lead to similarity between the two approaches. Situations where NRV or EV are the appropriate measures may be relatively rare as these permutations mean that an existing resource is not worth buying again as a replacement. Why would such an economically unattractive resource remain on the market? Thus, where historic cost represents a reasonable proxy for RC the economist and the accountant may indeed have cost ascertainment methods that have considerable compatibility.

The accountant does have to operate in the real world in a practical way. Time pressures and imperfections in information generation may well mean that the theoretical exactness of the economist may not be possible. To cope with the demands of providing a practical information service, the accountant often has to deal in proxies (Zimmerman, 1979) and heuristics (Baxter and Oxenfeldt, 1961). It is apparent already from a consideration of the nature of costs and cost management that the subject of the text is a challenging one. The chapters that follow reveal how accountants have attempted to meet this challenge. The book is divided into four themes, each of which has a distinct emphasis and which together encompass both the conventional and contemporary developments in cost management.

Cost control issues

Cost control has traditionally been a central part of the management accountant's work and in this area budgetary control has been the most prominent technique in the accountant's tool-kit. As David Marginson's chapter demonstrates this has been an enduring focus of research interest. In part this has been engendered by it being a topic where the technical is so closely related to the behavioural in the setting and use of budgetary information. The current preoccupation with the ideas of the 'beyond budgeting' school to replace traditional budget will no doubt ensure that it will continue to attract research interest. Providing an overarching philosophy for tight cost control is the concept of lean production. Thomas Kristensen and Poul Israelsen not only review this idea but also show in their case study some of the practical ways in which the accountant can produce the type of information that will help in pursuit of this cost control ideal. The use of software packages such as ERP has become increasingly common. They provide the opportunity to develop cost management information on a routine basis and Timo Hyvönen's chapter shows the potential contribution that this software can make. Japan and Germany are two of the strongest international competitors. John Innes, Takeo Yoshikawa and Peter Kajüter respectively review the cost control approaches that have enhanced their companies' competitiveness. Target costing has pushed the accountant outside the confines of their organization to find and internalize market intelligence and then support this practice by developing the information in cost tables and the commitment to cost reduction inherent in the kaizen approach. Takeo Yoshikawa and Reza Kouhy discuss the potential of kaizen costing. They do it by unfolding the philosophies and aims of kaizen costing along with a number of examples that show the practice of kaizen costing.

Cost management and decision-making

To manage costs effectively management should know the cost (and indeed the revenue) implications of their decisions. Consequently, awareness of the decision relevance of cost information is necessary. Samuel Pereira and Falconer Mitchell use mathematical analysis to provide the first complete specification of the conditions under which product costs are formally decision-relevant in both the short and long run. The implications of this for designing cost management systems are outlined. The most prominent of developments in product costing has been activity-based costing (ABC). One of its great strengths has been the wide range of decision applications that unit costs have. However, one of its great weaknesses has been the cost and administrative difficulty of its implementation and operation. Sophie Hoozée shows how this weakness can be overcome by using the most recent manifestation of ABC – time-driven ABC. David Dugdale reviews the thought-provoking ideas of the theory of constraints. This approach negates the value of much of the conventional cost management information and proposes the use of throughput measures to provide a basis for management decisions. It is a radical approach which casts doubt from a very practical perspective on much of what the accountant normally does. Trond Bjørnenak and Katarina Karbøe describe how cost management has inherent dynamics that show how the whole area is one where change and development has become a dominant feature. It is one which raises many important issues about how relevant managerial decision-making can best be supported by cost information in a fast-changing context. Finally, Lino Cinquini and Andrea Tenucci discuss one of the most important but challenging decisions that organizations have to make. That is the provision of capacity. Not only is it a challenging decision involving future forecasting of output volumes but it impacts greatly on the unitization of costs and therefore has the potential to influence pricing decisions and profit measurement. As the chapter shows, these uses have stimulated a lot of analysis and research on capacity cost.

Inter-organizational cost management perspectives

Ideas such as the value chain have ensured that cost management has a strong inter-organizational perspective. Willie Seal and Ian Herbert highlight this in analyzing the costs incurred by those supplying the services that comprise the overhead costs of an organization. Morten Jakobsen extends this notion to component suppliers and describes the collaboration obtained from the use of open book accounting. An increasingly common feature of the modern firm is the continual consideration and justification of what the organization does. Screening internal functioning against the option of outsourcing is another way in which external organizations can play a part in cost management. Lars Nielsen's chapter not only identifies the mechanics of outsourcing but also shows how the cost management ideas on the topic have been outpaced by developments in the broader management literature. In addition to the upstream part of the value chain, the downstream can also be considered. Trond Bjørnenak and Øyvind Helgesen do this in their analysis of how the customer can become a cost object by profiling customer profitability and using the results to revise relationships and identify those customers whose continued business is vital to the firm's ongoing success.

Strategy and cost management

The idea of the accountant becoming a business partner and thereby more heavily involved in strategy formulation and implementation is a topical one (CIMA, 2010). Cost management is an area where support for strategy can be quite direct, e.g. cost leadership. Many of the cost containment approaches outlined above can contribute to this type of strategic objective. However-as this theme shows, accounting can also offer support for other strategies and strategic activities. Chris Carr, Katja Kohlmainen and Falconer Mitchell use a contingency framework to identify different corporate typologies where strategic decision-making (and the accountant's role therein) may differ. Riccardo Giannetti shows how an activity that can be central to strategy – i.e. quality activity – can become a focus for accounting reports. Alessandro Marrelli highlights the work done to allow accounting and costing to aid the sustainability objective, which is becoming more and more significant to business. Performance measurement is necessary to manage strategies and to provide feedback to management. Rainer Lueg and Hanne Nørreklit show that decisions on strategic objectives should be linked to cost and profitability analysis.

Lino Cinquini, Falconer Mitchell, Hanne Nørreklit and Andrea Tenucci examine the methodology of performance measurement and show that managerial culture and style can be very different in a cost management context. Finally, Al Bhimani's chapter examines how the macro trends of globalization and digitization impact on the practices of the management accountant, including their efforts to manage costs.

Conclusions

Cost management is an activity that can play a major role in improving organizational performance. A wide variety of techniques have been developed (many in recent years) to provide the accountant with an extensive tool-kit for cost management. However, as the following chapters show, cost management is more than simply a technical matter. It is socio-technical in nature and encompasses issues such as management style, the role of the accountant, the stresses of cost reduction and the challenges of organizational change. Cost management means cost changes and the implications of these, both financial and behavioural, need to be understood as a foundation for management action. Hopefully this text will contribute to this understanding.

Bibliography

Arnold J., 1973, *Pricing and Output Decisions,* Accountancy Age Books, Haymarket Publishing, London.

Baxter W., 2003, *The Case for Deprival Value*, Occasional Paper, the Chartered Institute of Management Accountants, Edinburgh.

Baxter W. and Oxenfeldt A. R., 1961, 'Costing and Pricing: The Cost Accountant versus the Economist', *Business Horizons* 4(4), 77–90, reproduced in *Studies in Cost Analysis*, 1968, edited by Solomons D., Sweet and Maxwell, London.

Bonbright J. C., 1937, *The Valuation of Property*, McGraw Hill, New York.

Brinker B. (ed.), 1991, *Handbook of Cost Management*, Warren Gorham and Lamont, Boston.

Bromwich M., 1990, 'The Case for Strategic Management Accounting: The Role of Accounting in Competitive Markets' *Accounting Organisations and Society*, 1/2, 27–46.

Bromwich M. and Bhimani A., 1994, *Management Accounting: Pathways to Progress*, Chartered Institute of Management Accountants, London.

Drury C., 2008, *Management and Cost Accounting*, Thomson, London.

Shank J. K. and Govindarajan V., 1989, *Strategic Cost Analysis*, Irwin Inc., Homewood, Illinois.

Shank J. K. and Govindarajan V., 1993, *Strategic Cost Management: The New Tool for Competitive Advantage*, The Free Press, New York.

Simmons K., 1981a, *The Fundamentals of Strategic Management Accounting*, the Chartered Institute of Management Accountants, London.

Simmons K., 1981b, 'Strategic Management Accounting', *Management Accounting*, 26–29.

Yoshikawa T., Innes J., Mitchell F. and Tanaka M., 1993, *Contemporary Cost Management*, Chapman Hall, London.

Zimmerman, J. 1979, 'The Costs and Benefits of Cost Allocations', *The Accounting Review*, LIV(3), 504–521.

Part I
Cost control issues

2

Budgetary control

What's been happening?

David Marginson

Introduction

The subject of this chapter is budgetary control. Although not defined in the literature, budgetary control may be considered to represent how organizations seek to ensure the efficient and effective utilisation of financial resources. For the purposes of this chapter, *traditional* budgetary control refers to the idea of ensuring the efficient and effective utilization of financial resources through processes of monitoring, feedback, motivation, variance correction, and performance evaluation at the level of the individual responsibility centre. Budgets (resources) and budgeting (resource allocation) may be considered to form part of the overall budgetary control process.

Cost management, the broader subject of this book, is inexorably connected to budgetary control. For instance, both concern resource allocation, both implicate responsibility accounting as the framework for resource allocation, and both ultimately depend on 'people' for their execution. Cost management is essentially about controlling costs, and budgets, through responsibility accounting, are essentially about 'controlling costs through people' (Argyris, 1952). In short, budgetary control, involving budgets and budgeting, has traditionally represented one dimension of, or approach to, cost management.

The aim of the chapter is to review recent literature on budgetary control. A particular concern is to assess the literature published since around 2000 in terms of its contribution to our understanding of how organizations are seeking to control costs in an increasingly globalized economy. The term 'globalization' tends to be an all-encompassing phrase implying, for instance, hyper-competition, fast-moving environments, rapid technological advancement, increased market volatility, and – in terms of organizational architecture – a highly organic arrangement as a basis by which firms may seek to cope, through an emphasis on innovation and learning, with the demands of globalization. The point is that more complex and more flexible organizational arrangements, including 'modern' management philosophies such as flexible working and empowerment (Wilkinson, 2002), are recognized as holding non-trivial implications for traditional budgetary control practices and procedures (Otley, 1994; 1999; Libby and Lindsay, 2007a). This chapter therefore also aims to explore some of these implications, and what they may mean for how budgetary control can, is, and should be exercised in practice.

In terms of 'should', the now well-recognized and well-established Beyond Budgeting Roundtable (BBRT), is premised on the view that traditional budgets are no longer appropriate for today's organizations and should therefore be abandoned (Hope and Fraser, 2003). The BBRT represents a group, the members of which are individuals and organizations interested in managing without budgets. Membership in the BBRT is worldwide with the largest membership base in Europe (Libby and Lindsay, 2010). In this chapter, the term Beyond Budgeting (BB) Movement is used to represent both the BBRT and associated literature.

In terms of 'is', there is recent research which suggests that companies may be adapting their budgetary practices in favour of more flexible forms of resource allocation and budgetary control (see e.g. Neely, Sutcliff and Heyns, 2001; Marginson and Ogden, 2005; Østergren and Stensaker, 2010). In terms of 'can', survey evidence continues to suggest that traditional budgetary control practices may remain a key mechanism by which today's organizations seek to control costs (Libby and Lindsay, 2010), with budgetary information being used for the purposes of planning, communication, co-ordination, motivation, and/or performance evaluation (Dugdale and Lynne, 2004). The role(s) of budgets may also include benchmarking, and/or ritual/tradition (Hansen and Van der Stede, 2004). The use of traditional budgetary control procedures includes the continued use of traditional responsibility accounting frameworks. There is little evidence at present to suggest that firms are dispensing with such frameworks as a basis for allocating resources and exercising budgetary control (cf. Rowe, Birnberg and Shields, 2008). This mix of normative argument and empirical evidence raises questions about what we might know and might not know about the scope, practice and consequences of budgetary control in today's organizations. As part of its remit, this chapter will attempt to provide some insight into the current 'state of understanding'.

The chapter begins by outlining traditional budgetary control and responsibility accounting. The body of the chapter is devoted to reviewing recent literature on budgetary control. In this context, the chapter will raise some of the key issues, outline conceptual and practical developments (particularly notions of Beyond Budgeting and Better Budgeting), present the recent research evidence, and suggest areas for further research. To foreshadow the forthcoming discussion, and to borrow and adapt a famous phrase, the chapter concludes by suggesting that, rather than 'Beyond Budgeting' (Hope and Fraser, 2003) or even 'Better Budgeting' (Banham, 2000) what we may sometimes find in practice is 'budgetary control, but not as we know it'. A diversity of budgetary practices is noted. The extent of this diversity suggests that today's organizations may be identifying different ways of addressing how to exercise budgetary control for a globalized environment. A growing diversity of practice provides much scope for scholars to document and understand these practices and associated issues.

Traditional budgetary control and traditional responsibility accounting

A cursory read of 'standard' management accounting textbooks often reveals something of a disjuncture between how traditional budgeting is described and how responsibility accounting is explained. The two topics are often discussed separately, in separate chapters. This is surprising, given the inexorable link between the two. Traditionally, responsibility accounting has provided the structure or framework through which traditional budgetary control is exercised. To separate the two might give the impression that the two are disconnected. The following presents their nexus.

Exercising traditional budgetary control through traditional responsibility accounting

Normally, in a context where it is deemed necessary to decentralize at least some decision-making, it also becomes necessary to disperse decision-making authority over a proportion of the organization's financial resources. The manager must have the resources to do the job!

Amounts distributed to the major decision points in an organization will depend on all sorts of factors. These can include, for instance, organizational size and structure, organizational performance, strategy, top management views, organizational culture, and so on. Regardless of the amounts involved, the quid pro quo to resource allocation is normally that those given the financial resources to support their decision-making must account for how they then use these resources in, supposedly, the furtherance of organizational objectives. Budgeting has long been viewed as the cornerstone of management control (Otley, 1978; 1987). Management control refers to the idea of organizations attempting to ensure, through the use of information-based routines, systems and procedures (Simons, 2000), the cooperation of organizational participants (managers in our case) toward the achievement of organizational aims and objectives.

For some time now, both resource allocation (budgeting) and accountability (budgetary control) have been underpinned by notions of responsibility accounting. The concept of responsibility accounting is simple and appealing. It states that, in terms of accountability – which is normally discharged through performance evaluation – only factors under the manager's *control* should be considered when his/her performance is evaluated (Choudhury, 1986). Basically, responsibility accounting seeks: 'To identify those financial elements in a certain area of activity which form a controllable set and to appoint a person to be responsible for managing this set of financial elements' (McNally, 1980: 165).

The corollary of this and other similar definitions of responsibility accounting (e.g. Drury, 2000) is that a person or persons should *not* be held responsible for those financial elements they are unable to control. Nor should they be rewarded for revenues/cost savings that are not the result of their own efforts. This 'principle of controllability' is the fundamental tenet upon which the concept of responsibility accounting is based (Choudhury, 1986). The underpinning rationale is that it would be somehow unfair to hold people accountable for expenditures and/or revenues that they did not authorize or could not 'manage' in some way. For convenience, this chapter will focus on notions of expenditure as the basis for exploring budgetary control. We shall return to the issue of controllability later on in the chapter. The concept of responsibility accounting has an inherent appeal to equity, and is consistent with traditional organization theory, which advocates a relationship between authority, responsibility, and controllability (Filley and House, 1969; Urwick, 1939).

Responsibility accounting is traditionally or typically operationalized as a hierarchy of responsibility centres. The full extent of these centres can range from investment centre(s) at the apex of the firm, through profit centres, to revenue and cost centres at middle- and lower-ranking management levels. It is not my intention to explain these centres here. There are many adequate descriptions in standard management accounting textbooks (see e.g. editions of Drury, 2000; Garrison, Noreen and Brewer, 2008; Merchant and Van der Stede, 2007). The two fundamental points to make at this juncture are: (1) that single individuals are normally placed in charge of a given responsibility centre, and (2) that responsibility accounting is typically the basis by which budgetary control is both supposed and purported to operate (McNally, 1980). Responsibility accounting systems identify the budget-responsible manager to be held accountable for the resources under his/her control (Ezzamel and Hart, 1987).

Organizational context

Responsibility accounting's role as the framework for budgetary control can be traced to the development of the bureaucratic multi-division 'M-form' structure pioneered in the early part of the 20th century by organizations such as Du Pont and General Motors (Chandler, 1962; 1977). This type of organizational configuration was viewed as providing the stability, certainty, and clearly demarcated independence of managerial responsibility deemed essential for the execution of budgetary control through responsibility accounting. Responsibility accounting frameworks permit the decentralization of decision-making to major decision points in the firm based on the organization chart. Resources can be divided and sub-divided through this framework, and budgetary control exercised by holding the responsibility centre manager accountable for the resources allocated to his/her designated area of responsibility. In this context, budgetary control has traditionally proceeded via monitoring, feedback, motivation, and performance evaluation. The cybernetic model of control has long underpinned and informed budgetary control within the quintessentially bureaucratic 'M-form' organization (Bartlett and Ghoshal, 1993; Hofstede, 1978).

Challenges and critiques

While notions of responsibility accounting have their roots in classic organization theory (Ezzamel and Hart, 1987), the historical link between organizational architecture and responsibility accounting outlined above implies a contingent relationship (Donaldson, 2001). That is, if the organizational architecture changes, so should how budgetary control is organized and exercised (Bruns and Waterhouse, 1975; Waterhouse and Tiessen, 1978). Although not explicitly stated, this contingency argument underlies criticisms about budgeting and budgetary control (discussed in due course). Put another way, given the apparent dovetailing of organization structure, responsibility accounting framework and budgetary control process, the move, in some industries at least (e.g. electronics), to more complex and flexible organizational architectures is seen as representing a non-trivial challenge to traditional methods of budgetary control (Hope and Fraser, 2003).

The challenge includes a problematization of budget variance analysis. Traditional methods of budgetary control include the idea of conducting variance analysis at the level of the individual responsibility centre. As Ansari noted, however, as early as 1979, such a compartmentalized approach to budgetary control sits awkwardly with the jurisdictional and decisional interdependencies which characterize more 'open', organic organizational forms (Emmanuel, Otley and Merchant, 1990). The basis of Ansari's thesis is that, in the absence of clear-cut allocations of tasks and resources, organizations need to move away from 'isolated' variance analysis conducted at the level of the individual responsibility centre, and towards a more integrated or collective (potentially unit- or organizational-level) analysis of budget variances based on an understanding of strategic priorities vis-à-vis competitor actions. That is, an equally more 'open' approach to variance analysis is required, one which will likely necessitate cooperation rather than competition among managers, with regulation of the whole (organization) taking precedent over regulation of the parts (individual responsibility centres) (Ansari, 1979: 151). To encourage such behaviours, Ansari (1979: 151) advocated that performance should become 'more an exercise in problem solving and less a method of assigning responsibility'. For Ansari (1979: 149), variances computed under his proposed system 'more fully reflect the interacting nature of most organizations and provide better control information'.

Besides Ansari's (1979) critique of budget variance analysis, there exist a multitude of more general criticisms of traditional budgetary control. These more general criticisms include the following (this list is indicative, not exhaustive):

- that the exercise of traditional budgetary control through variance analysis, motivation and performance evaluation at the level of the individual responsibility centre constrains responsiveness and flexibility, and is a barrier to change;

- that traditional budgeting and budgetary control is unnecessarily time-consuming;
- that budgets are rarely strategic and are often contradictory;
- that traditional budgetary control encourages 'gaming' and perverse behaviours;
- that traditional budgets do not reflect new organizational forms and arrangements;
- that traditional budgets are developed and updated too infrequently, usually annually;
- that traditional budgets are often based on unsupported assumptions and guesswork;
- that budgets and budgetary control make people feel under-valued.

The above criticisms are well-rehearsed; complaints about budgets have been repeatedly voiced and documented ever since Argyris (1953) first identified 'human problems with budgets'. Fine; critique is a fundamental aspect of academic enquiry. Further, while clear conclusions have yet to be reached (Hartmann, 2000), there is considerable behavioural research in accounting to suggest that many of the 'human problems with [traditional] budgets' may well be justified (although later in the chapter, evidence is presented which suggests a more positive or psychologically functional role for budgets). Given these points, we might well have expected the budgetary control literature to offer alternative suggestions as to what could or should replace traditional budgetary control if traditional budgetary control procedures are seen as inappropriate for the increasingly prevalent N-form organization. (The term 'N-form' is often used to distinguish supposedly complex, highly organic, 'third-wave', knowledge-based, information-age companies operating in a globalized environment, from the more traditional 'M-form' archetype.) However, this is currently not the case. It is noticeable that the criticisms of budgets have generally not been matched with alternative suggestions. Ansari's (1979) study was discussed above as it is one of the very few studies to suggest how budgetary control could and should be conducted within organic organizational architectures. The other major exception is the BB Movement.

Of course, the BB Movement has also levelled a host of criticisms at traditional budgetary control. It continues to do so (BBRT; Libby and Lindsay, 2010; see also Libby and Lindsay, 2003a,b, for a rehearsal of the BB Movement's case against traditional budgeting). There is little which is new in these criticisms. Most if not all of the misgivings stated in the BB literature tend to reflect or rehearse the general and enduring discontent about budgets outlined above. Parker (2002), in his textbook analysis of budgets, outlines the critical discourse on budgeting in the 1930s and 1940s. He points out the stark similarities of this discourse to that presented by the BB movement some 60 years later.

What is different is that BB represents a systematic effort to create a conceptual antithesis to traditional budgeting and budgetary control. The BB Movement refines some of the criticisms, and, significantly, it *does* also offer potential 'solutions' to the perceived problems with traditional budgets. For instance, Hope and Fraser (2003a: xx) argue that traditional budgetary practices have degenerated into what is akin to 'fixed performance contracts' that 'force managers at all levels to commit to delivering specified outcomes, even though many of the variables underpinning those outcomes are beyond their control'. Hope and Fraser advocate a move away from focusing on individual responsibility and accountability (as via the 'tyranny of fixed performance contracts') and towards 'relative improvement contracts' which, in essence, emphasize a more integrated if still individual-level approach to budgetary control (the BB's 'solutions' and propositions are elaborated below; see Libby and Lindsay, 2003a,b, for a fuller coverage).

An oft-repeated criticism of traditional budgetary control is that the practice of budgeting reinforces vertical chains of command (made possible through the use of hierarchically-based responsibility accounting systems). As such, budgets are 'the primary barrier to contemporary organizational success' (Hope and Fraser, 2003), particularly for the 'third-wave' N-form organizational archetype. Today's N-form organizations do not need a strengthening of vertical chains of command; rather, the need is for flexibility and responsiveness, including – or particularly at – middle-management levels (Bartlett and Ghoshal, 1993; Hope and Fraser, 2003). Within the N-form organizational model, middle- and lower-ranking managers can be, and have been observed as being, the 'primary initiators' of entrepreneurial activity (Bartlett and Ghoshal, 1993; Marginson, 2002). Increasingly, it seems that middle-level managers are being charged with the task of creating and responding to new opportunities for the organization (Dutton et al., 1997). It is this more 'grassroots' approach to strategy-making (Marginson, 2002) which, according to many, should not be constrained by traditional budgetary control systems (Hope and Fraser, 1997; 2003). But, among other things, this is to ignore or downplay the role that budgetary controls may play in 'limiting innovative excess' (Dent, 1990).

Recent practitioner literature has also been highly critical of traditional budgetary control. Perhaps prompted by Hope and Fraser's 1997 article, a number of publications appeared in the period 1997 to 2003 advocating the demise of traditional budgets. The publications include: Anon (2000), 'Rethinking life without budgets'; Babbini (1999), 'Reality check: is traditional budgeting under siege'; Bunce (1999), 'Budgets: the hidden barrier to success in the information age'; Bunce and Fraser (1997), 'Beyond Budgeting'; Gurton (1999), 'Bye bye budget ... the annual budget is dead'; Gary (2003), 'Why budgeting kills your company'; Hendersen (1997), 'Does budgeting have to be so troublesome?'; Libby and Lindsay (2003a,b), 'Budgeting – an unnecessary evil'; Libby and Lindsay (2003c), 'Booting the budget: how the BBRT envisions a world without budgets'; Marcino (2000), 'Obliterate traditional budgeting'; Marshall (2003), 'Beyond budgeting'; and Oldham and Mills (1999), 'Abandoning traditional budgeting'. Jensen (2001; 2003) offers a more academic but no less forceful critique of traditional budgeting. He argues that: (1) 'Corporate budgeting is broken', so ' let's fix it' (2001), and (2) traditional budgets encourage 'people to lie' (2003). In addition, or more precisely at the center of the debate, there are, of course, the many articles by Hope and Fraser (Hope and Fraser, 1997; 1998; 1999a,b,c,d; 2000; 2001; 2003a,b,c; Fraser and Hope, 2001).

I have included titles to some of the articles to illustrate the emphasis or flavour of the practitioner debate. It is, or was, very much about problems with traditional budgetary control. Based on this sample of publications, it appears that the view of some at least is that, because of the problems they create, budgets should be abandoned. This implies that few see adaptation or modification as a practical alternative. Budgeting is budgeting; budgetary control either occurs in its traditional form or not at all. (As will be discussed below, it is not clear from the BB debate whether the issue is no budgeting whatsoever, or budgetary control of a different form. The catchy term 'Beyond Budgeting' signals something different. However, descriptions provided by the BB Movement may amount to little more than a repackaging of budgetary control procedures.)

Others, however, are more sanguine. This literature suggests that modification and adaptation *is* possible; what is needed is 'Better Budgeting', not necessarily the compete obliteration of budgets. Neely, Bourne and Chris (2003), for instance, question whether it should be BB or 'Better Budgeting'. Banham (2000) discusses the notion of 'Better Budgeting', as does Colman (2004). Cokins (2008) advocates simply 'Repairing the budgeting process'. More radically, in terms of 'Better Budgeting', Newing (1994) suggests 'Out with the old, in with the new'. Durfee (2006) considers 'Alternative budgeting'. Needleman (2005) suggests 'New tools make for better budgeting'. Orlando (2000) argues that 'budgeting pain' can be converted into 'budgeting gain'. Fanning (1999) speculates on 'Budgeting in the 21st century'. In contrast with Libby and Lindsay (2003a,b), Wallander (1999) refers to budgeting as 'a necessary evil'. Greenberg and Greenberg (2006) similarly suggest that firms need budgets, while Prendergast

(2000) even dares to suggest that '[traditional] budgets hit back'. Neely et al. (2001) document several organizations – including Borealis, BP, and Ford Motor company – that have apparently modified and adapted their budgetary control practices to meet organizational purpose and needs (some of the adaptations are outlined below). Neely et al. (2001: 2) further suggest that all 15 organizations involved in the research 'were actively seeking to improving their planning and budgeting, but for different reasons'. These reasons included (1) to enhance cost efficiency, (2) to improve forecasting ability, and (3) to encourage managers to think more strategically (Neely et al., 2001: 2). The reported developments and modifications are labelled as examples of 'Better Budgeting', but what is 'Better Budgeting'?

Better budgeting

'Better Budgeting' appears an all-encompassing concept, encapsulating a range of ideas. Indeed, Neely et al. (2001) suggest that 'Better Budgeting' can include:

Activity-based budgeting

Activity-based budgeting (ABB) is an approach to budgeting which builds on well-established ideas such as activity-based costing and activity-based cost management. The aim of ABB seems to be to ensure that resource allocation decisions are consistent with activity-based management analysis (to the extent this occurs; Connolly and Ashworth, 1994; Neely et al., 2001). More specifically, a 'Closed-Loop Model' of ABB (Consortium of Advanced Manufacturing [CAM-I], see Hansen and Torok, 2004) creates 'an explicit model of the organization's activities, processes, resources, and capacity that it uses to generate plans and budgets' (Hansen, 2010: 16). Hansen and Torek (2004) claim several benefits of the Closed-Loop ABB Model. These include the idea that the Closed-Loop Model can link resource capacity explicitly with resource demand, thereby helping to avoid building a budget solely on extrapolation of prior data. Other claimed benefits include a reduction in 'gaming', and a 'more meaningful' budget. Generally, ABB is meant to be computer-based, allowing for a quicker and simpler remodelling of budgetary needs as events unfold and the environment changes (Hansen, 2010). For these and other reasons, advocates claim that ABB can result in cost savings of between 10% and 20% through 'better methods of working and the elimination of bureaucracy' (Brimson and Antos, 1999; Brimson and Fraser, 1991).

Zero-based budgeting

Zero-based budgeting (ZBB) is, perhaps, better understood than ABB. Its inclusion as part of 'Better Budgeting' is interesting, not only because of the recognized limitations of ZBB (e.g. the degree of effort involved), but because neither ZBB nor ABB seem to address the documented shortcomings of traditional budgetary control, as set out above. For instance, just like traditional budgeting, ZBB can be enormously time-consuming (Wetherbe and Montanari, 1981)!

Rolling forecasts and budgets

A rolling budget is a forecast that maintains a constant forward-looking time horizon, normally between 12 and 18 months (Clark, 2007). Several potential benefits over traditional budgeting and budgetary control are claimed. They are that (1) planning can occur more often throughout the year rather simply at year end, (2) the less detail allows rolling budgets to be updated more easily, (3) changes can be quickly incorporated into the plan, and (4) managers can maintain a connection with a longer time horizon through the use of rolling forecasts and budgets (Hansen, 2010). There is evidence to suggest that organizations may be adopting – or at least contemplating adopting – rolling forecasts and budgets (Ekhom and Wallin, 2000; Comshare, 2001; Neely et al., 2001; Lynn and Madison, 2004). As with ABB, however, the purported benefits of rolling budgets have yet to be subjected to empirical analysis. This is despite the growing use of rolling forecasts, and in spite of the fact that the notion of rolling forecasts and budgets has existed for some considerable time (see Owen, 1949: 598).

Value-based management

Value-based management is described as having three core elements: beliefs, principles, and processes (Neely et al., 2001). The key to value-based management is that all expenditure plans 'should be evaluated as project appraisals and assessed in terms of the shareholder value they will create' (Neely et al., 2001: 10). It is the linking of planning and budgeting to strategy and shareholder value which enables value-based management to be seen as part of 'Better Budgeting'. To date, however, value-based management appears more of a concept (Burton, 1996) than an empirical practice. Its use in organizations has yet to be documented.

Profit planning

As the title suggests, profit planning is about planning, specifically planning and assessing the extent to which an organization's responsibility centres can and should generate sufficient cash, create economic value, and attract sufficient financial resources for investment. Again, however, few examples of its practical application have thus far been reported.

Beyond budgeting

To the extent that BB represents 'better budgeting', it is, perhaps, if 'better budgeting' means dispensing with traditional budgetary control. The main idea of BB, as envisaged by Jeremy Hope and Robin Fraser (1997; 2003), is to abandon budgetary contracts and accompanying ex ante performance targets. Instead, the key argument is that organizations should follow a set of principles that will 'set them free' from the 'annual performance trap' that is associated with traditional budgets (Hope and Fraser, 2003). The principles of BB include the following:

- the use of benchmarking and other forms of relative performance evaluation;
- the replacement of annual plans by rolling forecasts;
- increased decentralization of decision-making;
- other means of empowering managers and other employees (Hope and Fraser, 2003).

The principles of BB are expanded, developed, revisited and revised in a series of publications (Hope and Fraser, 1997; 2003). For instance, in terms of relative performance evaluation, Hope and Fraser (2003: 42) argue for the use of 'relative performance contracts' by which managers, although still expected to reach high standards, are nonetheless 'evaluated and rewarded after the event according to how they performed in the light of circumstances that actually prevailed and, perhaps more importantly, how they performed against their peers'. For a full elaboration of each of the principles of BB, the reader is referred to Hope and Fraser's 2003 publication. The point to highlight here is that these earlier publications (Hope and Fraser, 2000) show 12 principles of BB. Becker, Messner and Schäffer (working paper) chart the development of BB through a series of publications, showing how the associated principles are seen to develop and change over time (Hope and Fraser, 1997; 2000; Fraser and Hope, 2001; Bunce et al., 2001; Hope and Fraser, 2003).

Beyond budgeting, better budgeting, or diversity in budgetary control practice?

The BB Movement continues to promote its principles through the activities of the BBRT. The aims of the BBRT seem almost missionary: to persuade or convince as many organizations as possible to convert to the BB way of thinking and abandon traditional budgetary control (Daum, 2003). Given the attempts at persuasion, the persuasive nature of the principles, the fact that the BB message originates from practice (Libby and Lindsay, 2010), and the general and continuing disquiet with traditional budgetary processes – as documented in both practitioner and academic literatures – we might expect that the concept of BB would or should prove as practically popular as other management accounting initiatives, such as activity-based costing and the balanced scorecard. Yet, this appears not to be the case. Hope and Fraser support their arguments with evidence that a number of companies, particularly Scandanavian companies (e.g. Svenska Handelsbanken), have abandoned budgeting in its traditional form, and have remained successful, if not more successful, after so doing. That said, the number of examples of firms apparently abandoning budgets that the BB movement draws upon to support its assertions, while growing, still appears extremely limited, even after more than ten years of the BB message. Hope and Fraser, in their various publications, still draw heavily and often on just *one* company, Svenska Handelsbanken, as an exemplar of a firm operating BB. Interestingly, this firm's abandonment of traditional budgeting preceded rather than followed the development of the BB concept.

The apparently limited 'success' of the BB message also becomes apparent if we consider available survey evidence on the budgetary control and other management accounting practices and procedures employed by firms. Notwithstanding observed modifications (discussed below), survey evidence continues to suggest that traditional forms of budgeting and responsibility accounting persist throughout the organizational environment. The surveys indicate that the vast majority of responding companies in Europe (irrespective of country, industry or size) still operate with formal budgeting systems along hierarchical lines (see Eckholm and Wallin, 2000; Neely et al., 2003; Dugdale and Lyne, 2006). Evidence from North America also points to the retention of traditional budgeting and budgetary control as part of overall cost management (Umapathy, 1987; Libby and Lindsay, 2010).

This survey evidence raises an interesting question: given the apparently increasing prevalence of organizational architectures which problematize the exercise of traditional budgetary control, why is it that more firms are not following the advice of the BB movement and abandoning budgets as a form of cost control?

Perhaps one answer is that, rather than dispensing with budgeting and budgetary control altogether, firms are instead modifying and amending their practices and procedures as they see necessary (Epstein and Manzoni, 2002). The thoughtful and extensive report by Neely et al. (2001) documents several such cases. For example, the study reports how BP apparently no longer uses the term budgeting, and how, for this major multinational enterprise, planning is based around competitor and market expectations. In this context, broad targets are set top-down, while detailed operational plans are made bottom-up (Neely et al., 2001: 36).

Other examples documented by Neely et al. (2001) include Electrolux, which uses an annual planning cycle with rolling quarterly re-forecasting, Ford Motor Company, which has separated budgets from forecasts and cost control from the 'motivation cycle', and Volvo.

Volvo apparently uses 'performance planning' rather than budgets based on expectations of income, quality, product development, and projected sales volumes over a two-year planning horizon. All of the examples outlined in Neely et al.'s (2001) report suggest varying degrees of modification and adaptation of traditional budgetary control. Taken together, they suggest, not necessarily BB or 'Better Budgeting', but a possibly growing diversity of budgetary control practices and procedures. Indeed, it is difficult to say whether the examples outlined by Neely et al. (2001) represent either BB or 'Better Budgeting', not least because of the lack of precise criteria by which to judge what may be either BB or Better Budgeting. It is only possible to speculate that there may be a growing diversity of budgetary practices, given that extant research offers little insight into the previous 'state of play'.

Contribution of the academic literature

It would be useful at this juncture to turn to the academic literature in a bid to offer further insight into firms' developing budgetary control practices. As it is, recent academic literature has little to say on the subject of budgetary control practice. The author has at his disposal a file which, at the time of writing, contains over 350 *academic* references on budgets, budgeting and budgetary control. Of these, approaching 50 have been published since the year 2000. Of these, the vast majority continue to explore, revisit and finesse budgetary control issues first established in the 1950s, 60s and 70s. For instance, studies have continued to examine budget participation (Brown and Evans, 2009; Chalos and Poon, 2001; Chong, 2002; Chong and Bateman, 2000; Chong and Chong, 2002a,b; Chong, Eggleton and Leong, 2005a,b; 2006; Fisher, Frederickson and Peffer, 2000; 2002; 2006; Lau and Buckland, 2000; 2001; Lau and Lim, 2002a,b; Maiga, 2005a,b), budgetary slack (Davila and Wouters, 2005; Fisher, Maines, Peffer and Sprinkle, 2002; Lau and Eggleton, 2002; 2004; Stevens, 2002; Webb, 2002), and the link between budget participation and budgetary slack (Dunk and Lal, 1999; Lau and Eggleton, 2003; Maiga, 2005a). Several investigate the procedural and distributive fairness of performance evaluation procedures involving budgetary and other measures (Lau and Sholihin, 2005; Lau and Tan, 2006; Sholihin and Pike, 2009), while others consider the roles of budgets (Epstein and Manzoni, 2002; Hansen and Van der Stede, 2004), and the link with strategy (Abernethy and Brownell, 1999). Examining the behavioural aspects of budgeting remains a popular research topic (Emsley, 2001; Lau and Chong, 2002; Lau and Ng, 2003; Otley and Fakiolas, 2000; Otley and Pollanen, 2000; Quirin, Donnelly and O'Bryan, 2000; Quirin, O'Bryan and Donnelly, 2004; Subramaniam and Ashkanasy, 2001; Subramaniam and Mia, 2001; 2003; Tsui, 2001; Van der Stede, 2000; 2001; Walker and Johnson, 1999; Wentzel, 2002).

Such research is undoubtedly adding to our understanding of budgeting, particularly the behavioural and psychological aspects of budgetary control. At the same time, the focus of recent studies means that firms' budgetary practices and procedures have gone largely unexplored. In particular, little is currently known about whether these practices are changing in line with changing organizational architecture, and if so, what the developments may entail. Yet, based on the findings of a small but growing body of literature, there may be much more to learn, not only about how budgetary control may be exercised in today's organizations, but also about the behavioural consequences of any 'new' practices and procedures.

Contemporary budgetary control practices

Østergren and Stensaker (2010) is a recent study which explores 'Management control without budgets' (see also Libby and Lindsay, 2007 for a discussion of Svenska Handelsbanken). Based on a case study of a large Norwegian multidivisional oil and energy company with 30,000 employees worldwide, the authors document an example of what they claim is BB in practice by examining its implementation in two of the company's business units. Several issues are investigated and several features illustrated. Conceptually, Østergren and Stensaker (2010: 5) argue that, while 'Beyond budgeting consists of similar activities as budgeting, such as target setting, forecasting, and resource allocation', the difference is that, with BB, 'no budget is allocated in advance and the processes are separated in time'. The authors proceed to list a number of key differences between budgets and BB under the headings 'target planning', 'resource allocation', 'challenges', and 'benefits' (Østergren and Stensaker, 2010: 5, Table 1).

Empirically, Østergren and Stensaker (2010) offer insights into how the Norwegian multinational, pseudonym Oilco, is seeking to exercise management control without budgets. The company's management is reported as having decided, in 2005, to 'abolish budgets completely' and to instead 'introduce Beyond Budgeting' (Østergren and Stensaker, 2010: 8). The reasons proffered for this decision appear to echo the well-documented criticisms of traditional budgetary control. For example, one reason was that the budget was perceived as inflexible and inappropriate in fast-changing circumstances. The budget was also considered to have created a false perception that the future was manageable. Budgeting was viewed as an expensive and time-consuming process, while the budget was 'known' within the company to 'create a budgetary game when it came to resource allocation' (Østergren and Stensaker, 2010: 9). This game was expected to be eliminated with the removal of the budget.

BB at Oilco was introduced via a set of 'principles'. To some extent, the 'principles' applied reflect or rehearse the principles of BB. For instance, corporate management considered that 'performance should be about outperforming peers' (relative performance evaluation). Managers were empowered to act with flexibility, and respond with initiative and judgement to unfolding events (increased decentralization of decision-making), while a further principle was that resources 'should be available or allocated case by case' (removal of annual budgetary plans).

It is not clear from the study to what extent Oilco's corporate management was influenced by the BB literature. Irrespective of this, Østergren and Stensaker (2010) report several features of the company's approach to cost management which help to advance our understanding as to how firms may operate without traditional budgetary control procedures and practices. It is not within the scope of this chapter to repeat all of the features here; the reader is referred to Østergren and Stensaker (2010) for a full account. Perhaps the key ones to note are: (1) centralized target-setting involving strategically orientated targets, (2) a pursuit of these targets based on relative rather than fixed principles (where unit costs and the relationship between costs and revenues is key, rather than 'remaining within budget'), and thereby (3) resource allocation as a dynamic process 'that can happen any time during the year depending on whether sub-groups come up with a good project . . .' (Østergren and Stensaker, 2010: 16).

Østergren and Stensaker (2010) is the first study to explicitly investigate budgetary practices through the prism of BB. The authors note the current dearth of research into how alternative management control systems function in practice. Østergren and Stensaker (2010) present their study as a possible springboard for further research into BB practices and concomitant issues and challenges. Interestingly, while not explicitly presented as research into BB, several other studies do appear to offer insight into some of the issues and challenges which may arise from non-traditional budgetary practices.

Marginson (1999), for instance, reports how one organization, in a seemingly radical break with tradition, removed evaluation and accountability from the budgetary process for all managers except the most senior. There was a deliberate move away from respecting the controllability principle, in that, for example, the chief finance officer had financial accountabilities for achieving contribution and profit targets for the organization. Yet, neither his remit of authority nor his line-management responsibilities provided the necessary degree of formal decision-making authority to enable personal control over the activities necessary to achieve the expected contribution and profit targets. Instead, the company as a whole operated with a heavy emphasis on social controls and 'mutual accountabilities' as a basis for gaining the cooperation of managers towards pursuing organizational objectives (Marginson, 1999). In the context of this more informal and collective approach to management control, initial budgetary allocations could be revised and modified as events unfolded and circumstances changed during the budgetary period. This flexibility of resource allocation was supported by the use of rolling forecasts. Several of the organization's budgetary procedures documented by Marginson (1999) appear consistent with notions of BB.

Marginson and Ogden (2005) similarly describe a seemingly radical budgetary control process involving target-based flexibility and 'cost consciousness' as bases by which their case-study organization sought to manage the tension between the need to achieve 'tight' cost control on the one hand, and the need to pursue continued 'creative innovation' on the other (Simons, 1995; 2000). A key aspect of cost control at the research site was how managers were empowered to forgo pre-set budgetary targets for 'strategic reasons'. Interestingly, however, Marginson and Ogden (2005) analyse how a proportion of managers preferred instead to focus on achieving initial budgetary targets, not because of the 'threat of accountability or the promise of reward' (again, formal accountability and reward had been decoupled from the budgetary process), but for the reason that doing so offered a degree of structure and certainty to counter the experience of role ambiguity. Such evidence provides some initial insight into the potential behavioural consequences of BB-type practices. In the present case, it was described as a 'design-behaviour' paradox. 'Where strong reliance on budgets is no longer deemed suitable, or desirable, from an organizational point of view, managers may react, for psychological reasons, by maintaining or increasing their commitment to budgetary targets' (Marginson and Ogden, 2005: 451).

Retaining traditional budgetary control practices

In contrast to the above two studies, Frow, Marginson and Ogden (2005; 2010) document a major multinational organization which has largely retained traditional budgetary control practices and procedures, including the use of traditional responsibility accounting centres. The company does so in the context of attempting to promote continuous innovation and learning throughout the firm, given, for this organization, a *highly* globalized environment. As reported by the authors (Frow et al., 2005), one of the issues raised by the organizational circumstance again concerned controllability. Basically, managers faced the challenge of balancing their exposure to traditional budgetary controls and the imperative of achieving organizational-level financial targets, with the more broadly-based demands imposed by the need to pursue strategic initiatives. The 2005 study documents how managers were aided in this challenge by the embedding of budgetary control within a wider management control framework comprising various formal and informal procedures aimed at supporting 'negotiated' arrangements and 'shared' accountabilities. Nonetheless, a lack of individual-level controllability characterized the organization: individual responsibility centre managers acknowledged having partial and limited control over achievement of budgetary targets. Extant literature suggests that a lack of controllability will lead to dysfunctional consequences; for instance, increased job-related tension and stress (Dent, 1987; Merchant, 1987). This may have been so at the case study organization; the issue was not formally examined. That said, Frow et al. (2005) report how Astoria's managers at the least accepted – and in some cases, even seemed to relish – the challenge of fulfilling role requirements in the absence of controllability.

The suggestion that the organically configured multinational organization investigated by Frow et al. (2005; 2010) was continuing with traditional budgetary controls requires qualification. In the spirit of Ansari (1979), the company operated with a more 'open' approach to budget variance analysis. Individual responsibility centre managers were empowered to assess budget variances, not on a compartmentalized basis, but in terms of the potential effects on broader organizational strategy. The company also emphasized the importance of unit costs over budget allocations, while there was some attempt to align input with output. For example, initial budget allocations could be increased if the prognosis was that doing so would secure proportionally greater revenues in the medium- to longer-term. The budgetary processes operated by the company in question were observed to be embedded within a wider management control framework, and are conceptualized as an example of 'continuous budgeting' (Frow et al., 2010).

The above two studies suggest that traditional approaches to budgetary control may not be as problematic for organizations, and in particular highly organic ones, as is generally perceived. In a study of eight UK-based companies, Dugdale and Lyne (2006: 3) report, in contrast to the arguments of the BB Movement, that 'Most respondents were not critical of the budgeting process'. Such evidence raises a number of issues, one of which is the possibility that, in focusing so heavily on the perceived negative aspects of budgets and budgetary control, the academic literature could be accused of ignoring the more positive role(s) that budgets may play in organizations. After all, there may be reasons as to why organizations have persisted with traditional budgetary control procedures despite the 'very bad press' budgets have tended to receive over the years, especially in the academic literature. In this context, Hansen, Otley and Van der Stede (2003) note how research into budgetary control may have become misplaced, with scholars investigating issues of decreasing practical relevance to organizations.

A positive psychological role for budgets?

Adopting a more positive perspective, an emerging literature has begun to examine the positive psychological role that accounting and budgets may play in managers' work experience. Hartmann (2005), for example, shows how tolerance for ambiguity may moderate how managers view the appropriateness of accounting performance measures in conditions of uncertainty: the higher the tolerance for ambiguity, the greater the perceived appropriateness of accounting as a measure of performance. Marginson (2006) finds that increasing reliance on financial information may reduce role ambiguity. As mentioned, Marginson and Ogden (2005a, p. 437) show that managers may commit to achieving pre-set budgetary targets because 'doing so offers a sense of clarity and security' within a role subject to ambiguity and uncertainty. Marginson and Ogden (2005b) propose that budgets may enable managers to feel psychologically empowered. Finally, Hall (2008) examines the extent to which 'comprehensive performance measurement systems (PMS)' are related to both psychological empowerment (PE) and role clarity, with consequences for managerial performance. Hypotheses are based upon the assumption that a comprehensive PMS 'provides richer and more complete feedback about operations and results . . . which is expected to have positive effects' (p. 144). Defining comprehensive PMS in terms of information provision (to assist managers in managing firm operations) (Ittner, Larcker and Randall, 2003; Lillis, 2002), Hall (2008) reports support for his hypotheses. Hall's (2008) research is consistent with the argument that a broad range of measures, incorporating non-financial measures, overcomes the inadequacies of traditional narrowly based financial measures (see Ittner and Larcker, 1998; Ittner, Larcker and Meyer, 2003; Lau and Sholihin, 2005; Lau and Moser, 2008; Kaplan and Norton, 2001).

The literature examining a positive psychological role for budgets highlights an important point: that, despite the significant body of literature that has amassed on the subject of budgeting over the years, there may be yet much to learn, not only about how budgetary control may be exercised in practice, but also on the behavioural consequences of these practices. This point appears particularly pertinent regarding the role(s) played by budgets and budgetary control in settings which are traditionally seen as problematizing the effectiveness of traditional budgetary control practices and procedures. There are studies which challenge this orthodox view (see e.g. Chapman, 1998). There is even research which suggests that budgets may not necessarily stifle innovation and learning (Marginson and Ogden, 2004; Marginson and Bui, 2009; Frow et al., 2005; 2010), an oft-repeated criticism of traditional budgetary controls (Argyris, 1977; Bartlett and Ghoshal, 1993; Emmanuel, Otley and Merchant, 1990; Hedberg and Johnson, 1978; Hope and Fraser, 2003; Johnson and Gill, 1993). All this reinforces the point that, irrespective of the considerable research thus far undertaken into budgeting, there is still scope for further research. The following offers a few suggestions as to where such research may be directed.

Ideas for further study

A potentially useful way of considering the question of budgetary control in a modern context is to view the issue from what are perceived to be three core elements of the budget cycle: budget setting, budget implementation, and budget accountability (performance evaluation). Each is elaborated in turn.

For the purposes of this chapter, budget setting refers to the distribution of resources and the establishment of budgetary targets at the level of the individual responsibility centre (Horngren, Bhimani, Datar and Foster, 2002). Budget setting encompasses budget planning, to the extent that planning informs the distribution of resources. From a traditional perspective, budget setting is normally seen as a periodic process following, in the main, the solar cycle (i.e. occurring annually, although budget-setting may be conceived of as a more frequent process, through the use of rolling budgets for example). Traditional budget-setting procedures may be laborious and time-consuming (Neely et al., 2001). However, the setting of the annual budget, including the master budget, is viewed as a way of enabling top management's strategic plans to be 'cascaded' through the firm and translated into a series of financial targets at the level of the individual responsibility centre (McNally, 1980). In essence, budget setting is about establishing forthcoming budgetary requirements for each of the major decision points of the firm.

Budget setting is generally viewed as being enhanced through participation since participation enables the subordinate to reveal private information, thereby leading, it is presumed, to higher-quality budgets (Nouri and Parker, 1998; Shields and Shields, 1998). Participation is viewed as being particularly important in conditions of uncertainty, which reduces the relevance of historical data (Emmanuel, Otley and Merchant, 1990). Yet, as Marginson and Ogden's (2005) study shows, high levels of uncertainty need not necessarily be accompanied by high levels of budget participation. Rather, initial budget allocations may be imposed, simply because *all* managers are equally uncertain about future resource requirements in a fast-moving environment. Imposing budgets has generally been viewed as a way of de-motivating managers towards achieving budgetary targets (on the basis that participation is seen as a way of motivating managers towards achieving the budget – see Collins, 1982; Searfoss, 1976). Marginson and Ogden's (2005) study, however, again suggests this may not necessarily be the case. In place of an absence of participation, managerial commitment to the budget may be achieved on the basis of what an imposed budget offers: a sense of stability and structure in the face of considerable instability and uncertainty. The potential for certain budgetary issues/practices to act as substitutes for other issues and practices is a neglected topic that is worthy of further investigation.

Notwithstanding the above, and for the organization concerned, budgetary targets were imposed on the understanding that initial allocations could be revisited and revised as circumstances changed. The rationale involved appears similar to that reported by Ostergren and Stensaker (2010): target setting was simply a first step in a more flexible budgetary control process which involved potentially numerous budget adjustments and iterations as circumstances unfold. Budget setting as an imposed procedure merits further investigation, not least in terms of both why budgets may be imposed, and what issues might follow.

Budget implementation may be viewed as involving resource consumption in support of organizational activities; the money is spent (or at least committed to be spent). The control of resource consumption has traditionally been associated with the provision of variance information (Ansari, 1979). Reporting frequency may vary (e.g. weekly, monthly), but according to the cybernetic model of control on which traditional budgeting is based, corrective action should follow automatically from information received about budget variances (Ansari, 1979). This may, of course, be the case in all circumstances; regulatory action may be invoked which seeks to correct any deviations from budget. At the same time, of course, recent research (Frow et al., 2005; Marginson and Ogden, 2005) suggests managers may be encouraged to consider budget variances, not in isolation, but in the context of firms' strategic requirements, such as the possibilities of making improvements to ongoing projects as new information becomes available, notwithstanding the extent to which project modification often require additional resources. This may give rise to tensions and possible trade-offs involving budgets and broader strategic activities (Marginson, 2002), while questions also arise regarding the usefulness of responsibility-centred accounting control reports in these circumstances. Traditionally, accounting control reports provide information on performance against predetermined targets; they are not able (or used) to supply information on the financial implications of the strategic developments that occur during the period of budget implementation.

The above illustrates just a few of the issues that can arise with budgetary implementation in highly organic circumstances. Yet, of the various budgetary issues for investigation, the period of budget implementation currently remains one of the least researched. For instance, little is currently known about how tensions and possible trade-offs involving budgetary expenditure and other organizational activities are resolved during the implementation period, who may be involved, what influences are brought to bear, and indeed what role(s) accounting information may play in the decision processes that accompany or comprise budget implementation. The *process* of budget implementation has generally been treated as the proverbial 'black box', with the vast majority of academic research focused on investigating issues relating to the 'start' and 'finish' points of budgetary control: budget-setting and performance evaluation. The discoveries of recent research suggest this situation should not and cannot continue.

Finally, regarding the 'finish point' of budgetary control, it seems, on the basis of recent evidence, that more needs to be done to investigate the role of budgetary information in performance evaluation; or more precisely, how budgetary control may be achieved in the absence of accountability for budget performance. A key aspect of traditional budgetary control is to hold managers accountable for their budgetary performance (Hanson, Otley and Van der Stede, 2003). Budget-responsible managers may also be rewarded for meeting the budget (Horngren et al., 2002). This implies the use of budgetary information in performance evaluations (Otley, 1987). However, the idea of assessing individual managers' performance against pre-set standards by reference to accounting information is accepted as problematic in fast-moving, highly organic circumstances. Besides problems of controllability, the process presumes an ability to predict with accuracy managers' budgetary requirements at the budget-setting stage. By contrast, contemporary organizational settings demand that managers are able to take advantage of unfolding opportunities which promise longer-term payoffs, but which may require the sacrifice of short-term results (Laverty, 1996). *This* implies a reduced role for budgetary information as a performance indicator, to the extent that notions of formal accountability (and reward) for budgetary performance may be removed altogether for all but the most senior managers (Marginson and Ogden, 2005). In turn, this takes the issue beyond even 'performance evaluations based on relative performance contracts with hindsight' (Hanson, Otley and Van der Stede, 2003: 101), as there is no formal performance contract, flexible or otherwise (Hope and Fraser, 2003).

To the extent that the above is the case, it would be instructive to investigate how budgetary/cost control is exercised in circumstances where the familiar extrinsic motivators (accountability and reward) have been de-emphasized or removed altogether. Such actions seem almost heretical, as they strike at the very heart of traditional understandings of traditional budgetary control (Searfoss, 1976). Yet, not only have such radical steps seemingly been taken (Marginson, 1999; Marginson and Ogden, 2005), but the organizations concerned appear not to have suffered as a consequence. The removal of formal accountability and reward from the budgetary control process appeared motivated, in part, by organizational attempts to address controllability issues which arise from using traditional responsibility accounting frameworks within highly organic circumstances. These issues merit further attention, as does responsibility accounting (Rowe et al., 2008). Generally, the limited but no less revealing evidence further highlights the considerable scope for further research into the scope and practice of budgetary control.

Concluding comments

This chapter has attempted to weave a way through the recent literature on budgetary control, which covers a range of issues. There is continuing investigation of topics first researched some considerable time ago. The topics include: budget participation (Fisher et al., 2006), budgetary slack (Davila and Wouters, 2005), dysfunctional consequences of budgetary controls (Van der Stede, 2000), and the relationship between budgetary control systems and strategy (Abernethy and Brownell, 1999). There have been repeated calls for the demise of traditional budgeting (Hope and Fraser, 1997; 1999; 2003). There is research into management control without budgets (Østergren and Stensaker, 2010). There are now the established concepts of 'Beyond Budgeting' (Becker et al., 2010) and 'Better Budgeting' (Neely et al., 2001). There continue to be surveys of organizations' budgetary control practices and procedures (Libby and Lindsay, 2010), as well as the roles budgets may play in an organizational context (Hansen et al., 2003). There continues to be much conceptual criticism of traditional budgets, particularly in the practitioner literature (Hendersen, 1997). There is criticism of the focus of academic research on budgeting (Hansen et al., 2003). There are studies documenting developments in firms' budgetary practices (Neeley et al., 2001). There is research documenting budgeting's embedding within wider management control frameworks (Frow et al., 2005; 2010). There are a few studies highlighting seemingly radical approaches to budgetary control (Marginson and Ogden, 2005). There is limited evidence of developments in responsibility accounting arrangements (Rowe et al., 2008). Finally, there is an emerging literature which is beginning to document and understand the more positive psychological roles that accounting and budgets may play in managers' work experiences (Hall, 2008; Hartmann, 2005; 2007; Marginson, 2006; Marginson and Ogden, 2005).

This is quite a mix of issues, arguments, and investigations, with no obvious consistency of view/evidence. Perhaps, however, the one common theme we may take from the recent literature on budgeting is evidence of a growing diversity of budgetary control practice. Contingency theorists argue the need for control systems and processes to 'fit' the organizational context in which they operate. For some organizations at least, this organizational context is documented as having developed towards a more highly organic N-form-type arrangement. From a contingency perspective, therefore, it is not surprising to find changing budgetary control practices and procedures. At the same time, the apparent diversity of practice suggests that today's firms may be struggling to determine how best to exercise budgetary control in a globalized environment. The diversity of practice that is being documented appears to include some radical approach to budgetary control. It may still be, in many respects, budgetary control, but, to borrow from a famous phrase, not as we know it – or at least not as we used to know it. As a final comment, therefore, perhaps there is a growing need for textbook literature in management accounting to reflect the growing diversity of budgetary control practices. The idea that a standard approach exists may no longer apply, if it ever did.

Bibliography

Abernathy, M., and Brownell, P. (1999) The role of budgets in organizations facing strategic change: an exploratory study, *Accounting, Organizations and Society*, 24, 189–204.

Anon (2000) Rethinking life without budgets, *Harvard Management Update*, Harvard Business School.

Ansari, S.L. (1979) Towards an open-systems approach to budgeting, *Accounting, Organizations and Society*, 4(3), 149–161.

Anthony, R.N. (1965) *Planning and control systems: a framework for analysis*. Boston: Division of Research, Harvard University Press.

Argyris, C. (1952) *The impact of budgets on people: a study prepared for the Controllership Foundation, Inc*, Ithaca, New York: Cornell University, The School of Business and Public Administration.

Argyris, C. (1953) Human problems with budgets, *Harvard Business Review*, 31 (1), 97–110.

Austin, L.A., and Cheek, L.M. (1979) *Zero-based budgeting: a decision package manual*, United States of America: Amacon.

Babbini, C. (1999) *Reality check: is traditional budgeting under siege?* CMA Management, November, Hamilton.

Banham, R. (2000) Better budgets, *Journal of Accountancy*, February, 37–40.

Bartlett, C.A., and Ghoshal, S. (1993) Beyond the M-form: towards a managerial theory of the firm, *Strategic Management Journal*, 14, 23–46.

BBRT (2010) Beyond budgeting round table: enabling the lean, adaptive, and ethical enterprise principles. From http://www.bbrtna.org/principles.html

Becker, S., Messner, M., and Schäffer, U. (2010). *The evolution of a management accounting idea: the case of Beyond Budgeting*. Working Paper www.ssrn.com.

Bogsnes, B. (2009) *Implementing beyond budgeting: unlocking the performance potential*, Hoboken: Wiley.

Brimson, J.A., and Antos, J. (1999). *Driving value using activity-based budgeting*. New York: John Wiley.

Brimson, J.A., and Fraser, R. (1991) The key features of activity-based budgeting, *Management Accounting* (UK), 69 (1), 42–43.

Brown, J., and Atkinson, H. (2001) Budgeting in the information age: a fresh approach, *International Journal of Contemporary Hospitality Management*, 13 (3), 136–143.

Brown, J.L., and Evans, J.H. (2009) Agency theory and participative budgeting experiments, *Journal of Management Accounting Research*, 21, 317–345.

Bruns, W.J. Jr., and Waterhouse, J.H. (1975) Budget control and organizational structure, *Journal of Accounting Research*, 13 (2), 177–203.

Bunce, P. (1999) Budgets: the hidden barrier to success in the information age, *Accounting and Business*, March, 24.

Bunce, P., and Fraser, R. (1997) Beyond Budgeting, *Management Accounting*, 75 (2), 26–26.

Chalos, P., and Poon, M. (2001) Participative budgeting and performance: a state of the art review and re-analysis, *Advances in Management Accounting*, 10, 171–201.

Chandler, A.D. (1962) *Strategy and Structure*. Cambridge, MA: MIT Press.

Chandler, A.D. (1977) *The visible hand: the managerial revolution in American business*. Boston, MA: Harvard University Press.

Chapman C.S. (1998) Accountants in organisational networks, *Accounting, Organizations and Society*, 23 (8), 737–766.

Chong, V.K. (2002) A note on testing a model of cognitive budgetary participation processes using a structural equation modeling approach, *Advances in Accounting*, 19, 27–51.

Chong, V.K., and Bateman, D. (2000) The effect of role stress on budgetary participation and job satisfaction-performance linkages: a test of two different models, *Advances in Accounting Behavioral Research*, 3, 91–118.

Chong, V.K., and Chong, K.M. (2002a) Budget goal commitment and informational effects of budget participation on performance: a structural equation modeling approach, *Behavioral Research in Accounting*, 14, 65–86.

Chong, V.K., and Chong, K.M. (2002b) The role of feedback on the relationship between budgetary participation and performance, *Pacific Accounting Review*, 14 (2), 33–55.

Chong, V.K., Eggleton, I.R.C., and Leong, M.K.C. (2005a) The effects of value attainment and cognitive roles of budgetary participation on job performance, *Advances in Accounting Behavioral Research*, 8, 213–233.

Chong, V.K., Eggleton, I.R.C., and Leong, M.K.C. (2005b) The impact of market competition and budgetary participation on performance and job satisfaction: a research note, *The British Accounting Review*, 37 (1), 115–133.

Chong, V.K., Eggleton, I.R., and Leong, M.K.C. (2006) The multiple roles of participative budgeting on job performance, *Advances in Accounting*, 22, 67–95.

Choudhury, N. (1986) Responsibility accounting and controllability, *Accounting and Business Research*, Summer, 189–198.

Clark, P. (2007) The rolling forecast as a catalyst for change, *Accountancy Ireland*, 39 (5), 22–24.

Cokins, G. (2008) Repairing the budgeting process, *Financial Executive*, 12, 45–49.

Collins, F. (1978) The interaction of budget characteristics and personality variables with budgetary response attitudes, *The Accounting Review*, 53 (2), 324–335.

Collins, F. (1982). Management accounting systems and control: a role perspective, *Accounting, Organizations and Society*, 7 (2), 102–122.

Colman, R. (2004) Better budgeting, *CMA Management*, 11, 14–15.

Comshare (2001) The 2001 survey of top financial executives: planning and budgeting today. Available at: www.comshare.com

Connolly, T., and Ashworth, G. (1994) An integrated activity-based approach to budgeting, *Management Accountant*, 72 (3), 32–37.

Daum, J. (2003) Beyond budgeting on the move – report from the First Annual Beyond Budgeting Summit in London, 1–2 July 2003. From http://www.juergendaum.com/news/07_04_2003.htm#Pioneers

Davila, T., and Wouters, M. (2005) Managing budget emphasis through the explicit design of conditional budgetary slack, *Accounting, Organizations and Society*, 30 (7/8), 587–608.

Dent, J. F. (1987). Tension in the design of formal control systems: a field study in a computing company. In *Accounting and Management: Field Study Perspectives* (eds W. J. Bruns and R. S. Kaplan), 119–145.

Dent, J.F. (1990) Strategy, organization and control: some possibilities for accounting research, *Accounting, Organizations and Society*, 15, 3–24.

Donaldson, L. (2001). *The Contingency Theory of Organizations*, Thousand Oaks, CA: Sage Publications.

Drury, C. (2000). *Management and Cost Accounting* (5th edition). London: Thompson International Business Press.

Dugdale, D., and Lyne, S. (2006) Budgeting, *Financial Management* (November), 32–35.

Dunk, A.S. (2011) Product innovation, budgetary control, and the financial performance of firms, *The British Accounting Review*, in press.

Dunk, A.S., and Lal, M. (1999) Participative budgeting, process automation, product standardization, and managerial slack propensities, *Advances in Management Accounting*, 8, 139–157.

Dunk, A.S. and Nouri, H. (1998) Antecedents of budgetary slack: a literature review and synthesis, *Journal of Accounting Literature*, 17, 72–96.

Durfee, D. (2006) Alternative budgeting, *CFO*, 22 (7), 28.

Dutton, J.E., Ashford, S.J., O'Neil, R.M., Hayes, E., and Wierba, E.E. (1997) Reading the wind: how middle managers assess the context for selling issues to top managers, *Strategic Management Journal*, 18 (5), 407–425.

Ekholm, B.G., and Wallin, J. (2000) Is the annual budget really dead?, *The European Accounting Review*, 9 (4), 519–539.

Emmanuel, C., Otley, D., and Merchant, K. (1990). *Accounting for Management Control*. Chapman & Hall: London.

Emsley, D. (2001) Budget-emphasis in performance evaluation and managers' job related tension: the moderating effect of information completeness, *The British Accounting Review*, 33 (3), 399–419.

Epstein, M.J., and Manzoni, J.F. (2002) *Reconciling conflicting roles of budgets: review and survey of corporate practices*. Working Paper, Rice University and INSEAD.

Ezzamel, M., and Hart, H. (1987) *Advanced Management Accounting: An Organizational Emphasis*. London: Cassell.

Fanning, J. (1999) Budgeting in the 21st century, *Management Accounting*, 24–25.

Filley, A. and House, R. (1969) *Managerial Process and Organizational Behaviour*. Glenview, IL: Scott, Foresman and Company.

Fisher, J.G., Frederickson, J.R. and Peffer, S.A. (2000) Budgeting: an experimental investigation of the effects of negotiation, *The Accounting Review*, 75 (1), 93–114.

Fisher, J.G., Frederickson, J.R. and Peffer, S.A. (2002) The effect of information asymmetry on negotiated budgets: an empirical investigation, *Accounting, Organizations and Society*, 27, 27–43.

Fisher, J.G., Maines, L.A., Peffer, S.A. and Sprinkle, G.B. (2002) Using budgets for performance evaluation: effects of resource allocation and horizontal information asymmetry on budget proposals, budget slack, and performance, *The Accounting Review*, 77 (4), 847–865.

Fisher, J.G., Frederickson, J.R. and Peffer, S.A. (2006) Budget negotiations in multi-period settings, *Accounting, Organizations and Society*, 31 (6), 511–528.

Fraser, R., and Hope, J. (2001) Beyond budgeting, *Controlling*, 13 (8–9), 437–442.

Frow, N., Marginson, D., and Ogden, S. (2005) Encouraging strategic behaviour while maintaining management control: multifunctional project teams, budgets, and the negotiation of shared accountabilities in contemporary enterprises, *Management Accounting Research*, 16 (3), 269–292.

Frow, N., Marginson, D., and Ogden, S. (2010) 'Continuous budgeting': reconciling budget flexibility with budgetary control, *Accounting, Organizations and Society*, 35, 444–461.

Garrison, R.E., Noreen, E.W., and Brewer, P.C. (2008) *Managerial Accounting* (12th edition). Irwin, McGraw-Hill.

Gary, L. (2003) Why budgeting kills your company [online] http://hbswk.hbs.edu/item/3623.html

Gordon, L.A., and Miler, D. (1976) A contingency framework for the design of accounting information systems, *Accounting, Organizations and Society*, 1, 59–70.

Greenberg, P.S., and Greenberg, R.H. (2006) Who needs budgets? You do, *Strategic Finance*, 88 (2), 41–45.

Gurton, A. (1999) Bye bye budget, *Accountancy*, March, London.

Hall, M. (2008) The effect of comprehensive performance measurement systems on role clarity, psychological empowerment and managerial performance, *Accounting, Organizations and Society*, 33 (2/3), 141–163.

Hansen, S.C. (2010) A theoretical analysis of the impact of adopting rolling budgets, activity-based budgeting and beyond-budgeting, *European Accounting Review*, 1–31.

Hansen, S., and Torok, R. (eds) (2004) *The Closed Loop: Implementing Activity-based Planning and Budgeting*. Indianapolis, IN: Bookman.

Hansen, S., Otley, D.T. and Van der Stede, W.A. (2003) Practice developments in budgeting: an overview and research perspective, *Journal of Management Accounting Research*, 15, 95–116.

Hansen, S.C., and Van der Stede, W.A. (2004) Multiple facets of budgeting: an exploratory analysis, *Management Accounting Research*, 15, 415–439.

Hartmann, F.G.H. (2000) The appropriateness of RAPM: toward the further development of theory, *Accounting, Organizations and Society*, 25 (4/5), 451–482.

Hartmann, F.G.H. (2005) The effects of tolerance for ambiguity and uncertainty on the appropriateness of accounting performance measures, *Abacus*, 41 (3), 241–264.

Hedberg, B., and Jonsson, S. (1978). Designing semi-confusing information systems for organizations in changing environments, *Accounting, Organizations and Society*, 3 (1), 47–64.

Hendersen, I. (1997) Does budgeting have to be so troublesome, *Management Accounting* (UK), October.

Hirst, M.K., and Yetton, P.W. (1999) The effects of budget goals and task interdependence on the level of and variance in performance: a research note, *Accounting, Organizations and Society*, 24, 205–216.

Hofstede, G.H. (1968) *The Game of Budgetary Control*. London: Tavistock.
Hofstede, G.H. (1978) The poverty of management control philosophy, *Academy of Management Review*, 3 (3), July, 450–461.
Hope, J., and Fraser, R. (1997) Beyond budgeting ... breaking through the barrier to the 'third wave', *Management Accounting*, 75 (11), 20–23.
Hope, J., and Fraser, R. (1998) Measuring performance in the new organizational model, *Management Accounting*, 76 (6), 23–33.
Hope, J., and Fraser, R. (1999a) Beyond budgeting: building a new management model for the information age, *Management Accounting*, 77 (1), 16–21.
Hope, J., and Fraser, R. (1999b) Budgets: the hidden barrier to success in the new information age, *Accounting & Business* (March), 24–26.
Hope, J., and Fraser, R. (1999c) Budgets: how to manage without them, *Accounting & Business* (April), 30–32.
Hope, J., and Fraser, R. (1999d) Take it away, *Accountancy*, 123 (1269), 50–54.
Hope, J., and Fraser, R. (2000) Beyond budgeting, *Strategic Finance*, 82 (4), October, 30–35.
Hope, J., and Fraser, R. (2001) Figures of hate, *Financial Management* (February), 22–25.
Hope, J. and Fraser, R. (2003a) *Beyond budgeting: how managers can break free from the annual performance trap*. Boston, MA: Harvard Business School Press.
Hope, J. and Fraser, R. (2003b) Who needs budgets? *Harvard Business Review*, 81 (2), February, 108–115.
Hope, J., and Fraser, R. (2003c) New ways of setting rewards: the beyond-budgeting model, *California Management Review*, 45 (4), 104–119.
Hopwood, A.G. (1972) An empirical study of the role of accounting data in performance evaluation. Empirical Research in Accounting. Supplement to *Journal of Accounting Research*, 10, 156–182.
Horngren, C., Bhimani, A., Datar, S.M. and Foster, G. (2002). *Management and Cost Accounting* (2nd edition). London: Prentice Hall.
Jensen, M.C. (2001) Corporate budgeting is broken, let's fix it, *Harvard Business Review*, 79 (10), 94–101.
Jensen, M.C. (2003) Paying people to lie: the truth about the budgeting process, *European Financial Management*, 9 (3), 379–406.
Kahn, R.L., Wolfe, D.M., Quinn, R.P. and Snoek, J.D. (1964). *Organizational Stress: Studies in Role Conflict and Ambiguity*. New York: John Wiley and Sons.
Lau, C.M., and Buckland, C. (2000) Budget emphasis, participation, task difficulty and performance: the effect of diversity within culture, *Accounting and Business Research*, 31 (1), 37–55.
Lau, C.M., and Buckland, C. (2001) Budgeting – the role of trust and participation: a research note, *Abacus*, 37 (3), 369–388.
Lau, C.M., and Chong, J. (2002) The effects of budget emphasis, participation and organizational commitment on job satisfaction: evidence from the financial services sector, *Advances in Accounting Behavioral Research*, 5, 183–211.
Lau, C.M., and Eggleton, I.R.C. (2002) The effects of participation and evaluative style on the propensity to create slack, *Accounting Research Journal*, 15 (1), 23–41.
Lau, C.M., and Eggleton, I.R.C. (2003) The influence of information asymmetry and budget emphasis on the relationship between participation and slack, *Accounting and Business Research*, 33 (2), 91–104.
Lau, C.M., and Eggleton, I.R.C. (2004) Cultural differences in managers' propensity to create slack, *Advances in International Accounting*, 17, 137–174.
Lau, C.M., and Lim, E.W. (2002a) The effects of procedural justice and evaluative styles on the relationship between budgetary participation and performance, *Advances in Accounting*, 19, 139–160.
Lau, C.M., and Lim, E.W. (2002b) The intervening effects of participation on the relationship between procedural justice and managerial performance, *The British Accounting Review*, 34 (1), 55–78.
Lau, C.M., and Ng, J. (2003) The influence of organizational commitment on the use of financial measures for performance evaluation, *Pacific Accounting Review*, 15 (1), 17–48.
Lau, C.M., and Tan, J.J. (2005) The importance of procedural fairness in budgeting, *Advances in Accounting*, 21, 333–356.
Lazere, C. (1998) All together now – why you must link budgeting and forecasting to planning and performance, *CFO Magazine*, February, 28–36.
Libby, T. (2001) Referent cognitions and budgetary fairness: a research note, *Journal of Management Accounting Research*, 13 (1), 91–105.

Libby, T., and Lindsay, R.M. (2003a) Budgeting – an unnecessary evil, *CMA Management*, 77 (1), 30–33.

Libby, T., and Lindsay, R.M. (2003b) Budgeting – an unnecessary evil, *CMA Management*, 77 (2), 28–31.

Libby, T., and Lindsay, R.M. (2003c) Booting the budget: how the BBRT envisions a world without budgets, *CMA Management Magazine* (April), 28–31.

Libby, T., and Lindsay, R.M. (2007a) Beyond budgeting or better budgeting?, *Strategic Finance*, August, 46–51.

Libby, T., and Lindsay, R.M. (2007b) Svenska Handelsbanken: controlling a radically decentralized organization without budgets, *Issues in Accounting Education*, 22 (4), 625–640.

Libby, T., and Lindsay, R.M. (2010) Beyond budgeting or budgeting reconsidered? A survey of North American budgeting practice, *Management Accounting Research*, 21, 56–75.

Lynn, M.P., and Madison, R.L. (2004) A closer look at rolling budgets, *Management Accounting Quarterly*, 6 (1), 60–64.

Maiga, A.S. (2005a) Antecedents and consequences of budget participation, *Advances in Management Accounting*, 14, 211–231.

Maiga, A.S. (2005b) The effect of manager's moral equity on the relationship between budget participation and propensity to create slack: a research note, *Advances in Accounting Behavioral Research*, 8, 139–165.

Marcino, G.R. (2000) Obliterate traditional budgeting, *Financial Executive*, Nov./Dec., Morristown.

Marginson, D. (1999) Beyond the budgetary control system: towards a two-tiered process of management control, *Management Accounting Research*, 10, 203–230.

Marginson, D. (2006). Information processing and management control: a note exploring the role played by information media in reducing role ambiguity, *Management Accounting Research*, 17, 187–197.

Marginson, D., and Ogden, S. (2005a). Coping with ambiguity through the budget: the positive effects of budgetary targets on managers' budgeting behaviours, *Accounting, Organizations and Society*, 30 (5), 435–456.

Marginson, D., and Ogden, S. (2005b) Managers, budgets and organizational change: unbundling some of the paradoxes, *Journal of Accounting and Organizational Change*, 1 (1), 45–62.

Marginson, D., Ogden, S., and Frow, N. (2006) *Budgets and innovation*. CIMA Report, cimaglobal.com

Marshall, J. (2003) Beyond budgeting: how managers can break free from the annual performance trap, *Financial Executive*, 19 (5), July/August, 19.

McNally, G.M. (1980). Responsibility accounting and organizational control: some perspectives and prospects, *Journal of Business Finance and Accounting*, 7 (2), 165–181.

Merchant, K.A. (1981) The design of the corporate budgeting system: influences on managerial behavior and performance, *The Accounting Review*, 56 (4), 813–829.

Merchant, K.A. (1984) Influences on departmental budgeting: an empirical examination of a contingency model, *Accounting, Organizations and Society*, 9 (3/4), 291–307.

Merchant, K.A. (1987) How and why firms disregard the controllability principle. In *Accounting and Management: Field Study Perspectives* (eds W. J. Bruns and R.S. Kaplan), 316–338.

Merchant, K.A., and Van der Stede, W.A. (2007). *Management Control Systems: Performance Measurement, Evaluation and Incentives* (2nd edition). Prentice-Hall, Harlow.

Needleman, T. (2005) New tools make for betting budgeting, forecasting, *Accounting Today*, July/August, 24/27.

Neely, A., Sutcliff, M.R. and Heyns, H.R. (2001) *Driving value through strategic planning and budgeting*, New York, NY: Accenture.

Neely, A., Bourne, M. and Chris, A. (2003) Better budgeting or beyond budgeting, *Measuring Business Excellence*, 7 (3), 22–28.

O'Connell, B. (2000) Beyond budgeting and forecasting: new tools, strategies making an old job easier, *Business Finance Magazine*. Available at: http://businessfinancemag.com (accessed 15 August 2012.

Oldman, A., and Mills, R. (1999) Abandoning traditional budgeting, *Management Accounting*, 77, November, 26.

Orlando, J. (2000) Turning budgeting pain into budgeting gain, *Strategic Finance*, 90 (9), 47–51.

Østergren, K., and Stensaker, I. (2010) Management control without budgets: a field study of 'beyond budgeting' in practice, *European Accounting Review*, 19 (1), 1–33.

Otley, D. (1978) Budget use and managerial performance, *Journal of Accounting Research*, 16 (1), 122–149.

Otley, D.T. (1982) Budgets and managerial motivation, *Journal of General Management*, 8, 26–42.

Otley, D.T. (1987). *Accounting Control and Organizational Behaviour*. Published in association with the CIMA, London: Heinmann.

Otley, D.T. (1994) Management control in contemporary organizations: towards a wider framework, *Management Accounting Research*, 5, 289–299.

Otley, D.T. (1999) Performance management: a framework for management control systems research, *Management Accounting Research*, 10 (4), 363–382.

Otley, D.T. and Fakiolas, A. (2000) Reliance on accounting performance measures: dead end or new beginning?, *Accounting, Organizations and Society*, 25 (4/5), 497–510.

Otley, D.T. and Pollanen, R.M. (2000) Budgetary criteria in performance evaluation: a critical appraisal using new evidence, *Accounting, Organizations and Society*, 25 (4/5), 483–496.

Parker, L.D. (2002) Twentieth-century textbook budgetary discourse: formalization, normalization and rebuttal in an Anglo-Saxon environment, *European Accounting Review*, 11 (2), 291–313.

Player, S. (2003) Why some organizations go Beyond Budgeting, *Journal of Corporate Accounting and Finance*, 14 (3), March/April, 3–9.

Prendergast, P. (2000) Budgets hit back, *Management Accounting* (UK), 78 (1), 14–16.

Quirin, J.J., Donnelly, D.P. and O'Bryan, D. (2000) Consequences of participative budgeting: the roles of budget-based compensation, organizational commitment, and managerial performance, *Advances in Management Accounting*, 9, 127–143.

Quirin, J.J., O'Bryan, D. and Donnelly, D.P. (2004) A nomological framework of budgetary participation and performance: a structural equation analysis approach, *Advances in Management Accounting*, 13, 143–165.

Rickards, R.C. (2008) An endless debate: the sense and nonsense of budgeting received, *International Journal of Productivity and Performance Management*, 57 (7), 569–592.

Ronen, J., and Livingston, J.L. (1975). An expectancy theory approach to the motivational impact of budgets, *The Accounting Review*, 671–685.

Searfoss, D.G. (1976) Some behavioural aspects of budgeting for control: an empirical study, *Accounting, Organizations and Society*, 1 (4), 375–385.

Simons, R. (2000) *Performance Measurement and Control Systems for Implementing Strategy*. Englewood Cliffs, NJ: Prentice-Hall.

Steele, R., and Albright, C. (2004) Games managers play at budget time, *Sloan Management Review*, 45 (3), 81–84.

Stevens, D. (2002) The effect of reputation and ethics on budgetary slack, *Journal of Management Accounting Research*, 14, 153–171.

Subramaniam, N., and Ashkanasy, N.M. (2001) The effect of organizational culture perceptions on the relationship between budgetary participation and managerial job-related outcomes, *Australian Journal of Management*, 26 (1), 35–54.

Subramaniam, N., and Mia, L. (2001) The relationship between decentralized structure, budgetary participation and organizational commitment: the moderating role of managers' value orientation towards innovation, *Accounting, Auditing and Accountability Journal*, 14 (1), 12–29.

Subramaniam, N., and Mia, L. (2003) A note on work-related values, budget emphasis and managers' organizational commitment, *Management Accounting Research*, 14 (4), 389–408.

Tsui, J.L.S. (2001) The impact of culture on the relationship between budgetary participation, management accounting systems, and managerial performance: an analysis of Chinese and Western managers, *International Journal of Accounting*, 36 (2), 125–146.

Umapathy, S. (1987) *Current Budgeting Practices in the US Industry*. New York: Quorum Books.

Urwick, L. (1939) *The Elements of Administration*. New York: Harper and Row.

Van der Stede, W.A. (2000) The relationship between two consequences of budgetary controls: budgetary slack creation and managerial short-term orientation, *Accounting, Organizations and Society*, 25, 609–622.

Van der Stede, W.A. (2001) Measuring 'tight budgetary control', *Management Accounting Research*, 12, 119–137.

Walker, K.B., and Johnson, E.N. (1999) The effect of budget-based incentive compensation scheme on the budgeting behavior of managers and subordinates, *Journal of Management Accounting Research*, 11, 1–28.

Waterhouse, J.H., and Tiessen, P. (1978) A contingency framework for management accounting systems research, *Accounting, Organizations and Society*, 3 (1), 65–76.

Webb, R.A. (2002) The impact of reputation and variance investigations on the creation of budget slack, *Accounting, Organizations and Society*, 27, 361–378.

Wentzel, K. (2002) The influence of fairness perceptions and goal commitment on managers' performance in a budgetary setting, *Behavioral Research in Accounting*, 14, 247–271.

Wetherbe, J.C., and Montanari, J.R. (1981) Zero-based budgeting in the planning process, *Strategic Management Journal*, 2 (1), 1–14.

Wilkinson, A. (2002) Empowerment. In Poole, M., and Warner, M. (eds), *International Encyclopaedia of Business Management: Handbook of Human Resource Management*. London: International Thomson Business Press.

3

Management accounting system problems in context of Lean

Development of a proposed solution

Thomas Borup Kristensen and Poul Israelsen

Introduction

Lean manufacturing philosophy, based on Toyota's production system, has been around for years (Schonberger, 1986, 1990, 1996; Womack et al., 1991) and forwarded as an ideal – world-class manufacturing – system to enable companies to compete on quality, product variety, and timeliness in a cost-effective and profitable manner. As a manufacturing philosophy it combines Just In Time (JIT), total quality management (TQM), and total preventive maintenance (TPM). In this paper we are interested in how implementation of Lean interacts with the company's management accounting system.

In the words of Åhlström and Karlsson (1996) there are seven main principles of Lean manufacturing: (i) elimination of waste (i.e. all non-value-adding activities, e.g. inventory, transportation, unnecessary movements), (ii) striving for zero defects as a prerequisite for JIT, (iii) pulling instead of push manufacturing (i.e. production to order as opposed to forecast), (iv) creation of multifunctional teams around product-dedicated production cells (as opposed to single-skilled employees in a functional machine layout), (v) decentralization of responsibility to these multi-skilled teams (i.e. delegation of procurement, materials handling, planning and control, maintenance, and quality control), (vi) creation of vertical and horizontal information systems that provide timely information continuously and directly in the production flow, and finally (vii) creation of a continuous improvement culture where improvement towards perfection is the goal.

In these Lean principles there is no or very little mention of the implications for the company's cost and management accounting system. However, if we look into the authorship of Schonberger, cost accounting can actually be abandoned: "non-monetary process data are the lifeblood of improvement projects – [they] tell what needs to be done and, to a very large extent, prioritize those needs. Cost data are not part of that improvement methodology" (1996: 104), and further: "Don't try to pin down all cost. . . . Instead, drive costs down and quality, response time, and flexibility up by plotting quality, cycle time, set-up time etc. on large visible screens on the wall. This is the cost effective way there is for upper managers and line employees alike to size up results . . ." (1996: 113). In the eyes of Schonberger, cost accounting is a problem rather than a solution to Lean implementation (Mouritsen and Hansen, 2006: 271). In this reasoning non-financial process, data form input for decision-making on improvements and cost reductions will automatically follow. This is puzzling: is it always the case that improvement decisions based on non-financial performance measures will lead to cost efficient cost reductions? Will it lead to the same type of improvement initiatives as if the decisions had been informed by cost calculations? If financial as well as non-financial measures are in use at the cell level what happens if they are in conflict, and how can this conflict be resolved?

Extant case-based research papers on the interaction between Lean implementation and management accounting change are limited. Among these are three in-depth single case studies by Åhlström and Karlsson (1996), Lind (2001), and Kennedy and Widener (2008). These studies report on changes made during Lean implementation encompassing, for example, organizational structure (e.g. functional vs. product groups), control forms (e.g. output, behavioral vs. social controls), and elements of the costing system (e.g. standard vs. actual cost). In none of the companies have the cost accounting system been abandoned, but changes have been made. All three studies directly or indirectly confirm that responsibility accounting must shift from the performance of the individual and individual machines to the cell level/team to align the decision authority and aggregation level of information. All companies also have a mix of financial and non-financial performance measures, and Lind (2001: 61) concludes that "Non-financial measures became dominant for day-to-day control; for long-term control both financial and non-financial measures were used". This is part of our intellectual puzzle: does short-term control using non-financial performance measures automatically align with long-term financial measures? Additionally, in one of the studies (Kennedy and Widener, 2008) standard cost was given up in favor of using only actual cost whereas in the two other studies standard cost was kept but changed to accommodate the cellular structure. This widens our puzzle: why is standard costing a potential problem in Lean settings?

The above leads to our research questions: what are the problems that companies encounter when Lean implementation meets the company's cost and management accounting system? And based on this, which changes can be made to have the goals of Lean and the financial measures of the management accounting system better cohere?

In addition, we find our endeavor justified by Lindsay and Kalagnanam (1993) forwarding the concern that if management accounting is not able to measure the consequences of Just In Time and Lean, there is a danger that it will become a potential blocker of Lean.

The remainder of the paper is organized as follows. In the following section we introduce the research design – case method – and the three case companies investigated in this paper. The following section summarizes across cases the interaction problems identified between Lean and the companies' management accounting systems. Then, the main section, develops and describes a new cost measurement system which is coherent with Lean – Lean financial accounting. This new model is contrasted to value stream mapping (usually used in Lean) and traditional cost models in relation to the decision support they provide. The final section sums up the paper, identifies limitations of the model developed and points to avenues of further research.

Method

The case study method is chosen to allow us to thoroughly understand which interaction problems between Lean control and management accounting control companies face. Yin (2003) defines case study as an investigation of a contemporary phenomenon within its real-life context with the benefits of prior theoretical development to guide data collection and analysis. In this paper the "contemporary phenomenon" is the interaction between Lean and a company's management accounting system. These particular case studies have the advantage of being longitudinal and the researchers spent three years collaborating with the companies. It has taken many hours of dialog (approximately 200 hours) with different company actors to understand how their Lean control package and management accounting system clashes, and why they believed they needed to be integrated and adapted to fit their specific context. Using a longitudinal approach we have witnessed the development of the actors' understanding of the Lean and management accounting system interaction as implementation of Lean is an ongoing process. We entered all companies at the point where they began to discuss the research topic, and it soon became obvious that they all had somewhat similar discussions on how to measure the Lean implementation, and how to guide the implementation in a financially informed way.

Common to the selected companies is that they are concerned with their ability to measure the profitability of their Lean efforts. While still convinced of having substantial Lean benefit they have recognized what they believed to be shortcomings within their existing management accounting and control systems. In understanding and dealing with this we are inspired by seeing this as a first step in researching "a real problem" (Nørreklit et al., 2006), i.e. it is neither just a practical nor solely a theoretical problem (Henriksen et al., 2004). If this was the case, and it merely comprised a practical problem, the actors would already have found suitable tools for solving it, and yet it is not only a theoretical problem as the actors see it.

In order to work in a manner consistent with finding real problems in the interaction between the cost models used and Lean, we employ Merchant's (2006) six general criteria for a complete measurement system. In addition, we use the theory of coherent systems (Nørreklit, 2000) in understanding these problems.

Speaking of cost models, i.e. how they are constructed and used in the Lean organization, we use this term interchangeably with management accounting system (MAS). According to Chenhall (2003) MAS refers to a collection of practices – such as costing – used to achieve goals. In this paper the goals are those of Lean. This focus on MAS leaves out discussions of other controls, such as clan or personal control, referred to as organizational control (Chenhall, 2003).

Merchant (2006) presents six criteria against which a management accounting system may be evaluated. These criteria are used to understand how well a particular MAS is developed to comply with them. There may be trade-offs among the criteria in question, and if so, they can be used to understand the weight put on each. In the paper, we use the six criteria to describe why particular MAS causes problems when interacting with Lean.

The use of coherence theory serves the same purpose, i.e. understanding the problems caused by management accounting systems in the Lean organization, and indicating how to develop solutions.

The six criteria that Merchant (2006) believes to be generic are whether: (i) the MAS is congruent with the organizational objectives, (ii) it is controllable by the manager whose behavior is being influenced; and whether or not the information is (iii) timely, (iv) accurate, (v) understandable, and (vi) cost-effective.

Merchant (2006) argues that goal congruence is the most important of these criteria, since "good" actions should cause an increase in the measured performance, while the reverse ought to be the case for "bad" actions. If this criterion is not fulfilled, then all the other criteria seem irrelevant (Otley, 1999). It is important to note that it is not only necessary for the measurement to be congruent with one of the organizational objectives, ideally speaking; it should be congruent with all of them.

The second criterion describes the importance of controllability by the manager. If a manager or team is not able to control the level of a measure it cannot provide information on the desirability of actions. The third criterion, timeliness, is about closing the time-lag between actions and measurement feedback. Accuracy is the fourth criterion and consists of two dimensions: precision and objectivity. A measure is precise if it is free of noise. Noise is random variation in the level of the measure that cannot be attributed to a systematic change in actions. Objectivity refers to the freedom from bias, such as the ability to manipulate the measure. The ability to withstand manipulation would strengthen the accuracy of the measure in question. The measure should also be readily understandable, which is the fifth criterion. It should be clear what the measure conveys and how it is calculated. Furthermore, it should be clear how the actors influence the measure, i.e. how they can improve it. The last criterion involves the cost-effectiveness of the measure. Preferably, the cost of producing the measures should be as low as possible, and the benefits should exceed the costs of obtaining them.

As mentioned in the introduction we would expect the Lean organization in manufacturing to use a mix of financial and non-financial performance measures. It is this paper's intention to find out if these measures induce decision-making and improve behavior in the same direction – if they work together, if they cohere. For example, lead time is often an important measure in Lean (Kennedy and Brewer, 2005), but improved lead time does not always cause improved labor consumption variance in a standard cost model. On the one hand, while increasing the number of manpower hours on the production line will often cause improved lead time, it can also cause increased unfavorable time consumption variance, mainly due to increased available capacity not being used. On the other hand, a higher unfavorable time variance does not necessarily cause an improved lead time, as the faster processing time might just result in a longer stock time. Therefore, lead time and time consumption clearly have to be considered simultaneously in a balanced manner if the overall profit goal is to be improved. When the actors understand the nature of the mutual logical dependencies, and act to balance these in order to increase the overall goals, these relations become coherent (Nørreklit, 2000).

Research site selection

Space does not allow a thorough account of the case companies and our case-individual findings.[1] We introduce each of the three companies with a few lines below, and provide in section 3 a summary of findings across companies.

Case company A

Company A is the smallest of the three case companies, with around 2,000 employees. The headquarters is located in Scandinavia while its production facilities are located in Scandinavia, Eastern Europe, and the US. Company A produces a range of small electronic equipment for business customers. It is a family-owned company that has expanded immensely since the present owner introduced new products in the 1970s.

Since 2003, when several Lean tools such as JIT, Kanban, 5S, Lean office, Kaizen etc. were implemented, the company has been dedicated to Lean. The company also changed its organizational structure at this point in time. The new structure involved a product line for each product group resembling value streams even though all product groups still have some functions, inventory and packaging in common.

Case company B

With around 20,000 employees worldwide, case company B has its headquarters in the same country as the other two case companies. Company B is, unlike Company A, listed on the stock exchange.

While the company had a lot of financial difficulties a few years ago, today it is a profitable, heavy-duty industrial company with production facilities and sales offices in most regions of the world. In this case study we only focus on one of its production divisions employing around 2,500.

The company has been much engaged in Lean since 2005. In 2008 it won a prize for productivity improvement made through transition from birdcage production to flowline production. The company is working with most of the tools in the Lean tool-box (Bicheno, 2004), and Lean is perceived to be a necessary strategy if the company is to create sustainable growth. Although the company's value chain begins by casting some of the components themselves, it still buys approximately 90% of all components from outside, which end up in assembly and on-site delivery. Even though most of the value chain is controlled by Company B, it still has thousands of suppliers. With the implementation of a Lean strategy, Company B has accomplished many of its goals, such as major lead time reduction and increases in stock turns.

Case company C

Case Company C is in the fashion industry, employing around 10,000 workers worldwide, and has its headquarters in Scandinavia too. The company has a long value chain within its own legal control. Originally it also bred the very raw materials, animals, used in the leather tanneries under its control. Today, its control of the value chain begins in the tanneries and ends in its private consumer shops around the world. The business has been successful for many years and is well known for the quality of its products. In this case company our focus is on the factories at the end of the value chain, which have responsibility for the final four major process steps to finish the final product. Company C has to introduce new product collections twice a year in keeping with the trend amongst its competitors and the expectations of its customers. While some of the products may be in the product portfolio for several years, most are changed completely each season.

Having worked with Lean initiatives for several years, Company C is very aware of adopting a bottom-up approach to Lean implementation by educating many of its local employees to become Lean experts. Company C has tried to create a strong focus on the payback of Lean and has even hired a Lean controller to assess the general profitability of Lean. As within Companies A and B, Company C has had many internal discussions about the economic impact of Lean. Company C could see some improvements in lead time as various WIP stocks were reduced, but struggled to trace the lead time effects to improved cost efficiency. In this case, Lean implementation included a broad range of the Lean tools, primarily value stream mapping, Kanban, 5S, visual boards, Kaizen events and single piece-flow.

Identified interaction problems between Lean and MAS

The analysis of the three case companies can be summarized in a number of points. The ten points below cover the problems with the current cost models in the three case companies vis-à-vis Merchant's six principles and the theory of coherence. Points 9 and 10 identify the main behavioral effects.

1. The companies have difficulty in measuring the profit improvement achieved through Lean.
2. Companies have difficulty in measuring Lean progress in financial terms through multiple periods during which standard costs are inevitably changed.

3. Cost of quality in their currently implemented cost model does not contain all waste categories of Lean, and traditional notions of waste are not always equivalent to the concepts of waste forwarded by Lean thinking.
4. Cost of capital does not include imputed cost which hampers costing of lead time, e.g. stocks.
5. Some capacity costs are misleadingly allocated to the unit level, e.g. cost of water spiders, which impedes insights as to what drives costs. (Water spiders are personnel mostly working in the productions cells as helpers, planners and transporters.)
6. The rich data on deviations from takt time shown on the takt time boards (also called Andon boards) at the shop floor is not picked up and used in the management accounting system. (Takt time is the time between finished products leaving the production cell.)
7. Detailed process information, especially on waste, collected in the value stream maps,VSMs, is not used in the management accounting system. (VSM includes important information regarding process time, lead time, takt time, stock sizes, shared resources, shifts, and the process- and planning-flow (Rother and Shook, 1999).)
8. Normal learning curve effects are mixed with Lean improvements.
9. Line operators have no access to information stated in the traditional variance reports and, consequently, have no sense of ownership of the data registered to produce these reports, hampering data quality.
10. Traditional standard cost models support a management-by-exception way of thinking as opposed to Lean's continuous improvement; standard cost models focus on unexpected cost of waste whereas Lean looks for expected as well as unexpected cost of waste.

The case companies' currently used cost models are variations of textbook cost models, i.e. standard cost models and variance reporting. Thus, the findings offer some general cost model problems in which traditional cost models fail to fully complement the Lean journey. These shortcomings can be overcome using a new Lean financial model, outlined below.

Improved costing to support and assess Lean

The solution developed and presented is based on problems with the measurement systems found in the three companies. The solution presented uses a modified example from one of the case companies. The solution has been discussed in plenary sessions with representatives from all three companies, who found it useful as a source of inspiration, and contributed to making the proposed solution even more solid.

The example begins in Figure 3.1 with a flow layout providing the overview of how the products are physically moved and how machines and labor are located. In Table 3.1 an activity path is presented, describing in numbers what happens in the production flow. A visual board on a numerical example week (Table 3.2) presents all the problems the workers experienced during the week. The information on the visual board and in the activity path (together with input data in appendix 1) is the foundation of three different types of reporting: (i) a traditional cost-of-waste financial report, (ii) a regular Lean report showing lead time, and (iii) our developed Lean financial model showing more cost-of-waste categories than the traditional financial model. The latter guides the decision-makers towards relevant Lean waste types, and the enhanced insights obtained by the Lean financial model eliminate the problems identified with the two other models.

Figure 3.1's drawing of the production layout shows that the site consists of three buildings: stock 1, stock 2, and factory 1. Stocks, as well as the factory floor, are split between value streams

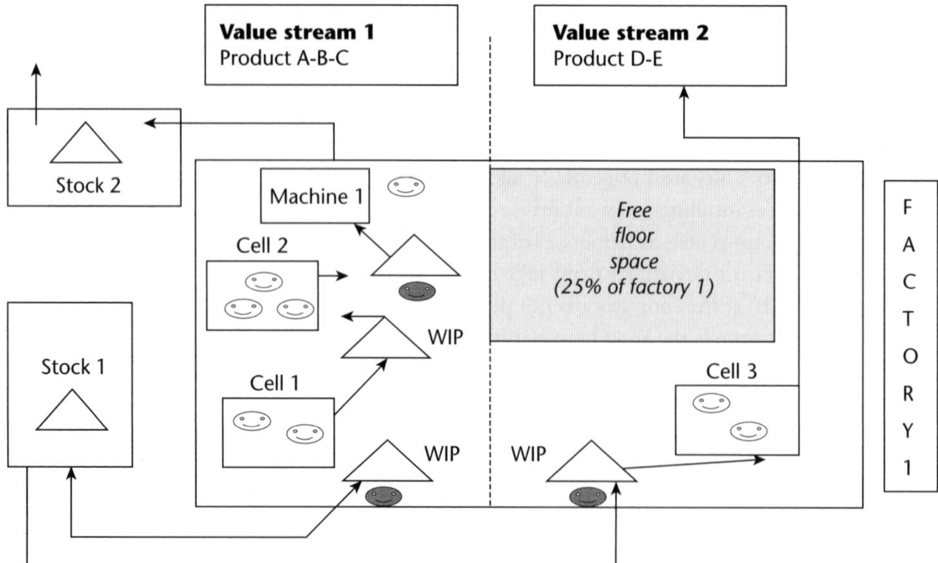

Figure 3.1 The flow layout and activity path in the example

1 and 2. The value streams are dedicated to products and thus a value stream refers to the processes and assets dedicated to producing products within a product group. Maskell (2004) describes this as the Lean way to organize, where resources are dedicated to individual value streams. In turn, these value streams are defined by products that have similar flow patterns. "Monuments", for example a machine, refers to shared resources across two or more value streams and are to be avoided in Lean as they will cause a "batch and queue" production (mass production [Womack et al., 1991]) instead of single-piece flow production. In order to keep the example short we focus on value stream 1 only.

The activity path, Table 3.1, shows the process steps to make the final products out of the raw materials. It shows the standard labor and materials consumption required to make each unit or batch. Labor is divided between that of operators and water spiders (grey in the layout diagram). As previously mentioned, water spiders mostly work in the cells as helpers, planners and transporters. The data on the activity path is part of the company's detailed value stream map, VSM, jointly created by operators and Lean change agents. They also jointly carry out the necessary updates as the VSM is improved.

In the traditional reporting presently employed within the companies, consisting of regular standard cost system output (Horngren et al., 1997; Horngren et al., 2010), the degree of information regarding the detailed processes within the individual cells is very modest. In fact, the company's traditional reporting only uses the total standard time registered for each cell. The reason is that the costing system is not integrated with the information contained in the detailed value stream map. According to the current system, the cell is considered the unit of responsibility and measured in terms of variances from the standard.

It is worth noting that cell operator 1 is the pacemaker (bottleneck) of value stream 1, as operator 1 is responsible for the process step with the longest time consumption, and that in traditional reporting the work carried out within the cells is termed "direct hours" and all other labor activities are considered indirect in nature.

Table 3.1 The activity path for value stream 1

Resource	*Activity path for value stream 1*	*Standard*
	Per unit – if not otherwise stated	
Stock 1	Stock 1 storage	5 days
Water spider	Transport of materials per batch	180 sec
Factory 1	Storage (average time)	1 hour
Water spider	Scheduling and planning per batch	2,500 sec
Water spider	Expected extra scheduling – rescheduling (rework) once every 5 batches	2,000 sec
Materials	Bill of Materials per unit	1 pc
	Cell 1 activities (per unit) – bottleneck (special tools)	
Operator 1	1. Shaping components	310 sec
Operator 2	2. Getting special power tools (movement)	10 sec
Operator 2	3. Surface treatment	250 sec
Operator 2	4. Transport materials to WIP	10 sec
Operator 2	5. Time expected for screwdriver problems (incorrect process)	10 sec
Operator 2	Cell 1 imbalance (1) (2+3+4+5)	30 sec
	Cell 1 total standard time	**620 sec**
Factory 1	WIP storage	2 hours
Water spider	Moving WIP into cell 2	15 sec
	Cell 2 activities	
Operator 1	1. Drilling holes	280 sec
Operator 1	2. Moving between two power tools	7 sec
Operator 2	3. Montage	200 sec
Operator 2	4. Moving around the product unit to get in right position	15 sec
Operator 3	5. Welding	300 sec
Water spider	6. Inspection	25 sec
Water spider	7. Transport materials to WIP	20 sec
Operator 2	8. Time expected for power tool problems (incorrect process.)	20 sec
Operator 1+2	Cell 2 imbalance (5) (1+2)+(5)-(3+4+8)	78 sec
	Cell 2 total standard time	**945 sec**
Operator 1+2+3	Cell 1 and 2 imbalance (bottleneck process time 310 sec)	30 sec
Factory 1	WIP storage (average time)	1 hour
	Machine 1 (23 painting slots in machine per batch)	
Water spider	Moving WIP into machine 1 – per Batch	300 sec
Operator	Loading machine with paint per batch	200 sec
Operator	Set-up of machine per batch	200 sec
Machine 1	Machine 1– painting the batch	4,500 sec
Operator	Managing and steering the machine per batch	4,500 sec
Operator/machine 1	Machine breakdown time expected per batch (waiting time)	200 sec
Water spider	Inspection of finished goods per batch	100 sec
	Machine 1 total standard time per batch	**5,500 sec**
Machine 1	**(Imbalance with cells) available time on machine 1 per batch**	**2,030 sec**
Materials	Paint used per batch in machine 1	10,000 ml
Materials	Paint wasted inside machine – not usable 2% per batch	20 ml
Operator	Adjusting – reworking some of the units per unit	13 sec
Water spider	Transport of finished goods to stock 2 per batch	300 sec
Stock 2	Storage (average time)	10 days
Materials	Scrap of finished goods by inspection per batch	1 pc

(Continued)

Table 3.1 (continued)

Resource	*Activity path for value stream 1*	*Standard*
Traditional reporting		
Direct hours	**Total operator/water spider direct (hours) standard time per unit – sec**	**1,795**
Lean reporting		
Unit hours	**Total operator/water spider standard time per unit without waste – sec**	**1,340**
Batch hours	**Total operator/water spider standard time per batch without waste – sec**	**7,200**

Visual board data of the example week

In the example, the company has now implemented visual boards on the shop floor. The visual boards are used by operators and foremen to follow on an hourly basis whether they are ahead of or behind their planned production targets, based on the takt time. They also use the boards in discussing how to handle deviations from plans. Hence, the visual board is a working tool in co-ordinating and fixing problems. In the process they also collect information on the nature (cause) of deviations. During discussions they write down their immediate analyses of causes of deviations. All these data are collected by the water spider and entered into the costing function of the company's ERP system to be used in relation to cost reporting weekly. This data collection is part of our solution. Hence, information is not lost when the visual boards are erased at the end of the week, and there is no need to have other types of registration in order to gather shop-floor data on deviations. In addition, the information gained from the visual boards is more precise, as operators and foremen themselves use this information to improve their work, which is therefore less prone to manipulation. Integration of the visual board and cost reporting also creates a more coherent reporting system as deviations reflected on the visual board are aligned with the cost reporting reflecting reality in a similar manner. As operators and foremen believe the data to be precise, cost reporting can also be used to improve decision-making at shop-floor level from a profitability (mainly cost-saving) perspective.[2]

Visual board data are very simple and cost-efficient to use in the company's cost accounting system – particularly since it is only necessary to register deviations, which is readily done as visual boards are a compulsory activity/tool in a Lean environment.

Table 3.2 The visual board

Visual board of this week's actual consumption	
Value stream 1	
Actual finished units (including scrap)	322
Actual finished batches	14
Scrap per batch	2
Total operator hours actual (6 operators, 8 hours a day, 5 days)	240
Total water spider hours actual (2 water spiders, 8 hours a day, 5 days)	80
Actual paint consumed less standard ml	100
Reported visual board deviations	
Problems with tools in cell 1 (incorrect processing) – working slower – 1 batch missed	2 hours
Cell 2 had trouble keeping up the pace and was 400 sec slower on one batch (no lost batch as this is not a bottleneck)	400 sec

In the example, the visual board shows that 322 units are completed in 14 batches. Scrapped are two pieces per batch compared to a standard scrap value of one per batch according to the activity path. Total hours for operators and water spiders are equivalent to the number of hours for which they are paid. Another registration in Table 3.2 shows that they had used 100 ml more paint than specified in the activity path. Furthermore, the foreman recorded a major problem with the tools in cell 1 (the pacemaker process) which caused them to work slower, hence missing a batch of 15 pieces of the product. Cell 2 reported some small problems with keeping up the pace of 400 seconds.

Traditional profit reporting

Table 3.3 shows what traditional reporting involves. This report is common to the three case companies and is an almost complete copy of the one used in Company C. Additionally, it is similar to that reported in a traditional standard cost regime (Atkinson et al., 2007; Cheatam and Cheatam, 1996).

Column 3 is the budget, column 1 the actual costs, and column 2 the flexible budget. The difference between columns 2 and 3 is caused by a lower number of units produced, as column 2 is calculated on the basis of the actual production volume multiplied by the standard costs per unit. The difference between columns 1 and 2 is the difference between actual and standard consumption for the actual volume. Appendix 1 contains the input data used to make the calculations.

The actual numbers come from the visual board. This is not the case in Company B, for example, where a scanning system of completed products provides the feed-in data for the calculations. However, we use the visual board data in the following to keep the comparison between the traditional and our new reporting simple.

Table 3.3 The traditional reporting format

	Value stream 1		
	1	*2*	*3*
	Actual production volume x actual price (consumption)	*Actual production volume x standard price (consumption)*	*Scheduled volume x standard price*
Revenue (equal production)	29,400	29,400	33,000
Direct labor (operator – water spider in cells)	3,718	3,666	4,115
Materials (bom + paint)	2,515	2,515	2,755
Contribution margin 1	*23,166*	*23,219*	*26,131*
Indirect variable costs (operators – water spiders)	3,932	4,160	3,599
Contribution margin 2	*19,234*	*19,059*	*22,532*
Materials loss (paint)	29	28	30
Scrap (materials)	234	117	125
Scrap (labor)	349	175	287
Contribution margin 3	*18,622*	*18,740*	*22,090*
Capacity costs	1,000	1,000	1,000
Depreciations	1,000	1,000	1,000
Profit before interest	*16,622*	*16,740*	*20,090*

Table 3.4 Cost of waste – traditional perspective

Cost of waste from a traditional perspective		
1 – 2	Direct labor (unexpected) fixing prod stop	53
2	Materials loss (expected)	28
1 – 2	Materials loss (unexpected)	1
2	Materials scrap (expected)	117
1 – 2	Materials scrap (unexpected)	117
2	Labor scrap (expected)	175
1 – 2	Labor scrap (unexpected)	175
1 – 3	Increase indirect labor (unexpected) 1 batch "lost"	334
	Total expected cost of waste	*319*
	Total unexpected cost of waste	*679*
	Total cost of waste	**998**

In the traditional regime, costs of scrap materials (materials used in the units not usable for sales), materials loss (paint not applied to the product units and "lost" in the machine or too much applied) and labor scrap (that used in completing scrapped units) constitute cost of waste. Notice, increase in indirect variable labor would be perceived as waste. This approach would lead to the cost of waste expressed in Table 3.4, where we differentiate between expected and unexpected. The standards multiplied by actual production volume (column 2's flexible budget) are an expression of expected costs. Consequently, unexpected costs are additional costs. Unexpected costs are unfavorable variances. Information regarding the cost of waste guides future Lean initiatives towards certain waste types and focus areas.

Viewing the cost of waste in the manner of Table 3.4 constitutes the predominant structure of the three case companies. It mainly perceives waste as something caused by failures or something going "wrong". Expected paint loss (materials loss) is the only exception to this, as this is a direct result of following process specifications and cannot be avoided no matter how much caution is pursued during execution or how much quality focus is exhibited in the process.

This report would guide Lean activities towards the increase in indirect costs and the fact that one batch was missed leading to a lower productivity level than standard. The latter would be interpreted as unexpected time consumption caused by the batch that was "lost" due to tool problems in cell 1. It would also provide focus for improving the unexpected waste of direct labor which has consumed more time than that specified in the standard. It would point to scrap being the main cost of waste from the traditional perspective.

In case company B the direct/indirect cost ratio was used as an expression of value-added vs. waste. In the current example, this ratio is 48.6% (3,718/(3,718+3,932)), as direct labor constitutes almost half the total number of hours. The example clearly shows that this does not reflect the available capacity, as presented in the section on Lean financial reporting below. In addition, it assumes that direct labor is entirely value-added, i.e. not waste, which is an incorrect assumption in terms of waste defined in Lean.

Value stream reporting from a strict Lean perspective

A strict Lean perspective would focus on non-financial measures. According to one of the founding fathers of the Activity Based Costing model, Johnson (1992), this model or any other financial model (Schonberger, 1990, 1996) is irrelevant, as this type of accounting information is too late, too aggregated and too distorted to be relevant for a manager's planning and control activity. This

Table 3.5 Lean KPI reporting

LEAN KPI reporting	
Lead time stock (materials and finished goods stock)	15 days
Lead time WIP storage	4 hours
Lead time process	2.1 hours

approach is equivalent to that presented in the Toyota house, where Lean tools are the foundation and pillars of improved profitability (Liker, 2004, 2006; see Appendix 2 for a picture of the house). And none of the Lean tools are management accounting tools. A main analytical tool in Lean is the value stream map (Rother and Shook, 1999), which focuses on lead time. However, lead time does not cost the same from one process to another; for example, a product sitting for one minute in inventory is much less costly than a minute in machining (Friis et al., 2007).

Using the lead time indicators in Table 3.5, Lean activities would focus on stocks, seeing that this entails by far the largest lead time. However, as a chief controller in Company B said: "These Lean activities always seem to be addressing lead time and this is easiest to cut either in terms of work-in-progress or finished goods but the cost impact is either low or difficult to trace."

Based on traditional cost reporting we concluded that Lean activities should focus on scrap. This is different to value stream mapping that would focus on reducing lead time in relation to both the materials and finished goods stock – or WIP. The economic benefits of reducing stock are difficult to track on the basis of traditional cost reporting. Evidently these two reporting tools are not working coherently; they have different perspectives on what are the best Lean initiatives to take, and hence create confusion within the organization.

Lean financial reporting – cost of waste from a Lean perspective

In the last 15 years new approaches to accounting for Lean have evolved based on critiques of the standard cost model (Kennedy and Widener, 2008; Kaplan and Cooper, 1998; Cunningham, 2003; Huntzinger, 2007; Fry et al., 1995). Maskell and Baggaley (2004), especially, create a costing model based on actual costs instead of standard costs in their approach to Lean accounting, and focus on the value stream as cost object. This approach is found to suit Lean in Kennedy and Widener's recent study (2008).

Contrary to Johnson (e.g. 1992) and Schonberger (1990, 1996), the approach by Maskell and Baggaley (2004) recognizes the fact that a cost model cannot be excluded from the Lean organization, but rather that the right fit would be an *actual cost* model.

There are two main types of critique against the standard cost model's fit with Lean. First, it motivates non-Lean goal-congruent behavior (Maskell and Baggaley, 2004). However, this critique is implicitly based on the assumption that the cost model is used in a coercive manner according to Kristensen and Israelsen (2010). They show that this assumption is not valid in all circumstances as the standard cost model can be used in an enabling manner, leading to Lean goal-congruent behavior.

The second critique of standard costing is that the technique is misleading in itself due to a confusing allocation of non-unit cost to the unit level. This critique assumes that standard costing is used in the full cost version and creates the over/under costing phenomenon we are familiar with from, e.g., ABC's critique of traditional full costing (Kaplan and Cooper, 1998). Yet, in the three case companies standard costing is not used in a full cost version for management accounting purposes.

In a third critique, standard costing is criticized for hiding waste within standards (Maskell and Baggaley, 2004). It is true that standards are often set without a distinction between the waste types known in Lean. This is similar to our observations in the three case companies. This is not a critique, we will argue, that cannot be solved within a model that works with standards. In our solution we present a model, Table 3.6, based on the principles of using standards which entail separate categories for each waste type in Lean.

In Table 6 we have incorporated the seven waste types presented by Liker (2006): rework/scrap, movement, transport, waiting time, incorrect processing, overproduction and inventory. In addition, we have added imbalance time – which is a form of waiting time – and inspection, which is sometimes also considered waste in Lean (Bicheno, 2004). We have also included set-up as a waste category even though we generally accept that without set-ups there can only be single-product production (Kaplan and Cooper, 1998). However, reduction of set-up time is essential in making Just In Time work, and in Lean certain tools have been developed to reduce set-up time, especially single-minute-exchange-of-die, SMED (Bicheno, 2004).

As depicted in the last two columns of Table 3.6 standards are clearly needed if we are to successfully complete budgets in which cost of waste is stated. Standards are formed within the value stream analysis which we labelled the "activity path" of a VSM. In order to understand how the cost of waste changes just because we change the product mix and volume in response to a given budget change, it is necessary to have standards. And, without standards it is not possible to assess how much capacity is available compared to process consumption and waste. Since the system of scanning actual time consumption has been abandoned we can only use standards and visual board information on exceptions in assessing available capacity.[3]

Cost of capital is introduced to address the problem of not having income statement consequences of stocks. This cost of capital does not reflect costs that can be traced back to company expenses – as do other costs; on the contrary, it is the rate of return required by investors and loan providers: weighted average cost of capital, WACC. The approach is similar to that of the residual income model. In our example the cost of capital is 15%. In calculating the cost of capital per value stream it is possible to address the financial value of reducing stock and thereby represent the financial value of lead time in stocks. Additionally, it is possible to evaluate the financial impact of lead time changes and to assess whether or not a reduction would result in sufficient gains in financial value compared to those achieved through adjustment of other waste types.

The Lean financial model also differentiates between unit-level cost drivers and batch-level cost drivers of waste, viz. Table 3.6. This is done in order to avoid the weaknesses in the traditional full cost model critiqued, for example, in the ABC (Kaplan and Cooper, 1998) and variability accounting literature (Israelsen, 1993, 1994). This way it is easier to predict the financial outcome of differently focused Lean kaizen events. Furthermore, it is possible to understand ex post why the cost of waste changes at batch level simply because of changes in the number of batches initiated.

A main advantage of our Lean financial model is the way in which it fully and clearly defines all waste types.[4] Addressing different waste types calls for the application of different Lean tools. For example, while reduction of stocks calls for increased work with Just In Time, reduction of scrap and rework requires improved human attention – poka yoke (Carriera, 2005). As we have seen in our case companies, every company must decide which aspects of Lean they wish to emphasize on their Lean journey. Resources for implementing Lean will always be scarce, therefore it is necessary to have the right decision-making support to optimize cost-benefit trade-offs. Without this guidance it is a blindfolded decision process.

Johnson's (1992) point of view is that all Lean tools constitute the right way to do things in any given situation. Even if one agrees with this proposition, we would still need some guidance

Table 3.6 Lean financial reporting

	Value stream 1		
	1	*2*	*3*
	Actual production volume x actual price (consumption)	*Actual production volume x standard price (consumption)*	*Scheduled volume x standard price*
Revenue	29,400	29,400	33,000
Unit-level labor (operators – water spider)	2,739	2,736	3,071
Unit-level materials (bom & paint)	2,515	2,515	2,755
Unit-level contribution margin 1	*24,146*	*24,149*	*27,174*
Unit-level materials loss (paint)	29	28	30
Scrap (materials)	234	117	125
Unit-level inspection	56	56	60
Unit-level movement	105	105	113
Unit-level transport	67	67	72
Unit-level scrap (labor)	261	130	140
Unit-level rework	29	29	31
Unit-level waiting time	350	0	0
Unit-level incorrect processing	117	67	72
Unit-level imbalance	309	309	331
Unit-level contribution margin 2	*22,590*	*23,241*	*26,202*
Batch-level labor (operators – water spiders)	700	700	750
Batch margin 1	*21,890*	*22,541*	*25,452*
Set-up	19	19	21
Batch-level inspection	10	10	10
Batch-level movement	29	29	31
Batch-level transport	47	47	50
Batch-level rework and rescheduling	39	39	42
Batch-level waiting time	19	19	21
Batch-level incorrect processing	0	0	0
Batch-level imbalance with cells	197	197	211
Batch margin 2	*21,529*	*22,180*	*25,065*
Value stream sustaining (avoidable operators)	1,425	1,425	1,425
Available labor operators – not bottleneck cell	56	345	58
Available labor operators on bottleneck cell (1)	28	172	29
Value-stream sustaining – (avoidable water spiders)	1,398	1,498	1,468
Depreciation for available machine time	240	290	240
Depreciation for wasted machine time	322	272	292
Depreciation for machine time consumed	438	438	469
Value stream capacity costs (engineer)	1,000	1,000	1,000
Profit before imputed interest	*16,622*	*16,740*	*20,090*
Raw materials stock – cost of capital	4	4	4
WIP storage materials – cost of capital	1	0	1
Finished goods – cost of capital	8	7	8
Stock facilities – cost of capital	87	81	87
Machine assets – cost of capital	29	29	29
Factory occupancy – cost of capital	288	288	288
Profit after imputed interest	*16,206*	*16,330*	*19,674*

on where to begin with Lean to achieve the biggest financial impact, and on how intensely each tool should be implemented. Stretching all Lean tools to their limit in every company would be the equivalent of perceiving Lean to be universally profitable. This is not true, of course, as companies work under different contingencies and need to adapt to these in different ways, which in turn involves different weighting of Lean tools. The waste types incorporated are those that Lean claim to be able to reduce by means of different tools. This is similar to knowing which actions (tools) will affect costs in a certain way, and this involves the controllability and accuracy principles of Merchant's approach. The goal of Lean is to reduce waste and monitor the progress of these reductions, something that can be rendered explicit by the measurements of the Lean financial model.

Finally, it is important to bear in mind that our Lean financial model is not aimed at supporting a "management by exception" culture. On the contrary, it aims to support a continuous improvement approach, for which reason we have made the expected cost of waste explicit in standards, as it is just as important to manage and focus on these in Lean activities as it is to manage and focus on the unexpected cost of waste. This way, it is possible to determine which Lean initiatives would be the best to pursue and where in the processes they ought to be activated in order to make the greatest financial impact.

The relativity measure as an indicator of Lean progress

While studying the three case companies it became apparent that they faced challenges in finding financial KPIs for their Lean progress. Assessing Lean progress from a traditional standard costing model perspective is difficult over multiple periods as standards change. Alternatively, actual costs could be compared to revenues or number of units (Maskell and Baggaley, 2004). Yet this too is difficult to compare, as we may experience product mix changes. Furthermore, costs are subject to inflation and if this varies over the years cost-to-unit/revenue ratios are affected.

Another difficulty using this ratio in measuring Lean progress is the non-explicit handling of available capacity. This is especially problematic during the first couple of years of Lean implementation where the effect of Lean mainly creates available capacity not yet consumed by sales growth (Cunningham, 2003). This aspect of making the cost of available capacity explicit is part of measuring Lean progress, as Lean is not about laying people off but rather a cost-efficient growth strategy (Womack and Jones, 2003).

Moreover, it may be difficult to compare revenues with actual costs as a measure of Lean progress if the company has powerful customers or the market is tightly controlled by competitors with successful Lean programs (Cooper and Slagmulder, 1999). In these situations it is likely that cost improvements will be more beneficial to customers than to the company itself (Lewis, 2000). So the result would be a reduction in revenues compared to costs, and the Lean progress would be perceived as unsuccessful – i.e. the margins of the company would not increase.

A final disadvantage of using actual costs as a Lean progress indicator is the lack of ability to identify areas in which the company could benefit the most from Lean initiatives. If the cost model does not show the cost of all waste types it cannot effectively show where Lean tools can potentially remove waste and which tools to pick for the job.

Inspired by Maskell and Baggaley (2004), we introduce the relativity measure. This consists of the relative percentage of costs for:

1. process consumed costs (neither available nor waste) – i.e. value-added;
2. cost of waste;

3. cost of available capacity;
4. value stream sustaining costs.

The process consumed costs are those found in the activity path as neither available nor waste. The cost of waste is based on the waste registered in Lean. The available capacity consists of both idle time at the bottleneck resource in cell 1 and idle labor in the other cells. Furthermore, the time assigned to imbalance time is also perceived as available time. The value stream sustaining costs consists of time consumed by activities such as breaks, meetings and the like. This time is standard and assigned according to Appendix 1. These activities could also be analyzed further in the same style as costs in the activity path; however, we do not pursue this as it would be more a study of Lean in administrative processes.

Our example reporting of the relativity measure is shown in Table 3.7 and summarized in Table 3.8.

Table 3.7 separates expected and unexpected costs and shows in some cases "negative" unexpected cost. This happens for instance in "bottleneck cell available labor" as a consequence of

Table 3.7 Cost of waste according to the Lean financial model and the relativity measure

	Unexpected	*Expected*	*Relativity measure*
1. Process consumed (not available nor waste)			
Materials	0	2,515	**90.5%**
Labor (slower pace)	3	3,436	**43.0%**
Machine time	0	450	**43.8%**
2. Cost of Waste			
Materials loss (paint)	1	28	
Scrap (materials)	117	117	
Cost of waste materials			**9.5%**
Inspection	0	66	
Movement	0	134	
Transport	0	114	
Scrap (labor)	130	130	
Rework	0	68	
Waiting time	350	19	
Incorrect processing	50	67	
Set-up	0	19	
Cost of waste labor			**14.4%**
Wasted machine time	50	280	**32.1%**
Stock cost	7	92	**100.0%**
3. Available			
Bottleneck cell available labor (operators)	–144	172	**0.3%**
Imbalance labor	0	506	**6.3%**
Machine available	–50	299	**24.2%**
Other labor operators available	–289	345	**0.7%**
4. Value-stream sustaining			
Operators	0	1,425	**17.8%**
Water spiders	–100	1,498	**17.5%**
Total cost of waste	**1,840**		

Table 3.8 Summary of relativity measure

	Material	*Labor*	*Machine*	*Stock*
Process consumed	90.5%	43.0%	43.8%	
Cost of waste	9.5%	14.4%	32.1%	100.0%
Available		7.4%	24.2%	
Value stream sustaining		35.3%		
Total	**100.0%**	**100.0%**	**100.0%**	**100.0%**

decreased costs. The actual costs are 144 less than the flexible budget costs. This means that the actual costs are 28 (172–144, figures from Table 3.6). We expected these costs to be 172 in the flexible budget column but the actual costs were 28. Hence, we have a (favorable) difference of 144.

Our relativity measure is divided between resource types, as opposed to Maskell and Baggaley (2004). In our example, we focus on two of these: "materials" and "labor". The division is necessary as the price per resource may have different inflation rates and thus separate effects.

The company can use the relativity measure to measure the progress of Lean over multiple periods from a cost perspective, and improvements are signalled in an increased percentage of resources used in the "process consumed" category, and a decreasing percentage in the cost-of-waste category in particular.

The Lean financial model and subsequent relativity measures make it easier to track changes arising from "lead time" registered in the cost model. The lead time measure can be tracked over multiple periods as one non-financial trend indicator of Lean progress (Maskell and Baggaley, 2004). Using the Lean financial model's relativity measure we can now compare cost improvements indicated by this measure (stock waste) with the lead time trend. This way, we are linking the logic between the costing scheme and the lead time measure, increasing coherence between these two measures in the control package.

The relativity measure can also help in analyzing Lean progress independently of the organization's normal learning curves. It is regularly assumed that operators learn how to work faster over time as they gain more practice. This effect is quite pronounced in Company C as, twice a year, it introduces new products which operators need some time to learn to operate in order to produce more rapidly. Let us assume that learning how to work faster would include both process-consuming (value-adding) and wasteful activities in the activity path, with equal pace. From this perspective the learning curve effect would not remove waste, just complete the wasteful activities faster. So, while total time consumed in completing a product unit would be reduced, the proportion of cost-of-process time and wasteful activities remains. . This is the reason why the relativity measure is unaffected (or only modestly affected) by the normal learning curve effect and therefore a strong measure of Lean activity benefits which in turn primarily directs improvement efforts to cost-of-waste categories. Subsequently, this would shift the relative distribution between the cost of waste and cost of process consumed towards more time being spent on the latter.

Comparing Tables 3.4 and 3.7 it is obvious that the total cost of waste is higher in our Lean financial model. According to traditional reporting the total cost of waste is 998 while in Lean financial reporting it is 1,840 (all expected and unexpected cost in Table 3.7's "2. Cost of Waste"). Lean financial reporting indicates a higher cost of waste as the standards are now transparent with regards to waste. According to Lean financial reporting, "movements", in the example, constitute the major type of waste. Movements could be the focus of Lean, addressed by specific tools such as cell layout and single piece-flow without WIP stocks (Liker, 2006). This constitutes a different focus compared to the one resulting from the conclusion of the value stream map (i.e., in the example, lead time on stocks), not to mention that arising from traditional financial reporting (i.e. scrap). Logically, Lean financial reporting forces decision-making to encompass a concern with all waste types, something which Lean is created to reduce and therefore increase the goal congruence between the analysis of Lean and the goals of Lean.

Available capacity and opportunity cost of waste

The Lean financial model renders different types of available capacity explicit. This is done intentionally in order to understand the potential use of this capacity. Acting on this we can improve time consumption.

We distinguish between available bottleneck capacity (cell 1 in the example), other labor-available capacity and imbalance capacity. Other labor-available capacity is the capacity available in non-bottleneck labor resources, and the imbalance idle capacity comes from the activity path in which cells cannot be balanced completely with each other, or in which cells cannot be balanced internally. Only if there is available capacity at the bottleneck is it possible to increase value stream activity. In the example schedule there is very little available capacity at the bottleneck resource, and not enough to run another batch. Therefore, as the tool problems registered on the visual board in cell 1 arise, and the cell loses time equal to one batch, it may be argued that the cost of waste in our model fails to represent the opportunity costs. Opportunity costs are by definition equal to the contribution margin lost with the above-mentioned batch. The increased scrap level reduces the contribution margin as there are (potential) customers for these goods. This in turn changes the cost of waste so that it becomes the opportunity cost of waste including the lost contribution margin. A calculation of opportunity costs would be fruitful in assessing the total cost of waste. Nonetheless, to keep the example simple we have not included the explicit calculations in this presentation.

Encoding activities as VA or NVA in the costing system or not – the literature debate

A main element of the Lean financial model presented is based on encoding actions that are perceived as waste within the Lean philosophy; it has been shown how the model benefits from this categorization. However, we acknowledge the literature debate on this topic and will briefly address it.

Banker et al (2008) confirm their hypothesis that the impact of Activity Based Costing on performance is mediated by world-class manufacturing (WCM, Lean). They argue that ABC facilitates a more accurate identification of cost drivers associated with non-value-adding manufacturing activities and as a result supports a better implementation of WCM through a more focused resource allocation and cost control. Kaplan and Cooper (1998) argue that encoding activities, in the form of value-adding or non-value-adding, are not enhancing decisions on cost reductions, the reason being that the cost reduction of value-adding activities is worth just as much as the cost reduction of non-value-adding activities. In addition, they believe it is no easier – a priori – to reduce the costs of non-value-adding activities than of value-adding activities, e.g. industrial engineers reduce costs in value-adding activities on a daily basis by increasing machine speed. Instead, they propose a four-category approach which divides the activities between those required by the products and those not required. The required activities are divided into whether they can be optimized or not, and the non-required activities into whether they can be eliminated in the short or long term. Bicheno (2004) points to the fact that non-value-adding activities can be divided between avoidable and unavoidable; similar to necessary and non-necessary. Even though the non-value-adding activities are divided into two categories, this does not capture Kaplan's and Cooper's category of required (value-adding) activities that can be improved.

We believe Kaplan and Cooper's analysis (1998) of the categorization between value-adding and non-value-adding and their a priori assumption is valid. Furthermore, we agree that it is very difficult to categorize activities as non-value-adding by assessing the value from the customers' perspective. Customers want the lowest process cost on both value-adding and non-value-adding activities in anticipation of a lower sales price.

In relation to Lean implementation though, there is a great need to distinguish between value-adding and non-value-adding activities. In the Lean context, non-value-adding activities are labelled waste. In Lean, waste is defined rather precisely in normative terms and thus not a subjective judgement of what creates value for the customer. In Lean, waste is defined in terms of the sevenfold typology used above (Liker, 2004). Thus, waste types define what characterize non-value-adding. Liker (2004) presents the overall goal of Lean as being waste reduction within the house of Lean. The Lean house also shows that the Lean tool-box has been developed in order to reduce this waste. Just In Time, Jidoka, value stream mapping and "5 Why's" are just some of the tools that have been created to reduce waste. If the cost system is to be able to assess whether the costs of waste types actually have been reduced it is necessary to have an explicit waste cost model. This cost system must be able to enforce actions that are directed at reducing waste. Hence it is necessary to know where waste is located and whether or not the actions are actually successful in reducing waste over time.

Summary of the Lean financial model

Lean is about removing waste and the tools in Lean are created to that end. Thus, Lean tools are the means to control and reduce the level of waste. To be logically close to the main goal of long-term profit a costing model that measures the Lean tools' ability to remove waste from within the organization is necessary. This would be goal-congruent and point towards goal-congruent actions. How to support this is the aim of the Lean financial model.

Results of the investigations at the case companies suggest that they are in need of a better cost model to measure (ex post) the progress of Lean, but also in need of improved costing methods in order to achieve more precise decision-making support on where to develop the organization with the aid of Lean tools. Using Merchant's six generic measurement system principles and the theory of coherent systems, we found several problems in the traditional standard costing model used in Lean organizations. The Lean Financial model addresses these problems and the model consists of several new features on how to configure a Lean organization's costing system. These features (indicated by letters) and their benefits (indicated by Arabic numbers) are summarized below:

A. The Lean financial model integrates information form the visual board used in Lean production.
   Benefits:
   1. It is a mandatory source in Lean and therefore an (almost) free resource to management accounting.
   2. It provides actual data on variances, making continuous registration of actual consumption unnecessary.

3. It improves data quality and creates one coherent system of variance calculations and increased chances of "one story of variance explanations".
4. It supports shop-floor people with information on cost-saving potential per waste type.

B. The Lean financial model's input on standards comes from value stream maps, VSMs.
Benefits:

5. VSM is mandatory in Lean and therefore cost-efficient to use in the management accounting system.
6. VSMs often contain detailed information on waste providing opportunity to calculate standards/expected cost of waste in many categories.
7. With the information from the visual board (item 1) and standards, the Lean financial model calculates unexpected variances.

C. Lean financial model vis-à-vis a traditional standard cost model:

a. The Lean financial model splits total cost and total variance into four main categories:
   (i) process-consumed costs
   (ii) cost of waste
   (iii) cost of available capacity
   (iv) value stream sustaining costs.
b. Within the waste category the model is open in resource categories (materials and labor) and in all Lean categories of waste (inspection, movement, rework etc.) showing maximum attainable cost savings per waste type.
c. Within the availability category the model distinguishes between (i) available capacity at the potential bottleneck (pacemaker), (ii) at other resources due to imbalance between resource workloads, and (iii) at resources other than the bottleneck.
d. Imputed interest is used to cast lead time in stocks in cost terms.
e. It separates unit and batch cost.
f. Water-spider costs are separate from labor cost to avoid confusion.

Benefits:

8. The four-category division in C-a provides the advantage of measuring Lean progress in terms of cost effects which comes logically closer to the overall long-term profit of the company than does any non-financial Lean KPI.
9. A relativity measure based on the four categories in C-a makes it possible to measure Lean progress over multiple periods.
10. The three availability categories in C-c are important measures in the Lean journey as there might be time-lags between creations of more availability and the productive use of this through increased sales.
11. Separating unit and batch cost in C-e is important since Lean entails a journey towards reducing batch sizes.
12. The model rules out most of the normal learning curve effects and therefore provides a more accurate measure of Lean progress.

Limitations and future research

As with most models there are also limitations to the Lean financial model presented. A potential limitation is the way it handles product mix changes stemming from introduction of new products to the value streams. New products may change the relative distribution between the four categories (viz. Tables 3.7 and 3.8), as some products may be designed to create less waste. The model implicitly assumes that new products in the same value stream entail approximately

the same relative distribution of costs between the four categories (see the vertical dimension in Table 8) of each resource type as the existing products. If new products contain less relative waste it will cause the value stream relativity measure to improve. And this improvement is not caused by operational improvements; it may be the result of more focus on Lean-"friendly" product developed in the R&D department.

Another limitation of our model is that is has not passed the 'put to use test' yet. However, we must think of different degrees of use, actually somewhat like companies using Activity Based Costing models. The simplest use is a stand-alone model in one department with manual data feed. A more advanced application involves a number of departments with the model using automated data feeds from ERP systems. The ultimate implementation is where the Lean financial model substitutes the previous traditional standard cost system and is totally integrated into the company's ERP system. For the latter to happen, however, every shop floor should use visual boards; this is Lean implemented company-wide. Even in the biggest and most well-run Lean companies this is rare. Hence, it is the more modest implementation we can hope for.

Appendices

Appendix 3.1 The inputs to computations in the example

Budget no. of batches	15
Budget finished unit (without scrap – scrap 15 units)	330
Operator indirect activities standard time – hours (value stream sustaining)	57
Bill of materials – 1pc EUR	4
Paint 1000 ml, EUR	10
Operator/water spider hourly wage EUR	25
Batch size, pcs	23
sales price per pc (no deviation between budget and actual)	100
1 engineer dedicated to each value stream – weekly costs	1,000
Depreciation – machine 1	1,000
Factory (building) 1 value EUR 50% of total value – driver = square meters	100,000
Machine 1 value 100% – dedicated to this value stream	10,000
Stock 1 materials value (5 days of production including scrap)	1,380
Stock 2 materials value (10 days of production without scrap)	2,700
WIP storage materials value (4 hours)	184
Stock 1 & 2 building value (50% of total value as standard-cost driver is square meters)	3,000
Total asset value – dedicated and allocated	*144,264*

Appendix 3.2 Toyota production system house

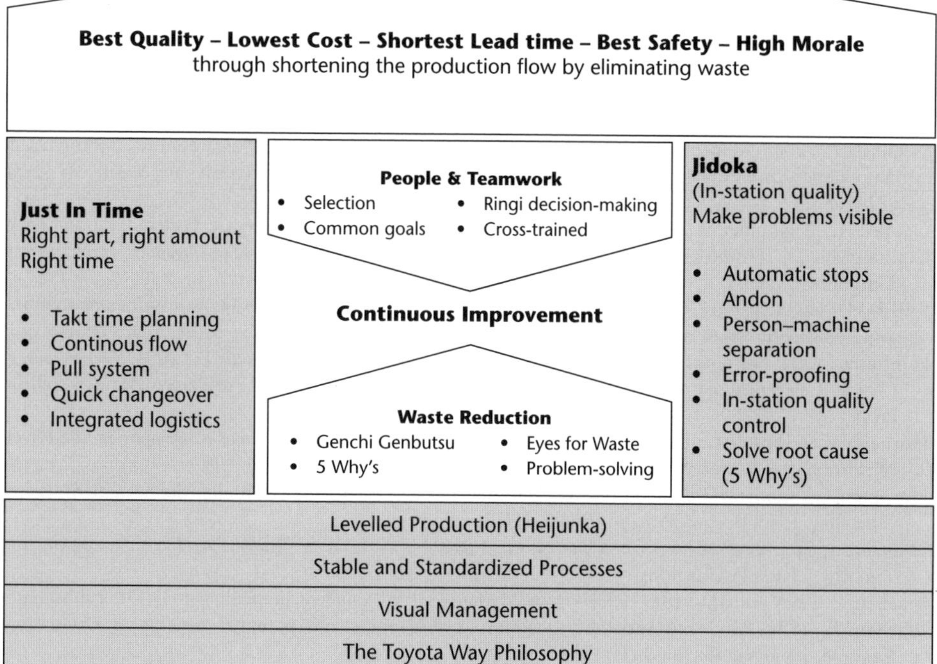

Source: Liker (2004), p. 33.

Notes

1 A ten-page account of our findings in the individual companies can be obtained by contacting the relevant author.

2 In Company C operators are taught about different types of waste cost to facilitate their decision-making process. This is similar to the findings of Lind (2001), in which a world-class manufacturing company decided not to abandon its budgeting system, while its shop-floor-level subordinates are able to discuss their daily activities with their superiors in budget terms, voicing budgetary arguments if necessary.

3 In our discussion of the relativity measure below, we point to the fact that Maskell and Baggaley (2004) employ something similar when they calculate available capacity. But as they operate solely with actual accounting, devoid of any form of time registration, they believe in using the value stream map to calculate available capacity. However, as the VSM does not contain any costing figures it would seem difficult to obtain a cost value for available capacity from the above without using standards as we do.

4 For illustrative purposes, the costs of waste presented in the Lean financial model can be drawn in a cost-time diagram as recommend by Bicheno (2004). The lead time would be represented on the x-axis and the accumulated cost of waste on the y-axis. All the data are available in the activity path and Lean financial model.

Bibliography

Åhlström, P., Karlsson, C. 1996. Change processes towards lean production. The role of the management accounting system. *International Journal of Operations & Production*, 16 (11), 42–56.

Atkinson, A., Kaplan, R.S., Matsumura, E.M., Young, M.S., 2007. *Management Accounting*. Upper Saddle River, NJ: Pearson Education.

Anderson, S., Widener, S., 2007. Doing Quantitative Field Studies. In Chapman, C.S., Hopwood, A., Shields, M.D. (eds), *Handbook of Management Accounting Research*, Oxford: Elsevier, 319–341.

Banker, R.D., Bardhan, I.R., Chen, T-Y. (2008). The role of manufacturing practices in mediating the impact of activity-based costing. *Accounting, Organizations and Society*, 33 (1), 1–19.

Bicheno, J., 2004. *The New Lean Toolbox – Towards Fast, Flexible Flow*. Buckingham: Picsie books.

Carreira, B., 2005. *Lean Manufacturing that Works Powerful Tools for Dramatically Reducing Waste and Maximizing Profits*. Amacom: American Management Association.

Cheatam, C.B., Cheatam, L.B., 1996. Redesigning cost systems: is standard costing obsolete? *Accounting Horizons* 10 (4), 23–31.

Chenhall, R., 2003. Management control systems design within its organizational context: findings from contingency-based research and directions for the future. *Accounting, Organizations and Society*, 28 (2–3), 127–168.

Cooper, R., Slagmulder, R., 1999. *Supply Chain Development for the Lean Enterprise*. Portland: Productivity.

Cunningham, J.E., Fiume, O.J., 2003. *Real Numbers Management Accounting in a Lean Organization*. Managing Times Press, USA.

Friis, I., Hansen, A., Vámosi, T., 2007. Koordination i en LEAN-virksomhed: grænser for værdistrømsanalysen som koordinationsmekanisme. *Økonomistyring & Informatik* 23(1), 33–68.

Henriksen, L.B., Nørreklit, L., Jørgensen, K.M., Christensen, J.B., O'Donell, B., 2004. *Dimensions of Change: Conceptualizing Reality in Organizational Research*. Copenhagen: Copenhagen Business School Press.

Horngren, C.T., Foster, G., Datar, S.M., 1997. *Cost Accounting – A Managerial Emphasis*. Upper Saddle River, NJ: Simon & Schuster, 9th international edition.

Horngren, C., Sundem, G.L., Straton, W.O., Burgstahler, D., Schatzberg, J., 2010. *Introduction to Management Accounting*, 15ed. Boston: Pearson Prentice Hall

Huntzinger, J.R., 2007. *Lean Cost Management: Accounting for Lean by Establishing Flow*. Plantation, FL: Timothy J. Ross Publications.

Israelsen, P., 1993. *Activity- versus Variability-Based Management Accounting*. Copenhagen: DJOF Publishing.

Israelsen, P., 1994. ABC and variability accounting: differences and potential benefits of integration. *European Accounting Review*, 3 (1), 15–48.

Johnson, H.T., 1992. *Relevance Regained*. New York: The Free Press.

Kaplan, R.S., Cooper, R., 1998. *Cost and Effect: Using Integrated Cost Systems to Drive Profitability and Performance*. Boston: Harvard Business School Press.

Kaplan, R.S., Norton, D.P., 1996. *The Balanced Scorecard – Translating Strategy into Action*. Boston: Harvard Business School Press.

Kennedy, F.A., Brewer P., 2005. Lean accounting: what's it all about? *Strategic Finance*, 87 (5), 26–34.

Kennedy, F.A., Widener, S.K., 2008. A control framework: insights from evidence on Lean accounting. *Management Accounting Research*, 19 (4), 301–323.

Lindsay, R.M., Kalagnanam, S.S., 1993. *The Adoption of Just-In-Time Production Systems in Canada and their Association with Management Control Practices*. Hamilton, Ont.: The Society of Management Accountants of Canada.

Kristensen, T.B., Israelsen, P., 2010. Standard costing in Lean organizations: enabling or coercive? Paper presented at MAR 2010 (EIASM), Ghent, June 20–23.

Lewis, M.A., 2000. Lean production and sustainable competitive advantage. *International Journal of Operations & Production Management*, 20 (8), 959–978.

Liker, J., 2004. *The Toyota Way*, USA: McGraw-Hill.

Liker, J., Meier, D., 2006. *The Toyota Way Fieldbook*. USA: McGraw-Hill.

Lind, J., 2001. Control in world-class manufacturing: a longitudinal case study. *Management Accounting Research*, 12 (1), 41–74.

Maskell, B., Baggaley, B., 2004. *Practical Lean Accounting*. USA: Productivity Press.

Merchant, K.A., 2006. Measuring general managers' performances: market, accounting and combination-of-measures systems. *Accounting, Auditing & Accountability Journal*, 19 (6), 893–917.

Mouritsen, J., Hansen, A., 2006. Management Accounting, Operations, and Network Relations: Debating the Lateral Dimension. In Bhimani, A. (ed.), *Contemporary Issues in Management Accounting*. Oxford: Oxford University Press, 266–290.

Nørreklit, H., 2000. The balance on the Balanced Scorecard: a critical analysis of some of its assumptions. *Management Accounting Research*, 11 (1), 65–88.

Nørreklit, L., Nørreklit, H., Israelsen, P., 2006. The validity of management control: towards constructivist pragmatism. *Management Accounting Research*, 17 (1), 42–71.

Otley, D., 1999. Performance management: a framework for management control systems research. *Management Accounting Research*, 10 (4), 363–382.

Rother, M., Shook, J., 1999. *Learning to See: Value Stream Mapping to Add Value and Eliminate MUDA*. Cambridge, MA: The Lean Enterprise Institute Inc.

Schonberger, R.J., 1986. *World-Class Manufacturing: the Lessons of Simplicity Applied*. New York: The Free Press.

Schonberger, R.J., 1990. *Building a Chain of Customers: Linking Business Functions to Create the World-Class Company*. New York: Hutchinson Business Books.

Schonberger, R.J., 1996. World-Class Manufacturing: the Next Decade. Building Power, Strength and Value. New York: The Free Press.

Fry, T.D., Steele, D.C., Saladin, B.A., 1995. The role of management accounting in the development of a manufacturing strategy. *International Journal of Operations & Production Management*, 15 (12), 21–31.

Womack, J.P., Jones, D.T., Roos, D., 1991. *The Machine that Changed the World*. New York: HarperCollins Publishers.

Womack, J.P., Jones, D.T., 2003. *Lean Thinking: Banish Waste and Create Wealth in your Corporation*. UK: Simon & Schuster.

Yin, R.K., 2003. *Case Study Research: Design and Methods*. Thousand Oaks, CA: Sage Publications.

4

ICT systems and cost management

Timo Hyvönen

Introduction

This chapter addresses a topic which has profoundly affected management accounting research during the last decade: the links between modern information and communication technology (ICT) and cost management. A starting point for that research tradition has been the two papers published in the *Harvard Business Review*, namely Davenport (1998) and Cooper and Kaplan (1998), in which the idea of a new kind of integrated information system was first presented. Since then, more attention has been paid to the relationship between information systems and management accounting, such as the possible impacts of ICT on management accounting and cost management practices and the roles of management accountants (Granlund, 2010).

The relationship between ICT and accounting has changed considerably during the last four decades. Even in the 1970s, only a small proportion of accounting functions were operated on computer-based information systems. These transaction-processing systems typically covered payroll, inventory and record-keeping. For instance, cost accounting, budgeting and all the other traditional cost management tasks were often organized manually at that time. According to Kaplan and Cooper (1998) these systems can best be described as (external) financial reporting-driven systems. In the 1980s, the role of computer-based information systems in financial management increased with the introduction of personal computers (PCs) and easy-to-use spreadsheet (e.g. Lotus 1–2–3 and Microsoft Excel) and database (e.g. Paradox and Microsoft Access) applications. This change also broke down the previous hegemony of a centralized mainframe computer-based ICT infrastructure. In addition, companies simultaneously started to create profit-centre organizations and decentralize their financial management functions.

However, the conventional mode of action at that time was still to develop a separate stand-alone system for every function of the organizations. Thus, this kind of best-of-breed (BoB) architecture easily led to a fragmented ICT infrastructure and to a situation where a company might easily have dozens of different software products from different vendors to maintain and update.

After the second half of the 1990s, virtually all large multinational organizations – and later on even many small- and medium-sized organizations and also public sector organizations (e.g. municipalities, universities and hospitals) – replaced their earlier home-grown (best-of-breed) legacy systems, and implemented wide-ranging and multifunctional integrated information systems and enterprise resource planning (ERP) systems (Cooper and Kaplan, 1998; Davenport, 1998). The roots of the ERPs can be found in the inventory management systems of the late 1960s. Material Requirement Planning (MRP), a part of which was the bill of material (BoM), was the very first attempt to control material resources by computer. The purpose of the MRP system was to make sure that enough parts would be found when needed. In the mid 1970s, the systems diversified when manufacturing resources came in, and thereafter the system was called Manufacturing Resource Planning (MRP II). This was a method for the effective planning of all the resources of a manufacturing company. Finally, after the MRP II was extended to all the other organization functions, such as sales and distribution, human resource management, financial management, product design and plant maintenance, the current ERP system was born (Vortman, 1999).

This kind of information system evolution also restored the power of centralized ICT infrastructure. The core of the ERP (e.g. SAP and Oracle) system is a central database that stores, standardizes and streamlines the collection, analysis and dissemination of data throughout the organization. There is no universally shared definition of ERP systems, but from the cost management perspective a well-known and often cited one has been put forward by Granlund and Malmi (2002, p. 303), according to which ERPs are defined as 'module-based integrated software packages that control all the personnel, material, monetary and information flows of a company'. Thus, in integrated ERP systems accounting and financial management are only one part of the large information system.

Quite soon, after having implemented new ERP systems at the beginning of the 2000s, some organizations also started to reorganize financial functions yet again. There was a movement from decentralized financial departments back to centralized organizations, either by establishing financial shared service centres, or in some cases even to outsourcing these functions. Modern ICT and especially integrated ERP systems enabled these organizational changes.

Typically, the motivation behind these investments – both technological and organizational – has been the need, as well as the will, to improve organizational efficiency, effectiveness and performance (e.g. Poston and Grabski, 2001). As the implementation of ERP systems often forces companies to re-engineer their business processes or organization structures, Sutton (2006, p. 1) has emphasized that modern integrated information systems 'have fundamentally re-shaped the way the business data is collected, stored, disseminated and used'.

The purpose of this chapter is to explore management accounting and cost management change in the ERP implementation context, and create a new kind of framework for ICT-oriented cost management research. The next section incorporates the relevant literature review of the respective topics. Then, the framework is presented. Finally, the contribution of this chapter to our knowledge of management accounting and cost management change in ERP implementation is outlined, and some possible new research areas are presented.

Earlier cost management research in the ERP context

The focus in this chapter is especially on integrated ERP systems; in practice, in the last ten years almost all studies concerning the relationship between ICT and management control and cost management have concentrated on ERP systems (Granlund, 2010). Recent management accounting literature shows increasing research interest in the effect of ERP systems on cost management practices. In their literature review Aernoudts et al. (2005) put existing empirical management accounting-oriented literature into two main categories. According to them, the studies in the group with a 'structural approach' focus on two main questions: how the implementation of ERP system will change the organization, and whether ERP implementation has an impact on organizational performance. The second empirical research category identified by Aernoudts et al. (2005) is 'processual studies'. These studies try to explain how the processes of change unfold and how their outcomes develop over time.

In their seminal study, Scapens and Jazayeri (2003) reported that, although the introduction of ERP systems had not caused fundamental changes in the nature of the management accounting information used, there were indeed some changes in the role of management accountants – in particular: (i) the elimination of routine jobs; (ii) line managers with accounting knowledge; (iii) more forward-looking information; and (iv) a wider role for management accountants. Notably, they did not claim that ERP was the driver of these changes; rather, it is argued that the characteristics of ERP (integration, standardization, routinization and centralization) opened up certain opportunities and facilitated changes already taking place within the company.

The next question of these processual studies covers the issue of the impact of ERPs on management accountants' working routines and represents an idea of accounting hybridization (Granlund and Malmi, 2002; Caglio, 2003; Newman and Westrup, 2005; Hyvönen et al., 2009). While Granlund and Malmi (2002) at the time their study was carried out found only modest changes, Caglio (2003) and Newman and Westrup (2005), however, reported on the adoption of a new ERP system challenging the definition of the expertise and roles of accountants within organizations, leading perhaps to new, hybrid positions. The hybridization in this case means a situation in which different professional groups have either divided their occupational tasks or struggled over power. The remainder of these studies focus on either the links between ERPs and innovative accounting practices, or the effects of ERPs on management control (Granlund and Malmi, 2002; Quattrone and Hopper, 2005). Besides that, Quattrone and Hopper (2005) found that while the adoption of an ERP system did not influence management control in one of their cases, in their other case financial management expressed concern at the loss of control.

As an outcome of their literary review, Aernoudts et al. (ibid.) observed that as a consequence of a variety of theoretical and methodological perspectives, the knowledge of the subject is rather fragmented, leading to the low degree of knowledge accumulated concerning the issue. One of their major concerns was that there is an important shortcoming of the extent to which research addressed the question 'how do accountability and control changes occur when ERP is adopted?'.

Dechow and Mouritsen (2005), in their literature review, also adopted the same kind of methodological starting point as Aernoudts et al. (2005). However, in addition to structural/processual classification they also added the third dimension, namely the 'learning curve'. According to that research approach, firms implementing ERP systems have to go through a learning curve in order to benefit from the ERP investment. Dechow and Mouritsen (ibid.) argue that this approach is based on the 'stage–maturity model' used as a basis for consultants' advice on ERP implementation. The purpose of that research genre is to bring to light the potential of instrumental rationality acting within and through ERP systems. The next approach (structural) in Dechow and Mouritsen's typology in the ERP literature focuses on performance by asking whether ERP works. Common features of these, usually survey-based, studies are that they suggest only very moderate impacts of ERP systems on management accounting (Boot, Matolscy and Wieder, 2000; Granlund and Malmi, 2002).

In contrast to the two approaches mentioned, the third one emerging (processual) is concerned with 'how ERP technologies are made to work as "systems"' (Dechow and Mouritsen, 2005, p. 692). The studies by Quattrone and Hopper (2001, 2005), Caglio (2003), Scapens and Yazayeri (2003), Lodh and Gaffikin (2003) and Newell et al. (2003) have in some cases identified remarkable effects of ERP systems both on the process of design, as well as on the process of use. In addition, these studies also explain why earlier surveys have been limited, and therefore unable to capture the essential features of the effects of the ERP systems on management control and cost management. In their own study Dechow and Mouritsen (2005) explored ERP as a promise of system integration, and as a result reported that full integration had never taken place.

The fourth approach coming to light just recently is a more critical perspective. The study by Caccio and Steccolini (2006) focused on accounting change in local governments, and the active role of CFO in the project, a part of which was also ERP implementation. The study by Dillard et al. (2006) was interested in ERP systems as an 'administrative evil', and Jack and Kholeif (2008) were interested in the contest to limit the role of management accountants in developing countries through ERP implementations. Finally, Teittinen (2008) in his dissertation suggested that integration in ERP means not only integration between the software modules and organizations, but also integration between invisible realities. The common feature of these studies is that they all see ERPs as either a pure managerial fashion or an unacceptable outcome of ever-increasing bureaucracy.

Summing up, the ERP-oriented management accounting and cost management literature can be presented using the framework proposed by Lukka and Granlund (2002). In their article, they distinguished three genres of activity-based costing (ABC) research (consulting research, basic research and critical research). As an outcome of the study, they demonstrated how fragmented the field of ABC research seems to be. Using the same framework, it is also possible to describe the different research genres in management accounting-oriented ERP research (see Figure 4.1).

In consulting research (e.g. KPMG Consulting, 1997; Deloitte Consulting, 1998) the focus is twofold: either the possibilities to develop organizations with ERPs are presented; or the interest is in critical success factors in the ERP implementation phase, often studied by statistical methods. In the basic studies, however, the research questions concentrate more on the possible impacts of ERP implementation on management accounting, management control, cost management or the changing roles of management accountants. Structural studies have typically found only moderate impacts, while processual studies have also reported remarkable, albeit contradictory, changes. Finally, critical studies as a basis will call into question the whole idea of ERP as integrated information systems. According to these, ERP systems will be seen either as

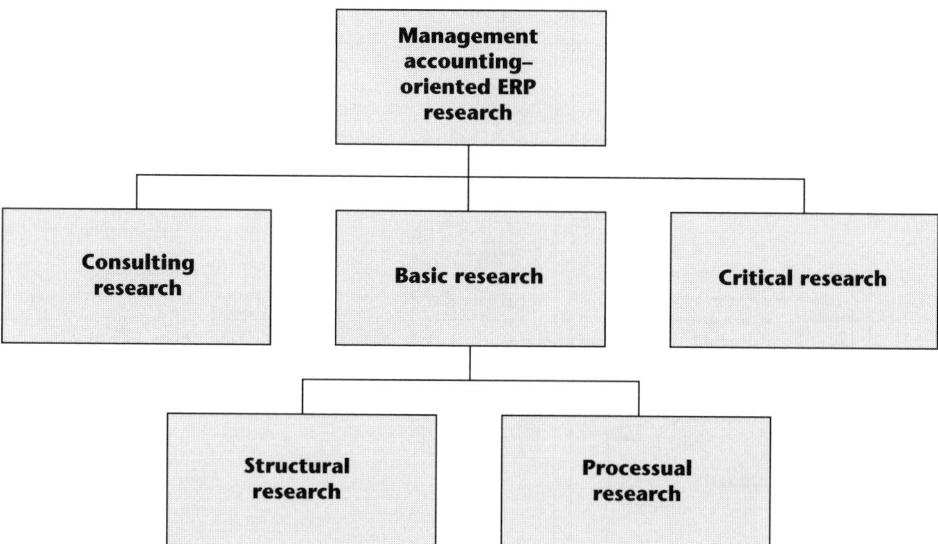

Figure 4.1 Research genres in management accounting-oriented ERP research

a form of managerial fashion or a labour processing issue, when these systems just offer a new device to forestall democracy by centralizing power on a small elite within the organization.

Four perspectives on cost management in the ERP context

In addition to the methodological classification presented in the preceding section there are other ways to describe and analyse the relationship between ICT and cost management. The overall purpose of this section is to study the role of ICT in the controlling process of the organizations (e.g. Ribeiro and Scapens, 2006; Dechow et al., 2007), and specifially how financial management is able to mobilize resources, control decision-making and manage meanings within the ERP implementation process. Thus, the purpose here is to present a new kind of framework and to shed light on management accounting change in the ERP systems context from four different perspectives: (i) cost management as a technology, (ii) cost management as knowledge, (iii) cost management as a control structure, and (iv) cost management as a profession. However, unlike in earlier studies, the focus here is on the implementation phase, not on the impacts of ERP systems on cost management.

First, the focus is on the technological role of ERPs when new management accounting or cost management systems are implemented. The elementary questions in that perspective are: why, and by whom, was the new information system implemented in the industrial units studied? The second, albeit secondary, aim in this perspective is to explore what kinds of impact the ICT infrastructure (BoB versus ERP) has had on the management accounting function and cost management systems between these two different configurations. The paper by Granlund and Malmi (2002) suggests that, in many cases, modern cost management systems have been implemented outside the ERP system by using separate off-the-shelf solutions. Therefore, the latter three perspectives will take into more profound consideration why and how modern multidimensional profitability and cost management systems have been created

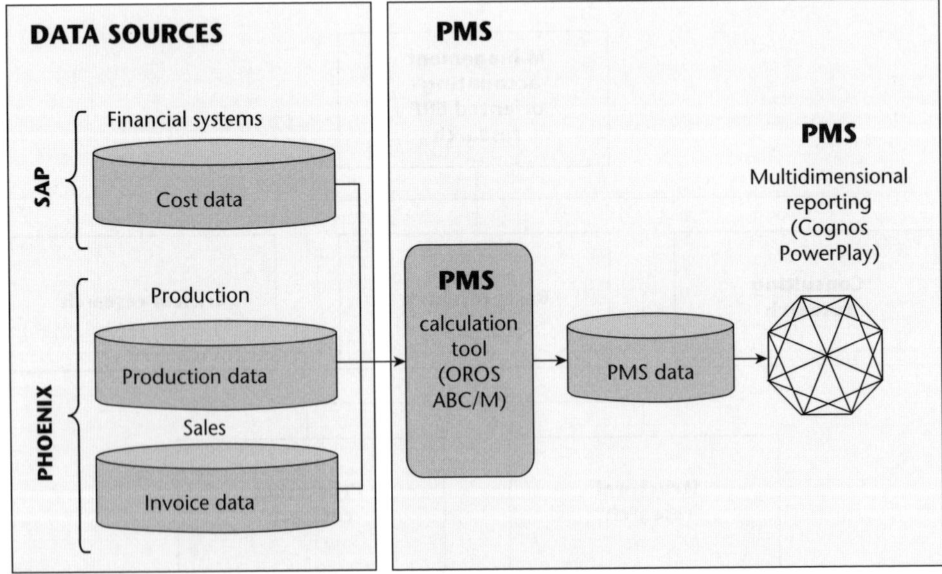

Figure 4.2 The structure of the new cost management system

in a big industrial enterprise with different cost management and management control off-the-shelf software packages (Oros ABC/M, which is currently known as SAS® Business Intelligence, and Cognos PowerPlay) by using an ERP system (SAP R/3) as a basic platform. The other important issue is what kind of reflection this has had on cost management, management control and the changing roles of controllers.

The second perspective approaches the issue from the aspect of knowledge transfer: how the standard software packages can help organizations to mobilize local cost management knowledge (cf. Vaivio, 2004 and his idea of mobilizing local knowledge with 'provocative' non-financial measures). In our case this means the roles of standards (Brunsson and Jacobsson, 2000; Giddens, 1990) when dis-/re-embedding management accounting knowledge within a company.

In the third perspective, the focus is on how a company managed to create a new management control system (called virtual organization) by using the technology mentioned earlier, when the purpose is to increase its headquarters' control and visibility over local business units. The essential point in that perspective is that when creating a new cost management structure the focus is on parallel processes and their social networks.

The last perspective concentrates on the management accounting profession and the role change of controllers. So far studies on the subject have concentrated either on the national or organizational level of change (the only exception being Baxter and Chua, 2008). In this case, the focus is on a single controller: how the aspiring controller (an active agency) managed to expand his role from 'bean counter' to create a new kind of role model for the organization by using the ERP-linked cost management development project as a stepping stone (cf. Järvenpää, 2007) in the early stage of the controller's career.

Cost management as a technology

The first perspective explores the differences between the adoption and use of modern enterprise resource planning (ERP) and traditional stand-alone best-of-breed (BoB) systems in practice.

The survey study (n = 99, response rate 33%) focuses on one grouping variable – the type of present information system, ERP or BoB (Hyvönen, 2003). This comparison is relevant because companies or units which do not have an ERP system still have a variety of stand-alone BoB systems. The results indicate that 47% of the respondents were using traditional BoB, and 53% had implemented the ERP system at least to some extent. According to the respondents, 67% of the units had updated both of their main IT platforms (financial and production control systems), 19% had updated only their financial systems and 14% had updated only their production control systems. Sixty-three per cent of the units that had updated both their main systems had selected ERP system as their IT infrastructure, while only 37% did so using BoB. When the unit had updated only its production control system there were no differences between the groups. Seventy-five per cent of the units which had updated their financial system only had done it with BoB, and only 25% with ERP.

The first research question addressed the background factors of the IS implementation and consisted of three sub-areas: (1) initiators of the new IS, (2) motives behind IS investment and (3) the need for system modification versus business process re-engineering. As the purpose of these research questions was to analyse the differences between BoB and ERP adopters, the variable (1) was compressed into three groups. In group A the initiator was the financial department alone, in group B the initiators were the financial department with some other departments, and in group C the initiators were other than the financial department. The results indicate that in 83% of the cases in group A the solution was BoB. In group B and group C the solution was more often ERP, 57% and 61% respectively. Thus, the results support the assumption that because of the historical background of BoB and the evolution of ERP, the members of financial departments were used to developing IT infrastructure more often with BoB than with ERP. This also emphasizes the role of active actors and different professions.

The articulated motives in the variable (2) were classified either as strategic or technological. In order to facilitate statistical analyses, the variables were therefore compressed into three groups. In group A the reasons for implementation were only strategic, in group B only technical and in group C both strategic and technical. The results proved that in groups A and B, when the motives were either technical or strategic, the solutions were more often BoB than ERP: 56% and 69% respectively. However, in group C, where articulated motives were technical and strategic, the solution was more often ERP (62%) than BoB (38%). The results therefore support the role of ERP as an important strategic platform: ERP is more than a mere technical or strategic renewal of IS, it is a company- (or unit-) wide strategic IS. The third factor (system modification versus business process re-engineering) indicated no statistical significance

The second research question addressed the changes in the problems of management accounting and cost management after new IS implementation. Some improvement had taken place in all issues studied, but the changes were quite moderate. The next step was to compare the issues between the two groups (ERP and BoB). The measurement device was a five-item Likert scale. As a result of the analysis, the Mann-Whitney non-parametric rank test indicated no statistically significant differences between the two groups of units. The only exception was budgeting: according to the analysis, ERP adopters have more problems with budget planning than units using only BoB systems.

The final research question focused on the adoption of modern cost management accounting techniques (activity-based costing, target costing, life-cycle costing, activity-based management and balanced scorecard) and the relationship to ERP and BoB. The results indicated that exclusive of life-cycle costing, modern management accounting applications were more frequently adopted within companies which had implemented ERP than BoB. However, the Pearson chi-square test indicated no statistically significant differences between the groups.

Cost management as knowledge

The second perspective aims to analyse how standard software packages provide divisionalized corporations with standards that can be used in achieving an efficient means of accounting knowledge transfer. In this case study (Hyvönen et al., 2006) the Oros ABC/M software package became an important 'medium of interchange' (Giddens, 1990) for cost accounting-related knowledge. The generic features of the ABM system could be quickly implemented at other locations, anywhere in the world. Such mediating of generic cost accounting knowledge was also possible without regard to the specific characteristics of ICT infrastructure, cost management system features, accountants or the managerial needs of any single mill location.

A key argument emerging from this study is that off-the-shelf software packages can be efficient drivers for management accounting change (Granlund and Malmi, 2002) as they can be viewed as 'best practice' standards that create trust in the new systems. In our case study, the ERP-linked ABM system had a key role in re-embedding the cost management knowledge that was needed to unify the existing systems whose heterogeneity was a result of recent company mergers and acquisitions. The new division level management accounting system can be considered as a 'shock' originating from outside and typically involving resistance to change. However, at the case unit, reaction varied from eagerness to indifference, and division-wide implementation across 11 mills in Europe was accomplished with relative speed (in only eight months). Although users of the new cost management system at the mill sites were to blindly trust that the cost management system would eventually provide them with superior cost and profitability information, our observations suggest a high level of commitment towards this new system.

The findings of our case also suggest that success in increasing the internal uniformity of a management accounting system can be explained not only by following bureaucratic rules (Burns and Scapens, 2000), but importantly by establishing internal accounting standards that leave room for voluntary choices (Brunsson and Jacobsson, 2000). The standards defining a uniform cost accounting model, together with the off-the-shelf software package, created a new expert system inside the case company (Giddens, 1990). This kind of system is flexible, and yet can be copied across all the mills. However, it is also a system that can easily become unquestioned and unchallenged.

Successful implementation of the new cost management system comprised three main elements:

1. a software package;
2. a standardized ABM methodology;
3. management accounting experts.

Different stages of the implementation project involved varying degrees of freedom to apply the standards. In the cost management design phase, ABM was chosen ahead of alternative cost management standards and, of the different cost management software solutions, SAP R/3 was abandoned and SAP-integrated Oros ABC/M adopted. With respect to the ICT infrastructure choices, the case findings complement the results obtained by Granlund and Malmi (2002), who reported that the majority of companies in their study had decided to implement ABC/M outside of the SAP system. However, in the case study the main reason for this was not related to the technical complexity of SAP R/3 (Lodh and Gaffikin, 2003), but rather to the faster rollout options offered by the competing solution. This argument was supported by the case company's growth strategy and was successfully mobilized by the management accounting professionals to support the project and the ICT infrastructure solutions.

In terms of introducing software packages at mill level, the freedom to apply standards was related to the extent of tailoring of the information systems, i.e. whether or not the systems should be implemented and/or whether the system should be at least partially tailored to 'fit' existing organizational practices. A common argument (Scapens and Jazayeri, 2003) is that by customizing standard software packages, a company will lose many of the essential advantages of purchasing such a software package. Our findings suggest that tailoring accounting software may have hindered the implementation of a new ICT system, the more so where the expert knowledge embodied in the cost management system was exposed to discussion and criticism. However, as the necessary tailoring was left to the division's ABM project group, such tailoring did not include the organizational benefits of using off-the-shelf software.

Even though there was considerable freedom at mill level in terms of adhering to the standards, total compliance was generally accepted as being the sensible choice. The division's standards were broad enough to allow mill-level personnel to introduce local information requirements in their reporting. Interestingly, at one stage the production site personnel expressed a wish for firmer divisional guidance. However, the introduction of very strict and detailed rules to varying situations has the potential to be a cumbersome solution. Moreover, it was also suggested that the creation of very detailed rules would have been too demanding for the experts, as this would imply that the division level had detailed knowledge of the production site-level cost accounting issues across all of the mills.

Earlier studies have indicated how important it is to trust both accountants and accounting information when evaluating corporate performance (Johansson and Baldvinsdottir, 2003). Our findings suggest further that voluntarism and 'blind' trust in experts and software packages are essential features of both dis- and re-embedding processes (Giddens, 1990).

Cost management as a control structure

In the third perspective, Actor Network-Theory is used to analyse the aspect of cost management as a control structure (Hyvönen et al., 2008a). Actor Network Theory-based research on management accounting has to date illustrated how little we know about the messy and continuously changing accounting information systems (AIS) realities in large organizations, and how the information systems influence management control and cost management. In this perspective the purpose is to draw on the heuristic framework of Quattrone and Hopper (2001) and present the development of a cost management system as a serendipitous process that illustrates the episodic nature of such processes. Actions are taken simultaneously in different geographical locations, with only a few key actors managing to hold the process together. For most of the time, the majority of actors are not connected, while new social actors emerge unobtrusively, in private or in small groups, using ICT. Only in a few instances is a larger association of actors formed, but although these associations can prove to be decisive, their outcome cannot be planned in advance.

The case findings suggest that ICT-based accounting solutions seem to shape the organization's social reality in two ways. First, the ICT solutions virtually force accountants to study the logic of the solution, and second, they challenge them to invent ways of combining accounting and management rationalities. Actors such as ICT solutions, accountants and management are connected. This collection of actors begins to create its own agency and rationality that is not only accounting, ICT or management, but also an emerging rationality. In this case, the actor that connected the local rationalities in different factories was the accounting software solution and the action (the cost management system project) that took place around it.

As in Quattrone and Hopper (2005), this case study evidences the imperialistic agenda of virtual integration to shrink the distance between geographically separated units by gathering detailed data on the factories and combining these into a virtual mill created by accounting reports. The case findings illustrate various local collections of AIS and other agents. A seemingly small assignment by the CFO to investigate the possibilities of utilizing ABM methodology in SAP triggered a series of events that eventually challenged the existing management control system and which had the capacity to create new agencies. Taking on the assignment, the divisional controller began by studying and comparing the opportunities provided by various off-the-shelf software solutions, which was the starting point for new a AIS agent that could create a local totality, i.e. an oligopticon (e.g. Latour, 2005). Then the agent, using the centralization theme as an incentive, persuaded top management to grant the right to compel factory accountants to associate and become part of the new agency. Central to this persuasion was the creation of representations of the management accounting software and the new visibilities that they enabled (see Bloomfield and Vurdubakis, 1997). The case findings suggest that, in addition to being visual images (e.g. PowerPoint slides), representations can also be lingual metaphors. For the division's top management, the representation was labelled 'virtual integration' while to factory accountants it was a 'profitability management system'. As the project was ongoing, these metaphors were visualized by PowerPoint presentations, including speculative calculations with hypothetical numbers (since the actual numbers were unavailable at the time). After the project ended, 'pipeline management' replaced the virtual integration metaphor.

This illustrates how framing activities become important in establishing ICT systems. The case findings illustrate the dynamic interaction between the idea of reorganization (centralized management control) and the representations of the ICT system. Important political choices were made with respect to how to represent the system through visual images and metaphors, and to whom it should be represented. In this political process it is extremely important to know the organization's history, e.g. what metaphors have been used previously and what concepts are tainted. These findings extend the studies by Quattrone and Hopper (2006) and Andon et al. (2006) by illustrating the nature of inter-company politics and management behaviour in ERP implementation.

Notably, the case organization made use of off-the-shelf accounting software packages. However, our findings prompt the question: how 'ready-to-use' and 'packaged' are these software packages? Even though a software package can offer ready-made solutions, the organization's actors must construct its meaning through action, and this meaning must be continuously renewed in order to continue its existence socially. The process of framing then 'customizes' the ready-made off-the-shelf solutions as an organizational practice. In this sense, ready-made ICT systems can provide competitive advantages, even though other companies are likely to have them, too. What counts in creating competitive advantage is not technical functionality, but how the system can serve management purposes – for instance, how the case organization managed to reorganize its management control.

Cost management as a profession

So far studies of cost management and management accounting professions, and the changing role of controllers, have concentrated either on the national or organizational level of change (the only exception being Baxter and Chua, 2008). In this case, the focus is on a single controller. Drawing on earlier literature, we have identified the areas where management accountants must excel in order to survive in the organizational jungle: command of both emerging cost management techniques and ICT, interest in developing business and social networking (Hyvönen et al., 2008b).

Järvenpää (2007) illustrated accountants' role change in a multinational conglomerate. One of his findings was that all accountants work on development projects at some stage in their careers. This case, however, illustrates the importance of a successful development project as a means of role change. Being able to surf the wave of new technology and to take full advantage of it made it possible to bypass many normal limits of role change. The importance of successful projects seems, in this case, to be at least partly explained by creating opportunities for social networking, as the project legitimates or even compels contact with production location and marketing managers, ICT professionals and senior management. This social network can be put to use in multiple ways: we call the controller's ability to take advantage of his network a 'good tactical eye'. It involves three aspects: willingness to take risks, the ability to react quickly to new opportunities, and the ability to understand other actors' vital interests. Regarding the ability to seize opportunities, we may point out that the project included challenges that, if not taken on by the controller, would have been taken on by someone else.

In this case the mill controllers' job descriptions became more focused on financial reporting and data inputting, while the controller at divisional HQ was able to take control of strategic systems. The divisional controllers were able to utilize the centralized integrated information systems (ERP and the related cost management system) while the mill accountants were left with the task of collecting and inputting the data. Even though some routine functions may have decreased at mill level as new information systems were implemented, more demanding analytical tasks did not seem to emerge (see Granlund and Malmi, 2002; Scapens and Jazayeri, 2003).

The third aspect of the controller's good tactical eye seemed to be understanding the motivations of other organizational actors. This often requires some work history in the organization, which enables an ability to interpret information – a sort of personal multiplier (see Vaivio and Kokko, 2006). Role change can also be seen in connection with the ability to link up with organizational discourses (Alvesson and Willmott, 2002). The discussion around the profitability management project also benefited from strategic discourses. The new business controller seemed able to utilize strategic concepts and claim ownership of 'profitability management' in the organization while actively avoiding accounting concepts such as ABM. However, the controller did remain in control of the new cost management system, and thus did not lose touch with management accounting tasks. Instead, the controller was able to operate in both spheres.

Thus, the influence of ERP was to polarize management accounting tasks. Just as Scapens and Jazayeri (2003) predicted, ICT eliminated many of the routine tasks – for the new business controller. For the mill accountants, there was little or no effect while new systems did not replace and/or integrate old reporting systems entirely, and the amount of data input and data transfers increased. The case findings suggest to us that for the mill accountants, the bean-counter role may actually have strengthened. For the line managers, future-oriented cost management information became more readily available, and they began including the new business controller – the information provider – in decision-making, thus increasing his business orientation. However, this new business-controller role was by nature focused on the efficiency and profitability of existing operations, rather than on the generation of new business opportunities.

Conclusions

As Granlund (2010) and Wagner et al. (2011) have pointed out, the ICT-oriented research on management control and cost management has so far been very diverse. Thus, the purpose of this chapter was to shed light from four different perspectives on management accounting change in the ERP systems context – (i) cost management as a technology, (ii) cost management as knowledge, (iii) cost management as a control structure, and (iv) cost management as a profession – and to present a framework for studying the relationships between ICT and cost management.

The contribution of the chapter to our knowledge of management accounting and cost management change in the ERP implementation context can be condensed into one entity: the role of ICT and especially ERP systems in management control change, and the importance of active individuals in this process. The framework presented here concentrates on how financial management as an active agency can exploit ERP implementation, which has already been accomplished in the organization. Drawing on Burns (2000), the chapter elaborates how an active agency (a single controller) mobilizes resources, controls decision-making and manages meanings when implementing the new cost management system in ERP environment (see also Caccia and Steccolini (2006)), and the active role of the CFO when implementing the new management accounting system.

This relates to the question of how it is possible, using a company-wide integrated information system, to mobilize local cost management knowledge to dis-embed it from local level to headquarters, and then globalize it by re-embedding the knowledge in all sites. According to the results obtained, it is easier to implement the new system when there is no need to open up the basics of the ICT system. Without opening up the system, the whole implementation is based on trust and the blind commitment of experts and technology. The study combines the idea of expert systems (Giddens, 1990) with the internal standards (Brunsson and Jacobsson, 2000) of the organizations, and shows how easy it is to hide away from the critics behind these standards.

Besides this, the chapter also shows that, on the one hand the company-wide information system created by using the standard software packages is not only a stable system but also a dynamic process (Dechow and Mouritsen, 2005; Quattrone and Hopper, 2006), while on the other hand, the case findings illustrate the dynamic interaction between the idea of reorganization (centralized management control) and the representations of the ICT system. Important political choices were made with respect to how to represent the system by visual images and metaphors, and to whom. In this political process, it is extremely important to know the organization's history, e.g. what metaphors have been used previously and what concepts are tainted. These findings extend the studies by Quattrone and Hopper (2006) and Andon et al. (2006) by illustrating the nature of inter-company politics and management behaviour in ERP implementation.

The findings also addressed the role of technology when increasing the centralized power over the mills. Earlier studies have suggested that the ERP systems may decrease the power of accountants by creating hybrid accountants (Newman and Westrup, 2005). In those cases other professions start working on traditional management accounting tasks. On the other hand, opposite suggestions have been made. In those cases, accountants broaden their sphere of operations, and expand their control to other business areas beyond financial management, either by using ERP systems (Caglio, 2003; Scapens and Yazayeri, 2003), or even without them (Burns and Baldvinsdottir, 2006). In any case, without ERP-integrated off-the-shelf systems it might be difficult, or even impossible, to build a division-wide center of calculation. The basic ERP system displays the views to everyone who has access to a certain part of the system. With off-the-shelf packages, it is easier to restrict the view offered to different professions in individual agencies by invoking the complicated technology as a reason (it is reasonable to limit the scope of the view because the system is so multidimensional and difficult to use).

In contrast to some previous management accounting studies (e.g. Hopwood, 1987), this suggests that instead of a panopticon, this kind of calculation center may be more like an oligopticon (Latour, 2005). The nature of the oligopticon, however, includes a propensity for errors (Latour, 2005) as its functioning depends on the existence of many accounting information system (AIS) agencies and the connections between them. For instance, a local and unexpected technical problem with (Excel) spreadsheets in one of the factories may cause the system to lose its rationality and visibility at the center, at least for a while. The same goes for version updates, or process changes that result in the inability of the system to produce interesting reports for top managers, who then start to lose their AIS-based rationality.

Finally, this chapter explains how technology by definition and implementation can help an accountant in his/her personal career. Järvenpää (2007) suggests that traditionally almost all accountants have to work in some kind of accounting system development project at some stage in their career. This case continues that discussion and illustrates the factors which are essential when creating something so valuable to the company that the person in charge of the project will be rewarded with a promotion. In that case, the technology simply serves as an enabler. Nevertheless, in order to normalize the change, as a part of daily action, the person in charge of the project must have not only skills in management accounting and business processes, but also a good tactical eye to help him/her combine different issues in a creative way. By so doing, it is possible to create a completely new, permanent position for a business controller based on the wave of new technology.

Besides that, the results of the study by Rom and Rohde (2006) indicate that ERP systems support the data collection and the organizational breadth of cost accounting better than SEM (strategic enterprise management) systems. SEM systems, on the other hand, seemed to be better at supporting reporting and analysis. In addition, modern management accounting techniques involving the use of non-financial data are better supported by an SEM system. Therefore the reasons why the companies are supplementing their ERP systems with separate stand-alone systems (ABM, BSC, budgeting, financial reporting) instead of ERP's SEM systems, will also need further investigation. The other research agenda in the near future will probably include the benefits of modern Business Intelligence (BI) solutions to cost management.

Bibliography

Aernoudts, R.H.R.M., van Der Boon, T.H., van der Pijl, G.J. and Vosselman, E.G.J. (2005) 'Management accounting change and ERP, an assessment of research', Paper presented at the inaugural joint workshop by MCA and ENROAC 'Research Conference on the Changing Roles of Management Accounting as a Control Systems', Antwerp, Belgium, 2005.

Alvesson, M. and Willmott, H. (2002) 'Identity regulations as organizational control: producing the appropriate individual', *Journal of Management Studies*, 39: 614–44.

Andon, P., Baxter, J. and Chua, W.F. (2007) 'Accounting change as relational drifting: a field study of experiments with performance measurement', *Management Accounting Research*, 18: 273–308.

Baxter, J. and Chua, W-F. (2008) 'Becoming the Chief Financial Officer of an organization: Experimenting with Bourdieu's Practice Theory', *Management Accounting Research*, 19: 212–30.

Bloomfield, B.P. and Vurdubakis, T. (1997) 'Vision of organization and organization of vision: the representational practices of information systems development', *Accounting, Organizations and Society*, 22: 639–68.

Booth, P., Matolcsy, Z. and Wieder, B. (2000) 'The impacts of enterprise resource planning systems on accounting practice. The Australian experience', *Australian Accounting Review*, 10: 4–18.

Brunsson, N. and Jacobsson, B. (2000) *A World of Standards*, Oxford: Oxford University Press.

Burns, J. (2000) 'The dynamics of accounting change. Interplay between new practices, routines, institutions, power and politics', *Accounting, Auditing & Accountability Journal*, 13: 566–96.

Burns, J. and Baldvinsdottir, G. (2005) 'An institutional perspective of accountants' new roles - the interplay of contradictions and praxis', *European Accounting Review*, 14: 725–57.

Burns, J. and Scapens, R. (2000) 'Conceptualising management accounting change: an institutional framework', *Management Accounting Research*, 11: 3–25.

Caccia, L. and Steccolini, I. (2006) 'Accounting change in Italian local governments: what's beyond managerial fashion?', *Critical Perspectives on Accounting*, 17: 154–74.

Caglio, A. (2003) 'Enterprise resource planning systems and accountants: towards hybridization', *European Accounting Review*, 12: 123–53.

Cooper, R. and Kaplan, R.S. (1998) 'The promise – and peril – of integrated cost system', *Harvard Business Review*, 76: 109–19.

Davenport, T.H. (1998) 'Putting the enterprise into the enterprise system', *Harvard Business Review*, 76: 121–31.

Dechow, N. and Mouritsen, J. (2005) 'Enterprise resource planning systems, management control and the quest for integration', *Accounting, Organizations and Society*, 30: 691–733.

Deloitte Consulting (1998) *ERP's Second Wave – Maximizing the Value of ERP-enabled Processes*, New York: Deloitte Consulting.

Dillard, J.F., Ruchala, L. and Yuthas, K. (2006) 'Enterprise resource planning systems: a physical manifestation of administrative evil', *International Journal of Accounting Information Systems*, 7: 107–27.

Giddens, A. (1990) *The Consequences of Modernity*, Cambridge: Polity Press.

Granlund, M. (2010) 'Extending AIS research to management accounting and control issues: a research note', *International Journal of Accounting Information Systems*, 12: 3–19.

Granlund, M. and Malmi, T. (2002) 'Moderate impact of ERPS on management accounting: a lag or permanent outcome?', *Management Accounting Research*, 13: 299–321.

Hopwood, A.G. (1987) 'The archaeology of accounting systems', *Accounting, Organization and Society*, 12: 204–234.

Hyvönen, T. (2003) 'Management accounting and information systems: ERP versus BoB', *European Accounting Review*, 12: 155–73.

Hyvönen, T., Järvinen, J. and Pellinen, J. (2006) 'The role of standard software packages in mediating management accounting knowledge', *Qualitative Research in Accounting & Management*, 3: 145–60.

Hyvönen, T., Järvinen, J. and Pellinen, J. (2008a) 'A virtual integration – The management control system in a multinational enterprise', *Management Accounting Research*, 19(2), 45–61.

Hyvönen, T., Järvinen, J. and Pellinen, J. (2008b) 'Struggling for a new role for the business controller', *Tampere Economics and Accounting Net Series*, WP 1.

Hyvönen, T., Järvinen, J., Pellinen, J. and Rahko, T. (2009) 'Institutional logics, ICT and stability of management accounting', *European Accounting Review*, 18: 241–75.

Jack, L. and Kholeif, A. (2008) 'Enterprise resource planning and a contest to limit the role of management accountants: a strong structuration perspective', *Accounting Forum*, 32: 30–45.

Järvenpää, M. (2007) 'Making business partners: a case study on how management accounting culture was changed', *European Accounting Review*, 16: 99–142.

Johansson, I-L. and Baldvinsdottir, G. (2003) 'Accounting for trust: some empirical evidence', *Management Accounting Research*, 14: 219–34.

Kaplan, R.S. and Cooper, R. (1998) *Cost & Effect. Using Integrated Cost Systems to Drive Profitability and Performance.* Boston, MA: Harvard Business School Press.

KPMG Consulting (1997) *Profit-focused software package implementation*, London: KPMG Management Consulting.

Latour, B. (2005) *Reassembling to Social. An Introduction to Actor-Network-Theory*, Oxford: Oxford University Press.

Lodh, S. and Gaffikin, J.R. (2003) 'Implementation of an integrated accounting and cost management system using the SAP system: a field study', *European Accounting Review*, 12: 85–122.

Lukka, K. and Granlund, M. (2002) 'The fragmented communication structure within the accounting academia: the case of activity-based costing research genres', *Accounting, Organizations and Society*, 27: 165–90.

Newell, S., Huang, J.C., Galliers, R.D., Pun, J.S. (2003) 'Implementing enterprise resource planning and knowledge management systems in tandem: fostering efficiency and innovations complementary', *Information and Organization*, 13: 25–52.

Newman, M. and Westrup, C. (2005) 'Making ERPs work: accountants and the introduction of ERP systems', *European Journal of Information Systems*, 14: 258–72.

Poston, R. and Grabski, S. (2001) 'Financial impacts of enterprise resource planning implementations', *International Journal of Accounting Information Systems*, 2: 271–94.

Quattrone, P. and Hopper, T. (2001) 'What does organizational change mean? Speculations on a taken for granted category', *Management Accounting Research*, 12: 403–33.

Quattrone, P. and Hopper, T. (2005) 'A 'time-space Odyssey': management control systems in two multinational organisations', *Accounting, Organizations and Society*, 30: 735–64.

Quattrone, P. and Hopper, T. (2006) 'What is IT?: SAP, accounting, and visibility in a multinational organisation', *Information and Organization*, 16: 212–50.

Ribeiro, J. and Scapens, R.W. (2006) 'Institutional theories in management accounting. Contributions, issues and paths for development', *Qualitative Research in Accounting & Management*, 3: 94–111.

Rom, A. and Rohde, C. (2006), 'Enterprise resource planning systems, strategic enterprise management systems and management accounting: a Danish study', *Journal of Enterprise Information Management*, 19: 50–66.

Scapens, R. and Jazayeri, M. (2003) 'ERP systems and management accounting change: opportunities or impacts? A research note', *European Accounting Review*, 12: 201–33.

Spathis, C. and Constantinides, S. (2004) 'Enterprise resource planning systems' impact on accounting processes', *Business Process Management Journal*, 10: 234–47.

Sutton, S.G. (1999) 'The changing face of accounting and the driving force of advanced information technologies', *International Journal of Accounting Information Systems*, 1: 2–6.

Sutton, S.G. (2006) 'Enterprise systems and the re-shaping of accounting systems: a call for research', *International Journal of Accounting Information Systems*, 7: 1–6.

Teittinen, H. (2008) Näkymätön ERP: taloudellisen toiminnanohjauksen rakentuminen [English summary: Invisible ERP. Construction of enterprise resource planning], *Jyväskylä: Jyväskylä* [Studies in Business and Economics]: 69.

Vaivio, J. (2004) 'Mobilizing local knowledge with "provocative" non-financial measures', *European Accounting Review*, 13: 39–71.

Vaivio, J. and Kokko, T. (2006) 'Counting big: re-examining the concept of the bean counter controller, *Finnish Journal of Business Economics*, 55: 49–74.

Vortman, J.C. (1999) 'Evolution of ERP systems'. In Bitici, S. and Carrie, A.S. (eds), *Strategic Management of the Value Chain*, 11–23, London: Springer.

Wagner, E.L., Moll, J. and Newell, S. (2011) 'Accounting logics, reconfiguration of ERP systems and the emergence of new accounting practices: a sociomaterial perspective', *Management Accounting Research*, 22: 181–97.

5
Functional analysis

Takeo Yoshikawa and John Innes

Introduction

Functional analysis is an adaptation of value analysis and value engineering techniques which were developed in the West over 50 years ago. In *A Functional Analysis System Technique Manual*, Creasy (1973) stated that Chrysler, Ford Tractors, General Electric and Univac-Sperry-Rand were among the early users of value engineering. Value engineering was defined by The Society of Japanese Value Engineering (1992, p. 1) as 'a systematic approach to studying the functions of products or services in order to achieve their necessary functions with minimum costs'. British Standard 3138 defined value engineering in a slightly different way as 'a systematic interdisciplinary examination of factors affecting the cost of a product or service in order to devise means of achieving the specified purpose most economically at the required standard of quality and reliability'.

Davila and Wouters (2006) reviewed management accounting research in the manufacturing sector into managing costs at the design and production stages. Cooper and Slagmulder (1997) explored the links between target costing and value engineering. Cooper and Slagmulder (2002, p. 5) argued that value engineering is used 'to identify ways to design the product so that it can be manufactured at its target cost'. In addition to value engineering, they suggested that design for manufacture and assembly and quality function deployment could be used to help product designers achieve the target cost. However, they considered that value engineering was the most important of these three techniques. Cooper and Slagmulder (2002, p. 6) suggested that value engineering 'tries to increase functionality and quality while at the same time reducing cost'. Where this type of value engineering is based on the functions of a product, it is known as functional analysis and management accountants support functional analysis with the provision of cost information.

Functional analysis is a cost management system that focuses on the various functions of each product or service. For example, the parts of a pen include the barrel, ink cartridge, tip and top but the functions of a pen include:

1. store ink;
2. flow ink;

3. make mark;
4. add colour;
5. prevent stains.

It is by concentrating on the functions of a product rather than on its parts that you can take a much broader view of the product. This broader view is extremely useful during both the design of new products and the redesign of existing products. For example, by thinking of the functions of an existing product (rather than its parts), the redesigned product may be very different from the existing product. Japanese organizations have found that the functional analysis process can also result in the development of new patents and even new products.

In one Japanese company functional analysis was developed in 1975 and introduced formally in 1976. The development of functional analysis in this particular company can be divided into four periods from 1976 to date. Firstly, from 1976 to 1979 functional analysis was applied to existing products. Secondly, from 1980 to 1982 functional analysis was broadened to include overhead areas. Thirdly, from 1983 to 1988 functional analysis was widened from existing products to new product design. During this period sub-contractors working for this particular company were involved in some of these functional analysis projects. Fourthly, from 1989 to date this Japanese company has tried to develop a functional analysis ethos. As one senior manager said, 'You have to develop a functional analysis mind with value for the customer and cost at the front of your mind.' During the first 20 years – from 1975 to 1994 – approximately 2,500 employees participated in functional analysis projects. This is an overview of the functional analysis experience of only one Japanese organization, but it illustrates how the approach can be developed.

The overall objective of functional analysis is not only cost management but also profit improvement. For example, functional analysis can identify product functions where customers are willing to pay more if these particular functions are improved. Similarly, functional analysis may show where new functions can be added to a product to make it more attractive to customers and lead to improved profits. Functional analysis is a group activity involving about six employees from different departments within the organization. This inter-disciplinary nature of the group is an important aspect of functional analysis. Many Japanese organizations have a small department that organizes and supports functional analysis activities. Japanese organizations tend to use several groups working independently on the same functional analysis project, to encourage competition between the groups and produce the most effective solution. Functional analysis also helps to develop strong teamwork among an organization's employees.

The functional analysis department sets specific objectives for each functional analysis project, such as reducing manufacturing costs by 25% (without reducing the quality of the product), and finding at least one new patent. Another important aspect of the Japanese system of functional analysis is that, when the project is completed, each group presents their results to a group of top managers.

Functional analysis contributes to cost management not only by identifying possibilities for cost reduction but also for improving products or services by adding new functions. In Western management accounting the most common cost object is the product or its parts, but in functional analysis the functions of the product or service are the cost object. The following section will concentrate on product design, but the principles of functional analysis can be applied also to the design of services.

Product design

Cost tables

A helpful technique that Japanese organizations use during their product design process is cost tables. Cost tables use the concept of cost drivers not only in relation to overheads but also in relation to direct costs. In other words cost tables assume that direct costs are driven not only by the volume of production but also by other factors. For example, cost tables reveal that one cost driver of the overall cost of a new motorbike is the size of the engine. Another example is that the costs of using a particular drilling machine may vary with the type of material used, the depth of the hole and the diameter of the hole. Cost tables are computerized databases used mainly to estimate costs and are particularly useful in estimating the costs of new products. There are two basic types of cost table. The first is the approximate cost table used mainly to estimate the cost of different functions during the planning and basic design stages of new products. The second type is the detailed cost table for the manufacture of existing products and also for purchasing (see Yoshikawa et al, 1990 for further details).

Japanese management accountants spend a great deal of time constructing, updating and maintaining these cost tables. Indeed, in Japan there are private firms that provide cost information which can be incorporated into an organization's own cost tables. This means that an organization can include information in their cost tables about materials, equipment and new technological developments that are not currently being used by that particular organization. Designers can use information from cost tables (often incorporated into their computer-aided design software) to estimate the cost of various alternative designs. For example, one large Japanese multinational company uses approximate cost tables together with a target cost management system to screen out unprofitable new product design proposals. The widespread use of cost tables in Japan is the result of many years of hard work and experience. However, if an organization wishes to develop cost tables, it is possible to develop approximate cost tables (rather than detailed cost tables) as a first stage in their development. Cost tables provide helpful information for functional analysis.

Steps in functional analysis

Functional analysis is a useful cost management approach not only at the design stage for new products but also at the redesign stage for an existing product. However, Japanese organizations have concentrated their use of functional analysis at the early design stage for a new product, where experience has shown that the greatest benefits are gained. Hiromoto (1988) and Monden and Sakurai (1989) have described the role of value engineering and functional analysis as part of the process of achieving target costs. Design decisions commit an organization to incurring costs. Design engineers know about direct material and direct labour costs but some design engineers do not fully understand what drives overhead costs. Functional analysis (in conjunction with cost tables) can help with this particular problem.

Functional analysis has 16 basic steps, namely:

1. select the project;
2. define the objectives for the project (including the target cost);
3. plan the timetable;
4. choose the team members;
5. collect relevant information;

6. define the functions;
7. draw a functional family tree;
8. calculate the cost of each function;
9. evaluate the value of each function for the customers;
10. assign the target cost to each function and identify problem functions;
11. generate alternative solutions;
12. evaluate alternative solutions in terms of the project's objectives;
13. decide on preferred solution;
14. present results to top management;
15. implement preferred solution;
16. audit results six months or one year after implementation.

The above 16 steps can be divided into three stages, namely, planning (steps 1–4), team exercise (steps 5–14), and implementation and audit (steps 15–16). These three stages will now be discussed in more detail.

Planning

The planning stage begins with the first step of selecting the project for functional analysis. This is a critical step in the process and the full-time functional analysis employee(s) play an important role in this selection process trying to determine where the greatest benefits are likely to be obtained. Various criteria can be used to select a particular product or component, such as: being very bulky (if space is at a premium) or very heavy (if weight is significant) or very complex (particularly for high-volume products or components) together with the total cost involved.

After selecting the product or component, the full-time functional analysis employees also set the objectives for this particular project. For example, the objective might be to reduce the weight of the part by 30% without affecting the quality of the part, while at the same time cutting the cost of the part by 40%. Such a cost reduction objective will usually be set within a target cost framework (discussed in another chapter of this book). Japanese organizations often combine functional analysis with target cost management. The important point for functional analysis is that a major aim is to meet a target cost objective. The objectives of the functional analysis project often appear impossible to achieve for Western managers without any experience of functional analysis. Yoshikawa et al (1995, p. 423) report in a Japanese case study of functional analysis the comments of one manager who compared reducing costs to squeezing a wet towel dry. This Japanese manager suggested that 'when the towel feels dry you keep on squeezing and get another bucket of water from it'. The Japanese experience of functional analysis projects is that very often the teams do more than just meet their objectives. Nevertheless, the demands of the target costing system and functional analysis objectives place pressure on the team members; Kato (1993) reports that the effects of such pressure can lead to dysfunction in some Japanese organizations.

The third step involves the full-time functional analysis employees deciding the appropriate timetable for this particular functional analysis project. The timetable set will depend on the complexity of the project and can vary from one week (for a small component) to several months (for a new product). However, most functional analysis projects can be completed in less than a month.

In the fourth step, the members of each team are selected by the full-time functional analysis employees. Each team usually consists of five or six members selected from different departments within the organization: accounting, design, engineering, human relations, manufacturing, marketing and purchasing, for example. The members of the team will be seconded temporarily from their normal jobs and one person will become the team leader. In Japan usually a full-time functional analysis employee will provide support and advice for the team. The mix of different skills and the interaction of team members are critical to the success of any functional analysis project. Some Japanese organizations involve their sub-contractors and customers in their functional analysis projects. For example, an employee from a sub-contractor or from a customer may be invited to join the functional analysis team.

Team exercise

After the teams have been selected, the detailed mechanics of the functional analysis can begin. The fifth step is for each team to collect relevant information about the product or component such as costs, marketing data and technical specifications. The costs would include analyses of material, labour, overhead, scrap and any other relevant costs. The marketing data would include not only data about the product (such as advertising, customers and market share) but also about the products of competitors. The technical specifications would include data not only about the detailed design of an existing or proposed new product but also manufacturing data such as machines used, the manufacturing process (including any capacity problems or the technology becoming out of date) and details of suppliers and sub-contractors (including any problems with the suppliers and sub-contractors).

The sixth step is to define the functions of the product. Many people find this very difficult at first. One problem is that employees in most organizations think of their products (both existing and new) in terms of parts rather than their functions. One helpful approach is to think of product functions in terms of a verb and a noun. For example, the primary function of a pen could be defined as 'make a mark', but supporting functions are also required. The different functions can be related to each other. One way to make such links is to ask the question 'how?' For example, how do you make a mark? The answer is 'by flowing ink'. There will be other supporting functions such as 'storing ink', 'preventing stains' and 'preventing loss'. It is also important at this stage to identify any government regulations and customer requirements.

Once the product functions have been defined, the seventh step is to draw a functional family tree. An example of a functional family tree for a propelling ballpoint pen is given in Figure 5.1 where the primary function is 'make mark', with secondary functions of 'add colour' and 'hold pen'. An indirect function (such as 'prevent loss') is denoted by a dotted line. Generally,

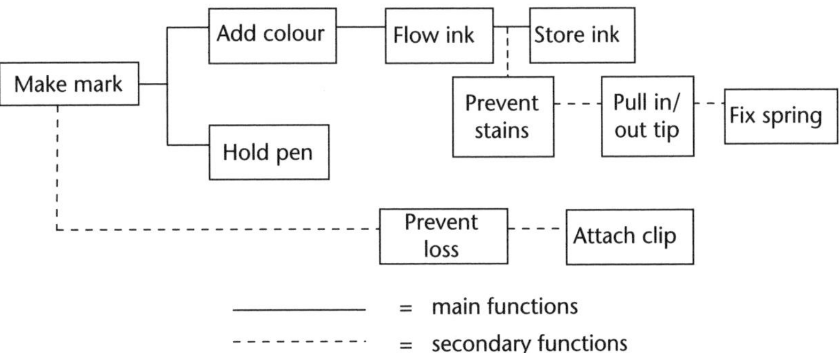

Figure 5.1 Propelling ballpoint pen functional family tree
Source: Adapted from Yoshikawa et al (1989, p. 15).

as you move to the right-hand side of a functional family tree the functions, such as 'fix spring' and 'attach clip', become less abstract and closer to the parts of the product. One advantage of drawing a functional family tree is that it forces the team to arrange the product functions in a logical order. Often this reveals a missing function that needs to be added. A helpful check of the logic of a functional family tree is to start at the right-hand side and ask the question 'why?' For example, why do you 'attach clip' – the answer is to 'prevent loss'. Similarly, why do you 'add colour' – to 'make a mark'.

After drawing a functional family tree, the eighth step is to calculate the cost of each function. Up to this point, a management accountant will have been operating simply as one of the members of the functional analysis team. However, management accountants (whether or not they are part of the team) provide their expertise in calculating the cost of each function. One problem for management accountants in the West is that usually the costing information is based on the parts rather than the functions of a product or component. Table 5.1 shows the cost of all the functions; for illustrative purposes the parts of the existing product are also included. Obviously, if this was a completely new product only the functions and the cost of the functions would appear and no parts would be included. In Japan, cost tables are usually based on the product functions and, therefore, cost tables can be used to cost the functions.

After calculating the cost of each function, the ninth step is to evaluate the value of each function for the customers. The best way to achieve this is to survey the customers to discover what they would be willing to pay for each function. However, if time does not allow for such a survey, the team members can all act as customers and value each function. After each team member has decided their customer values for all the functions, the different values for each function selected by the team members are discussed and, after this discussion, a consensus is reached on the monetary value for each function. Another approach to reaching the customer values for all the functions is to ask each team member to assess the relative value of each function in percentage terms – with all these percentages totalling 100. If this percentage method (rather than the monetary method) is used, again group discussion would then take place to finalize the agreed relative values for all the functions.

The tenth step involves assigning the target cost for the product to each function to determine the main problem functions of the existing product. Table 5.2 gives the example of a propelling

Table 5.1 Existing parts, functions and costs

Part no.	*Name of parts*	*Function*		*Cost £*
		Transitive verb	*Noun*	
1	Tip	Flow	Ink	0.80
2	Barrel	Hold	Pen	1.20
3	Cartridge	Store	Ink	0.30
4	Top	Store	Ink	0.20
5	Ink	Add	Colour	0.15
6	Cap	Prevent	Stains	0.12
7	Spring	Pull in/out	Tip	0.10
8	Stopper	Fix	Spring	0.08
9	Clip	Prevent	Loss	0.13
10	Screw	Attach	Clip	0.02
				3.10

Source: This table is adapted from Yoshikawa et al (1994b, p. 56).
Note: The costs are notional and have been selected by the authors purely for illustrative purposes.

Table 5.2 Costs and values of functions

Functions	*Actual cost* £ *(a)*	*Relative value to the customer (%) (b)*	*Assignment of target cost based on customers' relative function value* £ *(c) = £2.40 × (b)*	*Value ratio (d) = (c)/(a)*
Flow ink	0.80	25	0.60	0.75
Hold pen	1.20	50	1.20	1.00
Store ink	0.50	12	0.29	0.58
Add colour	0.15	2	0.05	0.33
Prevent stains	0.12	4	0.10	0.83
Pull in/out tip	0.10	1	0.02	0.20
Fix spring	0.08	1	0.02	0.25
Prevent loss	0.13	4	0.10	0.77
Attach clip	0.02	1	0.02	1.00
	3.10	100	2.40	

Source: This table is adapted from Yoshikawa et al (1994b, p. 57).
Note: The costs are notional and have been selected by the authors purely for illustrative purposes.

ballpoint pen where the existing pen has a cost of £3.10 but the target cost is £2.40 and the relative value of each function to the customers is used to assign this target cost. For example, the flow ink function in Table 5.2 has a value to the customers of 25 per cent and, therefore, 60 pence of the target cost of £2.40 (namely, 25 per cent) is assigned to this particular function.

Table 5.2 also shows the value ratio of the assigned target cost (60 pence for the flow ink function) as a percentage of the existing actual cost of 80 pence – namely 75 per cent. Where this value ratio is under 1.00, this means that the function's actual cost is greater than its assigned target cost. However, this value ratio needs to be considered together with the absolute cost of the function because if the absolute cost is very small – for example, two pence for the attach clip function – then there is relatively little scope for significant cost reduction in relation to the actual cost of the propelling ballpoint pen (£3.10). Table 5.2 shows that, in monetary terms, the biggest differences between the actual cost of a function and the assigned target cost are for flow ink and store ink functions, and in terms of the value ratio the lowest ratios are for the pull in/out tip, fix spring and add colour functions. These are the main problem functions of the existing propelling ballpoint pen.

The eleventh step is perhaps the most important in the entire functional analysis process: to generate alternative solutions for the most significant problem functions identified in the above tenth step. Basically this is a brainstorming session involving every member of the functional analysis team. At the initial stage no suggestion is rejected: experience has shown that what at first sight appears to be a silly suggestion can sometimes be the basis for the best solution. This is one of the stages in the functional analysis process where a team approach is critical. Team members have different backgrounds and experience; discussion among them can lead to new suggestions. For example, in the case of the propelling ballpoint pen, such a discussion can lead to suggestions for new patents or products such as the disposable pen. Another example is that new functions might be added to the product such as 'erase ink'. This example illustrates that functional analysis is not just about cost reduction but also profit improvement.

The twelfth step is to evaluate all the alternative solutions generated during the brainstorming session in terms of the objectives of the functional analysis project. These alternative solutions may include using new materials or new parts, using a different manufacturing method, deleting functions, adding new functions to the product to improve value to the customers, or combining functions. An example of combining functions for the pen example is to integrate the functions in Figure 5.1 of 'prevent stains' and 'prevent loss' into one function of 'prevent stains and loss'. Management accountants play an important role in helping to cost the alternative solutions generated by the team. It is at this stage that Japanese management accountants find their cost tables particularly helpful because these tables can provide answers to 'what if?' questions from the functional analysis team. Management accountants can, of course, cost the alternative solutions generated by the team without the use of cost tables, although this will usually involve more time and effort. These costs include not only the direct material, labour and other costs per unit but also any incremental overhead costs for each alternative solution. At this point an activity-based overhead costing system can be helpful. The net cost saving from each alternative can then be estimated as:

(variable cost saving per unit × total number of units) – incremental overhead

Some alternative solutions may also generate additional sales, and these would be included and the results reported in terms of net profit improvement.

The thirteenth step is to decide on the preferred solution from all the possible alternative solutions generated by the functional analysis team. The final decisions are made on the basis of the objectives of the functional analysis project, feasibility, customer need, environmental and social acceptability and profit. An example of the results for our propelling ballpoint pen example is given in Figure 5.2, which shows the revised functional family tree for, in effect, a new product – namely, a disposable ballpoint pen without the propelling element.

In Figure 5.2 some functions that were in Figure 5.1 – 'pull in/out tip', 'fix spring' and 'attach clip' – have been eliminated and the two separate functions of 'prevent stains' and 'prevent loss' have been combined into one function: namely, 'prevent stains and loss'. The new disposable pen now has only six parts (see Table 5.3) instead of the original ten parts (see Table 5.1). The cost has been reduced from £3.10 to £2.00, exceeding the target cost of £2.40. Obviously this is a simple illustrative example; another example of the functional analysis process for a staple remover can be found in Yoshikawa et al (2002, pp. 15–19).

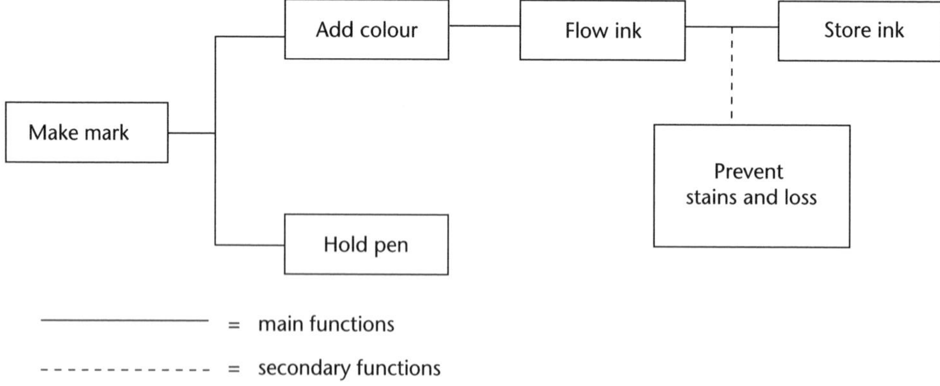

Figure 5.2 Disposable ballpoint pen functional family tree

Source: Adapted from Yoshikawa et al (1989, p. 17).

Table 5.3 Final parts, functions and costs

Part no.	*Name of part*	*Function*		*Cost £*
		Transitive verb	*Noun*	
1	Tip	Flow	Ink	0.50
2	Barrel	Hold	Pen	1.00
3	Cartridge	Store	Ink	0.20
4	Top	Store	Ink	0.10
5	Ink	Add	Colour	0.12
6	Cap	Prevent	Stains/Loss	0.08
				2.00

Source: This table is adapted from Yoshikawa et al (1994b, p. 58).
Note: The costs are notional and have been selected by the authors purely for illustrative purposes.

The fourteenth step is to present the results of this functional analysis project to top management. In Japan all the functional analysis team members present their findings, expected benefits and suggested changes to a few top managers in the organization. Such a presentation is very important in Japan because no team member wishes to lose face by not achieving the objectives of their particular functional analysis project. In addition to this formal presentation to top managers, the team also prepares a report on its functional analysis project and its results.

Implementation and audit

After the team project has been completed, the results from this functional analysis have still to be implemented and audited. The fifteenth step is for the organization to implement the team's preferred solution – assuming that top management has approved it. Obviously this step is outside the control of the functional analysis team, with all the team members returning to their different jobs in the organization.

The sixteenth and final step is to audit the actual results of implementing the solution chosen by the functional analysis team. This step is included in the functional analysis process to dissuade the team from overstating the predicted benefits from their preferred solution. In addition, this audit or review provides feedback so that future functional analysis projects can be improved. The results of this audit are reported to top management.

Overheads

This chapter has concentrated on the application of functional analysis to new or redesigned products or components. However, Japanese organizations also apply their functional analysis approach to the cost management of overheads. Instead of a product sold to external customers, overheads are services provided to internal customers – users of the overhead service. As with products, the objective is to improve the overhead service and not just to reduce cost. The process of applying functional analysis to overheads is basically the same as for products. For example, the criteria used to identify the overhead for functional analysis include complex procedures, increasing numbers of staff and increases in costs. The members of the functional analysis team for an overhead area would include a manager or user of the overhead service.

One example of applying functional analysis to the overhead of purchasing can be found in Yoshikawa et al (1994a); a case study of applying functional analysis to a process management system in a Japanese factory is in Yoshikawa et al (1995). This Japanese company has completed a number of successful functional analysis projects on overheads including the following:

1. improving a training programme;
2. revising a project management system;
3. rationalizing a control system.

Control

Mouritsen et al (2001) conducted case studies into controls between autonomous organizations engaged in cooperative projects. In one of these cases they found that design was outsourced and functional analysis became a significant aspect of the inter-organizational management control. Mouritsen et al (2001, p. 226) concluded that 'through attention to products' functionality, functional analysis creates a new form of transparency and facilitates new opportunities of control'. Furthermore, Mouritsen et al (2001, p. 231) found that functional analysis not only created a new form of control over suppliers but also 'became a resource in understanding what technology, strategy and organization were all about'.

Conclusions

Functional analysis is a helpful cost management technique during both the product design and redesign stages. This chapter has concentrated on the functional analysis of products but this approach can also be applied to both services and overheads. However, there are also some problems associated with functional analysis. Firstly, it is important to remember functions required for legal or safety reasons. Secondly, it can be difficult for customers to evaluate individual product functions or even to give a relative evaluation of these functions. Thirdly, the benefits from functional analysis projects may diminish over time when applied to the same product. In particular, repetitive functional analysis projects tend to concentrate on cost reduction rather than on profit improvement.

However, in our opinion, the advantages of functional analysis as a cost management approach far outweigh its problems. One advantage of functional analysis is that it forces employees to view products and components in more abstract terms – namely, in terms of their service potential rather than their physical parts. A second advantage is the team approach with its interdisciplinary aspect. Thirdly, although functional analysis can be used throughout the life cycle of a product, the greatest benefits from functional analysis are usually derived during the early planning and design stages of a new product. Functional analysis helps to ensure that non-design managers are also closely involved in the design process and can provide useful information for designers.

Fourthly, although functional analysis is a cost management tool, it incorporates the views of customers into the process. Functional analysis has an external perspective with its emphasis on both the market (target cost) and also customers' evaluations of a product's functions (assignment of target cost). Fifthly, functional analysis can be applied not only to products and components but also to services and overheads. Sixthly, functional analysis projects mean that, over a number of years, many employees within an organization participate in such projects, which is a useful training process and allows them to develop many skills, including teamwork, cost awareness and sensitivity to customer needs. Seventhly, functional analysis is a useful form of inter-organizational management control when autonomous organizations engage in cooperative projects. Eighthly, functional analysis results in improved competitive advantage for an organization with better-designed products and services.

Western organizations can certainly use functional analysis which, of course, was developed from Western value engineering. An important aspect of the Japanese approach to functional analysis is the use of multidisciplinary teams with members from different departments, or even from a sub-contractor or a customer. In Japan functional analysis is viewed as a management approach rather than an engineering technique. Functional analysis links closely with target costing and has a strong customer emphasis. In Western organizations the lack of both cost tables and cost information based on functions does pose problems, though they can be overcome. For example, the authors have conducted a very successful functional analysis project with a Scottish organization where the management accountant calculated the costs for the various alternatives generated by the team as special one-off exercises. This experience suggests that Western organizations can benefit from the multidisciplinary team approach to functional analysis incorporating customer expectations into the cost management process.

Bibliography

Cooper, R. and Slagmulder, R. (1997) *Target Costing and Value Engineering*, Portland: Productivity Press.

Cooper, R. and Slagmulder, R. (2002) Target Costing for New-product Development: Product-level Target Costing, *Journal of Cost Management*, July/August, pp. 5–12.

Creasy, R. (1973) *Functional Analysis System Technique Manual*, Irving: Society of Value Engineers.

Davila, T. and Wouters, M. (2006) 'Management Accounting in the Manufacturing Sector: Managing Costs at the Design and Production Stages', in Chapman, C.S., Hopwood, A.G. and Shields, M.D. (eds) *Handbook of Management Accounting Research*, Oxford, Elsevier, pp. 831–858.

Hiromoto, T. (1988) Another Hidden Edge – Japanese Management Accounting, *Harvard Business Review*, July/August, pp. 23–26.

Kato, Y. (1993) Target Costing Support Systems: Lessons from Leading Japanese Companies, *Management Accounting Research*, March, pp. 33–47.

Monden, Y. and Sakurai, M. (1989) *Japanese Management Accounting: A World Class Approach to Profit Management*, Cambridge, Massachusetts: Productivity Press.

Mouritsen, J., Hansen, A. and Hansen, C.Ø. (2001) Inter-organizational Controls and Organizational Competencies: Episodes around Target Cost Management/Functional Analysis and Open Book Accounting, *Management Accounting Research*, June, pp. 221–244.

Society of Japanese Value Engineering (1992) *VE Terminology*, Tokyo: Society of Japanese Value Engineering.

Yoshikawa, T., Innes, J. and Mitchell, F. (1989) Cost Management Through Functional Analysis, *Journal of Cost Management*, Spring, pp. 14–19.

Yoshikawa, T., Innes, J. and Mitchell, F. (1990) Cost Tables: A Foundation of Japanese Cost Management, *Journal of Cost Management*, Fall, pp. 30–36.

Yoshikawa, T., Innes, J. and Mitchell, F. (1994a) Functional Analysis of Activity-based Cost Information, *Journal of Cost Management*, Spring, pp. 40–48.

Yoshikawa, T., Innes, J. and Mitchell, F. (1994b) Applying Functional Cost Analysis in a Manufacturing Environment, *International Journal of Production Economics*, August, pp. 53–64.

Yoshikawa, T., Innes, J. and Mitchell, F. (1995) A Japanese Case Study of Functional Cost Analysis, *Management Accounting Research*, December, pp. 415–432.

Yoshikawa, T., Innes, J. and Mitchell, F. (2002) *Strategic Value Analysis*, London: Financial Times.

6

Target costing

Market-driven cost management

Peter Kajüter

Introduction

When Volkswagen developed the Beetle in the 1930s, it defined a price target of 990 Reichsmark. The reason for this price limit was the scarcity of foreign currencies required to pay for the parts and licences from abroad. Moreover, it was a price at which the car should be affordable for many people. In order to meet the price limit, Volkswagen examined alternative technical solutions for the various components of the car. As a result, the Beetle was not built with hydraulic brakes but with simpler cable brakes because this led to a cost saving of 25 Reichsmark (Franz, 1993).

Although the development of the Beetle can be seen as an early case of target costing, it was not until 1993/94 that Volkswagen systematically adopted target costing as a cost management technique in response to the competitive advantage that Toyota and other Japanese car manufacturers had gained. The Japanese firms integrated various elements of product cost management in the 1970s into a holistic, market-driven approach to profit and cost management called 'genka kikaku' or 'target costing' (Sakurai, 1989; Tanaka, 1989; Monden and Hamada, 1991). This structured approach to managing costs during product development did not attract any attention in other countries until the early 1990s when US and European firms tried to explore the reasons for the success of their Japanese competitors. However, Western companies in the automobile, electronics and mechanical engineering industries quickly realized the potential benefits of 'Japan's smart secret weapon' (Worthy, 1991, p. 48) and adopted the technique in one way or another. Subsequently, target costing has also gained significant interest in academia. As a result, a large body of literature has emerged over the past two decades dealing with technical issues of the method, its diffusion across industries and countries, its determinants and benefits as well as its behavioural and cultural implications.

In view of its relatively young age and multifaceted nature, it is not surprising that there is no common definition of target costing in literature. Although a broad consensus about the key elements of target costing prevails, its boundaries and its relationship with other management accounting tools are defined differently by different authors. While some take a broad view and regard target costing as a strategic approach to profit planning (e.g. Ansari et al., 1997; Cooper and Slagmulder, 1997), others view target costing primarily as a cost reduction technique (e.g. Fisher, 1995; Dekker and Smidt, 2003). In the broad view, however, cost reduction is a means of achieving profit targets. Focusing on its key elements, target costing can thus be defined as a market-driven approach to cost management that aims to reduce product costs over the entire life cycle.

This chapter pursues the objective of reviewing almost 25 years of academic research on target costing. Current achievements and directions for future research are outlined. The remainder of the chapter is structured as follows. Section 2 focuses on technical issues of the target costing concept. After that, section 3 presents empirical evidence of target costing practices. The chapter ends with a summary and conclusions in section 4.

Technical issues of the target costing concept

The target costing process

Target costing is a market-driven approach to cost management that reverses the traditional cost-plus pricing into a price-minus costing. It takes the market price and the profit margin as given and determines allowable costs according to the following formula:

Market price – target profit = allowable cost.

By comparing the allowable cost (target cost) with the estimated cost (drifting cost) a cost gap can be identified showing the need for a cost reduction.

To capture the concept more precisely, the CAM-I model defined six key principles for target costing: (1) price-led costing, (2) customer focus, (3) design centred, (4) cross-functional teams, (5) life-cycle orientation, (6) value chain involvement (Ansari et al., 1997). These principles become manifest in the target costing process, which comprises several steps (Figure 6.1).

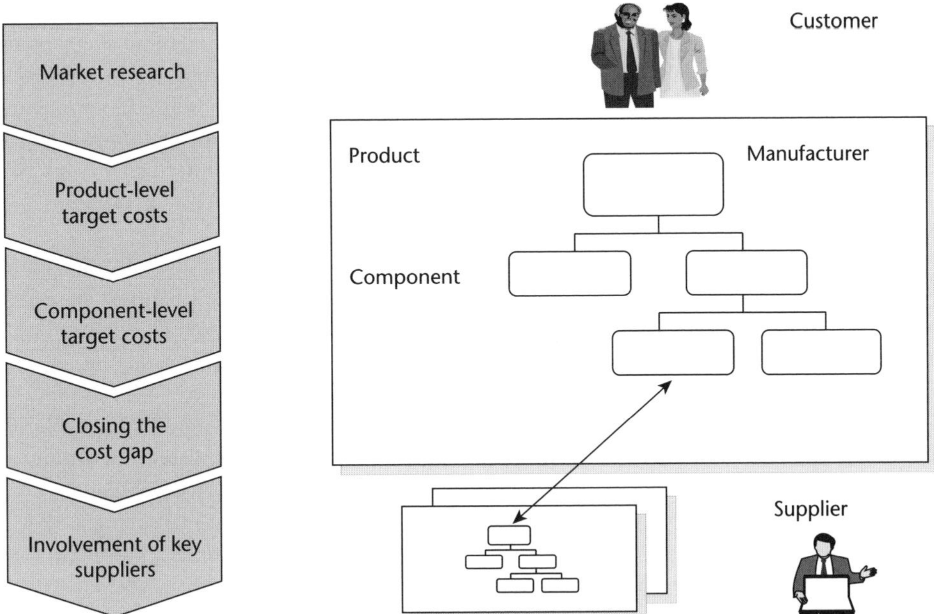

Figure 6.1 Target costing process

The first step is to understand customer needs and the customer's willingness to pay for certain product features. Hence, target costing does not take internal processes and technologies as a starting point, but rather requires comprehensive **market research**. This includes the use of various market research methods to analyse the needs of the target customers (e.g. conjoint analysis, see for instance Green and Srinivasan, 1990) as well as a solid competitive analysis to understand the competitors' pricing policies and product design.

The second step in the target costing process is **product-level target costing**. Based on the market price and a target profit margin, the allowable costs for the entire product are determined. Unless the allowable costs are unachievable even with hard effort, they equal the target costs of the product. By using cost estimation tools such as cost tables, drifting costs (viz. Feil et al., 2004) for the entire product have to be estimated and compared with the target costs in order to identify and quantify the cost gap.

The product-level target costs are too aggregated, though, and are not suited as an operational target for the product development teams that are only responsible for single components or parts. For this reason, the product-level target costs are decomposed. This third step in the target costing process is called **component-level target costing** (Cooper and Slagmulder, 1997, 1999a). The cost gap is thereby allocated to the various components and parts that make up the product.

To **close the cost gap**, cost reduction measures are initiated in the fourth step. They may refer to the design of the product and its components, the design of manufacturing processes or the materials used. Other cost management tools – such as value engineering, reverse engineering and activity-based costing – serve to identify potential cost reduction opportunities (Cooper and Slagmulder, 2002; Cokins, 2002). Thus, target costing is closely linked with other management accounting tools which are also considered to be an integral part of it (Ansari et al., 1997). In closing the cost gap, the **involvement of key suppliers** plays an important role, in particular if they develop and manufacture components specifically designed for the product. Close cooperation with these suppliers can offer opportunities to exploit cost reduction opportunities beyond the firm's boundaries. Open-book accounting is often an element of such inter-organizational cost management efforts (Kajüter and Kulmala, 2005, 2010). However, target costing can also be applied to these inter-organizational relationships. Component-level target costs may become the market price of the supplier which in turn starts a target costing process for its product. Hence, the target costing processes of manufacturing firms and their suppliers become linked (chained target costing). Thereby target costing transmits the competitive pressure upstream (Cooper and Slagmulder, 1997).

Target costing requires not only the involvement of key suppliers but also of other value chain partners such as dealers and distributors. These external value chain partners are often part of the cross-functional target costing teams comprising employees from all relevant business functions – product development, procurement, production, sales and marketing, as well as accounting.

Although the target costing process can be applied at all stages of the product life cycle, its main focus is on the product development phase because this offers the greatest opportunities to manage costs. As more and more costs are committed during product development, cost reductions become increasingly difficult to realize. However, focusing cost management efforts on the early stages in the product life cycle entails the problem of estimating the impact of design changes on future product costs (Monden, 1995).

The basic target costing concept outlined above focuses on the unit cost of a new product. The target costs per unit, however, also include costs for product development, investments in tools and, if applicable, recycling costs. In this way, all life cycle costs of a product are considered in the target costing process. This approach neglects the fact that the development of a new product is a multi-period project. Costs and revenues (better to say cash flows) occur at different points in time during the life of the project. Market prices, labour costs, raw material costs, etc. may change over time. The traditional basic target costing concept does not take this into account. It neglects the time value of money, assumes certainty, and uses average values. In view of these shortcomings, life cycle target costing concepts have been proposed in the German literature (Franz, 1997; Mussnig, 2001). These concepts consider the development of a new product as an investment project and use the net present value as a performance measure. As these life cycle target costing approaches do not decompose the target costs to single components, they may be used to complement rather than to substitute the basic target costing concept.

The basic target costing process described above looks fairly straightforward at first glance. However, a closer look reveals several technical issues throughout the entire process. The following two sections therefore discuss the most important technical issues of target costing at the product and component levels.

Target costing at the product level

Product-level target costing determines the cost reduction requirement for the entire product. It is based on a market-driven costing procedure (Figure 6.2). Each of the elements contains technical problems.

Determining the optimal **market price** for a product is a traditional domain of marketing. The price a customer is willing to pay depends, among others factors, on the product's attributes. Pricing has implications for volume and market share. All these aspects have to be considered when setting the market price for a product in the target costing process. In addition, there are a number of other issues to be taken into account. First, prices are not the same in all markets. Rather, they may differ for domestic and foreign markets. Thus, when determining the market price for products that are sold internationally, an average market price must be derived based on assumptions for the different prices and the expected volumes in the various markets. Second, as the product development often takes several years, inflation, exchange rates, pricing policy of competitors and other factors influencing future market prices have to be considered. Third, market prices vary over time. Especially in the case of high-tech products, prices usually decline over the product life cycle as competition from new products increases. Hence, an average price has to be calculated for the target costing process. Fourth, determining the market price is already quite challenging for the latest generation of an existing product (e.g. the subsequent model of the current Golf), but it is even more difficult for innovative products that do not yet exist. Fifth, the ability to determine the market price depends on the type of product. While suppliers of industrial goods usually know their (small number of) customers well and negotiate

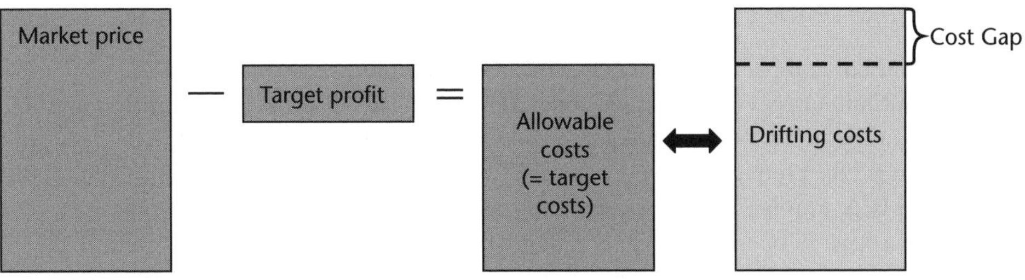

Figure 6.2 Product-level target costing

prices for a contract, it is more demanding for manufacturers of consumer goods to explore future market prices an anonymous group of customers is willing to pay.

In addition to the market price, the **target profit** must be determined. The target profit reflects the expectations of shareholders for an adequate return on their investment. Target costing is thereby ultimately a technique for value-based management. A minimum target for the ROI can be derived from the cost of capital: to create value, ROI must be higher than WACC. However, the target profit in the basic target costing concept is not a return on investment, but a return on sales (ROS), and therefore does not consider the amount of capital tied up in the product (Sakurai, 1989). Assuming a certain asset turnover, a minimum target profit margin can be derived from the cost of capital, though:

$$\text{WACC} = \text{ROI} = \text{ROS} \times \text{Asset Turnover}.$$

If, for instance, WACC is 10%, then ROI should be at least 10%, and – assuming an asset turnover of 2 – the target ROS is 5%. This target profit margin would be an average ROS for the entire company, which may be adjusted for different kinds of products. A firm's current profit margins – as well as medium-term profit plans – can be considered in setting the target profit margin for individual products (Kato, 1993; Kato et al., 1995).

Subtracting the target profit from the market price leads to the **allowable costs** per unit of the product. In general, the allowable costs equal the **target costs** of the product. If it turns out, though, that the allowable costs cannot be realized even with strong efforts and creativity, target costs may be set above allowable costs. In this case, the target profit margin is not achieved unless continuous cost savings are realized over the product life cycle so that the profit target is met on average.

Finally, when comparing target costs with drifting costs to determine the **cost gap**, two further issues arise. First, as target costs are full costs per unit, drifting costs must be determined as full costs as well. This requires sophisticated cost estimation tools for both direct and indirect costs. Estimating the latter is particularly difficult and requires the use of activity-based costing systems (Horváth et al., 1998; Cokins, 2002). The allocation of indirect costs also implies that different costing systems may lead to different drifting costs per unit and thereby result in different cost gaps. Using activity-based costing systems in the case of complex products may lead to a higher drifting cost per unit – compared to traditional costing systems, for instance. Second, as in all absorption costing systems, the full cost per unit depends on volume. This implies, for target costing, that the cost gap varies with different degrees of capacity utilization. Even if the cost gap is closed by the start of production due to cost reduction measures during product development, it may arise again at the manufacturing stage if the number of units sold is lower than expected.

Target costing at the component level

An important but complex and tricky element of target costing is to decompose the total target costs per unit into target costs for single components and parts of the product. It is important in order to identify the components and parts whose costs have to be reduced and to derive operational targets for the product development teams. It is, on the other hand, complex and tricky due to the often large number of components and parts and the various assumptions and subjective estimates that have to be made. While component-level target costing is already quite challenging for industrial products from assembly industries, it is even more so for services because their 'components' and 'parts' are activities and processes that are far less well documented and defined than the physical items of a product, which can be shown on a parts list. This also explains the lower adoption rates of target costing in service industries (see section on Adoption of target costing, p. 90).

There are two approaches for component-level target costing: the function method and the components method. The **function method** aims to systematically translate customer requirements into product components and parts. It assumes that a product can be considered to be a bundle of functions that the product fulfils to solve the needs of the customer. The relative importance of these functions (e.g. speed, safety) is measured by market research techniques such as conjoint analysis. The difficult step is to make a precise link between the functions and the components that contribute to deliver the functions. If, for example, 25% of a car's value originates from safety, and if several components contribute to achieving safety (e.g. brakes, seat belts, airbags, body), the target costing team has to make subjective estimates about the individual contribution of each component to the overall safety of the car. The total contribution of a component to the product's value is then the basis for decomposing the total target costs to the components. Thus, the function method assumes a linear relationship between the value created and the resources consumed. The more value a component contributes, the higher are its target costs.

While the function method works in the classroom using simplistic examples (e.g. Tanaka, 1989), it does not lead to reliable results in the case of complex products in practice. Although it may have the advantage of explicitly considering the voice of the customer, its practical application is limited to those elements of a product that the customer can see and evaluate. Moreover, the selection of product function, the judgements made regarding the contribution of components to these functions, as well as the simplifying assumption of a linear relationship between value creation and cost allocation to components – are critical issues that constrain the usefulness of the method. Little research exists that has tried to further develop this area of target costing.

Compared to the numerous technical issues associated with the function method, the **component method** is much more pragmatic. As its name indicates, it decomposes the total target costs directly to the components based on a cost structure of a reference product. Usually the reference product is a predecessor model, but it could also be a comparable product of a competitor. Thus, the component method requires the existence of a similar product to derive a cost structure which may be modified to consider changing customer needs or new technological developments. Customer requirements are taken into account more implicitly in this method. There is no reference to the functions of the product unlike the function method. This may entail the danger that the current design and the existing components are not questioned but rather carried over to the new product. However, the component method can be applied to all components and sub-components down to single parts.

The following example from Volkswagen illustrates the component method (Claassen and Ellssel, 2002; numbers are artificial). Based on existing products Volkswagen defines the cost structure of a new model comprising direct costs (60%), indirect costs (28%), a risk margin (2%) and a profit margin (10%). Given the average net selling price for the domestic and export markets of €12,397, respective absolute targets are derived for these four items (Figure 6.3). The indirect costs (€3,471) and some elements of the direct costs (€1,100, e.g. for warranty costs, direct sales costs) are not decomposed to single components and parts as they can hardly be influenced by engineers. What is further decomposed are direct material and direct labour costs (€6,338). For all other items target costs are defined not per unit but per cost category for the entire product.

Initially, six major components are distinguished: engine, gearbox, chassis, body, trim, electricals (Figure 6.4). The total cost of the current model (€8,000), the current costs of each component, as well as their relative share serve as a starting point for determining the target

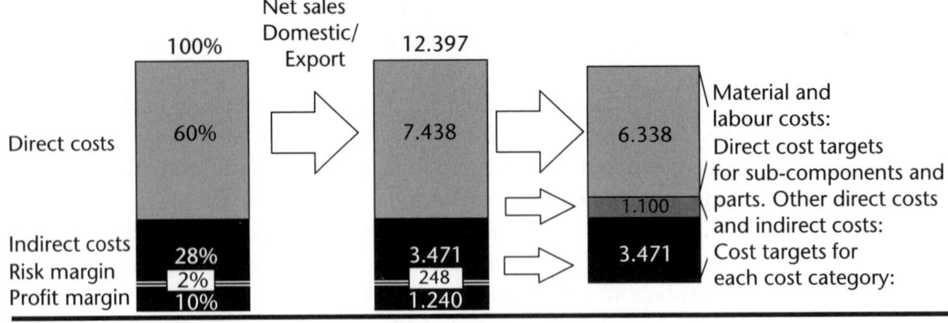

Figure 6.3 Component-level target costing at Volkswagen
Source: Claassen and Ellssel, 2002, p. 176.

costs for each component of the new product. For the new car model, additional features are planned to meet the increasing expectations of customers. Also, feedback received from customers in the form of complaints is taken into account when deciding on the design of the new model. The additional features not only lead to higher costs for the new model (€9,500), they also cause changes in the cost structure. The relative share of trim and electricals increased from 16% to 18% and from 20% to 22% respectively. These new relative shares, which reflect changing customer needs, are then applied to the target cost for direct material and direct labour (€6,338) to derive the target costs for the six components. This process is continued in the same way for sub-components and parts.

For some sub-components and parts it may be unrealistic to achieve the cost targets. If target costs for these are set above their initially derived value, it is necessary to compensate for these higher target costs by either lower target costs for other sub-components and parts or by reducing the targets for the indirect costs. Thus, setting the target costs for the sub-components and parts is an iterative process that ensures that the total target costs for the product are not exceeded.

Empirical evidence of target costing practices

Empirical research about target costing

As target costing is still a rather young management accounting technique, it is not surprising that the empirical research in this field is at an early stage. Compared to the large number of publications dealing with technical issues of target costing and the numerous experience reports of practitioners and consultants, there are far fewer empirical investigations. Most of them are single-site case studies (e.g. Shank and Fisher, 1995). Some multiple-site case studies have been conducted as well (e.g. Cooper and Slagmulder, 1997; Nicolini et al., 2000; Ellram, 2002). In addition, several field surveys analysed the adoption, determinants, goals and perceived benefits of target costing (e.g. Tani et al., 1994; Arnaout, 2001; Kim et al., 2002; Dekker and Smidt, 2003). As the data collection took place in the 1990s, these surveys do not provide an up-to-date picture of target costing practices. Due to the rather small samples, the studies also lack representativeness. Besides surveys specifically focusing on target costing practices, surveys covering general issues of management accounting and cost management have investigated target costing among several other aspects (e.g. Wijewardena and De Zoysa, 1999; Joshi, 2001; Kajüter and Kulmala, 2005). As a consequence, they were not able to analyse target costing in depth.

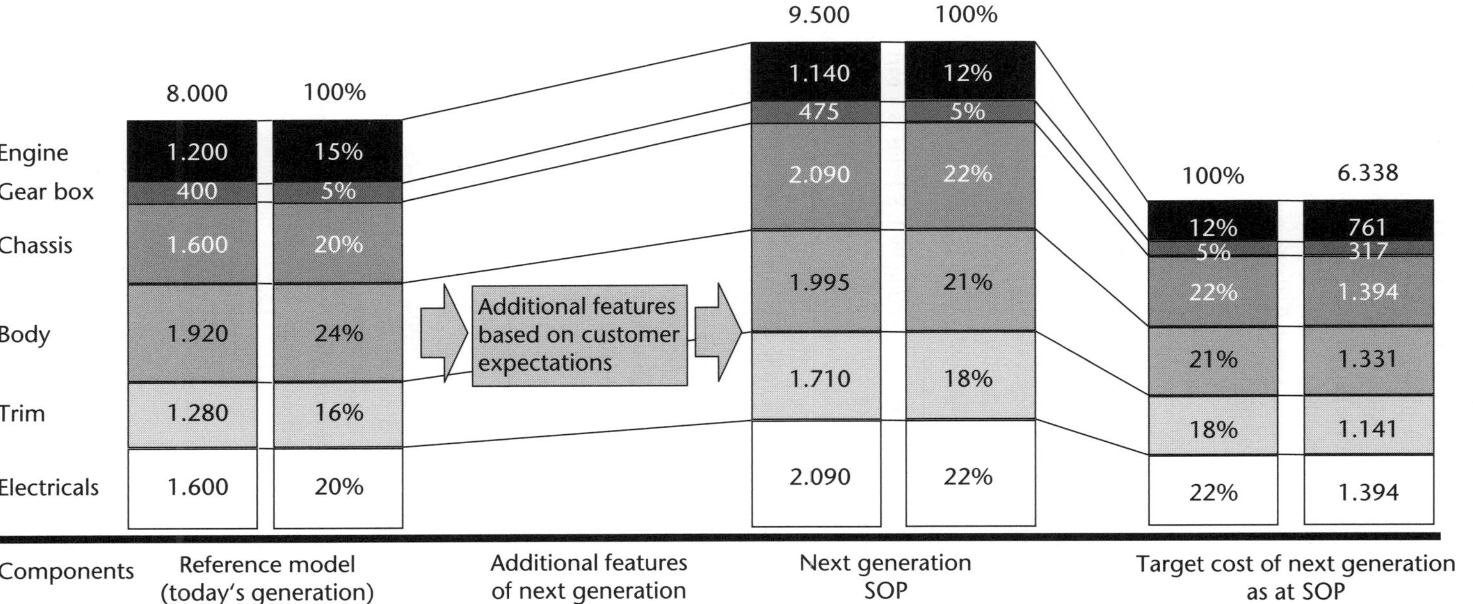

SOP = Start of Production

Figure 6.4 Component-level target costing at Volkswagen

Source: Claassen and Ellssel, 2002, p. 177.

Empirical research on target costing is therefore largely of an **exploratory nature**. The main focus has been to describe current practice and to gain a more comprehensive view of the adoption of target costing across different industries. Very little empirical research about target costing has attempted to test hypotheses. Monden et al. (1997), for example, tested hypotheses about the motivational impact of alternative participation and performance-evaluation methods on the cost reduction performance of product designers in the product development process. Consistent with the exploratory state of the research, there are also only a few experimental studies on target costing issues (e.g. Monden et al., 1997; Everaert and Bruggeman, 2002).

Adoption of target costing

Several surveys have explored adoption rates of target costing. A survey by Tani et al. (1994) investigated the use of target costing in Japanese manufacturing companies listed at the Tokyo Stock Exchange. The results indicate that 60.6% of the firms use target costing in one way or another. Further, 32.8% had implemented target costing company-wide, 18.3% used it in some divisions or departments, and 9.4% for particular projects. The adoption rates varied across industries, with the assembly sector being the most extensive user of target costing (Tani et al., 1994; Tani and Kato, 1994).

Kim et al. (2002) studied the adoption of target costing by US firms as a part of the CAM-I target costing project. Based on a sample of 120 mainly manufacturing firms they report an adoption rate of 40%. Most of the adopters had implemented target costing partially. Only 19% used it throughout the organization. As 50% of the adopting firms had used target costing for between one and three years, Kim et al. conclude that target costing is relatively new to many US companies.

In Germany, Kajüter (2005) revealed that 55% of German firms with more than 3,000 employees adopted target costing, and another 13% planned to implement it. All firms in the automotive and electronics industries claimed to use target costing. Adoption rates in the service sector were lower than in manufacturing industries. Target costing was also more intensively used in the latter.

In addition to Japan, the USA and Germany, the adoption of target costing has also been analysed in more or less detail in other countries. Drury et al. (1993), for example, find that 26% of British manufacturing firms apply target costing often or regularly. Dekker and Smidt (2003) conclude that 59.4% of the listed Dutch manufacturing companies use target costing practices. Joshi (2001) reports an adoption rate of 35% for target costing in Indian firms.

Although the survey results are difficult to compare because they are based on differently defined samples (in particular as regards firm size and industry) and relate to different points in time, some common findings can be observed. First, target costing is used by a significant number of firms, not only in Japan but also in other countries. Second, target costing practices seem to vary across firms, industries and countries. It is therefore necessary to analyse the determinants that influence the adoption of target costing.

Determinants of target costing

Empirical studies have analysed various factors that explain the use of target costing. Given the exploratory nature of the research, the factors emerged as common patterns across single- or multiple-site case studies or from survey findings. According to these findings, size, industry, product characteristics, and the nature of the firm's environment are key determinants for the adoption of target costing. They are traditional internal and external context factors from a contingency theory perspective.

Firm size tends to be positively associated with the use of target costing (Kim et al., 2002; Kajüter, 2005). This finding is consistent with extant literature on management accounting practices (e.g. Chenhall, 2003). Large firms usually have more resources to implement target costing and to tailor the concept to their specific needs. As target costing is considered to be a disciplining mechanism for product development (Cooper and Slagmulder, 1997), there is also an agency theory argument for the positive association between firm size and target costing adoption: information asymmetries increase with size, thus making control mechanisms more relevant.

A second major determinant is the industry. The target costing concept has been developed in the Japanese assembly industries (automotive, electronics, machinery etc.) and is therefore most widely applied in these sectors (Tani et al., 1994; Cooper and Chew, 1996; Cooper and Slagmulder, 1997; Bhimani and Neike, 1999; Koga, 2000; Kim et al., 2002; Dekker and Smidt, 2003; Swenson et al., 2003; Kajüter, 2005). The technical challenges inherent in the target costing concept are presumably easier to solve in these industries than in other areas of the manufacturing sector or in service firms. The latter, for instance, first have to define standard processes and allocate costs to them in order to apply target costing. Despite the primary focus on assembly industries, there is evidence from several case studies that target costing can also be adapted to the circumstances of other industries, such as textiles (Hergeth, 2002; Seuring, 2002), construction (Nicolini et al., 2000), banking (Zimmermann and Grundmann, 2001) and software (Sakurai, 1989).

Closely linked with industry are the characteristics of the product: its complexity, its life cycle, and the duration of its development process. Cooper and Slagmulder (1997) also list the firm's product strategy and supplier-base strategy as important factors influencing target costing practice. Kim et al. (2002) suggest an impact of corporate culture. However, it is largely unexplored how corporate culture actually affects target costing practice and how it interacts with other determinants.

By contrast, there is comprehensive evidence that a competitive and unpredictable business environment induces firms to adopt target costing practices (Cooper and Slagmulder, 1997; Kim et al., 2002; Dekker and Smidt, 2003; Hibbets et al., 2003). Target costing apparently enables firms to better cope with competitive pressures and yields benefits – especially in dynamic settings.

Benefits of target costing

Reports from practitioners and consultants regularly describe the positive results experienced from the successful application of target costing. Besides such anecdotal evidence, the empirical literature documents various goals and benefits resulting from the use of target costing. Cost reduction is the main goal when adopting target costing practices (Tani et al., 1994; Kim et al., 2002; Dekker and Smidt, 2003). However, adopters also pursue other objectives with the implementation of target costing; in particular, to reduce product development time, to improve quality and to enhance customer satisfaction (Tani et al., 1994; Kim et al., 2002; Dekker and Smidt, 2003).

The empirical results indicate that firms are able to realize benefits by achieving the pursued goals or at least by enhancing the goal achievement. Arnaout (2001) studied German target costing adopters and found that 60.7% of the sample firms consider the impact of target costing on improved profitability to be high, 21.3% even as very high. Franz and Kajüter (2002) reveal that German target costing adopters evaluate the performance of target costing to be high, higher than for other cost management tools such as activity-based costing or benchmarking for life cycle costing. Moreover, empirical evidence suggests that the potential benefits of target costing are related and come together as a package (Kim et al., 2002). They also tend to increase over time as experience with target costing matures (Kim et al., 2002).

Hence, extant research provides evidence that target costing yields positive benefits for adopters. Some caution is necessary, however, in interpreting the results due to the limitations inherent in the research design of the studies. First, when surveying target costing adopters the samples may be biased. Failures in implementing target costing are not reported to the same extent because firms are reluctant to admit poor results. Second, when the persons in charge of developing and implementing target costing are asked about its success, their evaluation may overestimate the benefits. To avoid such limitations, future research could analyse the reasons for abandoning target costing and might use dyadic research designs to assess the performance of target costing practices.

Organizational and behavioural issues

Empirical research has also analysed organizational and behavioural aspects of target costing practices. One of the key principles of target costing is cross-functional teamwork. Empirical studies confirmed that various functional departments are involved in the target costing process (Tani et al., 1994; Kim et al., 2002; Dekker and Smidt, 2003). Mixed results exist, however, as regards the degree of involvement of single functions. Kim et al. (2002) find, for US firms, that design engineering and manufacturing departments participate most intensively in the target costing process, followed by the accounting and finance function, purchasing and product planning. Tani et al. (1996), to the contrary, report a leading role for management accounting in the implementation of target costing in German firms. Ellram (2002) investigates the supply management's involvement in the target costing process in detail and concludes that it plays a substantial role throughout the entire process, especially when developing component-level target costs.

The purchasing and supply management functions hold close relationships to suppliers that may get involved in the target costing process as well. Thus, target costing can be a technique to extend cost management efforts beyond the organization's boundaries (Cooper and Slagmulder, 1999b; Seuring, 2002; Carlsson-Wall and Kraus, 2010). Kim et al. (2002) find that target costing adopters provide training for their suppliers (50% for value engineering, 38% for cost driver analysis). Bozdogan et al. (1998) list enabling factors for integrating suppliers in target costing, e.g. matching product features with the specialized technical skills of suppliers. Empirical research on the application of target costing in inter-organizational relationships is still scarce, however. The effects target costing might have on the development of dyadic relationships or networks are largely unexplored (Carlsson-Wall and Kraus, 2010).

Only a few studies have analysed the behavioural implications of target costing. Bhimani and Neike (1999) report that the implementation of target costing at Siemens led to greater employee empowerment. Kim et al. (2002) find that US target costing adopters seldom link target costing to employee rewards. Using an experimental research design, Monden et al. (1997) provide evidence that cost reduction by target costing is improved if product designers participate in target setting and are held accountable for cost items under their control. Also, Everaert and Bruggeman (2002) describe the positive effect of target costs on the behaviour of design engineers.

Similarities and differences of target costing across countries

Target costing practices have been developed in Japan since the 1970s in a specific institutional and cultural environment. Although elements of target costing – value engineering, for example – have also been used by US and European firms, it was not until the 1990s that

Western companies started to adopt target costing in a comprehensive and structured way. There are some empirical studies that discuss the diffusion of target costing from Japan to other countries. Tani et al. (1994) find that target costing teams in foreign subsidiaries of Japanese firms consist of more than 50% local employees. Bellis-Jones et al. (1999) report that US-based Japanese firms use target costing in a similar way to Japanese domestic companies. However, Japanese subsidiaries are also influenced by US practices in their implementation of target costing.

The similarities and differences of target costing practices across countries are investigated by comparative management accounting research (Kajüter and Moeschler, 2011). Only very few studies compare the application of target costing cross-nationally (Ansari, 2007). Exploring the importance attached to various management accounting tools by Japanese and Australian firms, Wijewardena and De Zoysa (1999) find a significant difference for the perceived relevance of target costing. While target costing was considered to be the most important management accounting tool in Japan, it was only ranked tenth in Australia. Tani et al. (1996) find some particularities in target costing practices of German firms compared to those in Japanese companies. First, the adoption of target costing has been initiated by management accountants in German firms whereas the engineering function played the leading role in developing target costing practices in Japanese companies. Second, German firms tend to apply target costing with a stronger customer focus (e.g. by using conjoint analysis) than their Japanese counterparts. Third, target costs are more market-driven in Germany whereas they are more frequently derived from long-term profit plans in Japan.

The existing empirical comparative management accounting research about target costing has several limitations. Wijewardena and De Zoysa (1999), for example, use differently defined samples of Japanese and Australian firms and do not control for size, industry or other variables. Moreover, they use the term 'target costing', which may be understood differently in each country. As Dekker and Smidt (2003) note, firms often apply techniques very similar to target costing but use a variety of different names for them. It is therefore hard to compare adoption rates or an overall assessment of target costing practices across countries if equivalence in terminology is not ensured. Similar shortcomings can be observed in Tani et al. (1996) who compare the results of a survey of Japanese firms with ten case studies of German target costing adopters. Thus, future research could attempt to explore similarities and differences of target costing practices cross-nationally and thereby sensitize practitioners to national specifics.

Summary and conclusions

Target costing was developed by Japanese manufacturing firms in the 1970s by integrating and further developing various elements of product cost management. It is a market-driven approach to cost management that focuses cost management efforts on the design stage of the product life cycle because the opportunities to influence costs decline as the product reaches the manufacturing stage. Whereas the basic idea of target costing is simple, there are numerous technical issues inherent in the concept that make its implementation a complex task.

A comprehensive review of extant literature reveals that most papers are targeted on practitioners. They describe successful cases of target costing practice. Academic research in the field of target costing is still at an exploratory stage. After extensive research efforts in the 1990s, target costing has gained less attention by academics in the past few years. In view of the technique's potential benefits and the large number of unexplored issues, target costing practices merit more research in the future. Research projects could focus on both technical aspects (e.g. adapting target costing to the specifics of service industries, setting target profits for individual products, decomposition of target costs) and behavioural issues (e.g. impact of target costing on individual behaviour or corporate culture, the link between target costing and incentive systems). More research is also needed into the interaction between target costing and other cost management tools (Dekker and Smidt, 2003). Moreover, longitudinal case studies could investigate the long-term effects of target costing on product differentiation (Ansari et al., 2007). To advance our knowledge base about target costing, further empirical research should not only attempt to describe practices but also test hypotheses about the determinants and consequences of target costing application. Hence, target costing provides many fruitful areas for future research.

Bibliography

Ansari, S., Bell, J. and Cam, I. Target Cost Group, 1997. *Target Costing. The Next Frontier in Strategic Cost Management*, Irwin Professional Publishing, Chicago.

Ansari, S., Bell, J. and Okano, H., 2007. Target Costing: Uncharted Research Territory. In: *Handbook of Management Accounting Research*, Vol. 2, edited by Chapman, C., Hopwood, A. and Shields, M.D., Elsevier, Amsterdam, 507–530.

Arnaout, A., 2001. *Target Costing in der deutschen Unternehmenspraxis*, Vahlen, München (in German).

Bellis-Jones, R., Oldman, A. and Mills, R., 1999. Trends in cost management practice, *Management Accounting*, 77 (7), 28–30.

Bhimani, A. and Neike, C., 1999. How Siemens designed its target costing system to redesign its products, *Journal of Cost Management*, 13 (4), 28–34.

Bozdogam, K., Deyst, J., Hoult, D. and Lucas, M., 1998. Architectual innovation in product development through early supplier integration, *R&D Management*, 28 (3), 163–173.

Carlsson-Wall, M. and Kraus, K., 2010. Target Costing in Inter-Organizational Relationships and Networks. In: *Accounting in Networks*, edited by Håkansson, H., Kraus, K. and Lind, J., Routledge, New York and London, 184–210.

Chenhall, R. 2003. Management control system design within its organizational context – Findings from contingency-based research and directions for the future, *Accounting, Organizations and Society*, 28 (2/3), 127–168.

Claassen, U. and Ellssel, R. 2002. Produkt Business Pläne als operative Umsetzung von Target Costing und Target Investment. In: *Kostenmanagement*, edited by Franz, K.-P. and Kajüter, P., 2nd edn, Schäffer-Poeschel, Stuttgart, 173–186.

Cokins, G. 2002. Integrating Target Costing and ABC, *Journal of Cost Management*, 16 (4), 13–22.

Cooper, R. and Chew, W.B., 1996. Control tomorrow's cost through today's designs, *Harvard Business Review*, 74 (1), 88–97.

Cooper, R. and Slagmulder, R., 1997. *Target Costing and Value Engineering*, Productivity Press, Portland.

Cooper, R. and Slagmulder, R., 1999a. Developing profitable new products with target costing, *Sloan Management Review*, 40(4), 23–33.

Cooper, R. and Slagmulder, R., 1999b. *Supply Chain Development for the Lean Enterprise. Interorganizational Cost Management*, Productivity Press, Portland.

Cooper, R. and Slagmulder, R., 2002. Target costing for new-product development: Product-level target costing, *Journal of Cost Management*, 16 (4), 5–12.

Dekker, H. and Smidt, P., 2003. A survey of the adoption and use of target costing in Dutch firms, *International Journal of Production Economics*, 84 (3), pp. 293–320.

Drury, C., Brand, S., Osborne, P. and Tayles, M., 1993. *A Survey of Management Accounting Practices in UK Manufacturing Companies*, The Chartered Association of Management Accountants.

Ellram, L.M., 2002. Supply management's involvement in the target costing process, *European Journal of Production & Supply Management*, 8, 235–244.

Everaert, P. and Bruggeman, W., 2002. Cost targets and time pressure during new product development, *International Journal of Operations & Production Management*, 22, 1339–1353.

Feil, P., Yook, K. and Kim, I., 2004. Japanese target costing: a historical perspective, *International Journal of Strategic Cost Management*, 2(4), 10–19.

Fisher, J., 1995. Implementing target costing, *Journal of Cost Management*, 9 (2), 50–59.

Franz, K.-P., 1993. Target Costing. Konzept und kritische Bereiche, *Controlling*, 5 (3), 124–130 (in German).

Franz, K.-P., 1997. Ein dynamischer Ansatz des Target Costing. In: *Marktleistung und Wettbewerb – Strategische und operative Perspektiven der marktorientierten Leistungsgestaltung*, edited by Backhaus, K. et al., Gabler, Wiesbaden, 277–289 (in German).

Franz, K.-P. and Kajüter, P., 2002. Kostenmanagement in Deutschland. In: *Kostenmanagement*, edited by Franz, K.-P. and Kajüter, P., 2nd edn, Schäffer-Poeschel, Stuttgart, 569–585 (in German).

Green, P. E. and Srinivasan,V., 1990. Conjoint analysis in marketing: new developments with implications for research and practice, *The Journal of Marketing*, 54(4), 3–19.

Hergeth, H., 2002. Target costing in the textile complex, *Journal of Textile and Apparel Technology and Management*, 2 (4), 1–10.

Hibbets, A., Albright, T. and Funk, W., 2003. The competitive environment and strategy of target costing implementers: Evidence from the field, *Journal of Managerial Issues*, XV (1), 65–81.

Horváth, P., Gleich, R. and Schmidt, S., 1998. Linking target costing to ABC at a US automotive supplier, *Journal of Cost Management*, 12 (2), 16–24.

Joshi, P.L., 2001. The international diffusion of new management accounting practices: the case of India, *Journal of International Accounting, Auditing and Taxation*, 10, 85–109.

Kajüter, P., 2005. Kostenmanagement in der deutschen Unternehmenspraxis, *Zeitschrift für betriebswirtschaftliche Forschung*, 57, 79–100 (in German).

Kajüter, P. and Kulmala, H.I., 2005. Open-book accounting in networks, *Management Accounting Research*, 16 (2), 179–204.

Kajüter, P. and Kulmala, H.I., 2010. Open-Book Accounting in Networks. In: *Accounting in Networks*, edited by Håkansson, H., Kraus, K. and Lind, J., Routledge, New York and London, 210–232.

Kato, Y., 1993. Target costing support systems: lessons from leading Japanese companies, *Management Accounting Research*, 4 (1), 33–47.

Kato, Y., Böer, G. and Chow, C.W., 1995. Target costing: an integrative management process, *Cost Management*, 9 (1), 39–51.

Kim, I.-W., Ansari, S., Bell, J. and Swenson, D., 2002. Target costing practices in the United States, *Controlling*, 14 (11), 607–614.

Koga, K., 2000. Analysis of Variation of Target Costing Practices in the Camera Industry. In: *Japanese Cost Management*, edited by Monden, Y., Imperial College Press, London, 123–160.

Moeschler, M., 2012. Cost Accounting in Germany and Japan: A Comparative Analysis (Münsteraner Schriften Zur Internationalen Unternehmensrechnung), Peter Lang GmbH, Frankfurt am Main.

Monden, Y., 1995. *Cost Reduction Systems. Target Costing and Kaizen Costing*, Productivity Press, Portland.

Monden, Y. and Hamada, K., 1991. Target costing and Kaizen Costing in Japanese automobile companies, *Journal of Management Accounting Research*, 3, 16–34.

Monden, Y., Akter, M. and Kubo, N., 1997. Target costing performance based on alternative participation and evaluation methods: a laboratory experiment, *Managerial and Decision Economics*, 18 (2), 113–129.

Mussnig, W., 2001. Dynamisches Zielkostenmanagement, *Controlling*, 13 (3), 139–148 (in German).

Nicolini, D., Tomkins, C., Holti, R., Oldman, A. and Smalley, M., 2000. Can target costing and whole-life-cycle costing be applied in the construction industry? Evidence from two case studies, *British Journal of Management*, 11, 303–324.

Sakurai, M., 1989. Target costing and how to use it, *Journal of Cost Management*, 3 (2), 39–50.

Seuring, S., 2002. Supply Chain Target Costing – An Apparel Industry Case Study. In: *Cost Management in Supply Chains*, edited by Seuring, S. and Goldbach, M., Physica, Heidelberg and New York, 111–125.

Shank, J.K. and Fisher, J., 1999. Target costing as a strategic tool. *Sloan Management Review*, 41 (1), 73–82.

Swenson, D., Ansari, S., Bell, J. and Il-Woon, K., 2003. Best practices in target costing, *Management Accounting Quarterly*, 4 (2), 12–17.

Tanaka, T., 1989. Cost Planning and Control Systems in the Design Phase of a New Product. In: *Japanese Management Accounting*, edited by Monden, Y.M. and Sakurai, M., Cambridge, 49–71.

Tanaka, T., 1993. Target costing at Toyota, *Journal of Cost Management*, 7 (1), 4–11.

Tani, T. and Kato, Y., 1994. Target Costing in Japan. In: Neuere Entwicklungen im *Kostenmanagement*, edited by Dellmann, K. and Franz, K.-P., Haupt, Bern, 191–222.

Tani, T., Horváth, P. and von Wangenheim, S., 1996. Genka Kikaku und marktorientiertes Zielkostenmanagement, *Controlling*, 8 (2), 80–89 (in German).

Tani, T., Hiroshi, O., Nobumasa, S., Iwabuchi, Y., Fukuda, J. and Cooray, S., 1994. Target cost management in Japanese companies: current state of the art, *Management Accounting Research*, 5 (1), 67–81.

Wijewardena, H. and De Zoysa, A., 1999. A comparative analysis of management accounting practices in Australia and Japan: an empirical investigation, *The International Journal of Accounting*, 34(1), 49–70.

Worthy, F.S., 1991. Japan's smart secret weapon, *Fortune*, 124 (4), 48–51.

Zimmermann, G. and Grundmann, R., 2001. Zur Anwendung des Target Costing in Kreditinstituten, *Kreditwesen*, (2), 79–85 (in German).

7

Continuous improvement and Kaizen Costing

Takeo Yoshikawa and Reza Kouhy

Definition and introduction

In the Japanese language Kaizen Costing is called 'Genkakaizen' with 'genka' meaning 'cost', 'kai' meaning 'change' and 'zen' meaning 'good'. In other words Kaizen means change to good ways and good results: in the West this is usually interpreted as continuous improvement. For example, Imai (1986) in his glossary of terms defines Kaizen in relation to the workplace as meaning 'continuous improvement involving everyone – managers and workers alike'. Imai (1986) argues that a Kaizen strategy involves relatively small improvements. Monden and Hamada (1991, p. 17) suggest that 'Kaizen Costing is the system to support the cost reduction process in the manufacturing phase of the existing product . . . Kaizen refers to continuous accumulations of small betterment activities rather than innovative improvement'. They also argue that target costing and Kaizen Costing can be linked together and 'constitute the total cost management system of Japanese companies' (ibid., p. 17). There is a separate chapter on target costing in this book. See Chapter 6.

However, there is some disagreement about whether or not Kaizen Costing covers only the cost reduction process during the manufacturing stage for existing products. For example, Cooper and Slagmulder (2006) in their case study of the Olympus Optical Company found that there was 'product-specific Kaizen Costing' and 'general Kaizen Costing'. According to Cooper and Slagmulder (2006) product-specific Kaizen Costing was only for those high-volume products that did not achieve their target cost and the focus was on product design and was ad hoc. By contrast, in the Olympus Optical Company general Kaizen Costing concentrated on cost reduction during the production process and was systematic. This book also has a chapter on cost management during the design stage (see Chapter 5, Functional Analysis). The current chapter will concentrate on Kaizen Costing as an approach used after the design process to reduce the cost of existing products or services.

From their case study of the Olympus Optical Company, which examined the life cycle of the Stylus Zoom camera, Cooper and Slagmulder (2004, p. 45) found that 'Olympus Optical achieves significant cost reductions in manufacturing, contradicting the widely held assumption that a larger percentage of costs are locked in during design'. They found in this case study that 'costs can be aggressively managed throughout the product life cycle' and Kaizen Costing can contribute to such cost management after the design stage for both products and services (ibid., p. 45). Modarress et al (2005) present a case study of Kaizen Costing in a division of the Boeing Commercial Airline Company showing a method of setting Kaizen Costs in a production context.

Some of the early Western literature on Kaizen Costing concentrated on cost reduction during the manufacturing stage for existing products. However, experience has shown that Kaizen Costing can be applied to a wide range of services as well as products. For example, Kaizen Costing has been used in Japan in charities, construction, distribution, government and hospitals, to list only a few areas of its application. Kaizen Costing is now used in many countries and many sectors. For example, Granja et al (2005) show how Kaizen Costing can have a big impact on both the cost and performance of construction contracts.

In Japan the Kaizen approach is very much regarded as a management, rather than a management accounting, technique. Indeed, in Japan it is often referred to as Kaizen Management or just Kaizen rather than Kaizen Costing. The word 'Costing' in Kaizen Costing is rather misleading because it is an approach involving several different cost management techniques – as distinct from a specific type of costing such as Activity-Based Costing or Standard Costing. Kaizen Costing can be referred to more appropriately as Kaizen Cost Management because it is an approach to managing costs with incremental cost improvements – namely, continuous improvement.

Philosophies, aims and critical success factors

Wakamatsu (2007) has written a book on the introduction of the Toyota way of Kaizen, emphasizing its three underlying managerial philosophies. Firstly, customers are the top priority and are at the centre of all Kaizen Cost Management. Secondly, the culture of the organization is very important, including the following:

1. The targets set must be challenging.
2. Solve problems by asking the 'five times why'. This means to keep asking 'why' – the answer is 'because'; then ask why for this 'because' and the answer is 'because', then again ask 'why' for this 'because' . . . keep asking 'why' at least five times.
3. Make everything as transparent and visible as possible.
4. Train employees to respect human nature.
5. Have an attitude of learning things without any arrogance; appreciate such learning.
6. Cherish teamwork.
7. Take into consideration all factors including safety, quality and environmental aspects while at the same time offering additional value to customers.

The third underlying managerial philosophy is the changing and dynamic nature of the organizational environment. Managers need to realize that the environment (both inside and outside the organization) is not stationary but is in a state of flux.

Wakamatsu (2007) suggests four aims for Kaizen. The first aim is to have the lowest cost while at the same time aiming for the highest quality and shortest delivery time. This first aim implies the elimination of waste and variances, the use of set work procedures, and clear roles and responsibilities for all employees. The second aim is to train the best employees, creating human assets (not just human resources). This aim emphasizes the importance of practical experience. Only the best employees can deliver an organization fit for the customers. Most organizations cannot exist without customers (or their equivalent, such as users of government services). To train the best employees means that employees must be trained to have:

1. the ability to think for themselves;
2. the power to perform for customers;
3. the ability to evaluate.

This training of employees is very much a long-term and ongoing process in the Kaizen approach.

The third aim is to ensure at least a minimum level of profit (or its equivalent in, for example, public sector organizations) regardless of any factors, such as recession. However, Kaizen is not just a management approach judged on the final financial results but rather a process including any necessary corrections (because the situation has changed) to ensure the expected results. This is why the Kaizen approach fits well with target cost management (discussed in another chapter in this book) because target costing begins with the selling price being decided by the customers (or market) rather than being a cost-plus approach to pricing. In other words the expected profit cannot be achieved simply by changing the selling price as costs increase. Instead, managers must respect the speed and timing of all the processes under their control, manufacture and deliver products based on sales orders, and always reduce their costs (including people costs, material costs, equipment costs, overhead costs and information costs).

The fourth aim is to respect and value the human nature of employees and to use all the experience and wisdom of employees. The Kaizen approach is very much a bottom-up approach rather than a top-down approach to continuous improvement, with all employees being actively involved. This is why all employees need to feel valued and be motivated, because without their suggestions the Kaizen approach will fail. The Kaizen approach means that the improvements made to any process are usually small incremental amounts rather than radical improvements through innovation or large-scale investment, although sometimes improvements will involve capital expenditure (a new machine, for example). Kaizen Cost Management involves everyone from the top management to shop-floor employees. Indeed in the Kaizen approach shop-floor employees are usually much more influential than top managers.

The fifth aim is not to sell the products made but to manufacture the products that sell (the same applies to services). This means not manufacturing products based on sales forecasts, but manufacturing products after receiving the sales orders. The detailed practical implications of achieving such an aim will be discussed later in this chapter in discussing the practice of the New Production System. Another implication of this aim is to make as many costs as possible variable rather than fixed. Teamwork is also critical to achieve this aim.

In relation to the above three managerial philosophies and five aims for the Kaizen approach, Wakamatsu (2007) highlights seven critical success factors. The first is preparation to win, namely, to learn the managerial approach to winning 'modestly'. The second critical success factor is to forget about past history and traditions: the Kaizen approach is *not* to do everything the same way as in the past but to improve continuously. The third critical success factor is to clarify the roles and responsibilities of the organization including making visible to all involved the costs of each department, process and product so that all such costs can be managed via continuous improvement.

The fourth critical success factor according to Wakamatsu (2007) is that the human nature of employees is valued, leading to very motivated employees. The fifth critical success factor is that everyone involved is always thinking about the Kaizen targets to be achieved. This includes not only all employees of the organization, but also employees of the suppliers and sub-contractors. The sixth critical success factor is that every single employee of the organization has the mindset that 'I myself can change the organization with my knowledge, skills and motivation.' However, even more important than this sixth critical success factor is the seventh (that was touched on under the above underlying philosophies of the Kaizen approach), namely, that the power of the group – teamwork – is stronger than the power of any individual.

Practices

The previous section on the underlying philosophies, aims and critical success factors is at a general level, but this is fundamental because the essence of Kaizen is a state of mind for all employees. Employee suggestions are at the core of the Kaizen approach and many of these suggestions will be informal comments from employees. Indeed Wakamatu (2007) suggests Kaizen practices that cover not only quality and safety but also the '5Ss', namely:

1. *Seiri*, meaning arrangement.
2. *Seiton*, meaning tidiness.
3. *Seisou*, meaning cleaning.
4. *Seiketu*, meaning preventative maintenance.
5. *Shituke*, meaning training.

To a Western mind the above five 'practices' seem to be at a very general level and again this emphasizes that for Kaizen Cost Management, the general approach is as important as the detailed techniques.

Monden and Lee (1993) present an interesting and detailed case study of how the Japanese car-maker, Daihatsu, uses Kaizen Costing to reduce costs. Monden and Lee (1993, p. 22) point out that 'Daihatsu defines Kaizen costing activities as those activities that sustain the current level of the existing car production costs, and further reduce it to the expected level based on the company plan'. The aim of the Kaizen approach in Daihatsu is to reduce the actual costs to a level below the existing standard costs. Monden and Lee (1993) compare Kaizen Costing concepts and standard costing concepts; one such comparison is that Kaizen Costing is about cost reduction, assumes continuous manufacturing improvement and achieves cost reduction, whereas standard costing is about cost control, assumes current manufacturing conditions and meets cost performance standards. Monden and Lee (1993) show that Daihatsu sets both variable cost improvement (using the actual cost per car from the previous year) and fixed-cost improvement and give detailed examples of how such improvement works in practice, and how Kaizen Costing links closely with Daihatsu's profit-planning process.

Monden and Hamada (1991) give an example of how Kaizen cost targets are set and evaluated during a Kaizen Cost meeting. These meetings are held at various levels (including divisional plant, process, department and section) with the cost reduction or Kaizen target being set at each level according to the specific situation involved and following discussion between managers and subordinates. The Kaizen approach is very participative and depends more on contributions from lower level employees than from top managers. Monden and Hamada (1991, p. 29) found that 'on the manufacturing floor, everyone is involved daily in Kaizen activities through quality control circles and suggestion schemes'. However, there are practices in addition to quality control circles and suggestion schemes that can help with the Kaizen approach, such as Just In Time, Kousuu, the Noren Wake system and the New Production System. These four practices will be discussed in the following four sections.

Just In Time

The Just In Time approach fits well with the Kaizen approach, basically because the holding of stocks can hide underlying problems for an organization. However, the Just In Time approach requires secure and efficient suppliers, almost no stoppages of the production line and the shortest possible processing time. Purchasing is organized so that the required materials are available just as the first department requires them. In some organizations daily or even hourly deliveries are arranged. The Kaizen approach means that continuous improvements are made not only to the production process but also to the supplier chain process. For example, production in a Just In Time organization is on a demand-pull basis, with the starting point being the customer's sales order. Production in each department is initiated only from a demand for its output from departments further down the production process. If stock is held, the problems in the production process can be hidden. However, with little or no stock, problems in the production process are highlighted and the Kaizen approach can be used to solve such problems and, once the initial problems are overcome, the Kaizen approach can then be used to improve the process further.

The Kaizen approach will help to eliminate any bottlenecks and to reduce production lead time (further details of how to reduce production lead time will be discussed later in this chapter under the heading The New Production System). In a Japanese organization using a combination of Just In Time and Kaizen, the following problems were highlighted and solved:

1. non-processing production time where the work-in-progress was lying idle on the factory floor;
2. excessive set-up times;
3. scrap and rework costs;
4. quality problems.

Just In Time is now a very well-known approach in the West, and in Japan the combination of Just In Time and the Kaizen approach is very powerful.

Kousuu

In contrast to Just In Time, Kousuu is a system that is little known in the West. Kousuu is helpful for the Kaizen approach as a reporting system that provides feedback on Kaizen attempts to reduce resource consumption within the organization. Kousuu are basically units of resource consumption expressed in physical terms – usually in terms of direct or indirect labour time or machine time. Kousuu covers all resource elements of conversion and support costs, including work production processes and overhead service functions such as maintenance and material handling.

In their case study of one particular Japanese organization, Yoshikawa et al (1997, p. 50) found Kousuu 'expressed in terms of the various time components of the work required to produce one unit of final output' – this is known in Japanese as 'Gentani'. A Gentani shows the conversion work resource consumption product by product and is, therefore, a performance measure. Some Japanese organizations use only these physical performance measures but others calculate a charge-out rate for each Kousuu (based on the relevant labour and equipment costs involved). Japanese organizations use Kousuu widely in sectors such as construction, defence and manufacturing (see Defence Equipment Society, 1989 and Government Buildings Department of the Ministry of Construction, 1991).

Table 7.1 gives an example of the detail included in a typical Kousuu report to managers in terms of labour working hours for a specific production process for a particular period of time. It shows the decomposition of working time into basic working hours that add value to this process and line management hours that are basically non-value-added activities. The table

Table 7.1 Working hours for Kousuu

Type of working hours			*Activities*
Working hours (WH)	Basic working hours (BWH)	Net working hours (NWH)	1. machine loading and unloading 2. working manually or operating machines 3. supplying parts daily 4. washing processed parts and finished products 5. measuring processed parts and finished products
		Incidental working hours (A)	1. walking between processes 2. dressing parts and products 3. loading parts on to automatic machines 4. adjusting machine tolerance 5. checking size of processed parts and finished products by random sampling 6. cleaning for checking size of processed parts and finished products by random sampling
	Line management hours (LMH)	Incidental working hours (B)	1. turning on and off the main switches 2. preparing parts for manufacturing 3. preparing and checking tools 4. checking machines and supplying oil 5. cleaning machines and floors 6. warming up machines 7. holding preliminary meeting and making contact with workers 8. checking the blueprint
		Incidental working hours (C)	1. changing cutting or grinding oil 2. changing running or lubricating oil
		Set-up hours (SU)	1. changing fitting and fixing tools 2. changing manufacturing tools
		Artificial delay hours (AD)	1. relating to abnormal shop-floor works 2. relating to factory management 3. relating to personal issues
		Waiting hours (W)	1. waiting for manufacturing parts and products

Source: Yoshikawa et al (1997, p. 51).

then analyses in more detail these two basic components of working hours into much more detail. Reports such as Table 7.1 give not only managers but also the machine operators themselves details of how resources are being consumed. Such a report helps everyone in a Kaizen environment to identify continuous operational improvements. These improvements can be monitored in terms of the improvement in the Kousuu performance measure both physically and financially.

Another performance measure ratio that is commonly reported in the Kousuu system is that of value-added time compared to non-value-added time. Employees try to reduce the non-value-added element of this ratio and during the Kaizen process this encourages their search for ways to eliminate or reduce non-value-added work time. However, some Japanese organizations have found that too much of this pressure on employees can become dysfunctional and Yoshikawa et al (1997, p. 52) concluded that 'Kousuu are therefore best used as a constructive support system for improvement rather than as a punitive control device'.

Yoshikawa et al (1997) provide detailed examples of five reports that form the core of the Kousuu-based reporting system. The first is a daily report highlighting the actual level of Kousuu achieved in an organization. The second report summarizes the savings made in Kousuu during the previous six months. The third report is a budget report for the organization's existing products for the forthcoming six months. The fourth report links the Kousuu reporting system to the Kaizen approach: an example is given in Table 7.2 which links back to the details shown in Table 7.1 above. In Table 7.2 the working hours are reported in terms of net working hours (in other words value-added hours), incidental working hours, set-up hours, artificial delay hours and waiting hours. Lines three to five in Table 7.2 report the actual Kousuu for three different production processes, namely, X, Y and Z. Line six gives the standard working hours and line seven summarizes the Kaizen proposals that have been made.

These Kaizen proposals are summarized in Table 7.3 under the headings net working hour variances (such as speed up work activity), incidental working hour variances (such as change work layout), set-up hour variances (such as adopt one-lathe tool changing system), artificial delay hour variances (such as rebalance work to staff) and waiting hour variances (such as reschedule throughput).

The fifth and final report is a Kousuu budget statement summarizing the planned Kaizen activities for the budget period. This report will summarize the Kousuu per unit at the beginning of the budget period and the planned Kousuu per unit to be saved during this periods. Yoshikawa et al (1997) found that Kousuu was particularly useful for organizations with an extensive product range and where the product life cycles were relatively short. In such organizations Kaizen proposals are a very important way of reducing the lead time to market and reducing the manufacturing time for new products. In general, the main test for any Kaizen proposal is elimination or reduction of the Kousuu.

Noren-wake system

For an English-speaking person 'wake' appears to be the opposite of 'sleep' but in fact it is pronounced in the same way as 'wacky'. In Japanese 'Noren' means 'company or section' and 'wake' means 'become independent' – the Noren-wake system aims to turn each department, production line, sales office etc. into an independent company with its own profit and loss account. Each department etc. becomes a profit centre. Furthermore, for every 'independent unit' there is a profit and loss account for every single day – to the Western mind, this seems to be an incredible amount of detail. This Noren-wake system can be useful for the Kaizen

Table 7.2 Kousuu for Kaizen activity statement

(1) Working hour structures	(NWH)	(A)	(B)	(C)	(SC)	(AD)	(W)
(2) Production process							
(3) Process X (actual working hours)	(NWH)	(A)	(B)	(C)	(SC)	(AD)	(W)
(4) Process Y (actual working hours)	(NWH)	(A)	(B)	(C)	(SC)	(AD)	(W)
(5) Process Z (actual working hours)	(NWH)	(A)	(B)	(C)	(SC)	(AD)	(W)
(6) Standard working hours (for each process)	(NWH)	(A)	(B)	(C)	(SC)	(AD)	(W)
(7) Kaizen activities proposal	1,2,3	1,2,3		1,2,3		1,2	1,2

Abbreviations are listed below and they correspond to those used in Table 7.1.
(NWH) = Net working hours, (A) = Incidental working hours of A, (B) = Incidental working hours of B, (C) = Incidental working hours of C, (SU) = Set-up hours, (AD) = Artificial delay hours, (W) = Waiting hours.
Source: Yoshikawa et al (1997, p. 55).

Table 7.3 Kaizen activities*

Net Working Hour Variances
1 Speed up work activity
2 Eliminate/reduce non-value-added activity
3 Introduce new machine

Incidental Working Hour (A) Variances
1 Change work layout
2 Increase productivity of lines
3 Introduce more automation

Incidental Working Hour (B), (C) and Set-up Hour Variances
1 Change approach
2 Adopt one-lathe tool changing system
3 Reduce number of changes

Artificial Delay Hour Variances
1 Reduce machine watch staffing
2 Re-balance work to staff

Waiting Hour Variances
1 Re-schedule throughput
2 Find alternative work for employees to do

*Numbers relate to those in Table 7.2, line 7.
Source: Yoshikawa et al (1997, p. 56).

approach because basically it encourages all employees to think how to improve the profit for their 'independent unit' and this leads to suggestions for continuous improvement. The Noren-wake system was used by Toyota, and some Japanese organizations use this Noren-wake system to help:

1. find a problem;
2. implement Kaizen activities;
3. reduce total costs;
4. raise profit awareness.

A Japanese case study will be used to illustrate the operations of a Noren-wake system. In the late 1980s and early 1990s this company was operating its production process on the basis of production lines when sales began to fall. This company found that it was very difficult to determine which product lines were profitable and which unprofitable. Furthermore, the monthly review was not sufficiently timely to take appropriate action. Following this decline in sales the company decided to introduce the Noren-wake system with a profit and loss account for each production line, for all the sales offices and for the head office.

The profit and loss account for each production line was calculated as follows. The sales for a production line consisted of the following two categories:

1. finished goods were treated as sold (for the purposes of the Noren-wake system) when the driver picked up the finished goods;
2. semi-finished products were treated as sold when these were transferred to another production line.

The costs and expenses for this profit and loss statement consisted of the following:

1. materials and parts when received in the store or when they arrived at the production line – whichever was earlier;
2. employee costs, overhead costs and interest.

The profit and loss statement for the head office consisted of the following:

1. sales were recognized (for this Noren-wake system) when the head office sold the finished products to a sales office;
2. the variable costs were the costs of products purchased from the factories;
3. the fixed costs were the head office employee costs, head office equipment costs (depreciation), head office electricity cost and other expenses.

The profit and loss statement for each sales office consisted of the following:

1. sales were recognized (for this Noren-wake system) when the sales office sold the finished products;
2. the variable costs were the cost of products purchased from the head office, sales promotion expenses, sales commissions and distribution expenses;
3. the fixed costs were costs of sales employees, sales equipment costs (depreciation), insurance and other costs associated with the sales office.

To help highlight the importance of profit to all employees, this company also used an internal money (or token) system. When materials for a production line arrive (usually at the production line but sometimes at the store), the production line buys these materials with red poker chips. Every two hours, when the fork-lift collects these 'finished goods' from the production line, white poker chips are handed over – the 'sale proceeds' for this production line. Employees on each production line can see these two piles of poker chips representing their sales and their costs and can see, therefore, whether the profit for their production line is rising or falling. This visual representation of the profit (or loss) has a great motivating effect on employees, who see this as their 'real profit' and who compete in profit terms against other production lines. Noren-wake is, therefore, a system that encourages the use of the Kaizen approach, with employees throughout the organization making many suggestions for improvements. A Kaizen approach can, of course, work without a Noren-wake system but some Japanese organizations have found that a Noren-wake system encourages employees to make even more suggestions for improvements. The Noren-wake system makes employees even more profit-conscious and even more willing to suggest improved ways to manage and reduce costs.

The New Production System

The approach of the New Production System has at least one similarity with the Noren-wake system in that a Kaizen approach can work without the New Production System but the New Production System motivates employees to make even more suggestions for continuous improvement. In Japan there is a New Production Study Group consisting of over 60 organizations (both manufacturing and service) with several supporting full-time instructors. These 60 organizations are divided into sub-groups of about 10 to 12, and in the Study Group there is no direct competitor so that confidential information can be discussed. For example, a sub-group may consist of organizations from the banking, brewing, electricity, electronics, furniture, house-building, leisure, motor vehicle, shipbuilding and wholesale sectors. The sub-groups of 10 to 12 organizations meet on a monthly basis at one of the organizations in the group to discuss a 'production' problem faced by that particular organization and hopefully to discuss a solution to this problem. The 60 organizations meet as an entire group to hear a summary presentation from the various sub-groups.

The basic idea underlying the New Production System is simple (but very difficult to achieve), and that is to reduce the 'production' cycle time (for both manufacturing and service organizations). The New Production System has three main themes. Firstly, it tries to eliminate three types of waste, namely:

1. waste from non-value-added activities;
2. waste from bad management;
3. waste from excess production capacity.

Secondly, the New Production System integrates business activities and also reduces the lead time between such activities. Thirdly, the New Production System manufactures products only for customer orders and not for stock purposes.

The New Production System has developed away from the system with stocks of raw materials, work-in-progress and finished goods. The first development was to eliminate the stock of finished goods with the goods being delivered from the end of the production line directly to the customers. The second development was to eliminate stocks of work-in-progress lying on the factory floor before each process. For example, after being machined, parts would lie on the factory floor waiting to be assembled but now the parts go straight from machining to assembly. To reach such a stage of development, the New Production System has four necessary conditions:

1. The lead time for the production cycle should be shorter than the customers' expectations.
2. The production system should be capable of manufacturing one unit of product.
3. It should be possible to purchase materials and parts whenever you wish and in the volume you want.
4. The quality of products should be perfect.

These four conditions seem very idealistic to the Western mind, and it is probably easier to understand the impact of the New Production System with an example.

In one of the organizations over a five-year period the sales increased from 48 million yen to 90 million yen while total stocks fell from 8 million yen to 3 million yen, meaning that stock turnover fell from 63 days to 12 days. Of course, such a reduction in stocks has many advantages, including:

1. reduced interest costs on stocks;
2. lower warehouse costs;
3. reduced employee costs in relation to stocks;
4. lower stock losses.

In fact this organization calculated that the total of such savings exceeded 3 million yen per year. Another very significant advantage from such a stock reduction is that it reveals problems that are hidden by higher levels of stock, such as:

1. poor yield rate;
2. machine down-times;
3. inefficient distribution channels;
4. long lead times for purchases.

The link between the New Production System and Kaizen is that usually the reduction in the production cycle time is achieved by a large number of small improvements. One advantage of the New Production System Study Group is that participants can learn from the experience of others. For example, a house-builder can learn from the experiences of a restaurant. This house-builder specializes in developing prefabricated houses – very different from the 1940s 'prefabs' in the UK. These houses are aimed at the upper end of the Japanese market, but built almost entirely in a factory and assembled at the building plots of the customers. This Japanese building company had reduced its production cycle time from more than one year to less than one month, from the placing of an order by a customer to final completion of the house on the customer's plot. In one room of this building company there are hundreds of small improvements documented around the four walls showing how this reduction in the production cycle time had been achieved. The New Production System has the three main themes listed above, but at the core of the system is the Kaizen approach, intended to achieve very significant reductions in the production cycle time.

Conclusions

This chapter has concentrated on Kaizen Costing as an approach introduced after the design process to reduce the cost of existing products or services through continuous improvement. The Kaizen approach can be used in almost any sector of the economy. Some of this continuous improvement comes from quality control circles and employee suggestion schemes but the philosophy (customers are the top priority, importance of the culture of the organization and changing nature of organizational environment), aims and critical success factors of the Kaizen approach are all important. Japanese organizations that have implemented the balanced scorecard have found that the Kaizen approach fits very well with it. Firstly, the cost-reduction objective of the Kaizen approach fits into the financial perspective of the balanced scorecard. Secondly, the philosophy of the Kaizen approach (that customers are the top priority) fits into the customer perspective of the balanced scorecard. Thirdly, the Kaizen improvements in the efficiencies of various business processes fit into the internal business process perspective of the balanced scorecard. Fourthly, the Kaizen philosophy of a changing and dynamic organizational environment and the Kaizen aims of training the best employees and using all the experience and wisdom of employees fit into the learning and growth perspective of the balanced scorecard.

The aim of Kaizen Costing in Daihatsu and many other organizations is to reduce the actual costs to a level below the existing standard costs. Kaizen Costing has cost-reduction targets that assume continuous improvement. This chapter discussed a number of techniques such as Just In Time, Kousuu, the Noren-wake system and the New Production System that can help with the Kaizen approach. By reducing stock the Just In Time approach can reveal problems. With the Just In Time approach an organization reduces stocks, and this can reveal problems that were previously hidden, and the Kaizen approach can help to solve such problems.

Kousuu are performance measures of units of resource consumption expressed in terms of direct or indirect labour or machine time, and sometimes converted into monetary measures. Kousuu give all employees details of how resources are consumed and where the Kaizen approach can gain the greatest improvements. The Noren-wake system has a daily profit and loss account for each department, production line, sales office and head office. Furthermore, an internal money (or token) system can be used so that all employees can physically see the profit (or loss) falling or rising. Again the Noren-wake system motivates all employees to generate even more suggestions for improvements. The theme of the New Production System is to reduce the length of the production cycle time and, basically, such reductions are achieved by using the Kaizen approach with a large number of relatively small improvements.

Just In Time, Kousuu, the Noren-wake system and the New Production System all encourage the use of Kaizen Costing and continuous improvement. However, employee suggestions for improvements remain at the core of the Kaizen approach. Employees know that such improvements may mean the end of their existing job but know that they will be given another job within the same organization. Sometimes the suggestions come from individual employees and sometimes from groups of employees, but the Kaizen approach depends on very highly motivated employees thinking every day about how to make improvements. Each improvement may be relatively small but the cumulative effect of hundreds (or even thousands) of such improvements is very significant. The Kaizen approach to continuous improvement is an important cost management tool that can be used in any organization.

Bibliography

Cooper, R. and Slagmulder, R. (2004) Achieving Full-Cycle Cost Management, *Sloan Management Review*, Vol. 46, Issue 1, pp. 45–52.

Cooper, R. and Slagmulder, R. (2006) Integrated Cost Management, in Bhimani, A. (ed.) *Contemporary Issues in Management Accounting*, Oxford, Oxford University Press, pp. 117–129.

Defence Equipment Society (1989) *Procurement Manual of Defence Agency Central Procurement Office*, Tokyo, Defence Procurement Studies Committee, pp. 159–246 (in Japanese).

Government Buildings Department of the Ministry of Construction (1991) *Cost Estimation Handbook for Building Preventative Maintenance in Industry*, Tokyo, Building Preventative Maintenance Centre (in Japanese).

Granja, A.D., Picchi, F.A. and Roberts, G.T. (2005) Target and Kaizen Costing in Construction, in Kenley, R. (ed.) *Proceedings of the 13th International Group for Lean Construction Conference*, Sydney, pp. 227–233.

Imai, M. (1986) *KAIZEN – The Key to Japan's Competitive Success*, New York, Random House.

Modarress, B., Ansari, A. and Lockwood, D.L. (2005) Kaizen Costing for Lean Manufacturing: A Case Study, *International Journal of Production Research*, Vol. 43, Issue 9, pp. 1751–1760.

Monden, Y. and Hamada, K. (1991) Target Costing and Kaizen Costing in Japanese Automobile Companies, *Journal of Management Accounting Research*, Vol. 3, pp. 16–34.

Monden, Y. and Lee, J. (1993) How a Japanese Auto Maker Reduces Cost, *Management Accounting* (US), August, pp. 22–26.

Wakamatsu, Y. (2007) *Introduction to the Toyota Way of Kaizen*, Tokyo, Diamond (in Japanese).

Yoshikawa, T., Innes, J. and Mitchell, F. (1997) Performance Measurement for Cost Management: The Nature and Role of Kousuu, *The Journal of Management Accounting Japan*, pp. 47–60.

Part II

Cost management and decision-making

8

Specifying conditions for cost systems generating relevant decision-making costs

Samuel C. A. Pereira and Falconer Mitchell

Introduction

The design of product cost systems has received considerable attention since the emergence of activity-based costing (ABC) in the late 1980s, as evidenced by the significant number of articles published in professionally oriented journals and, to a lesser extent, in academic journals (Lukka and Granlund, 2002; Bjornenak and Mitchell, 2002). Compared to the professional world, the reception of ABC by academia has been much more cautious and critical (Bjornenak and Mitchell, 2002). One distinct academic contribution which the ABC innovation has initiated has been the use of mathematical analysis to specify the conditions under which a costing system can generate relevant costs for decision-making. Such a specification provides the basis for assessing the validity of claims made for the advantages of activity-based and, indeed, other types of costing system.

Research on this specification in the management accounting literature has developed progressively, over the last two decades, in respect of both cost functions and technology. Noreen (1991) constitutes the first significant contribution. He focused on the theoretical foundations of an activity-based product cost system. These constitute conditions relating to cost functions: he derived three necessary and sufficient conditions for a product cost system to measure relevant costs for decision-making.[1] These are that (i) total costs can be divided into independent cost pools, each of which depends only on one activity, (ii) the cost in each cost pool is strictly proportional to the level of activity in that cost pool and (iii) the volume of an activity is simply the sum of activity measures utilized by the individual products. Christensen and Demski (1995), Bromwich (1997) and Bromwich and Hong (1999) have supplemented this work by developing a more fundamental analysis of the theoretical foundations of a product cost system, in the sense that they consider technology, apart from input prices, as the primary determinant of cost functions. This constitutes a perspective which, although well established in the production economics literature (e.g. Chambers, 1988), had been systematically absent in the management accounting literature. Christensen and Demski (1995) emphasize the concepts of separability and linearity of activity cost functions. Bromwich and Hong (1999) have shown that, in order for total costs to be partitioned into independent cost pools, technologies have to be both separable and non-joint (see also Bromwich, 2007).

One requirement for the results of mathematical analysis to be authoritative is that it must be complete. Its application to product costing systems, however, remains incomplete; the intention of this chapter is to rectify this defect. Its first purpose is to extend the analysis of product cost system decision-relevant costs to include consideration of an omitted characteristic of technology, i.e. output characteristics. This is done by deriving the necessary and sufficient conditions that support the construction of an aggregate output, in a context where the cost in each cost pool is strictly proportional to that output. The aggregate output is a single measure of output that fully captures the cost of the resources used by the various products within a cost pool. Moreover, the aggregate output in each cost pool is the sum of the activity measures utilized by the individual products. The point that must be emphasized here is that the management accounting literature above has taken the notion of aggregate output for granted, without deriving the necessary and sufficient conditions that support its construction. It remains therefore unclear under what conditions (i) the output in each cost pool is the sum of the activity measures utilized by the individual products and (ii) activity costs are strictly proportional to that output, two fundamental properties of a product cost system (Noreen, 1991). As demonstrated below, this analysis is necessary to complete a full specification of the conditions characterizing a product cost system which will generate relevant costs.

In pursuing the above aim, one further aspect of product costing is highlighted and incorporated into the analysis. The existing analytical research on decision-relevant costing is pursued in a long-run context, where all inputs are variable with output. A secondary purpose of this chapter is, therefore, to introduce the short-run structure of a product cost system. One of the major recognized innovations of ABC systems is the introduction of the distinction between the cost of resources used and the cost of resources supplied, where the difference between the two is given by the cost of resources not used (Cooper and Kaplan, 1992). It is in the short run, where some inputs are fixed, that this analysis has to be carried out. It is a notable deficiency of existing analyses that they only consider the long run. The significance of the restrictions on cost variability in the short run and the implications for a product costing system are, therefore, also investigated.

This chapter is organized into three further sections. The first investigates the theoretical foundations of an aggregate output. It assumes a long-run perspective, where all inputs are variable with output, i.e. there are no fixed costs. The second concentrates on the short-run structure of a cost system, i.e. fixed costs exist. The discussion, integration of the results obtained in this chapter with existing literature, implications for costing system design and conclusions are presented in the last section.

Theoretical foundations of an aggregate output

This section is organized as follows. Sub-section one describes the general production and cost models. Sub-section two discusses the accounting model. Sub-section three analyses some implications of the results derived in sub-section two.

Technology and costs

Bromwich and Hong (1999) show that, if a product cost system is to measure relevant costs for decision-making, technologies have to be both separable and non-joint. Separability means that activity cost pools and product technologies can be specified independently of each other. Formally, the technology is separable if the input mix used in a cost pool and by a product is not affected by the inputs used in other cost pools and by other products (see Bromwich, 1997). Non-jointness signifies that the cost of performing activities separately equals the cost of performing them together, i.e. there are no economies or diseconomies of scope between activities. Non-jointness also applies within cost pools, meaning that the amount of resources used by a product in a cost pool is independent of the amount of resources used by other products in the same cost pool. Therefore, the cost of producing separately the various product outputs equals the cost of producing them together, i.e. there are no economies or diseconomies of scope of producing jointly various product outputs.

To illustrate, suppose a company produces two products (P_1 and P_2) and imagine two possible cost pools of its cost system. The first one is a direct cost pool, corresponding to a direct labour activity. The second one is an overhead cost pool that corresponds to a set-up activity. The number of set-ups is the cost driver. This information, as well as benchmark costs, resource usage and total costs, is presented in Table 8.1.

Separability of the technology signifies that the direct labour and set-up activities can be performed independently of each other and specified individually for each product. Non-jointness means that the cost of performing separately the two activities equals the cost of performing them jointly. Non-jointness also signifies that the cost of producing separately the two products equals the cost of producing them together.

To pursue the analysis, it is necessary to introduce some structure. Suppose that p inputs are aggregated at cost pool t, which are used in the production of m products; in other words, we have a multi-output technology at cost pool t. There are r cost pools. In order to calculate the cost of producing separately each product, let $x^{t,j} = (x^t_{1,j}, \ldots, x^t_{p,j})$ represent a p-dimensional vector of inputs used by product j at cost pool t. Moreover, under the assumption that the technology is non-joint, the vector of inputs used at cost pool t when the m products are produced jointly is $x^t = (x^t_1, \ldots, x^t_p)$, where $x^t_i = \sum_{j=1}^{m} x^t_{i,j}$. Finally, let $y^{t,j}$ denote the output of product j at cost pool t. For example, $y^{t,j}$ can represent the number of set-ups of product j, the number of deliveries of product j or the total machine hours required to produce the same product.

Table 8.1 Values for benchmark costs, resource usage and total costs

Panel A: Benchmark costs

Activity		*Cost driver*	*Cost driver rate*
Direct labour		Hours of direct labour	£5/hour
Set-up		Number of set-ups	£10/set-up

Panel B: Resource usage

Product	*Production*	*Hours of direct labour (per unit)*	*Number of set-ups*
P_1	100 units	2 hours	20 set-ups
P_2	150 units	3 hours	10 set-ups

Panel C: Total costs

Activity	*Activity output*	*Total cost (P_1)*	*Total cost (P_2)*
Direct labour	650 hours (1)	£1000 = £5 × 100 × 2	£2250 = £5 × 150 × 3
Set-up	30 set-ups (2)	£200 = £10 × 20	£100 = £10 × 10
		£1200	£2350

(1) 650 hours = 100 units × 2 hours (P_1) + 150 units × 3 hours (P_2)
(2) 30 set-ups = 20 set-ups (P_1) + 10 set-ups (P_2)

The production function for product j at cost pool t is given by:

$$f_j^t(x^{t,j}) = y^{t,j} \tag{1}$$

We assume that $f_j^t(x^{t,j})$ is smooth, increasing and (strictly) quasi-concave.[2] We also consider that all inputs are essential to the production, in the sense that a positive amount of output cannot be produced without a strictly positive utilization of all inputs.

In general, the m product technologies at cost pool t will be different. For example, the technologies supporting, say, products j and k, j ≠ k, might be such that one and another use different input mixes within a cost pool. As will be shown later, the possibility that different products use different technologies has several important implications in relation to the conditions that allow the construction of an aggregate output in a cost pool.

The cost of producing output $y^{t,j}$ is given by:

$$c_j^t(w^t, y^{t,j}) \equiv \tag{2}$$

$$\min_{x_{i,j}^t} \sum_{i=1}^{p} x_{i,j}^t w_i^t$$

$$\text{subject to } f_j^t(x^{t,j}) \geq y^{t,j}$$

where $w^t = (w_1^t, \ldots, w_p^t)$ denotes a p-dimensional vector of strictly positive input prices. Problem (2) identifies the input vector that minimizes the cost of producing output $y^{t,j}$, when the input price set is w^t. For later reference, it is useful to represent problem (2) in terms of the *Lagrangean function*:

$$L(x^{t,j}, \mu) = \sum_{i=1}^{p} x_{i,j}^t w_i^t + \mu(y^{t,j} - f_j^t(x^{t,j})) \tag{3}$$

where μ is a *Lagrange multiplier*. The first-order conditions for the existence of a minimum imply the following:[3]

$$\frac{\partial f_j^t(x^{t,j})/\partial x_{i,j}^t}{\partial f_j^t(x^{t,j})/\partial x_{u,j}^t} = \frac{w_i^t}{w_u^t}. \tag{4}$$

Expression (4) is the well-known result that at an optimum the marginal rate of technical substitution of input i for input u ($MRTS_{i,u}^{t,j}$) equals the ratio of the corresponding input prices.

Finally, the cost of producing the m product outputs or the m-dimensional output vector $y^t = (y^{t,1}, \ldots, y^{t,m})$ at cost pool t is given by:

$$c^t(w^t, y^t) = \sum_{j=1}^{m} c_j^t(w^t, y^{t,j}). \tag{5}$$

While the left-hand side of expression (5) represents the total cost of producing the m outputs jointly, the right-hand side denotes the total cost of producing them separately. As observed above, this equality takes place if and only if the technology is non-joint. Applied across cost pools, expression (5) can be written as follows:

$$c(w^1, \ldots w^r, y^1, \ldots y^r) = \sum_{t=1}^{r} \sum_{j=1}^{m} c_j^t(w^t, y^{t,j}). \tag{6}$$

In other words, the cost of producing jointly activities and products, the left-hand side of expression (6), equals the cost of producing them separately, the right-hand side.

Accounting system

A fundamental property underlying the architecture of a product cost system is the application of average cost driver rates to cost outputs. This procedure can only be justified when cost functions are linear with output. Otherwise, average and marginal costs will differ. If this is the case, the cost reported by a product cost system does not measure incremental costs.

If the cost function for product j at cost pool t is linear with output, the cost of producing output $y^{t,j}$ is given by:

$$c_j^t(w^t, y^{t,j}) = y^{t,j}\, \phi_j^t(w^t) \tag{7}$$

where $\phi_j^t(w^t)$ is the average and marginal cost for product j at cost pool t. Moreover, by the envelope theorem, $\mu = \phi_j^t(w^t)$, i.e. the *Lagrange multiplier* in (3) is the marginal cost. Hereafter, we will refer to $\phi_j^t(w^t)$ as the cost driver rate for product j at cost pool t. For example, $\phi_j^t(w^t)$ can represent the cost per set-up of product j (as in the example of Table 8.1) or the cost per machine hour used in the production of the same product. The following Lemma is fundamental. It is based on the duality between costs and technology and shows that only linearly homogeneous technologies give rise to cost functions linear with output.

Lemma 1. *The cost function* $c_j^t(w^t, y^{t,j})$ *is linear with output if and only if the production function* $f_j^t(x^{t,j})$ *is linearly homogeneous.*

Proof. *By the Lemma of Shephard, the derived demand for input i,* $x_{i,j}^t$ *equals the derivative of the cost function with respect to the price of the same input,* w_i^t*. If we apply it to* (7)*, we obtain:*

$$\frac{\partial c_j^t(w^t, y^{t,j})}{\partial w_i^t} = y^{t,j}\frac{\partial \phi_j^t(w^t)}{\partial w_i^t} = x_{i,j}^t(w^t, y^{t,j}), \text{for all } i. \tag{A.1}$$

Condition (A.1) *shows that if the cost function for product j is linear with output, the optimal input-output relationships are also linear. For later reference, denote the rate at which the quantity of input i changes with output as:*

$$\frac{\partial x_{i,j}^t(w^t, y^{t,j})}{\partial y_{t,i}} = \frac{\partial \phi_j^t(w^t)}{\partial w_i^t} = \frac{1}{\alpha_{i,j}^t(w^t)}, \text{ for all } i \tag{A.2}$$

and the cost driver rate for product j as:

$$\phi_j^t(w^t) = \sum_{i=1}^{p} \frac{\partial x_{i,j}^t(w^t, y^{t,j})}{\partial y_{t,j}} w_i^t = \sum_{i=1}^{p} \frac{w_i^t}{\alpha_{i,j}^t(w^t)}. \tag{A.3}$$

Condition (A.1) *implies that, given the input price set, if the input combination* $x^{t,j}$ *is associated with the production of output* $y^{t,j}$*, the input combination* $\lambda\, x^{t,j}$ *is associated with the production of output* $\lambda\, y^{t,j}$.

What technologies give rise to such (optimal) input-output relationships? This requires that $f_j^t(x^{t,j})$ *is linearly homogeneous (since* $f_j^t(\lambda\, x^{t,j}) = \lambda\, f_j^t(x^{t,j})$*). Basically, all we need to show is that, given the input price set,* $x^{t,j}$ *and* $\lambda\, x^{t,j}$ *are the optimal input vectors when the outputs are* $y^{t,j}$ *and* $\lambda\, y^{t,j}$*, respectively.*

It is well known that if $f_j^t(x^{t,j})$ *is homogeneous of degree one,* $\partial f_j^t(x^{t,j})/\partial x_{i,j}^t$ *is homogeneous of degree zero* ($\partial f_j^t(\lambda\, x^{t,j})/\partial x_{i,j}^t = \partial f_j^t(x^{t,j})/\partial x_{i,j}^t$)*. Taking into account* (4)*, this implies that an increase of* λ *in all the p inputs does not change the* $MRTS_{i,u}^{t,j}$*. Therefore, given the input price set, if the first-order conditions are fulfilled by the input combination* $x^{t,j}$ *they must also be fulfilled by the combination* $\lambda\, x^{t,j}$*. Moreover, if the input combination* $x^{t,j}$ *produces output* $y^{t,j}$ *the input combination* $\lambda\, x^{t,j}$ *produces output* $\lambda\, y^{t,j}$ *(since* $f_j^t(\lambda\, x^{t,j}) = \lambda\, f_j^t(x^{t,j})$*). This completes the proof*. ■

It is well known that a linearly homogeneous technology is a special case of a more general class of technologies, called homothetic technologies. Specifically, a technology is homothetic if it can be written as $h_j^t(f_j^t(x^{t,j})) = y^{t,j}$, where $f_j^t(x^{t,j})$ is linearly homogeneous and $dh_j^t(f_j^t(x^{t,j}))/df_j^t(x^{t,j}) > 0$. The cost function dual to a homothetic technology takes the following form $c_j^t(w^t, y^{t,j}) = \varphi^t(y^{t,j})\ \phi_j^t(w^t)$, where $\varphi^t(y^{t,j}) = h_j^{t-1}(y^{t,j})/h_j^{t-1}(1)$ (see Jehle, 1991, 233).[4] This cost function is not linear with output and thus average and marginal costs are not, in general, constant. There is an exception, however, when $h_j^t(f_j^t(x^{t,j})) = f_j^t(x^{t,j})$, i.e when the technology is linearly homogeneous. This, of course, is the essence of the Lemma.[5]

Consider the set-up activity in Table 8.1 and assume that it aggregates two inputs, say indirect labour hours and litres of cleaning materials. The technology associated with product P_1 is linearly homogeneous if the two inputs change linearly with the number of set-ups. For example, if two indirect labour hours and five litres of cleaning materials are used to process one set-up, four indirect labour hours and ten litres of cleaning materials are used to process two set-ups, and so on.

The condition that product technologies are linearly homogeneous is necessary for the construction of an aggregate output. It is not sufficient, however. The construction of an aggregate output presupposes that a second condition is also verified. Basically, this second condition ensures that each cost pool depends on only one cost driver.

At this point, the question that should be asked is whether the various product outputs are or are not various volume levels of the same cost driver. They represent various volume levels of the same cost driver if they affect activity costs in the same way, more precisely, if the various (product) cost driver rates are equal. In this case, the various product outputs can simply be added together. For example, if the outputs of products j and k, $j \neq k$, are the same cost driver, $y^{t,j} + y^{t,k}$ constitute the aggregate output associated with both products j and k. If, however, they are not the same cost driver, $y^{t,j}$ and $y^{t,k}$ affect costs differently and so cannot be added together. Otherwise, and as will be shown, some cost distortion is introduced. The following definition can now be introduced.

Definition 1. *$y^{t,j}$ and $y^{t,k}$ are the same cost driver at cost pool t if $\phi_j^t(w^t) = \phi_k^t(w^t), j \neq k$. Similarly, they are not the same cost driver if $\phi_j^t(w^t) \neq \phi_k^t(w^t)$.*

In Table 8.1, the number of set-ups of products P_1 and P_2 represent two volume levels of the same cost driver if the cost per set-up of P_1 equals the cost per set-up of P_2. Proposition 1 shows that, in order to construct an aggregated output, all product outputs, at a given cost pool, have to represent various volume levels of the same cost driver.

Proposition 1. *$g^t(y^t) = \sum_{j=1}^{m} y^{t,j}$ is an aggregate output that accurately measures product incremental costs at cost pool t if and only if $y^{t,j}$ and $y^{t,k}$ are the same cost driver, for all $j \neq k$.*

Proof.

Sufficiency

The cost function for product h at cost pool t can be written as $c_h^t(w^t, y^{t,h}) = y^{t,h}\ \phi_h^t(w^t) = \sum_{i=1}^{p} x_{i,h}^t(w^t, y^{t,h})w_i^t$. If $y^{t,j}$ and $y^{t,k}$ are the same cost driver then $\phi_j^t(w^t) = \phi_k^t(w^t) = \phi^t(w^t)$, for all $j \neq k$. The cost allocated to product h at cost pool t is equal to:

$$y^{t,h}\frac{\sum_{j=1}^{m}\sum_{i=1}^{p}x_{i,j}^t(w^t,y^{t,j})w_i^t}{\sum_{j=1}^{m}y^{t,j}} = y^{t,h}\frac{\sum_{j=1}^{m}y^{t,j}\phi_j^t(w^t)}{\sum_{j=1}^{m}y^{t,j}} = y^{t,h}\frac{\phi^t(w^t)\sum_{j=1}^{m}y^{t,j}}{\sum_{j=1}^{m}y^{t,j}} =$$

$y^{t,h}\phi_h^t(w^t) = \sum_{i=1}^{p} x_{i,h}^t(w^t, y^{t,h})\, w_i^t$. *That is, the cost allocated to product h equals its incremental cost.*

Necessity

Suppose that $\phi_j^t(w^t) < \phi_k^t(w^t)$ *and* $\phi_k^t(w^t) = \phi^t(w^t)$, *for all* $k \neq j$. *Let also* $y^{t,h} > 0$, *for all h. The cost allocated to product h at cost pool t is now equal to:*

$$y^{t,h}\frac{\sum_{i=1}^{p} x_{i,j}^{t}(w^{t}, y^{t,j})\, w_i^t + \sum_{k\neq j}\sum_{i=1}^{p} x_{i,k}^{t}(w^{t}, y^{t,k}) w_i^t}{\sum_{j=1}^{m} y^{t,j}} = y^{t,h}\phi^t(w^t, y^{t,j}, g^t(y_{k\neq j}^{k}))$$

$$\text{where } \phi^t(w^t, y^{t,j}, g^t(y_{k\neq j}^t)) = \frac{y^{t,j}\phi_j^t(w^t) + g^t(y_{k\neq j}^t)\phi^t(w^t)}{g^t(y^t)} \text{ and } g^t(y_{k\neq j}^t) = \sum_{k\neq j} y^{t,k}$$

since $y^{t,h} > 0$ *and* $\phi_j^t(w^t) < \phi_k^t(w^t) = \phi^t(w^t)$, *then* $\phi_j^t(w^t) < \phi^t(w^t, y^{t,j}, g^t(y_{k\neq j}^t)) < \phi^t(w^t)$. *This implies that* $y^{t,h}\,\phi^t(w^t, y^{t,j}, g^t(y_{k\neq j}^t)) \neq y^{t,h}\,\phi_h^t(w^t) = \sum_{i=1}^{p} x_{i,h}^t(w^t, y^{t,h}) w_i^t$. *That is, the cost allocated to product h distorts its incremental cost.*

To sum up, the condition that $y^{t,j}$ *and* $y^{t,k}$ *are the same cost driver, for all* $j \neq k$, *is a necessary and sufficient condition for the construction of an aggregate output that accurately measures product-incremental costs at cost pool t.*

Remarks 1 and 2 follow directly from Proposition 1. While Remark 1 derives the fundamental relationship between product technologies, the aggregate output and activity costs, Remark 2 shows the consequences of using the output measure $g^t(y^t)$ to distribute costs when cost pool t depends on more than one cost driver.

Remark 1. *The cost function at cost pool t can be written as:*

$$c^t(w^t, y^t) = \sum_{j=1}^{m} c_j^t(w^t, y^{t,j}) = \sum_{j=1}^{m} y^{t,j}\phi_j^t(w^t) = g^t(y^t)\phi^t(w^t).$$

Proof. *The first equality results from the fact that the technology is non-joint, the second from the fact that product technologies are linearly homogenous and the third from the fact that* $y^{t,j}$ *and* $y^{t,k}$ *are the same cost driver, for all* $j \neq k$.

Consider again the example in Table 8.1. Processing separately or jointly the two products in the set-up activity costs the same, i.e. £300 (cost of producing jointly the two products) = £200 (cost of producing separately P_1) + £100 (cost of producing separately P_2)). Moreover, the total cost in the set-up activity is linear with the number of set-ups of the two products, i.e. £300 = 30 × £10, where £10 is the cost per set-up of product P_1 or P_2 and 30 the total number of set-ups (20 set-ups of P_1 + 10 set-ups of P_2).

Remark 2. *If* $\exists\, j \neq k$: $\phi_j^t(w^t) \neq \phi_k^t(w^t)$, *the cost function at cost pool t depends on more than one cost driver. In this case, distributing the cost at cost pool t based on the output measure* $g^t(y^t)$ *distorts product incremental costs.*

Proof. This follows directly from the demonstration of the necessity of Proposition 1.

Figure 8.1 summarizes the theoretical foundations of an aggregate output.

Further analysis

It was demonstrated that in order to create an aggregate output both product technologies have to be linearly homogeneous and all product outputs have to represent various volume levels of the same cost driver. As will be demonstrated, if product technologies are not only linearly

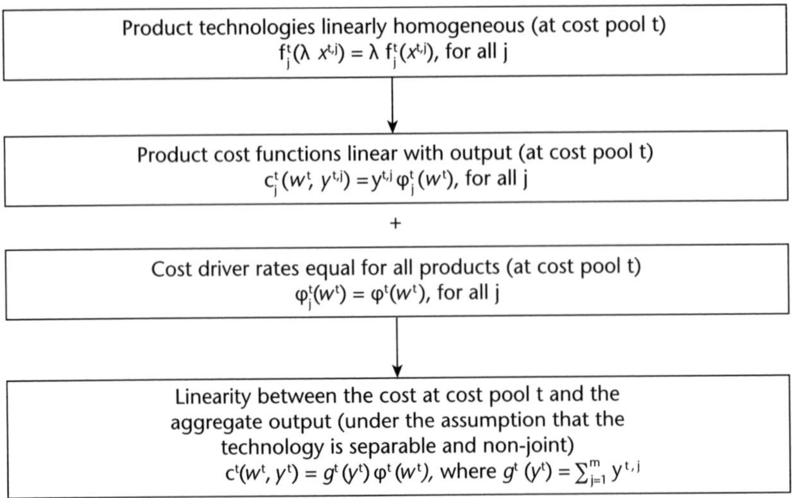

Product technologies linearly homogeneous (at cost pool t)
$f_j^t(\lambda\, x^{t,j}) = \lambda\, f_j^t(x^{t,j})$, for all j
Product cost functions linear with output (at cost pool t)
$c_j^t(w^t, y^{t,j}) = y^{t,j}\varphi_j^t(w^t)$, for all j
+
Cost driver rates equal for all products (at cost pool t)
$\varphi_j^t(w^t) = \varphi^t(w^t)$, for all j
Linearity between the cost at cost pool t and the aggregate output (under the assumption that the technology is separable and non-joint)
$c^t(w^t, y^t) = g^t(y^t)\varphi^t(w^t)$, where $g^t(y^t) = \sum_{j=1}^{m} y^{t,j}$

Figure 8.1 Theoretical foundations of an aggregate output

Source: adapted from Pereira, 2004.

homogenous but also identical, all product outputs represent various volume levels of the same cost driver. The contrary, however, is not true, as also will be shown. In other words, it might be the case that two product technologies are not identical while their outputs are still the same cost driver (at least for a particular input price set).

To pursue the analysis let us first assume that all product technologies are identical.

Assumption 1. $f_j^t(x^{t,j})$ *and* $f_k^t(x^{t,k})$ *are identical, for all* $j \neq k$.

It is obvious that when product technologies are identical the various product outputs represent different volume levels of the same output. In other words, we have a single output technology, as the various product technologies are indistinguishable. In this case, the various product outputs also represent different volume levels of the same cost driver (Remark 3).

Remark 3. *If* $f_j^t(x^{t,j})$ *and* $f_k^t(x^{t,k})$ *are identical,* $y^{t,j}$ *and* $y^{t,k}$ *are the same cost driver at cost pool t, for all* $j \neq k$, w^t. *In this case, any input aggregated at cost pool t can be used as an aggregate measure of output.*

Proof. *It follows directly from* (A.1) *and* (A.2) *that the optimal input-output relationships for product j at cost pool t are* $y^{t,j} = \alpha_{i,j}^t(w^t)\, x_{i,j}^t$, *for all i. Additionally, if all product technologies are identical, then:*

$$\alpha_{i,j}^t(w^t) = \alpha_{i,k}^t(w^t) = \alpha_i^t(w^t), \textit{for all } i, k \neq j, w^t. \tag{A.4}$$

Using (A.3) *and* (A.4), *we obtain* $\phi_j^t(w^t) = \phi_k^t(w^t) = \phi^t(w^t)$, *for all* $j \neq k$, w^t. *That is,* $y^{t,j}$ *and* $y^{t,k}$ *are the same cost driver at cost pool t. Moreover, any input aggregated at cost pool t can be used as an aggregate measure of output. More formally, using* (A.1), (A.2) *and* (A.4), *the cost driver rate at cost pool t when input u is used as a measure of output,* $\phi^t(w^t)_u$, *is:*

$$\phi^t\left(w^t\right)_u \equiv \phi_j^t\left(w^t\right)_u = \sum_{i=1}^{p} \frac{\partial x_{i,j}^t}{\partial x_{u,j}^t} w_i^t = \alpha_u^t\left(w^t\right)\sum_{i=1}^{p} \frac{w_i^t}{\alpha_i^t\left(w^t\right)}, \textit{ for all } j. \tag{A.5}$$ [6]

We still need to show the possibility that two product outputs are the same cost driver even though their technologies are not identical. An example will be sufficient to illustrate this point.

Example. Consider that cost pool t aggregates three inputs. Assume also that there are two products (P_1 and P_2). The production function for P_j can be represented as $f^t_j(x^t_{1,j}, x^t_{2,j}, x^t_{3,j}) = y^{t,j}$, where $y^{t,j}$ is the number of set-ups of P_j. Additionally, $f^t_j(x^t_{1,j}, x^t_{2,j}, x^t_{3,j}) = \min(\alpha^t_{1,j} x^t_{1,j}, \alpha^t_{2,j} x^t_{2,j}, \alpha^t_{3,j} x^t_{3,j})$, that is, the technology supporting P_j is Leontief, a special case of a linearly homogeneous technology that does not allow substitution between inputs.

The cost per set-up of P_j is $\phi^t_j\left(w^t\right) = \sum_{i=1}^{3} \frac{w^t_i}{\alpha^t_{i,j}}$, where $1/\alpha^t_{i,j}$ denotes the quantity of input i used to process one set-up of P_j. It is obvious that $\phi^t_1(w^t) = \phi^t_2(w^t)$ when $\alpha^t_{i,1} = \alpha^t_{i,2}$, for all i. However, it is no less obvious that even when $\alpha^t_{i,1} \neq \alpha^t_{i,2}$, for all i, we might have $\phi^t_1(w^t) = \phi^t_2(w^t)$, at least for some input price set. That is to say, it is possible that P_1 and P_2 use different input mixes while the cost per set-up of P_1 is still equal to the cost per set-up of P_2. If this is the case, the total number of set-ups is in fact an aggregate measure of output that accurately measures incremental product costs (i.e. $y^{t,1}$ and $y^{t,2}$ are the same cost driver).

Suppose then we consider using as an allocation base either the total number of set-ups or the quantity of input u. It might be the case that $y^{t,1}$ and $y^{t,2}$ are not the same cost driver ($\phi^t_1(w^t) \neq \phi^t_2(w^t)$) while $x^t_{u,1}$ and $x^t_{u,2}$ are the same cost driver ($\phi^t_1(w^t)_u = \phi^t_2(w^t)_u$).[7] Table 8.2 presents a numerical example to illustrate this point.

As Table 8.2 shows, if the total number of set-ups is the allocation base, activity costs are incorrectly distributed between P_1 and P_2 (since $\phi^t_1(w^t) = £120 \neq \phi^t_2(w^t) = £140$ – see Panel B and Remark 2). However, if input 2 is the allocation base activity costs are accurately distributed between P_1 and P_2 (since $\phi^t_1(w^t)_2 = \phi^t_2(w^t)_2 = £2$ – see Panel C).[8]

Finally, observe that, given the specific (heterogeneous) product technologies, the conclusion that $y^{t,1}$ and $y^{t,2}$ (or $x^t_{u,1}$ and $x^t_{u,2}$) are the same cost driver depends on the input price set. In other words, it might be the case (or not) that for some input price set $y^{t,1}$ and $y^{t,2}$ (or $x^t_{u,1}$ and $x^t_{u,2}$) are the same cost driver. Only when product technologies are identical, $y^{t,1}$ and $y^{t,2}$ (or $x^t_{u,1}$ and $x^t_{u,2}$) are the same cost driver for all the input price sets (see Remark 3).

The previous example implies that even when product technologies are heterogeneous – i.e. even when the various products use different input mixes – product cost distortions might be

Table 8.2 Product cost driver rates

Panel A: Parameters

$P_1 : 1/\alpha^t_{1,1} = 20;\ 1/\alpha^t_{2,1} = 60;\ 1/\alpha^t_{3,1} = 40$

$P_2 : 1/\alpha^t_{1,2} = 65;\ 1/\alpha^t_{2,2} = 70;\ 1/\alpha^t_{3,2} = 5$

$w^t = (w^t_1, w^t_2, w^t_3) = (£1, £1, £1)$

Panel B: Product cost driver rates (Allocation base: number of set-ups)

$$P_1: \phi^t_1(w^t) = \sum_{i=1}^{3} \frac{w^t_i}{\alpha^t_{i,2}}\ 20 \times £1 + 60 \times £1 + 40 \times £1 = £120$$

$$P_2: \phi^t_2(w^t) = \sum_{i=1}^{3} \frac{w^t_i}{\alpha^t_{i,2}}\ 65 \times £1 + 70 \times £1 + 5 \times £1 = £140$$

Panel C: Product cost driver rates (Allocation base: input 2)

$$P_1: \phi^t_1(w^t)_2 = \alpha^t_{2,1} \sum_{i=1}^{3} \frac{w^t_i}{\alpha^t_{i,1}}\ \frac{20 \times £1 + 60 \times £1 + 40 \times £1}{60}\ £2$$

$$P_2: \phi^t_2(w^t)_2 = \alpha^t_{2,2} \sum_{i=1}^{3} \frac{w^t_i}{\alpha^t_{i,2}}\ \frac{65 \times £1 + 70 \times £1 + 5 \times £1}{70}\ £2$$

small. Hwang et al. (1993) observe that product cost distortions, due to the use of an allocation base to distribute the cost of the inputs aggregated in a cost pool among the various products, increase when product technologies are significantly different. Although this can be accepted as a general observation, the preceding analysis shows that high product technology heterogeneity does not necessarily lead to high product cost distortions. We thus establish the following Remark.

Remark 4. *Even when* $f^t_j(x^{t,j})$ *and* $f^t_k(x^{t,k})$ *are not identical,* $y^{t,j}$ *and* $y^{t,k}$ *might still be the same cost driver (for some input price set).*

Overall, what Remarks 3 and 4 show is that even though it is true that when product technologies are identical (and linearly homogeneous) their outputs are the same cost driver, the contrary is not true. In other words, cost driver rates might be equal for two products even though their technologies are not identical (for some input price set). Nevertheless, it should be recognized that it is a very strong assumption that two product outputs are the same cost driver when their (linearly homogeneous) technologies are not identical.

Short-run structure of a cost system

The analysis undertaken in the last section has assumed a long-run perspective, where all inputs are variable with output. In the short run, however, some inputs are fixed. This section investigates the short-run structure of a cost system.

As was previously demonstrated, when product technologies are both linearly homogeneous and identical, cost pools depend on only one cost driver. The assumption that product technologies are identical is equivalent to imposing that, for a given cost pool, there is a single output technology. In other words, all product outputs represent various volume levels of the same output. This permits the visualization of the cost pool output as an intermediate input that is used by the various products. The analysis undertaken in this section explicitly assumes this (see Assumption 1).[9]

To incorporate the distinction between variable and fixed inputs, let us represent the vector of inputs supplied at cost pool t as $x^t_{(\text{supplied})} = (x^t_{f\,1}, \ldots, x^t_{f\,u}, x^t_{u+1}, \ldots, x^t_p)$, where u inputs $(i = 1, \ldots, u)$ are fixed and $(p - u)$ inputs $(i = u+1, \ldots, p)$ are variable. Let us also denote the short-run vector of inputs used at cost pool t as $x^{t(SR)} = (x^{t(SR)}_1, \ldots, x^{t(SR)}_p)$. Note that $x^{t(SR)}_i \leq x^t_{fi}$, $i = 1, \ldots, u$, i.e. in the case of the fixed inputs usage is lower than, or equal to, supply. In the case of the variable inputs, $x^{t(SR)}_i = x^t_i$, $i = u+1, \ldots, p$, i.e. usage equals supply. The short-run cost minimization problem is given by:

$$c^{t(SR)}(w^t, g^t(y^t), x^t_{f\,1}, \ldots, x^t_{f\,u}) \equiv \tag{8}$$

$$\sum_{i=1}^{u} x^t_{fi}\, w^t_i + \underset{x^{t(SR)}_i}{\text{Min}} \sum_{i=u+1}^{p} x^{t(SR)}_i w^t_i$$

$$\text{subject to } f^t(x^{t(SR)}) \geq g^t(y^t) \text{ and } x^t_{fi} \geq x^{t(SR)}_i,\ i = 1, \ldots, u$$

where $f^t(x^{t(SR)})$ is the production function at cost pool t and $x^{t(SR)}$ the input vector that minimizes the (short-run) variable cost of producing output $g^t(y^t)$. In order to characterize the optimal solution to problem (8) it is useful to represent its long-run counterpart:

$$c^{t(LR)}(w^t, g^t(y^t)) \equiv \tag{9}$$

$$\underset{x^{t(LR)}_i}{\text{Min}} \sum_{i=1}^{p} x^{t(LR)}_i w^t_i$$

$$\text{subject to } f^t(x^{t(LR)}) = g^t(y^t)$$

where $x^{t(LR)} = (x_1^{t(LR)}, \ldots, x_p^{t(LR)})$ denotes the input vector that resolves problem (9). In contrast with problem (8), all the p inputs are variable in problem (9). When $f^t(x^{t(LR)})$ is linearly homogeneous, the long-run cost function can simply be written as (see Lemma 1):

$$c^{t(LR)}(w^t, g^t(y^t)) \equiv \phi^{t(LR)}(w^t)\, g^t(y^t) \tag{10}$$

where $\phi^{t(LR)}(w^t)$ is the long-run marginal cost. Let us finally introduce the following assumption.

Assumption 2. *There is an output level, say* $g^t(y^t)^\bullet$, *such that* $x^t_{(supplied)} \equiv x^{t(LR)}$ *and thus* $c^{t(LR)}(w^t, g^t(y^t)^\bullet) = c^{t(SR)}(w^t, g^t(y^t)^\bullet, x^t_{f1}, \ldots, x^t_{fu})$.

The output $g^t(y^t)^\bullet$ is usually interpreted as the capacity of the activity undertaken in a cost pool. It corresponds to the output level for which long-run costs are minimized, i.e. long- and short-run costs coincide. Short-run fluctuations around this level of output imply that capacity is not optimal, i.e. the short-run cost will be higher than the long-run cost. Proposition 2 constitutes the main result of this section. It characterizes the optimal solution to problem (8).

Proposition 2. *The optimal solution to problem* (8) *exhibits the following properties:*

P2.(i) *All resources supplied in the short run are used.*

P2.(ii) *The short-run cost function is non-linear in output.*

Proof.

Property **P2.(i)**

The Lagrangean function for problem (8) *is:*

$$L\,(x^{t(SR)}, \lambda, \mu_1, \ldots, \mu_u) = \sum_{i=1}^{u} x^t_{fi}\, w^t_i + \sum_{i=u+1}^{p} x_i^{t(SR)} w^t_i + \lambda\left(g^t\left(y^t\right) - f^t\left(x^{t(SR)}\right)\right) + \sum_{i=1}^{u} \mu_i \left(x_i^{t(SR)} - x^t_{fi}\right) \tag{A.6}$$

where λ *and* μ_i *are Lagrange multipliers. The complementary slackness condition implies:*

$$\frac{\partial L(.)}{\partial x_i^{t(SR)}} = -\lambda \frac{\partial f^t\left(x^{t(SR)}\right)}{\partial x_i^{t(SR)}} + \mu_i = 0, i = 1, \ldots, u$$

$$\frac{\partial L(.)}{\partial x_j^{t(SR)}} = w^t_j - \lambda \frac{\partial f^t\left(x^{t(SR)}\right)}{\partial x_j^{t(SR)}} = 0, j = u+1, \ldots, p$$

or $$\mu_i = w^t_j \frac{\partial f^t\left(x^{t(SR)}\right)/\partial x_i^{t(SR)}}{\partial f^t\left(x^{t(SR)}\right)/\partial x_j^{t(SR)}} > 0. \tag{A.7}$$

Given that the μ_i*'s are positive, the restrictions* $x^t_{fi} \geq x_i^{t(SR)}$, $i = 1, \ldots, u$, *bind. Therefore, all resources supplied in the short run are used.*

Property **P2.(ii)**

Note first that the solution to the restricted problem (8) *cannot be better than the solution to the unrestricted problem* (9), *that is* $c^{t(SR)}(w^t, g^t(y^t), x^t_{f1}, \ldots, x^t_{fu}) \geq c^{t(LR)}(w^t, g^t(y^t))$. *Additionally, since* $c^{t(LR)}(w^t, 0) = 0$, $c^{t(SR)}(w^t, 0, x^t_{f1}, \ldots, x^t_{fu}) > 0$ *and* $c^{t(LR)}(w^t, g^t(y^t)^\bullet) = c^{t(SR)}(w^t, g^t(y^t)^\bullet, x^t_{f1}, \ldots, x^t_{fu})$, *short-run costs are non-linear in output (note that* $c^{t(LR)}(w^t, g^t(y^t))$ *is linear in output). Additionally, as the fixed inputs are fully used, the input mix changes with output.*[10] *This also implies that short-run costs are non-linear.*

Two points should be noted here. The first is that the above results hold whether the technology is linearly homogeneous or not. Thus, and in contrast with the long run, setting the requirement that technologies are linearly homogeneous no longer guarantees that short-run variable costs are linear with output – a fundamental property of a product cost system. The second is that the possibility of substitution between inputs plays a crucial role in Proposition 2.[11] In fact, one way of ensuring that short-run variable costs are linear with output is to restrict the possibility of substitution between inputs. For example, suppose that inputs are combined in completely fixed proportions, such as with a Leontief technology (a special case of a linearly homogeneous technology).[12] It is not hard to see that, in this case, short-run variable costs are directly proportional to output.[13]

Discussion and conclusions

Table 8.3 outlines a full specification of the conditions under which a cost system will generate relevant product costs for decision-making. It assumes a long-run perspective, where all inputs are variable with output. The conditions related to cost function have been derived by Noreen (1991). By considering technology, in addition to input prices, as the primary determinant of cost functions, Christensen and Demski (1995), Bromwich and Hong (1999) and the analysis in this chapter have together completed the specification of the conditions under which a product cost system will generate outputs relevant for decision-making.

The practice of dividing, in a product cost system, total costs into parts – among cost pools and within cost pools among products – presupposes that the technology is separable (condition (t.i)) and non-joint (condition (t.ii)). These two conditions guarantee condition (c.i) as well as the partition of costs among products within cost pools, an implication of conditions (c.ii) and (c.iii).

Separability signifies that activities and products can be processed in isolation, in independent processes or in specialized firms. This excludes, for example, processes that necessarily and simultaneously yield multiple products, i.e. joint processes. The question that should be posed in practice is whether such a separation of activities and products is possible, even if activities and products are being processed jointly.

Non-jointness signifies that performing jointly or separately activities and products costs the same. Non-jointness is a very strong assumption, since the economic rationale for the existence of a multi-product firm is the existence of economies of scope. That is, a multi-product firm exists when producing jointly two or more products costs less than producing them separately (Baumol et al, 1988; see also Bromwich, 1997).

Table 8.3 Foundation of a product cost system generating relevant costs for decision-making

Conditions related to cost functions	*Conditions related to technology*
(c.i) Total costs can be divided into independent cost pools (Noreen, 1991)	(t.i) Within and between cost pools the technology is separable (Christensen and Demski, 1995, and Bromwich and Hong, 1999, see also Bromwich, 2007)
(c.ii) The cost in each cost pool is strictly proportional to the level of activity in that cost pool (Noreen, 1991)	(t.ii) Within and between cost pools the technology is non-joint (Bromwich and Hong, 1999, see also Bromwich, 2007)
(c.iii) The volume of an activity is simply the sum of activity measures utilized by the individual products (Noreen, 1991)	(t.iii) Within each cost pool product technologies are linearly homogeneous
	(t.iv) Within each cost pool all product outputs represent various volume levels of the same cost driver

As observed, the conditions of separability and non-jointness of technology apply within and between cost pools. Within cost pools, two additional conditions, examined in this chapter, are necessary if a cost system is to measure product-relevant costs. These are that product technologies are linearly homogeneous (condition (t.iii)) and that all product outputs within a cost pool represent various volume levels of the same cost driver (condition (t.iv)). These two conditions – together with conditions (t.i) and (t.ii), which alone ensure the partition of costs within cost pools – guarantee conditions (c.ii) and (c.iii).

The condition that technologies are linearly homogeneous signifies that the relationship between inputs and outputs is linear. This ensures that costs change linearly with output and thus equality is guaranteed between the cost reported by a product cost system, an average cost, and marginal costs. The condition that technologies are linearly homogeneous is also a strong assumption, as it excludes effects such as production economies of scale or quantity discounts in input acquisition.

The condition that all product outputs within each cost pool represent various volume levels of the same cost driver necessarily holds when all products use the same (linearly homogeneous) technology. In a set-up activity – where the number of set-ups is the cost driver – identical product technologies amounts to saying that the set-up of one or another product is indistinguishable, in the sense that they use exactly the same combination of inputs (say indirect labour hours and litres of cleaning materials). The question that should be posed in practice is whether the various product outputs (the various set-ups, for example) are or are not distinguishable in terms of the way they use the inputs aggregated in a cost pool. If there are differences in the way products use the inputs aggregated in a cost pool, then it might be the case that cost pool activities depend on more than one cost driver, and so the practice of distributing the costs based on a single aggregate output or volume measure distorts product costs.

Introducing the possibility that within cost pools some inputs are fixed while others are variable and input substitutability is permitted, makes (short-run) variable costs non-linear (even if technologies are linearly homogeneous). One way of ensuring that (short-run) variable costs are linear with output is to restrict the possibility of substitution between inputs: a Leontief technology (a particular case of a linearly homogenous technology), where inputs are combined in completely fixed proportions. In many cases inputs are in fact combined in fixed proportions. For example, suppose a machine is supplied with material and requires an operator. Each input (the machine, the material and the operator) plays its own role in production and so cannot be substituted for another. That is, producing a given level of output presupposes the combination of one machine, one operator and a certain quantity of material, without the possibility of changing this input mix. But there are also cases where the substitution between inputs is allowed. For example, Ball and Chambers (1988) find evidence of significant input substitutions in the United States meat products industry. Thus, in practice, the relevant question is whether the substitution between inputs is or is not permitted when variable and fixed inputs are combined. Allowing for input substitutions is sufficient to make (short-run) variable costs non-linear and thus it violates a fundamental property of a product cost system generating relevant costs for decision-making.

Finally, it is interesting to note that the equation of capacity in ABC (Kaplan and Cooper, 1992) and, in particular, the existence of unused capacity, implicitly assumes that there are restrictions in terms of input substitutability. In fact, if inputs can be substituted for each other, (short-run) cost minimization implies that a firm should first use all the fixed inputs, before any variable input is acquired and used. That is, allowing for input substitutability implies that all the (fixed) inputs supplied are used – i.e. there is no unused capacity.

The set of conditions derived in previous studies and in this chapter form a basis to evaluate, in practice, the usefulness of the information generated by a cost system for the purpose of decision-making on final output variation. Deviations from these conditions will signify product cost information that is not consistent with necessary decision-relevant criteria and so it will be inadequate for the purpose of decision-making on the expansion or reduction of output of existing products, the introduction of new products or make-or-buy (outsourcing) decisions.

The analysis developed in this chapter also provides guidance for further research that empirically tests the set of conditions under which a cost system generates product-relevant costs. The investigation of cost distortions arising in situations where those conditions do not apply would be of particular relevance to those who wish to assess the utility of an existing costing system or who wish to design a new system. Gupta and Datar (1994), Gupta (1993), Hwang et al (1993), Christensen and Demski (1997) and Lavro and Vanhoucke (2008a, 2008b) have addressed some of the questions that the aggregation of inputs and the selection of cost drivers pose (see also Labro, 2006, for a nice review of this literature), but more research is necessary in this area. In particular, the analysis of situations where product technologies are not linearly homogenous (and are not identical) – and do not therefore permit the creation of a single aggregate measure of output for a cost pool – is likely to provide new insights.

Notes

1 In this chapter, decision-relevant is taken to mean relevant to decision-making on final output variation, e.g. the expansion or reduction of output of existing products, the introduction of a new product, make-or-buy (outsourcing) decisions or special orders. This is consistent with Noreen (1991).

2 The assumption that $f_j^t(x^{t,j})$ is smooth, increasing and (strictly) quasi-concave ensures that the first-order conditions are not only necessary but also sufficient for the existence of a (unique) minimum (see Chiang, 1984, 387–404).

3 More precisely, the first-order conditions are $\frac{\partial L}{\partial x_{i,j}^t} = w_i^t - \mu \frac{\partial f_i^t(x^{t,j})}{\partial x_{i,j}^t} = 0$ and $\frac{\partial L}{\partial \mu} = f_j^t(x^{t,j}) - y^{t,j} = 0$.

Dividing $\frac{\partial L}{\partial x_{i,j}^t}$ by $\frac{\partial L}{\partial x_{u,j}^t}$, $i \neq u$, establishes the result.

4 For example, consider the following homothetic production function:

$h_j^t(f_j^t(x^{t,j})) = \frac{1}{2} \text{Log } [f_j^t(x^{t,j})]^2$, where $f_j^t(x^{t,j}) = \sqrt{x_{1,j}^t x_{2,j}^t}$. The *Lagrangean function* can be written as $L = w_1^t x_{1,j}^t + w_2^t x_{2,j}^t - \mu\left(\frac{1}{2} \text{Log } x_{1,j}^t x_{2,j}^t - y^{t,j}\right)$ and the first-order conditions as $\frac{\partial L}{\partial x_{i,j}^t} = w_i^t - \mu \frac{1}{2x_{i,j}^t} = 0$, $i = 1, 2$ and $\frac{\partial L}{\partial \mu} = \frac{1}{2} \text{Log } x_{1j}^t x_{2,j}^t - y^{t,j} = 0$. After simplification we obtain $c_j^t(w^t, y^{t,j}) = 2\sqrt{w_1^t w_2^t} e^{y^{t,j}}$.

This cost function is not compatible with ABC (average and marginal costs are not constant). We thank Mark Tippett for suggesting this example.

5 This result is in sharp contrast with Bromwich and Hong (1999), who claim that homothetic technologies support, in general, a cost system.

6 Thus Remark 1 can be rewritten as

$$c^t(w^t, x_{u,1}^t, \ldots, x_{u,m}^t) = \sum_{j=1}^{m} c_j^t(w^t, x_{u,j}^t) = \sum_{j=1}^{m} x_{u,j}^t \phi_j^t(w^t)_u = x_u^t \phi^t(w^t)_u.$$

7 $$\phi_j^t\left(w^t\right)_u = \alpha_{u,j}^t \sum_{i=1}^{3} \frac{w_i^t}{\alpha_{i,j}^t}.$$

8 The same cannot be concluded when input 1 or input 3 is the allocation base.

9 As was shown, although the assumption that product technologies are identical, together with the necessary condition that technologies are linearly homogenous, is sufficient to construct an aggregate

output, it is not necessary. Only for the sake of analytical simplicity in the analysis of the short-run cost minimization problem, but without loss of generality, it is assumed here that product technologies at activity cost pools are identical.

10 By contrast, in the long run, the input mix is constant for a given input price set. Using both the *Lemma of Shephard* and (10), we obtain $\frac{x_i^{t(LR)}}{x_k^{t(LR)}} = \frac{\partial\phi^{t(LR)}\left(w^t\right)/\partial w_i^t}{\partial\phi^{t(LR)}\left(w^t\right)/\partial w_k^t}$, which is constant for a given input price set.

11 This is a direct implication of the fact that the marginal productivity of each input is positive, $\frac{\partial f^t\left(x^{t(SR)}\right)}{\partial x_i^{t(SR)}} > 0$.

12 That is, $g^t(y^t) = \text{Min}\,(\alpha_1^t x_{f1}^t, \ldots, \alpha_u^t x_{fu}^t, \alpha_{u+1}^t x_{u+1}^t, \ldots, \alpha_p^t x_p^t)$.

13 In particular, the rate at which short-run variable costs change is constant and equal to $\sum_{i=u+1}^{p} \frac{w_i^t}{\alpha_i^t}$, and $g^t(y^t) \leq \text{Min}\,(\alpha_1^t x_{f1}^t, \ldots, \alpha_u^t x_{fu}^t, \alpha_{u+1}^t x_{u+1}^t, \ldots, \alpha_p^t x_p^t)$.

Bibliography

Ball, V. E., and Chambers, R. (1982) 'An economic analysis of technology in the meat product industry', *American Journal of Agricultural Economics*, Vol. 64, 699–709.

Baumol, W. J., Panzar, J. C. and Willig, R. D. (1998) *Contestable Markets and the Theory of Industry Structure*, Orlando, Florida: Harcourt Brace Jovanovich Publishers.

Bjornenak, T. and Mitchell, F. (2002) 'An analysis of ABC literature 1987-2000', *European Accounting Review*, Vol. 11, 481–508.

Bromwich, M. (1997) *Accounting for overheads: Critique and Reforms*. Studia Oeconomiae Negotiorum 41, Uppsala University.

Bromwich, M. and Hong, C. (1999) 'Activity-based costing systems and incremental costs', *Management Accounting Research*, Vol. 10, 39–60.

Bromwich, M. (2007) 'Economics of Management Accounting', 137–162, in Chapman, C., Hopwood, A. and Shields, M. (eds), *Handbook of Management Accounting Research*, Elsevier, Amsterdam.

Chambers, R. (1988) *Applied Production Analysis: A Dual Approach*, Cambridge: Cambridge University Press.

Chiang, A. (1984) *Fundamental Methods of Mathematical Economics*, 3rd edition, New York: McGraw-Hill.

Christensen, J. and Demski, J. S. (1995) 'The classical foundations of "modern" costing', *Management Accounting Research*, Vol. 6, 13–32.

Christensen, J. and Demski, J. S. (1997) 'Product costing in the presence of endogenous subcost functions', *Review of Accounting Studies*, Vol. 2, 65–87.

Cooper, R. and Kaplan, R. S. (1992) 'Activity-based systems: measuring the costs of resource usage', *Accounting Horizons*, Vol. 6, 1–13.

Datar, S. and Gupta, M. (1994) 'Aggregation, specification and measurement error in product costing', *The Accounting Review*, Vol. 69, 567–591.

Gupta, M. (1993) 'Heterogeneity issues in aggregated costing systems', *Journal of Management Accounting Research*, Vol. 5, 180–212.

Hwang, Y., Evans III, J. and Hedge, V. (1993) 'Product cost bias and selection of an allocation base', *Journal of Management Accounting Research*, Vol. 5, 213–242.

Jehle, G. (1991) *Advanced Microeconomic Theory*, Prentice-Hall International.

Labro, E., 'Analytics of cost system design', in Bhimani, A. (ed.), *Contemporary Issues in Management Accounting*. Oxford University Press, pp. 217–242.

Labro, E. and Vanhoucke, M. (2008a) 'A simulation analysis of interactions among errors in costing systems', *The Accounting Review*, Vol. 82, 939–962.

Labro, E. and Vanhoucke, M. (2008b) 'Diversity in resource consumption patterns and cost system robustness to errors', *Management Science*, Vol. 54, 1715–1730.

Lukka, K. and Granlund, M. (2002) 'The fragmented communication structure within the accounting academia: the case of activity-based costing research genres', *Accounting, Organizations and Society*, Vol. 27, 165–190.

Noreen, E. (1991) 'Conditions under which activity-based costing systems provide relevant costs', *Journal of Management Accounting Research*, Vol. 3, 159–168.

Pereira, S. C. A. (2004) 'Towards a conceptual foundation of activity-based costing: theory and a simulation experiment', unpublished PhD dissertation, The University of Edinburgh.

9

Designing time-driven activity-based costing systems

A review and future research directions

Sophie Hoozée

Introduction

To achieve continuous improvements in the modern dynamic and hypercompetitive environment (D'Aveni 1994), companies must be agile (Goldman et al. 1995) and costing systems need to keep providing accurate cost information to managers, who base many decisions on reported product costs (e.g., Cooper and Kaplan 1988a; Shim and Sudit 1995). However, accurate cost information, by itself, does not invoke actions and decisions leading to improved profits and operating performance (Cooper et al. 1992). To identify improvement opportunities, a costing system should also encourage managers to pay more attention to reducing costs and trying to accomplish outcomes with fewer demands on organizational resources (Turney 1992). Hence, excluding inventory valuation, the purpose of costing is twofold. On the one hand, some cost analyses mainly require accurate information to improve the quality of decision-making (e.g., pricing, make-or-buy, product mix optimization, purchasing fixed assets, etc.). In this case we talk about *costing for decision-making*. On the other hand, cost analyses and performance reports may also assist managers in better controlling their departments (e.g., budgets, performance measurement and evaluation systems, etc.). This part is called *costing for control*. Referring to the first purpose, the focus of this chapter is mainly on the use of cost information to support decision-making. More specifically, the chapter includes a review of studies on when and why activity-based costing (ABC), as well as its recent extension, time-driven ABC, can benefit the use of management accounting for decision-making.

The remainder of this chapter is organized as follows. The next section summarizes the old debate on full or variable cost for decision-making. Then, the rise and fall of ABC is described. The following section elucidates the concept of time-driven ABC and, next, the research on time-driven ABC is reviewed. The last section offers conclusions and many fruitful areas for future research. Finally, in the Appendix, a worked example of time-driven ABC is provided.

The debate on full or variable costing for decision-making

Assuming that all cost objects have a knowable true cost (Babad and Balachandran 1993; Datar and Gupta 1994; Gupta 1993; Homburg 2001; Kaplan and Thompson 1971) (i.e. the monetary value of all the resources consumed by the cost object), when a costing system is used for decision-making, its purpose is to minimize the difference between the cost calculated by the costing system and the true cost of the cost objects, preferably with minimal costs of data collection, storage and processing (cf. Babad and Balachandran 1993). It should be noted, however, that only future costs that will change in response to a decision are relevant for decision-making.

According to classical economic theory, in the *short run*, a firm attempts to maximize profits by setting prices such that marginal revenue equals marginal cost. In particular, a profit-maximizing company should mark up its marginal cost by a factor determined by the price elasticity of demand. Adherents of the *profit maximization model* advocate the use of *variable costing* as a method of measuring product profitability. With variable costing, only those costs that are expected to vary with production volume are included in a product's cost.

To enable strategy as a continuous process in a fast-changing environment, managers do not only need cost and profitability information to determine the impact of decisions in the short run, but also to quickly assess the impact of new strategies on future profit. Therefore, opponents of variable costing argue that it understates the manufacturing cost by not measuring the fixed costs associated with actual production. In particular, according to the *satisfying model*, the primary objective of a business is not to maximize profits but to earn a satisfactory return on the assets that it uses. In order to obtain an adequate return, revenues must be large enough to recover all costs and gain a profit that provides a sufficient return on investment. This leads to *full cost* pricing as the normal practice. Proponents of full costing thus argue that cost allocation systems that properly capture consumption of fixed resources by products provide a better estimate of a product's *long-run* marginal cost (e.g., Cooper and Kaplan 1988b). Hence, whereas variable costing produces relevant cost and profitability information in the short run, in the long run such information loses its relevance: full costing is required because the decision to offer a product creates a long-term commitment to manufacture, market and support that product (Johnson and Kaplan 1987).

Both views may be reconciled by viewing a firm's capacity-planning and product-pricing problem as a trade-off between *opportunity costs*: at the time of acquiring capacity, opportunity cost is the best other investment opportunity foregone as a result of using money in this way; once acquired, opportunity cost is a function of the resource's alternative uses, which vary over time. Accordingly, if we are to deepen our understanding of the relation between allocated cost and economic decisions, the capacity-acquisition and product-pricing problems must be considered simultaneously rather than sequentially. The formulation of the joint capacity-planning and product-pricing problem implies that the decision-maker needs to specify a price for every future demand contingency at the time of resource acquisition (Balakrishnan and Sivaramakrishnan 2002). However, because managers are unable to estimate the demand curve (i.e. the quantity of products that will be sold at each possible unit price) and to search for all possible decision alternatives and select the one that maximizes profit, in practice they typically resort to easy-to-implement decision rules (Govindarajan and Anthony 1983). Hence, because the conditions for rational models rarely hold in practice, decision-making in organizations typically involves heuristics (Gigerenzer and Brighton 2009; Gigerenzer and Gaissmaier 2011) such as full costing. Besides, cost allocations can be valuable because they approximate the opportunity cost based on expected use at the time of resource acquisition (for a classic analysis of the 'cost accountant' versus the 'economist', see Baxter and Oxenfeldt 1961).

The rise and fall of activity-based costing (ABC)

The ABC paradox

Accepting that full costing can be a valid input to decision-making, particularly in the longer term, the question arises how to allocate indirect or overhead costs. Until the 1980s, when most products were mass-produced, traditional cost accounting systems were employed, which used direct labour hours, machine hours or material expressed in currency units to allocate overhead costs to products. As the direct labour content of products decreased, through automation and industrial engineering-driven efficiencies, the percentage of total costs represented by the arbitrary allocations of overheads had continually grown. As product diversity increased, the primary drivers of manufacturing overhead costs were (logistical, balancing, change and quality) transactions that involved exchanges of materials and/or information necessary to plan, organize and operationalize production but did not directly result in physical products (Miller and Vollmann 1985). Unable to capture the full complexity of business processes in which overhead costs are driven by variables other than production volume, traditional cost accounting systems provide a poor picture of the actual cost drivers when product diversity and indirect resource expenses are high. Hence, when overhead costs no longer rose in proportion to production volume (e.g., Banker and Johnston 1993; Banker et al. 1995; Datar et al. 1993), volume-based costing systems provided distorted cost information and became obsolete (Kaplan 1986).

Acknowledging that the primary drivers of manufacturing overhead costs are transactions that are not directly related to volume (Miller and Vollmann 1985), Cooper and Kaplan (1988a,b) introduced *activity-based costing (ABC)*. ABC systems focus on organizational activities as the key element for analysing cost behaviour by linking organizational spending on resources to the activities performed by these resources. Activity cost drivers, then, drive activity costs to the products, services and customers that create the demand for the organizational activities. Although it has been argued that ABC information can be used to support strategic and operational decisions (e.g., Cooper and Kaplan 1992; Narayanan and Sarkar 2002; Swenson 1995), the diffusion process for ABC has not been as successful as may have been expected (Gosselin 1997). In the next two paragraphs, several potential explanations for this 'ABC paradox' are developed.

Inaccuracy of ABC in complex business environments

A substantial body of research has focused upon errors in ABC. More specifically, researchers have scrutinized the accuracy of ABC by developing formal mathematical models that specify the implicit assumptions of ABC. For example, Noreen (1991) claimed that ABC provides accurate cost information for decision-making only under stringent conditions, more specifically: (1) no fixed costs at the cost pool level, (2) linear cost functions, and (3) absence of costs that are joint across activities. Accordingly, Noreen and Soderstrom (1994, 1997) and Anderson et al. (2003) have provided empirical evidence that suggests that cost functions are rarely linear. Others also have questioned the assumptions of linearity (e.g., Christensen and Demski 1997; Ittner and MacDuffie 1995; MacArthur and Stranahan 1998) and independence of production processes (e.g., Datar et al. 1993; Ittner et al. 1997). When these conditions are not met, cost estimates provided by ABC are not error-free. More specifically, Datar and Gupta (1994) state that, when designing an ABC system, the following three types of error may occur: specification, aggregation and measurement errors. A *specification error* arises when the wrong cost driver is used. An *aggregation error* occurs when costs are aggregated across heterogeneous activities to derive a single cost driver rate. A *measurement error* refers to measuring driver quantities and costs with error.

When using conventional ABC, it can be expected that growing *complexity* in a company's order, product and customer mix leads to increased aggregation and specification error. This can be addressed by splitting activities into smaller activities. However, referring to ABC, Datar and Gupta (1994) show that reductions in specification and aggregation errors from more disaggregated and better specified costing systems may actually increase total error, because by focusing on one type of error at a time, the offsetting effects of specification and aggregation errors can be removed (see also Christensen and Demski 1995). The simulation analysis of Labro and Vanhoucke (2007) provides more detail by showing regions for various types of errors where partial improvement in one error does not lead to an overall improvement in accuracy due to negative interactions between errors, most importantly when there is a high aggregation error in the activity cost pools and a high measurement error in the resource drivers. In addition, Cardinaels and Labro (2008) found a substantial endogenous trade-off between the magnitude of aggregation and measurement errors. Consider, for example, the activity of 'picking a delivery'. An aggregation error arises when the costs of manual picking (driven for example by the number of units to be picked manually) and the costs of layer picking (driven by the number of layers of equal units) are pooled within an activity cost pool and allocated to cost objects, based upon the number of pallets that have to be picked, because these are heterogeneous activities. Decreasing the aggregation error by splitting the activity into two separate activities – 'manual picking' and 'layer picking' – and using the specific drivers for each of the two activities may increase measurement error, because when aggregation is reduced, the task of providing estimates becomes cognitively more demanding. Hence, costing system designers that utilize conventional ABC are faced with a trade-off between aggregation and specification errors on the one hand, and measurement errors on the other, which suggests that refining conventional ABC systems does not necessarily lead to more accurate cost estimates.

Information economics arguments against ABC

Information economics is based on the notion that information will be generated when its benefits to decision-makers (in terms of profit generation) exceed its costs (e.g., Milgrom and Roberts 1992). As the number of activities in an ABC system increases, it becomes more costly to collect, store and process information. Hence, apart from the accuracy issues associated with ABC in complex business environments, information economics would also predict that ABC becomes problematic when activities are disaggregated.

The problem further exacerbates when, in addition to being complex, a company's order, product and customer mix also change with time. Generally defined, *dynamism* describes the degree to which the business environment remains basically static over time or is in a continual process of change (Duncan 1972). Such changes may be frequent (e.g., the customer mix changes every week) and/or drastic (e.g., new customers require totally new activities). In dynamic environments, the percentage times spent on activities change, so that the ABC model needs to be adapted frequently, which is costly and time-consuming.

In addition, when ABC information is used for decision-making (as opposed to control, see for example Dearman and Shields 2005; Zimmerman 2009), the cost of resources supplied should be distinguished from the cost of resources used. More specifically, allocations should be based on practical capacity and the responsibility for excess capacity should be assigned to the managerial level at which the capacity decision is made (Cooper and Kaplan 1992). Companies may experience predictable changes in the order, product or customer mix (e.g., due to seasonality), as well as unpredictable changes in capacity utilization (e.g., loss of an important customer). When a company's order, product and customer mix change frequently and in an unpredictable way – from an information economics perspective – it may again not be cost-efficient to keep the estimates of practical activity driver volumes up to date. Moreover, based upon their case study, Everaert et al. (2008b) suggest that when the business environment is characterized by high complexity and unpredictable changes in capacity utilization, splitting activities inflates the number of activities and creates difficulties in estimating the practical capacity for each activity. In a similar vein, Brüggen et al. (2011) found in their study of the North American auto industry that it is not uncommon for firms to use actual production capacity as the denominator for computing overhead rates. Hence, although theory suggests that the cost of excess capacity should be separated and treated as a period cost, in practice there is a tendency to absorb all costs, including excess capacity, into current production.

To conclude, in complex business environments, ABC is prone to different types of error; in dynamic business environments, revision is necessary for the estimated percentage mix of time spent on the different activities as well as the practical activity driver volumes. From an information economics perspective, it can be argued that it is not cost efficient to keep an ABC system up to date when a company's order, product and customer mix change frequently – especially when changes occur in an unpredictable way. Accordingly, due to the high maintenance costs (in terms of extra work, see for example Malmi 1997), many companies (especially large ones) either ceased updating their system or abandoned ABC entirely (Kaplan and Anderson 2004). Moreover, many organizations that had adopted and implemented ABC encountered difficulties during the implementation process and abandoned their ABC projects (Gosselin 1997; Innes et al. 2000; Kaplan and Anderson 2004). Finally, it is remarkable that there still is little empirical evidence that adoption of ABC has an impact on performance. Three exceptions should, however, be noted. In particular, (1) for a sample of UK firms, Kennedy and Affleck-Graves (2001) showed through an event study that the adoption of ABC significantly improved a firm's relative performance in terms of both market- and accounting-based measures; (2) through a cross-sectional mail survey of internal auditors in the US, Cagwin and Bouwman (2002) found a positive association between ABC and improvement in return on investment when ABC was used concurrently with other strategic initiatives, when implemented in complex and diverse firms, when used in environments where costs were relatively important, and when there were limited numbers of intra-company transactions; (3) and for a cross-sectional sample of US manufacturing plants, Banker et al. (2008) detected that world-class manufacturing practices mediated the effect of ABC on plant performance.

The concept of time-driven ABC

To overcome the difficulties inherent for conventional ABC in dynamic environments and to better capture the full complexity of activities, Kaplan and Anderson (2004, 2007c) developed a new approach for ABC, which they called *time-driven ABC*. With this new approach, time plays a pivotal role in allocating resources to cost objects. Although conventional ABC always has had the capacity to use time as a cost driver, time plays a different role in this newer version of ABC. Conventional ABC systems apply duration drivers in the second stage of a cost allocation process, whereas the new approach uses time to drive costs directly from resources to cost objects, passing over the stage of first assigning a department's resource costs to the multiple activities the department performs. Hence, with time-driven ABC, resources are not assigned to specific activities; they are pooled at a higher level. For each department or process, resource costs are directly assigned to cost objects using two sets of estimates: (1) the cost per time unit (or capacity cost rate) and (2) the process time (calculated by means of a time equation). A numerical example is given in the Appendix.

First, the *capacity cost rate* is calculated as overhead divided by practical capacity. The cost of resources supplied to an operating department (i.e. the numerator) consists of several elements: employees, supervision, indirect labour, equipment and technology, occupancy and other indirect and support resources. The practical capacity that has been supplied (i.e. the denominator) is the time available for productive work and can be obtained by removing unavoidable inefficiencies (e.g., breaks, training, education) from theoretical capacity; as a rule of thumb, it is usually assumed to be 80 to 85 per cent of theoretical capacity. Although capacity is often measured in minutes or hours supplied, it can also be measured in other units, such as space (e.g., for a warehouse), weight (e.g., for the capacity of transport) or gigabytes (e.g., for digital storage devices). It should be noted that a departmental cost rate is valid only if the mix of resources supplied is about the same for each activity and transaction performed within the department. If a department performs several processes, each requiring a different mix of resources, then the department must decompose departmental operations into two or more processes and calculate separate capacity cost rates for each process (for an example, see Öker and Adigüzel 2010). Finally, special treatment is required for resources handling peak or seasonal capacity. More specifically, the cost of capacity in the slack period should just be the capacity that would be required if only the slack-period demand were to be met; the capacity cost rate in the peak months should be more expensive and include both the cost of supplying capacity during the peak months as well as the cost of capacity resources supplied, but not needed, during the slack-demand period.

Second, time-driven ABC uses *time equations* to estimate resource usage and assign resource costs to the activities performed and transactions processed. A time equation is a mathematical equation that expresses the time required to perform a certain activity as a function of several time drivers, which can be discrete (e.g., the number of line items), binary (e.g., a new customer versus an existing customer) or continuous (e.g., weight or distance) variables. For each transaction, these time equations are used to determine the time needed to perform the activity for this transaction. Formally, the estimated transaction time based on k observable time drivers is expressed as:

$$\hat{t}_k = B_0 + B_1X_1 + \ldots + B_kX_k$$

with

$\hat{t}_k$ = estimated time for a particular transaction;
B_0 = estimated basic time, given by the personnel;
B_i = estimate for one unit time of driver i, given by the personnel, with $i = 1, \ldots, k$;
X_i = estimate for the volume of time driver i, as reported by the company's computer-based information systems, with $i = 1, \ldots, k$.

For example, the estimated order-processing time could be calculated as follows: the entry of basic order information involves 3 minutes (B_0); each line item (X_1) requires 2 minutes of data input (B_1); the input of new customer data (X_2) takes 15 minutes (B_2); and 10 additional minutes (B_3) are required in case of a rush order (X_3). Time-driven ABC allows for the calculation of cost estimates per specific transaction (i.e. one occurrence of an activity; so, a rush order consisting of five order lines from an existing customer takes 23 minutes). The cost allocated to the cost object is then obtained by multiplying this estimated time by a cost per time unit of the resources. In addition, since transactional data can be extracted from companies' computer-based information systems, it is possible to determine the estimated time required to perform all activities that are needed for the transactions over a certain period. Deducting this total time from the practical capacity delivers the estimated excess capacity for the period. Kaplan and Anderson (2004, 2007c) proposed this insight into capacity utilization as being one of the main advantages of time-driven ABC.

One may wonder whether time-driven ABC is actually that different from conventional ABC. Given that academics do not share a common view of what makes an accounting system an ABC system (Malmi 1999), the answer to this question depends on how both systems are defined. More specifically, ABC systems may differ in (1) their level of aggregation and (2) their treatment of unused capacity. With respect to the first distinction, Drury and Tayles (2005) argue that ABC systems can be classified along a continuum of complexity in which complexity is high when there are many activities and a new activity cost driver is defined for each activity. Because time-driven ABC pools resources at the level of departments or processes, a typical time-driven ABC model requires fewer equations than the number of activities used in a conventional ABC system (e.g., Dalci et al. 2010; Everaert et al. 2008b). However, conceptually, both systems may have an equal level of aggregation, namely when in a time-driven ABC system a new time equation with only one term is defined for each activity in a conventional ABC system. The second distinction is related to whether ABC is presented as a method to allocate overhead costs to products or as a method to assess resource consumption in organizations. When ABC is used for control purposes, idle capacity may be included in the cost figures because it can motivate managers/employees in firms to carefully consider capacity decisions and hence reduce costs (e.g., Zimmerman 2009). In contrast, as already mentioned, when ABC is used for decision-making, the cost of supplied resource capacity should be distinguished from the cost of used resource capacity (Cooper and Kaplan 1992). However, when people estimate how much time they spent on a list of activities handed to them, invariably they report percentages that add up to 100. Few individuals record a significant percentage of their time as idle or unused. Therefore, conventional ABC systems typically assign resources to activities based upon an estimated percentage mix of *productive* time spent on those activities. Next, activity driver volumes are calculated at practical capacity, rather than actual utilization, to exclude idle capacity from the cost figures. As already noted, increasing the number of activities in conventional ABC gives rise to cognitive (cf. Cardinaels and Labro 2008), practical (cf. Everaert et al. 2008b) and information-cost difficulties because the costs and resources must be assigned to more detailed activities, and more data must be collected on the volumes of the activity cost drivers. Time-driven ABC might thus be more likely to exclude the cost of idle capacity than conventional ABC. However, theoretically, both systems can reveal unused capacity because estimates in minutes can always be recalculated to percentages (and vice versa).

In conclusion, although conventional ABC and time-driven ABC may be theoretically equivalent, they differ substantially in their levels of aggregation. Essentially, time-driven ABC simplifies the first stage of cost allocation (i.e. there are typically fewer time equations in time-driven ABC than activities in conventional ABC) to allow more complexity in the second stage (i.e. there are typically more time drivers in time-driven ABC than activity cost drivers in conventional ABC). The second important distinction relates to the way in which information about the input parameters of both models is obtained. Rather than interviewing personnel about the estimated percentage of their time spent on a certain activity, in time-driven ABC this percentage is obtained by multiplying the estimated unit time required for one occurrence of the activity by the time driver volume obtained from the company's computer-based information systems – i.e. a 'bottom-up' approach.

Compared to conventional ABC, time-driven ABC is supposed to deliver more accurate and relevant cost and profitability information for decision-making and control, supporting continuous improvement of managers' business operations in a quickly changing setting. The next section reviews the articles on time-driven ABC that have been published up to 2011, to determine the current state of knowledge on the working and use of time-driven ABC.

A review of the research on time-driven ABC

To identify the articles published on time-driven ABC since its invention in 2004, the phrase 'time-driven activity-based costing' was entered in the Proquest ABI/Inform Global database. All the abstracts of the papers identified through this search were examined in order to delete irrelevant references to time-driven ABC. The final number of papers on time-driven ABC was surprisingly low: only 33 papers, from its first appearance in 2004 until 2011.

To distinguish these papers in terms of their development of knowledge, the consulting and basic research genres of ABC defined by Lukka and Granlund (2002) have been used. In a typical *consulting research* paper on time-driven ABC, based upon his participation in the development and implementation process, the author sells his ideas concerning time-driven ABC; the argumentation is uncritical and rather than using a rigorous method, a mixture of anecdotal empirical findings, visions of the future, logical pondering and a prescriptive and propagating style are employed. Contrary to a consulting research paper, a typical *basic research* paper on time-driven ABC relies on theory and is characterized by rigorous scientific analysis; rather than presenting uncareful claims, a much more neutral argumentation style is used, for example with respect to considerations on the effects of time-driven ABC systems on companies' profitability.

Table 9.1 divides the time-driven ABC articles referenced in Proquest up to 2011 into basic and consulting research, and summarizes the evidence-gathering approach that was undertaken in each article. Out of the 33 papers in the table, the vast majority (i.e. 31 papers) are classified

Table 9.1 Summary of time-driven ABC articles referenced in Proquest up to 2011

	Approach/Source of evidence	*Journal*
Basic research		
Cardinaels and Labro (2008)	Experiments on measurement errors in time-driven ABC	*The Accounting Review*
Hoozée and Bruggeman (2010)	Case study on the design process of a time-driven ABC system in four Belgian distribution warehouses	*Management Accounting Research*
Consulting research		
Cleland (2004)	Unrigorous arguments about the limitations of time-driven ABC and anecdotal evidence on how the contribution-based activity (CBA) method may complement time-driven ABC	*Financial Management*
Kaplan and Anderson (2004)	Propagating presentation of the technique of time-driven ABC	*Harvard Business Review*
Barrett (2005)	Logical pondering on the complementarity of time-driven ABC and conventional ABC	*Business Performance Management Magazine*
Thomson and Gurowka (2005)	Visions of the future of strategic costing best practices	*Strategic Finance*
Anderson et al. (2007a)	Anecdotal evidence on the profit impact of time-driven ABC through its use during due diligence processes	*Cost Management*
Anderson et al. (2007b)	See Anderson et al. (2007a), which is nearly the same article	*Journal of Private Equity*
Atkinson (2007)	Logical pondering on the complementarity of time-driven ABC and overall equipment effectiveness (OEE)	*CMA Management*

(Continued)

Table 9.1 (Continued)

	Approach/Source of evidence	*Journal*
Everaert and Bruggeman (2007)	Logical pondering on interactions between time drivers in time equations	*Cost Management*
Kaplan and Anderson (2007a)	Propagating arguments about the profit impact of time-driven ABC through its use during due diligence processes	*Business Finance*
Kaplan and Anderson (2007b)	Propagating presentation of the technique of time-driven ABC	*Cost Management*
Lambino (2007)	Uncritical book review of Kaplan and Anderson (2007)	*Government Finance Review*
Max (2007)	Propagating arguments about the benefits of time-driven ABC in the banking sector	*Journal of Performance Management*
Wegmann (2007)	Uncritical arguments about the usefulness of time-driven ABC	*Revue Française de Comptabilité*
Anonymous (2008)	Interview with Bob Kaplan on his book *The Execution Premium* (Kaplan and Norton 2008)	*Journal of Accountancy*
Everaert et al. (2008a)	Teaching case on time-driven ABC	*Journal of Accounting Education*
Everaert et al. (2008b)	Case study on the implementation of time-driven ABC and its taken-for-granted profit impact in a Belgian distribution company	*International Journal of Physical Distribution and Logistics Management*
Max (2008)	Propagating arguments about the benefits of time-driven ABC in the banking sector	*Journal of Performance Management*
Sharman (2008)	Interview with Bob Kaplan on the future of the management accounting profession	*Strategic Finance*
McGowan (2009)	Propagating arguments about the profit impact of time-driven ABC	*Accountancy Ireland*
Namazi (2009)	Unrigorous arguments about the limitations of time-driven ABC and logical pondering on how a performance-focused ABC system may extend time-driven ABC	*Cost Management*
Wegmann and Nozile (2009)	Unrigorous presentation of a typology of ABC systems and its application in the IT division of an international group	*Revue Française de Comptabilité*
Bendavid et al. (2010)	Case study on the use of a time-driven ABC-like approach in combination with radio-frequency identification (RFID) in the healthcare sector	*Business Process Management Journal*
Dalci et al. (2010)	Case study on the implementation of time-driven ABC and its taken-for-granted profit impact in a Turkish hotel	*International Journal of Contemporary Hospitality Management*
Öker and Adigüzel (2010)	Case study on the implementation of time-driven ABC and its taken-for-granted profit impact in a Turkish sheet metal and plastic parts manufacturer	*Journal of Corporate Accounting and Finance*
Zawawi and Hoque (2010)	Review of the literature on management accounting innovations published during the period 2000–2008	*Qualitative Research in Accounting and Management*

	Approach/Source of evidence	*Journal*
Ayvaz and Pehlivanli (2011)	Logical pondering on the complementarity of time-driven ABC and the analytic hierarchy process (AHP)	*International Journal of Business and Management*
Coulter et al. (2011)	Case study on the implementation of time-driven ABC and its taken-for-granted profit impact in an Irish energy company	*Accountancy Ireland*
Giannetti et al. (2011)	Case study on the implementation of time-driven ABC and its taken-for-granted profit impact in an Italian regional airport	*Cost Management*
Kim and Kim (2011)	Illustration of the use of time-driven ABC for calculating the costs associated with alternative quality inspection processes for sewer-pipe installations in Korea	*Construction Management and Economics*
Stout and Propri (2011)	Case study on the implementation of time-driven ABC and its taken-for-granted profit impact in a medium-sized consumer-electronics manufacturer	*Management Accounting Quarterly*
Zeller et al. (2011)	Teaching case on time-driven ABC	*Issues in Accounting Education*

within the consulting research genre; only two basic research papers on time-driven ABC have been published.

A common theme underlying the consulting research papers on time-driven ABC is the taken-for-granted effect on companies' profitability. Time-driven ABC mostly appears in practitioner journals (Zawawi and Hoque 2010). It is presented in a prescriptive fashion by its inventors as a simple model that expands linearly with increasing complexity (Kaplan and Anderson 2004, 2007b). Accordingly, Everaert and Bruggeman (2007) noted that a time equation not only accounts for the main effects of time drivers; it can also easily capture interactions between drivers when additional time needs to be taken into account to adjust for a multiplicative effect of several time drivers. For example, when picking a delivery, it may be that the time needed to wrap up a pallet increases as the number of boxes on the pallet is greater. The time spent performing a given subtask might also depend upon the occurrence of other subtasks. For instance, when processing an invoice, it is possible that a certain time per invoice line is only required for paper invoices, as opposed to EDI (electronic data interchange) invoices (see the Appendix for a complete example on invoicing). As another example, when determining the delivery time per drop, it may be that the subtask of accepting returned goods requires more time when no appointment has been made. In this instance, the requirement of accepting returned goods is a first time driver; whether or not an appointment has been made is a second time driver; and both time drivers can interact (for more examples, see Everaert et al. 2008b).

The majority of articles are replete with propagating arguments about the profit impact of time-driven ABC. For example, time-driven ABC is said to allow for a detailed examination of resource optimization (McGowan 2009). Moreover, when used during due diligence processes, it may offer prospective buyers a pricing advantage over competitors who bid based only on historical profits and cash flows (Anderson et al. 2007a,b; Kaplan and Anderson 2007a). In addition, with the increasing compliance with Sarbanes-Oxley requirements, banks have a ready supply of process flow documentation that they can translate into a time-driven ABC model (Max 2007), which may then be used as a 'cost reduction laser' (Max 2008). Finally, Thomson and Gurowka (2005) claim that, by accounting for idle capacity and simplifying data collection, time-driven ABC may navigate companies towards strategic costing best practices. A selling book review (Lambino 2007), interviews with Bob Kaplan (Anonymous 2008; Sharman 2008) and two teaching cases (Everaert et al. 2008a; Zeller et al. 2011) further shed a favourable light on time-driven ABC.

Case studies of time-driven ABC implementations have been performed in the distribution (Everaert et al. 2008b), manufacturing (Öker and Adigüzel 2010; Stout and Propri 2011), airport (Giannetti et al. 2011), hotel (Dalci et al. 2010), energy (Coulter et al. 2011), engineering (Kim and Kim 2011) and healthcare sectors (Bendavid et al. 2010). More specifically, the Belgian wholesaler studied by Everaert et al. (2008b) faced different customer groups that required a separate sales approach, various suppliers, considerable variation in terms of products, different kinds of package, seasonally dependent sales and short product-life cycles. The characteristics of the orders and the requirements of the customers caused significant variations in working method, which necessitated splitting activities and identifying separate activity cost drivers in a conventional ABC system. However, designing and maintaining a disaggregated model was too costly, so that the company shifted to time-driven ABC, which could capture multiple time drivers per activity by means of time equations. Assuming that the cost information provided by the time-driven ABC model was more accurate than the cost information provided by the conventional ABC model, the authors claim that time-driven ABC improved logistics decision-making because it enabled (1) improved insight into and analysis of customer profitability, (2) better capacity planning, (3) monitoring of the efficiency of the logistics processes, (4) internal benchmarking, and (5) increased cost awareness for sales and warehouse managers. Öker and Adigüzel (2010) performed a case study at a Turkish sheet metal and plastic parts manufacturer. Time-driven ABC was used to assign the cost of support departments to operating and manufacturing departments. The results were then employed to analyse product group profitability and capacity utilization. The supporting role of time-driven ABC for capacity management is also emphasized by Stout and Propri (2011), who highlight the additional granularity produced by time-driven ABC compared to conventional ABC at a medium-sized consumer-electronics manufacturer. In a similar vein, Giannetti et al. (2011) report the use of time-driven ABC at an Italian regional airport for the capacity management of all activities necessary to deliver services from an aircraft's arrival to its next take-off. Dalci et al. (2010) relied upon semi-structured interviews, direct observations and data obtained from cost reports and job descriptions to develop time equations for a Turkish hotel. Time-driven ABC was used to calculate and analyse the profitability of different customer segments and to balance the capacities supplied in different departments. Coulter et al. (2011) describe the implementation of time-driven ABC at an Irish semi-state company that operates within the energy sector. Time-driven ABC is proposed as an accurate costing technique that reduced the time spent on non-value-adding activities. Support of senior executives and the trust of lower-level staff appeared to be indispensable for a timely and successful implementation of the project. Kim and Kim (2011) illustrate the use of time-driven ABC as an evaluation tool for process re-engineering by quantifying the costs associated with two alternative quality inspection processes for sewer-pipe installations in Korea. Finally, Bendavid et al. (2010) employed a time-driven ABC-like approach to determine the time saved thanks to radio-frequency identification (RFID) in a hospital nursing unit. More specifically, for each specific role involved in the process under investigation (nursing staff, administrative staff, store personnel, etc.), time information was gathered based upon a time-and-motion study, and the average time was estimated by considering the frequency of the operation (replenishment) and the total number of storage locations visited.

Although most authors of consulting research papers do not question the beneficial outcomes of time-driven ABC, some criticism has nevertheless started to emerge. Time-driven ABC may be less appropriate for manufacturing companies as opposed to service companies (Öker and Adigüzel 2010; Wegmann and Nozile 2009) and for situations where the amount of time cannot be effectively predicted, such as (project-based) advisory work or consulting (Max 2007), or marketing and research and development (Wegmann 2007). Other proposed shortcomings of time-driven ABC are its costly design process (Cleland 2004; Kim and Kim 2011; Öker and Adigüzel 2010), the need for an effective enterprise resource planning (ERP) system (Stout and Propri 2011), the application of a uniform capacity cost rate for each department or process (Barrett 2005; Gervais et al. 2010; Namazi 2009), the exclusion of non-operational expenses (Cleland 2004), the use of time for measuring practical resources (Namazi 2009), the arbitrary determination of practical capacity as a percentage of theoretical capacity (Barrett 2005), the averaging nature of standard times (Giannetti et al. 2011), the unclear definition of the cost per time unit, and the problematic interpretation of idle capacity (Gervais et al. 2010). To address these weaknesses, alternative approaches have been suggested to replace time-driven ABC, such as the contribution-based activity (CBA) method (Cleland 2004) and performance-focused ABC (PFABC) (Namazi 2009). Other authors promote the leverage possibilities of time-driven ABC when used in combination with other initiatives, such as overall equipment effectiveness (OEE) (Atkinson 2007), business process re-engineering efforts and Six Sigma (Max 2007, 2008), the analytic hierarchy process (AHP) (Ayvaz and Pehlivanli 2011), or even conventional ABC (Barrett 2005). However, evidence supporting these 'hybrid' forms remains anecdotal. Finally, Lebas (2007) regrets that Kaplan and Anderson (2007c) followed a consultant approach in their book, avoiding any argument that would raise questions about time-driven ABC.

The two basic research papers on time-driven ABC focus on the design process of the costing system. Because unit time estimates, required for calculating time-driven ABC costs, are based upon interviews with operational employees and their managers, they may be subject to measurement error. Accordingly, Cardinaels and Labro (2008) examined the determinants of measurement error in time estimates through a computer-based lab experiment. Measurement error in time estimates was found to vary with (1) the level of aggregation in the definition of costing system activities, (2) task coherence, and (3) when notice is given that time estimates will be required – that is, in advance or after having performed the activities. In particular, participants generated lower measurement error when aggregation in the definition of activities was increased, when the activities that required time estimates presented themselves in a logical structure (as opposed to randomly), and when they were notified in advance that time estimates would be required before they performed their basic task. In addition, a strong overestimation bias was detected when participants provided estimates in minutes as opposed to percentages. Cardinaels and Labro (2008) warn that the presence of a large overestimation bias in the minutes estimation might undo time-driven ABC's intended benefit – revealing idle capacity by moving away from a percentage-based response mode. However, it should be noted that the respondents in their experiment were asked to estimate the total time spent on an activity as opposed to providing an estimate of the unit time spent on a transaction (i.e. one occurrence of an activity). Nevertheless, the results of the experiment highlight that costing system designers and decision-makers who use the figures produced by time-driven ABC should be aware of the extent of measurement error that impacts the accuracy of the cost figures.

Hoozée and Bruggeman (2010) investigated the antecedents of operational improvements in the design process of a time-driven ABC system. In their case study of four Belgian distribution warehouses, collective worker participation and appropriate leadership styles appeared to be indispensable factors. They showed that, for operational improvements to materialize, it is important that group discussions are guided by a leader with a considerate, people-oriented management style. When the group discussions are dominated by an autocratic leader, operational improvements may be hindered and the time-driven ABC system runs the risk of becoming merely another form of Taylorism. The case study also sheds light on how the search for accurate time equations and operational improvements are intermingled. In particular, during group discussions about time estimate accuracy, a negotiation process towards feasible time standards developed in an intertwined fashion. Hence, acknowledging that ABC may be used for various purposes and in various ways (cf. Malmi 1997), the case material extends the role of accuracy in time-driven ABC by evidencing that, at the case company, the main contribution of the time-driven ABC system was found in the control purpose of management accounting information.

Overall, the first study contributes to the costing error literature, which emphasizes the importance of accurate cost information to avoid making flawed decisions, while the second study complements studies that suggest decisions about error tolerance may depend upon the specific use of the costing system, to the extent that a more accurate costing system may even become unnecessary or undesirable (e.g., Alles and Datar 1998; Banker and Potter 1993; Callahan and Gabriel 1998; Kanodia et al. 2005; Merchant and Shields 1993; Mishra and Vaysman 2001). Overall, the results of these two papers provide insight into the use of time-driven ABC as a device for decision-making and control. In particular, by pointing out the determinants of measurement error in time estimates (Cardinaels and Labro 2008) and by revealing behavioural issues that may be encountered in the design of a time-driven ABC system (Hoozée and Bruggeman 2010), costing system designers, management accountants and managers are guided in improving the design process and the use of time-driven ABC information.

Conclusion and many future research directions

The review of time-driven ABC articles proved rather disappointing. With the exception of Cardinaels and Labro (2008) and Hoozée and Bruggeman (2010), most articles have a strong practical focus and merely offer anecdotal empirical evidence. Consequently, many opportunities for future research emerge: at least five fruitful areas can be distinguished.

First, future studies should *scrutinize the taken-for-granted profit impact of time-driven ABC.* As with conventional ABC, there still is virtually no empirical evidence showing that time-driven ABC adoption has an impact on performance. Empirical study is needed to provide evidence on the applicability and benefits of time-driven ABC (Zawawi and Hoque 2010). The case study results of Hoozée and Bruggeman (2010) offer some first insights. In particular, they suggest that time equations are equipped with specific characteristics that foster a detailed understanding of the work activities and the capacity utilization of resource pools, which manifested as very useful in identifying operational improvements. However, it is unclear whether such operational improvements actually result in higher profit. Following Banker et al. (2008), future research may disentangle whether time-driven ABC supports certain organizational capabilities, such as world-class manufacturing, that can be levered into significant improvements in plant performance.

Second, research efforts should be aimed at extending and complementing the findings of Cardinaels and Labro (2008). A first possible contribution to the costing error literature would be *to investigate the accuracy of time equations in greater detail.* Time equations are essentially composed of time parameters – which are estimated by operational employees and their managers – and of transactional data – which are exported from a company's computer-based information systems. Both may be subject to measurement error and consequently affect the accuracy of estimated transaction times. In addition to measurement (or estimation) error, the level of detail that is incorporated into the time equations may influence the accuracy of calculated transaction times (i.e. identification error). In particular, terms may be added to a time equation in an attempt to reduce the identification error in the transaction time estimate calculated using a time equation. However, due to measurement errors, adding terms may also add variance. Future research could explore this trade-off. Given that both conventional ABC and time-driven ABC operate at different levels of aggregation, a second possible contribution to the costing error literature would be to *compare and analyse the overall accuracy of both systems*, especially as a function of unused capacity (cf. Balakrishnan et al. 2011) and diversity in the time spent on activities. In particular, Gupta (1993) noted that diversity of variable values not only adds to costing error, but can also contribute to reductions in costing error through offsetting effects. This hypothesis was tested in the context of conventional ABC by Labro and Vanhoucke (2008) who provided more detail by identifying specific situations in which *less* diversity in resource consumption patterns increases the costing system sensitivity to unwanted errors. More specifically, they found that, while the intuition that increased diversity leads to increased sensitivity to errors holds for some aspects of diversity, decreasing diversity in the sharing of resources among activities and products across the whole of the costing system does not generally lead to decreased costing system sensitivity to errors. It may be noted that, next to increasing time-driven ABC system accuracy, the costs of designing and maintaining the costing system should also be considered. Future research could explore this trade-off and search for a balance between accuracy benefits and costs of data collection, storage and processing (cf. Babad and Balachandran 1993).

Third, future research can also investigate the *use of time-driven ABC for control*. Although time-driven ABC is not conceptually different from conventional ABC (see also Gosselin 2007), it is possible that equally accurate conventional ABC systems and time-driven ABC systems are perceived by decision-makers to differ in their usefulness, because of differences in presentation format between both systems. Therefore, it would be interesting to disentangle, for example, whether analytical versus heuristic decision-makers make more (or less) profitable decisions when cost information is presented through time-driven ABC versus conventional ABC (cf. Cardinaels 2008). Next, apart from the unintentional measurement error introduced by employees' best attempts to recall their time allocations, gaming behaviour may also distort time estimates in that employees supplying the data or managers using the data – anticipating how it might be used – may deliberately bias or distort the time estimates. Hence, as time-driven ABC supposedly produces more transparent cost information (Kaplan and Anderson 2007c), it may also be worthwhile investigating whether the use of time-driven ABC for budgeting will result in higher or lower budget slack compared to conventional ABC.

Fourth, a substantial body of research has analysed the *implementation* of conventional ABC systems. The first group of studies aimed at identifying the contextual and organizational factors that influence the decision to adopt and implement ABC. Examples of such factors include competition (e.g., Anderson 1995; Innes and Mitchell 1995; Malmi 1999), environmental uncertainty (e.g., Anderson 1995; Gosselin 1997; Innes and Mitchell 1995), centralization (e.g., Anderson 1995; Gosselin 1997), product diversity (e.g., Malmi 1999), complexity of manufacturing (e.g., Krumwiede 1998), size (e.g., Innes et al. 2000) and strategy (e.g., Gosselin 1997). Moreover, the degree of importance of these factors may vary by implementation stage (e.g., Baird et al. 2004). A second group of studies examined the determinants of success of ABC implementation, including top management support, linkage to performance evaluations and compensation, adequacy of resources (Anderson and Young 1999; Foster and Swenson 1997; McGowan and Klammer 1997; Shields 1995), training and linkage to quality (Foster and Swenson 1997; Shields 1995). Finally, several scholars have argued that issues of power and politics should not be neglected (e.g., Bhimani and Pigott 1992; Englund and Gerdin 2008; Major and Hopper 2005; Malmi 1997). An obvious avenue for future research would be to extend these studies to a time-driven ABC setting. More specifically, two research questions emerge: (1) what are the contextual and organizational factors that influence the decision to adopt and implement time-driven ABC, as opposed to conventional ABC?; and (2) do the determinants of success of conventional ABC implementation hold for time-driven ABC? Moreover, because the design process of a time-driven ABC system may be viewed as a target-setting process in which lower-level employees negotiate towards feasible time standards (Hoozée and Bruggeman 2010), time-driven ABC seems to be a return to standard costing (Gosselin 2007; Lebas 2007). Therefore, it would be worthwhile investigating which behavioural aspects, other than collective worker participation and leadership style (cf. Hoozée and Bruggeman 2010), play a role in the design process of a time-driven ABC system. Given the similarities of time-driven ABC to standard costing, future studies could also examine whether the same criticisms apply; for example: (1) can learning effects affect the accuracy of the system?; (2) can time encapsulate the intensity of resource use?; and (3) can idle capacity (slack) have positive functions (cf. Marginson and Ogden 2005)?

Finally, some authors have suggested that, with the advent of time-driven ABC, ABC has begun experiencing a resurgence in popularity (e.g., Barrett 2005). Survey research is needed to test this assertion. In addition, future research could reveal whether some industries (such as healthcare; Kaplan and Porter 2011) could reap increased benefits by investing in time-driven ABC.

Given that new 'hybrid' forms – combining time-driven ABC with other initiatives, such as overall equipment effectiveness (OEE) (Atkinson 2007), business process re-engineering efforts and Six Sigma (Max 2007, 2008), the analytic hierarchy process (AHP) (Ayvaz and Pehlivanli 2011), or even conventional ABC (Barrett 2005) – have started to emerge, it seems that the search for new acronyms is a never-ending journey. The innovation process for cost accounting continues (Gosselin 2007) and will probably keep feeding future research interests.

Appendix

This appendix describes a worked example of time-driven ABC. Assume operating expenses for an invoicing department are £101,250 per quarter. Five employees work in the department; each employee works 20 days per month (60 days per quarter) and is paid for 7.50 hours of work each day. Employees in the department spend about 75 minutes per day in breaks, training and education. The practical capacity for each employee is thus about 22,500 minutes per quarter and the cost per time unit of the invoicing department amounts to £0.90, which is the first estimate required for calculating time-driven ABC costs.

The second estimate is the time needed to process an invoice, which is calculated by means of a time equation. Suppose that interviews with employees in the invoicing department revealed that this time depends on: (1) whether the customer is British or not; (2) the number of invoice lines; (3) the invoice type (i.e. electronic data interchange (EDI) or not); and (4) the discount policy. This information results in the following time equation:

$$\text{time to process an invoice (in minutes)} = 0.40 + 0.60\,X_1 + 0.20\,X_2\,X_3 + 0.50\,X_4$$

with

X_1 = British customer: yes (0) versus no (1);
X_2 = number of invoice lines;
X_3 = EDI invoicing: yes (0) versus no (1);
X_4 = discount: yes (1) versus no.

For each transaction (e.g., a paper invoice consisting of 20 invoice lines for a French customer to whom no discount policy applies), the time equation is used to determine the time needed to perform the activity for this transaction (e.g., an invoice processing time of five minutes). The cost allocated to the customer is then obtained by multiplying this estimated time by the cost per time unit of £0.90. In addition, since transactional data can be extracted from companies' computer-based information systems, it is possible to determine the estimated time required to process all invoices over a certain quarter. Deducting this total time from the practical capacity of 112,500 minutes delivers the estimated excess capacity of the quarter.

Bibliography

Alles, M. and Datar, S. (1998) 'Strategic transfer pricing', *Management Science*, 44(4): 451–461.

Anderson, M.C., Banker, R.D. and Janakiraman, S.N. (2003) 'Are selling, general, and administrative costs "sticky"?', *Journal of Accounting Research*, 41(1): 47–63.

Anderson, S.R., Prokop, K. and Kaplan, R.S. (2007a) 'Fast-track profit models', *Cost Management*, 21(4): 16–28.

—— (2007b) 'Fast-track profit models: more powerful due-diligence process for mergers and acquisitions', *Journal of Private Equity*, 10(3): 22–34.

Anderson, S.W. (1995) 'A framework for assessing cost management system changes: the case of activity-based costing implementation at General Motors, 1986–1993', *Journal of Management Accounting Research*, 7: 1–51.

Anderson, S.W. and Young, S.M. (1999) 'The impact of contextual and process factors on the evaluation of activity-based costing systems', *Accounting, Organizations and Society*, 24(7): 525–559.

Anonymous (2008) 'Linking strategy to operations', *Journal of Accountancy*, 206(4): 80–82, 84.

Atkinson, A. (2007) 'Fixed factor fine tuning', *CMA Management*, 81(7): 42–46.

Ayvaz, E. and Pehlivanli, D. (2011) 'The use of time-driven activity-based costing and analytic hierarchy process method in the balanced scorecard implementation', *International Journal of Business and Management*, 6(3): 146–158.

Babad, Y.M. and Balachandran, B.V. (1993) 'Cost driver optimization in activity-based costing', *The Accounting Review*, 68(3): 563–575.

Baird, K.M., Harrison, G.L. and Reeve, R.C. (2004) 'Adoption of activity management practices: a note on the extent of adoption and the influence of organizational and cultural factors', *Management Accounting Research*, 15(4): 383–399.

Balakrishnan, R., Hansen, S. and Labro, E. (2011) 'Evaluating heuristics used when designing product costing systems', *Management Science*, 57(3): 520–541.

Balakrishnan, R. and Sivaramakrishnan, K. (2002) 'A critical overview of the use of full-cost data for planning and pricing', *Journal of Management Accounting Research*, 14: 3–31.

Banker, R.D., Bardhan, I.R. and Chen, T.-Y. (2008) 'The role of manufacturing practices in mediating the impact of activity-based costing on plant performance', *Accounting, Organizations and Society*, 33(1): 1–19.

Banker, R.D. and Johnston, H.H. (1993) 'An empirical study of cost drivers in the US airline industry', *The Accounting Review*, 68(3): 576–601.

Banker, R.D. and Potter, G. (1993) 'Economic implications of single cost driver systems', *Journal of Management Accounting Research*, 5: 15–32.

Banker, R.D., Potter, G. and Schroeder, R.G. (1995) 'An empirical analysis of manufacturing overhead cost drivers', *Journal of Accounting and Economics*, 19(1): 115–137.

Barrett, R. (2005) 'Time-driven costing: the bottom line on the new ABC', *Business Performance Management Magazine*, 3(1): 35–39.

Baxter, W.T. and Oxenfeldt, A.R. (1961) 'Costing and pricing: the cost accountant versus the economist', *Business Horizons*, 4(4): 77–90.

Bendavid, Y., Boeck, H. and Philippe, R. (2010) 'Redesigning the replenishment process of medical supplies in hospitals with RFID', *Business Process Management Journal*, 16(6): 991–1013.

Bhimani, A. and Pigott, D. (1992) 'Implementing ABC: a case study of organizational and behavioural consequences', *Management Accounting Research*, 3(2): 119–132.

Brüggen, A., Krishnan, R. and Sedatole, K.L. (2011) 'Drivers and consequences of short-term production decisions: evidence from the auto industry', *Contemporary Accounting Research*, 28(1); 83–123.

Cagwin, D. and Bouwman, M.J. (2002) 'The association between activity-based costing and improvement in financial performance', *Management Accounting Research*, 13(1): 1–39.

Callahan, C.M. and Gabriel, E.A. (1998) 'The differential impact of accurate product cost information in imperfectly competitive markets: a theoretical and empirical investigation', *Contemporary Accounting Research*, 15(4): 419–455.

Cardinaels, E. (2008) 'The interplay between cost accounting knowledge and presentation formats in cost-based decision-making', *Accounting, Organizations and Society*, 33(6): 582–602.

Cardinaels, E. and Labro, E. (2008) 'On the determinants of measurement error in time-driven costing', *The Accounting Review*, 83(3): 735–756.

Christensen, J. and Demski, J.S. (1995) 'The classical foundations of "modern" costing', *Management Accounting Research*, 6(1): 13–32.

—— (1997) 'Product costing in the presence of endogenous subcost functions', *Review of Accounting Studies*, 2(1): 65–87.

Cleland, K. (2004) 'As easy as CBA?', *Financial Management*, September: 28–32.

Cooper, R. and Kaplan, R.S. (1988a). 'Measure costs right: make the right decisions', *Harvard Business Review*, 66(5): 96–103.

—— (1988b) 'How cost accounting distorts product costs', *Management Accounting*, April: 20–27.

—— (1992) 'Activity-based systems: measuring the costs of resource usage', *Accounting Horizons*, 6(3): 1–13.

Cooper, R., Kaplan, R.S., Maisel, L.S., Morrissey, E. and Oehm, R.M. (1992) 'From ABC to ABM: does activity-based management automatically follow from an activity-based costing project?', *Management Accounting*, November: 28–31.

Coulter, D., McGrath, G. and Wall, A. (2011) 'Time-driven activity-based costing', *Accountancy Ireland*, 43(5): 12–15.

D'Aveni, R.A. (1994) *Hypercompetition: Managing the Dynamics of Strategic Maneuvering*, New York, NY: The Free Press.

Dalci, I., Tanis, V. and Kosan, L. (2010) 'Customer profitability analysis with time-driven activity-based costing: a case study in a hotel', *International Journal of Contemporary Hospitality Management*, 22(5): 609–637.

Datar, S.M. and Gupta, M. (1994) 'Aggregation, specification and measurement errors in product costing', *The Accounting Review*, 69(4): 567–591.

Datar, S.M., Kekre, S., Mukhopadhyay, T. and Srinivasan, K. (1993) 'Simultaneous estimation of cost drivers', *The Accounting Review*, 68(3): 602–614.

Dearman, D.T. and Shields, M.D. (2005) 'Avoiding accounting fixation: determinants of cognitive adaptation to differences in accounting method', *Contemporary Accounting Research*, 22(2): 351–384.

Drury, C. and Tayles, M. (2005) 'Explicating the design of overhead absorption procedures in UK organizations', *British Accounting Review*, 37(1): 47–84.

Duncan, R.B. (1972) 'Characteristics of organizational environments and perceived environmental uncertainty', *Administrative Science Quarterly*, 17(3): 313–327.

Englund, H. and Gerdin, J. (2008) 'Transferring knowledge across sub-genres of the ABC implementation literature', *Management Accounting Research*, 19(2): 149–162.

Everaert, P. and Bruggeman, W. (2007) 'Time-driven activity-based costing: exploring the underlying model', *Cost Management*, 21(2): 16–20.

Everaert, P., Bruggeman, W. and De Creus, G. (2008a) 'Sanac Inc.: from ABC to time-driven ABC (TDABC) – An instructional case', *Journal of Accounting Education*, 26(3): 118–154.

Everaert, P., Bruggeman, W., Sarens, G., Anderson, S.R. and Levant, Y. (2008b) 'Cost modeling in logistics using time-driven ABC: experiences from a wholesaler', *International Journal of Physical Distribution and Logistics Management*, 38(3): 172–191.

Foster, G. and Swenson, D.W. (1997) 'Measuring the success of activity-based cost management and its determinants', *Journal of Management Accounting Research*, 9: 109–141.

Gervais, M., Levant, Y. and Ducrocq, C. (2010) 'Time-driven activity-based costing (TDABC): an initial appraisal through a longitudinal case study', *Journal of Applied Management Accounting Research*, 8(2): 1–20.

Giannetti, R., Venneri, C. and Vitali, P.M. (2011) 'Time-driven activity-based costing and capacity cost management: the case of a service firm', *Cost Management*, 25(4): 6–16.

Gigerenzer, G. and Brighton, H. (2009) 'Homo heuristicus: why biased minds make better inferences', *Topics in Cognitive Science*, 1(1): 107–143.

Gigerenzer, G. and Gaissmaier, W. (2011) 'Heuristic decision-making', *Annual Review of Psychology*, 62: 451–482.

Goldman, S.L., Nagel, R.N. and Preiss, K. (1995) *Agile Competitors and Virtual Organizations: Strategies for Enriching the Customer*, New York, NY: Van Nostrand Reinhold.

Gosselin, M. (1997) 'The effect of strategy and organizational structure on the adoption and implementation of activity-based costing', *Accounting, Organizations and Society*, 22(2): 105–122.

—— (2007) 'A review of activity-based costing: technique, implementation, and consequences', in C.S. Chapman, A.G. Hopwood and M.D. Shields (eds), *Handbook of Management Accounting Research*, vol. 2, Oxford, UK: Elsevier.

Govindarajan, V. and Anthony, R.N. (1983) 'How firms use cost data in price decisions', *Management Accounting*, July: 30–36.

Gupta, M. (1993) 'Heterogeneity issues in aggregated costing systems', *Journal of Management Accounting Research*, 5: 180–212.

Homburg, C. (2001) 'A note on optimal cost driver selection in ABC', *Management Accounting Research*, 12(2): 197–205.

Hoozée, S. and Bruggeman, W. (2010) 'Identifying operational improvements during the design process of a time-driven ABC system: the role of collective worker participation and leadership style', *Management Accounting Research*, 21(3): 185–198.

Innes, J. and Mitchell, F. (1995) 'A survey of activity-based costing in the UK's largest companies', *Management Accounting Research*, 6(2): 137–153.

Innes, J., Mitchell, F. and Sinclair, D. (2000) 'Activity-based costing in the UK's largest companies: a comparison of 1994 and 1999 survey results', *Management Accounting Research*, 11(3): 349–362.

Ittner, C.D. and MacDuffie, J.P. (1995) 'Explaining plant-level differences in manufacturing overhead: structural and executional cost drivers in the world auto industry', *Production and Operations Management*, 4(4): 312–334.

Ittner, C.D., Larcker, D.F. and Randall, T. (1997) 'The activity-based cost hierarchy, production policies and firm profitability', *Journal of Management Accounting Research*, 9: 143–162.

Johnson, H.T. and Kaplan, R.S. (1987) *Relevance Lost: the Rise and Fall of Management Accounting*, Boston, MA: Harvard Business School Press.

Kanodia, C., Singh, R. and Spero, A.E. (2005) 'Imprecision in accounting measurement: can it be value enhancing?', *Journal of Accounting Research*, 43(3): 487–519.

Kaplan, R.S. (1986) 'Accounting lag: the obsolescence of cost accounting systems', *California Management Review*, 28(2): 174–199.

Kaplan, R.S. and Anderson, S.R. (2004) 'Time-driven activity-based costing', *Harvard Business Review*, 82(11): 131–138.

—— (2007a) 'The speed-reading organization', *Business Finance*, 13(6): 39–42.

—— (2007b) 'The innovation of time-driven activity-based costing', *Cost Management*, 21(2): 5–15.

—— (2007c) *Time-driven Activity-based Costing: a Simpler and More Powerful Path to Higher Profits*, Boston, MA: Harvard Business School Press.

Kaplan, R.S. and Norton, D.P. (2008) *The Execution Premium: Linking Strategy to Operations for Competitive Advantage*, Boston, MA: Harvard Business School Press.

Kaplan, R.S. and Porter, M.E. (2011) 'How to solve the cost crisis in health care', *Harvard Business Review*, 89(9): 46–64.

Kaplan, R.S. and Thompson, G.L. (1971) 'Overhead allocation via mathematical programming models', *The Accounting Review*, 46(2): 352–364.

Kennedy, T. and Affleck-Graves, J. (2001) 'The impact of activity-based costing techniques on firm performance', *Journal of Management Accounting Research*, 13: 19–45.

Kim, Y.-W. and Kim, S.-C. (2011) 'Cost analysis of information technology-assisted quality inspection using activity-based costing', *Construction Management and Economics*, 29(2): 163–172.

Krumwiede, K.R. (1998) 'The implementation stages of activity-based costing and the impact of contextual and organizational factors', *Journal of Management Accounting Research*, 10: 239–277.

Labro, E. and Vanhoucke, M. (2007) 'A simulation analysis of interactions among errors in costing systems', *The Accounting Review*, 82(4): 939–962.

—— (2008) 'Diversity in resource consumption patterns and robustness of costing systems to errors', *Management Science*, 54(10): 1715–1730.

Lambino, C. (2007) 'Time-driven activity-based costing', *Government Finance Review*, 23(4): 74–75.

Lebas, M.J. (2007) 'Book reviews – Time-driven activity-based costing: a simpler and more powerful path to higher profits', *European Accounting Review*, 16(4): 855–861.

Lukka, K. and Granlund, M. (2002) 'The fragmented communication structure within the accounting academia: the case of activity-based costing research genres', *Accounting, Organizations and Society*, 27(1–2): 165–190.

MacArthur, J.B. and Stranahan, H.A. (1998) 'Cost driver analysis in hospitals: a simultaneous equations approach', *Journal of Management Accounting Research*, 10: 279–312.

McGowan, A.S. and Klammer, T.P. (1997) 'Satisfaction with activity-based cost management implementation', *Journal of Management Accounting Research*, 9: 217–237.

McGowan, C. (2009) 'Time-driven activity-based costing: a new way to drive profitability', *Accountancy Ireland*, 41(6): 60–61.

Major, M. and Hopper, T. (2005) 'Managers divided: implementing ABC in a Portuguese telecommunications company', *Management Accounting Research*, 16(2): 205–229.

Malmi, T. (1997) 'Towards explaining activity-based costing failure: accounting and control in a decentralized organization', *Management Accounting Research*, 8(4): 459–480.

—— (1999) 'Activity-based costing diffusion across organizations: an exploratory empirical analysis of Finnish firms', *Accounting, Organizations and Society*, 24(8): 649–672.

Marginson, D. and Ogden, S. (2005) 'Coping with ambiguity through the budget: the positive effects of budgetary targets on managers' budgeting behaviours', *Accounting, Organizations and Society*, 30(5): 435–456.

Max, M. (2007) 'Leveraging process documentation for time-driven activity-based costing', *Journal of Performance Management*, 20(3): 16–28.

—— (2008) 'Bang for your buck: principles for improving your return on ABC', *Journal of Performance Management*, 21(3): 3–15.

Merchant, K.A. and Shields, M.D. (1993) 'When and why to measure costs less accurately to improve decision-making', *Accounting Horizons*, 7(2): 76–81.

Milgrom, P. and Roberts, J. (1992) *Economics, Organization and Management*, Englewood Cliffs, NJ: Prentice-Hall.

Miller, J.G. and Vollmann, T.E. (1985) 'The hidden factory', *Harvard Business Review*, 63(5): 142–150.

Mishra, B. and Vaysman, I. (2001) 'Cost-system choice and incentives – Traditional vs. activity-based costing', *Journal of Accounting Research*, 39(3): 619–641.

Namazi, M. (2009) 'Performance-focused ABC: a third generation of activity-based costing system', *Cost Management*, 23(5): 34–46.

Narayanan, V.G. and Sarkar, R.G. (2002) 'The impact of activity-based costing on managerial decisions at Insteel Industries - A field study', *Journal of Economics and Management Strategy*, 11(2): 257–288.

Noreen, E. (1991) 'Conditions under which activity-based cost systems provide relevant costs', *Journal of Management Accounting Research*, 3: 159–168.

Noreen, E. and Soderstrom, N. (1994) 'Are overhead costs strictly proportional to activity? Evidence from hospital service departments', *Journal of Accounting and Economics*, 17(1–2): 255–278.

—— (1997) 'The accuracy of proportional cost models: evidence from hospital service departments', *Review of Accounting Studies*, 2(1): 89–114.

Öker, F. and Adigüzel, H. (2010) 'Time-driven activity-based costing: an implementation in a manufacturing company', *Journal of Corporate Accounting and Finance*, 22(1): 75–91.

Sharman, P. (2008) 'Meet Bob Kaplan', *Strategic Finance*, 89(9): 19–20, 55.

Shields, M.D. (1995) 'An empirical analysis of firms' implementation experiences with activity-based costing', *Journal of Management Accounting Research*, 7: 148–166.

Shim, E. and Sudit, E.F. (1995) 'How manufacturers price products', *Management Accounting*, February: 37–39.

Stout, D.E. and Propri, J.M. (2011) 'Implementing time-driven activity-based costing at a medium-sized electronics company', *Management Accounting Quarterly*, 12(3): 1–11.

Swenson, D. (1995) 'The benefits of activity-based cost management to the manufacturing industry', *Journal of Management Accounting Research*, 7: 167–180.

Thomson, J. and Gurowka, J. (2005) 'Sorting out the clutter', *Strategic Finance*, 87(2): 27–33.

Turney, P.B.B. (1992) 'Activity-based management: ABM puts ABC information to work', *Management Accounting*, January: 20–25.

Wegmann, G. (2007) 'Analyse de quatre prolongements à la méthode ABC', *Revue Française de Comptabilité*, May: 28–32.

Wegmann, G. and Nozile, S. (2009) 'La méthode ABC au sein des services informatiques d'un grand groupe', *Revue Française de Comptabilité*, February: 36–40.

Zawawi, N.H.M. and Hoque, Z. (2010) 'Research in management accounting innovations: an overview of its recent development', *Qualitative Research in Accounting and Management*, 7(4): 505–568.

Zeller, T.L., Palzer, T.J. and Tressler, A.D. (2011) 'Fire the big box!?', *Issues in Accounting Education*, 26(2): 421–438.

Zimmerman, J.L. (2009) *Accounting for Decision-Making and Control*, 6th edn, New York, NY: McGraw-Hill.

10
The theory of constraints

David Dugdale

Introduction

The theory of constraints (TOC) originated as a management system that aimed to deliver product on time while holding relatively low levels of inventory. It therefore has some similarities with Just In Time production methods. However, the theory of constraints differs from JIT in two major ways. First, the aim is not to minimize inventory: indeed, an important element of the approach is to hold carefully calculated inventories at key locations. Second, the theory of constraints recognizes the crucial importance of plant bottlenecks and the need to maximize their utilization. The exploitation of bottleneck facilities led to the calculation of 'throughput per bottleneck minute', a similar idea to the management accountant's 'contribution per unit of limiting factor'. However, despite this similarity, cost accounting has been castigated by TOC enthusiasts because of the overhead included in product costs and the use of local performance measures such as efficiency ratios and variances. It is argued that these practices militate against optimal (or even good) production practices.

The method was first developed as a superior computer package for materials requirements planning (MRP[1]) that took account of the capacity constraint imposed by the plant bottleneck(s). However, as we will see, it has wider application, to project management, distribution and retailing as well as manufacturing. This chapter covers TOC principles and subsequent developments together with its implications for cost accounting and its relationship to linear programming and activity-based costing. The chapter ends with an evaluation of the competing arguments and recommends that management accountants take the theory of constraints and related ideas such as throughput accounting seriously.

The theory of constraints

Dr Eliyahu Goldratt introduced the theory of constraints to a wide audience by publicizing it in a best-selling novel, *The Goal* (Goldratt and Cox, 1984). Goldratt and his professional co-author expounded the theory of constraints through a fictional account of manager Alex Rogo's attempts to save his plant from closure. Alex takes advice from his old college professor, Jonah, as he identifies the bottlenecks in the plant and turns performance round by first concentrating on improving throughput and then breaking the bottlenecks. Along the way we see the futility of buying technology for its own sake (the robots that Alex is initially so proud of) and maximizing its use when the bottleneck is elsewhere.

Following the success of *The Goal* Goldratt developed the theory of constraints in three books, *The Race* (Goldratt and Fox, 1986), *The Haystack Syndrome* (Goldratt, 1990a) and *What is this Thing called Theory of Constraints and how Should it be Implemented?* (Goldratt, 1990b).

Noting that there is always a limit to performance Goldratt concluded that every system must have at least one constraint; so, first *(1) Identify the System's Constraint(s).* The second step follows logically – squeeze as much from the constraint(s) as possible: *(2) Decide How to Exploit the System(s) Constraint(s).* The third step recognizes that there is little point in over-producing from resources that are not constraints. In a manufacturing environment that would simply lead to a build-up of inventory without increased sales. The theory of constraints therefore requires *(3) Subordinate Everything Else to the Above Decision.* The fourth step, naturally enough, is to lift the constraint: *(4) Elevate the System's Constraint(s).* Fifth, recognize that, if a constraint has been broken, the whole system has changed and the process needs to begin again with step one: identify the (new) bottleneck. So, *(5) If a Constraint Has Been Broken, Go Back to Step One.*

Goldratt (1990a, b) provides advice on implementing the theory of constraints. The first step is to identify the constraint by calculating the anticipated load on each facility and comparing this to capacity. Equally, one could walk round the plant and look for the points where inventory piles up – or just ask an experienced manager.

The second step is to exploit the constraint. This involves (1) identifying the best product mix and (2) making sure that the constraint facility runs at its maximum capacity. To determine the best product mix Goldratt recommends the calculation of 'throughput per bottleneck minute' for each product and production of the highest ranking products. 'Throughput' is usually defined as revenue less purchased materials and services; a more restricted definition than the management accountant's 'contribution' because Goldratt does not believe that internal expenses such as 'direct' labour are variable. To ensure maximum utilization of the bottleneck Goldratt recommends that a buffer stock be held in front of it: if there are manufacturing problems in other parts of the plant, the bottleneck facility can continue to operate by running down the buffer stock.

The third step, subordination to the bottleneck, is achieved by restricting production on non-bottleneck facilities so that they produce only as much as the bottleneck can process. To produce more would simply lead to a build-up of inventory without increasing sales. It would also increase lead-time because of the inventory queuing ahead of any new work (and material earmarked for particular jobs might be 'stolen' in order to keep non-bottleneck processes operating). Subordinating everything to the bottleneck is at the heart of the 'Drum-Buffer-Rope' (DBR) method of production scheduling, set out in detail by Goldratt and Fox (1986). In the DBR method the bottleneck facility is the 'drum' and the whole plant moves to its 'beat' (the pace of the bottleneck). The 'buffer' is the buffer stock located ahead of the bottleneck. As the buffer is depleted, it is replenished by a metaphorical 'rope' pulling material from preceding facilities. The DBR system ensures that non-constraint facilities produce only what is needed to meet the needs of the bottleneck.[2]

The fourth and fifth steps in the TOC method are to 'elevate' or break the bottleneck and then to go back to the first step, identifying the new constraint. Goldratt emphasizes the importance of not allowing policy constraints or 'inertia' to hinder the search for even better solutions. In fact he extends the fifth step in the TOC method to: '*If in the Previous Step, a Constraint Has Been Broken, Go Back to Step One, but Do Not Allow Inertia to Cause a System's Constraint*' (Goldratt, 1990a, p. 62).

Critique of cost accounting

Cost accounting is regularly attacked in Goldratt's work and from the earliest days he saw 'Cost accounting as the number one enemy of productivity' (Goldratt, 1983).[3] According to Goldratt cost accounting has a number of pernicious consequences. First he notes that cost accounting leads to local performance measures such as labour efficiency and machine utilization. Such measures encourage a 'keep-busy' mentality that, on non-constraint facilities, leads to stock-building and longer production lead-times. Accountants also note that the financial accounting convention of including all production costs, including overhead, in the value of stock encourages stock-building. Second, Goldratt criticizes product costs; if an item were off-loaded from a constraint onto a less efficient but non-constraint facility, the product cost would increase and the switch might be vetoed (a negative 'switch variance' might reinforce this message in some companies). Third, Goldratt sees cost accounting in general and activity-based costing in particular as muddling variable costs (such as material and sub-contract costs) with operating expenses that do not vary with volume. He is scathing about activity-based costing: 'Yes, the allocation [into unit, batch, product and company-level costs] can be done in this way. But for what purpose? Anyhow we cannot aggregate them at the unit level or even at the product level. So why play all these number games?' (Goldratt, 1990a, p. 40).

Several of Goldratt's works draw attention to the negative consequences of the unthinking application of traditional product costs, overhead absorption, activity-based costing, efficiency variances/ratios and measures of utilization. In *Necessary but not Sufficient* Goldratt et al (2000) see technology as *necessary* for performance breakthrough but, given existing accounting measures, it is insufficient if not accompanied by changes in attitude and rethinking of the old measures. To achieve the promise of computerized DBR methods a culture shift is necessary. One of the characters summarizes: 'Every place I visited that got bottom-line results also changed the rules. They don't attempt to reach high efficiencies on every work centre. They don't behave as if releasing work orders early is the way to get early finish and they don't even think that the larger the batch the better it is' (Goldratt et al, 2000, pp. 128–129).

Origin of the theory of constraints

The theory of constraints emerged from the prior development of a computer software package, *Optimized Production Technology* (*OPT*)[4] designed to schedule manufacturing plants. The software was originally developed by Goldratt and his partners, working for Creative Output, Inc. and supported by the large US computer manufacturer, Control Data Corporation. Early developments were not trouble-free. Fox (2010: 2) writes: 'Creative Output's history was a roller-coaster ride that ended on a down note with a major dispute between Eli and his partners and the essential bankruptcy of the company.' Nevertheless, it was the development of OPT that led Goldratt to his wider theory of constraints so, to understand the origins of TOC, we first review the principles of OPT.

Goldratt (1987) explains that, working from first principles, the OPT bill of materials explosions and materials requirements calculation were more efficient than existing MRP software, which meant that OPT could employ more sophisticated scheduling algorithms. The early scheduling logic (circa 1978) was essentially 'automated Kanban': a batch would not be produced if it would result in inventory exceeding the 'station stock limitation (SSL)'. In late 1980 the more sophisticated HALT concept led to production being stopped if an operation 'fed paths in which more than one buffer was already filled' (Goldratt, 1987: 448). This led to the revelation that, typically, there was excess capacity at most work stations and appreciation of 'The vast importance of bottlenecks in determining the overall performance ...' (p. 448). In 1982 the software was again improved with a BRAIN module to schedule bottleneck facilities and a SERVE module that then scheduled non-bottlenecks. This was: '... a drastic conceptual departure from the Kanban logic and merged the good features of MRP and the finite scheduling approaches, while eliminating their major deficiencies' (Goldratt, 1987, p. 451).

Until the early 1980s Goldratt concentrated on technical matters. Then he started to appreciate the wider issues. Supervisors could always point to errors in the schedules when they wanted to discredit them and, because they were usually judged on the efficiency and utilization of men and machines, they tended not to favour schedules that required that production (on non-bottlenecks) be regularly halted. It was reflection on this behavioural problem that led Goldratt '... to attack what was at that time almost a sacred cow – cost accounting itself' (p. 451).

Goldratt's intellectual journey began with technical scheduling issues, moved on to the recognition that human and measurement factors could lead to apparently irrational behaviour, and to his conclusion that education was more important than expert software. Over a period of 30 years the theory of constraints has been central to Goldratt's work and, following the success of *The Goal,* he has regularly used novels to bring his ideas to a wide audience. The following section summarizes these novels, showing how the theory of constraints can be applied not only in manufacturing but also in marketing, project management, distribution and retailing.

Developments in the Theory of Constraints

The thinking processes: It's Not Luck *(Goldratt, 1994)*

After developing the theory of constraints, Goldratt worked on 'the thinking processes' – a generic method for analysing problems. It seems likely that Goldratt thought the 'thinking processes' a more powerful technique that subsumed TOC. He therefore marketed the technique through the Goldratt Institute and wrote a sequel to *The Goal* that developed the ideas and showed how they could be employed in a variety of situations. However, the new technique has not had the same impact as the theory of constraints and, though in theory it may be the more significant development, after *It's Not Luck* subsequent novels have focused on mainstream applications of TOC.

In *It's Not Luck* the hero of *The Goal,* Alex Rogo, now promoted to CEO of the 'diversified group', uses the thinking processes to address his wider responsibilities. The corporate strategy is to sell the companies in the diversified group and Alex needs a performance breakthrough in each of his group's three divisions: Cosmetics, Printing and Pressure Steam.

In Cosmetics the breakthrough is achieved by switching most of the division's inventory from regional warehouses to the manufacturing plants. Under the previous system retail branches and regional warehouses held inventory as protection against factory shortage, but now their stock is much reduced and replenished daily. Factory inventories are replenished on total rather than disaggregated, more variable, shop-based data; overall inventory is reduced and cash flow boosted. However, the change is not painless. Short-term profit is hit as production overhead in inventory falls and the accounting treatment of plants as profit centres that 'sell' to regional warehouses has to be replaced.

In Printing the wrappers department is unprofitable. The printing presses have short set-up times and can supply small-order quantities efficiently. However, they cannot compete with the competition's faster printing presses for large-order quantities. The solution exploits the dilemma facing the division's customers: to reduce prices by ordering large quantities or to reduce inventory by ordering small quantities. This 'cloud' is 'evaporated' by noting that small-order quantities lead to less inventory becoming obsolete: important because wrapper designs are often changed to meet regulations and/or the frequent marketing campaigns needed in dynamic markets. The recognition that small quantities can be more cost-effective allows the Printing division to put a persuasive proposition to its customers.

In Pressure Steam the breakthrough idea is to sell the steam itself, not the equipment and spare parts needed to produce the steam. A key element in the solution is the division's efficient handling of the spare parts inventory. This makes the proposition difficult for the competition to match.

There are two themes in the book. First, that after applying TOC in manufacturing, the constraint moves to the market place and 'breakthroughs' are needed in order to better target customers and increase sales. The examples, especially in Printing and Pressure Steam, emphasize the importance of analysing the problem from the customer's point of view. The second theme is the 'thinking processes', illustrated throughout the book in solving a number of home and business problems, including the derivation of the breakthrough solutions in each of the divisions. Somewhat disingenuously (because the thinking processes had not been invented) it is claimed that the thinking processes underpinned the bottleneck and inventory management techniques explained in *The Goal*. Referring to the turn-round of the Bearington plant, Alex reflects: 'That's when we met Jonah, and started to learn his Thinking Processes' (p. 38).

The thinking processes have not (yet) had the same impact as the theory of constraints. Fox (2010) recounts that, in 1991, 'Attendees who came to the Jonah course prepared to learn about bottlenecks and drum-buffer-rope scheduling were introduced to cause-effect trees evaporating clouds and several other techniques ...' The course was not a success, with some delegates, representing large companies, 'walking away'. However, with Goldratt's advocacy, some managers employ the thinking processes and Noreen et al. (1995) reported that, although in the TOC companies they visited very few managers routinely used the thinking processes, 'some were'.

Project management: Critical Chain *(Goldratt, 1997)*

This novel applies the theory of constraints to project management. Although there are references to evaporating clouds (pp. 97 and 99) and the thinking processes (p. 109), these are peripheral to the main theme of the book: the application of TOC to projects. Project management is a key management problem in many industries: students of engineering, production, management and management accounting are taught how to draw activity networks and identify the critical path. Then they meet the PERT technique, taking account of the probabilistic nature of activity durations and the mysteries of earliest/latest start dates and total, independent and freefloat. They are not told why, in view of all this theory, so many projects are late, over-budget and fail to meet original specification.

Critical Chain approaches this issue through a fictional university course in project management delivered by Professor Richard Silver, an associate professor seeking tenure. He engages his MBA class by discussing the various project management problems they face in practice.

A key issue is the uncertainty inherent in activity durations. The distribution of activity time is, typically, skewed, with a long tail – some activities take a lot longer than expected. As managers want to complete their activities within the scheduled time they build significant 'safety time' into their duration estimates. This is especially likely since, often, there is no incentive to finish an activity early, but a penalty for finishing late. Activity safety time is also increased for two other reasons. First, if a manager is responsible for linked activities, more safety time is likely to be added: for example, two activities requiring five hours each might require 12 hours when they are linked. This practice escalates if more layers of management are involved. Second, when the analysis is complete, senior managers often cut the total time allowed, so, in anticipation of this, managers inflate their activity time estimates.

All this safety time might be a good thing if it actually protected the intended project delivery date but, in practice, it does not. First, if an activity is completed ahead of time it will probably not be reported: to do so would invite pressure from senior management to cut time in future, and/or opprobrium from colleagues. 'In sequential steps . . . Delays accumulate, while advances do not' (p. 121). Second, for parallel activities, only *one* activity needs to be delayed for the next activity to start late. Third, if an activity seems to have plenty of time, there is a tendency not to start it: if problems are then discovered, some of the safety time has already been lost. Fourth, people or departments under pressure find that their efforts are regularly diverted: to other activities, projects, meetings, etc.

The next point concerns the measurement of progress. It is noted that progress is typically measured by the proportion of work completed, not the progress on the critical path. This measurement (which could be important to maximize progress payments) tends to lead to activities generally starting as early as possible. Starting everything as early as possible, or, indeed, as late as possible, leads to an unfocused style of project management.

Reaching a solution involves applying the theory of constraints in a project environment. The 'bottleneck' is now the project's critical path, and the key to completing the project on time is to protect the critical path. The crucial step is to take the safety time out of individual activities so that it protects the whole project. A project critical path should be changed as shown in Figure 10.1.

Of course, removing safety time from individual activities means that they are more likely to over-run, and a new philosophy is needed that does not penalize individual activity over-runs so long as all reasonable effort has been made to complete within the estimated time. No doubt persuading managers and engineers that they should cut the safety time out of each activity step and aggregate it into a 'project buffer' is the most difficult issue in implementing the 'critical chain' method.

In line with focusing on the critical path 'bottleneck' every effort should be made to ensure that resources needed on the critical path are ready at the appropriate time. The project buffer and more intense focus mean the critical path is much more likely to be completed on time. But a new danger arises: that a subordinate activity finishes so late that it delays the critical path. This problem is addressed by aiming to finish each subordinate activity with time to spare: a 'feeding buffer' is built into the time allowed for each chain of activities that feeds the critical path.

Two further issues are developed. The first relates to vendors and the traditional emphasis on negotiating the lowest price from them. Given the financial consequences of finishing a project late it is argued that it would be better to obtain shorter and more reliable lead-times and, for critical or near-critical activities, it is worth paying over the odds for the service. The second issue gives the book its title. Critical path networks recognize logical dependencies between activities but not dependencies that may arise because several activities compete for

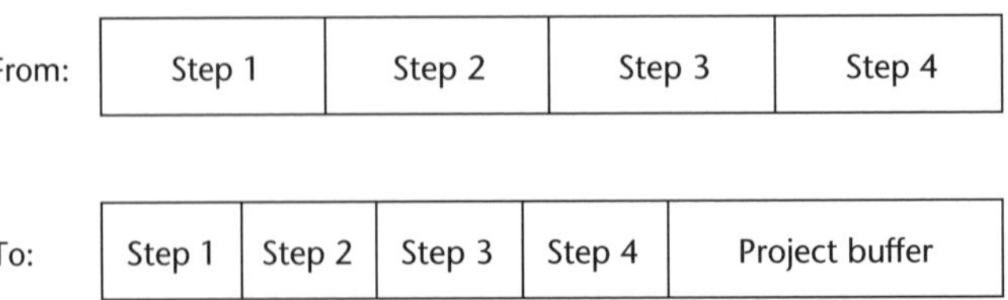

Figure 10.1 'Old' and 'new' critical paths
Source: Goldratt (1997: 157).

the same resource. The 'critical chain' is more sophisticated, taking account not only of logical dependencies but also of finite resource capacities.

Computing: Necessary But Not Sufficient *(Goldratt, Schragenheim and Ptak, 2000)*

This novel, set in the late 1990s, focuses on the exploits of a software supplier, BGSoft. This company supplies ERP[5] (enterprise requirements planning systems). The company has been growing fast but the whole industry is becoming mature, most large companies have ERP systems, and it seems unlikely that the rate of growth can be sustained. In fact the company is struggling to handle its existing level of systems implementations: only 20% of requested software modifications are approved because of their knock-on consequences on the increasingly complex ERP product.

Simultaneously, one of BGSoft's customers causes problems by asking for evidence that their ERP system has actually saved money. This is difficult to demonstrate because there have been no headcount savings. Reduced receivables and inventory and reduced shortages leading to slightly higher sales might justify the ERP system, but it is clear that introducing new computer systems does not directly impact the 'bottom line'. This leads BGSoft to consider Advanced Planning and Scheduling (APS) systems as a means of adding value, especially for mid-size companies.

One of BGSoft's customers successfully employs constraint management using drum-buffer-rope scheduling techniques. Bottlenecks are scheduled manually but the ERP system is needed to handle the consequential scheduling of non-bottlenecks. As usual, there are problems with measurements and the culture change necessary for a successful TOC implementation. Having seen this successful implementation, BGSoft arranges visits to more successful plants. In each case it is observed that the plant has not only changed its scheduling procedures but also its measurements and rules. It is this observation that gives the book its title, *Necessary But Not Sufficient.* Technology might be *necessary* for a step, change in efficiency and effectiveness, but it is not *sufficient.* For that there must also be a thoroughgoing culture change in which high efficiencies are not just pursued for their own sake, work orders are released only when needed and large batches are not automatically 'better'.

BGSoft purchases an existing software provider and improves its software by introducing inventory buffers ahead of bottlenecks and optimizing schedules only on bottlenecks. The revised software is then integrated into BGSoft's existing MRP system. Pierco, an important customer, provides a beta test site for the new ERP system and excellent results are obtained, especially as buffer management highlights those areas where the company can benefit most from the introduction of Lean management methods.[6] BGSoft now has a best-selling ERP/TOC product that adds value to the customer's bottom line and, in addition, adds many more factory-based 'concurrent users' – which leads to increased revenue for BGSoft. Working with TOC consultants who know how to sell the TOC ideas and educate prospective customers, the company begins to ramp up sales.

One further problem remains to be solved. As the plants at Pierco become more efficient and extra capacity is revealed by the TOC method, warehouse inventories start to rise with a devastating effect on cash-flow and on the space needed to house inventory. The solution is 'TOC in distribution', holding most of the inventory at the plants and replenishing warehouse inventory as it is used, day-to-day. This leads to further performance improvement and a smaller inventory.

The book concludes by alluding to future possibilities. BGSoft is preparing 'critical chain' software to address the problems faced by project-oriented companies and engineering departments. Thus the company is aiming for value-enhancing versions of its ERP software for production, distribution and engineering. The company's emphasis is now on value rather than technological sophistication: changing culture and devising appropriate measures and rules is now seen as the 'sufficient' condition which is just as important as the 'necessary' technological advance. Finally, the key actors in the book look to improving whole supply chains through better production and distribution management facilitated by interlocking ERP systems.

Retailing: Isn't It Obvious? *(Goldratt, 2010)*

In this novel Goldratt once again adopts his favoured Socratic method of teaching, demonstrating that the theory of constraints can be applied to retailing. Paul, a stores manager (who is also the son-in-law of the company president) has to deal with burst pipes at his store and the relocation of much of his inventory. The inventory is taken back by the regional warehouse and shipped only as needed on a day-to-day basis to the store. It turns out that less inventory, paradoxically, leads to fewer shortages because the regional warehouse has small amounts of 'leftover' inventory and, additionally, can arrange cross-shipments from other warehouses. This, combined with more space and better displays, leads to a much improved sales performance. In addition, the transfer of inventory to the warehouse means that the return on investment for the store shoots up. Eventually other store managers are persuaded to adopt the same system and the company's performance improves dramatically. The essence of the improvement comes from holding as much inventory as possible at regional warehouses instead of at retail stores. This reduces the variability of demand (because demands on individual stores are aggregated) and avoids shortages in some stores when others have surpluses. Eventually it is realized that a central warehouse should house the bulk of the company's inventory rather than it being dispersed to regional warehouses and stores.

Although not discussed explicitly in the book, the eventual solution follows the theory of constraints (and Just In Time) ideas as inventory is pulled down the chain only in response to demand. Inventory buffers are held in stores and warehouses and are replenished to meet demand. This idea is eventually pushed back into the supply chain as suppliers (now 'partners') hold dyed fabric in inventory but cut and sew into small batches only on demand from the retail chain.

TOC in manufacturing, project management, distribution and retailing

Goldratt's books demonstrate that the theory of constraints is not just about manufacturing bottlenecks. Perhaps unfortunately, the success of *The Goal* led to TOC being associated with manufacturing, and this may have been reinforced by *The Haystack Syndrome* where throughput per constraint minute is employed to determine the best product mix – again in a manufacturing context. Although Goldratt was heavily influenced by his knowledge of scheduling software in general and MRP (Materials Requirements Planning) systems in particular, he was always aware that TOC had wider applicability. For example, Goldratt (1990b) analyses why quoted delivery lead-times have remained high despite significant shop-floor improvements. Part of the problem rests in the design stage and the relevant manager is asked: 'Have you viewed the Goal in a more generic way? As a story about completing a task using a number of different resources?' (p. 74).

Goldratt (1990a) has also preferred to see the DBR buffers in terms of time rather than physical units. The time buffer is the 'interval of time that we release the task prior to the time we would have released if we assumed that Murphy [unpredictable problems] did not exist' (p. 124). In fact, in *The Goal* and *The Race* Goldratt uses troops of scouts and soldiers to explain the bottleneck idea in terms of time. In *The Goal* the slowest scout, Herbie, is placed at the head of the troop so that the whole troop is forced to move at the pace of the bottleneck. In *The Race* the lead soldier is tied to the slowest soldier so that he can never go faster than the slowest member of the troop. The length of the rope determines the buffer: the time that the slowest soldier would take to catch up with the lead soldier if the latter were temporarily incapacitated. Goldratt's emphasis on time buffers means that the ideas that led to the *Critical Chain* were always latent in previous work. In the DBR scheduling system the buffer can be interpreted as the safety *time* available to the constraint before the buffer is used up, while in the critical chain, safety time is allocated to the critical path and to the feeding buffers.

The size of the safety buffers and the related topic of non-constraint capacity have received considerable attention in Goldratt's writings. He finds the buffer-rope analysis useful because there is a close relationship between the 'rope' and the buffer: the longer the rope, the more buffer time (inventory) there is in the system. If the rope is long, jobs are released well in advance and pile up in the buffer ahead of the bottleneck; the constraint is well protected but at the cost of more inventory. If the rope is short, inventory is low, the system is very responsive but the constraint is poorly protected. Goldratt therefore sees sizing the buffers as crucial and: 'THE DECISION ON THE LENGTH OF THE BUFFERS MUST BE IN THE HANDS OF THE PEOPLE DIRECTLY RESPONSIBLE FOR THE OVERALL PERFORMANCE OF THE COMPANY' (Goldratt, 1990a, p. 126, emphasis as original).

To make sense of the various applications of the theory of constraints we need to recognize different configurations of plants and processes. Goldratt identified the generic types as I, V, A and T plants. An I plant produces a product through a sequence of processes; a V plant makes many products from a common material; in an A plant several assemblies, parts and components are assembled into the final product; and, in a T plant, one or several production lines feed several assemblies. These possibilities can be combined as in Figure 10.2.

The different production configurations are 'protected' by different types of inventory. The I, sequential, configuration may have a bottleneck facility in the sequence of connected work stations. This is the case that was addressed in the development of TOC: a buffer inventory should be placed in front of the bottleneck and other facilities in the I-chain should be subordinated to the bottleneck using DBR methods. The V configuration requires that inventory be held at point V. This is the case that applies to distribution and retailing, where the mistake would be to disperse inventory into the distribution chain or use it irreversibly in a product that is not yet needed. Goldratt shows how holding inventory centrally and releasing it only as needed leads to a more responsive system with less (total) inventory. The A configuration requires that several sub-assemblies are needed in order to complete an assembly; feeding buffers are needed to ensure that the final operation is not held up for lack of a single outstanding sub-assembly. This configuration also applies to critical chain project management. If several activities have to be completed before another activity can begin, each requires its own 'feeding buffer' to make sure all 'arrive' on time and the next activity begins on schedule.

The A, I, V analysis allows us to picture different process configurations and to understand why inventory is needed and where it should best be located. It also allows us to see that the development of TOC applications in project management, distribution and retailing are further applications of the basic ideas. Goldratt has expended considerable effort discussing the rationale for inventory, where it should be located and how much of it should be held. As we have seen, the amount of buffer inventory reflects a trade-off between protecting the bottleneck/final assembly or activity/distribution chain and the investment in inventory. In principle, it should reflect the inherent variability in the system and management's preferences for bottleneck protection versus responsiveness and inventory investment.

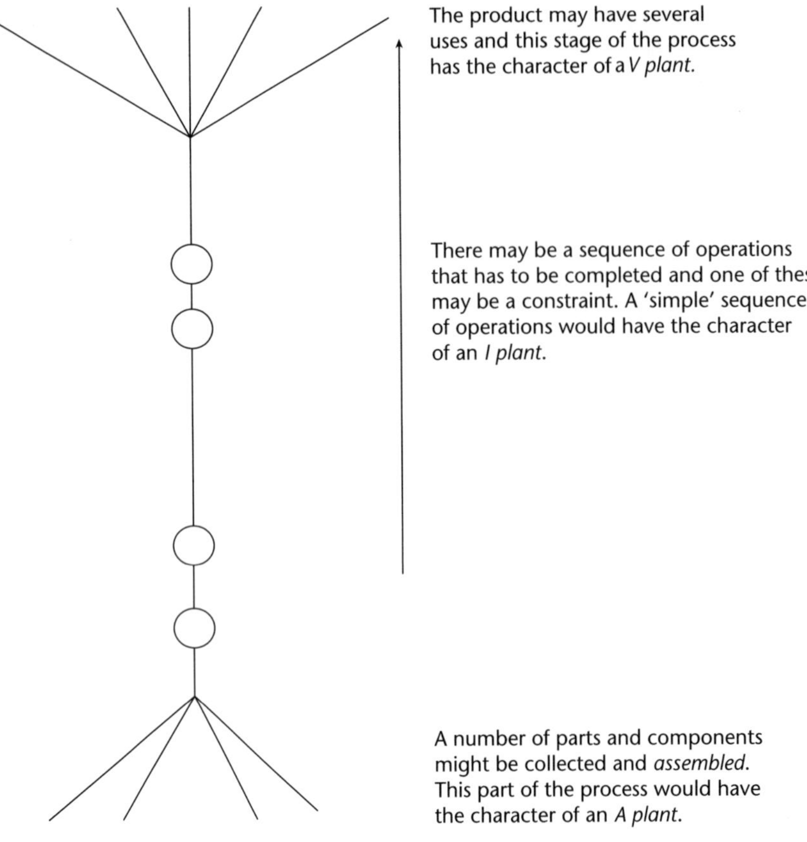

The product may have several uses and this stage of the process has the character of a *V plant.*
There may be a sequence of operations that has to be completed and one of these may be a constraint. A 'simple' sequence of operations would have the character of an *I plant.*
A number of parts and components might be collected and *assembled.* This part of the process would have the character of an *A plant.*

Figure 10.2 A, I and V processes

The Theory of Constraints and cost accounting

Goldratt refers to cost accounting as the number one enemy of productivity. His views can be traced to his belief that (1) many operational expenses are effectively 'fixed' and will not be affected by management decisions; (2) excess capacity on non-bottleneck facilities is 'free' because resource can be mobilized to utilize it at minimal cost, and (3) bottleneck capacity is very expensive because time lost on the bottleneck restricts sales and profit. Although management accountants might point out that the idea of 'contribution per unit of limiting factor' has been around for a long time and is very much in line with the theory of constraints, Goldratt would still attack typical cost accounting practices. He would say that cost accounting measures are institutionalized and do not take account of either the generally fixed nature of operating expense or the importance of bottleneck versus non-bottleneck facilities.

Product costing

Cost accountants attribute costs to product for a number of reasons. First, 'direct' costs are naturally associated with product. However, Goldratt does not accept that this treatment is appropriate even for some, so-called, 'direct' costs. He asks whether, even if labour costs can be directly traced to product, would they be eliminated if the product were not produced?

Goldratt would only unequivocally accept the attribution of direct material costs to product and, following this logic, even the accountant's contribution per unit of limiting factor can lead to an inferior product mix decision.

Second, financial reporting standards have long required the inclusion of *all* production costs (including all production overhead, whether 'variable' or 'fixed') in the value of inventory. This encourages stock-building and discourages stock reduction because reported profit is reduced in periods when inventory falls. Many management accountants would agree with Goldratt that this is unhelpful. Nevertheless, it is required for financial reporting purposes and it means that reported profit is higher when inventory is rising.

Third, the rise of activity-based costing has seen a strong rationale for attributing more and more overhead to products and other cost objects using a variety of cost drivers – some product volume-related, others related to number of batches, orders, products and so on. Goldratt considers the attribution of operating expense to product to be pointless; so naturally he feels that doing this in ever more sophisticated ways is even more futile.

How do we evaluate these arguments? In relation to variable costs it seems that Goldratt has softened his hard line that only materials and bought-out services should be attributed to products. According to Noreen et al. (1995), although the TOC literature usually defines throughput as revenue less direct materials, 'The official current definition of throughput is revenue less "totally variable costs"' (p. 13). This suggests that even Goldratt acknowledges that determining 'variable costs' might not be straightforward. Piece-work systems still exist: some companies introduce and lay off shift workers at short notice and, in the 2008/9 UK recession, there were many examples of companies reducing labour costs over relatively short periods. For example, Honda and other automobile manufacturers introduced short-time working. Goldratt may be right that labour costs are somewhat 'sticky', but they can be varied and assessment of which costs are variable over a given time scale needs to be undertaken on a case-by-case basis.

Goldratt and many management accountants are at one in regard to the unfortunate inclusion of fixed production overhead in inventory values. However, the significance of this can be overstated. Many managers are capable of seeing through the problem with short-term profit as inventories fall, especially as falling inventory leads to increased cash-flow.

Finally, Goldratt's attack on activity-based costing could be seen as an over-emphasis on short-run decisions. Activity-based costing supporters would point to supposedly 'fixed' costs increasing as businesses expand, and to the long-run variability of *all* costs. The Lehigh Steel teaching case (Narayanan and Donohue, 1998) provides an example that compares the use of TOC and ABC calculations in reaching a product mix decision relevant to a two to five year time scale. Over this time scale it was eventually decided that a number of ABC-derived costs should be included in the derivation of throughput/contribution as an input to limiting factor-style calculations.

Throughput accounting

The term 'throughput accounting' was introduced to a UK audience by two consultants, David Galloway and David Waldron (1988a, 1988b, 1989a, 1989b). They defined return-per-factory-hour as sales price less material cost divided by time on the key resource, and cost-per-factory-hour as total factory cost divided by the total time available on the key resource. The 'TA ratio' for a particular product was calculated as return-per-factory-hour/cost-per-factory-hour, and used in ranking products.

In fact, given that return-per-factory-hour is exactly the same as Goldratt's throughput per bottleneck minute/hour, and cost-per-factory-hour is the same for all products, Galloway and

Revenue

(Material cost of sales)

Throughput

(Operating expense)

Net profit

Figure 10.3 Proposed throughput accounting statement

Waldron are actually using Goldratt's recommended approach to ranking products.[7] David Waldron worked for the Goldratt Institute for a short period and his use of some of Goldratt's ideas led to tension between the consultants and the Goldratt Institute. It also means that the term 'throughput accounting' has an unclear meaning in the UK; does it refer to the theory of constraints and the main body of Goldratt's work, or to the ideas set out by Galloway and Waldron in the UK publication, *Management Accounting*?

In the US this problem does not arise and the term 'throughput accounting' refers to Goldratt's work. For example, Corbett's (1998) book, *Throughput Accounting*, provides a detailed exposition of the way that data relating to throughput, T (price less totally variable cost), operating expense, OE (all costs that are not totally variable), and the capacity constraint resource, CCR, can be manipulated to determine the best product mix. Corbett follows Goldratt's prescriptions exactly and, in the US, 'theory of constraints' and 'throughput accounting' often refer interchangeably to Goldratt's work.

It is a pity that the term *throughput accounting* may refer to the work of Galloway and Waldron in the UK or is simply a synonym for the theory of constraints in the US because, logically, the term could be used to describe a form of direct or marginal cost accounting based on Goldratt's very restricted definition of direct/variable/marginal costs. A throughput accounting statement would appear as in Figure 10.3.

Such a statement would, of course, be very similar to direct or marginal cost accounting statements but would take an extreme position in assuming that the only variable cost is materials. As Noreen et al. (1995) say, 'Most TOC companies use an extreme form of variable costing in which the only costs assigned to products are direct materials' (p. xxvii). Companies adopting 'throughput accounting' would value inventory at material cost only. Noreen et al. provide case studies of companies using such an approach, and UK examples are provided by Dugdale and Jones (1996, p. 36, see *Figure 3.1: Automek (UK) throughput P&L*) and Darlington et al. (1992).

Performance measures

As we have seen, Goldratt sees many of the performance measures associated with traditional cost accounting as unfortunate. In particular he regards measures of efficiency and utilization on non-bottleneck facilities as driving inappropriate behaviour: supervisors are rewarded for a 'keep-busy' mentality that achieves nothing but a build up of inventory. Goldratt has suggested that an appropriate measure would be inventory-dollar-days – a measure of the value of an order that is behind schedule. While there may be logic in such a measure it would likely lead to a large penalty being associated with a late order, and it is not clear how it would be used in practice or whether supervisors would take it seriously.

Revenue recognition

Goldratt has drawn attention to the unfortunate consequences of the accountant's tendency to recognize revenue as early as possible. In *Critical Chain* he points out that progress payments might be maximized by starting work as early as possible. Unfortunately this can lead to an unfocused style of project management that can neglect the critical path and its feeding activities. A second example arises in Goldratt's treatment of distribution and retailing, where the use of profit centres leads to 'revenue' being recognized as product and this is transferred down the (internal) value chain. While profit centres can help to motivate local managers, they can also lead to the 'sale' of product as soon as possible within the company. This, of course, is unfortunate as it leads to pre-emptive production and the commitment of product before necessary. As we know, in V-configured organizations inventory should be stored at the point of the V until it is needed further down the production/distribution chain.

Theory of Constraints versus linear programming

An early reaction (including that of the author) was to regard TOC as directly equivalent to simple management accounting 'contribution per unit of limiting factor problems' and an inferior version of linear programming (LP); inferior because linear programming can handle multiple, interacting process constraints. However, Luebbe and Finch (1992) suggest that, while (in their simple examples) the same solution is derived by either method, TOC has advantages compared with LP. First, TOC's throughput per minute/hour focuses on the desirability of particular products, while LP's shadow prices focus on the impact of making extra resource available. The product orientation of TOC is more useful in directing sales efforts. Second, LP is an optimization *technique* whereas TOC provides a wider approach to *management*. While both LP and TOC identify constraints or bottlenecks, TOC provides detailed guidance on their exploitation. In particular, the drum-buffer-rope approach helps in the management of the bottleneck through the use of buffer inventory and ensures that non-bottleneck facilities do not over-produce through the use of the 'rope' that limits release of work. Third, the authors argue that TOC automatically seeks new bottlenecks when old ones are broken in a process of ongoing improvement.

This analysis draws attention to the strengths of TOC; Luebbe and Finch are probably correct in their assertion that the idea of $ return/constraint minute is more intuitively understandable than a linear programming solution and is therefore more likely to be widely accepted and implemented. However, Luebbe and Finch overstate the advantages of TOC – if circumstances are relatively complex, TOC can lead to sub-optimal solutions. Balakrishnan and Cheng (2000) modify the Luebbe and Finch examples so that the optimal solution arises when *two* production constraints are binding. The TOC approach – which depends on finding *the* production constraint – therefore fails while LP – which is able to cope with multiple constraints – can identify the optimal solution. They conclude that LP can be applied, to '... ensure that the principles of TOC are applied correctly', adding that this should be straightforward because most spreadsheets now incorporate LP solvers.

We can ask whether it is better to adopt 'simple' TOC – which produces optimal solutions only when there is a single production bottleneck but provides valuable product-related information – or whether LP should be incorporated into the TOC method in order to ensure that optimal product mix solutions are reached? Technically, one could check by using both methods and, if they are the same or similar, a TOC-style presentation for managers. However, this might not be easy in practice and Goldratt argues that systems should be *designed* with only one bottleneck. If a production process includes a major, expensive facility, it makes sense to ensure that it is the *only* production bottleneck by investing in other areas. Goldratt also has a more technical rationale, discussed in the next section.

TOC versus activity-based costing

Kee (1995) set out to integrate activity-based costing with TOC. ABC does not take constraints into account, whereas identifying constraint(s) is central to TOC. Kee's suggestion is that ABC can be combined with the identification of constraints so that it incorporates the key insight from TOC. He takes a product mix problem with four products and sets out assembly labour, finishing labour, material, set-ups, purchasing and engineering costs for each product. Assuming capacity restrictions for labour, set-ups, purchasing etc., he demonstrates that this can be formulated as a mixed-integer programming problem and solves for the optimum product mix. We do not need to review this in detail but Kee assumes that the objective function should be based on the price of each product less material, labour and other unit-based costs, batch-related costs (assuming constant batch sizes for set-ups and purchasing) and product-related engineering costs. He also sets capacity restraints for a range of unit, batch and product-related variables. Kee's major contribution is therefore to show that, given the usual ABC approach, it is possible to introduce capacity constraints and solve product mix problems taking these into account.

It is doubtful, for two reasons, that Goldratt would agree this has 'integrated' TOC and ABC. First, he would argue that the inclusion of a range of costs in the objective function is faulty because many of these are, for practical purposes, 'fixed' operating expenses. Second, he would argue that the identification of many constraints is unnecessary because, in order to fully exploit a single constraint, other facilities must have significant excess capacity. He argues that, in order to protect a bottleneck, inventory should be placed in front of it. However, failure in the preceding operations will lead to this inventory being run down from time to time, and 'the feeding machines have not only to supply the ongoing rate of X [the bottleneck], at the same time they also have to rebuild the stock. Quickly, before Murphy [an unanticipated disruption] strikes again . . . which means that each of them must have more capacity than X' (Goldratt, 1997, p. 140).

Kee and Schmidt (2000) provide another comparison of TOC and ABC when making product mix decisions. Their data for products A and B are summarized in Table 10.1, together with capacity constraints for labour and machine hours. (Engineering resource is also included, but is not important in the example.)

First scenario: machine hours are non-discretionary

Given 600,000 machine hours and plenty of demand for both products, labour is the only important constraint. In these circumstances TOC provides the best solution and product

Table 10.1 Product and process data

	Product A	*Product B*	*Capacity*
Throughput	\$20 per unit	\$36 per unit	
Unit level profit	\$8 per unit	\$18 per unit	
Expected demand	500,000 units	300,000 units	
Labour (\$16 per hour)	0.5 hours per unit	1.0 hours per unit	240,000 labour hours
Machine (\$4 per hour)	1.0 hours per unit	0.5 hours per unit	600,000 machine hours

Source: Kee and Schmidt (2000).

A is best with throughput of $40 per labour hour compared with $36 per labour hour for product B.

Second scenario: cost of machine hours is 'discretionary' (variable)

Under this scenario it is argued that ABC provides the best solution because product B, with 'unit level profit' of $18 – compared with $8 for product A – is selected as best: concentrating on product B produces higher profit than concentrating on product A. We should note, however, that this result is fortuitous because the ABC calculation has not taken the labour constraint into account. In fact, if labour- and machine-related costs really are variable then TOC would provide the 'correct' answer because profit-per-labour-hour would be $16 for product A and $18 for product B. Whether material costs should be the only variable cost is slightly contentious in the TOC literature and Noreen et al. (1995, p. 13) suggest that 'The official definition of throughput is revenue less "totally variable costs". However, in most of the TOC literature, throughput has been defined as revenue less direct materials.' If the broader definition of throughput is accepted then it is TOC – not ABC – that provides the best solution.

Third scenario: 300,000 machine hours are non-discretionary but they are discretionary above 300,000

Kee and Schmidt formulate a 'general model' where they show that, if both labour and machine hours are constraints, the best solution is not generated by either TOC or ABC. If the non-discretionary machine-hour capacity is set at 300,000 then the best solution is 240,000 units of A and 120,000 units of B. This is a linear programming solution and it is not worthwhile breaking the machine-hour constraint – its shadow price is $2.66 per hour compared with the variable cost of $4 per machine hour. As one would expect, if the optimal product mix leads to multiple binding constraints, a mathematical programming technique is needed to identify the best product mix.

Conclusion

This chapter has reviewed developments in the theory of constraints. The idea of TOC is deceptively simple: focus on bottlenecks, exploit them, subordinate everything else, break bottlenecks and start again. The simplicity of the approach can easily lead to its power being underestimated, and companies that have adopted TOC and the associated DBR method have often improved performance significantly. Initially, TOC was seen as a manufacturing technique and this may have delayed its application in other fields. However, Goldratt's work over three decades has shown how TOC can be applied to marketing, distribution, project management and retailing. If process constraints are broken then, sooner or later, the constraint will move to the market. In *It's not Luck* he showed how adopting the customer's perspective together with TOC's inventory management techniques could lead to new marketing propositions that may well develop new business and expand markets. In *Critical Chain* Goldratt showed that, by treating the critical path as the project bottleneck and managing the buffer time, both in the critical path and in subsidiary paths, project management could be improved. In *Necessary but not Sufficient* Goldratt returned to his roots, scheduling software, by linking technological advance (enterprise requirements planning systems), TOC and DBR with the need for a culture change that eliminates unfortunate measures and attitudes. Finally, in *Isn't it Obvious?* Goldratt once again demonstrated that inventory should be held as far back in the production/distribution chain as possible and released only when it is needed.

The theoretical framework for Goldratt's work is provided by the I, V, A analysis of process configurations; the statistical consequences of demand aggregation/disaggregation; the trade-off between safety stock/time and responsiveness; and the importance of bottleneck and non-bottleneck capacity. TOC originally concentrated on the bottleneck in a sequence of processes (an I configuration) and Goldratt was clear that the amount of buffer inventory should reflect the views of senior managers concerning the trade-off between investment in inventory and responsiveness of the system. In a V configuration inventory should be held at the split-off point: for example, at manufacture rather than at regional depots or retail outlets. Demand is thereby aggregated and shows less variability than when reported at the retail level. In an A process – such as a project that is not complete until all activities are completed – the buffer time needs to reflect the inherent variability of the activity durations.

The theory of constraints is deceptively simple and academics have debated its merits against both mathematical programming methods and sophisticated costing techniques. It is easy to show that the theory of constraints generates a sub-optimal product mix in problems where several constraints are binding. Balakrishnan and Cheng (2000) and Kee (1995) provide examples designed to show the superiority of linear and other forms of mathematical programming over TOC. However, Goldratt argues that, in order to protect the bottleneck, sufficient protective capacity must be invested in non-bottleneck facilities: the system should be *designed* to operate with a single bottleneck. TOC is then sufficient to identify the best product mix and, once the planned product mix is known, the drum-buffer-rope system can be used to schedule non-bottleneck facilities. Linear programming and other sophisticated techniques are better in particular circumstances, but perhaps they should not be needed.

The theory of constraints has implications not only for operational practice but also for information systems and performance measurement, with Goldratt arguing that cost accounting can have pernicious effects. Product costing can mislead when used for short-run decisions because of the inclusion of essentially 'fixed' costs in the product cost. ABC is the extreme example of this tendency but Goldratt argues that even some, so-called direct, costs are essentially fixed in practice. Cost accounting leads not only to possibly misleading product costs but also to an incentive to build inventory because of its impact on overhead absorption, and to local measures of efficiency and utilization that can lead to sub-optimal behaviour. Interestingly, Goldratt's ideas also have implications for revenue recognition: logically, it is better to hold back production and distribution until a product's best use/destination is known. Unfortunately, profit centre managers will be tempted to 'sell' product down the internal chain as early as possible so as to record higher (internal) profits. A related problem arises in project-oriented firms that try to claim as much work completed as possible so as to maximize progress payments from the customer. This can lead to unfocused project management that overlooks the importance of the critical path (chain) and its feeding activities.

Of course, the theory of constraints has limitations. It has a short-term focus on existing bottlenecks, the current product mix and, sometimes, marginal cost pricing, with little to say about long-term product innovation, strategy or the control of operating expense. Operating expense is significant in many companies and TOC, implicitly, accepts its current level as both acceptable and 'fixed'. Despite Goldratt's antipathy to activity-based costing, ABC can help in understanding why operating expense was incurred, what it should be and how it might be controlled.

To conclude, while the theory of constraints is not a panacea, it can deliver benefits in a range of organizations; accountants should take TOC and its spin-offs – such as throughput accounting statements – seriously. Goldratt's attacks on cost accounting are, perhaps, overly virulent, but some accounting-based measures, systems and practices do have unfortunate consequences. If TOC is to be introduced, management accountants need to be aware of the need for revised measures that work with the method, not against it.

Notes

1 MRP or materials requirements planning systems became common in the 1970s and 80s. They are computer systems that take orders or forecasts for finished products and, using product bills of materials, calculate what materials are needed. Demands for the same material from different products are aggregated and a schedule of material purchases derived that takes account of the due dates for finished product, and plant and material lead-times.

2 Goldratt and Fox note that the two major twentieth-century production management breakthroughs, Henry Ford's production line and Ohno's (Toyota) Kanban system, can be analysed in TOC terms. The production line ties all the facilities together so they all operate at the same speed while the Kanban system restricts production by the physical size of the Kanban (bin) so that facilities only produce when demand for finished product 'pulls' material down the production line. Goldratt would argue that TOC is a more complete theory that includes the other two advances as special cases.

3 Goldratt has maintained his attack on cost accounting over many years. The hero of *The Goal*, Alex Rogo, is accused in *It's Not Luck* (Goldratt, 1994) of filling his listeners' ears with '. . . fierce attacks on cost accounting. Some even say that you call cost accounting "enemy number one of productivity"' (p. 127).

4 Optimised Production Technology, OPT, was subsequently sold to the UK company Scheduling Technology (STG) and is a registered trademark of that company.

5 ERP or enterprise requirements planning systems were introduced in the 1990s. These systems superseded MRP systems by extending their function outside purely manufacturing to other areas of the business such as purchasing and sales order processing as well as providing improved information for management.

6 Not only does TOC identify where Lean techniques might lead to the greatest gains; it can also guide investment decisions. An investment that breaks a bottleneck could lead to a significant increase in contribution. On the other hand, discounted cash-flow calculations can mislead at non-bottleneck locations where product cost savings are relatively worthless, and may even encourage inventory proliferation.

7 The particular advantage of the TA ratio might be that a ratio greater than one indicates a profitable product, whereas a TA ratio of less than one indicates a loss-making product.

Bibliography

Balakrishnan J. and Cheng C. H. (2000) Theory of constraints and linear programming: a re-examination, *International Journal of Production Research,* 38(6), 1459–1463.

Corbett T. (1998) *Throughput Accounting*, North River Press, Great Barrington, MA.

Darlington J., Innes J., Mitchell F. and Woodward J. (1992) Throughput accounting: the Garrett Automotive experience, *Management Accounting (UK)*, 70(4), 32–38.

Dugdale D. and Jones T. C. (1996) *Accounting for Throughput,* CIMA Publishing, London.

Fox R. E. (accessed 18/07/2010) The theory of constraints: fad or future? www.scribd.com/doc/40172564/TOC-Fad-or-Future.

Galloway D. and Waldron D. (1988a) Throughput accounting – 1: The need for a new language for manufacturing, *Management Accounting,* Nov, pp. 34–35.

Galloway D. and Waldron D. (1988b) Throughput accounting – 2: Ranking products profitably, *Management Accounting,* Dec, pp. 34–35.

Galloway D. and Waldron D. (1988c) Throughput accounting – 3: A better way to control labor costs, *Management Accounting,* Nov, pp. 32–33.

Galloway D. and Waldron D. (1988d) Throughput accounting – 4: Moving on to complex products, *Management Accounting,* Nov, pp. 40–41.

Goldratt E. M. (1983) Cost accounting: The number one enemy of productivity, *IPICS Conference Proceedings, American Production and Inventory Control Society,* 433–435.

Goldratt E. M. (1987) Computerized shop-floor scheduling, *International Journal of Production Research,* 26 (3), 443–455.

Goldratt E. M. (1990a) *The Haystack Syndrome,* North River Press, Great Barrington, MA.

Goldratt E. M. (1990b) *What is this Thing called Theory of Constraints and how Should it be Implemented?,* North River Press, Great Barrington, MA.

Goldratt E. M. (1994) *It's Not Luck,* Gower Publishing, Aldershot, England.

Goldratt E. M. (1997) *Critical Chain,* North River Press, Great Barrington, MA.

Goldratt E. M. (2010) *Isn't it Obvious?,* North River Press, Great Barrington, MA.

Goldratt E. M. and Cox J. (1984) *The Goal: A Process of Ongoing Improvement,* North River Press, Great Barrington, MA.

Goldratt E. M. and Fox E. F. (1986) *The Race,* North River Press, Great Barrington, MA.

Goldratt E. M., Schragenheim E. and Ptak C. A. (2000) *Necessary But Not Sufficient,* North River Press, Great Barrington, MA.

Kee R. (1995) Integrating activity-based costing with the theory of constraints to enhance production-related decision-making, *Accounting Horizons* (December), 48–61.

Kee R. and Schmidt C. (2000) A comparative analysis of utilizing activity-based costing and the theory of constraints for making product-mix decisions, *International Journal of Production Economics,* 63, 1–17.

Luebbe R. and Finch B. (1992) Theory of constraints and linear programming: a comparison, *International Journal of Production Research,* 30(6), 1471–1478.

Narayanan V. G. and Donohue L.E. (1998) *Lehigh Steel,* Harvard Business School Case 9-198-085.

Noreen E., Smith D. and Mackey J. T. (1995) *The Theory of Constraints and Its Implications for Management Accounting,* North River Press, Great Barrington, MA.

Shams-ur Rahman (1998) Theory of constraints: A review of the philosophy and its applications, *International Journal of Operations & Production Management,* 18(4), 336–355.

11

The dynamics of management accounting and control systems

Trond Bjørnenak and Katarina Kaarbøe

Introduction

In the management accounting literature increased dynamics has been emphasized for a long time. The message is that the world is changing, so management control systems (which encompass cost management systems) also have to change. In 1987 the US professors Thomas Johnson and Robert Kaplan wrote the book *Relevance Lost – the Rise and Fall of Management Accounting*. The book was a critique of how management accounting was taught in business schools, researched in academia and used in practice. The main point made by the authors was that the world had changed, but not the management control systems.

> In this time of rapid technological change, vigorous global and domestic competition, and enormously expanding information processing capabilities, management accounting systems are not providing useful, timely information for the process control, product costing, and performance evaluation activities of managers.
>
> *(Johnson and Kaplan, 1987, Foreword)*

The solution to this problem was the introduction of a number of new and different management accounting tools, such as activity-based costing (ABC) and the Balanced Scorecard (BSc). These innovations engendered increased empirical research, especially case studies. Characteristics of successful and less successful companies were described and, additionally, statistics were gathered through surveys on how many companies had adopted the new tools. Moreover, textbooks and teaching material were changed. An example is found in the concepts listed in textbooks, e.g. in Horngren's best-selling textbook *Cost Accounting* (co-authored by different US academics), more than 50% of the concepts were introduced between 1985 and 2005 (Ax and Bjørnenak, 2007). The new concepts were to a large extent related to the new tools which had arisen from the 'Relevance Lost' debate (e.g. activities, cost drivers and unused capacity related to ABC).

Changes occurring after the debate were not enough to stop the criticism of established practices. During the last decade a new relevance lost debate, called Beyond Budgeting, has emerged. Once again, it is the change in the environment that is the driver underpinning the need for improved management accounting and control systems. In his book *Implementing Beyond Budgeting* Bjarte Bogsnes – senior adviser at the oil company Statoil, also President of the Beyond Budgeting Round Table – expresses the dynamics of the operational environment in this way.

> Across almost all business, the operating environment has become radically more dynamic, unpredictable, and turbulent.
>
> *(Bogsnes, 2009)*

The argument is that, when the environment is unstable, the best solution is to abandon budgets and substitute a set of more dynamic management control systems. Thus, the control system is made more flexible and responsive to changes in the environment. This is not a new idea. The relation between uncertainty in the environment and challenges in the management control system was discussed in the 1960s and 70s. Then the discussion was in relation to the use of budgets. However, the argumentation has been reversed. The uncertainty in the environment is, in this case, the driver for introducing more budgeting to organizations. The Danish professor Palle Hansen has expressed it as follows:

> However, if the markets are uncertain there is an increased need for coordination of work processes and budgets are the best tool management can use to adjust actions under unstable market conditions.
>
> *(Hansen, 1975, p. 16)*

As these quotes illustrate, arguments on how organizations have to adjust to an uncertain environment have been a recurring theme. We can find examples in every decade – from the 1960s until the present time. Dynamic management control, understood as 'adjustments following changes', is not anything new. However, this does not mean that it is not important. In fact, repeating this message every decade clearly indicates the importance of a dynamic relationship between the need for information and the design of management accounting and control systems so that organizations can cope with environmental change.

Dynamic management accounting

The concept 'dynamic' comes from the Greek word *dynamikos*, which means 'power' (Oxford Dictionary of English, 2010). One definition is that it is a continuous and productive activity or change. The concept is also closely related to physics, where it characterizes energy in movement. The contrast is to be static. In physics, to understand dynamics is to understand why elements are moving and how change happens in these moving elements.

In a management accounting and control context the physical elements are sets of data about costs and performance that are provided to the organization for decision-making and control purposes. This is the focus of this chapter, and it is mainly two areas we want to discuss: first, dynamics in relation to *design*; and second, dynamics in relation to the *use* of management accounting and control systems. There should be a strong link between the two, i.e. how the system is designed and how it is used. The controller function in an organization is often responsible for ensuring this link exists.

Following the relevance lost debate, the demand for improved management accounting information has increased. Management accounting reports and analyses should be more informed by the manager's needs, and not mainly driven by the requirements of external reporting as has been claimed (Kaplan, 2011). The focus has moved from the reporting cycles of financial statements to the information needs of strategic decision-makers within the organization. This change has had a large influence on the role of controllers. They were supposed to change from producing standard reports and acting in a reactive manner, based on budget variances and financial performance, to a more proactive controller role focusing on organizational change and improvements. The concept *hybrid accounting* was introduced, indicating a more consultancy role for the controller (Burns and Baldvinsdottir, 2007). Hybrid accountants were expected to be an integral part of the team responsible for managing the information stream. They had to have both analytical skills and extensive knowledge about the business and strategic issues, along with the ability to communicate the results. The hybrid accountant operates out in the field – not only in finance departments. Another topical characterization of the extension of the management accountant's role is that of business partner: the management accountant places far more emphasis on the communication and use of information as opposed simply to its production.

Thus, dynamic management accounting and control systems are about the dynamics of what tools to use and how these tools and combination of tools are used in the organization. Dynamics therefore provides a focus that is insightful for activities such as cost management. The relationship between design and the use of tools is important in the rest of the chapter. In the following we present different perspectives on dynamics in management control systems. Based on conventional wisdom and the current academic debate, we have identified the following five forms of dynamics:

1. different cost for different purposes;
2. different scope and different tools for different purposes;
3. different periods of time;
4. different systems in scope and time;
5. different combinations of elements in a control package.

The first two forms of dynamics are commonly used in textbooks of management control and management accounting. The latter three are mainly discussed in academic journals and have therefore not yet become a part of the conventional wisdom expounded in textbooks. A focus is placed on costing examples to illustrate the different forms of dynamics.

Dynamics in cost information: different costs for different purposes

The change from 'cost accounting' to 'management accounting' in the 1960s was one of the first forms of dynamics seen in the literature. The difference between the two concepts is identified in at least two dimensions. First, cost accounting is mainly about collecting and organizing data for general purposes. It may be used for all financial accounting, controlling and decision-making purposes. By contrast, management accounting specifically emphasizes the use of accounting data. Focus is moved from recording, book-keeping and measurement to decisions and management issues. The second dimension is a consequence of the focus on decision-making. In cost accounting efforts centre on determining total costs and how they can be allocated to cost objects (typically, full costing methods), while in management accounting the focus is on understanding different costs for different purposes, i.e. a dynamic perspective on costs.

The dynamic element is closely related to management's decision situation. Arbitrary cost allocations are avoided and replaced with an understanding of the dynamics of costs in different situations and specific contexts. For example, in some cases costs can be avoided, in others this is not possible. Whether a cost is relevant is therefore dependent on what decision you are investigating.

The concepts of incremental cost and opportunity cost are, by definition, dynamic concepts. Incremental costs change according to a specific action, while opportunity costs are the contribution which is lost by not using limited resources in their next-best alternative use – thus the alternatives are dynamic. The opportunity cost concept is an extremely important driver for business dynamics, because this concept constantly reminds decision-makers that there are alternatives that have to be considered. Note that, for a given cost object, direct or indirect costs are normally described as static in relation to decisions; incremental costs and opportunity costs are not. In cost accounting, cost calculation and the related cost allocations are made independently of the use of the information.

One important observation is that more advanced cost calculation systems can be less dynamic. The reason for this is that advanced (complex) allocation methods may make it difficult to get a good overview of the total cost picture and therefore more complicated to adjust to a specific decision situation. For example, introducing activity-based costing (ABC) may lead to less dynamics when it comes to adjusting cost information to a specific decision. This was also an intended feature of the ABC model:

> Activity-based systems do not make decisions. Our ABC cases are not decision-focused. They illustrate the principle for designing general-purpose systems.
>
> *(Kaplan, 1990, p. 13)*

Thus, the ABC model can be seen as a return towards the general-purpose models of cost accounting. Making cost concepts dynamic in decision-making was too ambiguous according to Kaplan. It is difficult to systematize or routinize information that has to be tailored to the decision-maker's situation on an ad hoc basis. However, the adoption rates of ABC systems seem to have been rather low (Gosslin, 2007). Explanations for this may be that the systems became too comprehensive and focused too much on the technical issues related to cost allocation, definition of practical capacity, etc. and too little on how the information should be used to improve the performance of the company. The decision relevance of ABC information outputs has been downplayed among the complexities of design issues.

Dynamics in tools: different scope and tools for different purposes

As mentioned in the introduction, the result of the 'relevance lost' debate was a number of new tools within management accounting, and particularly the cost management areas of the discipline. *Activity-based costing* and the *Balanced Scorecard* are the most common examples, but other tools like *Target Costing*, *Performance Pyramid* and *Backflush Costing* were also introduced post relevance lost. The dynamics during the post-relevance lost period can be expressed in three ways: different tools for different purposes, different scope for a specific tool, and finally a debate on the fit between organizational characteristics and the benefits of different tools.

Costing systems can exemplify the first form of dynamics. During the 1990s a number of new costing techniques or methods were introduced to fit different purposes. To increase focus on bottlenecks and increased production flow 'Throughput Accounting' was introduced (see Chapter 10). The method highlights direct material costs as the main cost element that can be actively managed in the short term in pursuit of the goal of 'making money'. It can therefore be understood as an (extreme) form of the contribution margin model. For companies introducing *Just In Time*, the *Backflush Costing* method was suggested as a costing method for stock valuation, a very simple standard cost method which also only includes direct costs. For more advanced profitability analysis, activity-based costing was introduced, and for companies with a high degree of locked-in costs *Target Costing* was the new tool. In other words new costing tools for different purposes have been created as a means of improving cost management.

In addition to the extensive number of tools, the *scope* of the different tools has also increased. Scope may be related to the following dimensions: descriptive objects, i.e. the objects for which we are accounting; and causal variability factors, i.e. the causes of variation between the descriptive objects.

Again costing systems can serve as an example. It is possible to develop ABC systems to calculate profitability for customers, products, distribution channels etc. We call them descriptive objectives because one wants to describe characteristics (for example revenue and costs) for these objectives. For descriptive objectives, it is possible to use a number of different measures, including costs, profitability and other performance measures. These can also have various characteristics. For example, it is possible to use both financial and non-financial measures to describe the performance of a department. In addition, the focus on causality between the objects and different variables has also increased. This is another form of dynamics. A cost driver is a factor that describes variations in costs for an objective. Understanding cost drivers implies understanding the dynamics of costs. In the same way, there has been an increased focus on variations in performance measures related to a descriptive object. For example, for the object customer, some may claim that there is a causal link between increased customer satisfaction (measure A) and increased customer loyalty (measure B). Causal variability factors are used as a general concept to describe variables explaining variations in costs (cost drivers) and performance.

Finally, there is also an increased focus on the types of tool that fit the different characteristics of companies. Based on contingency theory the relation between variables – size, organization, technology, uncertainty, strategy and the effect of different tools – is emphasized. Nevertheless, there are no clear results from these studies (Chenhall, 2007). With size as an exception, it is difficult to find any clear relations between the characteristics of companies which adopt different tools and the performance effects of using them. The literature suggests three reasons for the difficulty in finding connections between accounting tool use, characteristics and benefits. First, it is difficult to identify what kinds of tool organizations use since the tools are continuously changing and may be designed and used differently in different organizations. Second, it is difficult to isolate the effect of the tools from other conditions that also influence performance. Third, it is difficult to say anything about causality. More profitable companies, for example, might adopt the Balanced Scorecard but it may not be the Balanced Scorecard that made them more profitable (see Nørreklit, 2002 for a critique of the logic behind the Balanced Scorecard). The use of such innovations might simply be symptomatic of a successful, progressive management style.

An interesting observation in the literature is that researchers have started to include the characteristics of adopters. For example Naranjo-Gil, Maas and Hartmann (2009) found that the age and tenure of CFOs affects the adoption rates of management accounting innovations. Younger and recently recruited CFOs tend to be more dynamic: in other words, they innovate more and change the control system. Less is known about the effect of this dynamic behaviour.

Dynamics in time: changing and loosening the link to the calendar's rhythm

We have so far discussed the dynamics of cost information, tools and the scope of tools as if they were dynamic elements in a management control system. These elements also have a time dimension – traditionally a year. A typical example is the budget year, where annual costs – or a part of them – are allocated to different objects. There are, however, many alternatives for modelling the time dimension: for example, historical or future periods (ex ante vs. ex post), calendar years or rolling years, and time rhythm de-coupled from calendar rhythm, shorter or longer than a year. One example of this is found in project management, where the project and the progression of the project is what the cost management is linked to.

Informed by contingency theory (Otley, 1980), it is possible to expect a relationship between the time period used and flexibility and uncertainty. Flexibility has to do with how easy it is to change the use of resources in an organizational unit. One example is the degree of locked-in costs, i.e. the ability to change resource usage if the company needs/wants to change their activities. In some cases – such as for the permanent staff at a business school – it is difficult to change the way personnel resources are used. If the demand for accounting courses is reduced and the demand for strategy courses increases, it can be difficult to change the knowledge and competences among the staff in order to give more strategy courses, at least in the short term. In an executive programme with a high proportion of temporary staff, the possibility of changing resources may be much higher. Hence, it is natural to have different management control systems for different programmes. In this case a longer cost management and planning horizon may be needed for permanent staff in the master programme than for the more flexible resource base in the executive programme.

The second concern is uncertainty in the market, regulations and other external conditions. If there is a low degree of uncertainty, organizations may have a longer planning horizon compared to those with higher levels of uncertainty, and vice versa. One example with a low degree of uncertainty may be public hospitals – though this may not be the picture we get from descriptions in the media. However, the type of treatments offered, costs and revenues are often relatively stable. This means that both demand and supply are relatively reliable in the short run (up to a year). Within any organization there can also be different degrees of uncertainty in its parts. Some departments may be almost protected from changes, while others do not know what and how much they will sell six months later. The difference can once again be illustrated with students in a business school and with the executive programme operating in the high-end market. The uncertainty in these two markets may be significantly different. A possible model to describe the adjustments to these two factors, or drivers of dynamics, is described below.

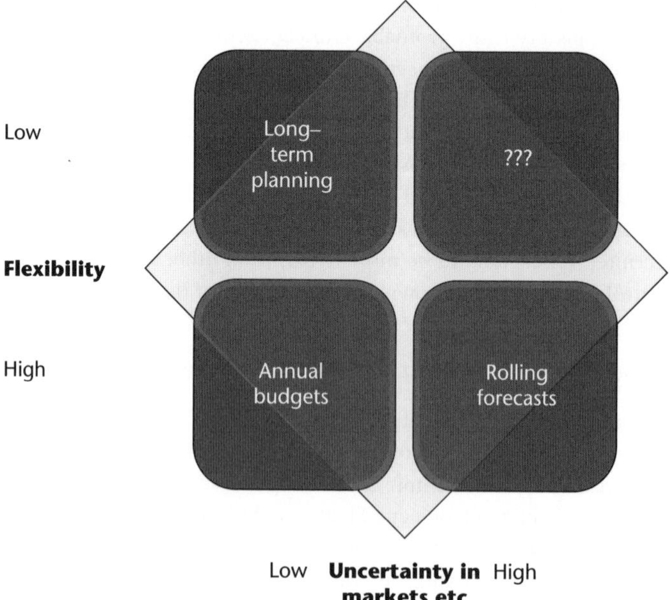

Figure 11.1 Time horizon and uncertainty/flexibility

Figure 11.1 shows different types of planning and control system, depending on different degrees of uncertainty and ability to influence or control the resource base. If the uncertainty is high but the organization is able to adapt, the planning horizon may be shorter and rolling forecasts can be used to give updated information on the effects of changing market conditions. This could, for example, be a marketing department in a cruise line company, where they have flexibility to change their marketing efforts depending on the demand from the customers. For a university hospital – where the uncertainty in the market may be rather low – the situation is different. On the other hand university hospitals may typically have a high degree of locked-in costs, resulting in a need for a management control system with a long planning horizon. Thus, the focus should perhaps be on structural costs and long-term planning. This indicates, according to Figure 11.1, that long-term budgets are suitable for university hospitals while the marketing department in a cruise line company may do better to use rolling forecasts in combination with a strong focus on accountability.

However, if the uncertainty is high and the ability to change is low, it does not help much to have dynamic management control systems. In this case, the solution may be to alter the organization so that it becomes more dynamic. This could mean a business school experiencing low enrolment to a specific program at the same time as they have a large permanent teaching staff. This is a difficult situation to resolve because it involves the need for large structural changes, e.g. layoffs of permanent teaching staff.

This discussion also relates to costing problems. If there is a high level of uncertainty in the markets then large and complex costing systems may easily become outdated. A simpler, more dynamic system might be better. Thus, a simplified time-driven ABC system (Kaplan and Anderson, 2004) may be better than a fully implemented traditional ABC system. A time-driven ABC system (see Chapter 9) may also be used for forecasting. If one is in the upper-left-hand corner of Figure 11.1 – with a high proportion of committed costs – target costing may be a good costing solution. A long-term view of cost variability is also consistent with this perspective.

Dynamics in systems: focus and time

The time dimension in the management control system is more than just the time horizon in a model or the time interval for the reports prepared. Time can also be used dynamically to focus on different areas at different points in time. This is not given much attention in the management accounting, control and cost management literature. One exception is Pike et al (2011) who show that activity-based costing – implemented as stand-alone or ad hoc systems – are seen as more useful than embedded ABC systems that are frequently updated and integrated with the financial reporting system. The reason for this is that the temporary system is understood as more target-oriented: trying to solve a specific problem. Still, organizations cannot only have temporary systems: some systems have to operate continuously. For all organizations it is important to find the right balance between temporary and continuous systems.

Another important dimension is whether the systems should be global or local. A global system is used by the whole organization – annual budgets or product costing systems – while local systems are developed and used only in a business unit or a smaller part of the organization. For large organizations, it is possible to have both global and local systems. In Figure 11.2 we illustrate different combinations of the two dimensions. The set core of the management accounting and control system is the fixed global set of cost and performance measures used throughout the whole organization. This can, for example, be a number of global and continuously measured financial (e.g., ROI) and non-financial (e.g., customer satisfaction) measures applicable to all business units. In addition, some business units or even smaller

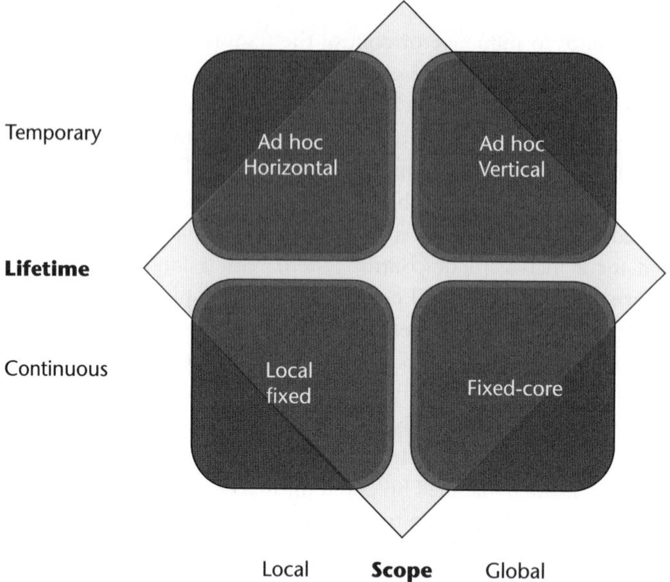

Figure 11.2 System dimensions

entities in the organization may have their local problems, e.g. there may be specific interest in a particular customer group which requires the profitability of that group to be identified, explained and understood. This may be done once in order to understand the cost development in that area. Therefore, a local and temporary system may be developed. An example of a mixed local and continuous system may be the benchmarking of particular activities continuously at a local level.

The main point is that systems can be differentiated and adjusted, i.e. they are dynamic and this dynamism is demonstrated in the way they can change to meet the needs of different users, their problems and their social systems. This also means that they typically become more focused on the decision-maker's dilemma. In many ways this is a return to management accounting and the dynamics of different costs for different purposes.

The essential point is to focus on the problem (decision) to be solved and to come up with a solution to that problem. This way of thinking is similar to the ideas found in the programming of IT systems. Agile programming, SCRUM and Dynamic System Development Method (DSDM) are examples of alternative approaches to problem-solving. To find new solutions to problems, the problem-solver is in close dialogue with the owner of the problem. The aim of this dialogue is to improve the understanding of the problem and to find a quick solution, rather than create a fully integrated system. One example of this is when the company tries to figure out which customers are the most profitable. This can be achieved by creating a fully integrated ABC model in an ERP system. Advanced resource allocation is not necessarily what creates the best understanding of variations in customer profitability. A more agile approach can therefore be to develop a simple alternative that gives you a 'good enough' picture of the situation. In addition, this can foster better communication between the developer of the system (the controller) and the user (the manager) of the system. The literature in management accounting/control has not emphasized these ideas. In many cases conventional wisdom in the discipline suggests the solution is in favour of the opposite type of solution, i.e. comprehensive global and continuous systems.

A more dynamic approach would be to make the development of the management control system more driven by the following two conditions:

1. Event-driven. When something changes in the environment, for example a large customer leaves the company or the market declines, this should lead to a change in what items are reported in the control system and the timing of their reporting.
2. Knowledge- and problem-driven. That implies that the content of the systems should be informed by the hypotheses of the controllers or managers. In most cases there are ideas about what should be analysed, e.g. 'we think prices are not optimal' or 'we have too many different products'. Such hypotheses should drive the development of new systems. This can be considered a user-sovereignty approach.

A dynamic way of thinking will incorporate both drivers of these dynamics. The control system should adapt to changes in the environment and acknowledge internal capacity and experience. This will put new demands on the controller's role, while at the same time all resources cannot be linked up to continuous local and global systems.

Dynamic control packages: from tool to management control package

So far we have only focused on the management control system as something de-coupled from other control systems in the organization. The financial part of the control system is often called the formal management control system. However, this formal part is dependent on the organization's other control systems – more informal systems (cultural values etc.), and the structure of the organization. How the organization develops performance measures has to be understood in relation to the degree of decentralization, culture etc. This is not a new idea. However, it has intensified with the new concept of the control package (Malmi and Brown, 2008).

The idea is that it is too simplistic to see the management control system as only dependent on the way characteristics fit with the environment – as was the case with traditional contingency studies. Instead, it is important to understand that challenges can be handled in different ways. If one goal is to underpin a performance culture in an organization it does not mean that there have to be more measures. This may also be approached with personnel controls (e.g. who they recruit), the way the business is organized, or the design of reward systems. The effects of the performance measures will be dependent on all these dimensions and possibly many others.

In this chapter we are concerned about the level of dynamics. We argue that increased dynamics is important when management control systems are designed. This way of thinking is not in contrast to the other types of dynamics mentioned earlier. Management control packages can pinpoint that when a management control system is designed it has to take into consideration all the parts of the control system, not just the formal parts. It has to consider both local and global systems. For example, it is difficult to have both annual budgets and the Balance Scorecard at the same time, since the two systems have different characteristics. The budget focuses on financial measures and short periods, aimed at making the decentralized manager accountable. The Balance Scorecard, on the other hand, focuses on additional, non-financial measures, and has a more long-term focus. Bourmistorov and Kaarbøe (2011) have shown that using both can create dilemmas from a management control perspective, leading to a confused picture when it comes to the outcome the company is aiming to achieve. By focusing on the whole control package top managers become more aware of which parts of the control package should be emphasized and how the different parts fit together. In the case described by

Bourmistrov and Kaarbøe (2011), different actors used different parts of the control package, which resulted in confusion and paradoxes.

Ax and Bjørnenak (2005) use the concept of bundling to discuss the mix of control elements, and combine this with the use of Balance Scorecards. In the Scandinavia Balanced Scorecard package, modifications to the original design emphasize the learning and growth perspective and employees' rights, in line with Scandinavian society's model. A control package perspective will help us to increase our understanding of the design and use of management control systems.

A control package, or a more holistic perspective, is also important for the design of costing systems. If you design an ad hoc ABC system in order to change your product portfolio, but have a sales budget and culture focusing on sales volume, the signals for the different systems may be in conflict. This conflict should be addressed before the design of the system. In both the costing and scorecard cases, a dynamic control package perspective would acknowledge that no perfect system exists, but highlight the importance of fitting the system to the social system and other practices over time.

Conclusion

In this chapter it has been shown that dynamic elements have received increasing attention in the current management accounting and control debates. Table 11.1 gives an overview of the different forms of dynamics and the corresponding dynamic elements in accounting systems. It is important to notice that there are two different forms of dynamics. The first one concerns the design of a control system and the other concerns the use of the control system.

The design dynamics focus has been, for example, on different costs for different purposes and the use of non-financial performance measures to give visibility to aspects of intangible assets. The dynamics are related to or driven by the manager's need for alternative information. This form of dynamics also includes the choice of descriptive objects and tools that can be used for different purposes. For the other type of dynamics the starting point is the problems, hypotheses and capacity of the users. The focus is on the need for new systems and the problems they try to solve. This need may or may not be driven by a change in the environment. The important driver is the manager's decision of what they want to emphasize at a certain point in time. The problem is emphasized: the solution may be both temporary and local.

Table 11.1 Different perspectives on dynamic management accounting and control systems

Type of dynamic	*Focus of dynamic*	*Dynamic elements*
Different cost for different purposes	Design of costing data	Incremental cost Opportunity cost
Different scope and tools	Choice of tools, objects and variability factors	Different tools Descriptive objectives Variability factors Different performance measures
Dynamics in time	Time horizon	Reporting period Forecasts Long-term budgets
Dynamics in systems	Different focus in time and scope	Local and global systems Temporary and continuous system
Dynamics in the design of control packages	Coupling between tools	Different solutions through different systems Interaction between systems

We believe that there is great potential for introducing more dynamic management accounting and control systems – especially when it comes to using the knowledge and competences in the controller function. Dynamics allows the controller to be more proactive by using a knowledge-driven search for solutions. The arguments about the increased intensity of change in the environment and the rapidity of changes in the market have existed for the last 50 years. In some cases this is true, in others it is not. Still, this is not an argument for not introducing more dynamics in the management control systems and the cost management systems they encompass. Maybe the largest challenge to increasing the dynamics of management control systems is the dominance of global, static and continuous control systems that hinder the more knowledge- (learning-)based dynamics. However, an awareness and understanding of the nature of dynamics in relation to management accounting is, in many ways, an important requirement in designing new accounting systems, and improving existing ones to provide better support for organizational management.

Bibliography

Ax, C., and Bjørnenak, T. (2005). Bundling and diffusion of management accounting innovations – the case of the balanced scorecard in Sweden. *Management Accounting Research*, 16, 1–20.

Ax, C., and Bjørnenak, T. (2007). Management Accounting Innovations: Origins and Diffusion. In T. Hopper, R.W. Scapens and D. Nortcott, *Issues in management accounting* (357–376). Essex: Pearson Education.

Bogsnes, B. (2009). *Implementing Beyond Budgeting: Unlocking the Performance Potential.* Hoboken, NJ: John Wiley & Sons. Inc.

Bourmistrov, A., and Østergren Kaarbøe, K. (2011). Tensions in Using Information from Budgets and Balance Scorecard: A Case Study of a Telecom Company in Distress. Working paper, Department of Accounting, Auditing and Law, Norwegian School of Economics.

Burns, J., and Baldvinsdottir, G. (2007). The Changing Role of Management Accountants. In C. S. Chapman, A.G. Hopwood and M.D. Shields, *Handbook of Management Accounting Research* (163–205). Elsevier Ltd, Amsterdam.

Chenhall, R.H. (2007). Theorizing Contingencies in Managmant Control Systems Research. In C.S. Chapman, A.G. Hopwood, and M.D. Shields, *Handbook of Management Accounting Research* (163–205). Elsevier Ltd, Amsterdam.

Gosselin, M. (2007). A review of activity-based costing: technique, implementation, and consequences. In C.S. Chapman, A.G. Hopwood and M.D. Shields, *Handbook of Management Accounting Research* (641–671). Elsevier Ltd, Amsterdam.

Hansen, P. (1975) (red). *Håndbog I Budgetering.* (*Handbook of Budgeting*) Valby: Institut for lederskab og og Lønsomhed.

Johnsen, T.H., and Kaplan, R.S. (1987). *Relevance Lost: The Rise and Fall of Management Accounting.* Boston, Massachusetts: Harward Business School Press.

Kaplan, R.S. (1990). Contribution margin analysis: no longer relevant/strategic cost management: the new paradigm. *Journal of Management Accounting Research*, 2, 2–15.

Kaplan, R.S. (2011). Accounting scholarship that advances professional knowledge and practice. *The Accounting Review*, 86(2), 367–383.

Kaplan, R.S., and Andersen, S.R. (2004). time-driven activity-based costing. *Harvard Business Review*, 82(11),131–138.

Malmi, T., and Brown, D. A. (2008). Management control systems as a package – opportunities, challenges and research directions. *Managment Accounting Research*, 287–300.

Naranjo-Gil, D., Maas, V.S. and Hartmann, F.G. (2009). How CFOs determine management accounting innovations: an examination of direct and indirect effects. *European Accounting Review*, 18 (4), 667–695.

Nørreklit H (2002) The balance on the balanced scorecard: a critical analysis of some of its assumptions. *Management Accounting Research*, 11 (1), 65–88.

Otley, D.T. (1980). The contingency theory of management accounting: achievement and prognosis. *Accounting, Organizations and Society*, 4, 413–428.

Pike, R.H, Tayles, M.E. and Mansor, N.N.A. (2011). Activity-based costing user satisfaction and type of system: a research note, *British Accounting Review*, 43 (1), 65–72.

12
Capacity usage

Lino Cinquini and Andrea Tenucci

Why capacity matters

When a company acquires a production factor, it becomes the owner of a resource capable of producing a specific output, whether tangible or intangible. More generally, the company can be considered a system of resources that exists for the production of goods or services. If we are talking of a resource of a company, the maximum amount of output that can be obtained from it is its maximum capacity. The level of resources needed is related to the 'potential income' that a company can obtain and therefore is a measure of its ability to create value (McNair, 1994).

The available capacity has an influence on several competitive dimensions, namely *quality*, *cost* and *time* (Ansari et al., 1997): product/service quality required by customers can be affected by the capacity available to fulfil demands for product/service features; investments in capacity create a cost structure that determines production efficiency; and capacity and output rates (production speed) contribute by achieving short time to market and adequate flexibility of production systems.

The root of the capacity issue lies in the fact that most of the resources in a business are *committed resources*. Organizations incur an actual cash outlay to acquire such resources needed for current or future activities. For example, the acquisition of buildings and equipment supplies a capacity for work in future years. The committed resources generate costs that represent long-term activity capacity. We can refer to this potential provision in term of the 'activities' these resources make it possible to perform in each of the periods considered, according to the following equation (Cooper and Kaplan, 1992):

Available Activities = Used Capacity + Unused Capacity

From an economic standpoint, the value of acquired resources is a *committed* cost that is independent from its level of use. The latter influences the level of profitability and of course will be the maximum (i.e. converging with the potential) when full capacity is used effectively. A level of less than optimum use gives rise to costs of unused capacity – missed opportunities, wasted resources. Capacity utilization, on the other hand, is not good per se: output produced has to be sold and revenues converted to cash in order to gain benefit and effective performance.[1]

The opposite of committed resource is *flexible resource*: material, energy, telecommunications services and employment, if used 'on demand' and not hired permanently. For these resources the organization may acquire the amount needed to meet short-term demand and the cost of acquiring them equals their cost of use (Kaplan and Cooper, 1998: p. 120ff.) – the issue of unused capacity does not apply.

However, capacity-related resource costs do become variable costs over long periods of time through a two-step procedure. First, the demands for the resources supplied can be changed because of the shifts in activity levels. For resources related to batch- and product-sustaining activities, the activity levels change because of increasing variety and complexity. Second, the organization changes the supply of committed resources, up or down, to meet the new level in demand for the activities performed by those resources. If the capacity-related resource costs fall, the organization must then manage the unused capacity of these resources out of the system.

In this respect, two main issues arise in dealing with capacity:

1. A managerial issue, related to the ways in which capacity can be understood and represented, and how resources can be exploited best.
2. A measurement issue, regarding the effects on costing of considering different capacity measures to allocate the costs of committed resources to objects.

These issues are certainly not new. However, they have assumed new significance in recent years with the development of new cost management proposals. In particular, the latest developments in Activity-Based Costing (ABC) and Time-driven ABC (TDABC) (Kaplan and Anderson, 2007) have shown the possibility of highlighting the cost of resources committed (or available) as the sum of the costs of resources used – and unused – according to the above equation.

A starting point is tackling the multifaceted concept of capacity. The following section introduces the multiple concepts of capacity and the different measures that can be used. Section three explains some costing issues related to capacity definitions, while the fourth presents the managerial implications from a cost management perspective. Section five develops implications in economic information for decision-making – such as pricing decisions and control – while section six closes the paper with some considerations of possible further research on the topic.

The multiple concepts of capacity and related measures

In general, capacity represents the maximum level of production obtainable from a resource or from a system. This concept can take many different forms. In the case of assets with a definite capacity (Dhavale, 1998) and in relation to the denominator (capacity base-line) we can speak of:

- theoretical capacity;
- practical capacity;
- normal capacity;
- expected (budgeted) capacity;
- current (actual) capacity.

The *theoretical capacity* can be defined as the maximum amount that a resource (or a system of resources) can achieve if used fully within a given period, i.e. with no waste and disruption due to maintenance, retooling, or lack of production orders from the market. In other words, we consider the maximum production capacity assuming that the system works 24 hours a day, 365 days a year.

There is a maximum of 8,760 available hours in a year: if a machine can produce, at best, one unit every ten minutes, its theoretical capacity would be 52,560 units of output. Precisely because it is theoretical, this figure is often criticized as unattainable and therefore de-motivating.

The *practical capacity* is at a lower level than the theoretical because it takes account of downtime due to maintenance, physiological declines in productivity, non-productive time due to non-working days, holidays, and so on. It is, essentially, the theoretical capacity reduced by 'unavoidable' downtime. In practice, engineering estimates normally reduce the theoretical figure by 30% as a first pass at establishing practical capacity limits. This limit therefore reflects both constraints from the market, from technical capabilities and, as in the case of regulated labour markets, from union rules. The practical measure is usually recommended to define the standards of production of a plant. Although this measure is preferred to the theoretical, it is often difficult to quantify and, above all, it leaves plenty of room for management discretion in its definition. In some cases it is possible to consider the interruption as scheduled and physiological. At other times, it is fixed arbitrarily as a percentage (70–80%) of theoretical capacity (Kaplan and Cooper, 1998). Anyway, there is not a common standard of reference.

To continue the above example, there are still 8,760 hours in a year, but now it is expected that a unit will be made every 14.3 (10/0.7) minutes (given the practical capacity as 70% of the theoretical). Practical capacity would, in fact, be set at around 36,755 units of output (8,760 times 60/14.3).

The *normal capacity* is based on the volume of output that reflects the average demand of the market over a long time period (say two or three years). This longer perspective is taken to exclude measurement fluctuations caused by market factors such as those related to the life-cycle of the product, seasonal factors, technical progress or learning improvements. Achieving the normal level could implicitly mean the creation of waste due to the purchase of capacity in excess of that absorbed by the market. Focus is moved from the capability of the machine or process to the way that asset is utilized. Let's now assume our machine is only run one shift per day: its normal capacity would be around 8,727 units (2,080 hrs times 60/14.3), or only 16.7% of the original capability.

The *expected or planned capacity* (budgeted capacity) results in the volume of expected output in the budgeted period. It is estimated taking into account the sales budget, the level of inventories held, and scheduled and other policies. Since it meets different requirements (for reporting purposes and practicality, all costs are allocated), this is the figure most frequently used (between 40% and 60% of cases[2]) and is especially suitable for the allocation of indirect costs.

Finally, the *actual capacity* refers to that currently in use. It represents therefore the production achieved with the asset for a given period.

The choice of a figure of capacity may lead to significant differences in the unit cost of a given cost object (a stage of processing, product, customer, etc.). It should be emphasized that these concepts are applicable not only to the capacity of production, but in all circumstances in which there are identifiable outputs connected to the activation of a resource or resource system, and also to processes and administrative tasks and support services for which this analysis can be useful. While the first two capacity figures express what a business or resource *can* do when exploiting its full potential, the latter three (normal, expected and actual) are concerned with what these resources have been planned to provide, or actually provide.

Managers tend to make decisions based not on the theoretical capacity of their assets, but on the relationship between normal and future expected demand (Watts et al., 2008). For example (Table 12.1), a manager who believes that future demand is going to require 111.1% utilization of assets behaves differently from one who perceives their utilization level to be 27.2%. In the former situation he/she may consider purchasing new assets to increase capacity. The way in

Table 12.1 Definitions of capacity

Capacity baseline	*Actual utilization*	*Utilization % (actual over baseline)*
Budgeted capacity (9,000 units)	10,000	111.1
Normal capacity (8,736 units)	10,000	114.5
Practical capacity (36,792 units)	10,000	27.2
Theoretical capacity (56,250 units)	10,000	17.8

which capacity is defined and presented within the firm's reporting system, therefore, influences management's decision-making.

The choice of the baseline capacity measure has an impact on the calculation of the cost of capacity and on overall capacity management policies.

Costing implication

From a theoretical point of view the definition of the level of capacity is crucial in the process of (fixed) overhead allocation and for the definition of the consequent level of unused capacity.

The study of capacity and costs is connected to the problems of variability in the unit cost of production and the allocation of indirect costs. Many authors claim that it is misleading to think that you can obtain the 'true' cost of a product, given the uncertainty in its determination particularly due to the variable impact of fixed production costs which depend on the volume of output (Drury, 2004). This causes a potential distortion of decisions (especially pricing) based on product costs when the allocation of fixed indirect costs occurs using allocation bases which are proportional to final volumes of output. In this sense, the issue of overhead allocation was widely addressed in the early 20th century in the American management literature. For example, Gantt (1915) observed the distortion resulting from the allocation of all indirect costs to products on the basis of variable levels of actual capacity. According to the author, the allocation to outputs should be based on maximum production levels, which he called the 'normal level' (referring to the average output level expected over the next several years). The error in calculating the cost of production occurs when the production drops below this level. Traditional theories on cost allocation continue to allocate all of the production overhead costs to the output regardless of volume, but Gantt (1915) asserted that this method inflates costs, provides managers with wrong information and consequently leads them to incorrect decisions.

Management accounting literature suggests four methods to calculate the denominator capacity level of overhead rates. As reported in the example of Table 12.2, the use of the configuration of Budgeted, Practical, Normal or Theoretical capacity creates four different potential overhead rates because of the different denominators of the ratio. The overhead rate is the ratio between the overhead costs and the chosen allocation base (capacity measure in this case as machine hours). Capacity measures therefore directly influence the determination of the overhead rate. Assuming the same amount of overhead costs (numerator), the overhead rate decreases when going from the theoretical capacity to the lower budgeted capacity. The variation of the overhead rate is caused by the fact that the overhead costs, which are fixed, are spread over a greater or lower amount of allocation base (machine hours in the example of the table).

We now consider the advantages and criticisms of the use of each capacity measure in the cost allocation process.

With the use of the (annual) *budgeted capacity*, each year's overheads are charged to the products realized in that year. This method is well known to companies as it is relatively easy

Table 12.2 Capacity configurations and overhead rates

Type of capacity	*Capacity measures (machine hours) (a)*	*Overhead costs (£) (b)*	*Overhead rate (£ per machine hour) (b/a)*
Theoretical	1,000	1,000	1
Normal	800	1,000	1.25
Practical	600	1,000	1.67
Budgeted	500	1,000	2

to estimate the annual level of activity (Drury, 2004). The use of this denominator is rejected by Cooper and Kaplan (1991) because they believe it can distort product costs and may lead to incorrect product decisions, since it is related to the short term. In this sense, there will be a fluctuation of the overhead rate when the budgeted capacity varies in a non-proportional relation to the overhead costs. As Cooper and Kaplan (1991) suggest, in periods of declining capacity the use of budgeted capacity in the denominator, complemented by a *cost-plus*-based approach in pricing, may lead to an unwanted event – the *death spiral*. Increases in overhead rates caused by the reduction of budgeted capacity, given the fixity of many overhead costs, lead to increases in product costs – which in turn cause increases in the selling price. This will be followed by a reduction in demand and consequently in budgeted capacity, followed by a further increase in the overhead rates and again in product costs and the selling price.

Using the *practical capacity* figure it is possible to distinguish between the cost of resources *available* for manufacturing, the cost of resources *used* in manufacturing and the cost of *unused* resources (Cooper and Kaplan, 1992). The cost of unused capacity is charged as a period cost to the income statement and is not allocated to the product. For such a reason, even if the budgeted capacity changes from period to period, there is no fluctuation of the level of product cost as in the former case when annual budgeted capacity is used. Similarly, Sopariwala recommends that

> . . . predetermined fixed overhead rates be computed using the maximum capacity that can be activated thereby producing fixed capacity rates that are not dependent on expected production. In addition, this method also provides an appropriate fixed overhead cost to assign to production, irrespective of whether the production was planned or resulted from new sales opportunities accepted during the year.
>
> *(Sopariwala, 1998)*

Two issues have been raised in relation to the use of practical capacity (Maguire and Heath, 1997). The first is that managers, within certain circumstances, can underestimate practical capacity, consequently overestimating the overhead rate and the product's cost. Second, there is the risk that managers do not adequately consider the flexibility requirements needed when deciding the capacity level to provide a quality service.

The use of *normal capacity* can be particularly useful as it provides an estimate of the long-run average capacity and consequently the effect of seasonal fluctuations is eliminated (Drury et al., 1993). The difficulty of estimating normal capacity is well recognized. This difficulty is also faced when valuing inventory, as required by IAS 2.[3]

The use of *theoretical capacity* is considered appropriate by McNair (1994), who suggests that capacity should be regarded as the ability of a company to create value for its customers.

Resources that do not add value are waste. Company improvement should be attained by minimizing waste and maximizing capacity and its use. There are at least two criticisms of this conception. The first is that such a capacity is unlikely to be achieved (Drury, 2004); secondly, the achievement of theoretical capacity may not be sustainable over the long run and may lead to a decline in customer service.

As demonstrated, a number of authors have advocated using full or practical capacity as the denominator for overhead rates to provide more accurate product costs and to avoid the 'death spiral' effect that can occur when planned or budgeted capacity is used. However, in the 'real' world many companies are still linked to such a capacity concept. A survey of Fortune 500 firms in Chiu and Lee (1980) revealed that approximately 57% of the 247 respondents used planned (or budgeted) production as the basis for calculating overhead rates, while 21.1% used practical capacity, 18.2% used normal capacity and only 1.6% used maximum (theoretical) capacity. In a similar trend a more recent survey by Brierley et al. (2006) revealed that 53.9% of the 219 respondents of 854 UK CIMA members currently use budgeted capacity as the denominator for calculating overhead rates, while 16.9% used practical capacity, 16% normal capacity and 1.8% theoretical capacity.

Managerial implication from a cost management perspective

Key concepts

The development of effective capacity management as a component of cost management requires the clarification of concepts in order to plan, assess and manage the deployment of a firm's value-creating potential to meet customer needs. Among these concepts, focus is now placed on the following crucial aspects in constructing a capacity management framework (CMA-IMA, 1996):

- capacity deployment;
- capacity utilization measures;
- time-frame;
- organizational level.

Capacity deployment

Effective capacity deployment requires an understanding of the following:

- *Productive capacity* - the capacity that provides value to the customer. Productive capacity is used to produce a product or provide a service. It must be based on the theoretical, or maximum, value-creating ability of the company's resources.
- *Non-productive capacity* - capacity neither in a productive state nor in one of the defined idle states. Non-productive capacity includes set-ups, maintenance and scrap; it may also be a *planned non-productive capacity* if we have capacity planned for use that is temporarily out of use due to process variability, such as the lack of materials, machine or process breakdown, or delays.
- *Idle capacity* - capacity not currently scheduled for use; *planned idle capacity* that might be planning for preventive maintenance; and *excess capacity*, which is permanently idle capacity that is not marketable or usable under existing operating or market or policy conditions.

Through effective deployment and design of work and daily management processes, organizations can productively use much of the capacity reserved for contingencies. This opportunity to adjust capacity is very attractive from a cost management viewpoint because it represents an exploitation of the inherent flexibility in existing capacity. For example, by reducing process flow time an organization effectively increases its available capacity with no investment in fixed assets. When making capacity decisions, organizations must balance the impact of the decision on customer value measurements – such as defect escapes, product delivery performance and product prices. Decisions to alter capacity utilization should be performed according to current and future market demands.

Capacity utilization measures

Once a process or system has been deployed, or placed into one of the key productive states, capacity cost management focuses on tracking and reporting current capacity utilization and its profit and cost implications.

The key factors in assessing capacity utilization include:

- *Throughput* – the total value obtained from a process during a specified time period; the rate at which a system generates revenues through sales.[4]
- *Activation* – the amount of time that a process is used or active during a period, whether or not the resulting output is required to meet customer needs (e.g., rework represents activation, not utilization).
- *Waste* – non-productive use of a company resource.
- *Efficiency* – total utilization as a percentage of baseline capacity.
- *Standby capacity* – excess capacity used as a buffer to absorb unplanned shifts in total activity and the impact of other variations of a process.
- *Actionable capacity* – capacity utilization that can be affected by a specific manager or management group, resulting in higher or lower total resource requirements.
- *Cost of capacity* – the total economic value of all resources needed to keep a process at a specific stage of deployment.

Capacity utilization costs are not limited to machine or asset depreciation charges. They include all of the indirect resources, or overhead, that are consumed in order to keep a process in a state of preparedness. The separation of *committed capacity costs* (unavoidable costs in the short to medium term) and *managed capacity costs* (avoidable in the short to medium term) is important in developing an effective capacity cost management system. When matched with the appropriate cost of capacity estimate, utilization measures provide management with detailed information on the efficiency and effectiveness of current operations as well as the potential for short-term, intermediate and long-term profit improvements.

Time-frame of analysis

Decisions on capacity have both short- and long-term implications. The time-frame of decision analysis has a major impact on a company's ability to change the cost of its capacity. As the time-frame extends, a company can act to change how a process operates. These changes can impact the theoretical capacity of the process, but only in the long run can the entire process be restructured. Eventually, it is possible to employ a wide range of techniques and costing approaches to support management's efforts to adjust capacity and its utilization.

Furthermore, in the long term a *strategic capacity management* approach in decision-making becomes appropriate. The choice of expanding capacity can employ investment cost analysis techniques such as Discounted Cash Flow and Net Present Value. However, acquiring new capacity is not the only eligible decision in this respect. Experience shows that sometimes such choices are the most expensive: '*A new plant means new constraints, not new opportunities*' (McNair and Vangermeersh, 1998: p.104). Different decisions may be considered: outsource to relieve current capacity constraints; lease plant and personnel; redesign existing products and processes to reduce the demand on the plant; pursue strategic alliances to increase the scope and availability of capacity – also, expand into new markets; and integrate forward or backwards in the value chain. These are some of the alternative options for managing capacity in the long term. Value creation, more than resource employment, should be the focus in decisions affecting long-term capacity.[5]

By contrast, in the short run theoretical capacity is constant; very little can be done to change the theoretical capacity of a process. Capacity cost management may substantially focus on improving the utilization of existing resources and processes (e.g., elimination of waste) but not on changing the overall level of capacity.

Organizational level

The issues impacting capacity cost management may also vary depending on the organizational level. The following specific levels may be considered:

- process;
- plant or sub-unit;
- company;
- value chain.

The first three levels are defined by an organization and its existing structure and capabilities. The *process level*, which can range from one task to an assembly line, focuses on individual units of output. The *plant or sub-unit level* suggests several processes and several unique types of outputs (e.g., different product lines). At the *company level* or strategic unit level, many different plants or sub-units (e.g. strategic business units) combine to create a complex organization that serves many markets with many different types of products and services. Finally, the *value chain level* returns to a product or product line focus, but shifts its attention to all of the activities and resources of all the organizations involved in delivering a good or a service to the consumer.

Cost management tools. The CAM-I capacity model

Several frameworks have been developed, and models and techniques proposed, to assist managerial decision-making with regard to capacity. These models and their adoption may allow firms to make the best use of their resources, to outperform their competitors and enable specific investigations which make capacity a *visible*, and hence an *actionable*, construct (Watts et al., 2008). Table 12.3 summarizes the main features of 12 frameworks according to a comprehensive inventory of capacity models provided by a CMA-IMA report (1996).

Among them, a brief description will now be provided of the CAM-I (Consortium for Advanced Manufacturing, International) capacity model, one of the most popular and most discussed in the last decade (Klammer, 1996; Ansari et al., 1997; Muras and Rodriguez, 2003; Sopariwala, 2006). In the 1990s CAM-I developed a robust and informative capacity

Table 12.3 A synthesis of capacity models (based on CMA-IMA, 1996)

Model	*Features*			
	Key points	*Capacity baseline emphasized*	*Primary time-frame of analysis*	*Organizational focus*
Resource Effectiveness Model	• Analyses economic impact of capacity management decisions; • Supports decisions across all time frames; • Assumes that zero waste is the goal; • Provides an integrated financial and operational analysis or resource decisions;	Theoretical capacity	Short- to long-term	Process/Plant/ Company levels
Capacity Utilization Model	• Focuses on waste as key capacity measure; • Separates causes of capacity waste by time frames and actionability; • Supports analysis and prioritization of key capacity issues; • Consists of systemic capacity measures;	Theoretical capacity	Short- to intermediate-term	Process/Plant/ Company levels
Capacity Variance Model	• Details actual performance against theoretical capacity; • Identifies causes of capacity losses; • Supports opportunity cost analysis; • Can be tracked against improvement goals;	Theoretical capacity	Short- to intermediate-term	Process/Plant levels
CAM-I Capacity Model	• Integrates capacity data among many dimensions; • Ties to the financial reporting system; • Details responsibility for capacity losses; • Uses time as a unifying measure;	Theoretical capacity	Short- to long-term	All levels (potential)
CUBES Model	• Integrates financial and nonfinancial data; • Builds from activity-based costs; • Uses Theory of Constraints, or constraints, logic; • Provides a dynamic analysis and least-cost solution;	Theoretical capacity	Short- to intermediate-term	Process/Plant/ Company levels
Cost Containment Model	• Focuses on support/service costs; • Supports/integrates with activity-based costing; • Builds on value added, market based models; • Supports analysis and cost containment across many settings;	Implicit theoretical capacity	Intermediate-term	All levels (potential)
Gontt Idleness Charts	• Efficiently highlights key capacity issues; • Summarizes performance in operational and financial terms; • Details costs and causes of idleness; • Is easy to implement and use;	Practical capacity	Short-term	Process level

Supplemental Rate Method	• Supports internal and external reporting; • Is easy to implement in existing systems; • Focuses on profit impact of idleness; • Provides summary statement of the total cost of idleness in a period;	Practical capacity	Short-term	Process/Plant levels
Theory of Constraints Capacity Model	• Emphasizes company profitability over keeping people/machines busy; • Highlights key constraints inhibiting process performance; • Is useful in plants or process using TOC in their management processes; • Provides solid baseline for action; • Has strong track record of effectiveness;	Practical capacity (marketable)	Short- to intermediate-term	Process/Plant/ Company levels
Normalized Costing Approach	• Asset depreciation is calculated on hours of machine use; • Abnormal expenses are eliminated from operational cost pools (e.g., plant modernization costs); • The behaviour of costs within a process is determined and defined within a formula that recognizes key elements affecting the cost of capacity within a process; • The capacity of the process is then determined, using practical capacity baselines set over a three- to five-year period; • Normalized cost is then determined by combining cost and capacity information to create a cost estimate under a given set of operating conditions;	Normal capacity	Intermediate-term	Process/Plant levels
ABC and Capacity Cost Measurement	• Fits into activity-based cost model; • Reports both the quantity and cost of idle capacity; • Supports analysis of alternative solutions to capacity issues; • Has strong emphasis on resources;	Normal capacity	Short- to intermediate-term	Process/Plant/ Company levels
Integrated TOC-ABC Model	• Uses mathematical modelling to solve for optimal capacity utilization; • Effectively combines both operational and financial views of the capacity problem; • Can be easily added to existing ABC applications; • When at least one bottleneck operation exists, provides a superior solution to a pure TOC or pure ABC methodology; • Uses marginal revenue as its decision basis.	Various	Short- to intermediate-term	Process/Plant/ Value-chain levels

reporting model which was able to utilize the more sophisticated data collection capabilities of modern manufacturing information systems. As Klammer states when introducing the CAM-I capacity model: '*Communicating idle capacity information is one priority of the capacity model*' (Klammer, 1996: 28).

In line with the concepts provided in paragraph 3.1.1, the model classifies available capacity into four major classes:

- *Rated capacity*, which is the same as theoretical capacity in the traditional model.
- *Productive capacity*, which is the time-available capacity used to produce products or services for customers. It may also include the time capacity used for essential production-related activities, such as product testing.
- *Non-productive capacity*, which is capacity that does not result in goods that can be sold. It occurs because of the nature of the production process.
- *Idle capacity*, which represents the time-available capacity not used because of policy decisions or market reasons.

Figure 12.1 shows the relationship of these four capacity categories. Note that productive, non-productive and idle capacity are measures of rated capacity. As shown in the figure, the basic CAM-I model is captured in a simple formula:

Rated capacity = idle capacity + non-productive capacity + productive capacity

In an expanded version, the model presents a more detailed analysis of the possible reasons behind the capacity categories addressed, providing a breakdown by the underlying causes (Figure 12.2).

There are four primary causes for non-productive capacity: set-ups, maintenance, standby, and waste. *Set-ups and maintenance* refer to time lost in setting up machines for new production batches or for routine maintenance; *standby* is a capacity buffer that helps the firm deal with variability caused by suppliers, customers or internal operations; *waste* may be scrap, rework, or other losses.

Unlike non-productive causes, the causes for idle capacity are rooted in policy decisions or market-related constraints. There are three major types of idle capacity: idle off-limits, idle marketable and idle non-marketable. *Idle off-limits* represents capacity not used because of holidays,

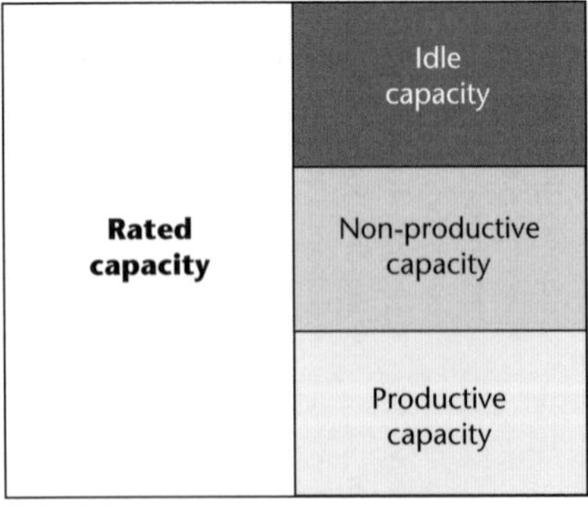

Figure 12.1 CAM-I capacity model

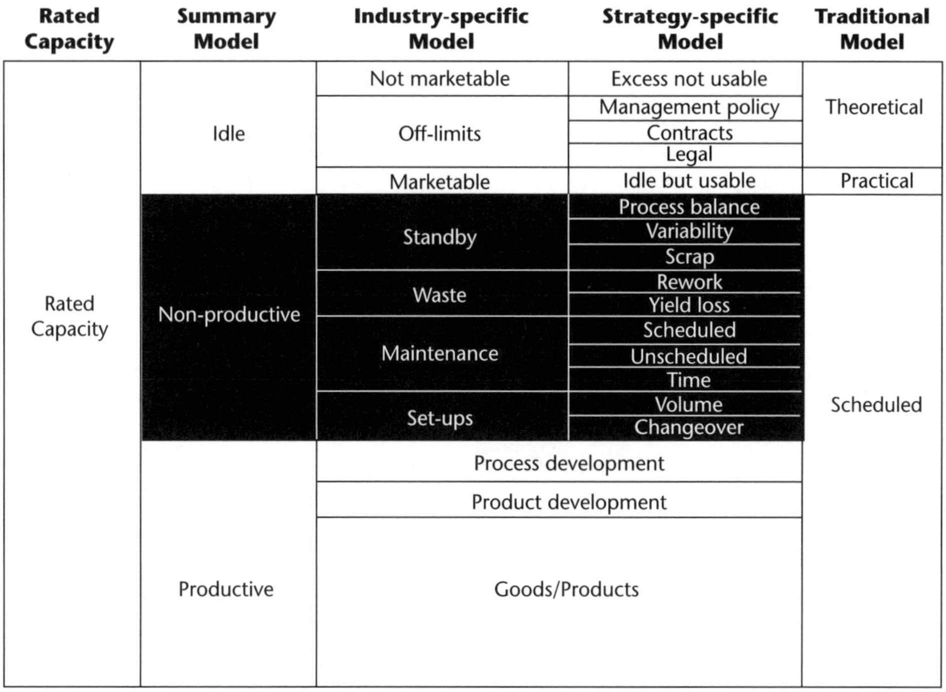

Rated Capacity	Summary Model	Industry-specific Model	Strategy-specific Model	Traditional Model
Rated Capacity	Idle	Not marketable	Excess not usable	Theoretical
		Off-limits	Management policy	
			Contracts	
			Legal	
		Marketable	Idle but usable	Practical
	Non-productive	Standby	Process balance	Scheduled
			Variability	
		Waste	Scrap	
			Rework	
			Yield loss	
		Maintenance	Scheduled	
			Unscheduled	
		Set-ups	Time	
			Volume	
			Changeover	
	Productive	Process development		
		Product development		
		Goods/Products		

Figure 12.2 The CAM-I expanded-capacity model

Source: Klammer, 1996.

contractual agreements or management policies, and remains off-limits until management changes policies or modifies contract terms. *Idle marketable* results from the inability of the firm to exploit the existing market for a product and represents measure of lost market share; *idle non-marketable* is physical capacity that cannot be used because there is no market for the product or because management chooses not to enter a market.

CAM-I model in action: a case study

Company SK is a paper producer.[6] It provides processed paper to other companies that refine it and then use it for several outputs (mainly packages). There are five lines of production (A, B, C, D, E) with different levels of automation and productivity – the latter measured in square metre of output (paper)/hour. Table 12.4 shows, for each product line on an annual

Table 12.4 Hourly productivity and cost of resources in Company SK

	Productivity (sq.m./h)	*Equipment (£)*	*People (£)*	*Power (£)*	*Total cost*
Line A	1,920	30,079	617,785	22,726	**670,590**
Line B	3,137	99,286	616,983	37,508	**753,777**
Line C	3,467	76,318	629,400	41,186	**746,904**
Line D	3,541	43,445	579,615	41,030	**664,090**
Line E	1,905	173,864	500,211	52,547	**726,622**
		422,992	**2,943,994**	**194,997**	**3,561,983**

Table 12.5 Capacity figures for each line (hours) (Company SK)

	Rated capacity	*Productive capacity*	*NP set-up*	*NP standby*	*NP waste*	*Idle OL*	*Idle NM*
Line A	8,760	1,585	1,108	1,040	46	960	4,020
Line B	8,760	2,617	1,214	520	115	960	3,333
Line C	8,760	2,873	942	532	153	960	3,300
Line D	8,760	2,862	634	654	66	960	3,583
Line E	8,760	3,666	608	508	36	960	2,981
		13,603	**4,507**	**3,254**	**417**	**4,800**	**17,219**

basis, the data related to the hourly productivity and costs for each line. Each resource (Equipment, People, Power) includes both direct and indirect cost elements allocated to a proper allocation driver.

In addition, the information system of operation provides time data (hours) of usage in each line. *Productive capacity* is the operating time of transformation of raw material into final output. *Non-productive set-up time* (NP set-up) is related to the need for change in production runs. *Non-productive standby time* (NP standby) is derived from the sum of waiting times, e.g. due to delays in receiving raw materials and due to events such as energy blackouts or bottlenecks. *Non-productive waste time* (NP waste) is due to unexpected machine breakdown. Other information provided is *Rated capacity time* related to full employment (24h × 365 days), *Idle off-limits* (Idle OL) time allowing 40 days of holidays and *Idle non-marketable* (Idle NM) as the difference between the rated capacity and productive, non-productive and idle off-limits capacities. Table 12.5 shows all this information.

According to the productivity in each line, the amount of capacity measured in square metres (sq.m.) of paper produced can be calculated. Table 12.6 shows the results in absolute and relative terms (%).

At this stage, it is possible to compare the capacity class rates of the different lines expressed in relative terms as represented in Figure 12.3. The introduction of cost information in this capacity analysis starts from the consideration of the amount of resources consumed by the figures taken from Table 12.4. To estimate the cost of capacity the following drivers are considered in Company SK:

- The cost of power is 100% allocated to the productive capacity.
- The cost in equipment is allocated among the different classes of capacity according to the percentages in Table 12.6.
- The cost of personnell is allocated using as a driver the estimate of the time of work effort shared among the activities based on a direct survey. The results are reported in Table 12.7.

As a result of the calculation based on the cost of resources and drivers, a specific capacity cost sheet can be produced for each line, and a graph report of results is shown in Figure 12.4.

The analysis shows the differences among the lines in terms of capacity cost according to the classification provided by the CAM-I model. Line A is clearly the bottleneck, with the highest NP set-up and NP standby, according to Figures 12.3 and 12.4. Such information may support both operational and investment decisions by (a) addressing the higher capacity cost categories to focus on running the plant more efficiently and (b) signalling a relevant economic issue in Line A to be considered in prioritizing plant investments by the company.

Table 12.6 Absolute and relative values of capacity (Company SK)

	Productivity (sq.m./h)	*Rated capacity*	*Productive capacity*	*NP set-up*	*NP standby*	*NP waste*	*Idle OL*	*Idle NM*
Line A	1,920	**16,819,200**	3,044,026	2,128,032	1,995,936	89,184	1,843,200	7,718,822
Line B	3,137	**27,480,120**	8,208,274	3,809,730	1,632,181	362,167	3,011,520	10,456,248
Line C	3,467	**30,370,920**	9,961,696	3,264,354	1,845,831	528,718	3,328,320	11,442,001
Line D	3,541	**31,019,160**	10,135,652	2,245,879	2,314,575	234,945	3,399,360	12,688,749
Line E	1,905	**16,687,800**	6,983,006	1,158,431	968,407	69,437	1,828,800	5,679,719

	Rated capacity	*Productive capacity*	*NP set-up*	*NP standby*	*NP waste*	*Idle OL*	*Idle NM*
Line A	**100.00%**	18.10%	12.65%	11.87%	0.53%	10.96%	45.89%
Line B	**100.00%**	29.87%	13.68%	5.94%	1.32%	10.96%	38.05%
Line C	**100.00%**	32.80%	10.75%	6.08%	1.74%	10.96%	37.67%
Line D	**100.00%**	32.68%	7.24%	7.46%	0.76%	10.96%	40.91%
Line E	**100.00%**	41.84%	6.94%	5.80%	0.42%	10.96%	34.04%

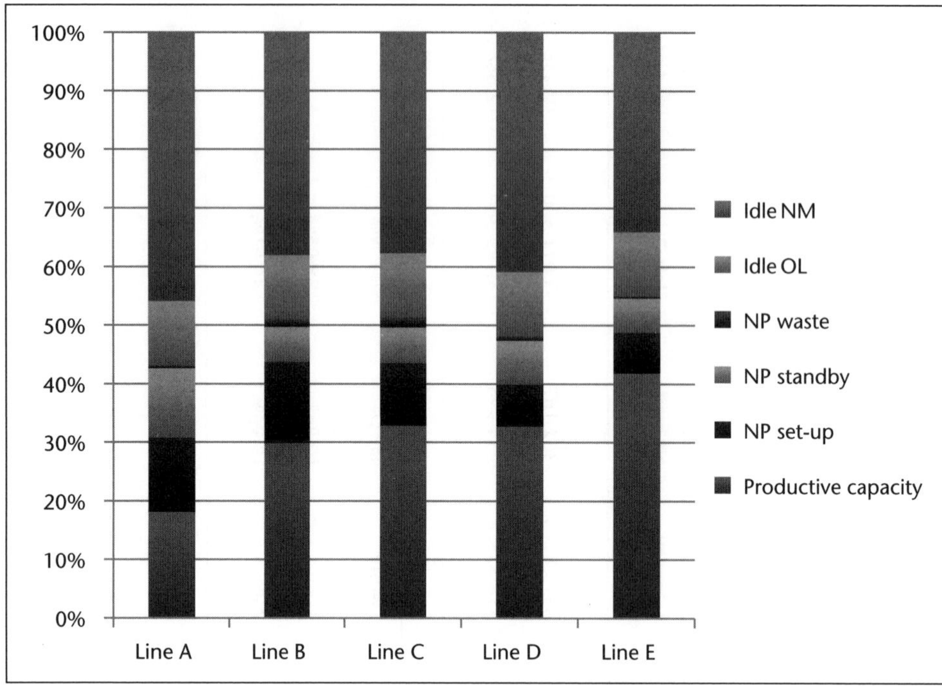

Figure 12.3 Capacity class rates of different lines (Company SK)

The measurement of capacity in terms of cost, though, may change the picture by addressing situations in which – given the same or a similar rate of unused capacity – capacity costs are different due to a different mix of resources employed and the amount of their cost. In our case, lines D and E show the same rate of NP set-up capacity (Figure 12.3) but a different cost and resource mix (Figure 12.4). This additional information on capacity cost segments per line may provide insights for managers for internal benchmarking initiatives, a prioritization in actions aimed at cost reduction, and an informative support for resource allocation in the budgeting process.

Implications in economic information for decision-making and control

There is sufficient reason to think that the issue of capacity is frequently not adequately considered in decisions made on the basis of product cost information. From the perspective of management control, the 'uncritical' use of standard cost information based on the budget could lead to sub-optimal behaviour. The literature on Japanese management practices shows clearly the opportunity to make systems-oriented improvement (Yoshikawa, Innes and Mitchell, 2002).

Table 12.7 Capacity as time-of-work effort (Company SK)

People capacity	*Productive capacity*	*NP set-up*	*NP standby*	*NP waste*
Line A	41.95%	29.32%	27.50%	1.23%
Line B	58.58%	27.19%	11.65%	2.58%
Line C	63.85%	20.92%	11.83%	3.39%
Line D	67.88%	15.04%	15.50%	1.57%
Line E	76.07%	12.62%	10.55%	0.76%

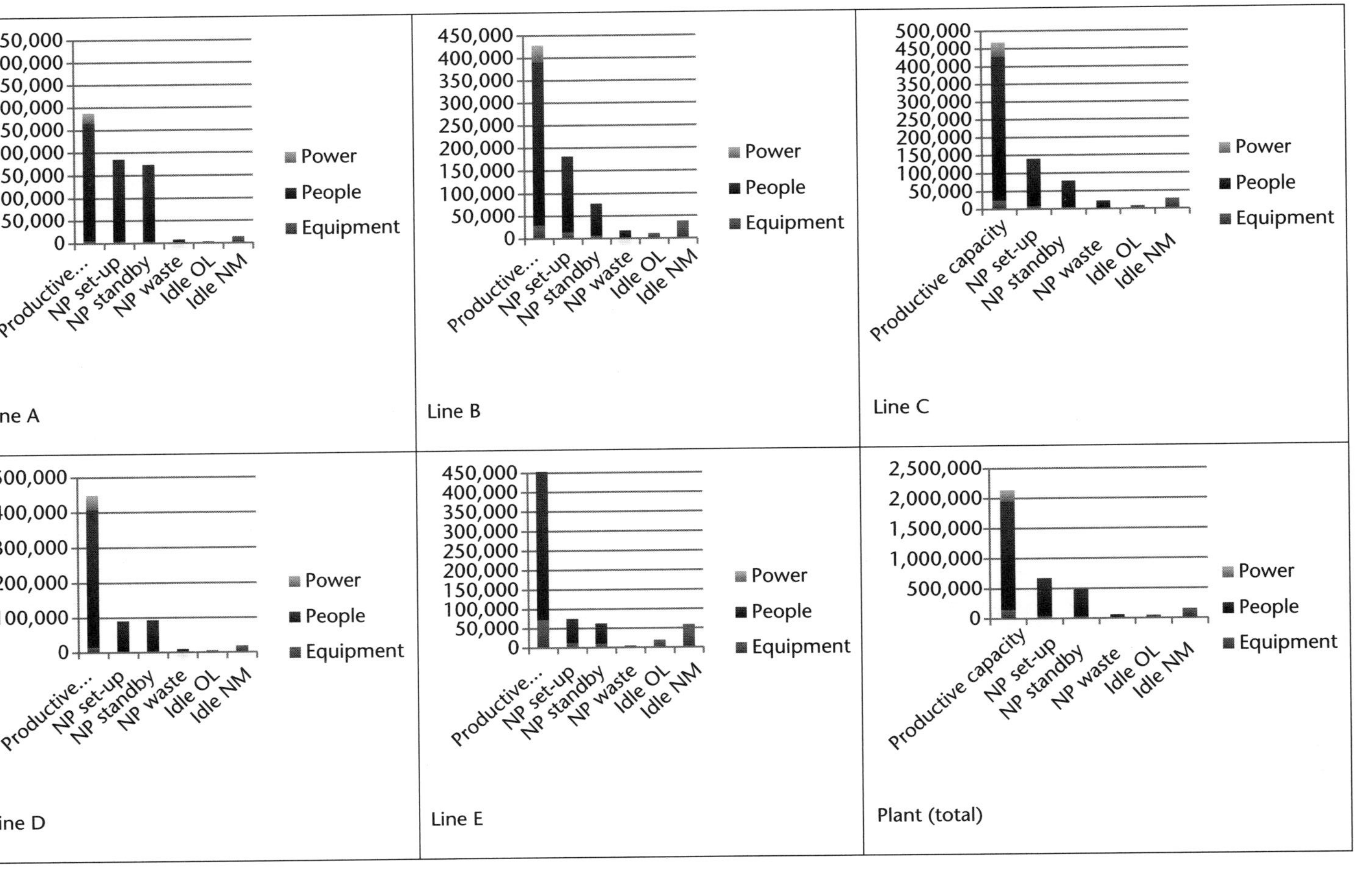

Figure 12.4 Capacity cost sheet per line (Company SK)

The conventional cost standard – which implicitly incorporates waste (McNair, 1993) – defines a limit to efficiency and even effectiveness. The application of benchmarking or best practice sometimes inhibits the search for innovative solutions.

What do these cases have in common? It is apparent that the results vary significantly according to the notion of capacity considered. The discussion here focuses on the reasons for these different assumptions. The concept of capacity to be used must take account of the strategic context in which the company operates (i.e. where this context is characterized by high competitive intensity, information is not cost-neutral or irrelevant to decision-making) and the specific goals and behaviours it expects from its members. This problem has been consigned to the margins in terms of importance and priority, and sometimes superficially dismissed with uncritical and mechanical considerations. This reflects the belief that the customer must still pay for the errors and inefficiencies of the company (this is particularly found in situations of growth, little competition and information asymmetry) and the influence of financial accounting regulations that govern costing practice and favour an allocation of costs based on what the company 'expects to do' and not on what it 'can do'.

The definition of the capacity volume of a resource (or system of resources, such as an activity, a department, a company) adopted in practice determines information outputs and inevitably affects decision-making. For example, what output volume is used in cost allocation? Is it based on existing or expected technological capabilities? Is it based on the sales budget? Or on the quantities produced? Is it a measure of the maximum that can be generated regardless of the volumes absorbed by the market? Each of these alternatives could lead to very different results in terms of unit cost, potentially affecting the effectiveness and impact of the decisions on pricing, production scheduling and product portfolio based on it. Ignoring the theoretical issues relating to capacity, the consequent adoption of a mechanical or uncritical approach risks alienating a company from the market. An awareness of economic significance of the capacity choice in information generation can be a powerful aid in supporting decision-making in the search for more competitiveness. Some of the relevant decisions and control issues in which capacity matters are considered below.

Pricing

Where cost information influences or even determines price, the capacity level, as a choice made before demand becomes known, is determined by the fixed cost of committed resources to be recovered by future revenues. This link of capacity with pricing has been widely dealt with in theoretical accounting (Banker and Hughes, 1994; Banker et al., 2002).

As seen in *product costing* the possible choice of the capacity level of overhead allocation base is essentially among practical, normal or budget output levels. In setting price on a cost-based approach, *practical capacity* is suitable for companies competing in highly competitive markets on the basis of the logic of price competition (Lawson, 2002). This is to avoid the 'death spiral' phenomenon and not to charge prices (and hence customers) that incorporate the costs of inefficiencies that could set the price higher than those of competitors.[7] However, the choice of the level of capacity should also be linked with the policy of the company, the customer service expected and competitors' pricing approaches (Cinquini and Silvi, 2003). Often, for example, service companies are equipped with extra capacity to promptly deal with requests from customers, and can obtain a premium price for the service provided (e.g. delivery within 24-36 hours). In these cases, the cost of excess capacity has a value (not only a cost) for the enterprise. In some cases, the application of the theoretical capacity might also be considered. For example, if competitors operate at or close to the total capacity absorption[8]

Table 12.8 Practical capacity in budgetary control

	Overhead cost (£)	*Amount of allocation base*
Practical capacity	280,000	5,000
Budgeted	280,000	4,000
Actual	273,600	3,800

the calculation of cost for pricing based on theoretical capacity may be needed to safeguard product competitiveness. The same considerations can be extended to the acceptance of orders or contracts. The consideration of the regime of price competition that confronts a company may therefore have an influence in the choice of the most appropriated figures of capacity to determine the allocation of costs.

Control

In budgetary control, the use of practical capacity to calculate allocation rates provides additional information about the 'budgeted cost of unused capacity' and hence more insightful variances can be reported. A simplified example in Table 12.8 makes the point.

If a company presents the above information on cost and capacity, then the cost allocation rate based on practical capacity will be £56.00 per base unit. Budgeted capacity of 4,000 (1,000 less than practical) means that the organization expects a level of activity 1,000 fewer than it could potentially handle, while the cost charged to products would be £212,800 (3,800 * 56.00). The cost of this *budgeted unused capacity* equals £56,000 (1,000 * 56.00). In addition, a *capacity variance* due to unexpected unused capacity is reported, as a consequence of 200 actual base units less than budgeted. The overall picture of variance analysis in this example, considering capacity information, is summarized in Figure 12.5.

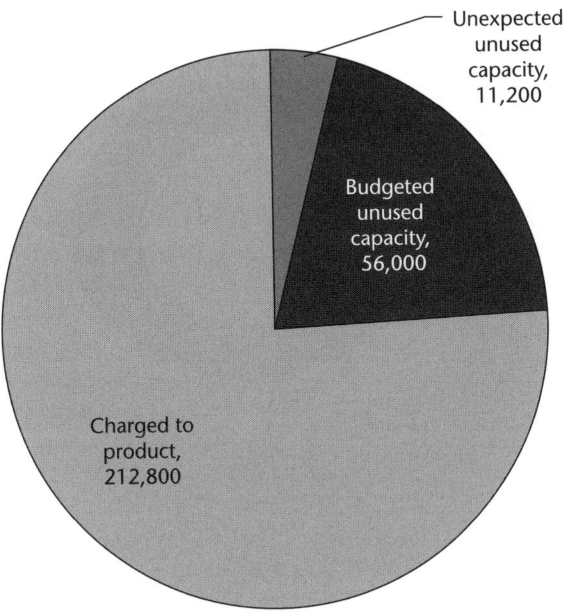

Figure 12.5 Variance analysis and unused capacity

This type of analysis can also be applied in an Activity-Based Costing framework,[9] where it puts into effect the basic equation: available activities = used capacity + unused capacity (Cooper and Kaplan, 1992; Kaplan, 1994; Mak and Roush, 1996; Kaplan and Cooper, 1998: pp. 111–136).

'Value Creation'

A recent development taking a strategic perspective on capacity information is that of 'value creation' for decision-making (McNair et al., 2000, 2001). They extended the models originating from the strategy and marketing literature and aimed at comparing customer preferences to the attributes of the product or service to determine the relative competitiveness of product. This was done by systematically connecting them with the cost structure of the firm. The results have yielded the development of a five-dimensional definition of cost within an organization: (1) customer value-added; (2) business value-added, current; (3) business value-added, future; (4) business value-added, administrative; and (5) non-value-added, or waste. These costs are inserted in a model that provides an interpretation of the value of resources in relation to value creation.

Figure 12.6 represents the model. Price can be seen as a boundary to what a firm can charge customers for a specific product or service given their objective of profit maximization. The costs of resources necessary to produce the product or service in addition to the profit represent the inner circles. The cost circles can be further broken down into the aforementioned value-added cost, business value-added costs (current and future), administrative or non-value-added cost and

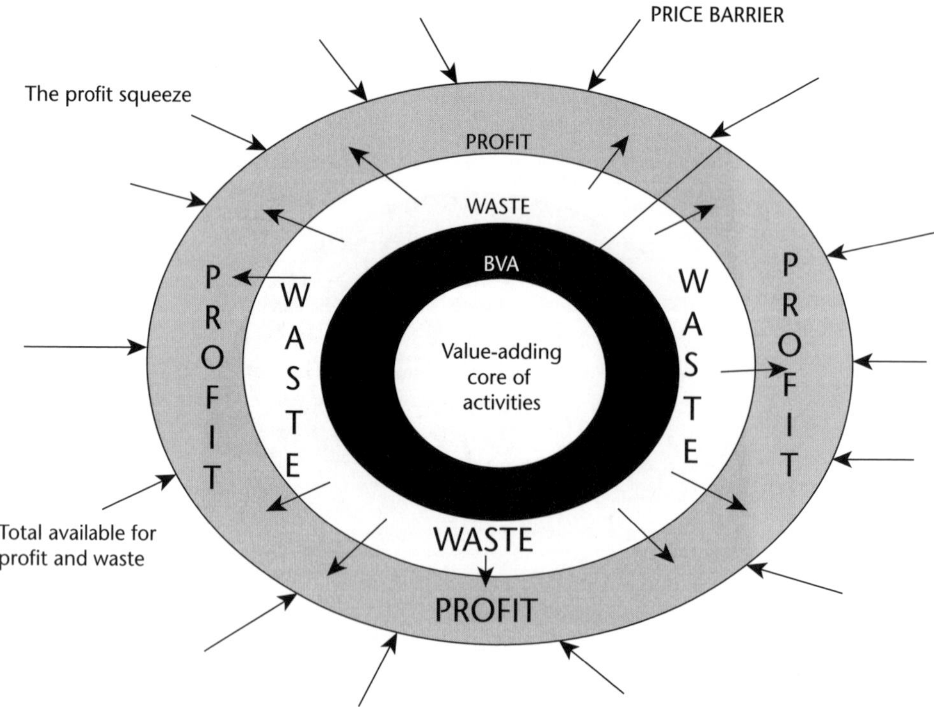

Figure 12.6 The value creation model

Source: McNair et al., 2001.

waste. Only *value-added cost* constitutes the monetary value of resources employed to directly satisfy the customer as a defined attribute of product or service. It is the root cause of revenues and consequently of profit for the firm. The remaining elements of cost create no value directly and, therefore, no revenue. Total revenues less total costs make up the operating profit of the firm. The relation between the percentage of value-added cost and revenues is critical and is defined as a 'value multiplier': it highlights the amount of cost focused on improving the firm's profit and how much value (revenue) is created for each monetary unit of value-added cost.

This analysis may support managerial decision-making by providing information about a new dimension of capacity – its ability to generate revenue growth or, in other words, the contribution of resource capacity to generating value for the firm. This can be considered a 'value creation-based capacity system' (Watts et al., 2008). It provides a complement to viewing capacity in terms of its cost implications.

Final considerations and emerging issues

Capacity reporting has been promoted as an important management tool, but there has been little empirical research evidence gathered to support this claim. In this respect, it is worthwhile to consider a study by Bucheit (2003). The study provides evidence that explicit capacity cost reporting leads to active capacity management that can either improve or worsen capacity decisions depending on the nature of demand. When demand is decreasing, capacity cost reporting highlights unneeded capacity and improves capacity decisions. By contrast, when demand is increasing, reporting unused capacity cost information may encourage cost containment to the extent that growth opportunities are partially lost. The effect of capacity reporting on managerial decision-making, and hence on performance, may therefore be ambiguous.

A further issue to be addressed is the challenge of applying capacity management in a service sector context. The importance of the service sector in many developed countries is great and growing, with over 70% of the gross domestic product due to the service and tertiary sectors (World Economic Forum, 2010). Furthermore, the diffusion of new information and communication technologies, and the new opportunities arising from their application, have boosted the relevance of 'service' far beyond the increase in the weight of the service sector in the overall economy. A different perspective on the essence of contemporary business has emerged in a new 'Service-Dominant Logic' (S-D Logic) (Vargo and Lusch, 2004). It has been proposed in marketing studies, and the process of 'servitization' is expanding as a competitive strategy in manufacturing (Vandermerwe and Rada, 1988; Oliva and Kallenberg, 2003). The S-D Logic refers to changing the view of the company as providing a service (rather than a product), as this is what creates value for the customer. Accordingly, goods are seen as mere means or delivery mechanisms of service provision. The 'servitization' process relates to the trend, especially in manufacturing companies, of transforming products into services and transforming the company from product manufacturer into service provider. For these reasons, the consideration of a service perspective on capacity considerations is worth serious attention.

Although it is perhaps not immediately apparent, a service company is likely to be tied more to its capacity than a manufacturing firm. It is probably not obvious because of how capacity is traditionally defined. There are at least two main reasons why capacity management is a fundamental issue in the service context (Corsten and Stuhlmann, 1998; Adenso-Diaz et al., 2002). The first is because of the impossibility of creating a service inventory for subsequent use – as can be done with the production of goods. The impossibility of synchronizing supply and demand, because of the fluctuations in the latter, produces potential loss due to the impossibility of attending to all the customers when demand is at its high point and the committed fixed resources are not enough to cope with this level of activity. A real loss is also produced when the demand is insufficient because the fixed costs of capacity are not covered. On the other hand fixed resources, committed to providing a certain level of service, need a flexible managerial pricing policy in order to maximize the relation between total revenues and the capacity resources used. In pursuit of this aim, *Yield Management* has been developed in service contexts to support pricing policies (Fitzsimmons and Fitzsimmons, 2008).

Demand fluctuation also underpins the second reason why capacity management really matters in service companies. This is for reasons of workforce allocation. Human resource planning is related to the assignment of the right number of people at the right place and time, in order to perform efficiently the job to be done, i.e. it is based on labour capacity provision. Given the high level of fixed costs in relation to total costs in service companies – mostly due to the cost of employees – it is crucial to plan correctly the workforce utilization and to manage the capacity (Brignall et al., 1991).

An example of how capacity management is important for decision-making, in particular for pricing decisions, is the Xerox company (Mont, 2001). Due to the recalled servitization phenomenon, the company no longer views itself as simply selling photocopiers. It retails document management capability. The main issue in this type of change is how to forecast the level of capacity usage in order to fix the price per copy.

The *servitization* process determines a crucial customer interaction transition for companies, from transaction-based to relationship-based. This implies a change in the way the service is priced, from a mark-up on labour and parts charged every time the service is provided, to a fixed price determined for a period of time. This change has important capacity management implications, as addressed by Oliva and Kallenberg:

> Relationship-based services centred around the product normally take the form of maintenance contracts priced in terms of operational availability and response time in case of failure. The move towards maintenance contracts is often triggered by a desire to make better use of the installed service organization. For the service provider, once the service organization is in place, it becomes a fixed cost and the main driver of profitability is capacity utilization. Established service contracts reduce the variability and unpredictability of the demand over the installed capacity, and allow a higher average capacity utilization.
>
> *(Oliva and Kallenberg, 2003: p. 168)*

These last considerations highlight that capacity management, historically an issue for manufacturing companies, is nowadays a new and relevant field of research which is highly relevant to management in the modern context of the service economy.

Notes

1 These aspects of capacity use have been exploited in the 'theory of constraints' and related 'throughput accounting': see Chapter 10 of this book.
2 For the North American experience, see the studies of Chiu and Lee (1980) and Brausch and Taylor (1997). Regarding UK experience, see Drury (1993).
3 IAS 2 defines 'normal capacity' as '… *the production expected to be achieved on average over a number of periods or seasons under normal circumstances, taking into account the loss of capacity resulting from planned maintenance*'.
4 See more detail on this topic in Chapter 10 of this book.
5 See on this issue also the subsequent para. entitled 'value creation'.

6 The case is based on a real study of the application of the CAM-I capacity model. Data have been slightly adjusted for explanatory purposes.

7 A thorough analysis of the approach to decisions by the use of 'practical capacity' is provided by DeBruine and Sopariwala (1994). On the issues of determining practical capacity in product costing see also Sopariwala (1998, 1999).

8 This may occur when competing with companies operating in countries or areas where it is easier to work in three shifts even during holidays or with short time for holidays.

9 See Chapter 9 of this book.

Bibliography

Adenso-Díaz, B., González-Torre, P., García, V. (2002), A capacity management model in service industries, *International Journal of Service Industry Management*, 13 (3), pp. 286–302.

Ansari, S., Bell, J., Klammer, T., Lawrence, C. (1997). *Measuring and Managing Capacity*. London: Richard D. Irwin Press.

Banker, R.D., Hughes, J. (1994), Product costing and pricing, *The Accounting Review*, 69, July, pp. 479–494.

Banker, R.D., Hwang, I., Mishra, B.K. (2002), Product costing and pricing under long-term capacity commitment, *Journal of Management Accounting Research*, 14, pp. 79–97.

Brausch, J.M., Taylor, T.C. (1997), Who is accounting for the cost of capacity?, *Management Accounting*, February, pp. 44–46.

Brierley, J.A., Cowton, C.J., Drury, C. (2006), Reasons for adopting different capacity-levels in the denominator of overhead rates, *Journal of Applied Management Accounting Research*, 4 (2), pp. 53–62.

Brignall, T.J., Fitzgerald, L., Johnston, R., Silvestro, R. (1991), Product costing in service organizations. *Management Accounting Research*, 2 (4), pp. 227–248.

Bucheit, S. (2003) Reporting the cost of capacity, *Accounting, Organizations and Society*, 28, pp. 549–565.

Chiu, J. and Lee, Y. (1980), A Survey of Current Practice in Overhead Accounting and Analysis, in Whittington, O.R. (ed.), *Proceedings of the 1980 Western Region Meeting of the American Accounting Association*.

Cinquini, L., Silvi, R. (2003), Relazioni tra costi e capacità produttiva: tra rilevanza nella prassi e teoria dimenticata (*Relationships between capacity and costs: relevance in practice and forgotten theory*). *Budget*, n. 33, pp. 73–94.

CMA-IMA (1996), *Measuring the Cost of Capacity*, Management Accounting Guideline 42, The Society of Management Accountants of Canada, Hamilton, Ontario.

Cooper, R., Kaplan, R.S. (1991), *The Design of Cost Management Systems: Text, Cases and Readings*, Englewood Cliffs, NJ: Prentice Hall.

Cooper, R., Kaplan, R.S. (1992), Activity-based Systems: Measuring the Costs of Resource Usage, *Accounting Horizons*, 6 (1), pp. 1–13.

Corsten, H., Stuhlman, S. (1998), Capacity management in service organisations, *Technovation*, 18 (3), pp. 163–178.

DeBruine, M., Sopariwala, P.R. (1994), The use of practical capacity for better management decisions, *Journal of Cost Management*, Spring, pp. 25–31.

Dhavalee, D. (1998), Capacity Costs Perspective – A, *International Journal of Strategic Cost Management*, Summer.

Drury C. (1993), *Management and Cost Accounting*, London, UK: Chapman & Hall.

Drury, C. (2004), *Management and Cost Accounting*, 6th edition, London: Thomson Publishing.

Drury, C., Braund, S., Osborne, P., Tayles, M. (1993), *A Survey of Management Accounting Practices in UK Manufacturing Companies*, Chartered Association of Certified Accountants, London.

Fitzsimmons, J.A., Fitzsimmons, M.J. (2008), *Service Management. Operations, Strategy, Information Technology*, New York: McGraw-Hill Irvin.

Gantt, H.L. (1915), *The Relation Between Production and Costs*, Buffalo, New York: American Society of Mechanical Engineers, Proceedings, pp. 109–128.

Kaplan, R.S., Anderson, S.R. (2007), The innovation of time-driven, activity-based costing, *Cost Management*, March-April, pp. 5–15.

Kaplan, R.S., Cooper, R. (1998), *Cost and Effect – Using Integrated Cost Systems to Drive Profitability and Performance*, Boston: Harvard Business School Press.

Kaplan, R.S. (1994), Flexible budgeting in an Activity-Based Costing framework, *Accounting Horizons*, 8 (2), pp. 104–109.

Klammer, T. P. (1996), *Capacity Measurement and Improvement: A Manager's Guide to Evaluating and Optimizing Capacity Productivity*, Chicago: Irwin Professional Pub.

Lawson, R.A. (2002), Managing the cost of capacity using process-based costing, *Journal of Cost Management*, November/December, pp. 24–29.

Maguire, W., Heath, D. (1997), Capacity management for continuous improvement, *Journal of Cost Management*, 11 (1), pp. 26–31.

Mak, Y.T., Roush, M.L. (1996), Managing activity costs with flexible budgeting and variance analysis, *Accounting Horizons*, 10 (3), pp. 141–146.

McNair, C.J. (1993), *The Profit Potential: Taking High Performance to the Bottom Line*, Essex Junction, Vermont, Oliver Wight Publications.

McNair, C. J. (1994), The hidden costs of capacity. *Journal of Cost Management*, Spring, pp. 12–24.

McNair, C. J., Vangermeersch, R. (1998), *Total Capacity Management*, The IMA Foundation for Applied Research, Inc., St. Lucie Press.

McNair, C.J., Polutnik, L., Silvi, R. (2000), Outside-In: Cost and the Creation of Customer Value, in *Advances in Management Accounting*, M. Epstein (Ed.), Vol. 9, pp. 1–12, Greenwich, CT.

McNair, C.J., Polutnik, L., Hertenstein, J., Vangermeersch, R. (2001), Capacity cost management, *Handbook of Cost Management*, Spring.

Mont, O. (2001), Introducing and Developing a PSS in Sweden, IIIEE Reports 2001:6, Lund University, Lund.

Muras, A., Rodriguez, M. (2003), A new look at manufacturing using CAM-I's capacity management model, *Journal of Corporate Accounting & Finance*, 14 (3), pp. 37–45.

Oliva, R., Kallenberg, R. (2003) Managing the transition from products to services, *International Journal of Service Industry Management*, 14(2), pp. 160–172.

Sopariwala, P.R. (1998), Using practical capacity for determining fixed overhead rates, *Journal of Cost Management*, September/October, pp. 34–39.

Sopariwala, P.R. (1999), Measurement of theoretical capacity as a first step to determining practical capacity, *Journal of Cost Management*, July/August, pp. 35–40.

Sopariwala, P.R. (2006), Capacity utilization: Using the CAM-I capacity model in a multi-hierarchical manufacturing environment, *Management Accounting Quarterly*, Winter, pp. 17–34.

Vandermerwe, S., Rada, J. (1988), Servitization of business, *European Management Journal*, 6 (4), pp. 314–324.

Vargo S.P., Lusch R.F. (2004a), Evolving to a new dominant logic for marketing, *Journal of Marketing*, 68 (1), pp. 1–17.

Watts, T., McNair, C.J., Baard, V., Polutnik, L., (2008), Structural limits of capacity and implications for Visibility, *Global Accounting and Organisational Change Conference*, Melbourne, 9–11 July.

World Economic Forum (2010), *The Global Competitiveness Report 2010–2011*, World Economic Forum.

Yoshikawa, T., Innes, J., Mitchell, F. (2002), *Strategic Value Analysis: Organize your Company for Strategic Success*, Financial Times Management.

Part III

Inter-organizational cost management perspectives

13

Cost management and the provision of support services in large organizations

Will Seal and Ian Herbert

Acknowledgement

The authors are grateful to the Charitable Trust of the Chartered Institute of Management Accountants for financial support for the research.

Introduction

This chapter analyses the cost management issues associated with the provision of finance, human resources, information technology, legal advice, and so on – all functions that might be regarded as 'support services' and thus distinct from the operations that deliver the primary products or 'front-line' services to the customers of an organization. In accounting terms, support activities may be seen as overheads or common costs that are difficult to allocate to a firm's products and departments. The process of cost management starts with analysis of the activity concerned in terms of its cost and added value. But support activities tend to be problematic, not least because the causal linkages with front-line activities are complex and varied but also because staff and associated resources are often embedded within operational management. Thus one option for analysing the cost of support activities is to unbundle staff and resources from their existing location in the hierarchy and move them to either a central location where they are *visible*, or alternatively, disperse them closer to operational management who are best placed to understand the cost/benefit issues.

In the 1980s and 90s, New Working Practices (NWPs) encouraged the unbundling of centralized support functions (often coalesced around mainframe computers) by relocating support staff within autonomous business divisions. The rationale was that front-line managers had knowledge of their support requirements and could manage the level of resources and cost in line with local needs, as would an independent entrepreneur. Desktop computing and spreadsheet technology enabled management accounting to develop a new sense of relevance to operational management – 'close to the customer' was the maxim. More recently, the globalization of production with consequential reductions in unit labour costs has challenged support services to make similar savings.

In the terminology of activity-based costing, support activities are generally seen as either facility- or organization-sustaining activities. Rather than pursue the activity-based costing route, which is premised on cost identification and casual understanding, this chapter focuses particularly on recent approaches to support service provision which may be described by the term corporate 'unbundling': services are made visible by migrating from local business or operating units and then repackaging via an in-house shared service organization (Janssen and Joha, 2006; Ulbrich, 2006; Rothwell, Herbert and Seal, 2011; Herbert and Seal, 2011) or outsourced to third-party providers (Helper and Sako, 2010).

The chapter is structured around the three main ways that cost management is implicated in the unbundling of support services. First, given that many of the organizational and processual changes are informed by attempts to reduce head-count and realize economies of scale and scope, cost management concerns are paramount. Indeed, the business transformation case could be seen as an elabourate and strategic version of the classic 'make-or-buy' puzzle. Second, the new structures have implications for the practice of accounting and control both within new support service facilities and between the different segments of the unbundled organizations: new reporting lines and new visibilities inside and outside the corporation as well as the management control of support service organizations.

Finally, the third theme of the chapter relates to the impact of corporate unbundling on the professional roles of the accountant-in-business. As a support service itself, the accounting function is frequently the *object* (or 'victim') of unbundling, disaggregation and work decomposition. Referring to *legal* services, Sako (2009) argues that '(W)hereas in the past, corporate legal departments were regarded as unavoidable overheads, now they are scrutinized for more cost-effective delivery, in the same way factories have been for decades' (2009, p. 31). Of course, Sako's comments could equally well apply to the professional work of the accountant-in-business.

Corporate unbundling as a make-or-buy decision: a strategic perspective

What is corporate unbundling?

In contrast to the copious literature on the vertical disintegration of *primary activities* (Porter, 1985; Gospel and Sako, 2010), there has been a relative neglect of the structures and processes associated with the provision of support services and a relative lack of conceptual development of the shared service model when support services are 'moved' but still retained within the corporation (Maatman, Bondarouk and Looise, 2010). Corporate unbundling is also very often (but not always) associated with a move to a single ERP model – the new technology both enables and is enabled by the centralization and standardization of business processes throughout the organization (Oliveira, 2010). The concept of corporate unbundling is derived from the strategic management discourse. For example, building on Porter (1985), Gospel and Sako state that:

> We may conceptualize some support activities as separable from primary value-adding activities, whilst other support activities are more complementary and coupled with primary activities. Thus, each corporate function consists of a hierarchy of activities which are tightly or loosely coupled to primary activities to varying degrees.
>
> *Gospel and Sako (2010, p. 7)*

More generally, capabilities may be typologized into lower-level operational capabilities to achieve technical fitness and higher-level dynamic capabilities to sustain evolutionary fitness (Teece, 2009). There is a sense that operational capabilities are more widely diffused in the firm and outsourceable, whilst dynamic capabilities are more concentrated and not subject to outsourcing (2010, p. 8).

This typology of capabilities suggests how service functions may be divided up into those which are to be sent to the SSM or outsourced and those which are to be retained 'on-site'. As much of the terminology implies, corporate unbundling usually has a strong *spatial* dimension. At the most mundane level, it implies a change from a user of support services just being able to 'pop their head round the door' or walk down the corridor, or even visit a location in the same building. The physical manifestation of unbundling involves moving support services to a special building, off-site or even offshore. The spatial reordering may also be a matter of layout in specialized buildings with a grouping together of 'end-to-end' process teams and a working environment which some critical researchers have characterized as 'service factories' (Taylor and Bain, 1999).

Some motives for unbundling

The usual assumption is that capitalist firms will have incentives to move activities to low-cost locations and that improvements in information and communication technology enable services to be relocated – just as, in an earlier phase, manufacturing was relocated. Although they may face political constraints on offshoring and outsourcing, non-profit-making governmental organizations may also pursue the shared services option. In the public sector, however, the rhetoric may be different, with talk about 'achieving cost reduction without damaging the front line.' As well as cost reduction, Gospel and Sako (2010) identified 'value-adding motives'. Citing their own empirical evidence, Gospel and Sako found in one case that internal HR managers are freed up 'to concentrate on less routine matters' (2010, p. 6) and, in another, the unbundling enables a 'further release of internal managers to concentrate on more value-adding activities' (ibid, 2010, p. 18).

Support service unbundling: captive or outsourced

Once the decision to unbundle support services has been taken, the next question is: should the unbundled services be provided through business process outsourcing (BPO) or through a captive shared service centre (SSM)? In this chapter, we compare these two alternative models of corporate unbundling, beginning with service outsourcing. The motives for service outsourcing are very similar to those that led to the creation of SSCs. The basic logics of both the shared service organization (SSO) and business process outsourcing are very similar from a company perspective; often the shared service option is seen as just a prelude to full outsourcing (Helper and Sako, 2010). In HR SSCs, Farndale, Paauwe and Hoeksema (2009) refer to two logics, *professionalism* – meeting the expectations of stakeholders, including customers – and *delivery* – cost-effective operations. Although part of the motive for corporate unbundling is to reduce the cost, other motives include the standardization of processes, freeing up operational managers' time, elimination of duplication, realization of economies of scale and scope, the migration of services to low-cost and/or high-skill locations, and improved knowledge management.

A schematic model of unbundling

Drawing on theories of corporate administration (Chandler, 1962), of transaction costs (Coase, 1937; Williamson, 1975), and of resources and capabilities of the firm (Teece, 2009) together with their own case study evidence, Gospel and Sako (2010) developed a schematic model of unbundling. As shown in Figure 13.1, they represented two dimensions of change – transformation

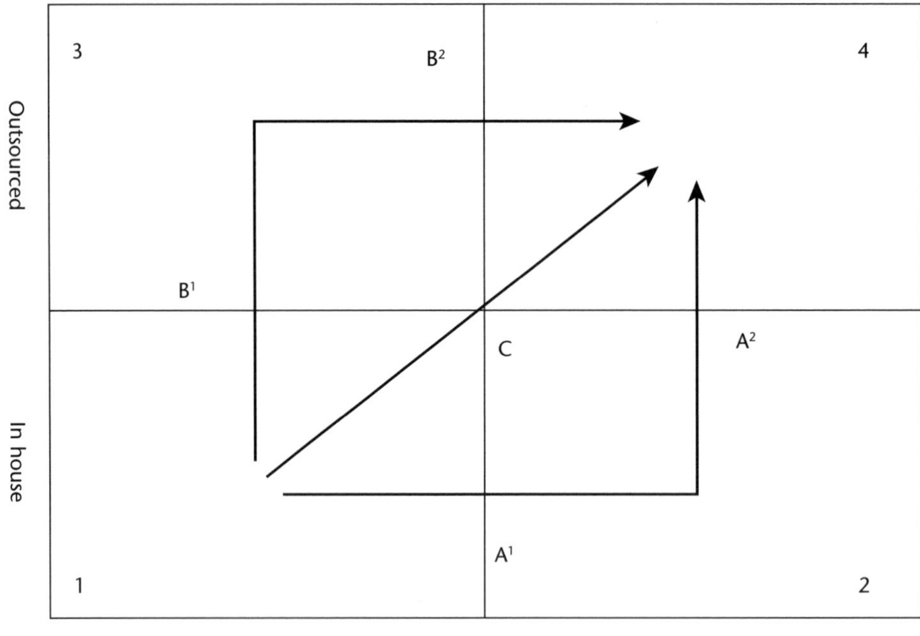

Figure 13.1 Transforming and outsourcing business processes

Source: Gospel and Sako, 2010, p. 20.

of the business process and in-house to outsourcing – as a two-by-two matrix. They then identified three possible paths that organizations can take on their unbundling journeys. Path A traces the move to a shared service centre which may follow through to full outsourcing. Path B goes straight to outsourcing without initial business transformation, while Path C is described as 'throw all over the fence' (2010, p. 20) with simultaneous transformation and outsourcing. Each approach has different implications in terms of start-up costs, the distribution of expertise and bargaining power between outsourcers and providers. The chapter proceeds with an initial consideration of paths B and C – the outsourcing destination.

Outsourcing support services: business process outsourcing (BPO)

The objectives for outsourcing can be various (Smith, Morris and Ezzamel, 2005) but might typically include: cost and head-count reduction, access to greater expertise and technology, a keener focus on core activities and better operational flexibility (Barnes, 2004; CIMA, 2001; Renner and Tebbe, 1998; Bromage, 2000; Rittenberg and Covaleski, 2001; Langfield-Smith and Smith, 2003; Bangeman, 2005). The act of disembedding and re-embedding both activities and personnel, (so-called 'lift and shift' in the vernacular of the consultants), provides an opportunity to break the psychological mould of previous operating regimes and facilitate transformational change. The aggregation of otherwise disparate activities may also provide an opportunity to leverage new information and communications technology (ICT), for example corporate intranets and Enterprise Resource Planning (ERP) systems. Such developments in system architecture can help to improve the co-ordination and effectiveness of the organizational overall (Schulman, Dunleavy, Harmer and Lusk, 1999; Leach, 2004).

The challenge of outsourcing

There have, however, been a number of notable failures of outsourcing in the UK (Centre for Public Services, 2006) and it is argued that where a particular activity is inappropriate, or the contract is badly negotiated in favour of the supplier, then outsourcing can increase costs, reduce flexibility and lead to reduced service quality (Caulkin, 2003; Davies, 2005). Together with sensitivities around security of employment, these concerns explain in part the emergence of a popular alternative to outsourcing, the Shared Service Centre (SSC), although this organizational form appears neglected in the academic literature. Recent problems with outsourcing initiatives in the UK have highlighted the risks of entering into long-term contracts with third parties for the supply of key support services (Caulkin, 2003; Davies, 2005). Perhaps this is not surprising as suppliers will likely be expert in framing and negotiating service contracts – compared, that is, to an outsourcer whose principal objective is to untangle itself from having to do an activity that it knows relatively little about (Caulkin, 2003; 2005).

Outsourcing involves lower-level, non-core support activities, such as security and cleaning; the usual motivation being cost reduction (Smith et al., 2005; Bangemann, 2005). However, some tasks that may *appear* unskilled and apparently peripheral to an organization's core competencies cannot, in practice, be readily standardized, routinized and farmed out to third-party contractors.

Hospital cleaning provides a good example of an activity that might normally be considered peripheral: undertaken by unskilled staff and comprising routines that can readily be made explicit and thus programmable, it seems a natural choice to outsource. Yet cleaning might be seen as an integral part of patient care, a vital role in the overall culture of healthcare, not simply a 'bolt-on' task added to nursing. The incidence of hospital-acquired infections, in particular the MRSA bug, has highlighted something of a polemical issue for government, health professionals and the public. After more than a decade during which outsourcing had been the vogue in the NHS, The Matron's Charter (NHS, 2004) repositioned cleaning as an essential core function that should be under the direct control of ward management. The incumbent Secretary of State for Health, John Reid, stated in the foreword to the Charter: 'cleanliness is everyone's responsibility, not just the cleaner's' (ibid, p. 3). Perhaps of greatest significance in the outsourcing debate is No. 9 of the 10-item charter, 'Nurses and infection control teams will be involved in drawing up cleaning contracts, and matrons have the authority and power to withhold payment' (ibid, p. 3). Giving such discretion to front-line staff would have been unthinkable only a decade ago, but it restores the connection between the service's process and outcomes.

The hospital cleaning example suggests that there may be something in *how* the work is done which requires tacit knowledge embedded within the organization's routines and/or embodied within individual workers. It may not always be possible to make such knowledge adequately explicit to enable a satisfactory outsourcing solution. The examples above lead us to further explore what defines an 'appropriate' task for outsourcing and what other factors might inform outsourcing decisions if common notions of marketization and core versus non-core skills are found wanting.

Core competences: a knowledge perspective

Whilst practitioner literature is still inclined to favour the external (outsourcing) approach (e.g. Bromage, 2000; Barnes, 2004; Hayward, 2002; Leach, 2004), a more balanced discussion was presented by Rittenberg and Covaleski (2001) in the context of outsourcing internal audit functions. The authors drew on the work of Matusik and Hill (1998), to suggest that in deciding what might be appropriate to outsource it is helpful to classify the knowledge inherent in performing the task as 1) *public or private*, 2) *architectural* (with understanding of the organization's culture and systems explicit) or *component* (with concrete operation of organization subsystems which can subsequently be viewed as core or non-core) and 3) explicit or tacit. Matusik and Hill (1998, p. 684) suggested that the use of contingent workers can create permeable boundaries through which a firm can gain or lose knowledge. A knowledge framework enables firms to be conscious of the need to maintain and keep private that knowledge which is architectural in nature and thus defines the firm. Earlier, Prahalad and Hamel (1990) had warned against unwittingly surrendering skills embedded within multiple divisions through outsourcing by mistakenly identifying non-core competencies as simply 'cost centre' activities when those very activities could become a core competence within the overall architecture of the organization.

The problematic aspects of the outsourcing route suggests that business transformation through shared services may be more feasible – path (A) in the model shown in Figure 13.1. The chapter proceeds by exploring and elaborating on this approach to support service provision.

Shared services as an alternative to BPO

In the shared service model (SSM)[1] support services are 'moved' but still retained or owned by the corporation (Maatman et al., 2010). In one version of the SSM, an organization's service functions (finance, legal, IT, procurement, etc.) are grouped together and supplied to the operating parts of the organization on a common basis. A related form of SSM pertains where a *single* function, such as finance, is supplied on a common basis to a number of geographically-dispersed business units.

SSMs have a similarity with outsourcing arrangements whereby the 'invisible hand' of a 'quasi-market' seeks to increase efficiency but, as a hybrid arrangement, SSMs also have the advantage of the continuing 'visible hand' of internal management when activities continue within the traditional organizational hierarchy (Chandler, 1977, pp. 6–12). Furthermore, support activities should have a greater level of cost transparency when untangled from divisional business units and reorganized into a separate centre. Figure 13.2 shows this change in structure schematically.

Perhaps the two key features of the SSM are that, in contrast to the traditional M-form approach articulated in the long-standing *strategy and structure discourse* (Chandler, 1962; Phillips et al., 2004; Whittington, 2002; 2007; Gospel and Sako, 2010; Helper and Sako, 2010), support services are subject to shared management systems across the various segments of the business. Second, there is a conscious rejection of formal, contract-driven provision because the services are still 'captive' or owned by the main operating company when relocated or even offshored. From a business policy perspective, the SSM offers an *alternative* to outsourcing and a new perspective on the traditional make-or-buy decision (Gospel and Sako, 2010).

Whilst corporate unbundling is often driven by a desire to obtain crude reductions in head-count in support services, it also potentially impinges on organization-wide co-ordination and control systems, the way that the organization learns and captures knowledge, and potentially even the way in which the organization thinks about its work and its identity (Gospel and Sako, 2010). As with outsourcing, the introduction of the SSM poses certain questions of design, about the core and periphery of the corporation and about its very *raison d'etre*.

The conceptualization of the SSM may be informed by a number of puzzles. For example, to what extent is the SSM a distinct and novel organizational concept, and how does it relate to broader work restructuring and outsourcing initiatives? If there are innovations, to what extent do these lie in organizational structures and/or in changed processes and work practices? These

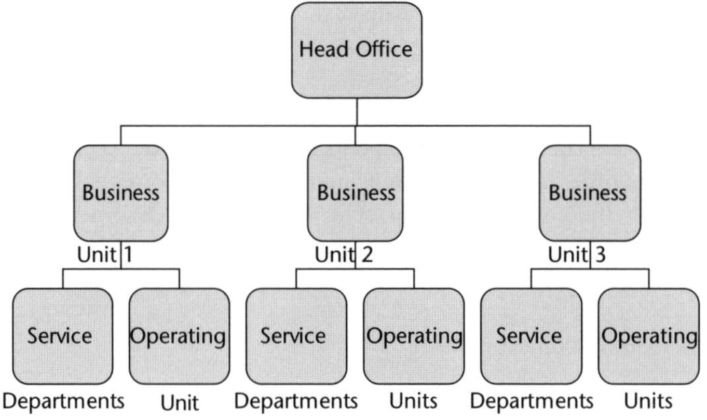

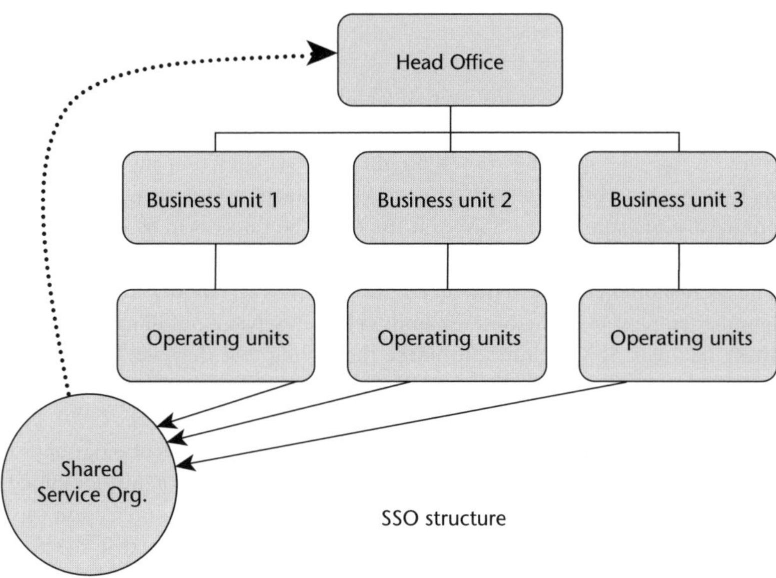

Figure 13.2 Moving to a shared service centre structure

questions and others can be addressed in a number of theoretical ways. For example, the SSM could be analysed in terms of production models and paradigms (Bartezzaghi, 1999), in terms of socio-technical systems (Dankbaar, 1997), through the lens of labour process theory (Adler, 2007) or through economic and strategy theories (Gospel and Sako, 2010).

The consultancy and practitioner agenda: analysing the managerial discourse

There is a particular type of practical discourse on the SSM produced by consultants and specialist service providers with texts written from a self-interested perspective (Schulman et al., 1999; Hagel and Singer, 1999; Quinn, Cooke, and Kris, 2000; Bergeron, 2003). As will be argued below, the practitioner literature forms an important body of texts that has thus far dominated the SSM discourse and thereby helped to frame managerial thinking and action. Indeed, the managerialist agenda is reflected in some of the definitions offered by consultants. Thus according to Schulman et al. (1999) an SSM is

> [T]he concentration of company resources performing like activities, typically spread across the organization, in order to service multiple internal parties at lower cost and with higher service levels, with the common goal of delighting external customers and enhancing corporate value.
>
> *Schulman et al. (1999, p. 9)*

Another source (Bergeron, 2003) argues that

> [S]hared services is a collaborative strategy in which a subset of existing business functions are concentrated in a new, semi-autonomous business unit that has a management structure designed to promote efficiency, value generation, cost savings, and improved service for internal customers of the parent corporation, like a business competing in the open market.
>
> *Bergeron (2003, p. 3)*

The managerial discourse for the SSM is written largely from the point of view of the parent company. Perhaps the most obvious advantage for the parent company is that by concentrating service activities on one site, specially chosen for the purpose, the company can reduce costs. Some authors have suggested that an 'easy' 25% to 30% reduction in costs is possible with the promise of progressive pressure on the SSM as it itself may be threatened by outsourcing to an even lower-cost location (Quinn et al., 2000). But it is also argued that there are more than cost advantages. The SSM should provide better service than the old service departments. There was always a danger that employees in the business units saw themselves as fulfilling low-status 'back office functions'. The new SSM culture can 'shake the feeling that they are "low value added employees" performing "cost centre" activities' because the culture of the SSM is affected by the knowledge that providing support service is its core business (Schulman et al., 1999). The SSM can focus its core competencies, standardize processes and apply the best technology appropriate to a service business. The appropriate technology may involve ERP systems combined with other technologies used in call centres which link voice, video and data-interaction capability (Schulman et al., 1999). The standardization and technology may mean that the SSM can possibly employ cheaper junior staff, but the scale and new focus of the organization should also enable it to recruit and concentrate on top experts and professionals.

A *knowledge management* perspective may further see the SSM as an opportunity attempt to repackage the intellectual capital of the company, redefine core competences and manage customer, human and structural capital (Bergeron, 2003). Although SSMs are usually associated with 'back-end processes' such as payroll, human resource management and billing, the SSM may also be used to provide some strategic services such as market intelligence, marketing, sales and customer support. A consultant's view of SSMs is shown in Figure 13.3, which represents a useful summary of the managerialist perspective of the roles of the SSM.

Weaknesses of the managerial discourse on the SSM

Consultant texts have picked up a number of issues relating to the SSM. The evolutionary nature of the SSM project (Deloitte, 2004) and choice of charging mechanism (Deloitte, 2007c); the relationship between the SSM and the business units (Deloitte, 2006); the value-adding potential

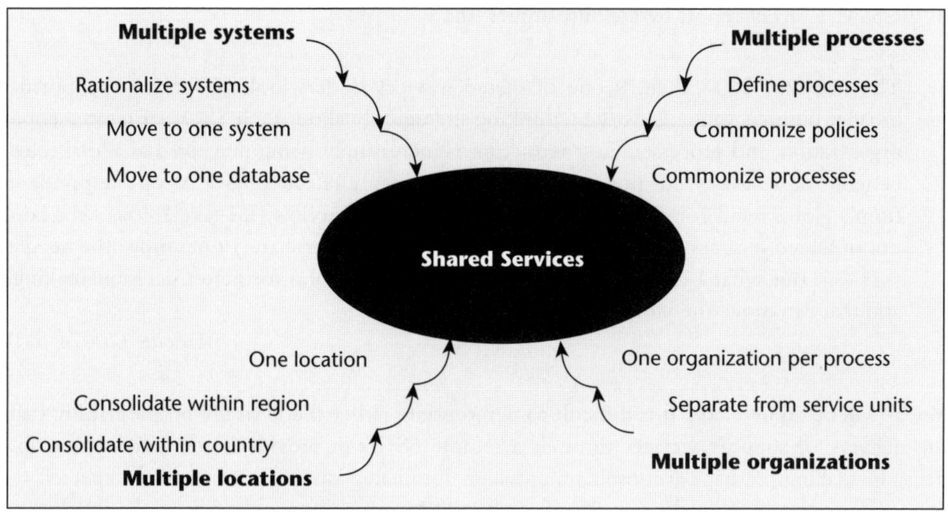

Figure 13.3 A consultant perspective on the SSM

Source: Deloitte (2004).

of the SSM (Deloitte, 2005; 2007a) are some of the potential problems (Deloitte, 2007b). Yet, the managerialist conceptualizations of SSCs suffer from a number of limitations. There is an understandable narrowness of perspective and a lack of reflection on concepts such as cost and efficiency. How are the costs and benefits measured, and if efficiency is enhanced, how can that be tested? In the formation of an SSO in a large electricity firm, Herbert and Seal (2011) found that the consultancy narrative had resonance with key actors although the rationalization of the SSO was largely justified by reductions in head-count from which cost savings were assumed to flow. The authors also noted that any savings could only have been assessed with data supplied from the divisions which had an obvious scope for political posturing. The language and outlook of the consultancy discourse seemed to represent native categories in the eyes of the managers in both the SSO and its user departments. They all suggested that the key motivation for the SSO was economic, or at least cost-saving. So that although from a research perspective the SSO needs to be interpreted via broader and more reflective perspectives, the chosen framework should acknowledge the pressures and opportunities of acting in a 21st-century capitalist environment. In short, it should be broad enough to understand as well as critique the functionalist perspective.

The managerialist literature can also be somewhat dogmatic about the precise nature of the SSM. For example, one of the problems in defining the SSM is trying to distinguish between an SSC and a more centralized head office. In addressing this issue, Schulman and co-workers state:

> The major distinctions between a back-office service that is simply consolidated and centralized and a shared business unit are that the delivery of service and governance are delivered together in a typical centralized business model. In contrast, the focus of the business unit is strictly on the delivery of service, with no policing by or governance of parent corporation employees involved . . . employees working with backend functions in the parent corporation deliver both governance and service.
>
> *Schulman et al. (1999, p. 87)*

In contrast to this narrow, 'subservient' view of the SSM, and reflecting the practical evolution of the SSM, a recent report by Deloitte argues that

> The story for 2007, then, is one of shared services leaders looking for ways to pursue broader business value delivery by thinking strategically about their SSOs' structure, scope, organization, and processes. Cost reduction is increasingly being perceived as a 'dial tone' benefit – a necessary but not sufficient goal for a truly effective SSO. As one respondent from a global retail company observed in a follow-up interview: 'If I take 100% of the cost out of shared services, it wouldn't even come to a penny per share. I can't move the needle that way. But what I can do is to provide better information for better decision-making, and that can move the [corporate] needle.
>
> *Deloitte (2007a, p. 3)*

Yet, as will be argued later, it is difficult to demonstrate either theoretically or empirically that the delivery of support services through a remote SSC can provide better information for decision-making. Perhaps a consultant/provider-dominated discourse cannot be expected to countenance the awful possibility that the entire SSM project not only fails to provide better information but may even lead to either a loss of intellectual capital or at least its relocation away from where it might be most productively deployed. These issues are beginning to be explored in the academic literature (Gospel and Sako, 2010; Maatman et al., 2010).

The SSM compared to outsourcing

Although SSMs have commonalities with third-party outsourcing there are, however, a number of points of difference. First, in the SSM, control is retained over processes, staff and operational knowledge (component and architectural). Second, the management time involved in negotiating and enforcing contracts with third-party suppliers is avoided. Third, contracts with outside parties can result in one partner to the deal (more likely the supplier) doing significantly better than the other; especially when operational circumstances change, such that the manner in which services are delivered also needs to change. Outsourcing might then be viewed as less flexible, or more costly if contract variations are subsequently necessary. Whilst lopsidedness in favour of either party in the original agreement might be mitigated by the *ex post* sharing of emerging benefits or costs between the parties, such appropriation requires accurate quantification of both the input costs and outcomes, together with proper cooperation between the parties at an operational level. Whilst contract outcomes will always be variable – 'some you win, some you lose' – in outsourcing, the risk to the outsourcer is likely to be significant due to the one-off nature of the deal. Outsourcing contracts are likely to be strategically significant and long-term, for example, providing an IT support service for, say, five years. Moreover, once outsourced, it is usually impractical to bring the service back in-house due to the loss of operational knowledge and organizational capability. Such asset specificity might apply equally to physical infrastructure (Williamson, 1975).

In the next section, we move on from considering the motives and types of corporate unbundling of support services and take a critical look at the management control of SSCs. This perspective seeks to open up the black box of the SSC. The imagery of the black box is particularly apposite as SSCs can appear to be forbidding, often housed in almost sinister buildings with high levels of security and internal surveillance – service factories rather than the white-collar ivory towers of the traditional office worker.

Management control in the shared service organization: some critical perspectives

Whatever the arguments for and against the various forms of corporate unbundling, once the new models were established, more critical texts have been produced – particularly including organizational 'voices' beyond the managers and consultants. Such an approach easily leads into a critical discourse as workers in the business units are often forced to move or lose their jobs completely. Dissident voices may be also found both in texts by non-managerial stakeholders – such as employers and customers – but also by considering criticisms from specific service functions – especially human resources (Farndale et al., 2009). Furthermore, if the SSM is conceptualized as a special type of call centre then an academic discourse can draw on the research on call centres and the extended organization (Colling, 2000; Marchington, Grimshaw, Rubery and Willmott, 2005). These perspectives introduce a far more complex view of contemporary trends in service work as being 'underpinned by dual logics of rationalization and customer-orientation ... [which] potentially lie in contradiction to each other' (Korczynski, 2004, p. 98).

Perhaps it is not surprising that critical views can be found when non-managerial voices are heard. Yet, it may be possible to criticize the SSM even from an efficiency perspective by building on dissident voices within the consultancy/practitioner community. In particular, the ideas of Seddon[2] (2005; 2008) are based on looking at the SSM in the context of more general notions of Lean production, Taylorism and systems theory. Seddon's critique of the 'command-and-control' philosophy of management is similar to Armstrong's critique (2002) in that they both point out the problems caused by separating management from knowledge of process – *context-free managerialism*.

The critical stance in these instances comes not from dissident voices outside management but from a critique that argues that corporate unbundling is not always the most efficient strategy. Seddon criticizes the SSM as follows:

> Unfortunately, most service centres are managed solely on production data, measuring activity rather than anything relating to purpose. Service centres appear as costs in top management's accounts. This is why managers are attracted by the idea of outsourcing. They hand over calls to an agency, whether in the same country or, more recently, in low-wage countries abroad, and pay per call for the service. The result is simply to outsource waste.
>
> *Seddon (2005, p. 29)*

The key critique is that shared service managers 'know about volumes and activity but little or nothing about the real nature of the work' (Seddon, 2005, p. 29). It is not the fault of the managers but rather that the design of the work process into front office/back office or primary and support inevitably fragments the end-to-process, leading to 'failure demand' – activity created by mistakes in the system. Even more worrying is the notion that the service work itself has been degraded in order to make it 'fit' into the abstract, context-free, managerialist mould (Armstrong, 2002). In general, if we (i.e. both practitioners and researchers) seek 'to understand the organizational forms we observe around us, we need to understand the work practices that these forms are designed to support' (Adler, 2007, p. 1313).

In the managerialist discourse, knowledge is seen as separable in a way that is similar to the Tayloristic division between 'brain and brawn'. Yet even from an efficiency perspective this simplistic view may be challenged. First, it ignores the dynamics of knowledge acquisition and deployment at the operational level of the organization, which is a feature of Lean production

(Womack, Jones and Roos, 1990). Second, it ignores the danger that the lack of expertise in the SSM may lead to the generation of so-called 'failure demand' – 'the demand caused by a failure to do something or do something right for the customer' (Seddon, 2005, p. 26).

Seddon's work (2005; 2008) is an excellent example of how the insights of the consultant can contribute to the development of a critical discourse on the SSM. Seddon's work is informed by the practical experience of the consultant together with an explicit conceptual framework. The conceptual basis for his critique of 'service factories' is Lean production, or what he terms a 'systems approach' (Seddon, 2005; 2008). Despite its reputation for work intensification and increased exploitation, Lean production *can* be given a radical twist (Adler, 2007). From a Lean perspective, the work processes and customer relationships associated with the SSM are more reminiscent of mass rather than Lean production. The organization is restructured through the SSM but the command-and-control and separation between managerial and shop-floor work is actually reinforced.

KPIs and benchmarking

One of the characteristics of the SSM is whether the company chooses to rely on recharging or uses some form of 'broad-brush' cost apportionment. Herbert and Seal (2011) noted that the KPIs used by the *Utlityco* SSO managers reflected a 'market-type mentality' with a big focus on customer satisfaction: internal users of the SSO were surveyed regularly. External benchmarking was a key feature of management control in the SSO. Indeed, benchmarking against the company's subsidiaries in the United States had actually informed the initial move to the SSO model with broad-brush measures such as the ratio of finance cost to sales and the head-count in individual plants and activities. Subsequently, more detailed benchmarks were developed for monitoring the *relative* performance of the SSO as it became established and developed as part of the wider business.

The benchmark was not service support quality *before* unbundling but tracking the progress (or otherwise) of the extant organizational configuration. In the early stages, the SSO managers participated in a 'round table' comprising a non-competitive peer group of SSOs. Next, the SSO was formally benchmarked by consultants against a database comprising a UK reference group and a 'world's best' figure. The objective of both exercises was to identify specific processing costs across a range of tasks, such as the cost of each purchase invoice processed, or cost per each £1,000 of receivables collected, and so on. At an even more advanced stage of the SSO, external consultants conducted ad hoc surveys of divisional customers. Inspection by the authors of internal performance statistics – which included an overall customer satisfaction rating – showed an improving trend for the Key Performance Indicators (KPIs). It was noted that there was a small bonus paid to staff in any month in which the rating improved.

The impact of corporate unbundling on the accountant in business

Smith et al. (2005) found that management accounting is likely to be affected by the use of outsourcing. Such new responsibilities may involve, typically: supporting management in deciding what activities are appropriate to outsource and supplier selection; framing and negotiating the contract; developing suitable performance measures and monitoring systems; managing the working relationship and post-project evaluation. Seal et al. (1999) reported that management accountants (MAs) were adopting new roles in managing external supply chain relationships and there may be similar implications in managing intra-firm relationships around a market-oriented SSC, albeit with internal rather than external customers. Consequently, there will be a need for MAs to adapt to an outward-facing role in selling and negotiating their accounting services, as opposed to simply providing a functional service out of head office. In other words, they must justify their existence and outputs to customers, who have some degree of power to demand value for money and relevance. Broadbent et al. (2004) suggested that MAs needed to make changes in their orientation in the context of the post-project evaluation of Public Finance Initiative contracts.

In Herbert and Seal (2011), the SSO caused three broad dimensions of change: (1) to the roles of MAs retained in divisions, (2) to the roles of MAs moving to the SSO and (3) through the creation of new relationships between the two groups, as one becomes a 'buyer' of accounting services, the other a 'supplier'. The MAs retained in divisions testified that they had been freed from the tedium of transaction processing and now enjoyed more 'space' to enhance the overall role of the management accounting function. The term 'business partner' was used by interviewees as an expression of the notion of finance, playing a proactive role in planning, decision-making and control within strategic and operational teams (see Baldvinsondottir et al., 2009; Gospel and Sako, 2010).

Herbert and Seal (2011) found that there was pressure on the MAs in the SSO to justify their existence through outputs to 'customers' who have the power to demand value for money and relevance. Conversely, having lost their core accounting transaction-processing function to the SSO, the divisional MAs were under pressure to justify themselves as business partners. A common expectation of MAs throughout the corporation was for them to manage *intra-firm* relationships around a market-oriented SSO, albeit with *internal* rather than external customers (Seal, Cullen, Dunlop, Berry and Ahmed, 1999). Thus, as a consequence of the SSO with its hybrid practices, there was a need for MAs to adapt to outward-facing roles in selling and negotiating their accounting services.

As mentioned earlier, the redesign of systems and business processes that accompanies the migration of accounting work to a SSC is often combined with the introduction of corporate-wide ERP systems. Indeed, research has shown that ERP systems can change the balance of tasks undertaken by management accountants in ways similar to those associated with the SSM. For example, the elimination of routine accounting jobs can, at least potentially, create a more value-adding role for the management accountant (Scapens and Jazayeri, 2003).

The challenge to professional notions of the 'career' posed by corporate unbundling

Rothwell et al. (2011) argued that corporate unbundling challenges the professional worker in First-World countries. Hitherto, protected by barriers to entry based on structured formation and progression, and secured by knowledge that is independent of organizational bonds, these professionals had a degree of perceived occupational security that had defied the apocalyptic predictions of late-20th-and early-21st-century career theorists (Handy, 1989; Baruch and Pieperl, 1997; Marchington et al., 2005; Wright, 2008). However, aside from the professional accounting work protected by statutory regimes, this past sense of security may yet prove to be ill-founded in the future. Rothwell et al. (2011) also noted anecdotal concerns about the emergence of a *development gap* (CIPD, 2004). For example, the next generation of high-level business partners may fail to acquire both the required 'nuts and bolts' experience of accounting routines and the inculcation into professional 'life'.

There may also be a problem if a significant number of technician-level workers experience problems in career progression. In one case history – *OilCo* – Rothwell et al. (2011) noted that the company had chosen to have an honest dialogue with their young mid-career workers in developing countries in which the management was explicit about the lack of opportunities for career progression within the company. A further scenario might emerge in *developed countries* where, if the technician-level jobs are relocated overseas, the opportunities for workers in developed countries to become senior managers may be damaged because they cannot acquire technical competences or experience professional life.

Overall, the imperative of cost reduction that is driving the reorganization, reconfiguration, redesign, relocation, commoditization and marketization of support services could, over time, lead to a hollowing-out of professional skill-sets (Rothwell et al., 2011). This is particularly problematic for those individuals who previously would have regarded themselves as professionals fulfilling what were integral – if not necessarily core – functions in organizations, but now find themselves in a narrower, more programmed role, and in a more transactional relationship with their employing organizations. The consequence may be an 'hour-glass' profession whereby the middle, comprised typically of recently qualified professionals, will be competing for tough-to-get promotion or aiming to leave with their experience 'passport stamped'.

Some conclusions

This chapter has reviewed research on the corporate unbundling of support services. It has been argued that cost management is involved in the logic of the unbundling decision (mode of delivery, location, etc.) and in the management control of the unbundled services. Outsourcing and in-sourcing via shared services have both changed the administrative structures and processes of multi-divisional organizations as corporate expertise is moved to new locations and delivered in different ways. This type of unbundling also has potential implications for the professional worker – especially the accountants, who are traditionally charged with cost management responsibilities. Indeed, there is even an element of the 'biter bit', as management accountants working in traditional cost management roles are becoming 'victims' of unbundling. Given that much of the academic research on unbundling has focused on the HR function, we would urge that a complementary research effort needs to be undertaken with respect to the accounting and finance function. Such an academic research effort should also serve to challenge the consultancy discourse that currently dominates the unbundling agenda.

Notes

1 The SSM refers to the general model in the context of the wider organization. The acronyms SSC or SSO refers to a specific sub-unit or specific site.
2 Seddon has academic links and thus straddles both academic and consultancy camps.

Bibliography

Adler, P. (2007) The Future of Critical Management Studies: A Paleo-Marxist Critique of Labour Process Theory, *Organization Studies*, 28, 1313–1345.

Armstrong, P. (2002) Management, Image and Management Accounting, *Critical Perspectives on Accounting* 13, 281–295.

Bain, P. and Taylor, P. (2000) Entrapped by the 'electronic panopticon'? Worker resistance in the call centre, *New Technology, Work and Employment*, 15(1), 21–28.

Bangemann, T.O. (2005) *Shared Services in Finance and Accounting*, Gower, Aldershot.

Barnes, P. (2004) Good going, *Financial Management*, October, CIMA, London.

Bartezzaghi, E. (1999) The evolution of production models: is a new paradigm emerging?, *International Journal of Operations & Production Management*, 19(2), 229–250.

Bergeron, B. (2003) *Essentials of Shared Services*, Wiley, New Jersey.

Broadbent, J., Gill, J. and Laughlin, R. (2004) *The Private Finance Initiative in the National Health Service: Nature, Emergence and the Role of Management Accounting in Decision-Making and Post-Decision Project Evaluation*, CIMA, London.

Bromage, N. (2000) Outsourcing: To Do, Or Not To Do, That Is The Question, *Management Accounting*, 78 (1), CIMA.

Caulkin, S. (2003) In-house and back on track, the *Guardian*, 29.11.03.

Caulkin, S. (2005) Outsourcing and out of control, the *Observer*, 28.8.05.

Centre for Public Services (2006) *Contract and Privatisation Failures*, Centre for Public Services, Sheffield. http://www.centre.public.org.uk/outsourcing-library/contract-and-privatisation-failures/ accessed 20.4.06.

Chandler, A.D. (1962) *Strategy and Structure: Chapters in the History of the American Industrial Enterprise.* Cambridge, MA: MIT Press.

CIMA (2001) *Contracting Out the Finance Function,* Technical Briefing, August, CIMA, London.

Coase, R. (1937) The nature of the firm, *Economica,* 4, 386–405.

Colling, T. (2000) 'The Extended Organization'. In Bach and Sisson (eds) *Human Resource Management*, Oxford: Blackwell.

Dankbaar, B. (1997) 'Lean production: denial, confirmation or extension of sociotechnical systems design?', *Human Relations,* 50(5), 567–583.

Deloitte (2004) *Shared Services: Implementing shared services is not a one-time effort it is a journey.*

Deloitte (2005) *Shared Services in a global economy: Expanding the shared services value proposition.*

Deloitte (2006) *Will the real customer stand up: The shared services myth that could be costing you big.* http://www.deloitte.com/assets/Dcom-Australia/Local%20Assets/Documents/DeloitteReal Customerfinal030106.pdf

Deloitte (2007a). *Shared Services Comes of Age: Pursuing broader business value on a global scale.* http://www.deloitte.com/assets/Dcom-UnitedKingdom/Local%20Assets/Documents/UK_C_SharedServicesComesof Age.pdf

Deloitte (2007b). *Is your shared services organization struggling with unfinished business?* http://www.deloitte.com/assets/Dcom-CostaRica/Local%20Assets/Documents/Industrias/CSC/070331-%28en%29_Building_an_Effective_SSC.pdf

Deloitte (2007c). *Shared Services: The price is right – or is it?* http://www.deloitte.com/assets/Dcom-CostaRica/Local%20Assets/Documents/Industrias/CSC/071211-%28en%29_Shared_Services_Pricing.pdf

Gospel, H. and Sako, M. (2010) The unbundling of corporate functions: the evolution of shared services and outsourcing in human resource management, *Industrial and Corporate Change*, 1–30.

Hagel, J. and Singer, M. (1999) Unbundling the corporation, *McKinsey Quarterly*, pp. 147–156. Reprinted from *Harvard Business Review*, March-April, 1999.

Handy, C. (1989), *The Age of Unreason*, London: Random House.

Hayward, C. (2002) Out of Site, *Financial Management*, February, 26–27.

Helper, S. and Sako, M. (2010) Management innovation in supply chain: appreciating Chandler in the twenty-first century, *Industrial and Corporate Change,* 19(2): 399–429. doi:10.1093/icc/dtq012.

Herbert, I.P. and Seal, W.B. (2011) Shared Services as a new organisational form: some implications for management accounting, *British Accounting Review* (forthcoming).

Janssen, M. and Joha, A. (2006) Motives for establishing shared service centres in public administrations, *International Journal of Information Management*, 26, 102–115.

Korczynski, M. (2004) Back-Office Service Work: Bureaucracy challenged?, *Work, Employment and Society*, 18(1), 97–114.

Langfield-Smith, K. and Smith, D. (2003) Management control systems and trust in outsourcing relationships, *Management Accounting Research*, 14 (3), 281–307.

Leach, R. (2004) Integrate Expectations, *Financial Management*, March, CIMA, London.

Maatman, M., Bondarouk, T. and Looise, J.K. (2010) Conceptualising the capabilities and value creation of HRM shared service models, *Human Resource Management Review* (in press).

Marchington, M., Grimshaw, D., Rubery, J. and Willmott, H. (eds) (2005) *Fragmenting Work: Blurring Organizational Boundaries and Disordering Hierarchies.* Oxford: Oxford University Press.

Matusik, S. and Hill, C. (1998) The utilization of contingent work, knowledge creation, and competitive advantage, *Academy of Management Review*, 23, 680–687.

NHS Estates (2004) *The Matron's Charter: an action plan for cleaner hospitals.* October, 2004, Department of Health, London.

Oliveira, J. (2010) *Power and organisation change: a case study*, Unpublished Doctoral thesis, University of Dundee.

Peiperl, M. and Baruch, Y. (1997) Back to square zero: the post-corporate career? *Organisational Dynamics*, 25, 7–22.

Porter, M. (1985) *Competitive Advantage: Creating and Sustaining Superior Performance*. New York: Free Press.

Prahalad, C.K. and Hamel, G. (1990) The core competences of the corporation, *Harvard Business Review*, May–June, 79–91.

Quinn, B., Cooke, R. and Kris, A. (2000) *Shared Services: Mining for Corporate Gold*. Harlow: Pearson Educational.

Renner, C.J., and Tebbe, D. (1998) Who Is Outsourcing and Why? *Management Accounting*, July, 80, 1, Institute of Management Accountants.

Rittenberg, L. and Covaleski, M.A. (2001) Internalisation of the internal audit function: an examination of the professional and organisational imperatives, *Accounting, Organisations and Society*, 26 (7–8), 617–641.

Rothwell, A., Herbert, I. and Seal, W. (2011) Shared services and professional employability, *Journal of Vocational Behaviour* (forthcoming).

Sako, M. (2009) Globalization of knowledge – intensive professional services. *Communications of the ACM*, July, 52, 7.

Scapens, R.W. and Jazayeri, M., 2003. ERP systems and management accounting change: opportunities or impacts? A research note, *European Accounting Review*, 12 (1), 201–233.

Schulman, D., Dunleavy, J., Harmer, M. and Lusk, J. (1999) *Shared Services: Adding Value to the Business Units*. New York: John Wiley.

Seal, W., Cullen, J., Dunlop, A., Berry, A. and Ahmed, M. (1999) Enacting a European supply chain: a case study on the role of management accounting, *Management Accounting Research*, 10, 303–322.

Seddon, J. (2005) *Freedom from Command and Control*, 2nd edition. Buckingham: Vanguard Press.

Seddon, J. (2008) *Systems Thinking in the Public Sector*. Axminster: Triarchy Press.

Smith, J.A., Morris, J. and Ezzamel, M. (2005) Organisational change, outsourcing and the impact on management accounting, *British Accounting Review*, 37, 415–441.

Taylor, P. and Bain, P. (1999) 'An assembly line in the head: work and employee relations in a call centre', *Industrial Relations Journal*, 30, 101–117.

Teece, D. (2009) *Dynamic Capabilities and Strategic Management*. Oxford: Oxford University Press.

Ulbrich, F., 2006. Improving shared service implementation: adopting lessons from the BPR movement, *Business Process Management Journal*, 12 (2), 191–205.

Whittington, R. (2002) 'Corporate Structure: from policy to practice'. In *Handbook of Strategy and Management*, edited by Pettigrew, A., Thomas, H. and Whittington, R., 113–138. London: Sage.

Whittington, R. (2007) Strategy practice and strategy process: family differences and the sociological eye, *Organization Studies*, 28(10), 1575–1586.

Williamson, O.E. (1975) *Markets and Hierarchies: Analysis and Antitrust Implications*. New York: Macmillan Free Press.

Womack, J.P., Jones, D.T. and Roos, D. (1990) *The Machine that Changed the World*. New York: Rawson Associates.

Wright, C. (2008) Reinventing human resource management: business partners, internal consultants and the limits to professionalization, *Human Relations*, 6, 1063–1098

14

Inter-organizational cost management

Morten Jakobsen

Introduction

Cost management has traditionally had an intra-organizational focus and has thereby had the firm as the main unit of analysis. Entities beyond the firm were perceived as 'opponents' with whom they traded in a more or less competitive market. In Chapter 15 Lars Bråd Nielsen discusses the strategic importance of business affiliates. As firms focus on increasingly smaller parts of the value chain, the necessity of cooperating with other companies on activities throughout the value chain has increased (Hopwood, 1996). This does not imply an increase in the number of partners that the company engages with. Often more intense cooperation with business partners is followed by a decrease in the number of partners (viz. Dekker, 2003). It is the complexity of the product and the increased dependency of these fewer partners that create the need for more intense co-ordination along the value chain and thereby require a more focused exchange of information than normal market transactions allow. Thus the managerial challenges and the conditions for cost management will change under such circumstances (e.g. Chenhall, 2003, p. 139).

This chapter illuminates the managerial accounting aspects of inter-organizational relationships as they progress. In this sense, it discusses some aspects of managing inter-organizational relationships when the strategic decision to outsource certain activities has been made. Thereby its focus becomes the execution of the outsourcing decision, and it represents a location for the application of cost management ideas where the technical and the behavioural issues are strongly interrelated.

An inter-organizational relationship is cooperation between two companies, where the interaction between the two parties exceeds arms-length transactions (Oliver and Ebers, 1998). Hence the relationship is more than buying and selling standard components. It involves organizational aspects such as joint product development, adjustment of existing products, production facilities and logistics. Interaction, co-ordination and exchange of information happen between the two organizations, and it is within the organizations – or at the boundary between them – that control of such organizational constructs takes place.

Networks are a concept related to this type of inter-organizational relationship. They are relationships between a company and two or more other organizations that are part of the environment in which the company conducts business (Oliver and Ebers, 1998). Networks typically consist of suppliers, customers, competitors, public authorities, etc. (Gulatti et al., 2000). The network concept has roots in the sociological area labelled economic sociology (e.g. Guillén, Collins, England and Meyer, 2002). This stream of research is built on the assumption that the actions of the actors are correlated and dependent upon the actions of other parties in the network; hence, economic activity has to be understood within a social context (Biggert and Castanias, 2001). It thereby provides a framework for understanding the possibilities that are part of the business environment of a company (e.g. Granovetter, 1985; Uzzi, 1997; Galaskiewicz and Zaheer, 1999). In this sense, the network perspective contains potential for managing the supplier selection process. However, this is beyond the ambition of this chapter.

Inter-organizational relationships can be given different labels: supply chain, outsourcing, joint-venture or network (Meira, Kartalis, Tsamenyi and Cullen, 2009), supplier partnerships, subcontracting and outsourcing arrangements and strategic alliances (Caglio and Ditillo, 2008). This chapter intends to include the central contributions from relevant academic scholars who use different labels for the overall concept of inter-organizational relationships as defined in the chapter.

The next section of this chapter outlines and discusses relevant cost management techniques for inter-organizational control. In addition to the techniques there is also an aspect of social control involving the concepts of trust and power; these are the focus of the third section. Finally the chapter is summarized in a fourth section.

Management and accounting techniques for inter-organizational control

Several accounting techniques for supporting the control process of inter-organizational relationships have been identified (e.g. Håkansson, Kraus and Lind, 2010). Often a contract is used as the overall framework for managing the inter-organizational relationship. In addition to the contract different types of management accounting techniques are also put into action. In this chapter target costing and open-book accounting are discussed. These techniques are employed in order to shed light on the cost structure of the acquisition cost of the product or component under consideration. However, buying through an inter-organizational relation can also have some indirect cost implications concerning control, shipment, duty, etc. that also have to be taken into account when the total cost of outsourced products is evaluated and managed.

Contracts

Inter-organizational relationships are almost always accounted for by a written document labelled a contract. According to Macaulay (1963, p. 56) a contract serves the purpose of:

- *rational planning of the transaction with careful provision for as many future contingencies as can be foreseen;*
- *the existence or use of actual or potential legal sanctions to induce performance of the exchange or to compensate for non-performance.*

Some branches of the literature suggest that use of contracts between partners in inter-organizational relationships can be inefficient: firstly because they are static – and hence incompatible with the request for flexibility, which is central in an inter-organizational setting (e.g. Hedberg et al., 2000, p. 135); secondly because they signal mistrust (viz. Granovetter, 1985; Bradech and Eccles, 1989; Gulattti, 1995; Uzzi, 1997). Despite these suggestions, Alvarez et al.

(2003) found that 98 per cent of the strategic alliances included in their study use contracts as a governance device.

Roxenhall and Ghauri (2004) give three reasons for drawing up contracts. The first reason is that contracts are regarded as communication tools. The second is that contracts are used to reduce uncertainty. And finally they state that contracts symbolize the existence of the business deal. So several reasons for employment of contracts can be found and, therefore, the existence of contracts per se is not the interesting topic. The interesting issue is how the involved parties employ contracts.

Cuganesan (2007) finds that the contract serves the role of an institutional mechanism for the formulation of expectations in the pre-commitment phase of the relationship. The involved parties feel familiar with the contract as a control device, and use it as a kind of check-list in order to make sure the relevant topics are discussed and written into the contract.

Roxenhall and Ghauri (2004) include in their case studies one company – a software case. The product delivered by the software company contains both intangible and tangible parts. A large number of people are involved during the negotiations, especially in what are labelled the verification phase, i.e. the phase where the discussions are further centred on technical issues. Roxenhall and Ghauri (2004) find that the contract is used to co-ordinate actions, direct attention to specific issues, exercise power, delegate responsibility and tasks and transmit knowledge. Thus, the contract is made primarily to serve as a means of communication.

It is difficult to give general guidelines for the content of a contract. However, usually it has at least four parts. An introduction outlines the general terms and goals of the business deal. It contains a section covering specification of the product. Then it has a section that concerns the price of the product. Finally, most contracts have a section covering terms of trade, how and when to pay and deliver, possible sanctions, place for legal judgments in case of insolvable disagreements, etc.

Jakobsen (2010) found that the contract served as a representation of the project at the centre of an inter-organizational relationship. The contract was the written account of all the details of the project. It initially functioned as the agenda for the negotiations, where the headlines to be discussed were technical specifications, price and terms of trade. In that way, the contract defined what topics to centre negotiations on. During negotiations people representing production, logistics and purchasing from both organizations participated in order to make the ends meet.

Though the contract may not seem to be a cost management instrument, the contract sets the framework for discussing aspects of the project or product in focus of cooperation. The contract facilitates the integration of the technical, logistical and economic aspects of the inter-organizational relationship. Hence cost management within inter-organizational relationships involves both actual cost awareness and accounts of costs written into the contract.

Target costing

Keeping the focus on costs within inter-organizational relationships can be done within the framework of target costing (viz. Cooper and Slagmulder, 1999). Target costing has its roots in the Japanese costing tradition (viz. Kato, 1993). It is often presented as a method to reach a certain sum of allowable costs derived from a market price minus a planned profit. However, target costing is more than that. It involves collaborative actions based on common and consensual decisions on how to reach the allowable costs (Bardy, 2006). This means that it is not sufficient to change cost allocation methods, reduce the quality level or squeeze the profit margin of a weak supplier, since these approaches will not bring sustainable cost reductions. Effective target costing requires substantial changes in choice of material, production methods, and logistical set-up. Consequently, negotiations that lead to the identification of allowable costs require inputs from many involved people who have to share their ideas. Allowable costs are hence a consequence of deliberate changes in the product and the activities that are involved in its production.

In an inter-organizational relationship target costing is challenged by the reduced access to cost data. A buying company that procures components from a supplier is not able to get direct insight into the costs and the factors that drive costs at this supplier. Such insight requires some kind of accounting that can serve as the foundation for further analysis. This type of accounting is labelled 'open-book' and will be discussed in the following subsection. However, if such accounting information is not shared among the parties, there is a risk that negotiations end up in price bargaining, and not as a dialogue concerning the substantial changes in activities that are central to the target costing principle.

Open books between companies in an inter-organizational relationship

Within inter-organizational relationships an account of the price of the product exchanged, in some instances, serves as the foundation for the negotiations in relation to target costing across organizational boundaries. This type of accounting is referred to as the open book. The open book contains different cost items, depending on the product that is under negotiation and the purpose of applying the open book as a cost management technique. Cooper and Slagmulder (1999, p. 106) find that many of the companies that they investigated employed open-book accounting in different ways, ranging from companies with full open-book policies, others partially open, some with one directional open book from supplier to buyer, and others with bidirectional sharing of cost information. Based on a case study within the automotive industry, Agndal and Nielsen (2008) find 17 examples of decision-making processes that are supported by open books. The 17 processes were found at different stages of the product life cycle. However they conclude that the formal uses of open books were especially important during pre-production stages where the details concerning the product and cooperation are being negotiated, so there is a coupling to the ideas contained in the target costing concept.

Common practice is that the supplying partner constructs a more or less detailed cost specification of the price of the product, and this is where the book becomes open. For a product development project an open book could be specified as in Table 14.1. This table is an example constructed in order to illustrate how the spending of relevant resources for a product development project can be represented in a cost account. In product development, human resources are the most important, and hence these are given the most attention. The use of

Table 14.1 A simple example to illustrate an open book concerning a product development project

Ressource	*Number of units*	*Unit cost per hour*	*Total cost €*
Senior engineer	55 Hours	200 €	11.000
Technical assistant	120 Hours	80 €	9.600
Administrative staff	30 Hours	60 €	1.800
Technical equipment	50 Hours	300 €	15.000
Material			2.200
General overhead			5.000
Contingencies (20 per cent of costs)			8.920
Profit			7.000
Price of product development project			60.520

different types of personnel and their corresponding hourly rates can be spelled out. Another possibility is that the specified usage of different types of machinery and their cost driver rates would be part of the open book. At this point cost information may not be that detailed – only represented as a fixed rate allocated to the specific contract or project. If the task is to produce a given product, the open-book account includes material used, probably specified according to the bill-of-material (BOM) and its corresponding unit prices in order to emphasize the importance of these aspects in that kind of project.

The open book, in its specified form, is a concrete starting point for negotiating the terms of the cooperation. This covers not only the price, but also the content of the product or service that is intended to be delivered. The open book discloses the invoice price, and creates a guide to the resources that are going to be used to produce the product or service. This creates a qualified foundation for constructive negotiations that can actually lead to substantial cost savings and improvements of the products, compared to a situation where the parties simply bargain over the price. With reference to the example in Table 14.1, questions from the buyer to the seller can easily be raised. For instance, why is the hourly rate for the senior engineer €200? Can some of his/her assignments be handled by the technical assistant? Can the administrative staff process some of the documentation and save time for the technical assistant? These types of questions have a cost focus, but they certainly also involve the product and its characteristics. Consequently negotiations initiated by costs become quality-functionality-price (QFP) trade-offs where the end result is somewhere between these three aspects of the product (viz. Agndal and Nilsson, 2009).

Cooper and Slagmulder (1999) illustrate the negotiation between the buyer and the supplier with a target costing triangle. In this triangle, functionality and allowable costs are managed through value analysis, including a qualified assessment of the value of each component and the function of the product – seen from the end customer's perspective. During this assessment process cost management is often supported by cost tables that give the product designers an estimate of the costs initiated by a certain design and technical solution.

Mouritsen et al. (2001) investigated open-book accounting in a company and found that it succeeds in bridging the focal company and its suppliers and thereby creates a mechanism for communication. It thus enables control from a distance. In addition to these inter-organizational changes, they also found that employing open-book accounting gave new insight into the internal processes of the competitiveness of the company. Achieving such a symbiotic effect normally requires both the supplier and the buyer to open their books. If they do not, then it is only the buyer who is able to raise questions during the negotiation process, indicating a disproportionate balance of power among the parties (Seal, Cullen, Dunlop, Berry and Ahmed, 1999).

Suomala, Lahikainen, Lyly-Yrjänäinen and Paranko (2010) have also documented how companies in practice apply open-book accounting and how the negotiations have impacted on the internal activities of the partners that are involved in the inter-organizational relationships. However, they also found that although the companies involved in their cases are dependent on each other, there is a lack of validity in the numbers they bring into the negotiations via the open book. The numbers were mainly based on speculation – they lacked hard evidence and the specific actions needed to meet the goals.

Jakobsen (2010) found that open-book practice, to a large extent, is able to define the playing field for the buyer-seller relationship. However, he also observed that the suppliers have strong incentives to inflate the cost information that they provide to the open book. Obviously, the suppliers have an interest in selling the products at as high a price as possible, and under such conditions it is naïve to believe that blindly sharing information has no consequences. Information obtained from suppliers is fragile, and it must be evaluated carefully during the negotiations. Such evaluation can take several forms including, for instance, one's own cost information from similar products, and knowledge from other inter-organizational relationships and industry data. Carr and Ng (1995) showed how Nissan provided their suppliers with cost information concerning second-tier suppliers in order to help Nissan's suppliers evaluate the costs for their suppliers. The data sources used for benchmarking suppliers can seldom provide sufficient foundation for evaluating a specific relationship. Therefore several aspects of the supplier have to be combined in order to construct a patchwork of information that can be used to evaluate the cost level of the present product or service.

Other studies on inter-organizational relationships (e.g. Håkansson og Lind, 2004; Kajüter and Kulmala, 2005) also documented that information did not float frictionless among the parties engaged in these relationships. Donada and Nogatchewsky (2006) found that in the case of a buying company that has limited bargaining power over their suppliers, co-ordination was primarily achieved via social control. The formalized exchange of information was only found where there was solid bargaining power in the buying company, a result congruent with, e.g., Frances and Garnsey (1996). Abbeelea, Roodhoofta and Warlop (2009) found, in an experimental context, that buyers with refined cost information were unable to benefit from this information because the suppliers tended to become reluctant in sharing information that could have contributed to a better product.

Though the open-book technique has the potential to highlight avenues for improving the product in focus – to the benefit of both parties – it can be difficult to provide the information that will form the foundation for the negotiations. The reason is that though the two parties in an inter-organizational relationship share interests in the product or project in focus, they have diverging interests. One of the parties may consider the profit distribution to be unfair – meaning that the price is either too high or too low. They may also be afraid that the information they share will be used against them in the future. No matter what, information cannot be expected to be shared in a frictionless way. The process of open-book accounting hence requires an ability to force through the sharing of information, and the ability to build a trusting atmosphere.

Inter-organizational relationships and social control

As discussed in the previous section, inter-organizational cost management often takes its starting point in modifying and utilizing existing process-oriented management accounting models in a way that fits the inter-organizational context (Tomkins, 2001). The fundamental difference is that cost data and information now has to be shared with parties outside the company. This creates the risk of misuse. Sharing information across organizational boundaries is not a technical problem; it is more a mental challenge. This section seeks to discuss these mental barriers. The discussions will focus on trust and power as means to deal with uncertainty concerning sharing information in an inter-organizational context.

Trust and exchange of managerial information within networks

Often a company will be reticent about the information they wish to share with the other company in an inter-organizational relationship, since it might be abused to the disadvantage of the company's interests (viz. Venkatesen, 1992; Welch and Ranganathan, 1992). On the other hand, sharing information is essential in order to co-ordinate activities, and thereby utilize the potential advantages of the inter-organizational relationship (e.g. Zaheer et al., 1998). Engaging in an inter-organizational relationship often depends on whether you trust the person in the other organization or not. This section deals with the concept of trust. A definition and an understanding of the concept will be provided and a discussion of trust and managing inter-organizational relationships will be presented.

Understanding the concept of trust

Though trust as a psychological phenomenon can be recognized by most people, there is not a general definition across academic disciplines. In an attempt to gather disciplines around this common phenomenon Rousseau et al. (1998, p. 395) define trust as: '. . . a psychological state comprising the intention to accept vulnerability based upon positive expectations of the intentions or behaviour of others'. This definition emphasizes that trust is an inter-personal affair but, as discussed by Tomkins (2001), trust can be applied in an inter-organizational setting too. Sako (1992) provides a framework for studying trust in an inter-organizational setting. In her framework trust is divided into three types: contractual, competence, and goodwill trust. Contractual trust refers to the ability to keep promises – either written or oral. Competence trust refers to the technical or managerial skills of the trusted person. And finally, goodwill trust refers to the open commitment between the parties and a willingness to do more than the other party expects. This typology highlights different aspects of trust and provides a more nuanced view of trust between parties in inter-organizational relationships (viz. Langfield-Smith and Smith, 2003).

Mayer et al. (1995) note that trust is often mixed up with similar concepts, such as cooperation, confidence and predictability. Even though trust often makes cooperation more efficient, it is not a necessary assumption for cooperation. It is possible to cooperate with someone you do not trust. All it takes is an ability to control the actions of this party, and to impose suitable sanctions if the agreement is not fulfilled. Trust may also be mixed up with confidence. If alternatives in relation to a specific partner are not considered, then you have confidence in this person. If, on the other hand, you actively choose a specific partner on the basis of specific criteria, then you have trust in this person. Hence trust is based on considerations, weighing, and choice of partner. Confidence is a blind action (see also Luhmann, 2000, p. 28). Finally, trust has to be more than the predictability of a person. A person who is one hundred per cent predictable does not contain any element of uncertainty. Therefore it is not necessary to have trust in a person if you can predict the future actions of this person with certainty. Consequently, trust is rooted in the fact that people are not one hundred per cent predictable; it is built on the foundation of experiences which tell you that you can rely on a person's intentions, and on that basis you can get involved with this person.

The relationship between information and trust

In the literature there seems to be a general agreement that the relevance of trust becomes of increased importance in an inter-organizational setting (e.g. Hedberg et al., 2000, p. 19). In absolute terms the importance grows due to an increase in the amount of uncertainty originating from a more complex business environment. In relative terms the increased uncertainty stems from no longer having direct influence on activities due to the strategic decision of outsourcing peripheral activities. Traditionally trust has been considered either as a substitute or as a complement to formal control mechanisms (Dekker, 2004).

A substitute relationship between information and trust means that managers can employ either trust or control (which is based on information) when they manage a given relationship (e.g. Das and Teng, 1998; Wicks, Berman and Jones, 1999). In line with theorists such as Lewis and Weigert (1985) and Luhman (2000), trust is associated with risk and is related to aspects of social life that you choose not to seek to control due to a 'calculated' belief that others will not act against your well-being. A manager facing the challenges of managing an inter-organizational relationship therefore has to choose between trusting the other party and seeking control based on information. The choice between trust and control are claimed to have consequences for the relationship between the parties. Contracts and formal cost management instruments – for example open-book accounting – are claimed to reduce trust within an inter-organizational relation (e.g. Seal and Vincent-Jones, 1997). If we accept the idea that trust is central for a fruitful relationship, insisting on getting access to the other parties' cost information will limit the efficiency of the inter-organizational relationship. Based on a number of case studies, Hedberg et al. (2000, p. 145) found that management of inter-organizational relationships based on the formal exchange of information is uncommon. Their studies revealed a certain amount of aversion to formal management of inter-organizational relationships. Within several of the relationships studied, cooperation was based on trust and a belief in the advantage of cooperation (Hedberg et al., 2000, p. 161). The rationale behind this approach is that the formulation of formal contracts and follow-up on these is difficult, due to both the problems of describing such a contract in detail, and the signal of mistrust implied. From their analysis of their empirical observations, Hedberg et al. (2000) stated that formal management of inter-organizational activities is a subject that could lead to more rewarding relationships. They suggested that management control can be carried out in two dimensions, i.e. the exchange of information and the evaluation of partners. The dialogue between the interacting parties appeared to be an important management instrument regarding the exchange of relevant information. The exchange of information can be made in the form of a number of indicators about the parties involved. It can be about customers, business associates, products – but information concerning cost structures is also relevant. In order to manage the indicators included and their interrelationship, a formalized management system could be developed to advantage. To a wide extent exchange of information concerns sharing knowledge of what you expect of the other party (often at an operational level). Correspondingly, evaluation involves strategic considerations about the individual partner. Evaluation of the relationship has to be made in order to determine whether the relations create value for both parties. It is essential to know whether the value is based on value added to the product in focus, or whether it is caused by access to new markets – potential business opportunities. It thereby becomes relevant to evaluate more aspects of the relationship than the price of the product in focus. Ittner et al. (1999) studied the performance level of two kinds of sub-supplier relationships: arm's-length (market transactions) versus close co-ordinative inter-organizational relationships. They specifically investigated different approaches regarding choice of sub-suppliers, exchange of information, evaluation of relationships, etc. They found that increased use of systematic evaluation processes had a positive effect on the performance of companies using close co-ordinative relationships, compared to companies primarily relying on arms-length transactions. Geitzman (1996) states that innovation and flexibility are most efficiently created in an environment based on non-contractual relations. Such relations require a certain level of knowledge of each other, and thus relations of a certain maturity. He states that the price of the product is not sufficient information to decide on relationships. To focus mainly on the price will even hinder efficient relationships.

Though it may be complicated and sensitive to share information within an inter-organizational relationship, companies who actively participate in networks must accept that management control is a necessary – but not sufficient – condition for success. However, new approaches have to be employed when performing management control. Managing inter-organizational relationships must be rooted in a dialogue between the parties involved about the content of the information that is to be exchanged. Likewise, an agreement about the conditions under which the exchange should take place has to be made.

A complementary relationship is the other extreme perception of the relationship between trust and control. This approach is based on the idea that as an inter-organizational relationship fosters trust, and information develops together (Reed, 2001). The foundation of this is that, before you begin to reveal important aspects of yourself, you must have a basic level of trust in the person you engage with. What happens is that when you show trust in a person, they will be more willing to share information with you and, in that way, show that they have trust in you. In that way the relationship turns into a positive spiral where both trust and the level of information exchanged will increase. Using a survey, Poppo and Zenger (2002) tested the relationship between trust and control, and they found support for a complementary relationship. Emsley and Kidon (2007) used the framework of trust by Sako (1992) in order to investigate the relationship between different types of trust and different types of information. Their case study indicated that competence trust and information related to the partner's qualifications had a complementary relationship, whereas goodwill trust and sharing of information did not show a clear picture. Their results supplement the ideas proposed by Tomkins (2001). He advocates that the relationship between trust and the requirement for information depends on the maturity of the relationship. Initially, the relationship is characterized by definite transactions carried out in accordance with the arms-length principle. If the relationship is maintained and there is a need for closer co-ordination the complexity, and thereby uncertainty, of the relationship increases. To absorb this uncertainty, the partners exchange relevant information. Simultaneously, trust is built up through successive interactions. As the relationship develops, the significance of the interaction becomes more important and the need for information increases. At the same time, the level of trust increases as people's knowledge of each other increases. That is, in the introductory phase of the relationship, both the level of information exchanged and the level of trust increase. At some point, the relationship has existed long enough and worked well enough, and the parties have built up a common understanding of each other. At that time the need for information in order to manage the cooperation declines, whereas the level of trust continues to increase.

The relationship between trust and control is ambiguous and is probably never either a substitute or a complementary relationship. Practitioners who must find their way through an inter-organizational relationship therefore have to be aware of the delicate balance between trust and control, and probably have to learn to trust their intuition of what is right in any given situation.

The weakness of trust

An important aspect of managing the inter-organizational relationship of a company is to maintain a dynamic environment of potential partners, and thereby keep up the strategic opportunities for development. However, maintaining the dynamics of inter-organizational relationships built on trust seems to be one of the more difficult challenges. There is a risk that the relationship becomes over-embedded (Uzzi, 1997). Over-embeddedness arises when the companies within an inter-organizational relationship becomes excessively interrelated. They construct a common perception of the business environment and – due to limited contact with companies outside the relationship – new information does not gain a footing inside the inter-organizational relationship. Hence, the companies slowly lose touch with the surrounding world. At the same time, feelings of obligation and friendship build up among the inter-organizational relationship members, making it even harder to open the inter-organizational relationship to new members and revised perceptions of the business environment. This paradox reduces the potential advantages of the inter-organizational relationship. People choose to cooperate with partners who they have worked with before, and with whom they have built up a relationship of trust. Renewal and flexibility are not utilized, and the companies end up forming closed relationships consisting of the same companies (Gulati and Gargiulo, 1999). An inter-organizational relationship that should have been characterized by dynamism and adaptability becomes static, and the advantages disappear. Maravealis (2001, p. 48) also discusses this problem. He proposes that it is the intensive interaction of the inter-organizational relationship that binds the members together. In this way the inter-organizational relationship becomes institutionalized and a state of inertia develops, causing the flexibility of the inter-organizational relationship to be lost over time. Ahuja (2000) finds that a well-established inter-organizational relationship enables trust, but at the cost of reduced input of new ideas – causing the relationship to become static. This condition may by appropriate in some situations, but for companies who entered inter-organizational relationships to achieve flexibility the paradox is likely to cause complications. Trust is a key parameter to understanding over-embeddedness. Inter-organizational relationship participants living in this steady state of flux will seek a solid foundation on which to build the business. Unfortunately, such a foundation is not directly available, and to compensate for this the members cling to partners with whom they have had positive experiences in order to reduce uncertainty. The trustworthy partners in a close inter-organizational relationship become landmarks that managers take account of – but they do so at the expense of flexibility. So, relying on trust as an uncertainty-absorbing mechanism requires stability, yet stability may not be present in an inter-organizational setting.

Another critique of trust as an uncertainty-absorbing mechanism is raised by Free (2008) in his case study of supply-chain accounting and trust among UK supermarkets and their suppliers. He finds that, on the surface, the relationship between the parties seems to be based on trust and trustworthiness, but in fact the trust rhetoric actually conceals domination, lack of alternatives and mutual dependency. Re-reading texts like Carr and Ng (1995) and Cooper and Slagmulder (2004) that explicitly use the concept trust through a set of power lenses actually supports the ideas raised by Free (2008).

Power as an alternative means of absorbing uncertainty

Though trust plays a role within inter-organizational relationships their existence does not necessarily imply trust – power can also have a bearing (Kumar, 2005; Free, 2008). Bachmann (2001) argues that in an inter-organizational context, power can be applied as a mechanism for reducing uncertainty; in that sense, power becomes an alternative to trust. Within his framework, power is related to the potential negative (re-)actions of the other party (Bachmann, 2001). These actions are not due to destructive intentions but are a natural consequence of two organizations pursuing different individual objectives (Hingley, 2005). Under such premises, actions that will bring one of the parties closer to its goals are often likely to be disadvantageous for the other party. Employing power as a strategy for managing inter-organizational relationships hence becomes a matter of defining desirable actions and mobilizing possible sanctions in case of detrimental actions. In these processes management accounting technologies can have significant impact (Jakobsen, 2010).

Power entails at least two advantages for managing inter-organizational relationships compared to trust. First, since trust requires that the parties interact and sound each other out in order to build sufficient trust, this strategy will not in all circumstances allow the potential of inter-organizational relationships to flourish, as the benefits of inter-organizational arrangements lie in their ability to create access to various resources (viz. Gulatti, 1995; Sabel et al., 1987; Castells, 2000; Burt, 1997). Assuming that strategies change faster than the ability of a firm to develop (Mouritsen and Thrane, 2006, p. 244), fast access to capabilities that can comply with these transitory strategies is crucial. It is under such circumstances that trust becomes problematic. Second, when you trust others, you invest a part of yourself in the relationship (Bachmann, 2001). This means that the field of interests, on a social level, evolve and converge. Accordingly, the boundaries between the parties erode as the relationship and trust develop. This is a highly desirable characteristic in many other social arrangements, for instance friendships and marriages, but in a business context – where the ability to access different external resources in different situations is essential – this characteristic is problematic. When you have invested in the relationship it becomes difficult to end it: you are likely to stay in the relationship even when it is no longer beneficial (viz. Uzzi, 1997; Gulati and Gargiulo, 1999; Maravealis, 2001; Ahuja, 2000). Power is different. Power requires no personal investment in the relationship, and hence it is possible to stop it without emotional cost when the commercial basis for cooperation is no longer present.

Traditionally, power has been defined as the ability to dominate, and power in that sense has been exemplified as A exercising power over B when A forces B to do things that are against B's interests (viz. Lukes, 2005). Some research within cost management and inter-organizational relationships shows that co-ordination and exchange of information seems most effective in settings with one dominating partner. For instance Frances and Garnsey (1996) show how UK supermarkets successfully controlled their supply chain by dominating their suppliers into delivering the proper information for optimizing the supply chain; a practice that was also found by Free (2008) in a later study also into the UK supermarket industry. Likewise Kajüter and Kulmala (2005), in the example of the automotive industry, showed that open-book accounting was carried out by dominating the auto-maker. As an alternative, they showed a Finnish inter-organizational relationship that did not have a dominating partner: in this situation open-book accounting did not seem to work. Consequently in settings where power cannot be exercised via domination, other perceptions and understandings of power are required.

In a setting characterized by individual companies that each seek to promote their own interests inspiration can be found in the concept of governmentality, where power is defined as *'actions on other's actions'* (Gordon, 1991, p. 5). Power is not meant in the sense of violence or of a ruler who has absolute domination over the subject (Foucault, 1982). Neither can power be possessed. It is exercised in the relation between free forces (Deleuze, 1999). Power is a mobilization of the free will, initiatives and resources of the subjects, but within the discursive frame of reference of what is true and what is not true (Dean, 1999). Freedom of the governed is a central element both because it requires the handling of the many possible actions of the governed and because it also contains possibilities for the future (Foucault, 1982). Thereby, actions taken in order to impose control are a matter of fencing in the possible actions of the other party that one intends to govern, and so structure the possibilities of others (Foucault, 1982). The intentions of governing become visible via the techniques applied for governing (Dean, 1999). The techniques, the inherent rationales and practices are what provoke certain actions.

In an inter-organizational relationship the contract and the request for open books are examples of how the buying company can impose a certain rationale among suppliers. The extent to which the buying company is able to make the supplier accept their rationale, the more powerful they are. Most often the supplier strikes back in one way or another; for instance, by bringing invalid information or by raising new proposals for the design or production of a product. Such input from the supplier challenges the position of the buying company but it also brings new ideas and possibilities into the relationship. Hence, the benefit from understanding the management of inter-organizational relationships through the concept of governmentality lies in its ability to create an awareness of the impact from certain management techniques on the possibilities of developing the relationship and the outcome thereof.

Concluding remarks

Inter-organizational cost management is both a mental challenge and a technical problem. The practice of inter-organizational cost management involves accounting techniques that are often well known at an intra-organizational level. However, in order to co-ordinate and manage relations, information has to travel across organizational boundaries – the practice we call open-book accounting. Open-book accounting takes several forms, ranging from full access to all cost information among the involved parties to nearly closed books that are only reluctantly opened. It has been discussed that opening the closed book can be done through building up trust among the parties until a certain level of trust is reached and exchange of information and control becomes a possibility. Power can be used as an alternative to trust in order to control the relationship. Finally, trust can function as a substitute for the exercise of control and the exchange of information. However, this alternative does not leave much room for inter-organizational cost management across organizational boundaries.

Bibliography

Abbeelea, A., Roodhoofta, F. and Warlop, L. 2009. The effect of cost information on buyer–supplier negotiations in different power settings. *Accounting, Organizations and Society*, **34**, 245–266.

Agndal, H. and Nilsson, U. 2008. Supply chain decision-making supported by an open books policy. *International Journal of Production Economics*, **116**, 154–167.

Agndal, H. and Nilsson, U. 2009. Interorganizational cost management in the exchange process. *Management Accounting Research*, **20**, 85–101.

Ahuja, G., 2000. Collaboration networks, structural holes, and innovation: a longitudinal study. *Administrative Science Quarterly*, **45**, 425–455.

Alvarez, S. A., Barney, J. B. and Bosse, D. A. 2003. Trust and its alternatives. *Human Resource Management*, **42**, 4, 393–404.

Bachmann, R. 2001. Trust, power and control in trans-organizational relations. *Organization Studies*, **22**, 2, 337–365.

Bardy, R. 2006. Management control in a business network: new challenges for accounting. *Qualitative Research in Accounting and Management*, **3**, 161–181.

Biggert, N. W. and Castanias, R. P. 2001. Collateralized social relations: the social in economic calculation. *American Journal of Economics and Sociology*, **60**, 2, 471–500.

Bradech, J. L. and Eccles, R. G. 1989. Price, authority, and trust: from ideal types to plural forms. *Annual Review of Sociology*, **15**, 97–118.

Burt, R. S. 1997. The contingent value of social capital. *Administrative Science Quarterly*, **42**, 339–365.

Caglio, A. and Ditillo, A. 2008. A review and discussion of management control in inter-firm relationships: achievements and future directions. *Accounting, Organizations and Society*, **33**, 865–898.

Carr, C. and Ng, J. 1995. Total cost control: Nissan and its UK supplier partners. *Management Accounting Research*, **6**, 347–365.

Castells, M. 2000. *The Rise of the Network Society*, 2nd edition. Blackwell Publishing, UK.

Chenhall, R. H. 2003. Management Control systems design within its organizational context: findings from contingency-based research and directions for the future. *Accounting, Organizations, and Society*, **28**, 127–168.

Cooper, R. and Slagmulder, R. 1999. *Supply Chain Development for the Lean Enterprise: Interorganizational Cost Management*. Portland, OR, Productivity Press.

Cooper, R. and Slagmulder, R. 2004. Interorganizational cost management and relational context. *Accounting, Organizations and Society*, **29**, 1–26.

Cuganesan, S. 2007. Accounting, contracts and trust in supply relationships. *Journal of Accounting and Organizational Change*, **3**, 104–125.

Das, T. K. and Teng, B. 1998. Between trust and control: developing confidence in partner cooperation in Alliances. *Academy of Management Review*, **23**, 491–512.

Dean, M. 1999. *Governmentality: Power and Rule in Modern Society*. Sage Publications, London.

Dekker, H. C. 2003. Value chain analysis in interfirm relationships: a field study. *Management Accounting Research*, **14**, 1–23.

Dekker, H. C. 2004. Control of inter-organizational relationships: evidence on appropriation concerns and coordination requirements. *Accounting, Organizations, and Society*, **29**, 27–49.

Deleuze, G. 1999. *Foucault*. The Athlone Press, London.

Donada, C. and Nogatchewsky, G. 2006. Vassal or lord buyers: how to exert management control in asymmetric interfirm transactional relationships? *Management Accounting Research*, **17**, 259–287.

Emsley, D. and Kidon, F. 2007. The relationship between trust and control in international joint ventures: evidence from the airline industry. *Contemporary Accounting Research*, **24**, 829–858.

Foucault, M. 1982. The subject and power. *Critical Inquiry*, **8**, 4, 777–795.

Frances, J. and Garnsey, E. 1996. Supermarkets and suppliers in the United Kingdom: system integration, information and control. *Accounting, Organizations, and Society*, **21**, 591–610.

Free, C. 2008. Walking the talk? Supply chain accounting and trust among UK supermarkets and suppliers. *Accounting, Organizations and Society*, **33**, 629–662.

Galaskiewicz, J. and Zaheer, A. 1999. 'Networks of competitive advantage', in *Research in the Sociology of Organizations*, ed. Andrews, S. B. and Knoke, D. Greenwich, CT: JAI Press, 16, 237–261.

Gietzmann, M. B. 1996. Incomplete contracts and the make-or-buy decision: governance design and attainable flexibility. *Accounting, Organizations, and Society*, **21**, 6, 611–626.

Gordon, C. 1991. 'Governmental rationality: an introduction', in Burchell, G., Gordon, C. and Miller, P., *The Foucault Effect – Studies in Governmentality*. The University of Chicago Press, Chicago.

Granovetter, M. 1985. Economic action and social structure. *American Journal of Sociology*, **91**, 3, 481–510.

Gulati, R. 1995. Does familiarity breed trust? The implications of repeated ties for contractual choice in alliances. *Academy of Management Journal*, **38**, 1, 85–112.

Gulati, R. and Gargiulo, M. 1999. Where do interorganizational networks come from? *American Journal of Sociology*, **104**, 1439–1493.

Gulati, R., Nohria, N. and Zaheer, A. 2000. Strategic networks. *Strategic Management Journal*, **21**, 3, 203–215.

Guillén, M., Collins, R., England, P. and Meyer, M. 2002. 'The revival of economic sociology', in Guillén, M., Collins, R. and England, P. (eds), *The New Economic Sociology: Developments in an Emerging Field*. Russell Sage Foundation, New York.

Håkansson, H. and Lind, J. 2004, Accounting and network coordination. *Accounting, Organizations and Society*, **29**, 51–72.

Håkansson, H., Kraus, K. and Lind, J. 2010. 'Accounting in networks as a new research field', in *Accounting in Networks*, edited by Håkansson, H., Kraus, K. and Lind, J. Routledge, UK.

Hedberg, B., Dahlgren, G., Hansson, J. and Olve, N. 2000. *Virtual Organizations and Beyond: Discovering Imaginary Systems*. Chichester, Wiley.

Hingley, M. K. 2005. Power to all our friends? Living with imbalance in supplier–retailer relationships. *Industrial Marketing Management*, **34**, 848–858.

Hopwood, A. G. 1996. Looking across rather than up and down: on the need to explore the lateral processing of information. *Accounting, Organizations, and Society*, **21**, 6, 589–590.

Ittner, C. D., Larcker, D. F., Nagar, V. and Rajan, M. V. 1999. Supplier selection, monitoring practices, and firm performance. *Journal of Accounting and Public Policy*, **18**, 3, 253–281.

Jakobsen, M. 2010. Management accounting as the inter-organizational boundary. *Journal of Accounting and Organizational Change*, **6**, 96–122.

Kajüter, P. and Kulmala, H. I. 2005. Open-book accounting in networks potential achievements and reasons for failures. *Management Accounting Research*, **16**, 2, 179–204.

Kato, Y. 1993. Target costing support systems: lessons from leading Japanese companies. *Management Accounting Research*, **4**, 33–47.

Kumar, N. 2005. The power of power in supplier–retailer relationships, *Industrial Marketing Management*, **34**, 863–866.

Langfield-Smith, K. and Smith, D. 2003. Management control systems and trust in outsourcing relationships. *Management Accounting Research*, **14**, 281–307.

Lewis, J. D. and Weigert, A. 1985. Trust as social reality. *Social Forces*, **63**, 967–985.

Luhmann, N. 2000. *Vertrauen – Ein Mechanismus der Reduktion Sozialer Komplexität*, 4th reprint, Stuttgart, Lucius and Lucius.

Lukes, S., 2005. *Power: A Radical View,* second edition. Palgrave Macmillan, Hampshire.

Macaulay, S. 1963. Non-contractual relations in business: a preliminary study. *American Sociological Review,* **28**, 1, 55–67.

Maravelias, C. 2001. Managing Network Organizations, Doctorial dissertation, Stockholm, School of Business, Stockholm University.

Mayer, R. C., Davis, J. H. and Schoorman, F. D. 1995. An integrative model of organizational trust. *Academy of Management Review,* **20**, 3, 709–734.

Meira, J., Kartalis, N. D., Tsamenyi, M. and Cullen, J. 2009. Management controls and inter-firm relationships: a review. *Journal of Accounting and Organizational Change,* **6**, 149–169.

Mouritsen, J., Hansen, A. and Hansen, C. 2001. Inter-organizational controls and organizational competencies. *Management Accounting Research,* **12**, 221–244.

Mouritsen, J. and Thrane, S. 2006. Accounting, network complementarities and the development of inter-organizational relations. *Accounting, Organizations and Society,* **31**, 241–275.

Oliver, A. L. and Ebers, M. 1998. Networking network studies: an analysis of conceptual configurations in the study of inter-organizational relationships. *Organization Studies,* **19**, 4, 549–583.

Poppo, L. and Zenger, T. 2002. Do formal contracts and relational governance function as substitutes or complements? *Strategic Management Journal,* **23**, 707–725.

Reed, I. 2001. Organization, trust and control: a realist analysis. *Organization Studies,* **22**, 201–228.

Rousseau, D., Sitkin, S. B., Burt, R. S. and Camerer, C. 1998. Not so different after all: a cross-discipline view of trust. *Academy of Management Review,* **23**, 3, 393–404.

Roxenhall, T. and Ghauri, P. 2004. Use of the written contract in long-lasting relationships. *Industrial Marketing Management,* **33**, 261–268.

Sabel, C. F., Herrigel, G., Kazis, R. and Deeg, D. 1987. How to keep mature industries innovative. *Technology Review,* **90**, 3, 26–35.

Sako, M., 1992. *Prices, Quality and Trust: Inter-Firm Relations in Britain and Japan.* UK: Cambridge University Press.

Seal, W. and Vincent-Jones, P. 1997. Accounting and trust in the enabling of long-term relations. *Accounting, Auditing and Accountability Journal,* **10**, 406–431.

Seal, W., Cullen, J., Dunlop, A., Berry, T. and Ahmed, M. 1999. Enacting a European supply chain: a case study on the role of management accounting. *Management Accounting Research,* **10**, 3, 303–322.

Suomala, P., Lahikainen, T., Yrjänäinen, J. L. and Paranko, J. 2010. Open book in practice – exploring the faces of openness. *Qualitative Research in Accounting and Management,* **7**, 71–96.

Tomkins, C. 2001. Interdependencies, trust and information in relationships, alliances and networks. *Accounting, Organizations, and Society,* **26**, 2, 161–191.

Uzzi, B. 1996. The sources and consequences of embeddedness for the economic performance of organizations: the network effect. *American Sociological Review,* **61**, 674–698.

Uzzi, B. 1997. Social structures and competition in interfirm networks: the paradox of embeddedness. *Administrative Science Quarterly,* **42**, 35–67.

Venkatesen, R. 1992. Strategic outsourcing: to make or not to make. *Harvard Business Review,* **70** (November–December), 98–107.

Wicks, A., Berman, S. L. and Jones, T. M. 1999. The structure of optimal trust: moral and strategic implications. *The Academy of Management Review,* **24**, 1, 99–116.

Zaheer, A., McEvily, B. and Perrone, V. 1998. Does trust matter? Exploring the effects of interorganizational and interpersonal trust on performance. *Organization Science,* **9**, 9, 141–159.

15

New directions for research on outsourcing decision-making

Lars Bråd Nielsen

Introduction

The *Harvard Business Review* lists outsourcing as one of the most important new management ideas of the 20th century (Sibbet 1997). Today companies of all kinds use outsourcing as a tool to focus and perfect company processes in a never-ending endeavor to improve the products or services they provide to customers. Indeed, outsourcing has changed the way in which firms compete in such diverse industries as automobiles, aerospace, telecommunications, computers, pharmaceuticals, chemicals, healthcare, financial services, energy systems, and software (Quinn 2000; Dahan and Hauser 2002; Carson 2007). In this process, the meaning and scope of outsourcing constantly develop as the strategic complexity of the elements considered for outsourcing grows.

Basically, outsourcing involves two aspects: the outsourcing *decision* and the *control* of the subsequent supplier-buyer relationship. Both aspects are important but, in this chapter, focus is on outsourcing decision-making as the role of management accounting in buyer-supplier relationships is largely dealt with in the chapter on inter-organizational relationships. Specifically, this chapter reflects on the existing treatment of outsourcing decision-making in the accounting literature and compares this with the emerging notions found in the management literature. The idea is: first, to provide an overview of the important literature on outsourcing decision-making; and second, to reveal the extent to which the costing literature in management accounting has remained a decisive tool in outsourcing decision-making as the understanding of outsourcing has been continuously shaped and redefined by developments in the management literature.

The remainder of this chapter is structured in the following way. Initially, the historical (conventional) treatment of make-or-buy[1] decision-making in the management accounting literature is reviewed. Subsequently, the most prominent theories of the firm found in the management literature are outlined in order to pinpoint changes in the fundamental unit of analysis when analyzing the boundaries of the firm. Based on this, new and promising trends in the costing literature are laid out and analyzed. The final section discusses whether management accounting's decisive role in the outsourcing decision process has remained intact and whether its current status is satisfying. As a part of this discussion, topics for further research on outsourcing are identified.

Traditional treatment of outsourcing in the management accounting literature

The conventional treatment of make-or-buy decision-making in the management accounting literature is tied to the notion of corporate planning which – throughout the 1950s and 1970s – represented a general enthusiasm among companies and academics for using scientific techniques for decision-making, including tools such as cost-benefit analysis, budgeting, and DCF appraisal in combination with mathematical methods such as linear programming, econometric forecasting, and macroeconomic demand management (Grant 2005). During this time period, in-sourcing was widely seen among managers as the proper way to organize business activities (Lonsdale and Cox 2000; Stigler 1951; Rumelt 1982). The prevailing belief was that internalization of all activities in the value chain would lead to economies of scale and that benefits related to superior market power (horizontal integration), improved insurance following from more extensive portfolios of goods and services (conglomeration), and better control of the value chain (vertical integration) could be exploited beneficially (Lonsdale and Cox 2000). For instance, 7-Eleven used to deliver its own gasoline and make its own candy and ice cream. In fact, the company even owned the cows that produced the milk that it sold (Gottfredson et al. 2005). Likewise, Ford Motor Company developed the concept of "Fordism" (Piore and Sabel 1986), which called for integrating into the firm not just car assembly activities and production of components but even the extraction of iron ore, and car dealerships (Mol 2007).

Within this notion of the boundaries of the firm, make-or-buy was mostly seen as a tool to improve cost efficiency. In the literature, the traits of corporate planning in outsourcing decision-making are found in the two classic papers: Higgins (1955) and Gross (1966). In Gross (1966), the starting point for the outsourcing decision is an estimation of the company's expected sales volume on the basis of a projection of the general market growth, which subsequently functions as the foundation for creating budgets reflecting capital investments (physical and human) and costs that can be used for comparison between the make-or-buy alternatives. Indeed, both Higgins (1955) and Gross (1966) stress the importance of proper cost comparison since the lower alternative cost applicable to either make-or-buy is believed to have the greatest impact on management's final choice, simply for the reason that the company's main objective is to maximize long-term profit.[2] Hence, costs are allocated to the "make" alternative using full cost, with overheads being distributed as a percentage of direct labor costs, while the cost of buying is determined as the supplier price (Gross 1966), possibly extended to include the cost of incoming freight and of search and inspection (Higgins 1955).

The cost comparison also plays a dominant role in the textbook treatment of make-or-buy during that time. For instance, the early versions of *Cost Accounting – A Managerial Emphasis* takes the perspective of a manufacturer confronted with the question of whether to make-or-buy a product (e.g. Horngren 1967, pp. 414–415). When internal production capacity is idle, the cost analysis focuses on a simple comparison between the relevant cost of internal production and the external quotation price, emphasizing the decision irrelevance of fixed overheads (e.g. depreciation, property taxes, and insurance) that will continue regardless of the decision.

However, unlike Higgins (1955) and Gross (1966), the main interest of Horngren (1967, pp. 415–416) is the demonstration of how opportunity cost can be operationalized and incorporated into the make-or-buy analysis as the measurable sacrifice in rejecting an alternative at constrained capacity.[3] The basic question asked is: what happens if production capacity is constrained and the company has to take into account how best to utilize its production facilities? Horngren (1967) gives the example that reducing internal production may create room for renting out capacity or for initiating different manufacturing activities. For instance, the decision to manufacture may entail the rejection of an opportunity to rent the given capacity to another

Table 15.1 Comparison between relevant cost of internal production and the quotation price when idle capacity remains

	Per Unit		Totals (10,000) units		
	Make	Buy	Make		Totals
	$	$	$		$
Direct material	1		10,000		
Direct labor	8		80,000		
Variable overhead	4		40,000		
Fixed overhead that can be avoided by not making	2		20,000		
Total relevant costs	15	16	150,000		160,000
Difference in favor of making	$1			$10,000	

Source: Horngren 1967, p. 415.

manufacturer for $5,000 annually. The opportunity cost of making the parts is now the sacrifice of the chance to get $5,000 rental. Hence, the difference in favor of making is now only $5,000 (see Table 15.1 and Table 15.2).

While acknowledging the analytical importance of opportunity cost at the conceptual level, Horngren (1967) also touches upon the inherent problem within management accounting of working with the concept in practice and on the basis of quantitative historical data:

> ... opportunity costs do not involve cash receipts or outlays. Accountants usually confine their recording to those events that ultimately involve exchanges of assets. Accountants confine their history to alternatives selected rather than those rejected, primarily because of the impracticality or impossibility of accumulating meaningful data on what might have been.
>
> *(Horngren 1967, p. 416)*

All the same, Horngren (1967) does not address the way in which this problem could be handled but leaves the question open-ended, thereby giving the impression that the possible opportunity cost included in the make-or-buy analysis only comes to represent those aspects that can be constructed on the basis of quantitative historical accounting data – and that this is acceptable for reasons of tractability.

This somewhat unresolved and simplified treatment transfers to other non-quantifiable aspects as well. Particularly, only a short paragraph is devoted to the importance of strategic factors:

> The qualitative factors may be of paramount importance. Sometimes the manufacture of parts requires special knowhow, unusually skilled labor, rare materials, and the like. The desire to control the quality of parts is often the determining factor in the decision to make

Table 15.2 The total cost under make-or-buy when opportunity cost exists

	Make		Buy
	$		$
Obtaining parts	150,000		160,000
Opportunity cost: rent foregone	5,000		
Total relevant costs	155,000		160,000
Difference in favor of making		$5,000	

Source: Horngren 1969, p. 416.

> them. On the other hand, companies hesitate to destroy mutually advantageous long-run relationships by the erratic order giving which results from making parts during slack times and buying them during prosperous times. They may have difficulty in obtaining any parts during boom times, when there are shortages of materials and workers and no shortage of sales orders.
>
> *(Horngren 1967, p. 414)*

Nevertheless, while the importance of the qualitative factors is stressed no directions are given as to how they should be incorporated into the analysis. A similar lack of integration is found in Higgins (1955) and Gross (1966) who both suggest, among other things, taking into account component quality and supplier access when evaluating either alternative. Again, however, both papers are silent as to how – if at all – these qualitative aspects are supposed to be incorporated into the costing and investment analysis, or – if not – whether they can tip the decision in favor of either alternative as stand-alone variables. Indeed, Gross (1966) seems more concerned with using the qualitative factors to intuitively emphasize the importance of estimating the quantitative factors (expected sales, costs, and investments) without actually working them into the analysis.[4] Hence, the absence of an underlying conceptual framework for understanding the boundaries of the firm (i.e. a theory of the firm) within the notion of corporate planning implies that the qualitative and quantitative factors are not incorporated into a comprehensive assessment of each alternative. Instead, outsourcing decision-making is somewhat reduced to a checklist of independent qualitative and quantitative issues to be investigated. Since the quantitative factors by nature are easier to record and handle than the qualitative factors, it leaves the impression that quantitative aspects automatically come to play a dominant part, possibly dictating the role and weight given to more qualitative-oriented aspects.

Moving to more recent times reveals that the textbook treatment of make-or-buy in management accounting has remained almost identical to that of the 1960s–70s. Indeed, the treatment in Horngren et al. (2000) has been extended to consider activity-based costing in determining the relevant cost of the make alternative. Yet, the lack of integration between qualitative strategic factors and the costing analysis remains intact. In fact Horngren et al. (2000) no longer make any note of the inherent problem that is related to the registration of opportunity in normal accounting systems. The question is then whether this conventional treatment is adequate and satisfies the evolving understanding and use of outsourcing as a concept. To discuss this, we will take a look at developments in the management literature.

The management literature: developing ideas on the theory of the firm

Over time several theories of the firm have emerged in the management literature. Specifically, this chapter draws attention to three distinct theories while simultaneously trying to display

Table 15.3 The historical shift in the focus of outsourcing decision-making as new theories of the firm have been introduced.

Elements of outsourcing decision-making	*Corporate planning*	*TCE*	*IV*	*RBV*
Fundamental unit of analysis	Production process	Transaction	Activity	Resource
Importance of intangible, strategic aspects	Low	Low (+)	Medium	High
Natural emphasis on conventional cost considerations	High	High (+)	Medium	Low

Note: + indicates a marginal increase.

and link these to the changes in the understanding and use of outsourcing. How practice has inspired and been inspired by these frameworks is complex and difficult to isolate and relate to single factors or theories; partly due to existing frameworks continuing to play a dominant role, and partly due to the time-lag that naturally exists between practice and academia, as theories are developed and later adopted and shaped by business practioners (see the cultural circuit of capitalism in Seal (2010) and Thrift (2005)). Still, linking the theoretical developments to business practice indicates an overall shift in the understanding of the boundaries of the firm. Keeping in mind this caveat, we study Transaction Cost Economics, the Industrial View, and the Resource-Based View.

Transaction cost economics

While the conventional treatment of outsourcing decision-making in the management accounting literature is still shaped by thoughts of corporate planning, outsourcing as a concept has developed greatly since the 1950–70s. At the onset of the 1980s, recognition was given to the fact that many large and diverse corporations underperformed the market. Rumelt (1974) examined the linkage between diversification and performance, and found that the highest levels of profitability were exhibited by companies having a strategy of diversifying primarily into areas that drew on some common skill or resource. In addition, the lowest levels of performance were those of vertically integrated firms following strategies of diversification into unrelated businesses. Moreover, turbulence in the business environment – partly caused by global recession – made it difficult for companies to plan their investments, new product introductions, and personnel requirements three to five years ahead (Grant 2005). The result was a shift in emphasis from corporate planning to strategy-making, where the focus was less on the detailed management of companies' growth paths than on positioning the companies in the markets and in relation to competitors in order to maximize the profit potential. Within this new understanding of business practice, outsourcing was given a more dominant position and seen as a *strategic* tool (Hätonën and Eriksson 2009). Still, in the early phase, the use remained identical to that of corporate planning as focus was on cutting operational costs and obtaining efficiency by contracting out non-core business processes.

The theory of the firm underpinning the increased importance assigned to outsourcing as a strategic tool is largely attributable to Williamson's Transaction Cost Theory (Williamson 1975, 1979, 1981, 1985), which builds on the ideas put forth in Coase (1937). In general, Transaction Cost Economics (TCE) analyzes situations in which transaction cost avoidance by firms may be particularly acute and focuses on exchanges in which opportunistic potential is significant (Conner 1991). Such potential exists when three conditions pertain simultaneously: asset specificity, small numbers of potential transactors, and imperfect information in combination with bounded rationality. Asset specificity imposes a condition of dependence upon the owner, A, of the specific asset because A's value depends on the presence of another input, B, to which the former is specific. Small numbers reinforce this dependence: A cannot costlessly find a replacement for B should B's services be withdrawn. Finally, imperfect information means that complete contingent contracts cannot be written, which in turn implies that a priori knowledge of B's later actions cannot be fully incorporated in determining A's ex ante hire price. Hence, A cannot nullify the risk of later opportunism by B through an ex ante adjustment of the price for A's services.

Consequently, Williamson argues that firms will come to exist when this opportunistic potential is significant, since firms (hierarchies) exhibit a joint profit-maximizing attitude that may help to deal with opportunism by vertically integrating the transaction (Williamson 1975). Indeed, the transaction cost of using the market may simply be too high and difficult to handle through an arm's-length contractual arrangement. This, in turn, favors internalization of the transaction. However, vertical integration is not optimal per se because firms lack a clear linkage between performance and reward, which reduces explicit incentives to perform. Therefore, if the opportunistic potential is limited due to low asset-specificity, large numbers, and perfect information, transactions between autonomous contractors will come to dominate as the market automatically provides these high incentives through the market pricing mechanism.

Accordingly, the preferred sourcing alternative is the governance structure that minimizes the production cost and transaction cost altogether – as Williamson somewhat vaguely defines transaction costs to be the cost of planning, adapting, and monitoring task completion under alternative governance structures (Williamson 1985, p. 2). Therefore, when outsourcing decision-making is framed by TCE, the fundamental unit of analysis becomes the individual transaction and the costs of making this transaction under either "make" or "buy". However, where production costs and the quotation price are by and large the predominant factors under corporate planning, the cost measures of both the make and buy alternatives are more complex when framed by TCE, since it includes all the costs of establishing and subsequently handling the transaction.

The industrial view

Whereas the 1980s introduced outsourcing as a viable strategy, contracting out really started to gain momentum during the 1990s (Morgan 1999). Positive experiences from early adopters encouraged other companies to follow (Lacity and Hirschheim 1993). Cost efficiency was no longer the main objective of outsourcing as companies started seeking external skills, competences, and knowledge to provide value to more complex and strategically important organizational processes. As a collective term for this, strategic outsourcing emerged (Quinn and Hilmer 1994) which, unlike the traditional (operational) outsourcing of previous times, emphasized that more strategy-oriented functions were being outsourced, based on closer relationships with suppliers. The thrust of these new thoughts carried into business practice partly came from the development of two new, competing theories of the firm – the Industrial View (IV) and the Resource-Based View (RBV).[5]

The fundamentals of the IV are laid out by Porter (1980) who argues that the industry and the relative position that the company holds in it are to be considered as the primary drivers of profitability. Particularly, five structural characteristics (forces) are identified to explain industry attractiveness, including entry barriers, threat of substitution, bargaining power of buyers, bargaining power of suppliers, and rivalry among competitors in the industry. Hence, the strength of these forces by themselves and in combination will decide the overall industry profitability. Furthermore, taking these characteristics into account, a firm can gain valuable insight into the dynamics of the industry and pinpoint possible competitive positions from which it can defend itself or influence key industry determinants to improve company profitability.

Building on these thoughts, Porter (1985) introduces the value-chain framework – the second cornerstone of the IV. In addition to the five structural industry forces, this framework sees an attractive position within an industry as a result of competitive advantage, stemming from the company's ability to handle the discrete activities which make up the company's value chain – such as products being assembled, salespeople making sales visits, or orders being processed. Porter stresses that often complex interdependencies between these activities exist. As a result opportunities for optimization and problems of co-ordination between activities are formed. Therefore, the company can create a competitive advantage by following one of two generic strategies, low cost or differentiation,[6] since an above-normal return can be obtained either by managing value-chain activities at a collectively lower cost or in a way that creates customer value, thus allowing for a price premium to be charged (Porter 1991). The essential question in the IV is, therefore, how the company can generate and sustain a competitive advantage over time, or, put differently, why some firms are simply able to perform particular activities at a lower cost than others or in ways that create superior value.[7] To answer this question, Porter introduces the concept of structural factors, essentially representing the structural differences among competitors in the cost of activities.[8] For instance, economies of scale can be a structural factor since obtaining economies of scale in a given activity holds the potential to reduce costs. Likewise, learning and spillovers can be a structural factor for a given activity as, over time, the company can strive to achieve learning-curve effects and thus improve cost-efficiency. Additionally, managing the linkages between activities within the company's internal value chain or between the company and the suppliers/buyers (vertical linkages) may constitute structural factors, which require careful attention in order to ensure a smooth workflow without costly extra steps or unnecessary interruptions. Also, Porter (1991) points out that moving to the level of structural factors sheds light on the important question of sustainability. In general, the mix and significance of individual structural factors vary by activity, by firm, and by industry. Therefore, a sustainable competitive advantage must be based on those activities in which a firm has proprietary access to scarce resources (e.g. skills, patents, assets, distribution networks, etc.).

All told, when outsourcing decision-making is framed by the IV, the fundamental unit of analysis is discrete company activity. Costs may still play a part in deciding between make and buy; yet the intangible, strategic aspects arising from a combination of external industry conditions and internal company circumstances are incorporated into the decisional context in a much more structured way than found in conventional management accounting analysis, and are thus given a more central position in the overall analysis.

The resource-based view

Turning next to the RBV, this theory rests on the work of Penrose (1959) on how firms make product decisions on price and manufacturing. In the RBV, the firm's main objective is the achievement of above-normal returns (e.g. Barney 1986; Wernerfelt 1984). Earning such returns requires the firm either to obtain a low cost position in the market when selling identical products in comparison to competitors (Ricardian rents), or to reduce competition by differentiating the firm's products from those of the rest of the market (monopoly rents) (Barney 1991; Peteraf 1993). Thus, the firm's crucial problem is how to maintain the distinctiveness of its product or, for identical products, its low cost position, while not investing so much in obtaining either of these distinctions to destroy the above-normal returns (Barney 1986). Distinctiveness in the product offering – or low cost – is tied directly to distinctiveness in the resources used to produce the product, which include: all assets, capabilities, organizational processes, firm attributes, information, knowledge, etc. controlled by the firm. Accordingly, the RBV emphasizes the combination and deployment of resources internal to the firm as the key driver of firm profitability and strategic advantage (Barney 1991; Conner 1991; Prahalad and Hamel 1990; Wernerfelt 1984).

A resource with the potential to create sustained competitive advantage has to fulfill the criteria put forth in Barney (1991). That is, the resource must enable the firm to meet factors critical to success in its business environment (value); it must be rare among the firm's current and potential competitors in order to minimize exploitation identical to that of the firm (rarity); it must not be easily obtainable for competitors (imperfect imitability); and finally, there should be no strategic substitutes for this resource that are valuable but neither rare nor imperfectly imitable, since this will allow other companies to implement the same strategy with different resources (no strategic substitutes).

Sometimes, and mostly in the consulting-oriented literature, the core competence approach is used to capture the ideas found in the RBV (Peters and Waterman 1982; Prahalad and Hamel 1990). Still, in spite of the change of wording, the message conveyed by the core competence approach remains the same: the company has to obtain, create, and develop certain capabilities in order to stay competitive (McIvor 2005). That is, the sources of competitive advantage are to be found in management's ability to consolidate corporate-wide technologies and production skills into competences that empower individual businesses to adapt rapidly to changing business opportunities. Thus, very similarly to the definition of a resource as holding the potential to create sustained competitive advantage in Barney (1991), Prahalad and Hamel (1990) suggest that a core competence has to meet the following three tests: it must enable the organization to provide fundamental customer benefits and make a contribution to customer-perceived value (customer value); it must be competitively unique and substantially superior to that of other competitors (competitor differentiation); and finally, it must provide potential access to a wide variety of markets – i.e. act as a gateway to future products and services (extendability). In effect, a core competence concerns those resources that are fundamental to a company's strategic position. Instead of developing a strategy based on only considering dominant markets (strategic business units), the core competence approach holds that it is more beneficial to think in terms of core competences, which will segment the organization in a totally different way compared to that of the IV.

In conclusion, proponents of the RBV claim that the fundamental unit of analysis comprises company resources when analyzing competitive advantages and thus the boundaries of the firm (e.g. Dierickx and Cool 1989; Teece 1976, 1980; Teece et al. 1997). Furthermore, the resource represents a further abstraction level to that of transactions and activities in which the intangible, strategic aspects are further emphasized as the most important factors when deciding in favor of make-or-buy.

Summary comparison of the three theories

Table 15.3 sums up the elements of analysis for each theory of the firm. Specifically, it shows how the unit of analysis has changed with the introduction of new theories of the firm. Correspondingly, a natural – or pre-specified – focus on costing with regard to outsourcing decision-making is no longer given. Instead, attention is increasingly directed to intangible, strategic aspects that are not incorporated into the conventional make-or-buy analysis depicted in the management accounting literature.

The management accounting literature: looking beyond the conventional treatment

Understanding that the notion of make-or-buy has shifted from a mere comparison of internal production costs with price towards contemplation of more intangible, strategic aspects, the key issue is whether management accounting still has an important role to play in the decision-making process and whether its current status is acceptable for management accounting as a discipline. In recent years, significant attention has been given to the *changing role* of the management accountant, from an independent, objective assessor to a business partner (hybrid accountant) who can engage in both operational and strategic decision-making at various levels in the organization (Burns and Baldvinsdottir 2005; CIMA 2009). However, while this transition is under way, it is less evident which tools the management accounting literature has to offer the hybrid accountant in this respect.

Focusing on outsourcing and acknowledging that the conventional treatment in the accounting literature has inadequacies in dealing with today's notion of outsourcing, we will look at some tools that may be further developed to bring management accounting up to speed with the theories of the firm emerging in the management literature. Accordingly, we focus on two promising areas: Total Cost of Ownership and Strategic Cost Management.

Total cost of ownership

In the accounting literature, a great deal of attention has been devoted to empirically explaining outsourcing decision-making on the basis of TCE (e.g. Anderson 1983; Bai et al. 2010; Balakrishnan et al. 2010; Widener and Selto 1999) while others suggest that companies have an inadequate or mistaken understanding of how to incorporate transaction costs into the analysis (Chalos 1995; Lamminmaki 2008). However, only a few scholarly pieces on TCE in the accounting literature offer prescriptive guidelines as to how transaction costs can be incorporated into the costing analysis in outsourcing decision-making. One exception is the literature on Total Cost of Ownership (TCO), which suggests an accounting proxy for transaction cost (Ellram 1993, 1995; Ellram and Maltz 1995).

Originally, the notion of TCO was hinted at in the literature on life-cycle costing (Harriman 1982; Jackson and Ostrom 1980). Yet, the emergence of Activity-Based Costing (ABC) during the 1980s (Kaplan 1983, 1984a, 1984b, 1985) made it possible to partly capture the complexity of transaction costs through the notion of TCO (Carr and Ittner 1992; Kaplan and Cooper 1998, pp. 206–209). Broadly defined, TCO is an approach that requires the buying firm to determine which costs are considered most important or significant in the acquisition, possession, use, and subsequent disposition of a good or service (Carr and Ittner 1992; Chalos 1995; Ellram 1995; Kaplan and Cooper 1998). One way to categorize the cost of ownership is based on the order in which the cost elements are incurred in the transaction sequence: pre-transaction, transaction, and post-transaction (Ellram 1993). Pre-transaction costs refer to the costs incurred prior to placing the order and comprise the costs of investigating alternative sources, qualifying and educating suppliers regarding the firm's systems and expectations, and adapting to the systems, styles, and delivery methods of new sources of supply. Moreover, the actual transaction cost elements are those items related to order placement and receipt which include the price of the item itself along with the costs associated with actually placing an order and getting the order into the firm or supply chain. In particular, this comprises the costs associated with preparing and placing the order (EDI, fax, phone, etc.), following up on the order, receiving, matching receiving data to the invoice, and paying the bill. Finally, post-transaction costs relate to those costs incurred when the item is owned or in the possession of the company. The actual occurrence of post-transaction costs may be soon after the order is received, or years later when the purchased item is in use or being modified, repaired, or disposed of. For this reason, such costs may be separated from the purchase by a great deal of time and thus difficult to track. More specifically, the costs may for instance include the costs of product repair in the field, routine and special maintenance costs, as well as those associated with replacement part scarcity and/or obsolescence.

The use of TCO in outsourcing decision-making is hinted at in both Drtina (1994) and Chalos (1995) as part of wider strategic frameworks. However, in Ellram and Maltz (1995) a more thorough and focused description is provided of how TCO can be incorporated into the make-or-buy analysis. Here, the first step in developing a complete understanding of the internal costs is to construct a flow-chart of the sequence of activities performed in the current system. Subsequently, key cost drivers are identified for each step in the flow-chart and costs are allocated accordingly using ABC, thus providing insight into the cost structure of the make alternative. The same procedure is then followed for the outsourcing alternative where the company in collaboration with the prospective supplier(s) try to establish a flow-chart of the steps and costs involved, should the transaction be handled by a third party. Based upon the respective cost studies, the outsourcing decision is approached as an incremental cost analysis, where the key to comparing the current and proposed alternatives is to examine: first, what current costs will change or be eliminated; and second, what additional costs will be added.

Ellram and Maltz (1995) illustrate this procedure for a case company where a number of key areas are identified as deviating between the make and buy alternatives. The approach has many similarities to the conventional treatment of make-or-buy in Horngren – as portrayed earlier in relation to corporate planning. The focus is still on differential cost; yet the relevant cost of each alternative includes a more holistic perspective on cost items than what is found in Horngren. To illustrate this let us return to the example in Table 15.1 and Table 15.2 and expand the costing analysis using some of the descriptions provided in Ellram and Maltz (1995). For instance, if outsourcing is chosen, savings on additional investments in capital and the cost recovered from disinvestments in existing assets may be deployed alternatively (the opportunity costs are added to the in-house alternative along with the already established rent revenue), transportation of the product may be handled by the supplier (the differential in transportation costs is added to the in-house alternative), orders will arrive in smaller quantities (the differential in obsolescence costs is added to the in-house alternative), and a higher price has to be paid compared to internal production costs alone (the differential in price, \$16 – \$15 = \$1, at volume, is added to the outsourcing alternative).

In total, adding up the cost increments for each alternative elucidates whether making or buying is cheapest. In this example the third-party supplier now ranks as the preferred alternative when evaluated on the basis of cost alone. Hence, in accordance with Williamson (1975, 1979, 1981, 1985), an essential point in Ellram and Maltz (1995) is that a simple comparison of internal production costs with price may lead to the wrong outsourcing decision, simply for the reason that important and inevitable extra costs related to each alternative are not taken into consideration.

In general, however, it still remains unclear what role a cost estimate based on TCO is left to play in an outsourcing decision-making process framed on the basis of TCE. The reason is that TCE is abstract and concerned with the transaction cost-minimizing *ability* of each governance structure while TCO is concrete and focuses on the *size* of the transaction costs. For tractability,

Table 15.4 Adding up the cost increments under make-or-buy when the costing analysis is based on TCO

	Make \$		*Buy* \$
Obtaining parts (price difference)			10,000
Logistic costs (transportation)	5,000		
Batch size (orders)	2,000		
Opportunity cost:			
Rent forgone	5,000		
Savings on additional investments in capital	10,000		
Savings from disinvestments	5,000		
Total relevant costs	27,000		10,000
Difference in favor of buying		\$17,000	

the TCO model suggested by Ellram and Maltz thus analyzes each sourcing alternative as a static relationship that will remain in place after a given governance structure has been chosen. As hinted in a case study by Drtina (1994), this implies that the reported transaction costs to a large extent come to resemble the expected production, logistical, and administrative costs under each alternative, since these costs are the easiest to quantify and measure. Consequently, the outsourcing alternative is analyzed as if the third-party supplier will never break the relationship or behave in an unreasonably opportunistic manner after the contract has been established – so the costs allocated to the outsourcing alternative primarily concern supplier selection, supplier education, and transfer of the good/service from the supplier to the company. However, as pointed out earlier, a strategic framing of the outsourcing decision, based on TCE, considers the potential risk associated with the transaction-specific investments – which the company carries into the relationship – as absolutely crucial when deciding on the optimal governance structure. Therefore, if the TCO procedure by Ellram and Maltz really builds on TCE, it has to account for the potential loss that the company faces on its transaction-specific investments insofar as the supplier behaves opportunistically and perhaps exits from the relationship after contract initiation. Still, the cost of risk is, ceteris paribus, very difficult to measure as it necessitates assessing both the likelihood of the supplier behaving opportunistically as well as the value of the transaction-specific assets in alternative use. The same problem characterizes the make alternative, where TCO encompasses the expected costs related to production, logistics, and administration, yet fails to explicitly consider the expected costs of inefficiency assumed to naturally encumber the hierarchy in TCE.

Indeed, these difficulties are not conceptual problems of TCO since theoretically nothing precludes the expected costs of inefficiency and a risk premium which is added to the relevant alternatives. Instead, they relate to the inherent obstruction within management accounting in "accumulating meaningful data on what might have been" – as previously pointed out in relation to make-or-buy decision-making under corporate planning. While the breadth of the TCO analysis is extended compared to that of corporate planning and the notion in Higgins (1955), Horngren (1967), and Gross (1966), conservatism still restricts the calculative elements included in the analysis and constrains it to considerations that only partially capture the essence of TCE. In effect, it is questionable what weight the TCO costing estimates – as it is currently portrayed in the management accounting literature – will carry in the final outsourcing decision when framed on the basis of TCE.

Strategic cost management

Focusing next on the later developments in the management literature – the value-chain framework (from the IV) and the RBV – the management accounting response to both notions falls under the umbrella of Strategic Cost Management (SCM).[9] Originally, SCM dates back to the early 1980s and the work of Simmonds (1981), although the concept has since then been developed by several academics (see e.g. Bromwich 1990; Shank and Govindarajan 1989). However, so far no agreed definition of SCM exists; Shank and Govindarajan (1994) describe it in very broad terms as: *The blending of the financial analysis elements of three themes from the strategic management literature – value analysis, strategic positioning analysis, and cost driver analysis* (Shank and Govindarajan 1994, p. xiii).

Generally, SCM embraces the idea of incorporating strategic reflections on competitors, customers, and suppliers into the cost analysis to develop superior strategies that can help a company gain a sustainable competitive advantage, in keeping with theories from strategy literature. Nevertheless, in the management accounting literature this idea has, so far, only been sporadically touched upon in case study illustrations, while a comprehensive scholarly work linking strategy and accounting at a theoretical level has still to emerge (Shank 2007; Langfield-Smith 2008). In effect, it is difficult to give a description that covers all aspects of SCM.

Interestingly, however – and as hinted in the quote above – the treatment of SCM in the mainstream accounting journals tends to build on Porter's IV (e.g. Bromwich 1990; Shank and Govindarajan 1989, 1992, 1994) while the ideas of the RBV have yet to be included. Some rather vague reflections on accounting and the RBV are available in the professional journals (e.g. Bromage 2000; Kralovetz 1996; Rogers and Blenko 2006; Stacey 1998), but none of these offer any explicit guidelines on how accounting can actually be incorporated into the outsourcing analysis to evaluate the financial conditions of each alternative. Venkatesan (1992) outlines a practical framework for outsourcing decision-making based on the RBV in which accounting is indicated to play several roles. Still, the focus is more on the management aspects – Venkatesan remains silent as to how accounting is actually supposed to fill out the roles specified. A rather similar approach depicting a simple matrix relationship (see Figure 15.1) between core competences and cost performance is found in McCormick and Duff (2009). Here, activities are plotted in the diagram according to their core competence potential and their effect on the collective costs of the company in order to obtain an overview of the strategically most important activities. However, while this may be useful during the initial phase of the outsourcing decision-making process, when sorting out possible outsourcing candidates, it leaves unanswered how to handle the outsourcing question when the situation becomes complex. More specifically, no directions are provided as to how the effect of being core is reflected in the cost performance evaluation.

If we instead direct our attention to the treatment of SCM building on Porter's IV (the mainstream academic treatment), nothing has been written specifically on outsourcing decision-making. Still, interesting insights are offered into how accounting can be incorporated into strategic analysis, which can quite easily be transferred to the case of outsourcing decision-making. In fact, although not elaborated upon, Shank and Govindarajan (1992) point out that value-chain analysis – in combination with SCM – can be used to ask make-or-buy questions pertaining to each value activity. Hence, in what follows we will try to combine the explanations provided in Porter (1985) with the mainstream treatment of SCM to indicate how the make-or-buy costing analysis may be extended to incorporate some of the elements of SCM.

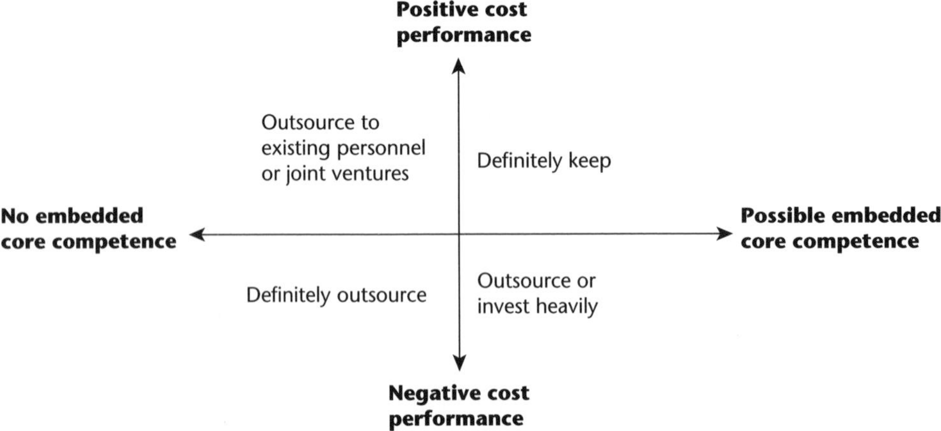

Figure 15.1 The outsourcing decision matrix

Following the general concepts of the IV, Shank and Govindarajan (1989) illustrate how the initial step in SCM is a five-forces study of the industry in which the company operates. Accordingly, management accounting may take on the role of empirically investigating such factors as the size and number of suppliers and buyers, barriers to entry, average cost of products, types of substituting products, etc. in order to provide information for decision-making. The results from the industry analysis may immediately qualify low cost or differentiation as the right company strategy to follow – in which case the role of SCM becomes the identification of how best to implement this generic strategy.[10] However, if the results are unclear, SCM may take on the additional challenge of revealing information that can rule in favor of either alternative. This information may come in various forms, yet in keeping with the focus on costs in previous sections and to stay true to the descriptions provided in the management accounting literature, we attend to the case where the company – on the basis of the industry analysis – has decided to follow a low-cost strategy.[11] Particularly, we stick to the outline in Porter (1985) and divide SCM into a sequence of four steps.

First, the company has to define its value chain, possibly on the basis of the well-known generic value chain (see e.g. Porter 1985, p. 37), from which each generic category can be further divided into discrete value activities specific to the company. Especially, defining relevant value activities requires that activities with discrete technologies and economics are isolated. Consequently, broad functions such as manufacturing and marketing are subdivided into activities. The appropriate degree of disaggregation depends on the economics of the activities and the purposes for which the value chain is being analyzed. In this respect, the basic principle is that activities should be isolated and separated if they (1) have different economics (i.e. cost behaviour), (2) have a high potential impact on differentiation, or (3) represent a significant or growing proportion of cost. For outsourcing in particular, it is thus natural to aim at a successively finer disaggregation of the activities immediately on either side of the activity considered for outsourcing, in order to gain accurate insight into how outsourcing affects the dynamics of the value chain.

Second, having defined the activities in the value chain, assets and operating costs need to be assigned accordingly. The necessity to assign assets to activities reflects the fact that the number of assets in an activity and the efficiency of asset utilization are frequently important to the activity's cost. Specifically, operation costs should be allocated to the activities in which they are incurred, while assets should be assigned to the activities that employ, control, or most influence their use. Porter (1985) does not specify which costing principles to use;[12] yet ABC seems like a natural choice of method, as it centres on allocating resource costs to activities using so-called resource cost drivers – the first basis for distribution in ABC.

The third step is to identify the structural factors that explain variations in the cost of the value activities compared to competitors. That is, the company's cost position results from the cost behaviour of its value activities which, in turn, are fundamentally shaped by a number of underlying structural factors. Understanding and dealing with these factors is thus important. Hence, as explained in relation to the description of the IV, the company has to search for such underlying causes of cost differences as economies of scale, learning and spillovers, and the handling of the linkages in the value chain.

After completing the three initial steps, the company, finally, has to evaluate the results of these to decide where a competitive advantage can potentially be generated either through controlling the structural factors better than the competitors or by reconfiguration of the activities in the value chain. Focusing on outsourcing, the company must therefore evaluate the activity considered for contracting out on the basis of the structural factors identified, as well as the costs allocated to it through ABC. That is, the company has to question how outsourcing will affect the other activities in the value chain, both internally and externally. For instance, it may be that the costs allocated to an in-house activity are higher than the price offer from the third-party supplier. Yet, as a result of linkages between activities (a structural factor), outsourcing may inflict extra costs on the rest of the activities in the internal value chain due to additional inspections, adjustments to the current activity set-up, or the like. Also, if possible, the cost reduction from the potential learning-curve effect of maintaining production in-house should be quantified – or at least debated. Thus, calculating these extra costs effectively amounts to determining the TCO, as discussed in the previous section; yet the factors included tend to have a more *strategic* focus. However, SCM goes even further than this. Shank and Govindarajan (1992) point out that it may be essential for decision-making also to contemplate the *external* part of a company's value chain. Particularly, they argue that:

> Management accounting, as explained in leading textbooks, usually takes a "value-added" perspective, starting with payments to suppliers (purchases), and stopping with charges to customers (sales). The key theme is to maximize the difference – the value-added – between purchases and sales, under the assumption that this is the only way a firm can influence profits. We argue that the value chain – not value added – is the more meaningful way to explore strategic issues.
>
> *(Shank and Govindarajan 1992, p. 182)*

Thus, according to Shank and Govindarajan, the conventional costing analysis starts too late and stops too soon, thereby leaving out many essential elements from the analysis. For example, in the context of outsourcing, it is not difficult to imagine that contracting out a given activity in the internal value chain may generate extra costs in a later activity belonging to one of the company's customers. In turn, this may lead the customer to demand a price reduction from the company, which should be taken into account when evaluating the outsourcing alternative. Adding to the previous analysis from Table 15.4, the effects from a SCM study may supposedly be an augmentation of the make-or-buy evaluation with the following cost items.

In this case, adding the extra cost of the expected, external price reduction and the learning-curve effects once again tips the make-or-buy costing analysis in favor of the make alternative.

However, while the importance of calculating the cost effects of strategic factors is easily appreciated, it may prove very challenging to estimate such factors in practice. Also, the nature

Table 15.5 Adding up the cost increments under make-or-buy when the costing analysis is based on SCM and the value-chain framework

	Make $		*Buy* $
Obtaining parts (downstream: price difference)			10,000
Logistical costs (transportation)	5,000		
Batch size (orders)	2,000		
Opportunity cost:			
Rent forgone	5,000		
Savings on additional investments in capital	10,000		
Savings from disinvestments	5,000		
Price reduction (upstream: customer)			10,000
Estimated learning-curve effects			11,000
Total relevant costs	27,000		31,000
Difference in favor of making		$5,000	

Table 15.6 Typical measures of learning

Proxy driver for rate of learning	*Explanation*
Cumulative volume in an activity	Typical for determining machine speed or reject rates in fabrication operations
Time in operation	Typical for work-flow layout in assembly
Cumulative investment	Typical for plant efficiency
Cumulative industry volume	Typical for product design improvements that lower cost where spillovers are high
Exogenous technical change	Typical for basic process improvements

Source: Porter 1985, p. 75.

of these effects is often company-specific – for which reason it is difficult to provide general guidelines. Still, to hint at how such factors may be dealt with let us focus on learning-curve effects. Porter (1985, pp. 73–5) describes how learning-curve effects may be driven by different proxies for the *rate of learning*, depending on the activity and the industry at hand. Table 15.6 lists some of the most typical measures.

The appropriate measure of learning reflects the specific learning mechanisms that account for the fall in costs over time in a value activity. For instance, in a value activity where learning influences cost behaviour through improving worker efficiency the rate of learning may be tied to the cumulative volume in that activity. In this case, the rate of learning is correlated with scale because high scale makes learning accumulate rapidly. Hence, volume may be used either *directly* as a very rough proxy for learning (thus in principal assuming away other factors contributing to the reduction in costs as volume increases) or, on the basis of further analysis, *indirectly* as a given percentage (thus acknowledging the contribution of other drivers to the cost reduction as volume increases). In either case, when the proxy is identified, the approximated relationship between the affected cost items and the proxy driver is estimated. This procedure is illustrated in Figure 15.2 for a hypothetical linear case. Finally, the accumulative cost reduction may be determined for the expected total of the proxy.

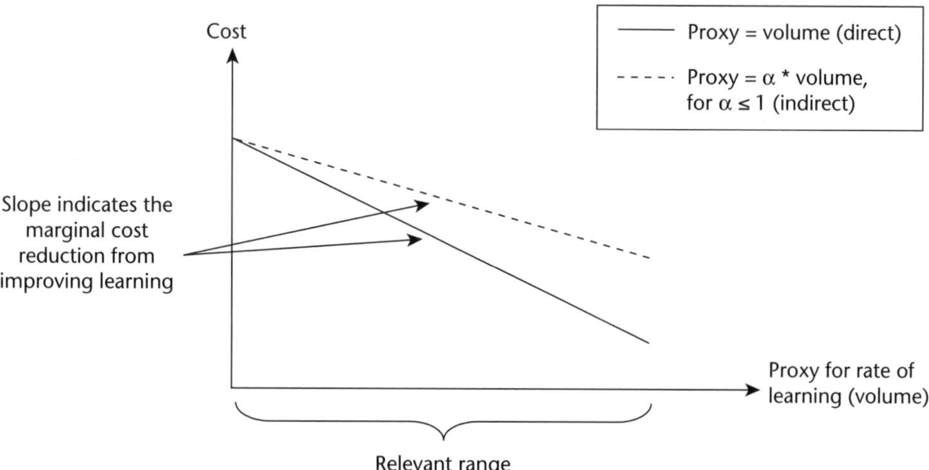

Figure 15.2 Approximation of the cost reduction from learning on the basis of volume as both a direct and indirect proxy for the rate of learning

On a more general level, however, the procedure described clearly illustrates the subjectivity and inevitable inaccuracy of incorporating cost effects that stem from structural factors into the make-or-buy analysis, since similar intricacies exist in respect to the remaining structural factors previously mentioned. Indeed, the analysis could have been refined; yet the cost estimates will still be flawed by uncertainty and excessive simplicity. Even so, they represent an attempt at improving the *relevance* of cost analysis in the decision-making process. Therefore, the SCM literature based on the IV is best seen as a change in the perception of cost accounting's role in decision-making – a new way of thinking that tries to abandon conservatism and instead subscribe to the guiding motto first formulated by J.M. Keynes: "it is better to be roughly right than precisely wrong" (Corazza 1999). In fact, Shank and Govindarajan (1992) do not regard SCM as an exact science, but more as an "art" of strategic analysis in which substantial subjectivity is involved when decoupling the supply chain and allocating assets and costs. So they reason that despite the calculational problems, every firm should attempt to estimate its value chain as the process of doing so by itself may prove quite instructive and force managers to carefully evaluate how the company activities add value to their customers who use their products (services). Accordingly, the mere fact that it not always possible to carry out a meaningful analysis does not negate its significance when it is possible.

Nevertheless, in total, the review of the SCM literature in this chapter inevitably serves as evidence of the fact that – in its current shape – SCM is underdeveloped and does not provide much guidance in relation to outsourcing decision-making when framed either by the RBV or the IV. That is, although intentions are worthy, the reality is that the contemporary management accounting literature provides little or no answer to most of the aspects deemed important within the RBV in particular – but also the IV. Consequently, as the fundamental unit of analysis has increased in complexity with the emergence of new, more strategically focused, theories of the firm, the costing analysis portrayed in the management accounting literature has gradually lost terrain as a decision support tool.

Conclusion and discussion

In summary, the literature review carried out in this chapter reveals that the current treatment of make-or-buy decision-making in the management accounting literature only partially reflects the developments in the management literature. Whereas previously accounting information carried a natural and decisive weight in the final decision – because of the way the outsourcing problem was perceived – a gap has come to exist over time between the information that accounting models can supply and the information deemed relevant for decision-making within the developing theories of the firm in the management literature. On the one hand, in the management literature the fundamental unit of analysis has grown ever more complex – increasingly emphasizing the importance of qualitative, strategic aspects in the outsourcing decision. On the other hand, the management accounting literature has, for a long time, stayed with a rather conservative and simplistic approach – not striving to incorporate into the analysis factors that are not immediately quantifiable.

Does this disparity create a problem? Empirical studies on high failure rates in outsourcing arrangements suggest that this may be the case. For instance, three-quarters of US managers surveyed by the American Management Association reported that outsourcing outcomes had failed to meet expectations (Bryce and Useem 1998). Additionally, Barthélemy (2001) reports a survey based on 50 companies where approximately 14% of all outsourcing operations were deemed to be failures due to hidden costs. Companies stated that they entered an outsourcing agreement believing that they understood all major costs. They even agreed that some expenses would be incurred in relation to activities – such as finding a vendor, drafting the contract, and managing the effort (i.e. transaction costs) – but they thought that these expenses would be negligible. Ex post of the outsourcing transition, however, most companies found that these costs were not negligible – in some cases, they actually halved or cancelled-out the company's potential savings from outsourcing.

Obviously, the reasons for outsourcing failures can be many and may be related to poor management of the outsourcing relationship. However, taken together the examples also indicate that many companies seem to underestimate the consequences of outsourcing and are equipped with inadequate decision tools to reveal the hidden costs before making the final decision. In this respect, there is tremendous scope for research on outsourcing decision-making in management accounting.

First, the gap that has come to exist between strategy and accounting has to be further explained and reflected upon. As hinted in this chapter, the research into accounting decision-models attempting to bridge the gap between traditional accounting and strategy has so far been fairly limited and most noticeably amounts to the work on SCM done by Bromwich, Govindarajan, and Shank – dating back several years. In fact, Shank (2007) points out that SCM in general seems to suffer from an "unraveling of the pieces", suggesting a collection of isolated texts rather than evidence of an emerging discourse:[13]

> By 2000, there was a fifteen-year history of great "beginnings", "pilot" projects, and "cameo" appearances for SCM, but not much more. It has been a great topic on the lecture circuit and in cost management symposia. In military parlance, "it briefs well"! But the topics had not been gaining traction in mainstream academe or in the corporate world . . .
>
> *(Shank 2007, p. 359)*

It appears that inherent conservatism in management accounting simply makes it difficult to keep pace with developments in strategy, since only certain types of information are considered credible for make-or-buy decision-making and therefore worked into the analysis. The end result may well be that the costing literature is essentially discarded by practioners as inadequate as they attempt to deal with the increasingly sophisticated ideas from the management literature when considering outsourcing. Indeed, they may still regard costing to be an important issue, but will have to develop their own ad hoc models.

However, if management accounting is an ambitious discipline and wants to influence practice, this is not a viable path to follow (Kaplan 2011). There thus seems to be a great need for taking the research on SCM to the next level in order to increase, if possible, the relevance of make-or-buy costing analysis for outsourcing decision-making. Indeed, management accounting must remain the "watchdog" that continuously checks up on strategic constructs with hard-headed (costing) reflections to ensure that the often diffuse strategic objectives coincide at least partially with the real world. In order to fulfill this task, management accounting research needs to lose its reluctance to deal with matters that do not immediately qualify as incontrovertible empirical facts.

As a part of this transition towards greater relevance, a more comprehensive look at and understanding of the outsourcing decision-making process may prove important. As reflected in the descriptions in this chapter, the process is usually portrayed in the management accounting literature as a typified *choice activity* between two alternatives: make-or-buy. In general, however, a decision-making process often involves several stages before the final choice is made. For instance, according to Simon (1977, pp. 40–41) a decision-making process consists of four phases. The first phase – the intelligence activity – is about scanning the environment for conditions which require decisions; the second phase – the design activity – relates to inventing, developing and analyzing possible courses of action. Following this, the third phase – the choice activity – concerns the evaluation and selection of a particular course of action from those available. Finally, in the fourth phase – the review activity – the choice is assessed.

In the current treatment of outsourcing in the management accounting literature, the "triggering" stages (in particular phases one and two) are highly neglected. Hence, instead of focusing only on the final choice situation, increasing attention could be given to the preceding phases in order to further understand how quantitative and non-quantitative aspects can come together to form a comprehensive basis for decision-making. Also, in addition to broadening the perspective on the outsourcing decision-making process, this may help distinguish between different outsourcing situations. For instance, a decision situation in which the activity considered for outsourcing is already established in-house may be very different from a situation where the make alternative is a new possibility for the company to pursue and where investments have yet to be made.

To further examine all of these aspects, a first step may be a study of how consultant firms tackle strategic outsourcing problems. Since these firms operate in the mixed zone between strategy and accounting there is a good chance that such insights can provide a solid preliminary awareness of how and to what extent the available theories of the firm are used as a platform for analyzing the outsourcing situation.[14] Based on this, a second step could be carefully selected case studies of how outsourcing decision-making is actually handled in companies, both in relation to the structure of the decision-making process but also in relation to how people (using human intuition) interact with rigid models when producing information for decision-making. The latter may possibly hold the key to understanding how qualitative and subtle aspects can be further incorporated into the information material for outsourcing decision-making. Consequently, the objective should not be a simple description of the procedures followed, if any, but instead a critical examination of how companies apply and combine the theoretical concepts and techniques. Essentially, what is called for is a more phenomenological treatment of outsourcing decision-making, rooted more in professional practice than is currently the case. This will extend current knowledge and provide a basis for improving management accounting practice in support of the outsourcing decision.

Notes

1 In this chapter, make-or-buy is taken to be synonymous with outsourcing and thus given an equal footing.
2 The strong focus on costs in the make-or-buy analysis is also found in Capettini and Salamon (1977) who provide a specific example of the internal versus external acquisition of services using maths (simultaneous equations) and economic theory.
3 Generally, there was a growing interest in opportunity cost during the years of corporate planning (1950s–1970s) (see e.g. Anthony 1964, p. 569; Mathews 1962, pp. 453–454; Oxenfeldt and Baxter 1961).
4 See for instance the discussion on the qualitative aspect of management having the necessary know-how to undertake and handle outsourcing in a given industry (Gross 1966, p. 753).
5 The IV was developed in stages. The competition with the RBV is mainly related to thoughts on the value-chain framework laid out in Porter (1985).
6 Porter also introduces a third generic strategy, called focus. However, since this strategy is merely a modified version of low cost or differentiation, it is not discussed further in this chapter.
7 According to Porter (1985, pp. 16–17), the two generic strategies are, ceteris paribus, not compatible. That is, if a firm engages in both generic strategies at the same time, there is a great risk of being "stuck in the middle".
8 To be precise, Porter (1985, p. 70) refers to structural factors as cost drivers. However, to avoid confusion with the definition of a cost driver in ABC, this usage is avoided.

9 Sometimes SCM is also referred to as Strategic Management Accounting (SMA) (Langfield-Smith 2008).
10 Usually a firm must make a choice between low cost or differentiation, or it will become stuck in the middle (Porter 1985, p. 17).
11 What is defined as strategic cost analysis in Shank and Govindarajan (1989, pp. 40–41) is described in relation to a generic strategy based on low cost in Porter (1985, pp. 62–118).
12 Porter merely states that "the costs and assets of shared value activities should be allocated initially to the value chain of the business unit using whatever methodology the firm currently employs, typically based on some allocation formula" (Porter 1985, p. 66).
13 Seal (2010) takes this even further and stresses that SMA (and hence SCM) has "failed" as an academic discourse even before it could influence the wider managerial discourse.
14 According to Shank and Govindarajan (1989) "there is a billion dollar a year market in strategic cost analysis consulting services dominated by such firms as Bain & Company, Boston Consulting Group, Booz Allen & Hamilton Inc., McKinsey & Company, and Monitor, Inc.".

Bibliography

Anderson, P. A. 1983. Decision-making by objection and the Cuban missile crisis. *Administrative Science Quarterly* 28 (2): 201–222.

Anthony, R. N. 1964. *Management Accounting*. Homewood, IL: Irwin.

Bai, G., F. Coronado, and R. Krishnan. 2010. The role of performance measure noise in mediating the relation between task complexity and outsourcing. *Journal of Management Accounting Research* 22: 75–102.

Balakrishnan, R., L. Eldenburg, R. Krishnan, and N. Soderstrom. 2010. The influence of institutional constraints on outsourcing. *Journal of Accounting Research* 48 (4): 767–794.

Barney, J. B. 1986. Strategic factor markets: Expectations, luck, and business strategy. *Management Science* 32 (10): 1231–1242.

———. 1991. Firm resources and sustained competitive advantage. *Journal of Management* 17 (1): 99–120.

Barthélemy, J. 2001. The hidden cost of IT outsourcing. *MIT Sloan Management Review* 42 (3): 60–69.

Bromage, N. 2000. Outsourcing: To do or not to do, that is the question. *Management Accounting (CIMA)* 78 (1): 22–23.

Bromwich, M. 1990. The case for strategic management accounting: The role of accounting information for strategy in competitive markets. *Accounting, Organizations and Society* 15 (1/2): 27–46.

Bryce, D. J., and M. Useem. 1998. The impact of corporate outsourcing on company value. *European Management Journal* 16 (6): 635–643.

Burns, J., and G. Baldvinsdottir. 2005. An institutional perspective of accountants' new roles - the interplay of contradictions and praxis. *European Accounting Review* 14 (4): 725–757.

Capettini, R., and G. L. Salamon. 1977. Internal versus external acquisition of services when reciprocal services exist. *The Accounting Review* 52 (3): 690–696.

Carr, L. P., and C. D. Ittner. 1992. Measuring the cost of ownership. *Journal of Cost Management* (Fall): 42–51.

Carson, S. J. 2007. When to give up control of outsourced new product development. *Journal of Marketing* 71 (1): 49–66.

Chalos, P. 1995. Costing, control, and strategic analysis in outsourcing decisions. *Journal of Cost Management* (Winter): 31–37.

CIMA. 2009. *Improving Decision-making in Organisations: The Opportunity to Reinvent Finance Business Partners*: Chartered Institute of Management Accountants.

Coase, R. H. 1937. The nature of the firm. *Economica* 4 (16): 386–405.

Conner, K. R. 1991. A historical comparison of resource-based theory and five schools of thought within industrial organization economics: Do we have a new theory of the firm? *Journal of Management* 17 (1): 121–154.

Corazza, M. 1999. Merton-like theoretical frame for fractional Brownian motion in finance. In *Current Topics in Quantitative Finance*, edited by E. Canestrelli. Heidelberg: Physica Verlag, 37.

Dahan, E., and J. R. Hauser. 2002. Product development: managing a dispersed process. In *Handbook of Marketing*. Thousand Oaks, CA: Sage Publications, 179–222.

Dierickx, I., and K. Cool. 1989. Asset stock accumulation and sustainability of competitive advantage. *Management Science* 35 (12): 1504–1515.

Drtina, R. E. 1994. The outsourcing decision. *Management Accounting (USA)*, March: 56–62.

Ellram, L. M. 1993. Total cost of ownership elements and implementation. *International Journal of Purchasing and Materials Management* 29 (4): 3–11.

———. 1995. Total cost of ownership: an analysis approach for purchasing. *International Journal of Physical Distribution & Logistics Management* 25 (8): 4–23.

Ellram, L. M., and A. B. Maltz. 1995. The use of total cost of ownership concepts to model the outsourcing decision. *The International Journal of Logistics Management* 6 (2): 55–66.

Gottfredson, M., R. Puryear, and S. Phillips. 2005. Strategic sourcing: From periphery to the core. *Harvard Business Review* 83 (2): 132–139.

Grant, R. M. 2005. *Contemporary Strategy Analysis*. 5th ed. Oxford: Blackwell Publishing Ltd.

Gross, H. 1966. Make-or-buy decisions in growing firms. *The Accounting Review* 41 (4): 745–753.

Harriman, N. F. 1982. *Principles of Scientific Purchasing*. 1st ed. New York: McGraw-Hill.

Higgins, C. C. 1955. Make-or-buy re-examined. *Harvard Business Review* 33 (2): 109–119.

Horngren, C. T. 1967. *Cost Accounting: A Managerial Emphasis*. 2nd ed. Englewood Cliffs, NJ: Prentice-Hall, Inc.

Horngren, C. T., G. Foster, and S. M. Datar. 2000. *Cost Accounting: A Managerial Emphasis*. Upper Saddle River, NJ: Prentice-Hall, Inc.

Hätonën, J., and T. Eriksson. 2009. 30+ years of research and practice of outsourcing - exploring the past and anticipating the future. *Journal of International Management* 15 (2): 142–155.

Jackson, D. W., and L. L. Ostrom. 1980. Life cycle costing in industrial purchasing. *Journal of Purchasing and Materials Management* 16 (Winter): 8–12.

Kaplan, R. S. 1983. Measuring manufacturing performance: A new challenge for managerial accounting research. *The Accounting Review* 58 (4): 686–706.

———. 1984a. The evolution of management accounting. *The Accounting Review* 59 (3): 390–419.

———. 1984b. Yesterday's accounting undermines production. *Harvard Business Review* 62 (4): 95–102.

———. 1985. Accounting lag: the obsolescence of cost accounting systems. In *The Uneasy Alliance: Managing the Productivity-Technology Dilemma*. Boston, MA: Harvard Business School Press, 195–226.

———. 2011. Accounting Scholarship that Advances Professional Knowledge and Practice. *The Accounting Review* 86 (2): 367–383.

Kaplan, R. S., and R. Cooper. 1998. *Cost and Effect: Using Integrated Cost Systems to Drive Profitability and Performance*. Boston: Harvard Business School Press.

Kralovetz, R. G. 1996. A guide to successful outsourcing. *Management Accounting (USA)* 78 (4): 32–38.

Lacity, M. C., and R. Hirschheim. 1993. The information systems outsourcing bandwagon. *Sloan Management Review* 35 (1): 73–87.

Lamminmaki, D. 2008. Accounting and the management of outsourcing: An empirical study of the hotel industry. *Management Accounting Research* 19 (2): 163–181.

Langfield-Smith, K. 2008. Strategic management accounting: how far have we come in 25 years? *Accounting, Auditing & Accountability Journal* 21 (2): 204–228.

Lonsdale, C., and A. Cox. 2000. The historical development of outsourcing: the latest fad? *Industrial Management & Data Systems* 100 (9): 444–450.

Mathews, R. 1962. *Accounting for Economists*. Cheshire, Melbourne: F. W. Cheshire Pty. Ltd.

McCormick, T., and D. Duff. 2009. *Strategic Cost Reduction: Cutting Costs without Killing your Business*. Longford, Ireland: Turner Print Group.

McIvor, R. 2005. *The Outsourcing Process: Strategies for Evaluation and Management*. Cambridge: Cambridge University Press.

Mol, M. J. 2007. *Outsourcing: Design, Process and Performance*. 1st ed. Cambridge: Cambridge University Press.

Morgan, J. 1999. Purchasing at 100: Where it's been, where it's headed. *Purchasing* 127 (8): 72–94.

Oxenfeldt, A. R., and W. T. Baxter. 1961. Approaches to pricing: Economist vs. accountant. *Business Horizons* 4 (4): 77–90.

Penrose, E. 1959. *The Theory of the Growth of the Firm*. Oxford: Oxford University Press.

Peteraf, M. A. 1993. The cornerstones of competitive advantage: A resource-based view. *Strategic Management Journal* 14 (3): 179–191.

Peters, T. J., and R. H. Waterman. 1982. *In Search of Excellence: Lessons from America's Best-Run Companies*. New York: Harper & Row.

Piore, M. J., and C. F. Sabel. 1986. *The Second Industrial Divide: Possibilities For Prosperity*: New York Basic Books.

Porter, M. E. 1980. *Competitive Strategy: Techniques for Analyzing Industries and Competitors*. New York: Free Press.

———. 1985. *Competitive Advantage: Creating and Sustaining Superior Performance*. New York: Free Press.
———. 1991. Towards a dynamic theory of strategy. *Strategic Management Journal* 12: 95–117.
Prahalad, C. K., and G. Hamel. 1990. The core competence of the corporation. *Harvard Business Review* 68 (3): 79–92.
Quinn, J. B. 2000. Outsourcing innovation: the new engine of growth. *MIT Sloan Management Review* 41 (4): 13–28.
Quinn, J. B., and F. G. Hilmer. 1994. Strategic outsourcing. *Sloan Management Review* 35 (4): 43–56.
Rogers, P., and M. Blenko. 2006. Who has the D? *Harvard Business Review* 84 (1): 52–61.
Rumelt, R. P. 1974. *Strategy, Structure, and Economic Performance*. Boston, MA: Harvard Business School Press.
———. 1982. Diversification strategy and profitability. *Strategic Management Journal* 3 (4): 359–369.
Seal, W. 2010. Managerial discourse and the link between theory and practice: From ROI to value-based management. *Management Accounting Research* 21 (2): 95–109.
Shank, J. K. 2007. Strategic cost management: upsizing, downsizing, and right(?) sizing. In *Contemporary Issues in Management Accounting*. Oxford: Oxford University Press, 355–379.
Shank, J. K., and V. Govindarajan. 1989. Concepts in Value Chain Analysis: The "Famous" Crown Cork and Seal Company Case. In *Strategic Cost Analysis –The Evolution from Managerial to Strategic Accounting*: Homewood, Illinois: Irwin, 39–59.
———. 1992. Strategic cost management: The value chain perspective. *Journal of Management Accounting Research* 4: 179–197.
———. 1994. *Strategic Cost Management. The New Tool for Competitive Advantage*. New York: Free Press.
Sibbet, D. 1997. 75 Years of Management Ideas and Practice. *Harvard Business Review* 75 (5): 2–12.
Simmonds, K. 1981. Strategic management accounting. *Management Accounting* 59 (4): 26–30.
Simon, H. A. 1977. *The New Science of Management Decision*. New Jersey: Prentice-Hall.
Stacey, M. 1998. Outsourcing: how organisations need to prepare in order to realise the full potential benefits. *Management Accounting* 76 (5): 14–16.
Stigler, G. J. 1951. The division of labor is limited by the extent of the market. *The Journal of Political Economy* 59 (3): 185–193.
Teece, D. J. 1976. *The Multinational Corporation and the Resource Cost of International Technology Transfer*. Cambridge, MA: Ballinger Pub. Co.
———. 1980. Economies of scope and the scope of the enterprise. *Journal of Economic Behavior and Organization* 1 (3): 223–247.
Teece, D. J., G. Pisano, and A. Shuen. 1997. Dynamic capabilities and strategic management. *Strategic Management Journal* 18 (7): 509–533.
Thrift, N. 2005. *Knowing Capitalism*. London: Sage Publications.
Venkatesan, R. 1992. Strategic sourcing: To make or not to make. *Harvard Business Review* 70 (6): 98–107.
Wernerfelt, B. 1984. A resource-based view of the firm. *Strategic Management Journal* 5 (2): 171–180.
Widener, S. K., and F. H. Selto. 1999. Management control systems and boundaries of the firm: Why do firms outsource internal auditing activities? *Journal of Management Accounting Research* 11: 45–73.
Williamson, O. E. 1975. *Markets and Hierarchies: Analysis and Antitrust Implications*. New York: Free Press.
———. 1979. Transaction-cost economics: The governance of contractual relations. *Journal of Law and Economics* 22 (2): 233–261.
———. 1981. The economics of organization: The transaction cost approach. *The American Journal of Sociology* 87 (3): 548–577.
———. 1985. *The Economic Institutions of Capitalism*. New York: Free Press.

16

Customer relations and cost management

Trond Bjørnenak and Øyvind Helgesen

Introduction

The management control and cost management literature have traditionally focused on two types of cost objects: organizational units and products. The first type focuses mainly on responsibility centres – such as departments or business units – and the task of controlling costs and profitability. The second is typically more decision-oriented, e.g. on pricing and product mix decisions. In both cases the information generated is for internal users and based on internal data sources, e.g. internal production data from internal processes. In some countries the term 'internal accounting' is used to describe such an information system, but it is better known as management accounting in the Anglo-Saxon literature.

The purpose of collecting information on departments, activities and products is to improve operational and strategic decision-making. Product cost information may be used for decisions regarding the number of products, the design of products or make-or-buy decisions, i.e. whether parts of the process should be produced internally or outsourced to others. This type of decision relates to the company's strategic positioning and represents the strategic use of cost information. However, information on costs related to responsibility centres and products may also be used for operational improvements, such as continuous improvement of processes or managing bottlenecks in the production. These are examples of the operational use of cost information.

Technological changes and increased global competition have increased and altered the focus on the design and use of cost management information. Large initial investments in, for example, the oil sector have highlighted the importance of controlling the cost in the design phase. When the oil platform is operating, only a minor part of the cost can be affected. When costs are locked in at an early stage, it becomes more important to understand the customer's need. What attributes is the customer willing to pay for? If this is not understood before the design of the product, it may be costly to change at a later stage. The consequences of making bad decisions are also more dramatic when competition is fierce and margins are low. Thus, increased competition and globalization increases the importance of controlling your costs and knowing your profitable and unprofitable products.

These changes have also highlighted the importance of the customer and the understanding of how the company generates value for the customer. When a company invests in customer-specific technology, it is more important to understand how the customer values this investment. Increased competition also implies more focus on the 'best' customers. If one company knows better who they are as compared to its competitors, this may be used for decisions on customer portfolio and marketing investments.

In this chapter we are going to take a closer look at how customer information may be designed and used in a management control system. First we focus on customer profitability analyses (CPA) and how these costing systems can be used to increase the value creation in a company. The second section looks into the design stage and the importance of understanding the customers' needs and willingness to pay. In the third section we discuss the use of customer-related performance measures. The concluding part discusses the link between strategic positioning, customer relations and the design of the control system. Much of the information proposed in the chapter can support important management decisions, particularly in the sense of attention-directing that will alert management to decision-relevant issues that might otherwise remain invisible.

Customer profitability analyses

An increasing share of a company's total costs is related to market- and customer-based activities (Helgesen and Voldsund, 2009), and marketing cost differences exist both between industries and within industries. Different customers may make different demands on these activities. This implies that the company's profitability may differ even if two customers buy exactly the same products in the same quantity at the same prices. Some customers may have a demand behaviour that drives more costs than others. Some customers may be difficult to attract, thus resulting in different acquisition costs, or they may ask for certain customer-specific adjustments. Some customers may have a demanding ordering pattern, or they may return a lot of the goods they have bought. Thus, owing to increased competition, knowing the customer-specific costs and the profitability of different customers and segments may be vital for the profitability of the company. If your competitors have better knowledge about costs and profits than your company, they may systematically approach these customers and leave you with a less valuable customer base.

Some tele companies are, for example, using customer profitability figures to direct their marketing activities and to differentiate services between customers, e.g. if two persons are calling the call centre at the same time the most profitable one may get priority. The telephone number is used to identify the customer, and the customer profitability system gives the identity a priority class. In the more advanced systems, this is not only related to how much you call, but to the revenues, discounts and customer-related costs.

How to approximate customer costs

Customer profitability is the difference between customer revenues and customer costs. This may sound simple but it is often hard to estimate real profitability. One challenge is the variation in revenues and cost through time. Customer groups in a bank can serve as an example. Students may not generate much revenue when studying, while their costs may be significant, e.g. related to a high number of transactions. So, why are (some) students still very attractive customers to banks? The reason is very simple. After finishing their studies, the students may get very well-paid jobs, and at the same time become borrowers. When settling down the former students have to make investments (houses, cars, etc.), thus becoming profitable customers for the bank. Is it therefore meaningful to call the student an unprofitable customer? Well, that depends on the total cash-flow through the lifetime of the customer (Gupta and Lehmann, 2005; Kumar, 2008; Rust et al., 2000; Ryals, 2008). Theoretically, this should be done using a life-cycle budget for the customer and calculating the net present value (NPV) of the customer (t is the period of time):

$$NPV = \sum_t[(\text{customer revenues} - \text{customer costs}) / (1 + \text{cost of capital})^t]$$

We do not see many calculations of this type in practice. A bank has many customers and it would be extremely time-consuming to set up a lifetime budget for each customer. The level of uncertainty in the customer relationship may also be high. We do not know how large the loans will be and the risk or the duration of the relationship. However, ideally we should know the cash-flow related to each customer. Most often this is not possible since the cash outflow is not separable among the customers. The solution to this problem is to estimate customer costs for each customer. The quality of the customer profitability reports is then dependent on the quality of the proxies.

The typical approach to approximating the cost is to do a cross-sectional analysis of the customers, i.e. to calculate the costs of all or a group of customers at a certain point in time and for a certain period of time, e.g. the previous quarter or year. The main problem in this approach is to trace the costs to the customer. Some costs are directly attributable to the customers, e.g. cost of goods sold, transport and distribution costs, quantity discounts, campaigns, bonuses and cash discounts. The amount of costs directly attributable to customers varies from company to company based on differences in cost structures. However, it is also related to the quality of the cost registration and classification systems.

Other customer-related costs are indirect and have to be allocated to the customer based on a chosen allocation base. Activity based costing (ABC) or time-driven activity-based costing (TDABC, see Chapter 8) may be useful approaches to customer costing (Cooper and Kaplan, 1999; Kaplan and Anderson, 2007). The basic principle in these approaches is to group the customer-related costs in homogeneous cost pools (activities) and allocate the costs to customers based on the cost driver, i.e. the factor (time) that describes how the customers generate workload for the cost pool and thus are driving the costs (Demeere et al., 2009; Everaert et al., 2008a; 2008b; Stouthuysen et al., 2010).

Thus, the estimation of the profitability of each customer in the customer portfolio of a business unit is based on an understanding of how the customers are causing (driving) the costs in different parts of the organization (Everaert et al., 2008a; 2008b; Helgesen 2006a; 2007; 2008; Kaplan and Anderson, 2004; 2007; Storbacka, 1995). If all customers are causing the same workload in an activity, the problem is simple. We can just allocate costs based on the number of customers or volume (dependent on which factor drives the cost). It gets more complicated when the customers are more heterogeneous:

- some customers may ask for adjustments of the standard products;
- some customers are systematically buying more of the most profitable products, and others may buy more of the less profitable ones;
- some customers need credit checks and more credit control;
- some customers demand extra services and higher quality;
- some customers have many engineering change orders;
- some customers have high levels of complaints and returns;
- some customers want to be involved in new product development;
- some customers are not predictable and thus costly to handle;

- some customers are located at places with high sales and distribution costs;
- some customers always pay their bills on time, are predictable and handle all the distribution.

This list gives only some examples. The point is that many of these important issues are not taken into account either when customer profitability is discussed and presented, or in price negotiations. Product cost information does not take these differences into account, because they are driven by the customers, not the products. However, the competitive situation – resulting in increased market- and customer-orientation – will also increase the need for more information on the cost of serving the customer and for the rationale for price differentiation.

Most often the design and use of customer profitability accounting will be industry-specific. In the banking industry, the attention will usually be on the pricing of deposits and loans, the customer's product portfolio and the use of different services (transactions). For a producer of fertilizer production batches, sales orders and distribution costs may be important elements in the customer profitability report. Thus, it is natural that industry-specific cost and profit drivers are modelled in the analyses. Nevertheless, there are some common concepts that may help in the design of a customer profitability report:

- customer revenues;
- customer revenue reductions;
- net customer revenues;
- direct customer product costs;
- customer product profits/margin;
- customer costs (direct and indirect);
- customer operating margin;
- customer financial costs;
- customer profits.

Customer revenues represent the sum of all revenues of all the transactions (invoices, etc.) during the chosen period of time (month, quarter, etc). (The amounts of the other items of the customer accounts are found analogously.)

Customer revenue reductions represent quantity discounts, campaign discounts, rebates, bonuses, etc. (Cash discounts are usually addressed as financial costs.)

Direct customer product costs are the estimated costs of products delivered to the various customers, and consist of purchasing costs, inward freights and brokers' commissions, production costs, packaging costs, etc.

Customer costs (direct and indirect) are costs caused by the customer, and are either directly traced to the customer or allocated to the customer, based on a factor signalling how these costs are caused by the customer. For an exporting company for example, the direct costs may comprise a lot of items such as sales and distribution costs (outward freights, transport assurances, agent commissions, etc.); losses and activities established in order to reduce losses (losses on account receivables, costs related to credit insurance, commercial letters of credit, etc.); post-sale service costs (training, support, complaints, etc.); the treatment of customers and markets (travelling, representation, exhibitions, advertisements and advertising campaigns, etc.); other marketing costs (charges related to exportation, duties, taxes, etc.). In order to trace the direct costs it is necessary to go into details. This implies the need to study all accounts, all vouchers and all items. The remaining costs may be treated as indirect costs (fixed costs that are divisible) and allocated to the different levels of the cost hierarchy provided by ABC/TDABC

(Cooper and Kaplan, 1999; Kaplan and Anderson, 2004; 2007). The assignment of costs to the different cost groups depends on different aspects, such as the understanding of costs and the effort carried out in order to trace costs according to this understanding (Demeere et al., 2009; Everaert et al., 2008a; 2008b; Stouthuysen et al., 2010). By working meticulously through each account it may be possible to trace a relatively large proportion of the customer costs (Helgesen, 2007).

Customer financial costs consist of discounting costs, and imputed interest cost on capital (stock, receivables etc.) related to the customer relationship.

The main purpose of the customer profitability analyses is to estimate the customer profits for the chosen period of time by linking the customer revenues to the customer's consumption of resources in all parts of the organization.

Reporting the results of customer profitability analyses

When analysing the financial aspects of the customer portfolio of a business unit, a starting point could be an exploration of the customer revenues. Some insight may be obtained by describing the typical customer or the average customer of the customer base and the variation from the average revenue, e.g. standard deviation, as well as other statistics. However, this kind of information is often of limited value and is really not very well suited for communication and discussion. Additional insight could thus probably be obtained by examining ordered distributions of customer revenues. Such distributions (Lorenz curves) can be used to measure the sensitivity of customer portfolios as they indicate how dependent business units are on a few customers.

Figure 16.1 presents an example of a Lorenz curve representing the revenues of 176 customers. On the horizontal axis the customers are ranked according to their customer revenues from low to high. On the vertical axis all customers are represented by their own shares of the total customer revenues. Thus the graph consists of 176 points. The first point of the curve represents the customer with the lowest revenues for the chosen period of time, the second point represents the two customers with the two lowest customer revenues and their accumulated share of the customer revenues, etc. As long as the customers are ordered in accordance with increasing revenues, the gradient of the Lorenz curve gradually increases. Of course, the end point of the curve represents 100% of the customer base and 100% of the customer revenues. It should be underscored that the Lorenz curve follows the diagonal of Figure 16.1 if the customer revenues are just the same for all customers.

Figure 16.1 shows that the customer revenues are unequally distributed:

- about 1% of the customer revenues are coming from about 25% of the customer base;
- about 50% of the customer base results in about 10% of the customer revenues;
- about 5% of the largest customers represent about 30% of the customer revenues.

In order to get an even better understanding of the variations regarding customer revenues, some economic key measures can be estimated. The Gini coefficient (G) is often used to describe how equally distributed the observations are, and can be calculated as, viz. Figure 16.1:

$G = 2 \star A$ (where A represents the area between the Lorenz curve and the diagonal)

If the customer revenues are equally distributed – implying that the Lorenz curve follows the diagonal of Figure 16.1 – the Gini coefficient is 0 (zero). If the customer revenues are very unequally distributed – implying that one of the customers represents almost 100% of

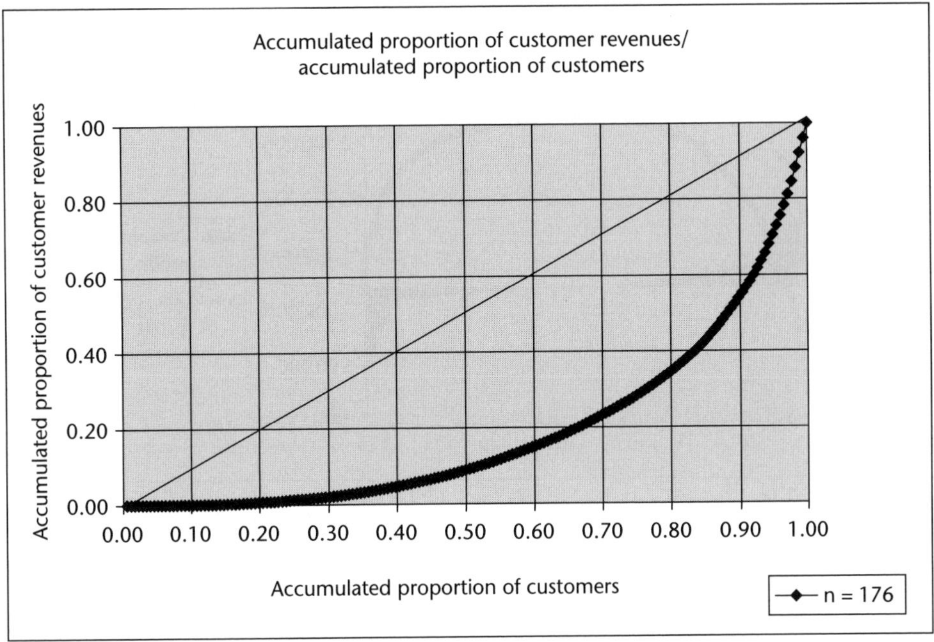

Figure 16.1 The Lorenz curve of customer revenues of a sample of 176 customers

the customer revenues – the Gini coefficient is close to 1. Thus the Gini coefficient will be somewhere between 0 and 1. The lower the obtained value of the Gini coefficient, the more equal the distribution of the customer revenues is. In this example (Figure 16.1), the Gini coefficient is estimated to be 0.63.

Thus, the Gini coefficient can be used as a measure of how dependent a business unit is on a certain number of customers. The higher the estimated figure (the closer to 1), the more vulnerable the customer base is to a loss of a small number of customers. Perhaps this is even easier to see when estimating another economic key figure – the 'Vulnerability factor revenues' (VFR) – which is defined as follows:

> VFR (Vulnerability factor revenues) = the proportion of customers below the average customer revenue.

Thus the measure called the 'Vulnerability factor revenues' (VFR) represents the proportion of customers of the customer base having customer revenues below the average. This economic key measure is also between 0 (zero) and 1. If the customer revenues are just the same for all customers, the VFR coefficient is 0 (zero). If the VFR coefficient is close to 1, this implies that the business unit's revenues are based on the customer revenues of only a few customers. Thus the business unit is very vulnerable regarding these customers with respect to volumes. In this example (Figure 16.1), the VFR coefficient is estimated at 0.72. This implies that the slope of the Lorenz curve is the same as the slope of the diagonal at this point, representing about 72% of the customers.

However, customer revenues and customer profits are different concepts. Thus it is even more interesting to study variations in customer profits. Customer profits can be analysed both in absolute figures (Figure 16.2) and in relative figures (Figure 16.3).

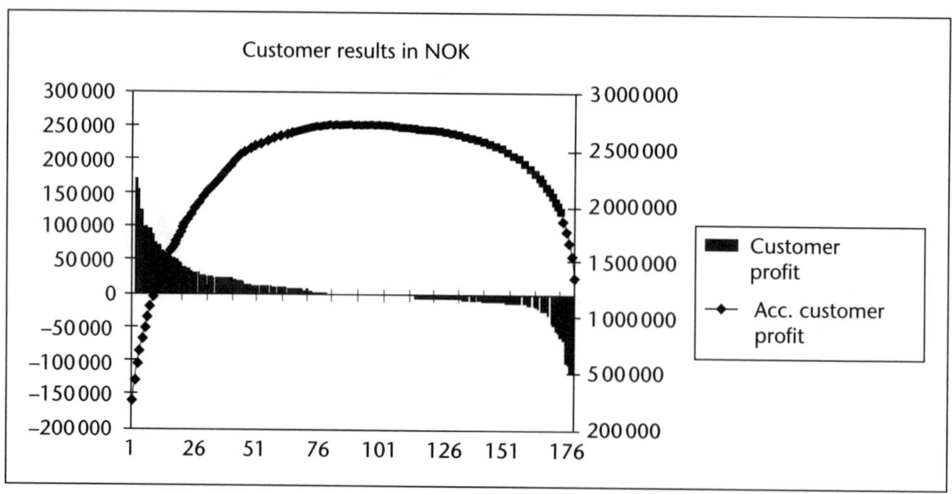

Figure 16.2 Customer profits in NOK ranked descending – per customer and accumulated

Figure 16.2 presents customer profits in absolute figures (NOK–Norwegian Kroner) per customer and accumulated for the whole sample. The customers are ranked according to absolute customer profits obtained during the period of analysis. This implies that the customer that contributed most to the total customer profit during the period is listed first, then the second most profitable customer, etc. The customer that is ranked last represents the lowest customer profit obtained, i.e. a considerable loss.

Figure 16.2 has two graphs. On the left axis the customer profits of the individual customers are measured and on the right axis the accumulated customer profits for the period are measured.

Out of the total sample of 176 customers there were 86 with positive customer profits and 90 with negative customer profits. The customer profit of the most profitable customer was about NOK 250 000 and customer profit of the second most profitable customer was about NOK 160 000, resulting in an accumulated customer profit of about NOK 410 000. The least profitable customer resulted in a loss of about NOK 200 000. During the period of time the accumulated customer profit was about NOK 1350 000. However, without unprofitable customers the final customer profit could have been about double (about NOK 2 700 000).

So far the figures have shown that the range of profitability (customer profits) is enormous, and that the negative customer profits reduced the accumulated customer profits quite a lot. This may be analysed further by way of ordered distributions based on relative customer profits (Figure 16.3).

Figure 16.3 presents the Stobachoff curve[1] for the sample. Both of the axes represent proportions. On the horizontal axis the customers are ordered according to their relative profitability, i.e. customer profit as a proportion of customer revenue. The most profitable customer is ordered as no. 1. The second most profitable customer is considered next and the customer profit of this customer is added to the customer profit of the first customer. The vertical axis shows the accumulated customer profit as a proportion of the total customer profit of the period. As long as the analysis is based on proportions, the end point of the Stobachoff curve has to be (1.1). The curve shows, for instance, what proportion of the customer revenues represents 100 per cent of the total customer profits. For the additional customer revenues the sum of the customer profits is equal to zero. The curve also shows the proportion of the

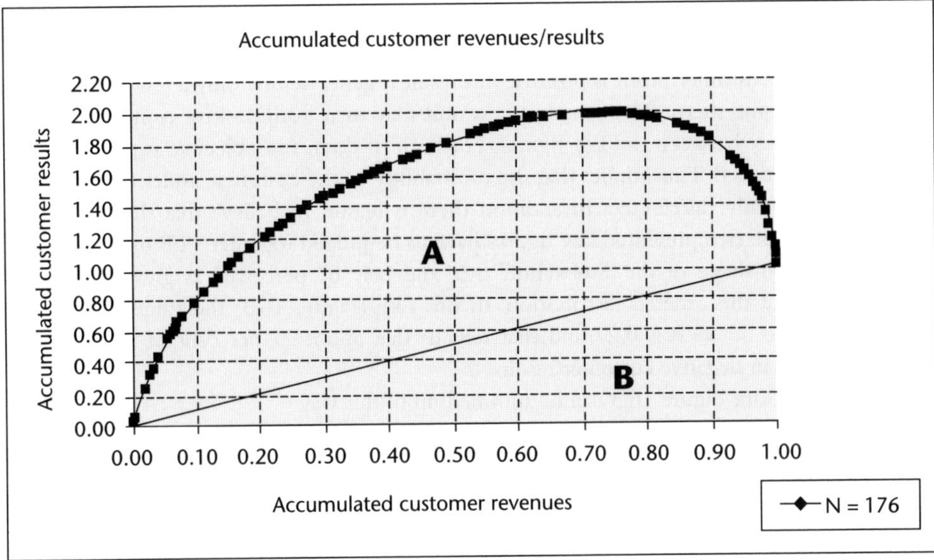

Figure 16.3 The Stobachoff curve for the customer sample

customer revenues which is profitable and the increase in the profitability that could have been obtained if the business did not have unprofitable customers. If all customers produce the same relative profitability, the Stobachoff curve follows the diagonal of Figure 16.3. If the relative profitability is different for different customers, the curve rises above the diagonal first, then levels out, and later falls until at last it reaches the (1.1) point.

Figure 16.3 may be elaborated in this way:

- estimate the customer profit for all customers, e.g. by using a TDABC approach;
- estimate the relative customer profit (the proportion customer profit/customer revenue) for each customer;
- based on the relative customer profits, rank the customer from the highest to the lowest;
- let the horizontal axis represent the proportion of customer revenues, implying that the proportion of the total line (distance) that the customer gets depends on the customer's share of the total customer revenues;
- the vertical axis presents the accumulated customer profits measured as a proportion of the accumulated customer profits for the period of time that is analysed.

The graphic representations of relative customer profits may be combined with economic key measures, e.g. Stobachoff coefficients (STC) and Vulnerability-factor profit (VFP). Referring to the labelled areas in Figure 16.3, the Stobachoff coefficient is defined as the ratio A/(A+B). The value of this coefficient will be between 0 and 1. The closer to 0, the more evenly the customer profits are distributed. In that case the A-area is small compared to the (A+B)-area. The closer the coefficient is to 1, the more unevenly the customer profits are distributed. However, different Stobachoff curves may produce the same Stobachoff coefficient. Thus, there is a need for another key figure. The Vulnerability-factor profit (VFP) is simply defined as the proportion of the customer revenues resulting in negative customer profits. Thus, the VFP gives the proportion of customers which results in negative bottom lines. Also this coefficient will be between 0 and 1. If each of the customer profits is positive, the coefficient will be 0. If the coefficient is close to 1, this implies that the business may be said to be vulnerable. Even if the aggregated customer profit is positive, this result is generated by only a few customers. If these customers quit, the profit of the business unit may turn from positive to negative. Thus, there is consistency between the key figures. For both of them the objective is to keep them as close as possible to 0. This implies that the profitability of the customer under consideration is positive and evenly distributed. In addition there is reason to believe that the situation is not vulnerable. The two presented key figures have to be judged together. VFP only represents a precision of the shape of the 'Stobachoff area' and may be perceived as giving additional information about the ordered distribution. In this case (Figure 16.3) the value of the STC is 0.67. The value of VFP is 0.27 and that tells us that about 27 per cent of the customer revenues resulted in negative customer results.

The findings from Figure 16.3 can be summed up in this way:

- about 100 per cent of the customer profits originated with about 15 per cent of the customer revenues;
- about 73 per cent of the customer revenues resulted in about 200 per cent of the customer profits ('summit');
- about 27 per cent of the customer revenues resulted in negative earnings and diminished about 100 per cent of the accumulated customer profits.

It should be underscored that the findings don't imply that the obtained total customer profits of the period would have been the same by concentrating the market activities towards the 15 per cent most profitable customers. As far as the customer margin (CM) of a customer is positive, the customer at least partly covers the indirect costs.

Lorenz curves, Gini coefficients, Stobachoff curves, Stobachoff coefficients and vulnerability factors (both regarding revenues and profits) may be used for various customer portfolios (as well as for other profitability objects). Stobachoff curves including economic key measures may for instance be used in order to compare various customer portfolios of a bank, e.g. the various customer portfolios for each of the customer-responsible employees. Differences regarding the shapes of curves as well as key measures can be discussed. In this way additional knowledge regarding revenues, costs and profits can be obtained among colleagues by learning from each other.

Often business people want to take appropriate action regarding various customers. In order to simplify this work it may be useful to group the customers based on predefined attributes or characteristics. Thus customer profitability accounts can be further analysed by assigning customers to customer segments.

Market (customer) segmentation – some financial approaches

Traditionally the goal of market segmentation is to identify product markets comprised of people, businesses or other organizations with similar characteristics and thus similar needs. Various characteristics are used as segmentation variables for both consumer and business markets. Most of the traditional approaches of market segmentation are based on non-economic characteristics of the customers such as geographic, demographic, psychographic and behavioural characteristics regarding consumer markets (Palmer, 2004). For business markets additional types of segmentation have been introduced, for instance based on industry sector, buying process characteristics (e.g. formality), structure of procurement, or buyer-seller relationships

(Macfarlane, 2002). However, some approaches to marketing segmentation, based on financial variables, have been introduced. These may be divided into two groups: one-dimensional and two-dimensional approaches (Helgesen, 2006a).

Regarding one-dimensional approaches, one approach suggests that customers should be assigned to one of four groups based on profitability analyses (Rust et al., 2000; Zeithaml et al., 2001): (1) 'The Platinum Tier' includes all the most profitable customers; (2) 'The Gold Tier' differs from the 'The Platinum Tier' in that profitability levels are not as high; (3) 'The Iron Tier' contains essential customers whose profitability is not substantial enough for special treatment; and (4) 'The Lead Tier' consists of the customers who are costing the business money. Other approaches exist (Ambler, 2003; Doyle, 2000).

Regarding two-dimensional or matrix approaches, Shapiro et al. (1987) assert that it may be useful to think of customers in two dimensions: net-price-realized and cost-to-serve. They introduce a matrix with cost-to-serve on the horizontal axis and net price on the vertical axis.

Figure 16.4 is similar to this matrix approach, though based on relative figures. Each customer is placed into one of four groups based on the averages of the relative costs to serve and the relative customer product margins. The segmentation procedure implies that the base of customers is divided into four groups: (I) customers that are 'demanding, but willing to pay', (II) 'aggressive customers', (III) 'transaction-oriented', or (IV) 'passive customers'. Customers that are categorized as (I) 'demanding, but willing to pay' (upper right) cost a great deal to serve, but the customers are willing to pay, (II) 'aggressive customers' (lower right) demand the highest product quality, the best service, and the lowest prices, (III) customers that are 'transaction-oriented' (lower left), are sensitive to price and relatively insensitive to service and quality, and (IV) 'passive customers' (upper left) can be served cheaply and are willing to accept higher prices.

Figure 16.5 shows another matrix approach. Each customer is placed into one of four groups based on the average of the customer revenues and the level (plus or minus) of the relative customer results of the period under consideration: (I) 'majors', (II) 'problems', (III) 'minors', and (IV) 'potentials'. The chosen names of the various customer segments implicitly describe the tactics or strategies that the business unit should consider with respect to the four segments.

The two matrix approaches presented above give differentiated insight (Helgesen, 2006a). It should be underlined that such matrixes only give an overview of the situation. It should also be mentioned that the chosen graduations of the matrixes may split customers that in reality are very similar. Therefore all the customers should be analysed and studied separately.

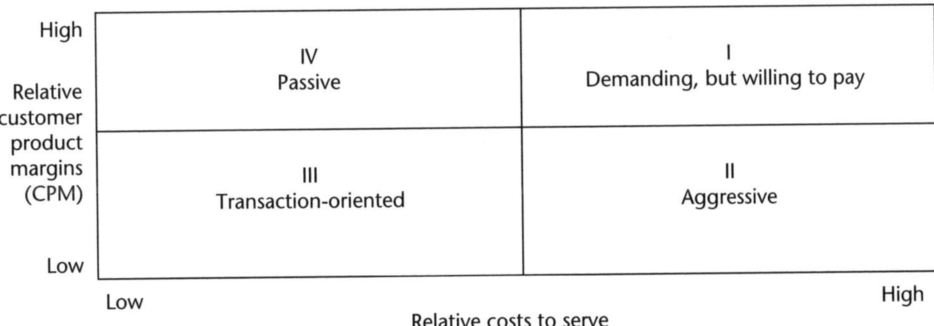

Figure 16.4 Customer segments based on relative customer product margins and relative costs to serve

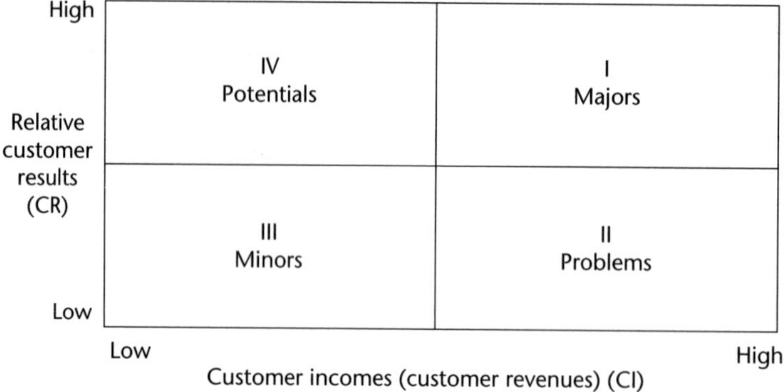

Figure 16.5 Customer segments based on customer revenues and relative customer results

Why do customer profitability analyses?

Market-oriented business units have two main objectives: (1) to satisfy the customers' needs, by offering products and services which accommodate the desires, requests and demands of the customers, and (2) to satisfy the business unit's needs, by carrying out exchanges that result in long-term profitability. Thus, it may be asserted that a company's implementation of the marketing concept is not in accordance with the original intentions if the company's efforts are only concentrated towards the customers and their needs, wishes and requests. In order to claim market-orientation, the self-interest of the business also has to be fulfilled, i.e. the customers have to be profitable. Thus the principal aim for implementing customer profitability accounting may be expressed in this way: to increase the market- and customer-orientation of the business by focusing on customer value (customer satisfaction) and economic customer value (customer profitability) (Helgesen, 2006b; 2007).

The creation of customer value and economic customer value may be related to various decision situations. Thus, there is a close connection between the formulated principal aim and decision-making, implying that market-oriented management accounting may be related to the following objectives: (1) to provide updated accounting information and profitability analyses concerning various profitability objects (accounts, orders, customers, customer segments, markets, products, etc.), (2) to provide profitability analyses adjusted to various decision situations, and (3) to arrange the data in such a way that ad hoc analyses may be carried out efficiently and easily.

Based on the statements above the objectives of the implementation of customer profitability accounting (CPA) and customer profitability analyses (CPA) can be formulated more specifically, for example as follows:

- to estimate the profitability of various profitability objects such as customers for a chosen period of time, e.g. each month;
- to estimate the profitability of various profitability objects for more than one period of time (time series);
- to estimate the financial value of a profitability object, e.g. the financial value of a customer, i.e. the lifetime financial value of a customer;
- to pay attention to the most profitable customers and offer the customers the products and services they want, as well as expert advice and guidance, i.e. to offer them the appropriate time;

- to try to make unprofitable customers profitable;
- to eliminate customers that cannot be made profitable (provided that this does not result in negative externalities);
- to include estimates of positive externalities, e.g. regarding reference customers, in the customer profitability accounts;
- to establish budgets for customer accounts as well as specified goals regarding customer profits;
- to establish portfolios of customers based on customer profits and credit risks based on customers' credit rating codes (Helgesen, 2008);
- to give decision-makers decision support regarding pricing decisions;
- to control costs of various activities, e.g. different support activities regarding order handling;
- to develop a market- and customer-oriented offer that can maintain or preferably increase the profitability of the business unit in the long term;
- to establish customer profitability based on key measures that can be included as part of a Balanced Scorecard;
- to include such key measures in business models.

Thus customer profitability analysis (CPA) should be included as a natural part of a managerial accounting system. When introducing a market-oriented accounting system, the context of the business unit has a lot to say. All industries are not similar. There are differences between for example the financial industries, the manufacturing industries, and the service industries. Even in the same industry there may be different approaches, just as in other areas of management accounting (Cooper and Kaplan, 1999; Demeere et al., 2009; Everaert et al., 2008a; 2008b; Foster et al., 1996; Helgesen, 2007; Kaplan and Anderson, 2007; Noone and Griffin, 1999; Ryals, 2008; Storbacka, 1995; van Raaij et al., 2003). Thus, there is not only one way for elaborating customer profitability accounts and doing customer profitability analyses. Therefore, when establishing a market-oriented managerial accounting system, it is necessary to know the context fairly well. The management accountants and the marketers should engage when problem areas concerning market-oriented managerial accounting are discussed in a business unit. Preferably, they should contribute heavily when the system is elaborated. At least they should demand market-oriented reports, graphical presentations, financial key measures, etc., so that the necessary decision-relevant information is included and easily available.

Customer value and product attributes

To the customer a product is often seen as a set of product attributes. For example, a specific car is seen as a combination of safety, comfort, environment friendliness, status and other attributes. Different customers may have different willingness to pay for different levels of these attributes. This is given a lot of attention in the marketing literature. However, significantly less attention is given to the costs of providing different levels of attributes. Exceptions are models like target costing (Ansari and Bell, 1997) and the value creation model (McNair, Polutnik and Silvi, 2001) that specifically focus on the trade-off between what the customer is willing to pay for a set of product attributes and the cost the firm bears to provide what the customer desires. This trade-off is illustrated in Figure 16.6.

The figure is based on a company which tried to differentiate its products based on the two dimensions of customer value and cost of proliferation. The company tried to build their strategy platform on the 'expensive proliferation' corner. These were product attributes with

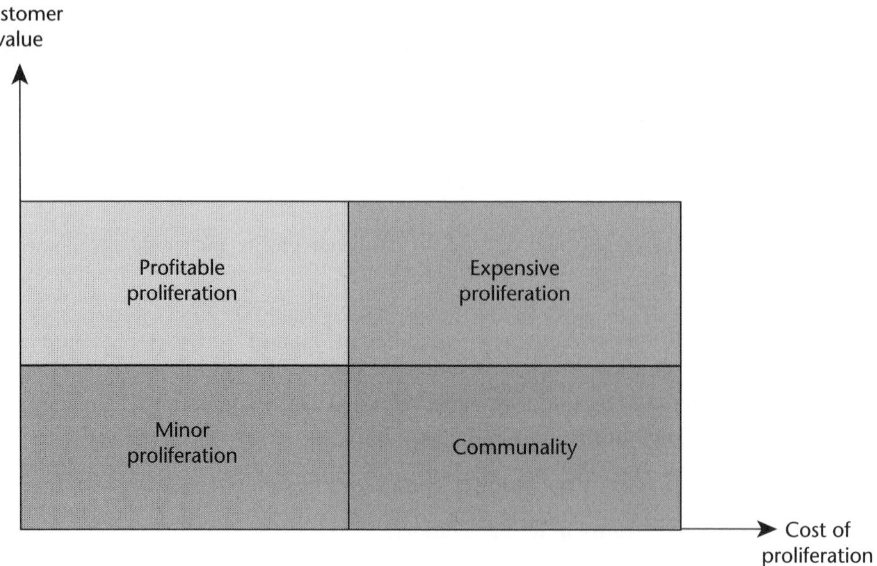

Figure 16.6 Matching customer value and value-added costs

high customer value, but also with high costs. At the same time these high costs gave them a barrier against its major competitors. It was also important to avoid putting too many resources into the 'communality' box.

In order to estimate the customer value, a company needs to identify a group of target customers. This group should have some common characteristics and homogeneous preferences for the most important attributes. When mapping the preferences it is important to identify the willingness to pay, which may be difficult to quantify in absolute measures. An alternative is to rank the attributes according to the value.

The value creation model provides another pragmatic approach to match costs and customer value. In this model the total value of the product or service is allocated to product attributes based on customer's value preferences. These preferences are based on survey data or interviews and expressed as customer weights. The average weight for a set of customers is used for the allocation. The following example may illustrate the approach:

Assume that a student pays 40 000 euros for an Executive MBA programme. A target group of students are asked to weight the following 'product attributes' of the programme:

Table 16.1 Weights and values of attributes in an Executive MBA programme

Programme attributes	*Customer weights*	*Value share*
Lectures	50%	20 000
Supervision	20%	8 000
Exam/evaluation	10%	4 000
Guest lectures from practice	10%	4 000
Administrative support	5%	2 000
Food	5%	2 000
Total	100%	40 000

Table 16.2 Calculating value multipliers

Programme attributes	*Value share (1)*	*Costs (2)*	*Value multipliers (1/2)*
Lectures	20000	8000	2.5
Supervision	8000	2000	4
Exam/evaluation	4000	5000	0.8
Guest lectures from practice	4000	4000	1
Administrative support	2000	4000	0.5
Food	2000	2000	1
Total	40000	25000	1.6

Note that this is a pragmatic approach. Lectures are activities rather than product attributes. The customers/students are looking for attributes like 'relevant knowledge' or 'information on how to improve my business'. However, these attributes are difficult to relate to the cost of providing the customers' desires. Activities are used as representatives for the attributes. In physical products, components may represent the attributes. The seats in a car may represent comfort or driving experience.

The next step in the analysis is to calculate the cost of attributes or their representatives. This may be done using activity-based costing or other costing methods. Dividing value shares by costs gives us value multipliers. This can be illustrated using the Executive MBA example.

Assume the total cost of the Executive MBA programme is 25 000 euros. Thus, the total contribution from the programme is 15 000 euros. An analysis of the total cost is shown in Table 16.2.

Interpreting the value multipliers should be done with care. One cannot conclude that administrative support should be reduced, even though the multiplier is low. The multipliers may be used as a platform for questions such as:

- Should more resources be allocated to teaching and supervision activities?
- Is it possible to simplify or change the exam and evaluation activities?
- Do we need to spend so much on food?
- What is the effect of reducing the local administrative support?
- Should we reallocate resources from guest lectures to supervision?

These type of design-related discussions are particularly important when the production process is characterized by a high level of locked-in costs. Car producers are often used as examples of this type of industry. However, costs are also often locked in early for service industries such as business school MBA programmes.

Customers and performance measures

Balanced Scorecards and other performance measurement models have attracted widespread attention in both academia and practice. We are not going to give a full description of these models, but only focus on how customer profitability can be linked to other customer-related performance measures.

In the previous section we highlighted the importance of understanding both costs and customer value. A third dimension in a control system is to measure the customer's view of how the company delivers in the important dimensions. Three different aspects are important to emphasise:

- the customer's view of the products and services provided by the company; this can be split into attributes or product components;
- the company's image and brand value, e.g. by measuring the relative rank of the company to important competitors;
- customer relations, i.e. how the customer is served by the company.

If we relate this to our Executive MBA example, we may measure the students' satisfaction with the different activities (product attributes) listed in Tables 16.1 and 16.2. We may also ask them to rank our programme compared to our closest competitors'. In the third group we may identify and measure critical performance indicators on how we treat our customers, e.g. the number of complaints.

Traditionally, market share has been a dominating performance indicator in the customer dimension. Different measures of customer satisfaction and customer loyalty have increased their popularity in the last decades. As described before, we may measure the student's satisfaction with different parts of an MBA programme. However, a better indicator may be whether the student has actively recommended the programme to any of his colleagues or friends. A third alternative is to measure the employer's perceived benefits from sending students to the Executive MBA programme.

The problem is that we may have high values for all these measures and still not be generating any value, simply by setting the prices below the costs of what we offer. Thus, it is of critical value that these measures are related to customer profitability, as we have described in previous parts of this chapter.

Customer measures and strategic positioning

Customer relations and how we generate value for the customer are decisive for a company's strategic positioning. If price is the vital point for the customer, cost management becomes the key issue in the control system. If the company believes it can generate added value it is important that this added value is understood. If the source of the added value lies in the product attributes, it is important to identify the attribute values and match them to the costs of providing the attributes to the customers. If the products are similar but the difference lies in the treatment of the customer, it is important to give customer relations particular attention.

Table 16.3 shows examples of how the control system can be adapted to a company's strategic positioning.

Table 16.3 The design of control systems and strategic positioning

Strategic positioning	*Cost leader*	*Product leader*	*Customer lock-in*
Example	Norwegian (low-cost airline)	Volvo (car producer)	DnB (bank)
Focus in the control system	Cost-efficient processes (activities)	Product attributes	Customers
Customer profitability object	Customer segments and routes	'Target Customer' for new models	Individual customers
Examples of performance measurement	Punctuality – price – brand identity	Satisfaction with product attributes	Satisfaction with customer relations and customer loyalty

The airline company Norwegian is used as an example of a cost leader. The main focus is on controlling the cost of different activities and keeping high-capacity utilization. Profitability analyses are done on flight numbers (routes) rather than by individual customer. However on an ad hoc basis different customer segments may be analysed and used for market positioning and marketing. Performance measures are selected based on what are seen as key profit drivers.

For car manufacturers it is important to both build an identity through a differentiation strategy and at the same time control costs and profitability. A product-attribute approach is combined with a target costing approach.

In the bank's case, the products are not very different from what other banks offer. Thus, it is important to pay specific attention to how the customer is treated and how to keep the most profitable customers loyal. In order to do this, the company needs to have a customer profitability system combined with measures of loyalty.

It is important to note that strategic positioning affects the focus and attention of the control system. It is of course also important for Norwegian to have satisfied and loyal customers. Both Volvo and DnB may also have activity-based management systems to benchmark cost-efficient processes. However, the focus of the system should always be informed by the strategic positioning of the company.

Conclusion

Management accounting and cost management systems have traditionally had an internal production bias. However, in the last two decades the customer's perspective has gained increased attention. Customer profitability analyses are introduced in more companies and are often considered more important than product costing. They not only provide management information on who the profitable customers are, but also why they are profitable, or not. This knowledge may be used in a number of different ways to build competitive advantages.

Viewing the products as sets of attributes is not a new thought. However, still only a few companies have systematically used such information to estimate value multipliers and to explore the potential profit related to the design of products and services.

On the other hand, the use of customer satisfaction indexes and other non-financial indicators has become widespread. We warn against such a simplistic view of customer relations in companies. While we acknowledge the importance of a satisfied customer, we warn against seeing this as synonymous with customer profitability.

Comparing a textbook from the 1980s with today's textbooks shows the increased attention given to the customer. However, there is still a strong product-focus bias. It is our impression that this is even more so in companies. Exploring the customer dimension may give the company a competitive advantage.

Note

1 This analysis may not be elaborated as presented if the accumulated customer result is negative.

Bibliography

Ansari, S.L. and Bell, J.E. (1997). *Target Costing: The Next Frontier in Strategic Cost Management*. New York: McGraw-Hill.

Ambler, T. (2003). *Marketing and the Bottom Line: The Marketing Metrics to Pump up Cash Flow*. Second edn. Harlow, UK: Pearson Education Ltd.

Cooper, R. and Kaplan, R.S. (1999). *The Design of Cost Management Systems.* Second edn. Englewood Cliffs, NJ: Prentice Hall.

Demeere, N., Stouthuysen, K. and Roodhooft, F. (2009). Time-driven activity-based costing in an outpatient clinic environment: Development, relevance and managerial impact. *Health Policy*, 92(2–3), 296–304.

Doyle, P. (2000). *Value-Based Marketing: Marketing Strategies for Corporate Growth and Shareholder Value.* West Sussex, England: John Wiley & Sons Ltd.

Everaert, P., Bruggeman, W. and De Creus, G. (2008a). Sanac Inc.: From ABC to time-driven ABC (TDABC) – An instructional case. *Journal of Accounting Education*, 26(3), 118–154.

Everaert, P., Bruggeman, W., Sarens, G., Anderson, S.R. and Levant, Y. (2008b). Cost modeling in logistics using time-driven ABC: Experiences from a wholesaler. *International Journal of Physical Distribution & Logistics Management*, 38(3), 172–191.

Foster, G., Gupta, M. and Sjoblom, L. (1996). Customer profitability analysis: challenges and new directions. *Journal of Cost Management*, 10(1), 5–17.

Gupta, S. and Lehmann, D.R. (2005). *Managing Customers as Investments: The Strategic Value of Customers in the Long Run.* Upper Saddle River, NJ: Pearson Education, Inc.

Helgesen, Ø. (2006a). Customer segments based on customer account profitability. *Journal of Targeting, Measurement and Analysis for Marketing,* 14(3), 225–237.

Helgesen, Ø. (2006b). Are loyal customers profitable? Customer satisfaction, customer (action) loyalty and customer profitability at the individual level. *Journal of Marketing Management*, 22(3–4), 245–266.

Helgesen, Ø. (2007). Customer accounting and customer profitability analysis for the order handling industry – A managerial accounting approach. *Industrial Marketing Management,* 36(6), 757–769.

Helgesen, Ø. (2008). Targeting customers: A financial approach based on creditworthiness. *Journal of Targeting, Measurement and Analysis for Marketing*, 16(4), 261–273.

Helgesen, Ø. and Voldsund, T. (2009). Financial decision support for marketers in the Norwegian fishing and furniture industries. *British Food Journal*, 111(7), 622–642.

Kaplan, R. and Anderson, S.A. (2004). Time-driven activity-based costing. *Harvard Business Review*, 82(11), 131–138.

Kaplan, R. and Anderson, S.A. (2007). *Time-Driven Activity-Based Costing: A Simpler and More Powerful Path to Higher Profits.* Boston, MA: Harvard Business School Press.

Kumar, V. (2008). *Managing Customers for Profit: Strategies to Increase Profits and Build Loyalty.* Upper Saddle River, NJ: Pearson Education, Inc.

Macfarlane, P. (2002). Structuring and measuring the size of business markets. *International Journal of Market Research,* 44(1), 7–30.

McNair, C-J., Polutnik, L. and Silvi, R. (2001). Cost management and value creation: the missing link. *European Accounting Review*, 10(1), 33–50.

Noone, B. and Griffin, P. (1999). Managing the long-term profit yield from market segments in a hotel environment: a case study on the implementation of customer profitability analysis. *International Journal of Hospitality Management*, 18, 111–128.

Palmer, A. (2004). *Introduction to Marketing: Theory and Practice.* Oxford, UK: Oxford University Press.

Rust, R.T., Zeithaml, V.A. and Lemon, K.N. (2000). *Driving Customer Equity: How Customer Lifetime Value is Reshaping Corporate Strategy.* New York, NY: The Free Press.

Ryals, L. (2008). *Managing Customers Profitably.* West Sussex, England: John Wiley & Sons Ltd.

Shapiro, B.P., Rangan, V.K., Moriarty, R.T. and Ross, E.B. (1987). Managing customers for profits (not just sales). *Harvard Business Review,* Sept.-Oct., 101–108.

Storbacka, K. (1995). *The Nature of Customer Relationship Profitability. Analysis of Relationships and Customer Bases in Retail Banking.* Helsingfors: Svenska Handelshøgskolan.

Stouthuysen, K., Swiggers, M., Reheul, A-M. and Roodhooft, F. (2010). Time-driven activity-based costing for a library acquisition process: A case study in a Belgian University. *Library Collections, Acquisitions & Technical Services*, 34(2–3), 83–91.

van Raaij, E.M., Vernooij, M.J.A. and van Trist, S. (2003). The implementation of customer profitability analysis: A case study, *Industrial Marketing Management*, 32(7), 573–583.

Zeithaml, V., Rust, R.T. and Lemon, K.N. (2001). The customer pyramid: Creating and serving profitable customers. *California Management Review*, 43(4), 18–142.

Part IV
Strategy and cost management

17

A new framework for strategic cost management

An empirical investigation of strategic decisions in Britain, the USA and Japan

Chris Carr, Katja Kolehmainen and Falconer Mitchell

Acknowledgements

The authors wish to acknowledge their gratitude to *Management Accounting Research* for giving permission to further disseminate the findings presented in our recent article – 'Strategic investment decision-making practices: A contextual approach' – which was published in *Management Accounting Research* in September 2010, and for which *Management Accounting Research* has full copyright. The authors also wish to acknowledge the many helpful comments they received on previous versions of this paper from participants at the EIASM 5th Workshop on International Strategy and Cross-Cultural Management, held in Istanbul in September 2007, at the 31st European Accounting Association Annual Congress, held in Rotterdam in April 2008, at the Academy of International Business Conference, held in Milan in June 2008, at the HSE Management Accounting Research Seminar, held in Helsinki in May 2009 and at a staff seminar held in the University of Edinburgh in September 2009. Constructive comments were also received from Robert Scapens, Tom Brown, Alison Kennedy, Teemu Malmi, Juhani Vaivio and the anonymous referees of *Management Accounting Research*. The authors wish to thank the Institute of Chartered Accountants of England and Wales, the Chartered Institute of Management Accountants and the Helsinki School of Economics Foundation, who all provided funding for the study.

Introduction

An identification of the determinants of practice has been one of the central quests for management accounting researchers. Within the strategic cost management (SCM) field, Oldman and Tomkins' (1999) empirical examination of SCM practice in five well-known companies has presented one of the most serious attempts to shed light on the contextual nature of SCM practice. It suggests that companies' decisions to apply SCM approaches can be attributable to two key contingencies – the extent to which a company is market-orientated, and the extent to which a company faces a need for a turnaround. Their study presents evidence of each of the four contextual situations constituted by using these two key contingencies, as the axis exhibits different SCM practices: for example, a strongly market-orientated company with no immediate need for a turnaround may draw benefits from using an externally orientated target costing approach. A less market-orientated company with no immediate need for a turnaround may, on the other hand, benefit from using a more internally orientated Kaizen costing approach. Finally, a weakly market-orientated company with a strong need for a turnaround may choose to utilize activity-based costing (ABC) as a way to enhance necessary product-pruning objectives.

Despite these valuable results, Oldman and Tomkins' (1999) contextual findings have received only limited attention from subsequent studies on SCM – and strategic management accounting (SMA) in general. Their study is, however, one of the most developed approaches to explaining differences in SMA practices. It is also one of the few SMA studies that are supported by several substantial and detailed case studies. Although focusing on explaining variation in SCM practices, their contextual approach is built on the broader contextual discourses within the strategic management and SMA literature – suggesting that their four-state Cost Management Model has broader applicability to explaining differences in other areas of SMA, as well.

This paper builds on Oldman and Tomkins' (1999) four-state Cost Management Model to develop a new contextual framework to explaining differences in practice. Our contextual framework's principal aim is to explain differences in another sub-set of SMA: namely strategic investment decision-making (SID) practices.[1] Similarly to Oldman and Tomkins' (1999) original model, our framework is built on the broader strategic management and SMA literature. It modifies Oldman and Tomkins' original *market orientation* and *need for a turnaround* axes to include a broader set of company and business sector-level variables, as well as to include a longer-term, more multidimensional concept of performance. This new framework is essentially an extended version of Oldman and Tomkins' original model: it integrates a wider range of generally acknowledged contextual variables into a single contextual framework. While focusing on explaining differences in SID-making practices, the general nature of this framework contributes to showing that the framework can also have potential for explaining variation in other SMA practices, including SCM practices.

This paper is to a large extent based on our recent article 'Strategic investment decisions: A contextual approach', published in *Management Accounting Research*.[2] As a consequence, the majority of the paper's empirics focus on explain differences in SID-making practices: by first developing a systematic contextual framework to explain differences in practice, and then by exploring this framework's potential for explaining SID-making practices through 14 case studies of UK, US and Japanese companies operating in vehicle component and telecommunications sectors. The broader implications of the study – including those regarding research on SCM – are addressed in the concluding section of the paper.

The remainder of the paper is structured as follows. The following section presents an overview of research related to SID-making practices, highlighting also the voids in the literature that our study seeks to address. Then, the explanatory contextual framework for SID-making practices is constructed and followed by a description of the research method. The research findings related to contextual SID-making practices are then presented, first in respect of potential contextual differences in the use of capital budgeting techniques, and second in respect of the companies' overall approaches to SIDs. The conclusion comprises a summary of the findings, a discussion of their broader implications, and a suggestion of areas for further research.

Literature overview on SID-making practices

Capital budgeting techniques

The literature on SID-making practices has provided ample evidence of the general use of capital budgeting techniques, such as DCF (e.g. Alkaraan and Northcott, 2006; Arnold and Hatzopoulos, 2000; Farragher et al., 1999; Graham and Harvey, 2001; Pike, 1996). Most research in the field has focused on the use of capital budgeting techniques in particular country contexts, addressing the use of techniques inter alia in the UK (e.g. Alkaraan and Northcott, 2006; Arnold and Hatzopoulos, 2000; Pike, 1996), the US (e.g. Farragher et al., 1999; Graham and Harvey, 2001; Klammer et al., 1991), continental Europe (e.g. Carr and Tomkins, 1996; 1998; Carr et al., 1994), and Japan (e.g. Carr, 2005; Carr and Tomkins, 1998; Jones et al., 1993; Kim and Song, 1990; Shields et al., 1991; Yoshikawa et al., 1989). Research findings demonstrate cross-country differences in the use of capital budgeting techniques. For example, the use of DCF techniques is more extensive among Anglo-Saxon companies (e.g. Arnold and Hatzopoulos, 2000; Graham and Harvey, 2001; Pike, 1996). Japanese, continental European and Scandinavian companies may, on the other hand, sometimes rely more on less sophisticated techniques, such as the payback period when making decisions on SIDs (Carr and Tomkins, 1996, 1998; Sandahl and Sjögren, 2003; Shields et al., 1991; Yoshikawa et al., 1989).

A limited amount of research has been conducted on the potential association between the use of capital budgeting techniques and contextual variables, other than the country context (Chen, 1995, 2008; Haka, 1987; Verbeeten, 2006). The relationship between corporate size and the use of techniques has been the most extensively covered topic. There is consistent evidence that large companies are more likely to use sophisticated techniques, such as DCF (Farragher et al., 1999; Graham and Harvey, 2001; Pike, 1996).[3] Available empirical evidence also suggests that the use of sophisticated techniques is more common among companies that operate in predictable as opposed to unpredictable business environments (Chen, 1995; Ho and Pike, 1998), among highly leveraged companies (Graham and Harvey, 2001; Klammer et al., 1991) and among companies that face financial uncertainty (Verbeeten, 2006). Companies facing a challenging financial situation have also been found to set tighter financial targets (Van Cauvenbergh et al., 1996).

Broader approaches to SIDs

Field study-based research on SID-making practices indicates that there are cross-country differences also in the extent to which SIDs are based on strategic versus financial considerations. Research findings suggest that UK companies may have a tendency to overlook strategic considerations and focus strongly on financial analyses, while Japanese and German companies may downplay financial evaluation and emphasize strategic considerations. US companies may, on the other hand, have a more balanced approach, paying attention to both strategic and financial considerations (e.g. Carr, 2005; Carr and Tomkins, 1996, 1998; Jones et al., 1993).

Corresponding evidence of differences in the extent to which SIDs are based on strategic versus financial considerations have also been documented among companies in the same country. For example, Sandahl and Sjögren (2003) found that some large Swedish companies base their decisions solely on sophisticated financial analysis while many of the companies promoting the traditional payback period technique tend to emphasize strategic considerations. Research evidence from the UK points to variation in the financial and strategic emphasis, as well (Alkaraan and Northcott, 2006; cf. Butler et al., 1991).

These documented differences in the balance of strategic versus financial considerations within the same country context indicate that contextual variables other than the country context are important influences on practice. However, available empirical evidence indicating an association with other contextual variables is very limited. There is some evidence to suggest that the higher levels of integration in manufacturing investment do attract a greater strategic emphasis (Abdel-Kader and Dugdale, 1998; Meredith and Hill, 1987).

Consequently, researchers have advocated the need for more contextually-based research studies designed to explain differences in SID-making practices (Haka, 1987; Ho and Pike, 1998; Slagmulder et al., 1995; Verbeeten, 2006). This study aims to address this gap by developing an explanatory contextual framework for SID-making practices. It seeks to explain contextual differences, not only in regard to which techniques are being used, but also in regard to why these techniques are used, and how they influence decision-making on strategic investments. The development of this framework is outlined in the following section.

Towards a contextual approach for SID-making practices

Oldman and Tomkins' contextual framework: the contexts of market orientation and the need for a turnaround

The development of the framework takes Oldman and Tomkins' (1999) four-state Cost Management Model as a starting point as it provides one of the most developed approaches to explaining differences in SMA practice. Their framework focuses on a sub-set of SMA, i.e. SCM, and proposes a theoretical framework that encompasses important contextual variables. Their study is also one of the few SMA studies that are supported by several substantial and detailed case studies. It provides evidence that companies' SCM practice variation can be explained by a four-state Cost Management Model that categorizes companies into four categories based on the extent of their *market orientation* and their *need for turnaround* (Figure 17.1).[4]

Although they do not explicitly address SID-making practices, they find differences in the type of investment favoured across their four contextual categories. This suggests that their framework may also have some relevance for explaining differences in SID-making practices (Chen, 1995; Klammer et al., 1991).

The strategic management, SMA and SID literature give direct support for the pertinence of Oldman and Tomkins' (1999) *market orientation* and *need for turnaround* contextual variables for explaining differences in SID-making practices. This literature suggests that financial turnaround shifts companies towards a greater financial orientation (Bibeault, 1981; Carr et al., 1994; Slatter, 1984), and that financial uncertainty and high leverage are associated with the use of more sophisticated capital budgeting techniques (Graham and Harvey, 2001; Verbeeten, 2006). Companies facing a difficult financial situation are also likely to operate a more formal investment decision-making process and will set tighter financial targets (Van Cauvenbergh et al., 1996). In addition, substantial literature arguing for a distinction between market and financial orientations (Barwise et al., 1989) suggests that companies with a weak market orientation are likely to put more emphasis on financial considerations, while strongly market-orientated companies will emphasize strategic considerations.

Modifying Oldman and Tomkins' contextual framework

Although *market orientation* and *the need for turnaround* are pertinent in explaining differences in SID-making practices (see, e.g., Bibeault, 1981; Doyle, 1992; Graham and Harvey, 2001;

	Strong turnaround need	No turnaround need
Strong market orientation	**Radical innovation** Focused investment	**Continuous market innovation** Growth investment
Weak market orientation	**Product pruning** Minimum investment/ divestment	**Continuous-process improvement** Process/maintenance investment

Figure 17.1 Oldman and Tomkins' (1999) four-state cost management model

Verbeeten, 2006), the strategic management, SMA, and SID literature suggest that Oldman and Tomkins' (1999) framework may need to be modified to explain adequately differences in SID-making practices. These modifications are discussed below by focusing on the two axes of their framework (see Figure 17.1 above).

Modifying the need for turnaround axis

SIDs involve long-term decisions, while turnaround is likely to be an inherently transitory circumstance. Companies may not be willing to change their SID-making practices frequently as this would destroy any consistency in their approach to these decisions. Companies may thus be more likely to adjust their SID-making practices in response to a more long-lasting decline in performance. For the analysis of SIDs, performance might, therefore, be better conceived in terms of some longer term, more multidimensional concept of performance.

This, in turn, requires recognition that goals and objectives will primarily reflect shareholder influence. However, it is possible that in some cases this may be extended to encompass other stakeholders (Johnson et al., 2008: 153–163) and so could modify the pure shareholder value pursuit implied by Rappaport (1996), particularly in stakeholder-driven societies such as Japan. Indeed, no theory exists to explain performance in absolute terms. In classical, formal strategic planning processes it is the *gap* between performance and shareholder goals and expectations which triggers any top-level strategic reviews or controls (Argenti, 1974). Empirical evidence suggests that SID practices reflect *perceptions* of shareholder or other stakeholder demands, which in turn vary widely across and even within different country contexts. Frequently, it is these somewhat subjective *perceptions*, rather than considerations of finance theory alone, which motivate any differences in practices, such as those relating to the tightness of financial targets (Carr et al., 1994).

We would expect weakly performing companies to be highly constrained by tough financial targets, as compared to strong performers, who may have more discretion to emphasize strategic considerations (Bibeault, 1981; Slatter, 1984; Van Cauvenbergh et al., 1996). Any perception of high shareholder demands would add further to such financial constraints.

Modifying the market orientation axis

Although *market orientation* is likely to be relevant for explaining differences in the extent to which strategic versus financial considerations are being emphasized (Barwise et al., 1989; Doyle, 1992), the strategic management and SMA literature suggests that *market orientation*'s influence on SID-making practices may be moderated or reinforced by a company's strategic orientation (Gupta and Govindarajan, 1984; Miles and Snow, 1978; Porter, 1980), management style (Goold and Campbell, 1987), and the attractiveness (Brownlie, 1985; Robinson et al., 1978) and dynamism of the market in which they operate (Cheung, 1993).

Association between a company's strategic orientation and SMA practices has been well documented in the SMA literature (e.g. Cadez and Guilding, 2008; Chenhall and Langfield-Smith, 1998; Govindarajan and Gupta, 1985; Guilding, 1999; Simons, 1987). However, the research findings in this area are rather fragmented (Fisher, 1995; Langfield-Smith, 1997) as SMA scholars have made use of several different strategy typologies, most notably generic strategies (Porter, 1980), strategic configurations (Miles and Snow, 1978) and strategic missions (Gupta and Govindarajan, 1984). Research findings do indicate that there may be general differences in the SMA practices between the more entrepreneurial strategy archetypes of *prospector* (Miles and Snow, 1978), *differentiator* (Porter, 1980) and *builder* (Gupta and Govindarajan, 1984), as compared to the more conservative strategy archetypes of *defender* (Miles and Snow, 1978), *cost leader* (Porter, 1980) and *harvester* (Gupta and Govindarajan, 1984; see Chenhall, 2003 and Langfield-Smith, 1997 for reviews on SMA literature).

Though popular in the SMA literature, in practice only two of Miles and Snow's (1978) four categories have usually been applied, *prospectors* and *defenders*; the remaining two, *analysers* and *reactors*, have usually been omitted (see e.g. Cadez and Guilding, 2008; Chen, 2008; Simons, 1987). Only Guilding (1999) noted all four categories in his research sample, but even he only reported differences in respect to *prospectors*. This may be because *analysers* are defined as a hybrid under which companies operate in silos, utilizing *prospector* configurations for some types of business and *defender* configurations for other types as they act in different environmental contexts. This compromises the coherence of the categories given in that their concepts are predicated upon integrated, consistent approaches to strategy, structure and organizational processes.

The *reactor* category is also problematic. Such companies are typically failing in terms of performance, having not adapted in any consistent manner to environments perceived as highly uncertain. Whilst Oldman and Tomkins (1999) also emphasize poor performance as an additional dimension, it is not clear why this should only arise in relation to uncertain environments. No SMA contributor has so far used more than the basic continuum as between *prospector* and *defender* extremes. Finally, in respect to strategic investment decision-making practices, Chen (1995, 2008) and Haka (1987) make no mention of the last two *analyser* and *reactor* categories.

Available evidence on the association between a company's strategic orientation and SMA practices suggests that the more entrepreneurial business strategy archetypes may be associated with stronger strategic orientation (Govindarajan and Gupta, 1985) and a broader use of planning information (Guilding, 1999; Simons, 1987) as compared to the more conservative business strategy types. Although the SID literature has not yet presented any direct evidence for an association between a company's strategic orientation and SID-making practices (Chen, 1995, 2008; Haka, 1987), the broader strategic management and SMA literature suggests that a company's tendency to emphasize strategic versus financial considerations may be moderated or reinforced by its strategic orientation.

The strategic management literature indicates, further, that a tendency to emphasize strategic versus financial considerations in SID-making practices may be moderated or reinforced by a company's management style, which can be categorized as *strategic planning*, *strategic control*, and *financial control* styles (Goold and Campbell, 1987). Although a management style principally depicts the way a corporate centre attempts to control other parts of the organization (for example by intervening in strategic planning and monitoring strategic performance, as in the *strategic planning* style, or by engaging in tight financial monitoring, as in the *financial control* style), such styles are also likely to be reflected in the way SIDs are approached. It would be expected that *strategic planning* styles will drive companies to put more emphasis on strategic considerations and on setting less challenging financial targets while *financial control* styles generate a stronger financial emphasis and tighter financial targets.

Finally, prior strategic management and SID research suggests that the business sector in which the company operates is likely to be associated with companies' SID-making approaches. Available evidence indicates that companies operating in stable business sectors may be more likely to use sophisticated capital budgeting techniques (Chen, 1995) and that they may also gain higher benefits from using such techniques as compared to companies operating in dynamic business sectors (Haka, 1987). Volatile business sectors may drive companies towards a greater emphasis on strategic considerations (Cheung, 1993), although the formality of their strategic analysis may be influenced by business sector dynamism (Eisenhardt and Sull, 2001; Mintzberg, 1994). A tendency to emphasize strategic considerations is likely to be further moderated or reinforced by market attractiveness. Companies operating in attractive business sectors that provide favourable prospects for growth and profitability are likely to put more emphasis on strategic considerations and to set less challenging financial targets as compared to companies operating in less attractive markets (Brownlie, 1985; Robinson et al., 1978).[5] We view such variables as likely to contribute further to market orientation,[6] and a tendency to emphasize strategic considerations.

A contextual approach to SID-making practices

The previous discussion indicates that Oldman and Tomkins' (1999) framework provides a useful starting position for explaining differences in SID-making practices. However, their original *market orientation* and *need for turnaround* dimensions do require modification to take account of key contextual variables pertinent to SIDs. Figure 17.2 integrates all these key contingencies into an overall contextual framework that explains differences in SID-making practices in terms of a company's '*market orientation*' (which, as explained above, is an extension of the definition for this term used by Oldman and Tomkins, 1999) and its '*performance in relation to shareholder expectations*'.[7]

The proposed new framework gives rise to four broad contingency positions, which we categorize as *market creators*, *refocusers*, *value creators* and *restructurers* to illustrate their different situational contexts.[8] Well-performing *market creators* are relatively free of short-term financial constraints and can therefore emphasize long-term market development and positioning. They

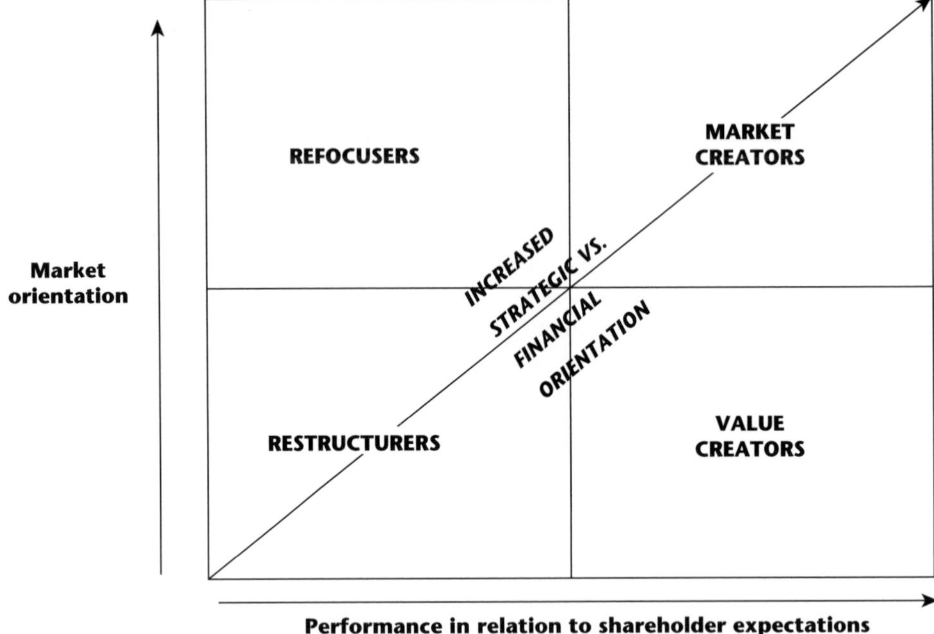

Figure 17.2 Contextual framework for strategic investment decision-making practices

will put a strong emphasis on strategic considerations in their SID-making approach, and will be relatively flexible in their use of financial targets. Similarly disposed, but experiencing greater short-term pressures to perform, *refocusers* are likely to be forced into greater conservatism and serious refocusing, while still having to protect crucial intangible assets, including brands and technology. Thus, *refocusers* will pay attention to both strategic and financial considerations in their SID-making approach and set moderately tight financial targets for their SIDs. Well-performing *value creators* emphasize internal efficiencies and 'value creation' for their customers, often through superior cost control. As with *refocusers*, *value creators* will pay attention to both strategic and financial considerations in their SID-making approach, and set moderately tight financial targets. Finally, *restructurers* engage in radical restructuring and cost-cutting due to strong short-term pressures to perform. *Restructurers* will put strong emphasis on financial considerations, set very tight financial targets for their SIDs and, in general, will be very conservative in their SID approaches.

In summary our working hypothesis is as follows: the SID orientation of a company may be predicted by the four-archetypes model reflected in Figure 17.2.

The counterfactual is that such differences in practices may be more effectively explained by one or other of our single variables taken in isolation, for example, Miles and Snow's (1978) major strategic configurations, or even by cross-country differences. A further issue in operationalizing the proposed framework is that, while a set of variables can be identified, there is an absence of any theoretical or empirical evidence suggesting that any particular individual variable is more influential than another. Consequently, in this exploratory analysis, variables are integrated on an unweighted basis. Again the counterfactual is that such a seemingly random approach is unnecessary; and that it is therefore preferable to stay with just one, more theoretically established, categorization approach.

Research approach and methodology

In order to empirically explore the above proposed framework's explanatory power over SID-making practices, matched comparative case studies on company SID practices have been undertaken. These cases were particularly pertinent to our research objective for two key reasons. Firstly, they provided rich enough data to enable scoring along the several variables identified above as relevant, and to explore overall SID approaches in considerable depth. Secondly, they enabled comparison of the SID practices across the four contextual categories described above.

To explore the influential dimensions of the four contingency-based typologies, companies representing diverse business sector and shareholder-influence contexts were selected. These comprised companies from the telecommunications sector (at the time of study an attractive, dynamic business sector) and vehicle components (at the time of study a relatively stable, less attractive sector). To extend the range of shareholder influence contexts, the vehicle component sample covered Japanese as well as UK and US companies. Earlier studies had indicated that Anglo-Saxon and Japanese companies exhibit substantial differences in shareholder influences (Carr, 2005; Carr and Tomkins, 1998). The resulting sample included four matched telecom companies (two UK, two US) and ten matched vehicle component companies (three UK, four US and three Japanese). All case study companies were large, multinational companies, operating in several countries, and among the global or regional leaders in their industries.

Interviews with senior executives, who had been personally involved with SIDs, formed the basis of the 14 case studies (see Appendix A). In seven out of the 14 cases, interviews were conducted with several company representatives. The interview approach was predominantly one of discussion around broad themes, aimed at obtaining managers' own perceptions of practices and events. An interview guide was used to ensure cross-case comparison of specific themes, e.g. in the use of capital budgeting techniques. We also prompted managers to give their explanations of the wider aspects of management control, strategic planning and the competitive situation. Interviews averaged approximately 2.5 hours and all were taped and transcribed.

The empirics were exploratory in nature and were drawn from an international study on SID practices conducted by one of the authors between 1994 and 1997. Although over a decade old, the data remains appropriate for an initial assessment of the corporate typologies developed in the paper. These typologies are expected to be enduring in nature, similar to those of Miles and Snow (1978) which have been in research use for over 30 years. Moreover, in three of the companies (one from each country), some further data, gathered between 2001 and 2003, was available and was used to confirm the longitudinal durability of the typologies. For example, in all three of these cases the principal capital budgeting techniques had remained the same and the hurdle rate targets had likewise remained largely unchanged.

Data analysis involved several phases. To enable positioning of the companies in the context of the proposed explanatory framework, investigated companies were first scored on a scale between one and nine on all contextual variables. To analyse our composite strategic orientation variable, we reviewed the quotations for all the four sub-variables (market/financial orientation, strategic configuration, generic strategy and management style) individually. The assessment was theoretically informed and entailed searching for quotations that would provide an indication of, for example, a *prospector*-type strategic configuration. The scores were assessed by two researchers working independently through all transcripts. Key quotations underlying the judgements were then collated to facilitate cross-case comparison across all variable scores. After joint analysis and comparison, the two researchers agreed on their final scores. To assess the validity of our scoring, we asked for independent reviews from experienced academics in the field from two different universities, working independently of each other. This analysis resulted in almost identical scores. The first researcher's initial scores diverged one point from our original scores in two instances. The second researcher agreed on all scores. The scores used in the study were confirmed after discussion with the authors. This independent analysis resulted in no material differences in the scores, or changes in the categorization of companies.

Where appropriate, use was made of secondary research data based on publicly available information. Performance scores were determined using a detailed financial benchmarking of companies, against each other and their worldwide sector peers. As the performance score aimed to capture companies' long-term financial and strategic performance, benchmarking was based on five-year average sales growth percentage, five-year average ROCE percentage (Y1994, Y1999 and Y2004), and relative market share (Y1996). The details of the financial benchmarking are elaborated in more detail in Appendix B. Market attractiveness scores were determined by assessing the five-year average sales growth percentage and five-year average ROCE percentage for the two business sectors, as elaborated in Appendix C. Finally, market dynamism scores were assessed, first for the telecommunications and vehicle component sectors overall. After this, the scores for individual companies were determined in the light of evidence that particular companies experienced more or less dynamic environments as compared to their sectors overall.

All of the interview transcripts were then reviewed to identify potential differences in the SID practices across the contextual categories. The transcripts were first examined for any potential differences in the use of capital budgeting techniques, hurdle rates, and other specifics related to the use of techniques. As well as analysing differences across the four contextually based categories, a systematic cross-check was made for differences against every composite contextual variable on a one-by-one basis. These analyses addressed the counter-hypothesis of whether our framework does have further explanatory power than that possessed by any individual variable. For example, do we really need all our new categories, rather than say just Miles and Snow (1978)'s strategic configurations? Checks were also made for differences in the SID practices of Anglo-Saxon and Japanese companies. This analysis addressed the other counter-hypothesis that country context, rather than contextual category, might afford a more convincing explanation of differences observed. Since our analyses included only 14 cases, these analyses were inevitably very tentative, but provided, nonetheless, some indication of the individual variable and country influences.

Thereafter, the transcripts were reviewed and analysed again, this time with an attempt to identify emergent themes that would characterize the overall SID approaches of the four corporate types. Finally, the transcripts of the three follow-up interviews were analysed and compared with initial interview transcripts to assess any changes in SID practices subsequent to initial interviews.

Research findings

Positioning companies in terms of our contextual framework

Table 17.1 presents the scores used for positioning investigated companies against our earlier proposed framework. Scores for the market context and strategic orientation variables are aggregated first to provide overall positioning on the vertical axis (*market orientation*). The scores for the performance and shareholder influence variables are then aggregated to provide positioning along the horizontal axis (*performance in relation to shareholder expectations*). The scores for the market context and strategic orientation dimensions are themselves averages from component elements, drawn from our overall framework, and are detailed separately in Table 17.1.

Table 17.1 Analysis of contextual positions of investigated companies

	BritTel1	*BritTel2*	*AmTel1*	*AmTel2*	*BritComp1*	*BritComp2*	*BritComp3*	*AmComp1*	*AmComp2*	*AmComp3*	*AmComp4*	*JapComp1*	*JapComp2*	*JapComp3*	*Mean score*
Market orientation															
Market context															
1=extremely stable environment 9=extremely dynamic environment	8.0	7.0	7.0	7.0	4.0	3.0	3.0	3.0	3.0	3.0	3.0	4.0	3.5	3.0	4.4
1=very low market attractiveness 9=very high market attractiveness	8.0	8.0	8.0	8.0	4.0	4.0	4.0	4.0	4.0	4.0	4.0	4.0	4.0	4.0	5.1
Average market context	8.0	7.5	7.5	7.5	4.0	3.5	3.5	3.5	3.5	3.5	3.5	4.0	3.8	3.5	4.8
Strategic orientation															
1=very strong financial orientation 9=very strong market orientation	3.0	5.0	5.0	3.0	5.0	2.0	5.0	5.0	5.0	5.0	6.0	9.0	9.0	9.0	5.4
1=purely cost leadership 9=purely differentiation	7.0	5.0	5.0	5.0	6.0	4.0	8.0	3.0	5.0	6.0	7.0	4.0	6.0	8.0	5.6
1=extreme defender[a] 9=extreme prospector	9.0	3.0	4.0	6.0	8.0	5.0	4.0	6.0	6.0	6.0	7.0	6.0	7.0	7.0	6.0
1=extreme financial control style 9=extreme strategic planning style	5.0	5.0	2.0	6.0	5.0	3.0	4.0	8.0	6.0	5.0	5.0	9.0	7.0	8.0	5.6
Average strategic orientation	6.0	4.5	4.0	5.0	6.0	3.5	5.3	5.5	5.5	5.5	6.3	7.0	7.3	8.0	5.7
Market orientation	7.0	6.0	5.8	6.3	5.0	3.5	4.4	4.5	4.5	4.5	4.9	5.5	5.5	5.8	5.2
Performance in relation to shareholder expectations															
Performance															
1=severe financial crisis 9=very high performance above expectations	9.0	7.0	6.0	4.0	8.0	2.0	3.0	3.5	4.5	7.0	5.5	8.0	6.0	4.0	5.5
Shareholder influence															
1=very high shareholder influence 9=very low shareholder influence	3.0	5.0	2.0	2.0	5.0	3.0	3.0	7.0	5.0	6.0	4.0	9.0	9.0	8.0	5.1
Performance in relation to shareholder expectations	6.0	6.0	4.0	3.0	6.5	2.5	3.0	5.3	4.8	6.5	4.8	8.5	7.5	6.0	5.3

[a]Similarly to most SMA and SID studies applying Miles and Snow's (1978) typology, we have operationalized their typology simply as a continuum between defender and prospector (see e.g. Cadez and Guilding, 2008; Chen, 2008).

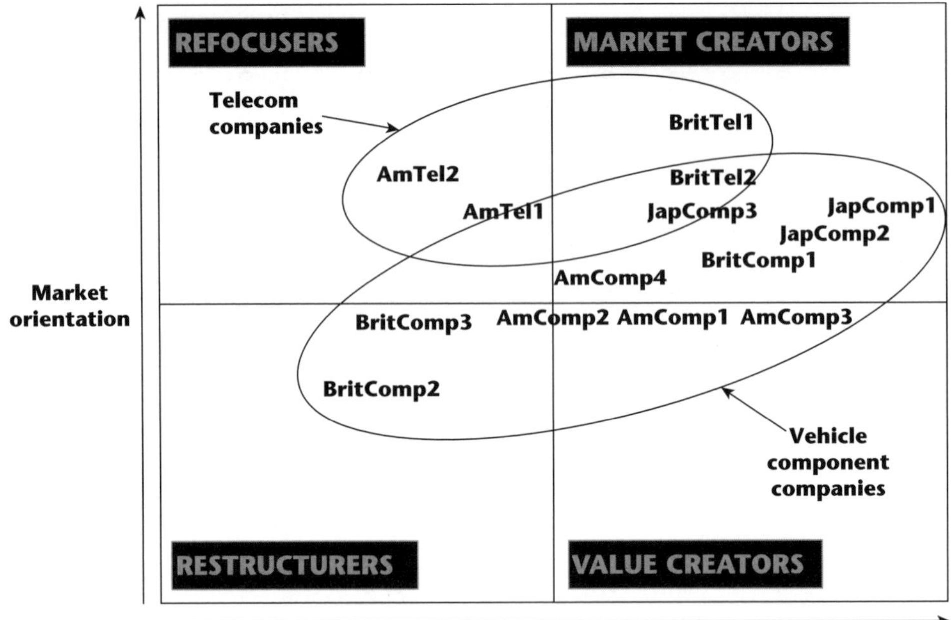

Figure 17.3 Contextual positions of investigated companies

Note: Pseudonyms are used throughout, prefixes 'Brit', 'Am' and 'Jap' indicating British, American and Japanese origins, and 'Tel' and 'Comp' indicating telecommunications and vehicle component sectors.

Figure 17.3 draws on the analysis from Table 17.1 to position the investigated companies within the proposed framework. Vehicle component companies operating in a stable and less attractive business sector, and exhibiting diverse market orientation, performance and shareholder influence contexts are spread among the *market creator*, *value creator* and *restructurer* categories. Telecom companies operating in a dynamic and attractive business sector and showing a general tendency to be market-orientated are, on the other hand, clustered exclusively in the upper *market creator* and *refocuser* categories. Although substantial differences are evident for the two sectors, there is nevertheless a significant level of overlap, particularly in the *market creator* category, suggesting that some companies, even located in such different sectors, are subject to similar overall contextual influences.[9]

Analysis of capital budgeting techniques for contextual categories

Our analysis in Table 17.2 shows little systematic variation in terms of the actual choice of specific capital budgeting techniques employed. Companies typically employ about four different techniques, DCF techniques and particularly IRR being the most popular and also the most influential. Any differences by category are generally subtle. *Value creators* and *market creators* most frequently prioritize some form of DCF technique; they downplay the traditional payback method, sometimes preferring return on capital methods. *Refocusers and restructurers,* by comparison, are distinctive only in that all of them utilize EPS growth targets, a technique utilized by no *value creators* and just one *market creator.* All *refocusers and restructurers* also perceive substantial shareholder pressures, so this may be the reason for the more extensive use of EPS growth targets. *Refocusers* and *value creators* utilize a greater number of capital budgeting techniques, as will be discussed later.

Table 17.2 Use of capital budgeting techniques by contextual categories

Categories	*Capital budgeting technique most frequently prioritized*	*Other techniques applied (listed in the order of prioritization)*	*Average number of techniques applied*
Market creators	IRR	Return target, NPV, payback, EPS growth, sensitivity analysis	3.4
Value creators	IRR/NPV/return target	Payback, sensitivity analysis	4.3
Refocusers	NPV/EPS growth	IRR, return target, payback, sensitivity analysis	5.0
Restructurers	IRR/payback	EPS growth, sensitivity analysis	3.5
All companies	IRR	NPV, return target, payback, EPS growth, sensitivity analysis	3.9

Table 17.3, on financial targets and time horizons adopted in applying capital budgeting techniques, exhibits more systematic differences among the contextually based categories. IRR hurdle rates rise as we move from the strategically orientated *market creator* category towards the more financially orientated *restructurer* category. The average hurdle target rates are 16% for *market creators,* 18% for *value creators,* 20% for *refocusers,* and 22% for *restructurers.*[10] These differences in the hurdle rates appear to reflect differences in the cost of capital, as we find the premium set over cost of capital to show less systematic difference across our contextual categories. The most noteworthy difference here is that the most strategically orientated *market creators* appear to be willing to accept lower premiums. The payback target and time horizon figures for the *market creator, value creator* and *refocuser* categories are, on the other hand, remarkably similar.

Reflecting their weak performance and strong shareholder influence, *restructurers* exhibit a consistent, distinctly conservative approach. Their IRR target hurdle rates are correspondingly higher, averaging 22% compared to 18% average for our whole sample. Similarly, their payback targets are shorter, averaging 2.5 years compared to four years for our whole sample. Their time horizons are even more distinctive, averaging only three years, compared with nine years for our whole sample.

Overall SID approaches

More in-depth analysis of the qualitative interview data suggests more profound differences in the overall SID approaches across our four contextual categories. Most significantly, the data suggests systematic, expected differences in the extent to which SIDs are based on strategic as opposed to financial considerations. As expected, *market creators* exhibit a strong emphasis on strategic considerations and use financial analysis in a supportive role. *Restructurers*, on the other

Table 17.3 Financial targets and time horizons by contextual categories

Categories	*IRR target, %*	*Premium over cost of capital, %*	*Payback target, years*	*Time horizon years*
Market creators	16	6.3	5	8
Value creators	18	8.5	4	11
Refocusers	20	9.5	5+	10
Restructurers	22	8	2.5	3
All companies	18	7.4	4	9

hand, tend to put strong emphasis on financial considerations and pay very little attention to strategic analysis. *Value creators* and *refocusers* demonstrate a more balanced emphasis on both strategic and financial considerations, but exhibit other marked differences in their overall SID approaches. The overall SID approaches of our four contextual categories are portrayed in more detail in the following sections.

Market creators

Consistent with the contextual framework, *market creators* tend to put strong emphasis on strategic considerations when making decisions on strategic investments. Although *market creators* often also conduct financial analyses, these analyses tend to have a secondary, supportive role in their strategic investment decision-making. Executive Vice-President of Operations at AmComp4 explained: *'We will still argue for strategic decision-making as the dominant basis for investment strategy after going through all this generation of (financial) valuation . . . Financial people are support people, not decision-makers.'* The strategic emphasis is also reflected in the fact that *market creators* often determine specific strategic criteria for evaluating their strategic investments.

Market creator companies are also willing to allow for significant flexibility in the use of financial targets. If an investment is viewed as strategically significant, there could even be attempts to modify financial valuations in order to meet the set financial criteria. The Executive Director at BritTel1 explained: *'If we saw IRRs which are low, then frankly we wouldn't be very interested in investing there . . . if the first cut is not looking right, but you still feel deep down it is an interesting investment, we will still try to justify it financially.'* Strict financial targets could be seen as a hindrance for achieving the rather aggressive growth targets of many *market creator* companies. The Head of Strategic Planning at BritTel2 commented: *'Any fool can put in a big hurdle rate but what that does is – you know – if X has a lower hurdle rate than me, they will accept growth opportunities that I will reject.'* Some very prospectively oriented *market creator* companies have also adopted very bold attitudes towards incorporating synergies into calculations. They consider potential investments as part of their global investment portfolio, and pay strong attention to getting synergies out of these businesses at an operating level. In contrast, some less prospective *market creators* have a more cautious, yet open, attitude towards calculating synergies. They take into account synergies that can be measured in advance.

Value creators

Value creators tend to take a more balanced approach to SID-making by paying attention to both strategic and financial analysis. Central to the *value creator* approach tends to be an intention to provide decision-makers with a multifaceted, thorough analysis. The Vice President of Financial Administration at AmComp1 explained this approach: *'I think AmComp1 culture is, we want to make every analysis as accurate as possible, and then react and use the data to make decisions.'* Reflecting the intention to conduct profound analysis, *value creators* are often not content with using only standard strategic techniques, and have developed other, complementary techniques to assist strategic evaluation. This was exemplified by the comment of the Vice President of Financial Administration at AmComp1: *'We'll think about it (BCG, Five Forces), but we are not rigorous to say those are the only things we are going to think about . . . We have got methodologies that we have developed over time.'*

As the strategic investment decisions of *value creators* are influenced by strategic considerations, *value creators* are, like *market creators*, willing to stretch their financial targets if investments are viewed as strategically significant. The Senior Vice President of AmComp2's automotive business noted: *'We wouldn't want to [go below the return target], but in a few cases we have, rarely, but we have . . . I could tell you that I have never gone into single digits, but I have on occasion looked at something in the 10% range.'*

Value creators tend to take a rather open attitude towards synergies when evaluating their strategic investments. The director responsible for acquisitions, divestitures and joint ventures at AmComp3 commented: *'We look at all the kind of cost- and sales-based synergies, technology, product, you name it; we look at it fairly broadly and rigorously, speculating of potential synergies, probably putting more weight on cost base because that's more in our control . . .'*

Refocusers

As with the *value creators*, the two *refocusers* in our sample pay attention to both strategic and financial analysis. Whereas *value creators* tend to put specific emphasis on the thoroughness of their strategic analysis, the two *refocusers* in our sample exhibit a tendency to strive towards very sophisticated financial analysis. The Corporate Development Director at AmTel1 explained their approach: *'Yes, strategy is important and it has to fit . . . otherwise we won't do it, but that is only the first cut and the first threshold decision criteria. It is always in the end going to come down to, "Is it financially attractive for us to do?"'*

Striving towards very thorough and sophisticated financial analysis is reflected in *refocusers'* attempts to conduct their analysis in accordance with the latest financial theory, for example by calculating the cost of capital on a continuous basis. The corporate development director of AmTel1 explained: *'You see, our philosophy is to determine the cost of capital as best we can and recognize there is going to be some fluctuation. We try to keep abreast of what's going on in the financial theory as much as possible and we try to use it as much as practical.'* The Vice President of Strategic Management at AmTel2 stated: *'They re-assess the cost of capital, I think on an hourly basis in our financial organization, so that it is always going on . . . we try to analyse those situations, we try to model those situations and run sensitivity analysis.'*

High shareholder influence, which is typical of *refocuser* companies, is reflected in shareholder value creation being viewed as a primary driver when making decisions on strategic investments. The Vice President of Strategic Management at AmTel2 explained: *'We have all the primaries (financial analysis) you ever want to see, but essentially if you boil it down to its least common denominator . . . you have to build growth on earnings per share.'* Perhaps reflecting the high shareholder influence, *refocusers* tend to take a much more cautious attitude towards calculating synergies than their *market creator* and *value creator* peers. They incorporate synergies into calculations only when there is a very high probability for these synergies to materialize.

Restructurers

As suggested by the contextual framework, *restructurers* exhibit a very strong financial emphasis. Strategic considerations are given very little attention. The Deputy Marketing Director at BritComp2 commented bluntly: *'We are going in to make money, and to return cash. We are not just doing it for strategic reasons. Hence, the emphasis is on the financial side when looking at these projects . . . So we don't accept their [the Germans'] view which is that strategy is what counts in any conflict with the financials. From our perspective, this would be "nuts".'*

Potentially influenced by their low performance and high shareholder influence, *restructurers* tend to set very tight financial targets for their SIDs. The director responsible for finance and acquisitions at BritComp3 explained: *'We use the sensitivity analysis and we use the gap between the*

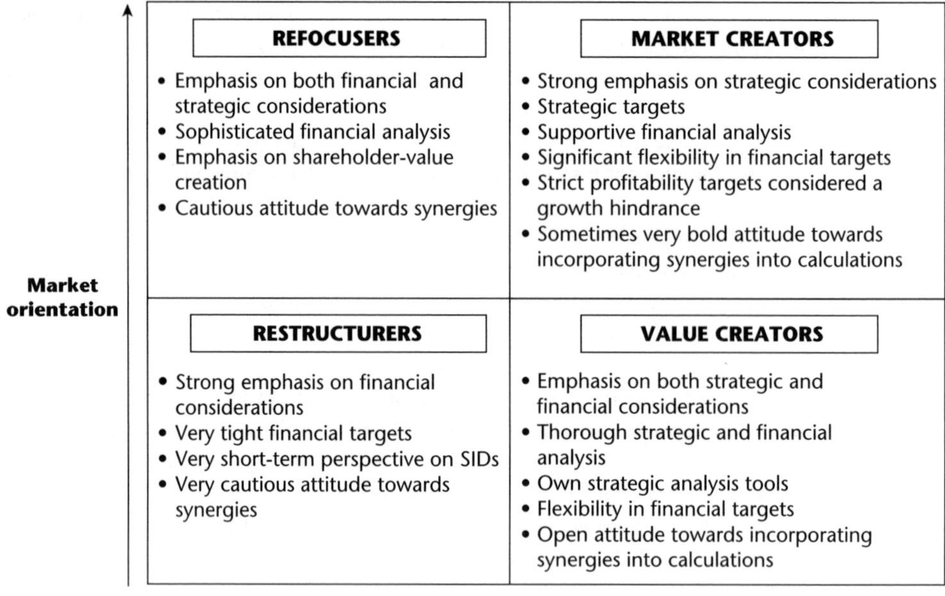

Figure 17.4 Contextual strategic investment decision-making approaches

two hurdle rates, you might say we are ultra-conservative . . . Now that means that we are more likely to turn down deals that they would go forward with, and we have experience of that.'

The financially constrained position of *restructurer* companies also tends to drive them to take a very short-term perspective in evaluating SIDs. As expected, *restructurers* are very cautious in their attitude towards calculating synergies when evaluating strategic investment decisions. The cautious attitude towards synergies is driven by the high shareholder influence encountered by *restructurers*. The director responsible for finance and acquisitions at BritComp3 explained, *'When you have built a successful business to date and the shareholders are behind you and you have a good market rating, to bring in the unquantifiables into your next year you are running a very big risk, because it is not only the risk for the acquisition to the brink of benefits you thought it was going to get, but it is the impact it has on your total business because all of a sudden the confidence in the management by investors goes and so your market rating goes. Overall the loss of value to shareholders is very, very significant, so if you like, we are cautious.'*

To conclude, the qualitative data analysis provides significant evidence confirming expected differences in the extent to which SIDs are based on strategic as opposed to financial considerations across our four contextual categories. We also find other marked differences in the contextual SID approaches. These are summarized in Figure 17.4.

Discussion

This study provides evidence of substantial differences in the way companies make their decisions on strategic investments. These differences are not revealed simply in regard to the *choice* of capital budgeting techniques, but are also particularly apparent in the *way* the techniques are used, and in how they *influence* decision-making on strategic investments.

Given reports of the widespread use of capital budgeting techniques such as DCF, the extent of convergence in the choice of techniques is not surprising (see e.g. Graham and Harvey, 2001; Sangster, 1993). What makes this more notable is the fact that, in the research design of this study, key contextual variables have been deliberately extended (e.g. market context and country/shareholder influence context). Yet, the degree of convergence in the use of capital budgeting techniques remains high. This is despite the international nature of the study and prior evidence of cross-country differences in the use of capital budgeting techniques (e.g. Carr and Tomkins, 1996, 1998; Jones et al., 1993).

Nevertheless, close observation of the manner in which these techniques really influence SIDs reveals differences in approaches that do, indeed, vary in accordance with the contextual framework proposed. Correspondingly, *market creators* exhibit the most strategically orientated approach to SIDs. Financial analyses have a more supportive role and they are likely to be overridden or even manipulated by decision-makers. At the other extreme, *restructurers* emphasize financial considerations and are more rigid and conservative when handling targets and non-quantifiables. As expected, *value creators* and *refocusers* pay attention to both strategic and financial considerations. They also emerge as the most thorough and also the most active in terms of the number of techniques utilized. *Refocuser* practices reflect perceived pressures to improve shareholder value, with a heavy emphasis on EPS growth targets; *value creators* do not use such targets at all and, by comparison, are more amenable to strategic arguments.

Correspondingly, from Figure 17.2, a consistent pattern of IRR rates is apparent, increasing as we move from the most strategically orientated *market creator* category to the most financially orientated *restructurer* category. *Restructurers* are also unique in adopting far shorter-term time horizons and payback targets, whilst all other categories here exhibit very similar practices.

The counter-argument to using the four-typology framework developed is that differences in SID-making practices may be explained more simply and plausibly, by an individual variable. This counter-factual was addressed by systematically cross-checking for differences against every contextual variable on a one-by-one basis. Since the analysis included only 14 cases, the results must be interpreted with care but, given this caveat, individual variables do appear to provide only a partial indication of why SID practices differ. For example, the variables included in the composite strategic orientation variable (strategic configuration, generic strategy, market/financial orientation and management style) were each found to have different impacts on SID practices. None of the individual variables appeared to dominate other explanatory variables.

Considering Miles and Snow (1978) in isolation, our *market creators* versus *value creators* at first sight seem similar to more traditional *prospector* versus *defender* typologies. However, our tentative univariable analysis indicates that the latter categorization does not predominate over other explanatory variables. Furthermore, the Miles and Snow model does not handle the issue of poor/failing performance well. For Miles and Snow only *reactors* (an entirely different category not endorsed in other SMA studies) are associated with poorer performance. Our poorer-performing cases might conceivably have been classified as *reactors* had they all grouped just above the mid-way vertical axis given their uncertain environments, offset by ill-adaptive market orientations. We observed, by contrast, two groups, one relatively higher and the other relatively lower on our vertical '*market orientation*' axis. Thus, poorly performing types do not conform to just one single *reactor* typology. Moreover, these two groups (differently positioned in our framework as respectively *refocusers* and *restructurers*) exhibit different SID-making behaviours, and these would have been inexplicable if Miles and Snow's typology were used. Finally, the hybrid *analyser* position, halfway between *prospector* and *defender*, can also be accommodated in our framework.

The strongest counter-argument to our more complex categorization is that differences in country contexts alone may explain differences in practice. Here, the literature suggests a strong convergence in practice within Anglo-Saxon countries – such as the UK and the USA – and differentiation in countries such as Japan (Carr, 2005; Carr and Tomkins, 1998). When comparing the cross-country influence to the explanatory power of our contextual framework, our tentative analysis of 14 cases indicates that the country context does have a particularly strong influence on the number of capital budgeting techniques and the level of IRR target hurdle rates, but the proposed contextual framework better explains differences in the time horizon adopted. When addressing the broader SID-making approaches, we find our contextual framework has a much stronger explanatory power when compared to the cross-country influence. Although all three Japanese companies in our sample fall into the more strategically oriented *market creator* category, this category also includes companies from the Anglo-Saxon UK and US contexts, providing evidence that companies from quite different country environments are subject to similar contextual influences and exhibit similar behaviour in terms of SID-making practices. The thesis of cross-country influence would also fail to explain the intra-country differences in SID-making practices that have been found (see Figure 17.2 for the contextual positions of investigated companies and Figure 17.4 for the contextual SID-making approaches).

Each of the individual variables used in the study do appear to contribute, in part, to the explanation for differences in SID-making practices. However, when combined into the four contextual categories, explanation is enhanced considerably. The proposed corporate typologies model also affords recognition of country context effects as extreme as those found in Japan, in so far as these are effectively transmitted through the indirect country effects included in the framework (see e.g. Carr, 2005; Carr and Tomkins, 1998).[11] The proposed model thus has the virtue of wider applicability than models that omit these important indirect country effects. It is suggested here that researchers should use universal frameworks with some appreciation and understanding of cultures quite different from their own.

While the use of the four firm types developed in this paper does contribute to the understanding of how contextual factors can help explain SID practice (as demonstrated above), their novelty and limited testing means that their generalizability has yet to be fully established. Fourteen cases categorized into four typologies composed from a wide range of variables cannot aspire to statistical rigour. The justification for limiting the number of cases is that our research is exploratory, case-based and involves considerable attention to contextual considerations (Butler et al., 1993; Marsh et al., 1988). Nowhere is this more important and nowhere is survey-based, statistically orientated research more vulnerable than in decision-making at a genuinely strategic level. Confidentiality considerations, and the sheer difficulty of responding to complex, strategically oriented questions, compromise the generation of reliable data from forced-choice scales.

Conclusion and directions for future research

Empirical research in management accounting (MA) consistently demonstrates that both similarities and differences arise in the intrinsic nature of techniques and in the way in which they are applied. Identifying the determinants of practice is a central quest for MA researchers. Without such knowledge, explanations and understanding of the discipline will be defective and prescription hazardous. One way of tackling this quest is the route followed in this paper. MA variation can be accounted for as a response to a set of situational characteristics which can be used to define explanatory contexts and categorize corporate behaviur. This is an approach widely adopted in the investigation of how strategy impinges on MA practice.

The contribution of this paper has been to encompass a wide range of acknowledged variables into a single overall contextual framework and to explore this framework's potential for explaining differences in SID-making practices. The empirical aspect of the research comprised an exploratory set of 14 matched field-case studies from the UK, US and Japan, providing coverage of the vehicle component and telecommunications sectors. Application of the contextual categories in the framework provided a successful explanation of variation in companies' overall SID approaches and the specific decision-support techniques adopted.

The findings indicate substantial differences in approach across the four firm typologies, particularly in terms of the emphasis on strategic versus financial considerations, the thoroughness and rigidity of financial analysis, and the attitudes towards incorporating less easily quantifiable factors such as synergies into calculations. Additionally, IRR target rates are higher in the most financially orientated *restructurer* category as compared to the most strategically orientated *market creator* category. Choice of specific investment techniques exhibits more moderate systematic variation, but this can be explained by the near-universal adoption of discounting techniques in large firms.

Thus the empirics, although limited in scale, do support the potential of the proposed framework to explain SID practice. In order to confirm this potential and to more fully investigate the utility of the typology, further research is needed. First, there is a need for deeper organizational field studies to verify and further develop understanding of the nature of SID-making practices and further elaborate the implications of the firm types for the finance function. While covering three continents and 14 cases, the scope of the empirics precludes study of the related underlying organizational processes as proposed by Miller and O'Leary (2005, 2007). It would also be desirable to have more longitudinal studies to explore further the question of consistency of SID-making practice and the applicability of the four proposed firm types over time. Further larger-scale studies are also needed to provide a more rigorous statistical analysis of the utility of the new corporate typology brought forward in this paper. Our latest – still unpublished – research within Nordic companies indicates that our framework's capability to explain differences in practice stands also more rigorous statistical analysis.[12]

Finally, the developed contextual framework may have a wider applicability for explaining differences in SMA (as opposed to merely SID) practice. The framework may be particularly relevant to explaining differences in SCM practice: it is based on Oldman and Tomkins' (1999) four-state Cost Management Model, which has been found to have explanatory power over variation in SCM practices. The new contextual framework proposed in this paper includes a more comprehensive set of generally acknowledged contextual variables that have been found to influence SMA practice. First, it complements Oldman and Tomkins' generic market-orientation dimension with a more comprehensive set of strategic archetypes. This provides a more multifaceted conceptualization of strategy: it accounts for the fact that although strategic archetypes share some common elements, there are also significant differences between the archetypes, which should be taken into account when analysing their contextual influence on practice (see Chenhall, 2003, p. 152). This new contextual framework also acknowledges the influence of the business sector context. It takes into account that companies operating in dynamic and attractive business sectors may draw benefits from other SCM practices than those operating in stable and non-attractive business sectors. Dynamic and attractive business sectors may reinforce companies' tendency to apply externally oriented SCM approaches, such as target costing. Stable and unattractive business sectors may, on the other hand, reinforce companies' tendency to apply SCM approaches – such as ABC – that support their objectives related to product pruning. (See Oldman and Tomkins (1999) for a general discussion about the contextual situations in which target costing and ABC appear to be most appropriate.) Finally, this new contextual framework applies a longer-term, more multifaceted concept of performance than that originally applied by Oldman and Tomkins. This takes into account that managers may not be willing to change their accounting practices in response to temporary decline in performance. Setting new SCM systems involves considerable time and costs, implying that managers may be willing to adjust their SCM practices only in response to more long-lasting decline in performance. These conclusions – related to our framework's potential applicability for explaining differences in SCM practices – are, of course, hypothetical at this stage. Our empirical examination has focused on another significant sub-set of SMA, namely SID-making practices. Further empirical investigations are needed to verify our contextual framework's explanatory power over variation in SCM practices. The generic nature of our contextual framework suggests, however, that such empirical endeavours could be worthwhile – and advance our understanding of the contextual nature of SCM practices.

Appendix A. Background information about the interviews and SIDs discussed[a]

Company	*Persons interviewed*	*Date of the interview*	*Estimated length in minutes*	*Length of the transcripts in words*
Initial interviews				
BritTel1	Executive Director	04 Sep 97	75	5600
BritTel2	Head of Strategic Planning	11 Sep 97	120	8456
AmTel1	Director, Corporate Development; Director, Financial Planning; Controller	06 Sep 94	150	37105
AmTel2	Vice President, Strategic Management	28 Jul 94	100	7184
BritComp1	Manager responsible for BritComp 1's operations in the US	09 Sep 94	80	4307
	Manager responsible for BritComp 1's operations in France	03 Jun 98	150	15624
BritComp2	Deputy Marketing Director, Group Financial Controller	22 Aug 97	75	3775
BritComp3	Director responsible for finance and acquisitions on a corporate level	28 Aug 97	150	13948
AmComp1	Vice President, Fin. Administration; Director, Fin. Analysis; Gen. Man., Sector X Operations	24 Aug 94	150	26884
AmComp2	Senior Vice President and Controller of AmComp2, automotive business	01 Seo 94	150	34511
AmComp3	Director responsible for acquisitions, divestitures and joint ventures	12 Aug 94	100	18956
AmComp4	Executive Vice President, Operations; Assistant to Executive Vice President	07 Sep 94	180	44011
JapComp1	Several senior executives involved in SIDs	31 Aug 95	100	8298
JapComp2	Director responsible for investment decisions	30 Aug 95	125	12206
JapComp3	General Manager; Corporate Planning Officer	01 Aug 95	155	11894
Total (initial interviews) in minutes and words			1820	252759
Follow-up interviews				
BritComp1	Strategic Planner	21 Jan 01	80	9534
JapComp1	General Manager of Corporate Planning Department	20 Sep 02	70	2266
AmComp1	Head of Finance; Financial President of a major business	17 Sep 03	70	12562
Total in minutes and words			2040	277121
Estimated total number of interview hours			34	
Estimated average interview time per company (in hours)			2.43	

[a] Pseudonyms are used throughout, prefixes 'Brit', 'Am' and 'Jap' indicating British, American and Japanese origins; 'Tel' and 'Comp' indicating telecommunications and vehicle component sectors.

Appendix B. Analysis of the performance scores

Company	*Score*[a]	*Long-term financial performance*						*Market position*	*Additional comments*
		5-Year average sales growth %			*5-Year average ROCE %*			*Relative market share*[b]	
		Y2004	*Y1999*	*Y1994*	*Y2004*	*Y1999*	*Y1994*	*Y1996*	
BritTel1	**9.0**	1390.63	313.84	211.49	–5.23	30.04	46.20	0.30	
BritTel2	**7.0**	29.95	31.38	3.67	10.29	14.53	13.37	0.15	
AmTel1	**6.4**	–19.52	49.75	20.35	11.84	11.34	9.18	0.24	
AmTel2 (merged corp.)	**4.0**	114.88	140.54	20.46	11.17	15.27	5.82	n.a	Mergered after the interview.
Av Tel (top 28 w'wide)		101.44	194.43	307.48	6.89	10.24	9.23		
BritComp1	**7.0**	35.27	67.64	–17.96	13.15	27.02	6.93	0.16	Worldwide no. 1. Long-term survivor. High margins.
BritComp2	**2.0**			29.62			5.21	0.04	Showed losses even with extraord. items.
BritComp3	**3.0**		452.26	643.59		12.58	3.16	0.01	Acquired subsequently by a failed company.
AmComp1	**3.5**	34.66	47.51	28.33	5.19	9.80	3.70	0.17	
AmComp2[c]	**4.5**	50.56		17.60	16.42	23.10	5.56	0.28	Auto division subsequently divested.
AmComp3	**7.0**	48.18	50.53	26.88	9.14	13.88	8.60	0.22	Consistency in performance over the years.
AmComp4[d](tyre division)	**5.5**	–5.22	56.52	61.89	7.45	12.89	16.18	0.17	We evaluate the figures sceptically, as these figures relate only to the tyre business.
JapComp1	**8.0**	96.99	–2.60	36.57	5.34	5.28	5.03	0.43	No. 1 v. c. company in Japan, no. 2 globally.
JapComp2	**6.0**	183.03	–8.35	56.59	1.88	4.21	2.92	0.07	ROCE over local cost of capital; excellent long-term growth.
JapComp3	**4.0**	45.44	–6.17	58.33	0.85	1.50	2.25	0.03	Figures show negative performance, but include business unrelated to vehicle components.
Av Comp (top 42 w'wide)		49.30	242.75	70.20	5.26	11.35	6.20		
Average (sample)	**5.5**	167.07	99.40	85.53	7.29	13.96	9.58	0.17	

[a] The scores for performance determined intuitively by taking into account long-term financial performance, market position and additional comments.
[b] Relative market share calculated by dividing 1996 sales by that for the largest player in the industry; as BritTel1 operates in a different segment, BritTel1 evaluated against the largest player in that segment; as AmTel1 operates both in the segments of BritTel1 and BritTel1, we have calculated AmTel1's relative market share by using the average sales figure of the largest companies in both segments.
[c] The figure for 5-year average ROCE 1994, and the figures for 5-year sales growth for 1994 and 1999, based on the data for former AmComp2.
[d] Tyre division, figures for AmComp4 (corporate).

Appendix C. Analysis for the market attractiveness scores

Company name	*Averaged 5-year sales growth for the industry[a] Y 1996*	*Averaged 5-year ROCE % for the industry[b] Y 1996*	*Scores[c,d]*
BritTel1	44	10	8
BritTel2	44	10	8
AmTel1	44	10	8
AmTel2	44	10	8
BritComp1	9	8	4
BritComp2	9	8	4
BritComp3	9	8	4
AmComp1	9	8	4
AmComp2	9	8	4
AmComp3	9	8	4
AmComp4	9	8	4
JapComp1	9	8	4
JapComp2	9	8	4
JapComp3	9	8	4
Average (our sample of 14 companies)			5

[a] Averaged 5-year sales growth calculated by dividing the total averaged 5-year sales growth of all companies in the industry by the number of companies in the industry.
[b] Averaged 5-year ROCE calculated by dividing the total averaged 5-year ROCE for the whole industry by the number of companies in the industry.
[c] The scores market attractiveness determined intuitively by taking into account average 5-year sales growth and ROCE % figures.
[d] The scores for telecommunications industry based on 52 companies listed on the Thompson database, the scores for the vehicle component industry based on 638 companies listed on Thompson.

Notes

1 The term strategic investment decision (SID) refers to a decision on a substantial investment which has a significant effect on long-term performance and the organization as a whole (Carr and Tomkins, 1996, 1998). Capital budgeting literature has not always distinguished more strategic types of investment (e.g. Graham and Harvey, 2001; King, 1975; Klammer, 1972; Klammer and Walker, 1984; Pike, 1983; Sihler, 1964); but a substantial body of research now attests to the importance of this distinction (Alkaraan and Northcott, 2006; Butler et al., 1993; Marsh et al., 1988; Oldcorn and Parker, 1996). Some researchers on SMA exclude SIDs from the field of SMA (e.g. Guilding et al., 2000; Roslender, 1995). Bromwich and Bhimani (1994) and Tomkins and Carr (1996) position SIDs, however, as a central field within SMA. The significance of SIDs is also reflected in that the March 1996 Special Issue on Strategic Management Accounting included several articles on SIDs (Carr and Tomkins, 1996; Van Cauvenbergh et al., 1996; Shank, 1996).

2 Carr, C., Kolehmainen, K. and Mitchell, F. (2010), 'Strategic investment decision-making practices: A contextual approach', *Management Accounting Research*, 21: 167–184.

3 We draw on Haka et al. (1985) to use the term 'sophisticated techniques' to refer to capital budgeting techniques such as Net Present Value (NPV) and Internal Rate of Return (IRR) that consider the risk-adjusted discounted net cash-flows expected from a project.

4 For the purposes of further discussion related to the development of our own contextual framework, we have transposed Oldman and Tomkins' (1999) original axes here so that *need for turnaround* appears on the horizontal axis, and *market orientation* on the vertical axis.

5 Building on Robinson et al. (1978) and Brownlie (1985) we use the term 'market attractiveness' to refer to the extent to which a business sector exhibits high profit and growth potential.

6 Strictly speaking this may imply a broader concept of market orientation than is sometimes used in the marketing literature (e.g. Doyle, 1992).

7 Contingency studies on management accounting (MA) practices have rarely conceptualized performance as an independent variable, having an influence on MA systems/practices. This study

draws on Oldman and Tomkins (1999) to consider performance as one of the key variables influencing MA practices.

8 Perceptive readers will recognize that our framework subsumes the well-known Directional Policy Matrix framework (see e.g. Brownlie, 1985; Hussey, 1978; Robinson et al., 1978), which in turn yields *build*, *hold*, and *harvest* strategy typologies of notable interest to e.g. Gupta and Govindarajan (1984), Langfield-Smith (1997) and Cadez and Guilding (2008).

9 Most companies were well distinguished by our four contextual categories, but for three, positions were less clear-cut. This grouping virtually on the border between *market creators* and *value creators*, nevertheless, lay distinctly apart from *market creator* companies in our sample, and exhibited distinctive SID-making practices.

10 Please note that this data was gathered in the 1990s. These hurdle rates may hence seem high in comparison with current interest rate levels.

11 Previous studies have provided evidence for significant cross-country differences in shareholder influence, market orientation and management style, in particular between Anglo-Saxon and Japanese companies (see e.g. Carr, 2005; Carr and Tomkins, 1998).

12 After presenting our new contextual framework in the recent *Management Accounting Research* article, we have sought to validate this framework's explanatory power with a larger database. During spring 2010, we conducted an internet survey targeted at the CFOs of Nordic listed companies. The survey was sent to 947 CFOs, from which we received 59 responses (response rate 6.2%). Although the number of responses was only 59, our analysis resulted in statistically significant differences in a tendency to emphasize strategic versus financial considerations across the categories. The findings of this new study were, overall, very much in line with our initial findings – for example, in regard to the contextual differences in the sophistication of financial and strategic analysis. The results of this internet survey have, so far, been published as an MA thesis: Ansio, J. (2010), 'Validating the contextual framework for strategic investment decision-making practices: quantitative evidence from the Nordic countries', unpublished thesis. Helsinki: Aalto University School of Economics. http://hsepubl.lib.hse.fi/FI/ethesis/id/12312

Bibliography

Abdel-Kader, M.G. and Dugdale, D. (1998) 'Investment in advanced manufacturing technology: a study of practice in large UK companies', *Management Accounting Research*, 9: 261–284.

Alkaraan, F. and Northcott, D. (2006) 'Strategic capital investment decision-making: a role for emergent analysis tools? A study of practice in large UK manufacturing companies', *British Accounting Review*, 38: 149–173.

Ansio, J. (2010) 'Validating the contextual framework for strategic investment decision-making practices: quantitative evidence from the Nordic countries', unpublished thesis. Aalto University School of Economics.

Argenti, J. (1974) *Systematic Corporate Planning*, New York: Wiley.

Arnold, G.C. and Hatzopoulos, P.D. (2000) 'The theory-practice gap in capital budgeting: evidence from the United Kingdom', *Journal of Business Finance & Accounting*, 27: 603–626.

Barwise, P., Marsh, P.R. and Wensley, R. (1989) 'Must strategy and finance clash?', *Harvard Business Review*, 67: 83–90.

Bibeault, D.B. (1981) *Corporate Turnaround*, New York: McGraw-Hill.

Bromwich, M. and Bhimani, A. (1994) *Management Accounting: Pathways to Progress*, London: the Chartered Institute of Management Accountants.

Brownlie, D. (1985) 'Strategic marketing concepts and models', *Journal of Marketing Management*, 1: 157–194.

Butler, R., Davies, L., Pike, R. and Sharp, J. (1991) 'Strategic investment decision-making: complexities, politics and processes', *Journal of Management Studies*, 28: 395–415.

Butler, R., Davies, L., Pike, R. and Sharp, J. (1993) *Strategic Investment Decisions: Theory, Practice and Process*, London: Routledge.

Cadez, S. and Guilding, C. (2008) 'An exploratory investigation of an integrated contingency model of strategic management accounting', *Accounting, Organizations and Society*, 33: 836–863.

Carr, C.H. (2005) 'Are German, Japanese and Anglo-Saxon strategic styles still divergent in the context of globalization?' *Journal of Management Studies*, 42: 1155–1188.

Carr, C. and Harris, S. (2004) 'The impact of diverse national values on strategic investment decisions in the context of globalization', *International Journal of Cross-Cultural Management*, 4: 77–99.

Carr, C. and Tomkins, C. (1996) 'Strategic investment decisions: the importance of SCM. A comparative analysis of 51 case studies in UK., US and German companies', *Management Accounting Research*, 7: 199–217.

Carr, C. and Tomkins, C. (1998) 'Context, culture and the role of the finance function in strategic decisions. A comparative analysis of Britain, Germany, the USA and Japan', *Management Accounting Research*, 9: 213–239.

Carr, C.H., Tomkins, C.R. and Bayliss, B. (1994) *Strategic Investment Decisions: A Comparison of UK and West German Practices in the Motor Components Industry*, Aldershot: ICAEW/Avebury.

Chen, S. (1995) 'An empirical examination of capital budgeting techniques: impact of investment types and firm characteristics', *The Engineering Economist*, 40: 145–170.

Chen, S. (2008) 'DCF techniques and nonfinancial measures in capital budgeting: a contingency approach analysis', *Behavioral Research in Accounting*, 20: 13–29.

Chenhall, R.H. (2003) 'Management control systems design within its organizational context: findings from contingency-based research and directions for the future', *Accounting, Organizations and Society*, 28: 127–168.

Chenhall, R.H. and Langfield-Smith, K. (1998) 'The relationship between strategic priorities, management techniques and management accounting: an empirical investigation using a systems approach', *Accounting, Organizations and Society*, 23: 243–264.

Cheung, J.K. (1993) 'Managerial flexibility in capital investment decisions: insights from the real-options literature', *Journal of Accounting Literature*, 12: 29.

Doyle, R. (1992) 'Marketing and strategic management', in *Marketing Manager's 1992 Yearbook*, London: AP Information Services.

Eisenhardt, K.M. and Sull, D.N. (2001) 'Strategy as simple rules', *Harvard Business Review*, 79: 106–116.

Farragher, E. J., Kleiman, R.T., Sahu, A.P. (1999) 'Current capital investment practices', *Engineering Economics*, 44: 137–149.

Fisher, J. (1995) 'Contingency-based research on management control systems: categorization by level of complexity', *Journal of Accounting Literature*, 14: 24–53.

Goold, M. and Campbell, A. (1987) *Strategies and Styles: the Role of the Centre in Managing Diversified Corporations*, Oxford: Blackwell.

Govindarajan, V. and Gupta, A.K. (1985) 'Linking control systems to business unit strategy: impact on performance', *Accounting, Organizations and Society*, 10: 51–66.

Graham, J.R. and Harvey, C.R. (2001) 'The theory and practice of corporate finance: evidence from the field', *Journal of Financial Economics*, 60: 187–243.

Guilding, C. (1999). 'Competitor-focused accounting: an exploratory note', *Accounting, Organizations and Society*, 24: 583–595.

Guilding, C. and McManus, L. (2002) 'The incidence, perceived merit and antecedents of customer accounting: an exploratory note', *Accounting, Organizations and Society*, 27: 45–59.

Guilding, C., Cravens, K.S. and Tayles, M. (2000) 'An international comparison of strategic management accounting practices', *Management Accounting Research*, 11: 113–135.

Gupta, A.K. and Govindarajan, V. (1984) 'Business unit strategy, managerial characteristics, and business unit effectiveness at strategy implementation', *Academy of Management Journal*, 27: 25–41.

Haka, S.F. (1987) 'Capital budgeting techniques and firm-specific contingencies: a correlational analysis', *Accounting, Organizations and Society*, 12: 31–48.

Haka, S.F. (2007) 'A review of the literature on capital budgeting and investment appraisal: past, present, and future musings', in Chapman, C., Hopwood, A.G. and Shields, M.D. (eds) *Handbook of Management Accounting Research*, Oxford: Elsevier.

Haka, S.F., Gordon, L.A. and Pinches, G.E. (1985) 'Sophisticated capital budgeting selection techniques and firm performance', *The Accounting Review* 60: 651–669.

Ho, S.M. and Pike, R.H. (1998) 'Organizational characteristics influencing the use of risk analysis in strategic capital investments', *The Engineering Economist*, 43: 247–268.

Hussey, D.E. (1978) 'Portfolio analysis: practical experience with the directional policy matrix', *Long-Range Planning*, 11: 2–8.

Johnson, G., Scholes, K. and Whittington, R. (2008) *Exploring Corporate Strategy: Text and Cases*, 8th edn, Essex: Prentice Hall.

Jones, T.C. and Dugdale, D. (1994) 'Academic and practitioner reality: the case of investment appraisal', *British Accounting Review*, 26: 3–25.

Jones, T.C., Currie, W.L. and Dugdale, D. (1993) 'Accounting and technology in Britain and Japan: learning from field research', *Management Accounting Research*, 4: 109–137.

Kaplan, R. and Norton, D.P. (2001) *The Strategy-Focused Organization*, Boston: Harvard Business School Publishing Corporation.

Kim, U.-W. and Song, J. (1990) 'US, Korea and Japan: accounting practices in three countries', *Management Accounting*, 72: 26–30.

King, P. (1975) 'Is the emphasis on capital budgeting misplaced?' *Journal of Business Finance and Accounting*, 2: 69–82.

Klammer, T.P. (1972) 'Empirical evidence of the adoption of sophisticated capital budgeting techniques', *Journal of Business*, 45: 387–397.

Klammer, T.P. and Walker, A.C. (1984) 'The continuing increase in the use of capital budgeting techniques', *California Management Review*, 26: 137–148.

Klammer, T., Koch, B. and Wilner, N. (1991) 'Capital budgeting practices – a survey of corporate use', *Journal of Management Accounting Research*, 3: 113–130.

Langfield-Smith, K. (1997) 'Management control systems and strategy: a critical review', *Accounting, Organizations and Society*, 22: 207–232.

Marsh, P., Barwise, P., Thomas, K. and Wensley, R. (1988) S*trategic Investment Decisions in Large Diversified Companies*, London Business School: Centre for Business Strategy Report Series.

Meredith, J.R. and Hill, M.M. (1987) 'Justifying new manufacturing systems: a managerial approach', *Sloan Management Review*, 28: 49–61.

Miles, R.E. and Snow, C.C. (1978) *Organizational Strategy, Structure and Process*, 1st edn, New York: McGraw-Hill.

Miller, P. and O'Leary, T. (2005) 'Capital budgeting, coordination, and strategy: a field study of interfirm and intrafirm mechanisms', in Chapman, C. (ed.) *Controlling Strategy*, Oxford: Oxford University Press.

Miller, P. and O'Leary, T. (2007) 'Mediating instruments and making markets: capital budgeting, science and the economy', *Accounting, Organizations and Society*, 32: 701–734.

Mintzberg, H. (1994) *The Rise and Fall of Strategic Planning*, New York: The Free Press.

Oldcorn, R. and Parker, D. (1996) The *Strategic Investment Decision: Evaluating Opportunities in Dynamic Markets*, London: Pitman.

Oldman, A. and Tomkins, C. (1999) *Cost Management and its Interplay with Business Strategy and Context*, Aldershot: Ashgate.

Pike, R.H. (1983) 'A review of recent trends in formal capital budgeting processes', *Accounting and Business Research*, 51: 201–208.

Pike, R.H. (1988) 'An empirical study of the adoption of sophisticated capital budgeting practices and decision-making effectiveness', *Accounting and Business Research*, 18: 341–351.

Pike, R.H. (1996) 'A longitudinal survey on capital budgeting practices', *Journal of Business Finance & Accounting*, 23: 79–92.

Porter, M.E. (1980) *Competitive Strategy: Techniques for Analyzing Industries and Competitors*, 1st edn, New York: The Free Press.

Rappaport, A. (1996) *Creating Shareholder Value: the New Standard for Business Performance*, New York: John Wiley & Sons Inc.

Robinson, S.J.Q., Hichens, R.E. and Wade, D.P. (1978) 'The directional policy matrix – tool for strategic planning', *Long Range Planning*, 11: 8–15.

Roslender, R. (1995) 'Accounting for strategic positioning: responding to the crisis in management accounting', *British Journal of Management*, 6: 45–57.

Sandahl, G. and Sjögren, S. (2003) 'Capital budgeting methods among Sweden's largest groups of companies. The state of the art and a comparison with earlier studies', *International Journal of Production Economics*, 84: 51–69.

Sangster, A. (1993) 'Capital investment appraisal techniques: a survey of current usage', *Journal of Business Finance & Accounting*, 20: 307–332.

Shank, J.K. (1996) 'Analysing technology investments – from NPV to strategic cost management (SCM)', *Management Accounting Research*, 7: 185–198.

Shields, M.D., Chow, C.W., Kato, Y. and Nakagawa, Y. (1991) 'Management accounting practices in the US and Japan: comparative survey findings and research implications', *Journal of International Financial Management and Accounting*, 3: 61–77.

Sihler, W.W. (1964) 'The capital investment analysis and decision process at the plant level of a large diversified corporation', unpublished thesis, Harvard Business School.

Simons, R. (1987) 'Accounting control systems and business strategy: an empirical analysis', *Accounting, Organizations and Society*, 12: 357–374.

Slagmulder, R., Bruggeman, W. and Van Wassenhove, L. (1995) 'An empirical study of capital budgeting practices for strategic investments in CIM technologies', *International Journal of Production Economics*, 40: 121–152.

Slatter, S. (1984) *Corporate Recovery: Successful Turnaround Strategies and their Implementation*, London: Penguin Books.

Tomkins, C. and Carr, C. (1996) 'Reflections on the papers in this issue and commentary on the state of Strategic Management Accounting', *Management Accounting Review*, 7: 271–280.

Van Cauvenbergh, A.V., Durinck, E., Martens, R., Laveren, E., and Bogaert, I. (1996) 'On the role and function of formal analysis in strategic investment decision processes: results form an empirical study in Belgium', *Management Accounting Research*, 7: 169–184.

Verbeeten, F.H.M. (2006) 'Do organizations adopt sophisticated capital budgeting practices to deal with uncertainty in the investment decision? A research note', *Management Accounting Research*, 17: 106–120.

Yoshikawa, T., Innes J. and Mitchell, F. (1989) 'Japanese management accounting: a comparative survey', *Management Accounting*, 67: 20–23.

18
Quality Costing

Riccardo Giannetti

Introduction

This chapter deals with the fundamentals of quality costing. The measurement and management of quality costs is an interesting issue for several reasons. First of all, quality costing is a cost management tool which requires a strong integration of accounting with other specialisms. These specialisms often have a functional background, for instance engineering. Second, there is potential for many organizations to use this tool due to its great potential impact on performance: an impact that can be found both in relation to revenue, since quality can be used to position the products, and in relation to net cost reductions. Although there is strong evidence of quality costing in practice (e.g. Dale and Plunkett, 1999; Shotmiller and Campanella, 2007; Tenucci et al., 2010), it does not exist, by any means, in all companies and there may be scope for its greater use. Third, there are well-known, predictable relationships among categories of quality costs on which managers can base their quality cost-reduction initiatives.

The first part of the chapter examines the basic concepts proposed in the literature about quality costs, i.e. their definition, classification, and the relationships among the categories of costs for prevention, appraisal and failures. The second part analyzes the value and use of quality costing in practice. Finally, some conclusions are drawn and future research considered.

Quality cost concepts

A definition of quality costs is critical for measuring them and for their effective communication. However, there is no agreement on a broad definition of quality costs and on the constituent elements (Dale and Plunkett, 1999; Schiffauerova and Thomson, 2006).

Dale and Plunkett (1999) and Williams et al. (1999) note that the constituents of quality cost have changed over time. In the early 1980s, quality costs were perceived as the costs of quality assurance, scrap, rework, testing and warranty. At the end of the 1990s quality costs were considered to be the costs incurred in design, implementation, operation and maintenance of an organization's quality management system, plus the cost of organizational resources committed to the process of continuous improvement, the costs of system, products and services failure, non-value-added activities and wastage in all its forms. Furthermore, in the literature it is

Box 18.1 Description of quality costing

Juran and Gryna (1988) consider "quality costs" as the cost of poor quality and describe these costs through the categories of prevention, appraisal and failure (internal and external) costs.

According to Feigenbaum (1991: 110) quality costs include "(. . .) *two principal areas: the costs of control and the costs of failure of control. These are producer operating quality costs, or those costs associated with definition, creation, and control of quality as well as the evaluation and feedback of conformance with quality, reliability, and safety requirements, and those costs associated with the consequences of failure to meet the requirements both within the factory and in the hands of customers*".

Campanella (1999: 5) defined quality costs as " (. . .) *the difference between the actual cost of a product or service and what the reduced cost would be if there were no possibility of sub-standard service, failure of products, or defects in their manufacture*".

Crosby (1979: 12) says that cost of quality "(. . .) *is the expense of doing things wrong. It is the scrap, rework, service after service, warranty, inspection, tests, and similar activities made necessary by nonconformance problems*".

possible to find numerous similar terms (see Box 18.1) that could produce confusion (Campanella, 1999). Some authors, such as Harrington (1987) and Juran and Gryna (1988) used "*poor quality cost*" and "*cost of poor quality*"; the USA Department of Defense has adopted "*costs related to poor quality*"; Campanella (1999) calls these costs "*quality costs*" of the "*cost of quality*". In this chapter all these terms are considered interchangeable. When speaking of quality costing we will refer to the costing systems adopted for measuring and supporting quality costs management (Ansari et al., 1997).

Feigenbaum (1956), Masser (1957) and Freeman (1960) were among the first to describe quality costs through the traditional categories of prevention, appraisal and failure (Campanella, 1999). This distinction gives the familiar prevention, appraisal, failure (internal and external) model (PAF) reported in many articles and textbooks. Prevention costs are incurred in order to avoid defects in design and development, purchasing, producing or delivering products/services. Typical costs included in this category are: reviews/checks (e.g. for design and engineering specifications), product qualifications, process capabilities studies, training (e.g. for suppliers and operation workers), zero defects program, preventive maintenance and the quality maintenance of patterns and tools. Appraisal costs are incurred to verify if products and services conform to the requirements coming from the market and engineering specifications. They include items such as prototype inspection/testing, product conformance analysis, supplier surveillance, receiving control/testing, product acceptance testing, process control acceptance, packaging inspection, status measurement and reporting. Internal failure costs are incurred because poor quality comes up before the product or services arrive to the customer. In this category there are costs due to: reworks, scrap, loss of revenue because of a downgrade in quality product, penalties deriving from process failures (e.g. penalties for delays due to unplanned maintenance on equipment or unplanned machine downtime). External failure costs are incurred when customers experience poor quality of products/services. These costs include items such as customer complaints and returns, rework on returned items, cancelled orders, freight premiums, product recalls and warranty claims (Campanella, 1999; Venters, 2004). Total quality costs are the sum of the prevention, appraisal and failure costs. Hence the economic effects of poor quality include: a) costs incurred to avoid consequences of poor quality, and b) the additional costs and loss of revenue caused by poor quality. As will be illustrated below, quality costing could be designed to measure and manage all these effects or just some of them.

The quality costs management system

In order to understand how to manage quality costs, Ansari et al. (1997) depict the relationship of quality costs to the quality management system. This relationship is explained through the following six most relevant activies carried out in managing quality.

1. *Understand customer requirements*: what customers want and how important the various dimensions of performance are for them is determined in this step.
2. *Establish quality goals*: here customer requirements for product/service are translated into appropriate quality goals (Six Sigma is one way to express quality goals).
3. *Set work processes to meet quality goals*: in this step processes are designed to ensure production is at the required quality level; prevention costs could be incurred here to avoid defects later.
4. *Perform work and monitor output*: in this step the output is checked to see if quality corresponds to the planned goals; appraisal costs are incurred because of the activities done that make certain that final output conforms to standards set, and hence it is possible to have failure costs due to defective units.
5. *Deliver product and monitor customer experience*: in this phase customers could discover product/services with defects and consequently external failure costs are incurred.
6. *Perform root causes analysis*: root causes analysis permits one to discover causes for internal and external failures; findings of root causes analysis may be used to redesign work processes in order to avoid the same problems.

The process is recursive: after the last step it restarts. Quality costs are used within this process for supporting continuous improvement effort, giving a monetary measure of resources consumption due to quality issues. Briefly, through quality costs managers gain information useful to select and to justify investment in quality.

Malmi et al. (2004) note that, despite the fact that management accounting literature provides models to address the practical problem concerning investments in quality improvement, the problem still exists because management accounting research has not extensively considered the issue of costing for poor quality and the related management process. Malmi et al. (2004) propose a collaborative approach for managing quality costs in a project business environment, see Figure 18.1. This approach is focused on project businesses and is grounded on these key elements: point-score heuristics, intermediate causes, prospective values and probabilities of occurrence, and use of workshops.

In the first phase (assessment workshop) the main problems causing quality costs are identified and ranked using point scores. The basic assumption is that workshop participants possess enough experience and tacit knowledge to select problems and make good judgments. In order to save both time and effort in this phase monetary information is not prepared, and quality costs are calculated only if there is not agreement on the main causes of poor quality. The output of this phase is a fishbone chart illustrating the main causes and, if possible, root causes for the cost of poor quality.

In the second phase (algorithm workshop) elements of poor quality are valued giving three values or a range, and each value is associated with a probability of occurrence. Only costs of poor quality that are considered significant are determined. Furthermore, the focus is on

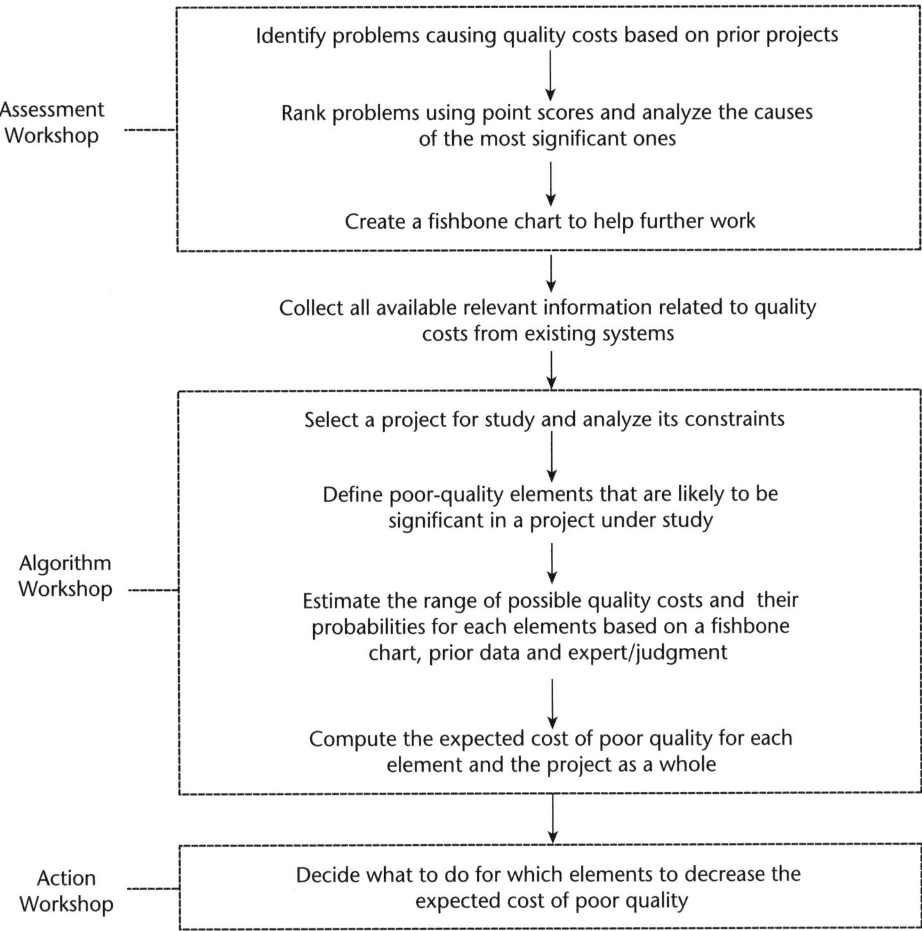

Figure 18.1 A collaborative approach for managing project cost of poor quality

Source: Malmi et al., 2004.

intermediate causes, and not necessarily on root causes. This is because sometimes it is not possible to divide problems neatly into elements connected by a causality relationship. A two-way, self-reinforcing system loop or just a probability relation may exist. Thus, the research for the ultimate root cause of cost of quality may be ineffective, while it could be more productive in finding causes that are both observable and controllable by organizational members.

In the final step (action workshop) decisions are taken on how to reduce the expected costs of poor quality.

Interestingly, Malmi et al.'s (2004) approach is based on the argument that quality costs can be managed without an extensive cost of poor-quality calculation. Although potentially less accurate than figures that can be computed by other methods, which are more focused on quality costs quantification, the figures produced by this approach have a clearer meaning and are designed to initiate managerial action. Finally, Malmi et al.'s (2004) proposal does not include quality costs measurement to monitor the continuous improvement process because they found cross-project measurement of these costs difficult in project business environments due to changing constraints.

The prevention–appraisal–failure cost model

Until the categorization into prevention, appraisal and failure (PAF), the concept of quality costs remained a theory (Jaju et al., 2009). The categorization of quality costs identified relevant cause-and-effect linkages among different categories. Relationships between these categories have been questioned (Burgess, 1996; Campanella, 1999) and can be analyzed by considering the "old" cost-of-quality model (or classical model) and the "new" cost-of-quality model (or modern model).

The old cost-of-quality model

The "old cost-of-quality model", see Figure 18.2, is Juran's first contribution, developed together with Lundvall and published in Juran (1951) (Freiesleben, 2004).

According to this model increasing appraisal plus prevention costs determine reductions in failure costs. Due to the behavior of these costs an optimal point is reached where the

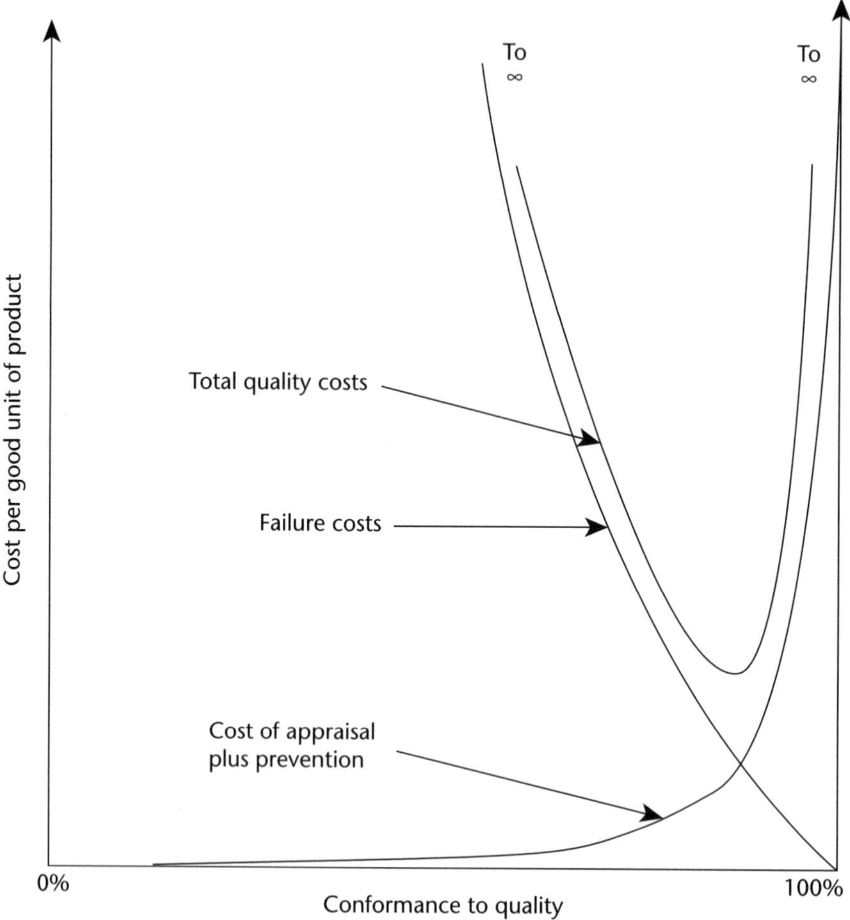

Figure 18.2 The old cost-of-quality model

Source: Juran and Gryna, 1988.

total cost of quality (that is to say appraisal plus prevention plus failure costs) is at the minimum level.

Before the optimal point, appraisal plus prevention costs increase with quality conformance, while failure costs decrease more. Hence, the total cost of quality per unit of good product decreases. After the cost, minimum point prevention and appraisal costs increase more than the reduction in failure costs, thus the total cost of quality per unit increases. It is evident that the lowest total quality cost per unit occurs before perfection, is attained (100 per cent conformance to quality).

The existence of an optimal point has been debated (Plunkett and Dale, 1988). Freiesleben (2004) underlines that there is a discrepancy between this model and the striving of organizations to approximate perfection, as the successful quality concept Six Sigma demonstrates in leading companies (Hahn et al., 2000). Freiesleben (2004) points out that failure costs are assumed to decrease approaching the level of perfection. This tendency is acceptable, as in attaining perfection there will be zero defects thus failure costs will disappear. Vice versa, failure costs increase exponentially if conformance to quality decreases. This tendency is again reasonable because the function is based on per-unit cost, hence reducing quality levels means the number of good products decreases, failure costs in total increase and as a consequence failure costs per unit will rise. Starting from a poor-quality situation, organizations can increase the number of good products placed on the market and so reduce external failure costs, which are often several times higher than internal failure costs (Bohan and Horney, 1991; Tannock, 1997 in Freiesleben, 2004).

As concerns appraisal costs, they include costs for inspecting process outputs and for monitoring production processes. These costs are assumed to increase exponentially when perfection is approximated. Possible explanations for this tendency rely on the assumptions that the old model is based on companies with a poor quality level. An engagement in continuous improvement over time permits organizations to be more efficient and effective in prevention and monitoring activities by adopting a leaner inspection system (Ittner, 1996). For a company which is just starting to incur the cost of quality implementation it would be too costly to find and solve all the root causes of poor quality. Thus, the optimum quality level will be below perfection. Furthermore, the model does not consider progress in technology which makes it more feasible to find and remedy the root causes of poor quality.

Another explanation for the exponential increase of appraisal costs could be the assumption that a certain level of defects will remain. Hence, it is possible to reach perfection only by employing an extensive inspection system that will be very costly. However, it is important to underline that this argument is based on the assumptions that prevention cannot avoid all defects and that appraisal costs are mostly inspection costs.

Starting from these considerations, Freiesleben (2004) finds that the old model of quality costs cannot depict the business reality because:

1. It considers organizations already in a situation of poor quality and doesn't fit organizations engaged in quality improvement starting from a higher quality level.
2. It is founded on a certain level of technology and does not take into account that technology progress permits the selection of the root causes of poor quality and the adoption of monitoring systems at lower costs.
3. It doesn't consider learning for the organizations engaged over time in quality improvement initiatives.
4. It is rooted in the "inspection mentality" of management (according to which a high level of quality is mainly associated with a strong commitment to inspection activities).
5. Excluding a company with a poor quality situation, it is unrealistic to have an exponentially growing total quality cost per unit approximating perfection because at a high level of

quality conformance there are more units of good products which are bearing an (unlikely) increase in appraisal costs.

The new cost-of-quality model

Figure 18.3 shows the "new" cost-of-quality model based on Juran and Gryna (1988). In this model the costs of achieving good quality have a tendency to increase in contrast to the old model. The increase in these costs stops by correspondence with zero defects. This tendency is justified by new technological solutions which make process-monitoring feasible. In addition, there is a prioritization of prevention initiatives.

The failure costs curve maintains the same shape as the old model. Thus, the resulting total quality cost per unit represents a negatively sloped curve with the minimum a zero defects point.

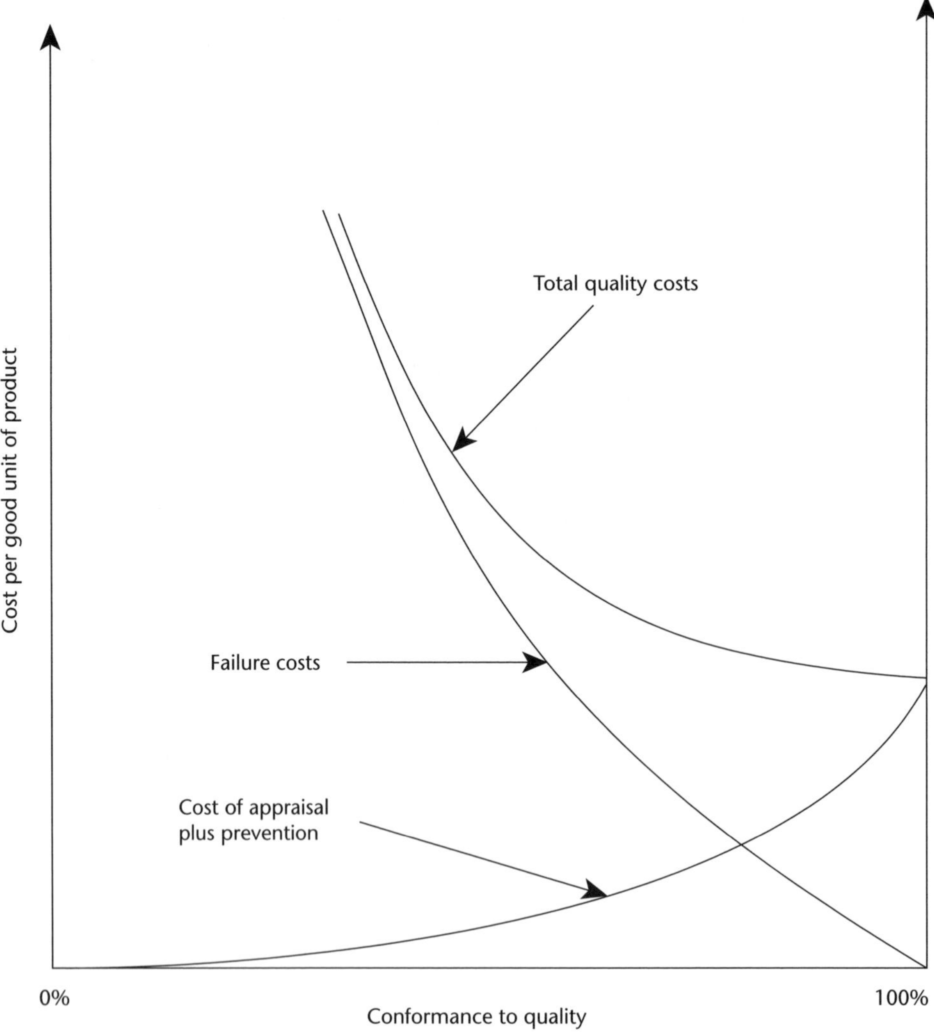

Figure 18.3 The new cost-of-quality model

Source: Juran and Gryna, 1988.

Also different from the old model is that the new minimum cost is reached with perfection. However Juran and Gryna (1988) argue that perfection is the goal for the long run but it does not imply that it is the most profitable goal for the short run and for every situation. According to Freiesleben (2004) this assumption shows that prevention costs have decreasing returns and they depend on the quality level already reached, on technological solutions available, and on learning over time.

It is interesting to recall that the new model is aligned with Deming's arguments. Deming (1986) argues that the cost of selling outputs with poor quality to customers is so high that the only logical purpose for minimizing quality costs it is to reach zero defects or total-quality conformance. Accepting this assumption, Deming does not see any reason to measure quality costs.

On the new model Freiesleben (2004) observes that:

1. time is not an explicit parameter and thus the model may again be a snapshot view of a high-quality producer which has a high percentage of prevention costs, adopting a certain technology for making feasible quality intervention on root causes;
2. due to the previous point the model is situation-dependent but this unnecessarily reduces the explanation scope (it is clear that the appropriate objective should be zero-defect);
3. perfection is the most desirable goal in order to minimize costs and if this goal cannot be reached in the short run, this fact does not reduce the importance of organizations striving to obtain it.

It is relevant to recall that Juran and Gryna (1988: 4.21) point out that both the old and new models apply to a variety of industries but with some exceptions:

- *industries producing goods that have a critical impact on human safety* – e.g. the generation of nuclear power or development of drugs, as such industries have to achieve quality at almost any cost;
- *highly automated industries* – here it is possible to obtain low defects by adequate planning, and automated inspection makes 100 per cent inspection economically feasible;
- *companies selling to affluent clients* – these customers can pay a premium price for perfect quality;
- *companies striving to optimize the user's cost* – when costs incurred by the user, due to failures, are added to the costs of failures which the manufacturer has incurred (reported in Figure 18.3), the optimum point shifts towards zero defects; the same happens if lost sales income to the manufacturer is included in the failure costs.

Integration of the old with the new cost-of-quality model

Freiesleben (2004) argues that neither the old nor the new cost-of-quality models can be used to determine an economically optimal quality level. Freiesleben (2004) suggests the models are extremes in a continuum. One extreme is for poor-quality conformance levels; here the situation could be depicted by the old quality costs model. The other extreme is for a high-quality level and here the new quality costs model is applied. Between these extremes, several intermediate situations exist and for each one there is an economically optimum quality level. Thus, from poor to high quality a company goes through several optimal quality points. Figure 18.4 depicts this transition considering a company which starts by adopting a quality costing system in a situation of poor quality.

Starting from the left of Figure 18.4 (poor-quality situation), the appraisal costs rapidly rise until they approach performance perfection, due to the diminishing return of prevention

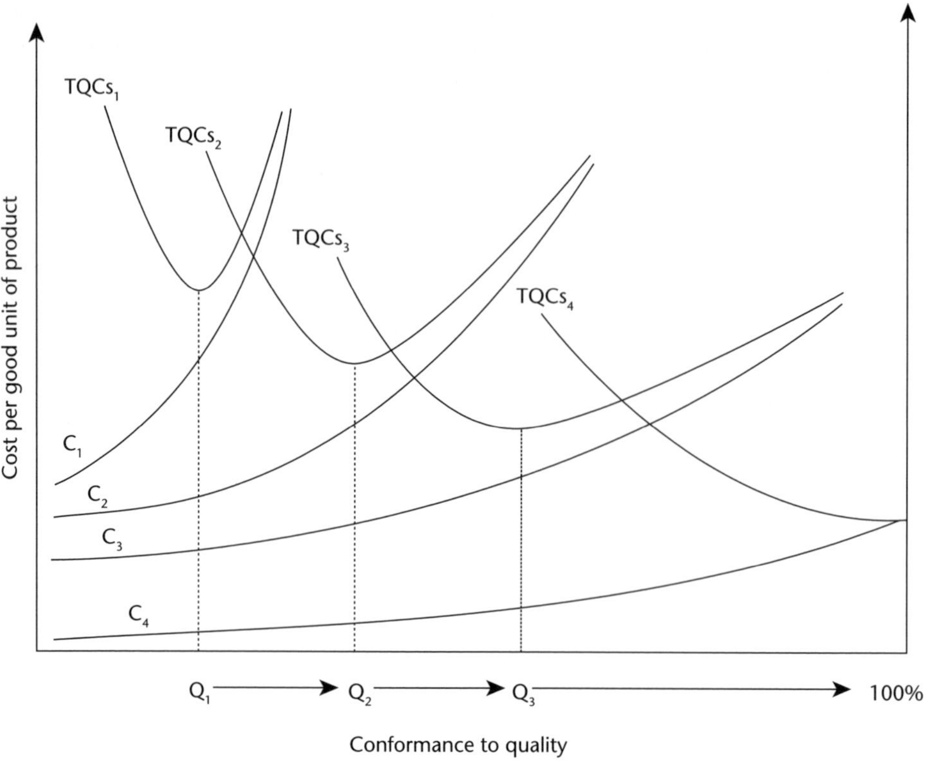

Figure 18.4 An example of change of costs per unit of good product over time

Source: Freiesleben, 2004.

initiatives (curve C_1). Capabilities and technological solutions that the organization employs during that time determine the diminishing returns for prevention, and the total quality costs (TQCs) are represented by curve $TQCs_1$. Due to the diminishing returns of prevention costs the first optimal point is Q_1. Here, some root causes are not eliminated because of the increasing prevention plus appraisal costs (curve C_1). After this first improvement the company learns how to be more effective and efficient in prevention. In addition, probably there will be new technological remedies for non-quality root causes. Thus, the return from prevention will improve and the curve for appraisal and prevention costs will become C_2 and that for total quality costs will be $TQCs_2$. Now, for the company it is convenient to arrive at the conformance quality Q_2. Repeating this logic, it is possible to define several intermediate states until the situation displayed in the new model of quality costs is reached (on the right of Figure 18.4). The failure costs function is not included in Figure 18.4 because it is assumed that it is not affected by the continuous improvement.

Ittner (1996) did a study which, in several ways, is aligned with Freiesleben's (2004) proposal. Ittner tests the hypothesis that conformance costs (prevention plus appraisal costs) must increase over time in order to obtain a reduction in non-conformance costs (internal and external failures). Results show that, in many of the plants observed, there have been significant reductions in non-conformance costs while conformance costs remained constant or diminished. These results are inconsistent with the assumption that a reduction in failure costs should lead to a continuous increase in conformance costs.

Thus Ittner (1996) provides empirical support for the continuous improvement model and shows that a quality learning effect took place over time. However, he concludes by saying that although the evidence of his study is inconsistent with the traditional or "old" cost-of-quality model and supports continuous improvement and quality-based-learning models, they do not invalidate the traditional cost-of-quality model. Data and econometric limitations of his study make it difficult to definitively test the competing models of quality-cost behavior.

However, even if quality-based learning models correctly depict quality-cost behavior over time, the old model of quality costs may still be an accurate static representation of quality costs. Adopting a multi-period dynamic perspective and considering organizations embracing a continuous improvement approach to quality, it is possible to have reduction in non-conformance costs while maintaining or even reducing conformance costs. Furthermore, the static and dynamic perspectives suggested by Ittner (1996) are consistent with Freiesleben's (2004) proposal to integrate old and new quality-cost models.

The impact of technology on the model is another relevant aspect. Technology influences the costs and benefits of quality improvement but also the amount of quality costs included in each category of the PAF model and the relationships among these categories. In Box 18.2 there is an example of the impact of nanotechnology diffusion on quality costs.

Concluding this section on quality costs relationships, it is interesting to recall a well-known contribution from Plunkett and Dale (1988). They analyze the quality-economics models presented in the literature by grouping them in five groups[1]. They underline that these models are notional and sometime inaccurate, and more research is needed to avoid misleading representations. From that paper several articles have been published, and their conclusions are clear and seem still relevant.[2]

> *"Everyone would like to have a valid model which they could use to assess their present situation and predict the effects of changes. So far as is known there are insufficient data available to construct such a model, though there should be enough collective experience available to make a reasonable hypothesis as to the shape and the relative proportions of the constituents costs in the diagram. For example, there are reasonably good grounds for believing that optimum quality, if it exists, is near to the highest attainable standard of quality."*
>
> *(Plunkett and Dale, 1988: 1725)*

Box 18.2 The impact of nanotechnologies on costs of quality

Dutta and Lawson (2006) point out that through nanotechnology diffusion the distribution of quality costs among well-known categories of prevention, appraisal and failures will dramatically change. In a nanotech environment, production or replication is perfect, with minimum possibility of errors during the production phase. Much more attention should be given to the prototyping phase. The finished product is identical to the prototype; hence it is fundamental to have a prototype with no flaws in order to avoid external failures. More emphasis should be placed on prevention costs, while appraisal and internal failure costs will be very low. With regard to a company's production process the molecular engineering process will ensure that no additional flaws are introduced. The need to test finished product prior to shipment won't be necessary and continuous improvement efforts will focus on design. Of course, during this change to quality costs connected to the manufacturing processes organizations will have to maintain improvement efforts to non-manufacturing processes.

The hidden quality costs

Poor quality can cause some costs that usually are not recorded through the traditional PAF model. These costs in literature are "hidden" or "invisible".[3] According to Dahlgaard et al. (1992) the term "hidden" is used due to the fact that, sometimes, failure costs are inadequately recorded and/or never discovered. Such costs could comprise costs incurred because of quality problems that go beyond evident activities such as inspection, testing, rework and improvement (Chiadamrong, 2003). Hidden quality costs can include items such as lost sales, loss of goodwill, extra inventories, over-quality design, or loss of productivity. These costs are not recorded as costs of poor quality due to both the inadequacy of cost accounting techniques and/or because they are not explicitly included in the cost-of-quality categorization adopted.

Hidden quality costs can be significant (Kume, 1985). According to some researchers they could be more than three times the level of the visible costs (Giakatis et al., 2001; Han and Lee, 2002). By knowing the amount of these costs, managers can gain a more comprehensive picture of the costs and benefits associated with quality improvements (Juran and Gryna, 1988). Several authors have formulated a categorization for hidden quality costs. Below, some contributions are summarized in order to show the main characteristics of hidden quality costs and the related proposals for accounting and managing them.

Sandoval-Chavez and Beruvides (1998) consider the costs of quality formed by the traditional prevention-appraisal-failure costs plus the opportunity losses. Opportunity losses have been broken down into three categories: capacity under-utilization, inadequate material handling and poor delivery service. Their study was conducted in a firm whose production process was continuous (the company produces concrete blocks for the construction industry). They found that the costs of quality expressed as lost revenues were mainly explained by the opportunity variables. The same variables explained costs of quality quantified as profit not earned. Usually PAF models do not embrace lost revenues due to poor quality. In the case study that Sandoval-Chavez and Beruvides (1998) analyze, the conformance of finished product is 100 per cent. Thus, it doesn't seem economically justified to invest more in voluntary costs such as prevention and appraisal costs. However, considering opportunity costs, that is to say lost revenues, the picture changes. In particular they apply a wider approach to the quality, such as Total Quality Management or Company-Wide Quality Control. In this wide approach not only the product level of conformance to the technical requirements is relevant, but also defects at the delivery stage (e.g. unit of product broken, or late delivery) or orders cancelled due to poor delivery service. These deficiencies caused waste and customer dissatisfaction. The effects of these problems are equal to those of failures. Thus, there is a case for considering them as failures in the prevention-appraisal-failures approach.

Sandoval-Chavez and Beruvides (1998) realized that the opportunity costs they considered did not fall into the categories used in the literature they analyzed (British Standard BS 6143 and ASQC taxonomy). Given that all the products were sold, the opportunity losses have been determined in the following way:

1. *Opportunity cost caused by poor delivery service (PDS):*
   (Total units solicited by purchase order − real quantity of units delivered) × weighted average selling price per unit (or "× weighted average profit per unit").
2. *Opportunity cost caused by inadequate materials handling (IMH):*
   (Total units broken because of inadequate material handling in the plant + Total units broken because of inadequate material handling during delivery) × weighted average selling price per unit (or "× weighted average profit per unit").

3. *Opportunity cost caused by installed capacity under-utilization (ICU):*
   (Total down and idle time × installed capacity per plant expressed as producible units per hour) × weighted average selling price per unit (or "×weighted average profit per unit").
4. *The total cost of quality is:*
   Prevention + appraisal + failures + losses caused by opportunity factors (determined as PDS + IMH + ICU).

Sandoval-Chavez and Beruvides (1998) raise some interesting issues from their case study. The first concerns the magnitude of the opportunity costs. Without these components, costs of quality represented roughly 8 percent of sales. However, their inclusion (calculated as lost revenues) caused costs of quality to increase to around 47% of sales. The second concerns the usefulness of considering customer perception in addition to quality conformance at the end of the manufacturing process. By so doing, costs of quality give a more complete measure of the impact of quality improvement on profit. Third, opportunity costs could become more and more important due to the changes in technology and the critical role of intangible factors. Finally they show that 100 percent of conformance could be obtained at a finite cost.

Giakatis et al. (2001) deal with hidden quality costs, distinguishing quality costs from quality losses:

> *"Quality cost is the cost for the company of every effort that sustains or improves the certainty that the product meets or will meet the specified requirements. On the contrary, quality loss is the money spent because a quality cost failed to sustain or improve certainty and hence nonconformances occur."*
>
> *(Giakatis et al., 2001: 181)*

Giakatis et al. (2001) identified the following categories of quality losses which are added to the traditional prevention, appraisal, internal and external failures ones (see Table 18.1).

It is interesting to note that quality losses could also affect prevention and appraisal activities. Another relevant point is that, given the presence of manufacturing and design losses, the cost of quality could decrease (apparently) – not because the root causes have been removed and

Table 18.1 Definitions of quality costs and quality losses

	Quality cost	*Quality loss*
Prevention	Money spent on a successful prevention activity	Money spent on an unsuccessful prevention activity plus the sequential losses
Appraisal	Money spent on a successful appraisal activity	Money spent on an unsuccessful prevention activity plus the sequential losses
Failure		All failures
Manufacturing		The decrease of the production equipment efficiency in order to decrease failures (e.g. reducing of production speed in order to reduce quality costs)
Design		The money spent to achieve more than required product quality (e.g. in a product design a material is changed to another more expensive one that is not subjected to the process of instability)

Source: Giakatis et al., 2001.

an improvement has been realized, but because there is an inefficient use of resources (e.g. a reduction of equipment production speed in order to avoid quality problems). If quality costs and losses are not distinguished, the total amount of negative effects coming from poor quality and the related main drivers[4] are unclear. Furthermore, some losses (above all those which differ from evident failures) could remain hidden.

Giakatis et al. (2001) also distinguish operating and idle losses. Operating losses derive from wasted time as a result of manufacturing losses and from time lost due to failures. Idle losses generally are more evident than operating losses. Idle losses derive from inactivity and typically frequent stoppages are evident. Operating losses could be less obvious because they are incurred during production and derive from activities that have been considered unmodifiable and/or unavoidable (while they could be redesigned in a more effective way).

The classification proposed by Giakatis et al. (2001) also impacts on the process for quality cost reduction. Applying the new categorization the sequence would be as follows (Giakatis et al., 2001: 189).

Step 1: Decrease of prevention loss.
Step 2: Decrease of appraisal loss.
Step 3: Decrease of failure loss.
Step 4: Decrease of hidden failure loss, manufacturing loss, design loss.
Step 5: Decrease of appraisal cost.
Step 6: Decrease of prevention cost.

The first step should be for the prevention losses because usually they have large and long run effects.[5]

Quality costing's usefulness

Tenucci et al.'s (2010) Italian survey on the diffusion of Advanced Management Accounting (AMA) techniques and their perceived usefulness placed quality costing in the third position. Three per cent of respondents considered quality costing not useful at all, 12% could not express an answer and 85% attributed some degree of usefulness to quality costing (more precisely, usefulness was distributed as: 14% little, 22% moderately, 16% very, 33% extremely). Hence, quality costing has a considerable range of perceived usefulness in practice. Some possible explanations for this are considered below.

The rationale behind quality costing

First of all, the potential usefulness of a quality costing system can be based on the rationale underlying the system. This rationale can be explained by three major objectives (Mevellec, 2009: *managing resources, interacting with the environment and orienting behavior*).

Resources can be managed at the points of their acquisition and/or their usage. A quality costing system will record cost elements representing resources employed for quality purposes. Since resources are used inside responsibility centers, quality costing provides knowledge of where in the companies the costs of quality are generated. Furthermore, quality costing gives cost information on resource usage that helps with finding and managing cost drivers. If a quality costing system can produce data aggregated for products, it could be useful for supporting management in assessing profitability and/or giving priority to investments oriented to reduce the negative effects of poor quality. Broadly speaking, quality costing helps managers to justify and monitor investment in quality programs. Otherwise, the cost of quality related to objects such as departments, training in quality, warranty interventions, or downgrade of product due to poor quality, would remain unknown as they are hidden in wider aggregates (e.g. manufacturing overhead) or not recorded at all (e.g. sales lost due to customer disappointment).

Sjoblom (1998) investigated the usefulness of quality costs and quality-related financial information in a way that could be useful for illustrating how and why quality cost information could be employed for managing resources. Sjoblom (1998) carried out a survey, informal discussions and interviews with quality managers. The sample was limited to the electronics industry. Sjoblom (1998) considers that financial information and cost of quality can be used for the following purposes:

1. flagging quality problems;
2. selecting and prioritizing quality-improving projects;
3. choosing correcting actions.

With regard to the first purpose, results shows that physical internal failure measures, such as yield, are the most commonly used variables (tracked by 86% of the sample). The comments of some respondents were as follows:

- "*We don't wait to see the impact of poor quality on our financial variables. It is too late by then.*"
- "*It is impossible to track financial variables to the responsible process sequence.*"
- "*Cost of quality is imposed by management, but not useful.*"

The difference in appreciation between non-financial and financial information is small. However, the respondents always rank non-financial information as more important than financial information (physical information has the advantages of reliability, timeliness and relevance).

In selecting which quality problem to pursue, the most important factor was the impact of the project on customer satisfaction. The financial impact and the frequency of defects were the most important factors after customer satisfaction. During the follow-up question it emerged that key reasons for financial analysis were to create awareness and to motivate plant management. Furthermore, for choosing corrective actions financial information and costs of quality are potentially useful (selection and justification of investments in improvements). However, the three most common outcomes (quick-fix process, changes in training methods and change in workmanship standards) should require relatively small financial sacrifice.

Sjoblom (1998) notes that the majority of respondents are using non-financial indicators to address the three purposes related to quality problems and they perceived these measures as good proxies for the financial impact.

According to the second major objective of a quality costing system (i.e. interacting with the environment), one of the reasons most often put forward in cost calculation is to set price. Viger and Anandarajan (1999) investigated the relevance of quality cost information on the pricing decisions by an experimental study with marketing managers. They explored the relevance of quality cost information in pricing decision. The results show that quality cost information is relevant because the decisions made by managers who received quality cost information were different from those made by managers who did not have this information. Moreover, the information on quality costs became particularly relevant when managers faced particularly sensitive situations (e.g. when they perceived a high level of competition and or when buyers were highly sensitive to price variation).[6] Additionally, quality cost information can be used for price bargaining with suppliers (Reeve, 2005) and/or to find and realize opportunities for cost reduction in inter-organizational relationships.[7]

Finally, according to the third major objective (i.e. orienting behavior), quality costing could be useful due to the orienting behavior effect that the measurement of quality costs could have. Providing quality costs to managers helps to emphasize the importance of quality for business performance and, consequently, will help to influence employee behavior and attitudes at all levels in the organization toward continuous improvement (Dale and Plunkett, 1999). For this rationale quality costing should be designed taking into account that it has an influencing role rather than purely an informative one. Thus, for this purpose, the accuracy of information could be less important (Merchant and Shields, 1993).

Quality costing and quality system maturity

Quality costing is a fascinating topic because, among other things, there isn't agreement on its relevance for supporting decision-making (Emsley, 2008). Many Japanese companies recorded failure costs, but few of them can completely describe their quality costs. Instead, in Western companies, it has seemed that quality control activities cannot exist without a formal quality costing system (Kume, 1985).

Shank and Govindarajan (1994) point out that it is possible to draw out four "quality management schools" which put different emphasis on quality costs, i.e. Juran's model, Deming's model, Crosby's model, and the Japanese model. Juran's model considers quality costing as a management control tool. The cost of quality categorized distinguishing costs according to the PAF model. Recording costs provides a basis for seeking the optimum level of quality costs. Deming's approach is completely different. According to his view, it is not relevant to measure quality costs, because the costs of poor quality are so high (in terms of lost customer goodwill and major internal costs) that investment in quality is always economically justified. It is productive to do things right the first time and the proper target from this perspective is to attain zero defects. Crosby's approach is also based on the notion that the minimum cost of quality is incurred by making things right first time, and a proper target is zero defects. But in his approach there is space for measuring quality costs. Crosby (1984) divides the cost of quality into (a) the price of conformance which includes the quality-related costs incurred in order to do things right the first time (such as costs for all prevention efforts and quality education) and (b) the price of nonconformance which includes all the costs incurred because things are not done right the first time (for example costs incurred to correct the product). Additionally, he proposes a "Quality Management Maturity Grid" which distinguishes different steps in quality management adoption: uncertainty; awakening; enlightenment; wisdom; certainty. Each stage is differentiated from the others according to several dimensions: management understanding and attitude; quality organizations status; problem handling; cost of quality as per cent of sales; quality improvement actions; and summation of quality company posture.

Crosby disagrees with Juran about quality costing as management tool, as he proposes measurement of these costs in order to better understand where the company stands in the Quality Management Maturity Grid.

Finally, Shank and Govindarajan (1994) recall the Japanese approach to quality management. Although Japanese companies do not apply a single quality system, this last approach is characterized by two basic notions: 1) quality is a journey rather than a destination; 2) quality enhancement is a way of life and not a business target. According to Shank and Govindarajan (1994), as the quality programs develop, the cost of quality can take different forms. For instance, approaching Total Quality Management for the first time a company might benefit by adopting a quality cost model such as Juran suggests (hence reporting explicitly quality costs) but when quality becomes part of the way of life of the organization, the cost-of-quality reports could become unnecessary (Deming's approach). Thus, Shank and Govindarajan (1994) show that at a certain point in time, quality costing could have different roles that could be roughly reconciled with Juran, Crosby and Deming's approaches. This means there could be a life cycle of quality costing where quality costs could have a different role and hence a changing potential usefulness over the life cycle.

Sower et al. (2007) conducted a study linking quality system maturity and quality cost usage. The maturity of the organization's quality system was assessed using the ANSI/ISO/ASQ Q9004-2000 performance maturity level classification system. Sower et al. (2007) provide evidence for possible benefits coming from quality costing adoption, and also gives insights into why some firms decide not to use quality costing. As the old and new models of cost of quality show, the amount and composition of costs of quality change. One of the main variables that could influence the content and amount of costs of quality is the quality system maturity. Sower et al. (2007) examined this issue using empirics gathered from a sample of USA professionals working in manufacturing. The main results indicated the following:

1. total quality costs decrease over time for organizations with quality systems adopting cost-of-quality techniques, however, the reduction of quality costs diminishes the longer the quality system has been in place;
2. an organization's quality cost distribution will change as the organization's quality system matures;
3. external failure costs decrease as a percentage of total quality cost as the organization's quality system matures;
4. external failure costs decline with increases in appraisal costs;
5. both internal and external failure costs decrease with increases in prevention costs;
6. as a company's quality system matures, external failure costs decrease as a percentage of total quality costs concurrent with increases in internal failure and appraisal costs;
7. higher growth rates in sales and/or profits are not associated with the maturity level of an organization's quality system or with tracking of quality costs.

Hence, the study confirms that when quality system maturity increases, the distribution of quality costs changes, highlighting an increase in the percentage of total quality costs spent on prevention activities and a decrease in the proportion spent in external failure. However, in the short term, the total cost of quality increases as an organization moves from a very low level of quality system maturity to a higher level. Another interesting result is that fewer organizations than expected systematically track quality costs.

The reasons for not identifying quality costs are: lack of management support and interest, the absence of adequate tracking systems, a lack of knowledge of how to track cost of quality and the life cycle position of the organization.[8]

Quality costing and other cost management techniques: analysis of some possible integrations

Quality costing may be based on the adoption of different cost accounting approaches and it may also be integrated with other cost management techniques. This section deals with the implementation of quality costing using an activity-based costing approach and it will also consider some proposals concerning the use of quality costing during the design stage of a product.

Activity-based costing and quality costing

If an organization decides to identify, collect and monitor quality costs it needs to have an appropriate cost accounting system. Sometimes, traditional costing systems cannot provide acceptable information for measuring quality costs and supporting continuous improvement. Frequently there are not specific departments dedicated to poor quality, and thus the costs of quality could be hidden (Cokins, 2006). In these cases an activity-based costing system (ABC) could be a remedy. An ABC system encompasses two main stages. First, the costs of resources used are traced to activities; second, the costs of activities are traced to output cost objects. The basic idea is that cost objects demand activities and by so doing generate costs. Consequently, costs of activities lie at the core of ABC systems.

As regards direct costs (with respect to the unit of product or service), usually in the traditional costing systems they are traced to the cost object using standard costs. Nevertheless standard costs for labor or material could include costs for non-value-added activities (e.g. waiting for missing assembly parts to arrive) that remain hidden (Campanella, 1999). Tracing direct costs to the activities carried out for each unit of product (or service) makes it possible to show how resources are used and this could be useful both for identifying inefficiencies and revising standards.

ABC can also be useful for assigning and managing overhead costs (indirect costs), which are a most significant part of quality costs. Overhead costs comprise costs that are difficult to trace to the unit level. They are first assigned to activities and then to the selected cost objects. Each activity will have a cost driver identified for it. This is normally a transaction measure of the work done in the activity, and together with the activity cost a cost driver rate can be computed and used to cost the cost object.

Figure 18.5 provides an example of activities that could be included inside the traditional cost of quality classification. Examples of cost drivers are training hours (quality education), number of inspections (appraisal activity), number of defects (defect removal) and number of complaints (complaint administration).

Figure 18.6 outlines a scheme proposed by Campanella (1999) where ABC is used for apportioning internal failure costs between two products (shafts and housings). First of all internal failure costs are assigned to the activities (rework and removal of scraps). Then the activities are traced to the products, and finally causes of activity costs are identified and reported in the last column on the right.

There are two levels of driver. The first level represents the activity drivers and the second represents the root causes of the costs of activities assigned to the products. The approach

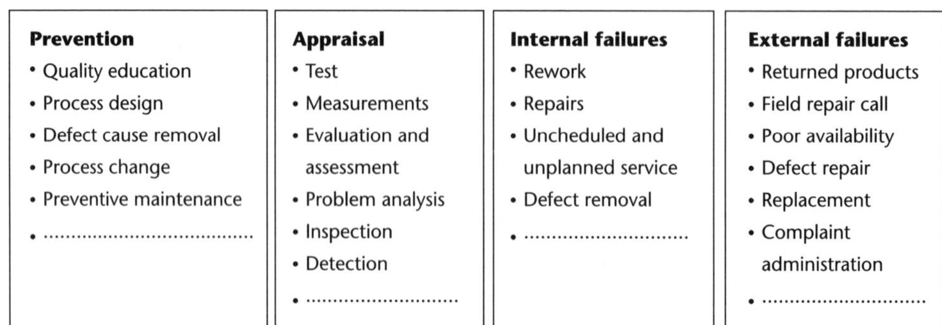

Prevention	**Appraisal**	**Internal failures**	**External failures**
• Quality education • Process design • Defect cause removal • Process change • Preventive maintenance •	• Test • Measurements • Evaluation and assessment • Problem analysis • Inspection • Detection •	• Rework • Repairs • Uncheduled and unplanned service • Defect removal •	• Returned products • Field repair call • Poor availability • Defect repair • Replacement • Complaint administration • ....

Figure 18.5 Example of activities classified according to the PAF model

Source: Cokins, 2006.

thus connects costs per activities to the causes of costs. An ABC system can be made even more powerful if it is implemented along with activity-based management (ABM). ABM uses ABC information to obtain two important goals (Turney, 2005), first to improve the value received by the customer, and second to improve the profits earned from providing this value (or in the case of non-profit organizations, to improve the cost-effectiveness of the value to the clients).

Activity-based cost management (ABCM) system use ABC information to improve products, services and processes by identifying product/service costs, possibly revising product prices, eliminating non-value-added activities, reducing cycle time and, above all, improving overall profitability of the companies (Gupta and Baxendale, 2008).

The ABCM system is compatible with a continuous improvement philosophy and it provides information about each process or activity (through which a product moves) as a potential area

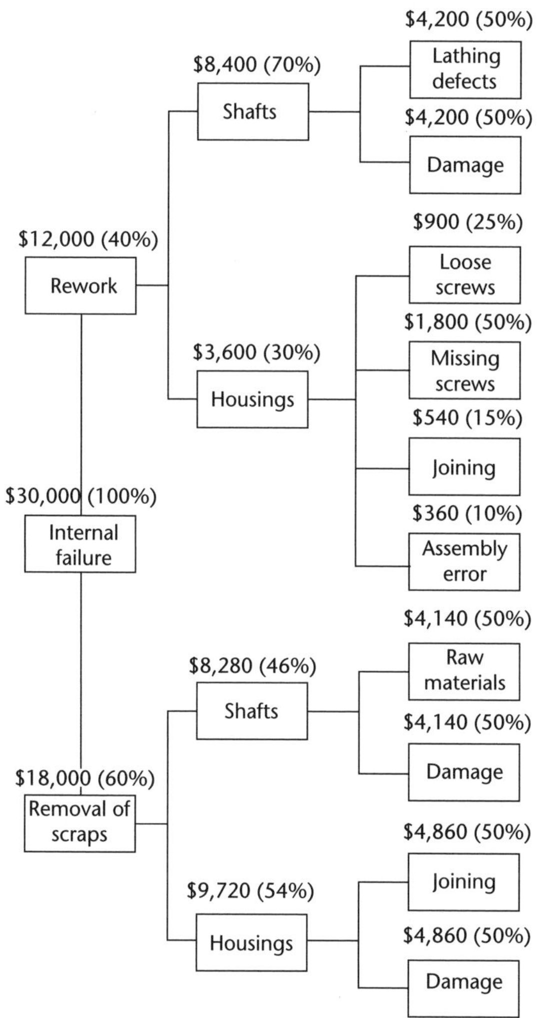

Figure 18.6 An example of internal failure costs breakdown through ABC

Source: Campanella, 1999.

for improvement, attention and control. The ABCM system has been recognized as a powerful tool in assessing the cost of not doing things right the first time.

Gupta and Baxendale (2008) report that in a large telecommunications company an activity analysis determined that approximately thirty per cent of personnel time was spent on rework. The cost of this internal failure activity had not been identified by conventional accounting reports and was thus never debated. By applying ABCM analysis the causes of the rework were identified and eliminated. As a consequence almost one fourth of the shop's workers became available for other activities.

ABCM also has the potential to find activities that are not adding value to the customers. Additionally, unnecessary work opportunities to "get it wrong" are reduced (Turney, 2005). Implementation of an ABCM system can be complicated and expensive. Yet a wide variety of service and manufacturing firms use simplified ABC concepts to identify non-value-added activities and quality improvement opportunities, without the time and expense required to implement a full ABC system (Gosselin, 1997; Ittner, 1999).

Ittner (1999) describes three levels of activity analysis used by a major telecommunications firm to identify and categorize quality-related expenditure. These three levels are differentiated by the level of detail. The first is the simplest and is based on current knowledge. The second is based on additional data. The third requires a highly detailed analysis. The analysis level therefore varies in terms of data and time requirements, but each follows the following five-step approach (Ittner, 1999):

1. define activities;
2. assign activities to the quality cost categories (the firm described used these activities categories: essential work, which encompasses value-added activities required to produce a product or service right the first time; prevention activities; appraisal activities; rework and failure activities);
3. assign costs to each activity;
4. determine improvement opportunities with the largest potential payback (not only quality failure costs for prioritizing improvement projects were considered: the firm also assessed three other factors: a) the seriousness or urgency of the problem as perceived by the external customer; b) the degree to which the quality improvement team controls the process and the required solution to the selected quality problem; c) the relative difficulty in terms of time required to solve the problem and in terms of the amount of resources requested);
5. make improvements and monitor results.

It has been found that ABCM can be considered as a valuable support system to implement Total Quality Management (TQM)[9] and to strengthen the operations strategy of a company by measuring its process improvements and customer satisfaction efforts (Gupta and Baxendale, 2008). Determining costs of poor quality by activity analysis and classifying these activities according to the cost of quality categories gives great insights for cost driver identification and cost management (Cokins, 2006).

Quality costing and cost management into design stage

The PAF model emphasizes importance of early intervention (prevention) for managing quality costs. As mentioned above Giakatis et al. (2001), in dealing with losses, identify the reduction of prevention loss as a first step in the management of quality costs. Many costs are committed

Table 18.2 Quality costs in the product development and design stage

Product life cycle stage	*Quality costs category*	*Items of quality costs*
Product development and design	Prevention costs	Engineering design and engineering data analysis
	Appraisal costs	Certification of production process
	Internal failure costs	Problems in the pilot run process (waste of resources)
	Extra resultant costs	Costs for downtime and delay delivery due to design change
	Estimated hidden costs	Extra expenses in the over-quality
		Company's reputation damage due to design problems

Source: Yang, 2008.

Note: Yang (2008) classifies hidden quality costs as "extra resultant costs" and "estimated hidden costs". Extra resultant costs are caused by failures or errors that can be traced and counted. For instance, if a product must be scrapped, costs incurred for this product (such as costs for components, raw materials, labor) represent failure costs already recorded in the traditional approach. However, the error giving rise to these costs might damage other parts of the company and additional resources will be wasted. Yang (2008) proposes to call these effects "extra resultant costs". These costs are not recorded as connected to the initial failure and for this reason could be considered "hidden". Numerous items might be included in the category of extra resultant costs, for instance: loss of productivity; additional labor hours; extra inventory; premium freight costs; increased engineering time. Estimated hidden costs include cost items that are difficult to analyze and quantify (for example, lost sales and loss of reputation as a result of poor quality in the past).

during the first pre-production stage of the product life cycle (Anderson and Sedatole, 1998). A similar view can be taken of quality costs.

Yang (2008) analyzed traditional (PAF model) and hidden costs of quality within the product life cycle stages, including the design stage. An example of typical PAF costs for the design stage is reported in Table 18.2.

Design has a significant influence on quality achievement. In particular, it can play an important role in prevention activities. If design does not provide a basis for products that meet the quality standards required by the market it will be difficult to achieve success. Hence, the first purpose is to design a product/service that will sell. Therefore, it will be important to check quality after and during the design stage in order to ascertain if the requirements recorded by market research activities are correctly translated into the product design and development.

The PAF model, in principle, could be applied to both the design and manufacturing stages. However, costs included in the cost-of-quality analysis are limited typically to manufacturing costs. Anderson and Sedatole (1998) review existing approaches to quality management with the conclusion that accountants provide adequate support for managing "conformance quality" but propose few contributions to "design quality".[10] As Taguchi et al. (1989) point out, there are two types of prevention activity: off-line and on-line. Off-line prevention activities are carried out prior to the production and include iterative processes of product design, process design and experimental prototyping. On-line prevention activities take place at the manufacturing stage and include activities such as quality training and manufacturing equipment maintenance. Both activities fit within the quality costs framework. However quality costing generally focuses on manufacturing costs, omitting off-line prevention activities. In these cases quality costing systems primarily promote conformance of quality.

Anderson and Sedatole (1998) proposed applying the cost of quality to the design stage. In this way the cost of quality would contribute to defining design characteristics of products according to a financial perspective. In particular, quality costs would provide information useful for the assessment of costs and benefits of design change. Costs will be determined by new designs and new choices in terms of processes and materials. Benefits would derive from failures avoided and from the positive changes in revenues achieved by effective designs. Achievement of "design quality" could be enhanced by using cost management tools such as target costing, ABC with traditional engineering cost estimation methods.

Anderson and Sedatole (1998) identify three ways for involving accountants in the provision of design quality. First, engineers and accountants should develop an integrated accounting and cost estimation system for having a dynamic representation of firm capabilities (distinct technical systems, skills, and managerial systems). Second, accountants improve product costs in the area of quality losses by supporting the robustness of product designs. Third, ABC and quality costing should be extended to design activities permitting a comparison of manufacturing and design-quality costs.

Conclusions

This chapter has shown the potential range of different practices in quality costing and the potential benefits that they offer to adopters. Research has confirmed the value of this type of cost management information as an attention-directing tool – a basis for monitoring quality performance and for quality-planning and delivering quality improvement.

Although much has therefore already been delivered from quality costing, there remain several challenges for research and many research questions still to be answered (e.g. Kume, 1985; Freiesleben, 2004; Dutta and Lawson, 2006). Does minimizing quality costs always mean profit enhancement? Can a preoccupation with quality mean neglect of other important aspects of business? What are the external effects (for example in customer satisfaction and revenues) of changes in quality levels? Can information on "hidden" costs be systematically produced? How do possible variations in quality costing practice match different practice settings (for example, industrial sectors or different technologies)? How does quality cost information fit into the broader performance and reward systems of the firm? Questions such as these ensure that quality costing will retain considerable research interest in the future.

Notes

1 Group (A) includes notional diagrams adopted in standard textbooks to indicate the principles of reducing failure and appraisal costs by increasing prevention costs.
Group (B) includes diagrams based on actual data published.
Group (C) covers models from Lockyer (1983) and the training literature of a leading automotive manufacturer; both are based on experience. In this group there is also a model constructed with data taken from a case developed by Veen (1974).
Group (D) encompasses notional diagrams having similar characteristics and taken from publications devoted specifically to quality costs (e.g. BS 6143 (1981)).
Group (E) contains models which are similar in principle to the others but different in an important detail (i.e. the position of the optimum point in the quality range).
2 See also Plunkett and Dale, 1999.
3 Hidden quality cost is a huge topic. For further in-depth analysis see also: Taguchi et al., 1989; Campanella, 1999; Harrington, 1999; Yang 2008. In particular Taguchi proposed a loss function as a means of estimating quality costs which are typically "hidden" by the accounting system. According to this function, losses occur not only when a product is outside specifications, but also within.
4 In addition it is relevant to remember another point connected to the previous arguments. Sometimes firms decide to maintain extra capacity and/or more inventories for facing the risk of poor quality. These costs are classified as indirect costs (Feigenbaum, 1991).
5 According to the BS 6143 Part 2 model, first it must be reduced failure costs, at the same time appraisal and prevention costs will rise slightly. When the quality awareness is increased all three quality cost categories mentioned in BS 6143 Part 2 decrease (in Giakatis et al., 2001).

6 A connection between quality costing and prices has been reported also in Cheah et al., 2011.
7 For a review of the theoretical and empirical literature on inter-firm management control and a critical evaluation of the corresponding achievements, see Caglio and Ditillo (2008).
8 Dale and Plunkett (1999) report that the two main reasons for the lack of a formal system of quality costs collection are: i) lack of resources and ii) current data and report are not in a form suitable to extract cost information.
9 On this argument see also Larson and Kerr (2007).
10 Anderson and Sedatole (1998) say that "design quality" refers to the intrinsic fit between a product's design specifications and customer needs, while "conformance quality" refers to how consistently manufacturing produces the product to stated design specifications.

Bibliography

Anderson, S.W. and Sedatole, K. (1998). Designing quality into products: The use of accounting data in new product development. *Accounting Horizons: American Accounting Association*, Vol. 12, No. 3, September, 213–33.

Ansari, S., Bell, J., Klammer, T. and Lawrence, C. (1997). *Measuring and Managing Quality Costs*. Series Editor. Shahid Ansari in *Management Accounting. A Strategic Focus*. McGraw-Hill, New York.

Bohan, G. P. and Horney, N. F. (1991). Pinpointing the real cost of quality in a service company. *National Productivity Review*, Summer, 309–17.

BS 6143, (1981). *Guide to the Determination and Use of Quality Related Costs*, BSI, London.

—— (1990): Part 2. Guide to the Economics of Quality – Prevention, Appraisal and Failure Model, BSI, London.

Burgess, T. F. (1996). Modelling quality-cost dynamics. *International Journal of Quality & Reliability Management*, Vol. 13, No. 3, 8–26.

Caglio, A. and Ditillo, A. (2008). A review and discussion of management control in inter-firm relationships: achievements and future directions. *Accounting, Organizations and Society*, Vol. 33, 865–98.

Campanella, J. (1999). *Principles of quality costs. Principles, Implementation and Use*, 3rd edn, ASQ Quality Press Milwaukee, Wisconsin.

Cheah, S.J., Shahbudin, A.S.M. and Taib, F.M. (2011). Tracking hidden quality costs in a manufacturing company: an action research. *International Journal of Quality & Reliability Management*, Vol. 28, No. 4, 405–25.

Chiadamrong, N. (2003). The development of an economic quality cost model. *TQM & Business Excellence*, Vol.14, No. 9, 999–1014.

Cokins, G. (2006). Measuring the cost of quality for management. *Quality Progress*, September, 44–51.

Cooper, R. and Kaplan, R.S. (1991). Profit priorities from activity-based costing. *Harvard Business Review*, May-June, 130–35.

Crosby, P.B. (1979). *Quality Is Free. The Art of Making Quality Certain*. McGraw-Hill, New York.

Crosby, P.B. (1984). *Quality Without Tears*, McGraw-Hill, New York.

Dahlgaard, J.J., Kristensen, K. and Kanji, G.K. (1992). Quality costs and total quality management. *Total Quality Management*, Vol. 3, No. 3, 211–21.

Dale, B.G. and Plunkett, J.J. (1999). *Quality Costing*. 2nd edn, Gower, Brookfield.

Deming, W.E. (1986). *Out of the Crisis*, 2nd ed, Cambridge University Press, Cambridge.

Dutta, S. and Lawson, R. (2006). The coming nanotech revolution – accounting challenges. *Cost Management*, May/June (electronic version).

Emsley, D. (2008). Different interpretations of a "fixed" concept. Examining Juran's cost of quality from an actor-network perspective. *Accounting, Auditing & Accountability Journal*, Vol. 21, No. 3, 375–97.

Feigenbaum, A.V. (1956). Total quality control. *Harvard Business Review*, 34, 6, 93–101.

—— (1991). *Total Quality Control*. 3rd ed., McGraw-Hill, New York.

Freeman, H. (1960). How to put quality costs to use. Transactions of the Metropolitan Conference, ASQC.

Freiesleben, J. (2004). On the limited value of cost of quality models. *Total Quality Management*, Vol. 15, No. 7, September, 959–69.

Giakatis, G., Enkawa, T. and Washitani, K. (2001). Hidden quality costs and the distinction between quality cost and quality loss. *Total Quality Management*, Vol. 12, No. 2, 179–90.

Gosselin, M. (1997). The effect of strategy and organizational structure on the adoption and implementation of Activity-Based Costing. *Accounting, Organizations and Society*, Vol. 22, 105–22.

Gupta, M. and Baxendale, A.S. (2008). The enabling role of ABC Systems in operations management, *Cost Management*, September/October (electronic version).

Hahn, G. J., Doganaksoy, N. and Hoerl, R. (2000). The evolution of Six Sigma. *Quality Engineering*, Vol. 12, No. 3, 317–26.

Han, C. and Lee, Y.H. (2002). Intelligent integrated plant operation system for Six Sigma. *Annual Reviews in Control*, 26, 27–43.

Harrington, H.J. (1987). *Poor-Quality Cost*, ASQC, Quality Press, Milwaukee.

—— (1999). Performance improvement: a total poor-quality cost system. *The TQM Magazine*, Vol. 11, No. 4, 221–30.

Ittner, C.D. (1996). Exploratory evidence on the behavior of quality costs. *Operations Research*, Vol. 44, No. 1, Special Issue on New Directions in Operations Management (Jan.-Feb., 1996), 114–30.

—— (1999). Activity-based costing concepts for quality improvement. *European Management Journal*, Vol. 17, No. 5, pp. 492–500.

Jaju, S.B., Mohanty, R.P. and Lakhe, R.R. (2009). Towards managing quality cost: a case study. *Total Quality Management*, Vol. 20, No. 10, October, 1075–94.

Juran, J.M. (1951). *Quality-Control Handbook* (1st edn). McGraw-Hill, New York.

Juran, J.M. and Gryna, F.M. (1988). *Juran's Quality Control Handbook*, 4th edn. McGraw-Hill, New York.

Kume, H. (1985). Business management and quality cost: the Japanese view, *Quality Progress*, May, 13–18.

Larson, P.D. and Kerr, S.G. (2007). Integration of process management tools to support TQM implementation: ISO 9000 and activity-based costing. *Total Quality Management*, Vol. 18, Nos. 1–2, 201–7, January–March.

Lockyer, K.G. (1983). *Production Management*. Pitman, London.

Malmi, T., Järvinen, P. and Lillrank, P. (2004). A collaborative approach for managing project cost of poor quality. *European Accounting Review*, Vol. 13, No. 2, 293–317.

Masser, W.J. (1957). The quality manager and quality costs. *Industrial Quality Control*, Vol. 14, 5–8.

Merchant, K.A. and Shields, M. (1993). When and why to measure cost less accurately to improve decision-making. *Accounting Horizons*, American Accounting Association, Vol. 7, No. 2, June, 76–81.

Mevellec, P. (2009). *Cost Systems Design*. Palgrave Macmillan, New York.

Plunkett, J.J. and Dale, B.G. (1988). Quality costs: a critique of some "Economic Cost of Quality" models. *International Journal of Production Research*, Vol. 26, No. 11, 1713–26.

Reeve, J.M. (2005). *Logistics and Marketing Costs*, in Weil, R.L. and Maher, M.W., *Handbook of Cost Management*, 2nd edn. Wiley, New Jersey, 329–49.

Sandoval-Chavez, D.A. and Beruvides, M.G. (1998). Using opportunity costs to determine the cost of quality: a case study in a continuous-process industry. *The Engineering Economist*, Vol. 43, No. 2, 107–24.

Schiffauerova, A. and Thomson, V. (2006). A review of research on cost of quality models and best practices. *International Journal of Quality & Reliability Management*, Vol. 23, No. 6, 647–69.

Schotmiller, J.C. and Campanella, J. (2007). Quality for profit. *Quality World*, May, 30–5.

Shank, J.K. and Govindarajan, V. (1994). A strategic cost management perspective. *Journal of Cost Management*, Vol. 8, Summer, 5–17.

Sjoblom, L.M. (1998). Financial information and quality management – is there a role for accountants? *American Accounting Association Accounting Horizons*, Vol. 12, No. 4, December, 363–73.

Sower, V.E., Quarles, R. and Broussard, E. (2007). Cost of quality usage and its relationship to quality system maturity. *International Journal of Quality & Reliability Management*, Vol. 24, No. 2, 121–40.

Taguchi, G., Elsayed, E. and Hsiang T. (1989). *Quality Engineering in Production Systems*. McGraw-Hill, New York.

Tannock, J.D.T. (1997). An economic comparison of inspection and control charting using simulation, *International Journal of Quality & Reliability Management*, Vol. 14, No. 7, 687–99.

Tenucci, A., Cinquini, L. and Giannetti, R. (2010). Implementation and Perceived Usefulness of Advanced Management Accounting Techniques: A Survey on Italian Firms. In Shil, N.C. and Pramanik, A.K. (eds.), *Contemporary Research in Cost and Management Accounting Practices: The Twenty-First Century Perspective*, 109–27, North American Business Press, Atlanta, GA.

Turney, P.B.B. (2005). *Common Cents. How to succeed with Activity-Based Costing and Activity-Based Management*. McGraw-Hill, New York.

Veen, B. (1974). Quality costs. *Quality* (EOQC publication), No. 2, 55–59.

Venters, V.G., CCC, (2004). *Cost of Quality*. AACE International Transactions, Morgantown, WV.

Viger, C. and Anandarajan, A. (1999). Cost management and pricing decisions in the presence of quality cost information: an experimental study with marketing managers. *Cost Management*, January/February 1999, 21–28.

Williams, A.R.T., van der Wiele, A. and Dale, B.G. (1999). Quality costing: a management review. *International Journal of Management Reviews*, Vol. 1, No. 4, 441–60.

Yang, C.C. (2008). Improving the definition and quantification of quality costs. *Total Quality Management*, Vol. 19, No. 3, 175–91.

19

Environmental cost management for green production

Alessandro Marelli

Introduction

Increasing interest has recently been apparent in environmental management accounting. One of the possible reasons for this is the continuous environmental degradation produced by company activities. Another reason is the mounting complexity of the administrative and managerial problems associated with this degradation. This interest is found not only in developed countries but also in many developing nations. In businesses and in markets, environmental and social impacts generate rises in costs of cleaner investments and the need to manage the 'bureaucratic activities' effectively and efficiently. There is a growing need to classify these new types of costs and their drivers. Several researchers have studied the opportunities and limits associated with enhancing traditional management accounting systems in this way. In this new milieu, a key role in highlighting the importance of environmental information is played by 'management fashion setters'. The management gurus, consultancy firms, business schools and universities and the mass media (reporting the debate over greenhouse gasses, global warming, human rights, deforestation, land degradation and pollution) operate to pursue the spread of 'management green fashion'. It is common to find a more accountable approach emerging in the communication of sustainability performance and sometimes even in 'greenwashing' business activities. Consequently, there is a large, varied and growing body of literature on different concepts and practices, and this 'green accounting' movement has produced, quite suddenly, innovation in corporate reports to supply ethical, social, and environmental information (Schaltegger, 1998; Burritt, Hahn and Schaltegger, 2002).

The movement towards integrating these issues into internal and external reports is evidenced by the publication of more comprehensive corporate sustainability reports supported by guidelines such as those of the Global Reporting Initiative (2011) labelled as the 'triple bottom line.' A contemporary development is the G3.1 which is an update and completion of the third generation of GRI's Sustainability Reporting Guidelines. Triple bottom line reporting contains three types of performance: financial (or economic), social and environmental; it is a comprehensive reporting process focused on a broader range of stakeholders, including various environmental and social interest groups. Social performance refers to the impact of an organization's behaviour regarding society including the broader community, employees, customers, and suppliers. Environmental performance refers to the impact of company performance concerning the environment, including the damaging effects on land, air and water as well as on people and living organisms.

However, the fact that 'traditional accounting systems' and 'ecological accounting systems' continue to be separate accounting and management systems in the companies working in Europe (Bartolomeo, Bennett, Bouma, Heydkamp, James and Wolters, 2000), should not be an obstacle to the 'integration' of their separate findings and results. The 'integration' of traditional accounting (divided into three main sub-systems: cost and management accounting, financial accounting and other traditional accounting) with ecological accounting (divided into three main sub-systems: internal ecological accounting, external ecological accounting and other sustainability accounting) would facilitate both the calculation of eco-efficiency and the process of decision-making by management and stakeholders (Schaltegger, 1998: 277). On the other hand, environmental accounting is part of a huge and complex system called sustainability accounting. Parker (2011), in his paper on 21 years of social and environmental accountability studies, points out that in the period between 1988 and 2003 studies on environmental accounting prevailed, while in the period between 2004 and 2008 papers devoted purely to environmental accounting declined but did continue to be presented either alone or in conjunction with social research. The environmental accounting research was not replaced by sustainability accounting research because, as Gray (2010) has recently stated,

> . . . any simple assessment of the relationship between a single organization and planetary sustainability is virtually impossible. The relationships and interrelationships are simply too complex. Furthermore, to assume that the notion of 'sustainability' has tangible meaning at the level of organisation is to ignore all we know about sustainability. Sustainability is a systems-based concept and, environmentally at least, only begins to make any sense at the level of eco-systems and is probably difficult to really conceptualize at anything below planetary and species levels. So whatever else organisational 'accounts of sustainability' are, they are probably not accounts of sustainability (Gray and Milne, 2002; Gray and Milne, 2004; Milne, Ball and Gray, 2008) . . .
>
> *Gray (2010: 48)*

In this chapter the literature on sustainability will be explored and attention will be focused on environmental cost accounting and the role of financial information in the managerial decision-making processes within 'green companies'.

Environmental management accounting and environmental costs in management accounting

The first consideration is the new role of traditional tools of management accounting (MA) for the manager who wants to be a 'player' in the 'green economy'. Recently, management accounting has been innovative, but at the same time reliance also remains on conventional tools to provide the necessary data for managerial decision-making.

The 'green accounting' movement has quite suddenly produced innovation and a push for different implementations in budget activities, capital investment decisions and key performance indicator systems to achieve more profitable solutions. Within environmental accounting (which describes with a statistical framework the relation between national/global economies, public policies and the environment), the role played by studies on environmental management accounting (EMA)[1] is becoming increasingly important. The growth of interest in EMA is closely linked to a broad development of environmental management systems (EMS). EMS are systems that companies implement to manage their environmental performance. An EMS may include recycling systems and systems to monitor and control levels of liquid, material and atmospheric discharge and waste. An important moment in this process is 1996, when the ISO 14001 was released, which is an international standard for environmental management systems and their audit.

In the last two decades, scholars have been developing a comprehensive framework linking business people and management tools (Burritt et al., 2002). The proposed framework can encourage the process of integration of two major components of environmental management accounting:

- MEMA: monetary environmental management accounting;
- PEMA: physical environmental management accounting.

Within this framework the possibility for managers to apply different tools for past/future and short- or long-term time managerial decisions is described (see Figure 19.1).

EMA is related to process costing (and can therefore be considered as environmental cost accounting) as well as focusing on environmental performance and management systems and on physical and economic information. It measures the flow of energy, water, products and materials used. If well designed and implemented, EMA helps to ensure better internal management and decision-making for investment appraisal, cleaner production, improving eco-efficiency and calculating within organizations. In a green company, the role of EMA is also relevant to improving the relationships with its stakeholder groups, in particular public institutions and Non-Government Organizations (NGOs). The data produced through the EMA serve as a basis for external accounting and reporting (Jasch, 2006).

Through environmental cost accounting the company collects data on its past and future environmental costs. The environmental costs measure private, internal or company costs. These are the costs that have a direct impact on a firm's bottom line. Alternatively, public, social or external environmental costs are environment costs, social costs or economic costs, relevant to society as a whole (Schaltegger and Burritt, 2000: 96–102). To date, attempts to concentrate on better tracking and allocating environmental costs within management accounting frameworks have predominantly focused on private costs because it is more difficult to evaluate external costs (Gray, 2006).

Figure 19.2 illustrates the richness of drivers that in different times and in different locations/nations can justify changes of status between internal and external environmental costs and the complexity of an evaluation of external costs.

In order to measure environmental costs managers have to find the main drivers. However, some environmental impacts of current decisions and operations can be difficult to recognize and report because the future issues are not yet known; in particular there are many work practices that will have future environmental and social impacts that we are not able to currently assess. Moreover, practical usefulness of environmental accounting tools is constrained by its oversimplification (Gluch and Baumann, 2004). A third generic category of environmental costs (Bennett and James, 1998) can be defined as the 'environmental opportunity costs'. These costs can be identified as the costs related to the best unrealized pollution prevention alternative (Schaltegger and Burritt, 2000: 103).

Environmental cost accounting permits the grouping together of the elements of the cost of resources employed in coping with environmental problems. They are cost elements that entail a particular method of analysis, both in terms of identification of the activities and in terms of quantification of costs. The need arises to measure environmental costs on this different basis and

Proposed comprehensive framework of environmental management accounting

		Environmental management accounting (EMA)			
		Monetary environmental management accounting (MEMA)		Physical environmental management accounting (PEMA)	
		Short-term focus	Long-term focus	Short-term focus	Long-term focus
Past-Oriented	Routinely generated information	1. Environmental cost accounting (e.g. variable costing, absorption costing, and activity-based costing)	2. Environmentally induced capital expenditure and revenues	9. Material and energy flow accounting (short-term impacts on the environment – product, site, division and company levels)	10. Environmental (or natural) capital impact accounting
	Ad hoc information	3. Ex post assessment of relevant environmental costing decisions	4. Environmental life cycle (and target) costing Post investment assessment of individual projects	11. Ex post assessment of short-term environmental impacts (e.g. of a site or product)	12. Life cycle inventories Post investment assessment of physical environment appraisal
Future-Oriented	Routinely generated information	5. Monetary environmental operational budgeting (flows) Monetary environmental capital budgeting (stocks)	6. Environmental long-term financial planning	13. Physical environmental budgeting (flows and stocks) (e.g. material and energy flow; activity-based budgeting)	14. Long-term physical environmental planning
	Ad hoc information	7. Relevant environmental costing (e.g. special orders, product mix with capacity constraint)	8. Monetary environmental project investment appraisal Environmental life cycle budgeting and target pricing	15. Relevant environment impacts (e.g. given short-run constraints on activities)	16. Physical environmental investment appraisal Life cycle analysis of specific project

Environmental cost accounting (arrow pointing to boxed cells 1 and 3)

Figure 19.1 EMA framework

Source: Burritt and Saka, 2006.

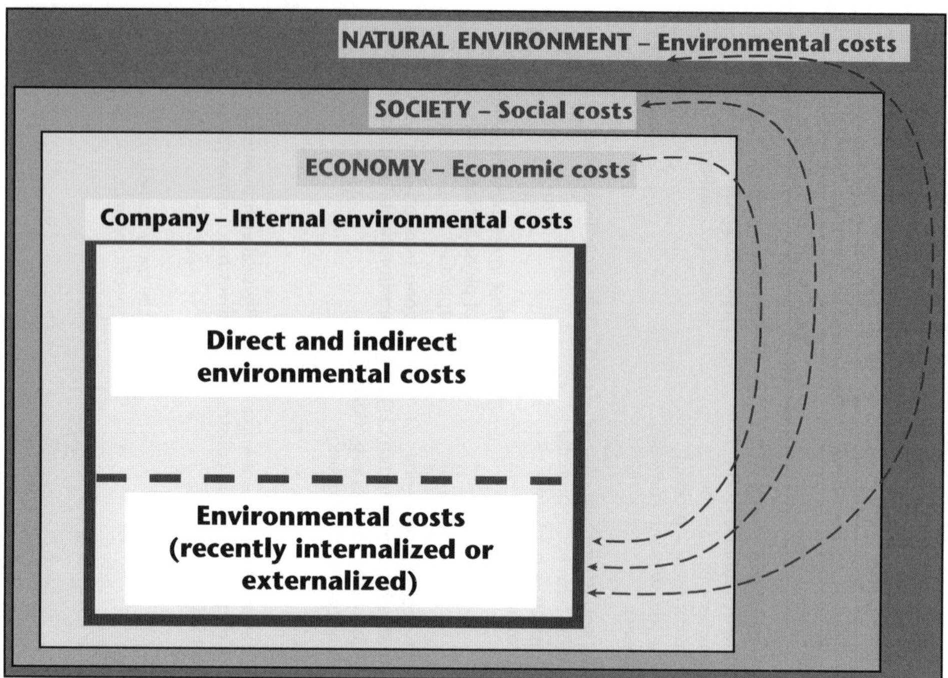

Figure 19.2 Changes of status between internal and external environmental costs

method of analysis in order to identify them and extract them from the grouping of indirect industrial costs and overheads. So 'environmental product costing' involves tracing direct and indirect environmental costs to products, and covers the costs of waste management, permits and fees, and recycling activities. Under EMA there is an emphasis on tracking environmental costs and benefits directly to the specific processes and products that cause those costs or benefits, rather than spreading them across all products. The thinking is that the environmental costs are often underestimated; this hypothesis is put to the test with several case studies. Conventional management accounting excludes the measurement of many environmental costs. In some companies the costs remain hidden, even though they may be substantial. Some organizations do measure some of these 'forgotten costs' (Langfield-Smith, Thorne and Hilton, 2006: 813), but other organizations trace them to products without adopting any cause-and-effect relationship base. Therefore these costs can be allocated to various cost centres or responsibility centres with 'less sophisticated' cost allocation methods. Thus some internal environmental costs are 'forgotten' or misallocated in the grouping of overheads, as can be seen in the example of Figure 19.3.

Tracing environmental costs permits the measurement of the use of resources and facilitates the interpretation of the economic results with greater clarity. The likely reason this is not commonly employed in practice can be attributed to the high administrative cost and complexity of costing systems. In fact companies incur administrative costs not only in gathering data, but also in taking the time necessary to educate management about the chosen system (Horngren, Bhimani, Datar, and Foster, 2005). Moreover, the design of the cost-allocation system is also influenced by other contextual factors (size, location, typologies of organizations, etc.).

In the case of the leather industry (Box 19.1), we can see that environmental cost accounting is not an independent item, but is designed to work coherently with the other costing practices.

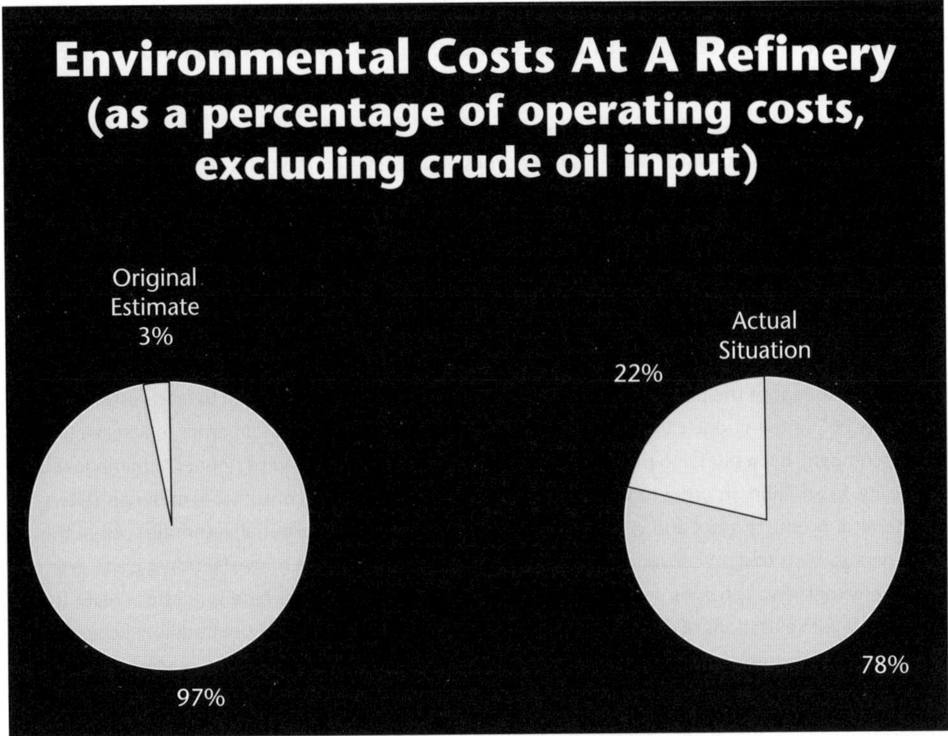

Figure 19.3 Original and actual environmental costs at a refinery

Source: Green Ledgers: Case Studies in Corporate Environmental Accounting. World Resources Institute, May, 1995.

It addresses, concurrently, two different economic values which are linked to one another, i.e. (more) environmental costs and (fewer) operational costs.

Company risk assessment and environmental issues

The increasing pressure exerted by stakeholders, the greater sensitivity of customers, and the new demands of stockholders about long-term problems that the company may create, have increased the need for information to:

- reduce product and process costs;
- minimize business risks which translates into savings in attracting capital funding;
- increase the value generated for customers and shareholders.

Uncertainty increases the risks with environmental issues and the long-term profitability of the firm. Then, the control of environmental costs can become a 'distinctive competence' that is useful for strengthening competitive financial strategies. This is so particularly for companies which operate in environmentally sensitive fields such as: the chemical industry; electrical energy production; the steel industry; waste and reclamation services. The growing development of operating initiatives aimed at experimenting with new operating methods based on sustainable growth fosters experimentation of certifications of EMS (for example, ISO 14001) which facilitate the introduction of methods to provide government agencies

Box 19.1 The case of 'underestimated' environmental costs in the leather industry

Let us analyse the case of a tanning company (Marelli, 2009: 234–235) in the Tuscan district of Santa Croce sull'Arno which performs three types of processes on the hides. The company uses a conventional full costing system of cost analysis. The production cost has a significant percentage of costs directly attributable to it. These include the costs of the leather to be treated, the costs of the direct labour dedicated to production and the costs of the chemical products employed. In addition, the company has indirect transformation costs not specifically attributable to the different products, such as: the cost of the salaries of the employees who control the phases of the production processes, the cost of electrical energy and the cost of maintenance. The company is required to reduce the pollutants in the sludge generated during production to levels established by law before the sludge can be released into the public sewage system. In order to achieve this, the company has a purifying plant with an operating unit of specialized personnel to manage this facility. In addition, in order to operate, this plant requires specific consumable materials (filters, chemical products, etc.) and is subject to regular inspections by external authorities. All of this generates costs that, in conventional accounting, are included in the normal product costs. From the environmental analysis, it was found that two out of three of the hide processes create the greatest concentrations of dangerous substances in the sludge since they use traditional chemical products. By contrast a third ecologically designed process follows innovative procedures using substances of low polluting substances that could avoid the necessity of on-site pre-treatment of the waste by the company prior to releasing it into the public sewage system. Thus, cross-subsidization is apparent since traditional analytical accounting attributes to all three processes direct costs, which are higher for the ecological process and lower for the two traditional processes. They have fewer direct costs because of the lower quality of the chemical agents employed and the lower direct labour costs. The labour costs are lower because, although the two traditional processes pollute more, they are simpler and have shorter production times. The indirect conversion costs are attributed to the processes on the basis of production volumes. This basis does not take into account the distinction between environmental costs and the resources dedicated to bringing the traditional production processes up to the standards required by law. Consequently, the attribution of the indirect costs with a system of traditional accounting penalises the ecological process, placing its use in an unsustainable competitive position (with low profit margins). This occurs even though it is ecologically superior and does not require purifying treatment. The attribution of costs through an environmental cost accounting system which detects the environmental costs would avoid assigning the indirect environmental costs to the ecological process, thus providing managers with clearer and more accurate information on the economic validity of the three processes.

with new means of guaranteeing compliance with the laws of environmental protection (for example, EMAS-Ecolabel). The challenge is to identify the points and the times of these linkages. The interdependence between a company and society takes two forms (Porter and Kramer, 2006). A company produces effects upon society through its operations in the normal course of business. These are inside-out linkages. Every activity in a company's value chain touches on the communities in which the firm operates, creating either positive or negative environmental consequences. While companies are increasingly aware of the environmental impact of their activities (such as hiring practices, emissions, and waste disposal), these impacts can be more variable than many managers realize. For one thing, they depend on location. The same manufacturing operations will have different social and environmental consequences in one of the BRIC economies than in the United Kingdom. A company's impact also changes over time, as social standards and scientific knowledge evolve. Not only does corporate activity affect society, but external social conditions also influence corporations, for their environmental costs. These are called the outside-in linkages.

The following list underlines the growing risks that can be the future drivers for new environmental costs:

- regulatory risk (e.g. Kyoto target-emissions or the European target on greenhouse gas emissions);
- supply chain risk (e.g. indirect risks for suppliers of an oil-refining process);
- product and technology risk (e.g. changes in the market due to environmental problems);
- litigation risk (e.g. legal actions coming from products and processes with asbestos);
- reputation risk (e.g. public opinion and image);
- physical risk (e.g. damage from typhoons or climate changes).

Green-washing practices and management accounting

Some studies show that companies also try to confront these risks by developing green-washing practices. The green-wash is defined as the act of misleading consumers regarding the environmental practices of a company or the environmental benefits of a product or service (Terrachoice, 2010). Schaltegger and Burritt (2010), reviewing the literature on sustainability accounting, distinguish different interpretations of sustainability accounting. In particular, they describe an interpretation as 'an illusion and buzzword' that is used as a 'window-dressing or a green-washing' (Schaltegger and Burritt, 2010: 379). The same problem can be found in environmental cost accounting practices. The reason can be derived from the motivation of management simply to signal concern and to collect data for communicating and reporting rather than to improve their real environmental performance.

Behavioural and cultural pathways in the green accounting paradigm

The 'win–win' green paradigm

The main reason for corporate adoption of environmental information in the internal decision-making processes is that it provides a framework for linking economic and environmental decision-making to strategy. Several scholars have indicated the need to study 'green strategies with the associated costs' (Parker, 2000a, 2000b). The greening of the organization emphasizes the relationship between environmental improvements and cost, arguing that pollution is a form of economic inefficiency and, thus, reductions in pollution increase productive efficiency and thereby reduce total costs (King and Lenox, 2002; Porter, 1991; Porter and van der Linde, 1995a, 1995b). This competing hypothesis challenges traditional cost management: it reflects an underlying 'win–win' green paradigm. Thus, the emerging environmental issues are considered relevant from a strategic point of view (Porter and van der Linde, 1995a, 1995b). If adopted, the green cost management is useful not only in satisfying stakeholder demands, but also in taking into account the internal decision processes (strategic decisions). This possible double application underlines the possibility of improving the economic performance of environmentally proactive companies (Ditz and Ranganathan, 1997). In the mid-1990s some researchers produced empirical reports based on case studies (De Simone and Popoff, 1997; Ditz, Ranganathan, and Banks, 1995; Epstein, 1996; Gray et al., 1993; Schaltegger, 1996; Spitzer and Elwood, 1995) underlying this 'win–win' paradigm. This selective set of case studies demonstrates that environmental management strategies are being declared and pursued, seeing the relevance of the relationship between environmental strategies and environmental costs, and such strategies are being 'normalized' into managerial thinking and decision-making (Parker, 2000a: 45). Recently, the viability of this approach has been confirmed by Porter and Kramer (2006), who indicate that corporations are not responsible for 'all the world's problems, nor do they have the resources to solve them all' (Porter and Kramer, 2006: 92). However, each company can identify the particular set of company problems that it is best equipped to help resolve and from which it can gain the greatest competitive benefit. More broadly, environmental studies can support stakeholders who wish to minimize an 'intergenerational conflict' caused by the operations of their companies (Grant, 2007: 11). However, it once again appears that, for many, the classification of and accounting for environmental costs has not yet begun or is only in its 'infancy' at operational-plant levels and management functions. The literature also points out that the accounting profession has not played a significant role in the development of environmental cost management systems (Bebbington et al., 1994; Parker, 2000b). This neglect occurs despite the 'win–win' green paradigm and the wide diffusion of managerial practices in EMS and corporate social responsibility reporting. Moreover, recent research has found that a large number of CEOs and CFOs believe that environmental issues are not the chief concern of controllers/accountants but of technical-engineer managers (Wilmshurst and Frost, 2001; Greig et al., 2006). The controllers and management accountants therefore have a low level of involvement in their companies' environmental activities.

Social and environmental accounting and environmental management accounting literature

The concept of environmental accounting has been used to cover different perspectives of analysis (at global, national and firm level), processing different typologies of financial and non-financial information and measuring in financial terms different damage costs (internal and external). Two approaches can be considered for our study and for the problem of decision-making in the company. The first comes from a financial accounting approach and the need to ensure a positive and broader impact of company activities on society and the environment. Social and environmental accounting (SEA) literature has been largely responsible for prompting many companies to produce corporate social responsibility reporting in the last few decades. However, there is a second approach in the literature, usually defined as a 'managerialist approach' (or 'management accounting approach'), that provides information analysis on how to support internal decision-making (environmental management accounting literature – EMAN). In practice, these two approaches often overlap each other and the question of a 'managerialist approach' exists and requires more definition.

Social and environmental accounting approach

The social and environmental accounting approach is very important and has been growing in the accounting research literature over the past 40 years, moving from the margins of accounting literature to centre stage in recent years (Parker, 2011). The critical time of transformation was at the end of the 1980s. In that period the SEA research considered the emergence of environmental accounting and auditing issues as an important perspective and it is characterized by significant key research developments (Owen, 2008). A predominantly managerialist approach is discernible in much of this research, witnessed by the almost complete displacement of the social dimension, along with an apparent desire to promote accounting and reporting systems in ways where the environmental dimension may be conveniently captured in the interests of promoting economic efficiency. A more critical problem also became important, i.e. the internalization of external environmental costs, via full-cost accounting methods (Antheaume, 2007), in the evolution of life cycle costing tools (Gluch and Baumann, 2004), and in the introduction of the social aspects as eco-justice issues.

Since businesses started discovering 'sustainability' as an issue of key concern, as part of a broader issue of competitiveness, companies have been attracted by innovation and opportunities for product and process changes. This phenomenon is evidenced in part by the growth in popularity of 'triple bottom line' reporting (Elkington, 1997), or 'sustainability' reporting (Global Reporting Initiative, 2002), encompassing the social and economic as well as the purely environmental dimension (Owen, 2008). SEA investigates the use of management accounting within organizations where environmental accounting can be mobilized as a means of encouraging them to change and reduce company unsustainability. This perspective, called 'organizational change', debates the efficacy and the need for EMA. In the beginning EMA was considered only an environmental management tool designed to trace and track environmental costs and physical environmental flows (Bennett and James, 1998), but the debate on developments in sustainability accounting and reporting shows the necessity to integrate external with internal reporting. Two main pathways are identified: the first based on an entirely new system of accounting while the second is a development of conventional financial, cost, or management accounting. The first is not yet considered to be at a practical level but the second is closer to practice because piecemeal changes to traditional accounting can stress an organization's practices less and produce new elements useful for solving complex managerial challenges. Some authors suggest that a 'managerialist' application of accounting techniques could solve the perceived crisis of SEA tools (Epstein, 1996; Gray and Bebbington, 2001). Other studies suggest that environmental accounting is a necessary but insufficient step in reshaping corporate behaviour (Gray et al., 1995a, 1995b; Bebbington, 1997). In these studies the authors have highlighted the failure of accounting to bring about functional environmental change (Gray et al., 1995a, 1995b; Larrinaga-Gonzalez and Bebbington, 2001). Despite the lack of confidence in accounting to produce sustainable organizational actions, SEA scholars are still 'reluctant' to suggest that accounting has no ability to effect positive changes (Larrinaga-Gonzalez and Bebbington, 2001: 286). Critical accounting scholars observe that the diverse perspective and traditional metrics are untranslatable in describing environmental problems (Lehman, 1999; Bebbington and Gray, 2001). Gray (2002), after reviewing SEA research, calls for researchers to develop new future possibilities employing radical approaches to drive innovation in SEA policy and practice. At the same time, Parker (2005) pinpoints the need for more qualitative research and inductive theorizing and he suggests that the risk for SEA scholars is to be confined to 'the halls of academe' (Parker, 2005: 856). Some scholars (Spence et al., 2010), reflecting upon SEA and Social and Environmental Reporting (SER), indicate that these theories have been developed in isolation from, and in contradistinction to, other organizational literatures. This self-referential production has precluded consideration of whether accountability is a realistic or desirable demand to make of corporations. In seeking to enhance the practical impact of SEA, Owen (2008) considered the relevance of studies devoted to the topic of engagement with organizations in pursuit of improved sustainability accounting and performance. In more recent years, however, the SEA literature is rebalancing its attention between social and environmental accounting. This reflects Gray's calls for an expansion in research efforts in the area of social responsibility (Parker, 2011) with a methodological mix of traditional and emerging methods (content analysis, statistical relationship, action and ethnographic research).

Managerialist approach (EMAN approach)

The managerialist approach was presented in the 1970s but found a more defined pathway of analysis with the creation of a pattern based on EMA. In fact EMA was defined, after an interesting debate only at the end of 1990s, as a set of tools that includes internal monetary and internal physical accounting in order to stress the necessity of integration of ecological and monetary issues (Schaltegger et al., 2000; Burritt et al., 2002). EMA became interesting for internal decision-making processes because it affects management control systems (MCS) and performance measurement. In fact some studies show direct links between MCS and corporate social and environmental reporting (Gray, 2002; Patten, 2002; Al-Tuwaijri et al., 2004). The longitudinal analysis conducted by Burnett and Hansen (2008) indicates that in electricity utility plants proactive environmental management can reduce environmental costs.

In addition to those concerns, eco-efficiency concepts have emerged. The relationship between EMA and economic performance has been developed, based on the socio-economic theory (Birkin and Woodward, 1997a, 1997b). However, within this pathway the information requirements and the scope of implementation depend on the type of efficiency that is being considered. Single efficiency measures profitability and ecological efficiency but the most important cross-efficiency figures are eco-efficiencies (Schaltegger et al., 2008). Eco-efficiency measures the cross-efficiency between the economic and ecological dimensions, or, in other words, the 'economic-ecological efficiency'. It is defined as the ratio of value-added, created by a company, to the resulting environmental impact added – more generally, economic performance achieved per environmental impact caused (Schaltegger, 1998):

Eco-efficiency = Value Added / Environmental impact.

Correct information derived from management accounting is a prerequisite for determining eco-efficiency. But in calculating the profitability (value-added) of products, it is essential not to mix internal and external costs and not to use incomplete cost information concerned with the incomplete tracking, tracing and allocation of environmental costs (Schaltegger, 1998). Eco-efficiency claims that it is possible to increase productivity and thus reduce costs while simultaneously improving environmental performance (Bebbington, 2001; Lehman, 2002; Stone, 1995). The practice highlights the difficulties in using the eco-efficiency ratio. However, it is important that some studies have produced evidence useful for research concerning the eco-efficiency approach. Al-Tuwaijri, Christensen and Hughes (2004) examined a sample of 198 firms from the Standard and Poor's 500. The survey shows the significantly positive relation between environmental performance and economic performance. In particular, they find a statistically significant positive association between a toxic-waste measure (toxic waste recycled/total toxic waste generated) and market returns. The eco-efficiency paradigm has implications for environmental management accounting and environmental cost management. This is consistent with the 'win–win' green paradigm that innovative solutions can promote improvement in competitiveness and in environmental concerns. This statistical analysis also supports a voluntary eco-efficiency approach, rather than formally specified guided eco-efficiency, since there is no specific regulatory act mandating a reduction of toxic waste for the firms studied. Guided eco-efficiency, however, finds a statistical validation in another study of 92 firms in the sugar industry in India (Murty and Kumar, 2003). The results demonstrate that the degree of technical efficiency increases with the degree of compliance with environmental regulations and water conservation efforts.

The early evidence encourages further promotion of EMA. However, there is still more to be done to understand better the gaps in relation to monetary environmental management accounting (MEMA) and economic performance. Within the comprehensive framework of EMA, the analysis of MEMA findings is closer to traditional management accounting practices. Physical environmental management accounting (PEMA) is highlighted because MEMA renders the environmental consequences of manager decisions more 'visible' and comparable. The implementation of MEMA, in fact, can be justified as a dynamic diffusion of managerial (and accounting) innovation. According to the efficient-choice perspective in the diffusion of innovation (Abrahamson, 1991), the main force driving the adoption of new management techniques is explicitly and implicitly the need for solving challenges and complex managerial tasks. Consequently, MEMA can be considered for adoption to help companies achieve their goals, to avoid environmental and social risks and to improve poor economic performance.

The two approaches are enriching the literature on environmental cost accounting, showing not only the limitations of practice but also emphasizing the opportunities for companies and society. The idea that a managerialist contribution can be useful to the improvement of SEA research is both necessary and inevitable if researchers want to have any real influence on organizational practice. At the same time, caution is necessary due to the lack of evidence on internal environmental cost accounting practices and on the reasons for internal stakeholders' use of them.[2]

Measuring and reporting environmental costs: examples from literature and practice

The attributes of environmental costs

The techniques of environmental cost accounting are based on identifying, gathering and processing information on the cost of resources used or consumed in coping with environmental issues.

As suggested above, such resources are mainly used for three reasons:

1. Legal or regulatory reasons. The regulations require companies to adopt behaviour that promotes the safeguarding of the environment and the safety of its employees and the natural habitat.
2. Societal or cultural reasons. Environmental culture changes from country to country. There are companies that have a well-established environmental awareness and aim to recycle materials and employ the cleanest of technologies, while in others these practices develop more slowly.
3. Customer or business reasons. The market requires, with different degrees, products designed for recycling from the outset and which have a low environmental impact during their life cycle.

Environmental cost may be classified in measurement-based categories and according to industrial sectors. Figure 19.4 illustrates different drivers that may generate different classifications of cost (Schaltegger and Burritt, 2000; Bennett and James, 1998).

Who is responsible	Difficulties to measure	Time	What are the activities responsible for?	Physical elements and energy flows
Societal	Hidden	Past and present	Past environmental activities	Air
Private	Conventional	Potential/future	Present environmental activities for future environmental targets	Water
			Improvement activities	Land
				Waste

Figure 19.4 Different typologies of criteria to classify environmental costs

The tiers of environmental costs: EPA model

A well-known classification system is suggested by the US Office of Pollution Prevention (EPA 742-R-95-001, 1995). The EPA suggests mainly four tiers (Langfield-Smith et al., 2006):

1. Conventional costs which are 'usual' costs of equipment, labour and material used in 'end-of-pipe activities'.
2. Hidden costs which are costs of compliance, other hidden regulatory costs from activities such as monitoring and reporting of environmental activities and emissions, the costs of searching for environmentally-responsible suppliers.
3. Contingent costs which are liability-based costs such as costs arising from the failure to clean up contaminated sites, fines and penalties for non-compliance with regulations.
4. Relationship and image costs that are 'less tangible' costs such as costs related to consumer responses and perceptions, employee health and safety, company's image and community relations.

The EPA also recognizes Tier 5 costs, societal costs that are generated by company environmental and societal impacts. They are difficult to measure because the cost of estimating these impacts, and the awareness that company controllers should have about these impacts, cannot also be provided by law.

In Figure 19.5 a relationship is described between the difficulties in tracing these categories of environmental costs and the strategic relevance for improving future profit and reduce the numerous categories of risks.

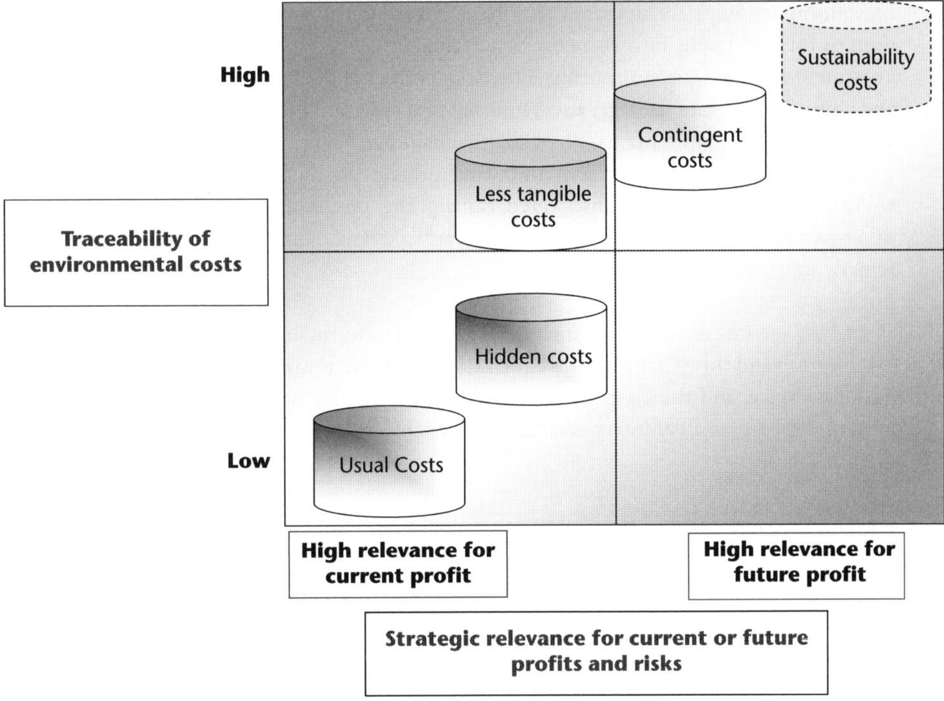

Figure 19.5 Trade-off between traceability of environmental costs and the strategic relevance for current and future profits/risks

Source: Marelli, A., 2005.

From quality cost management practices to environmental quality costs and activity-based costs

Another important pathway for analysis of environmental cost is linked with the 'quality costing approach' (Russell Skalak and Miller, 1994; Roth and Keller, 1997; Bennett and James, 1998; Langfield-Smith et al., 2006). This approach aims to measure, in financial terms, the benefits of good quality management. The idea is that financial measures increase the pressure and stimulate motivation to reduce costs of quality failure. The same framework of quality costing can easily be applied to the environmental costs. When developing this framework to measure environmental costs the goal is the overall control and reduction of these costs. In order to carry out this analysis an activity-based costing method can be useful. In fact, environmental costs should be traced to the activity that causes them. For example, the costs of handling and treating toxic waste brought about by the production of, say, product X should directly and exclusively be allocated to product X. Understanding activity cost drivers and allocating costs accordingly (de Beer and Friend, 2006) is the conceptual cornerstone of ABC. The advantage of activity-based costing (ABC) is that it enhances the understanding of the business processes associated with each product (United Nations, 2001). ABC improves internal cost calculation by allocating costs, typically found in overheads, to the polluting activities and products that are determined by the quantitative life cycle assessment procedures. So, following the conventional quality costing scheme and applying the ABC method, three main types of activity are defined:

- prevention activities are designed to solve environmental problems before they occur, or even to turn problems into competitive advantage;
- assessment activities (or monitoring activities) to observe the level of environmental impacts and control – measure damage, assess internal processes and products/services supplied, and audit environmental performance of supply chain partners;
- failure activities that can be split into two sub-categories: control activities to correct environmental breakdowns discovered during the production and in the products, in other words activities facing internal failure; and external failure activities to put right and remedy external company impacts.

In this analysis environmental costs include several that are intangible and/or changing from different location and times. With this categorization the focus is mainly on the costs of preparing the product/service, and the costs during production and after distribution for customer care activities (under legal and voluntary warranties). Considering these activities, the environmental quality costs can be:

- prevention costs, coming from prevention activities, which can be considered as investments that can provide a long-term cost/technical/reputation advantage over direct competitors;
- appraisal costs, coming from assessment activities, which are costs that measure depreciation of equipment, resources used in monitoring, external certification and audit, personnel department, etc.;
- internal failure costs (coming from control activities);
- external failure costs (coming from failure activities).

Material flow cost accounting (MFCA)

Another recent approach is defined by the term 'cleaner production approaches', that is in line with eco-efficiency strategies and ecological approaches. The most important tool which deals with eco-efficiency issues is material flow cost accounting (MFCA) (Jasch, 2009). It includes other important monetary information needed to cost-effectively manage environmental performance. Material flow costs comprise the purchase cost of materials that eventually become waste or emissions. The related capital and personal costs to produce waste and emissions may be added, thus calculating production costs of waste. The physical accounting side of MFCA provides the needed information on the amounts and flows of energy, water, materials and wastes to assess these costs (Jasch, 2009).

The determinants of environmental costs, the purpose of environmental activities and the attributes of an environmental cost system are developed in practice and in literature, but research pinpoints both opportunities and gaps in using this monetary information.

Decision-making and monetary environmental management accounting role

The reasons for using MEMA in managers' decision-making

Recently there has been a focus on the intersection between strategic decisions and MCS (Simons 1995; Langfield-Smith, 1997, 2005). The MCS contains a package or combination of controls (Abernethy and Chua, 1996; Simons, 1995). This includes controls that are cybernetic in nature and are about goals, standards, measures, valuation and variances. It represents a more traditional view of the nature of MCS. In addition to the traditional pathway, there is the perspective related to the administration of the organization, which may be more structurally governance-oriented or bureaucratically based (Abernethy and Chua, 1996). Then there is management control that is influenced by social aspects such as culture and values (Alvesson and Karreman, 2004). So it is important to study the reasons for managerial practices. The management accountant has often been associated with two main functions: decision-making and decision-influencing contracting. Other important roles are also linked with management accounting, i.e. planning and co-ordination; attention directing and legitimizing. The reasons for using MEMA in the manager's decision-making are based on the idea that MEMA renders environmental consequences of manager decisions more 'visible'. So environmental accounting information can be useful for both purposes: decision-making and decision-influencing contracting. Burritt (2004) suggests that the issue is what tools to use in EMA and MEMA, but also the identification of the circumstances in which they should be used and should be of benefit to the business. Hence, the reasons listed below summarize the ever-growing interest of managers (Burritt and Saka, 2006):

- environmental regulations imposing requirements on companies and asking for new information to be recorded to demonstrate compliance;
- an increase in voluntary acceptance (self-regulation) by managers: increasing the importance of managing business environmental impacts and information needs to be recorded as part of the responsibility-accounting process;
- promotion of EMA by international, national and regional governments and some educational institutions: the 'management fashion setters' identify best practices and encourage a wider development and use;
- eco-efficiency improvement and cleaner production: the growing adoption among technical managers (engineers) as a logical driver for implementing a sustainable approach in regional company management and consequently a way of enhancing strategies that promote, maintain or repair social legitimacy.

Burritt and Saka (2006) consider the possibility of also using qualitative information provided by EMA tools. They conclude, however, that the practice of linking eco-efficiency measurement with EMA information is incomplete, and environmental information is under-utilized, as shown by EMA cases in Japan.

Other research (Marelli and Miolo-Vitali, 2009) shows some positive circumstances that help the introduction of EMA information in the decision-making processes. They comprise regular production of environmental reports, working in a critical environmental sector, systematic communication of environmental certification, relevant presence socially and economically for the local country, past experience and cultural background principally concerning technical engineering and quality programme certification, and consciousness of the characteristics of the input and output of material flow, in particular product and 'non-product' output (waste and pollution). However, from the findings of this research the EMA's choices in decision-making and in selecting investments for the company are mainly to comply with regulatory requirements, avoid or mitigate environmental liabilities and manage environmental risk. The data also show that very little consideration is given to strategic decisions and company competitiveness in order to gain market advantage, improve profitability and broaden ethical stance. The findings are consistent with expectations, derived from the literature review, of a narrow view concerning the relevance of environmental issues for their investment decisions.

The reasons for using environmental costs

Environmental costs are leading indicators of MEMA outputs' effectiveness. So, the reasons for managing environmental cost in decision-making processes assume importance. These traditional organizational rules and cost accounting practices are often not able to validate the Porter hypothesis that pollution is equivalent to economic inefficiency. The validity of the eco-efficiency approach would entail the necessity of significant modifications to the way current cost accounting and internal reporting is done. The eco-efficiency approach requires two types of information in order to develop internal decision-making (Burnett and Hansen, 2008; United Nations, 2001):

- physical information relating to use and flows of materials, water, energy, wastes;
- monetary information relating to environmental costs, earnings and savings.

Some scholars emphasize (Epstein, 1996; Joshi et al., 2001; Burritt et al., 2002; de Beer and Friends, 2006) that conventional accounting systems typically underestimate internal environmental costs. Moreover, most companies lack adequate integrated systems for measuring and managing environmental costs (Burritt, 2004). Therefore, the availability and use of a wider set of accounting information relative to the economic consequences of production is an important task. The effort of integrating technical and environmental performance with economic measures is quite clear; positive relevance should be given to environmental costs in 'standard costs and budgeting'. In fact the reasons for using environmental costs to supply financial information to management regarding the environmental impact of the organizations' activities (Langfield-Smith et al., 2006) should enrich the information related to the following managerial decisions: environmentally-induced capital expenditures (e.g. capital investment decisions needed to comply with regulations) and improving performance measure systems (e.g. with environmental costs, cost of waste management systems, environmental training, legal activities and fines).

Conclusions

The case studies regarding environmental cost information and the way in which this type of information is used are insightful. Researchers have emphasized that environmental costs can potentially offer qualified information to improve efficiency and profitability analysis. They render the environmental consequences of manager decisions more 'visible'. The integration of production information with environmental costs can be viewed as a diffusion of managerial (and accounting) innovation. According to the efficient-choice perspective in the diffusion of innovation (Abrahamson, 1991), innovative costing could enrich decision-making processes through the important roles of co-ordination, attention-directing and legitimizing. However, from the literature analysis described in the chapter, it emerges that the environmental information flow is currently under-utilized. The results only evidence a limited awareness of the potential help that cost information and new practices of cost management might be able to offer in decision-making processes regarding strategic competitiveness and profitability. One of today's management accounting problems is the disconnection between the local measurements that managers and teams can influence and the subsequent organizational results and reports produced by the headquarters (Schaltegger and Burritt, 2000). This issue can be best addressed through the implementation of MEMA to promote environmental issues both in strategic decisions and in operational ones. These managerial ideas, which are not completely accepted by practitioners and academics, address the study of EMA tools that can enhance management control systems.

The need to go beyond conventional management accounting and the growing interest in environmental issues opens the way to inter-functional scientific interest in MEMA, which is designed to understand the role played by EMA information in internal decision-making processes due to revaluation and changes of strategy. Further research is needed to indicate useful and sufficiently more inclusive models of different information for management decision-making.

However, the conclusions coming from the literature review pinpoint different perspectives of analysis. Despite this there is general agreement on the necessity for innovating management accounting practices and the necessity to improve the qualitative research on the practices that can help pinpoint more clearly the right tools. To progress in this direction a number of constraints have first to be addressed:

- the limited integration of environmental management systems with environmental performance management;
- the links among management control systems (MCS) and corporate social and environmental reporting. Environmental Management Accounting (EMA) became interesting for internal decision-making processes because it affects MCS and performance measurement. Some studies pinpoint direct links between MCS and corporate social and environmental reporting (Gray, 2002; Patten, 2002; Al-Tuwaijri et al., 2004). Operationally in companies, how can sustainability be defined when even researchers have difficulty in finding an agreed definition for it?
- the completeness and credibility of the environmental reports (internal for the company management) (Adams, 2004);
- the process of developing key performance indicators (KPIs) for measuring sustainability performance and the way in which sustainability KPIs are used in decision-making, planning and performance management (Adams and Frost, 2008);
- the links between environmental costs, financial accounting and risk assessment.

Finally, managers feel the need to highlight a growing awareness by them of a positive relationship between environmental stance and company strategy. However, it is not easy to find the mapping of environmental drivers that can improve company competitiveness. The second positive aspect is that the different approaches of studies with a wide utilization of methodological tools are trying to stimulate valuable interdisciplinary debate on these issues.

Notes

1 Environmental Management Accounting (EMA) has been promoted by the Working Group on EMA of the United Nations Division for Sustainable Development, UN DSD EMA WG, and the publications commissioned by it (United Nations, 2001; United Nations, 2002). Recently, the International Federation of Accountants (IFAC) has published a guidance document on EMA (International Federation of Accountants – IFAC, 2005) that explains its application to accountants.

2 It is important to say that recently the Environmental and Sustainability Management Accounting Network (EMAN) and the Centre for Social and Environmental Accounting Research (CSEAR) are developing workshops together. The last workshop was the 22nd International Congress on Social and Environmental Accounting Research and the 13th EMAN Conference on Environmental and Sustainability Management Accounting at the Gateway, University of St Andrews, Scotland, September 1–3, 2010.

Bibliography

Abernethy, M.A., and Chua, W.F., 1996. A field study of control system 'redesign': impact of institutional process on strategic choice. *Contemporary Accounting Research*, 13(2), 569–606.

Abrahamson, E., 1991. Managerial fads and fashions: the diffusion and rejection of innovations. *Academy of Management Review*, 16(3), 586–612.

Adams, C.A., 2004. The ethical, social and environmental reporting-performance portrayal gap. *Accounting, Auditing & Accountability Journal*, 17(5), 731–757.

Adams, C.A., and Frost, G.R., 2008. Integrating sustainability reporting into management practices. *Accounting Forum*, 32(4), 288–302.

Al-Tuwaijri, A.S., Christensen, T.E. and Hughes, K.E., 2004. The relations among environmental disclosure, environmental performance, and economic performance: a simultaneous equations approach. *Accounting, Organizations and Society*, 29(5–6), 447–471.

Alvesson, M., and Karreman, D., 2004. Interfaces of control. Technocratic and socio-ideological control in a global management consultancy firm. *Accounting, Organizations and Society*, 29(3–4), 423–444.

Antheaume, N., 2007. Full cost accounting. Adam Smith meets Rachel Carson?, in *Sustainability Accounting and Accountability*, edited by Unerman, J., Bebbington, J. and O'Dwyer, B., Routledge, London.

Bartolomeo, M., Bennett, M., Bouma, J.J., Heydkamp, P., James, P. and Wolters, T., 2000. Environmental management accounting in Europe: current practice and further potential, *European Accounting Review*, 9(1), 31–52.

Bebbington, J., 1997. Engagement, education and sustainability: a review essay on environmental accounting. *Accounting, Auditing & Accountability Journal*, 10(3), 365–381.

Bebbington, J., 2001. Sustainable development: a review of the international development, business and accounting literature. *Accounting Forum*, 25(2), 128–157.

Bebbington, J., and Gray, R.H., 2001. An account of sustainability: failure, success and a reconceptualization. *Critical Perspectives on Accounting*, 12, 557–587.

Bebbington, J., Gray, R.H., Thomson, I., and Walters, D., 1994. Accountants' attitudes and environmentally-sensitive accounting. *Accounting and Business Research*, 24(94), 109–120.

de Beer, P. and Friend, F., 2006. Environmental accounting: a management tool for enhancing corporate environmental and economic performance, *Ecological Economics*, 58, 548–560.

Bennett, M., and James, P., 1998. The Green Bottom Line, in Bennett, M. and James, P., *The Green Bottom Line: Environmental Accounting for Management: Current Practice and Future Trends*, Greenleaf Publishing, Sheffield.

Birkin, F., and Woodward, D., 1997a. Management accounting for sustainable development Part 5: accounting for sustainable development. *Management Accounting (UK)*, 75(10), 52–54.

Birkin, F., and Woodward, D., 1997b. Management accounting for sustainable development Part 2: from economic to ecological efficiency. *Management Accounting (UK)*, 75(7), 42–45.

Burnett, R.D., and Hansen, D.R., 2008. Ecoefficiency. Defining a role for environmental cost management. *Accounting, Organizations and Society*, 33(6), 551–581.

Burritt, R.L., 2004. Environmental management accounting: roadblocks on the way to the green and pleasant land. *Business Strategy and the Environment*, 13, 13–32.

Burritt, R.L., and Saka, C., 2006. Environmental management accounting applications and eco-efficiency: case studies from Japan. *Journal of Cleaner Production*, 14(14), 1262–1275.

Burritt, R.L., Hahn, T., and Schaltegger, S., 2002. Towards a comprehensive framework for environmental management accounting – links between business actors and environmental management accounting tools. *Australian Accounting Review*, July, 12(2), 39–50.

De Simone, L.D., and Popoff, F., 1997. *Eco-efficiency: The Business Link to Sustainable Development*. MIT Press, Cambridge, MA.

Ditz, D., and Ranganathan, J., 1997. *Measuring Up: Toward a Common Framework for Tracking Corporate Environmental Performance*. World Resources Institute.

Ditz, D., Ranganathan, J., and Banks, R.D., 1995. *Green ledgers: Case Studies in Corporate Environmental Accounting*. World Resources Institute.

Elkington, J., 1997. *Cannibals with Forks: The Triple Bottom Line of 21st-Century Business*. Capstone, Oxford.

Epstein, M.J., 1996. *Measuring Corporate Environmental Performance: Best practices for Costing and Managing an Effective Environmental Strategy*. Irwin, Chicago.

Global Reporting Initiative, 2002. *Sustainability Reporting Guidelines*. Boston, MA.

Global Reporting Initiative, 2011. G3.1. Available at (accessed October, 2011): http://www.globalreporting.org/ReportingFramework/G31Guidelines/

Gluch, P., and Baumann H., 2004. *The life cycle costing (LCC) approach: a conceptual discussion of its usefulness for environmental decision-making.* Building and Environment, 39, 571–580.

Grant, J.H., 2007. Advances and Challenges in Strategic Management. *International Journal of Business,* 12(1), 11–31.

Gray, R.H., 2002. The social accounting project and accounting organizations and society privileging engagement, imaginings, new accountings and pragmatism over critique? *Accounting, Organizations and Society*, 27(7), 687–708.

Gray, R.H., 2006. Social, environmental and sustainability reporting and organisational value creation? Whose value? Whose creation? *Accounting, Auditing & Accountability Journal*, 19(6), 793–819.

Gray, R.H., 2010. Is accounting for sustainability actually accounting for sustainability ... and how would we know? An exploration of narratives of organisations and the planet. *Accounting, Organizations and Society,* 35, 47–62.

Gray, R.H., and Bebbington, J., 2001. *Accounting for the Environment.* 2nd ed., Sage, London.

Gray, R.H., and Milne, M., 2002. Sustainability reporting: who's kidding whom? *Chartered Accountants Journal of New Zealand*, 81(6), 66–70.

Gray, R.H., and Milne, M., 2004. Towards reporting on the triple bottom line: Mirages, methods and myths. In A. Henriques and J. Richardson (eds), *The Triple Bottom Line: Does it All Add up?* (Chapter 7, 70–80). London: Earthscan.

Gray, R.H., Bebbington, J. and Walters, D., 1993. *Accounting for the Environment.* Paul Chapman, London.

Gray, R.H., Kouhy, R., and Lavers, S., 1995a. Corporate social and environmental reporting: a review of the literature and a longitudinal study of UK disclosure. *Accounting, Auditing & Accountability Journal*, 8(2), 47–77.

Gray, R.H., Kouhy, R., and Lavers, S., 1995b. Constructing a research database of social and environmental reporting by UK companies. *Accounting, Auditing & Accountability Journal,* 8(2), 78–101.

Greig, J.T., Lord, B.R., and Shanahan, Y.P., 2006. Environmental management accounting. A survey of implementation in New Zealand. *International Journal of Environmental, Cultural, Economic and Social Sustainability,* 2(3), 153–163.

Horngren C.T., Bhimani A., Datar S.M., and Foster G., 2005. *Management and Cost Accounting.* 3e, Prentice-Hall, Harlow.

International Federation of Accountants (IFAC), 2005. International Guidance Document of EMA. IFAC, New York, http://www.ifac.org

Jasch, C., 2003. The use of environmental management accounting (EMA) for identifying environmental costs. *Journal of Cleaner Production*, 11(6), 667–676.

Jasch, C., 2006. How to perform an environmental management cost assessment in one day. *Journal of Cleaner Production*, 14, 1194–1213.

Jasch, C., 2009. *Environmental and Material Flow Cost Accounting. Principles and procedures.* Springer – IOW – EMAN, New York.

Joshi, S., Krishnan, R., and Lave, L., 2001. Estimating the hidden costs of environmental regulations. *The Accounting Review,* 76(2), 171–198.

King, A. and Lenox, M., 2002. Exploring the locus of profitable pollution reduction. *Management Science*, 48(2), 289–299.

Langfield-Smith, K., 1997. Management control systems and strategy: a critical review. *Accounting, Organizations and Society*, 22(2), 207–232.

Langfield-Smith, K., 2005. What do we Know about Management Control Systems and Strategy? In Chapman C.S. (ed.), *Controlling Strategy: Management, Accounting and Performance Measurement*, Oxford University Press, Oxford.

Langfield-Smith, K., Thorne, H. and Hilton, R.W., 2006. *Management Accounting. Information for Managing and Creating Value*, 4e, McGraw-Hill,

Larrinaga-Gonzalez, C., and Bebbington, J., 2001. Accounting change or institutional appropriation? A case study of the implementation of environmental accounting. *Critical Perspectives on Accounting,* 12(3), 269–292.

Lehman, G., 1999. Disclosing new worlds: a role for social and environmental accounting and auditing. *Accounting, Organizations and Society*, 24(3), 217–241.

Lehman, G., 2002. Global accountability and sustainability: research prospects, *Accounting Forum*, 26(3), 219–232.

Marelli, A., 2009. I costi ambientali (Environmental costs). In Miolo-Vitali, P., *Strumenti per l'analisi dei costi – Percorsi di cost management (Tools for Cost Analysis – Pathways of Cost Management)*, Vol. III, Giappichelli, Torino, Italy.

Marelli, A., and Miolo-Vitali, P., 2009. Reasons for Environmental Management Accounting Implementation: a Call for Costing Innovation. Paper presented to the Workshop 'Innovating Management and Accounting Practices', SDA Bocconi, Milan, 1–2 December, 2009.

Milne, M., Ball, A., and Gray, R.H., 2008. Whither Ecology? The Triple Bottom Line, the Global Reporting Initiative, and the Institutionalization of Corporate Sustainability Reporting. Paper presented to the American Accounting Association, Anaheim, August 2008.

Murty, M.N., and Kumar, S., 2003. Win–win opportunities and environmental regulation: testing of the porter hypothesis for Indian manufacturing industries. *Journal of Environmental Management*, 67, 139–144.

Owen, D.L., 2008. Chronicles of wasted time? A personal reflection on the current state of, and future prospects for, social and environmental accounting research. *Accounting, Auditing & Accountability Journal*, 21(2), 240–267.

Parker, L.D., 2000a. Environmental costing: a path to implementation. *Australian Accounting Review*, 10(3), 43–51.

Parker, L.D., 2000b. Green strategy costing: early days. *Australian Accounting Review*, 10(1), 46–55.

Parker, L.D., 2005. Social and environmental accountability research. A view from the commentary box. *Accounting, Auditing & Accountability Journal*, 18(6), 842–860.

Parker, L.D., 2011. Twenty-one years of social and environmental accountability research: a coming of age. *Accounting Forum*, 35, 1–10.

Patten, D.M., 2002. The relationship between environmental performance and environmental disclosure. *Accounting, Organizations and Society,* 27(8), 763–773.

Porter, M. E., 1991. America's green strategy. *Scientific American* (April), 168.

Porter, M.E., and Kramer, M.R., 2006. Strategy and society. the link between competitive advantage and corporate social responsibility. *Harvard Business Review,* December, 78–91.

Porter, M.E., and van der Linde, C., 1995a. Toward a new conception of the environment-competitiveness relationship. *Journal of Economic Perspectives*, 9(Fall), 97–118.

Porter, M.E., and van der Linde, C., 1995b. Green and competitive: ending the stalemate. *Harvard Business Review* (September–October), 120–134.

Roth, H.P., and Keller, C.E., 1997. Quality, profits and the environment: diverse goals or common objectives? *Management Accounting* (US) July, 50–55.

Russell, W.G., Skalak, S.L., and Miller, G., 1994. Environmental cost accounting: the bottom line for environmental quality management. *Total Quality Environmental Management*, 3(3), 255–68.

Schaltegger, S., 1996. *Corporate Environmental Accounting*. Wiley, Chichester.

Schaltegger, S., 1998. Accounting for Eco-efficiency. In Nath, B., Hens, L., Compton, P., Devuyst, D. (eds), *Environmental Management in Practice*, Vol. I, 272–287, Routledge, London.

Schaltegger, S., and Burritt, R.L., 2000. *Contemporary Environmental Accounting. Issues, Concepts and Practice*. Greenleaf, Sheffield.

Schaltegger, S., and Burritt, R.L., 2010. Sustainability accounting for companies: catchphrase or decision support for business leaders? *Journal of World Business,* 45(4), 375–384.

Schaltegger, S., Hahn, T., and Burritt, R.L., 2000. *Environmental Management Accounting – Overview and Main Approaches*. Centre for Sustainability Management (CSM), Lüneburg.

Schaltegger, S., Bennett, M., Burritt, R.L., and Jasch, C., 2008. *Environmental Management Accounting for Cleaner Production*. Springer Science, Dordrecht.

Simons, R., 1995. *Levers of Control*. Harvard Business School Press, Boston, MA.

Spence, C., Husillos, J., and Correa-Ruiz, C., 2010. Cargo cult science and the death of politics: a critical review of social and environmental accounting research. *Critical Perspectives on Accounting,* 21(1), 76–89.

Spitzer, M., and Elwood, H., 1995. *An introduction to environmental accounting as a business management tool: key concepts and terms*. Washington, DC: EPA (EPA 742-R-95-001).

Stone, D., 1995. No longer at the end of the pipe, but still a long way from sustainability: a look at management accounting for the environment and sustainable development in the United States. *Accounting Forum,* 19(2–3), 95–110.

Terrachoice, 2010a. Greenwashing Report 2010. Available at (accessed October, 2011): http://sinsofgreenwashing.org/

Terrachoice, 2010b: *The Sins of Greenwashing* Home and Family Edition,

United Nations, 2001. *Environmental Management Accounting, Procedures and Principles*. United Nations Publications, United Nations Division for Sustainable Development – UNDESA/DSD. New York/ Geneva, http://www.un.org/esa/sustdev/sdissues/technology/estema1.htm

United Nations, 2002. *Environmental Management Accounting: Policies and Linkages*. United Nations Publications, United Nations Division for Sustainable Development – UNDESA/DSD. New York/ Geneva, http://www.un.org/esa/sustdev/sdissues/technology/estema1.htm

Wilmshurst, T.D., and Frost, G.R., 2001. The role of accounting and the accountant in the environmental management system. *Business Strategy and the Environment,* 10, 135–147.

20

Performance measurement systems – beyond generic actions

Rainer Lueg and Hanne Nørreklit

Introduction

Over recent decades, academics and practitioners have discussed the weaknesses of traditional and advanced financial performance measures which incorporate cost considerations. In particular, return on investment (ROI) – as a ratio based on historical accounting information – has major shortcomings in measuring the financial results of organizational units and in motivating management. First, it ignores the financial value of intangible assets such as research in progress, human resources and the competitive position. Due to asset valuation, depreciation policy and lack of instruction about the cost of capital, ROI furthermore has serious dysfunctional implications for investment decisions (Copeland, Koller, and Murrin, 2000; Dearden, 1969: 292; Nobel, 1990). To address some of the weaknesses of ROI, EVA has been advocated as an advanced alternative (Stewart, 1991). One of the strengths of EVA is the inclusion of opportunity costs in the performance assessment and hence in managerial decision-making. Additionally, EVA requires detailed adjustments of earnings and invested capital to move away from historical accounting principles towards more economic-based principles. Yet, empirical evidence shows that EVA has only marginally higher explanatory power in explaining stock returns than unaltered accounting figures (Biddle, Bowen, and Wallace, 1997). However, since the figure relies on past accounting information and disregards many other expectations of market participants, we suggest that the singular focus on such a narrow definition of shareholder value could distort financial performance measurement, and motivate management to undertake dysfunctional, short-term actions or gaming at the expense of long-term profitability. Finally, it should be noted that the conventional wisdom of accounting advocates NPV to be used for managerial decision-making. However, the success of the NPV technique depends on the ability to estimate cash flows and the project-specific weighted average cost of capital. When evaluating possible investments, many companies tend to focus on cost savings only and hence neglect the measurement of (in-)tangible benefits, the opportunity costs of the decision and the project-specific risk (Kaplan and Atkinson, 1989; Nobel, 1990).

Overall, the recognition of the weaknesses of ROI, EVA and NPV has created a need for PMSs providing more future-oriented accounting information, thereby overcoming the historical nature of financial performance measurement. This demand has been reinforced by the increasing dominance of strategic management. Responding to this trend, initiatives have been launched to develop PMSs with non-financial indicators that directly relate to competitive strategy. In particular, there has been increasing interest in the use of PMSs or comprehensive 'packages'/'systems' combining financial and non-financial measurement such as the 'performance pyramid' and the Balanced Scorecard (BSC). It is of utmost importance to note that financial PMSs like ROI, EVA or NPV are strategy-neutral. They only measure the influence of company strategies and actions on financial performance. According to this view, the choice of strategies and actions is always related to the circumstances of the specific company. The management of the company is supposed to develop specific strategies and actions based on in-depth knowledge of the business model of the company. The purpose of financial PMSs is to provide information for the evaluation of strategies and action from the point of view of the institutional formula of accounting. Consequently, most non-financial PMSs are not strategy-neutral. PMSs like the BSC embed empirical postulates of generic strategic actions driving successful business performance and make specific prescriptions for managerial action.

Generic strategies offer strategic action for any given state of the environment whose execution leads to financial success. One of the most prominent approaches to generic strategies is that of Porter (1980). In the book *Competitive Strategy*, Porter (1980) introduces a set of techniques to analyse any competitive setting, and then to decide on the appropriate generic strategy for developing the competitive position of a company. Drawing on a rationalist methodology, he proposes the following three typologies of generic strategies to obtain competitive advantage: cost leadership, differentiation and segmentation. Companies 'stuck in the middle' of these three options will not become successful. This paper takes a more action-oriented approach to the BSC and generic strategy. Inspired by the BSC's assumptions, we are concerned about cause-and-effect relationships between generic types of strategic actions and profitability. In this view a 'generic relationship'/'cause-and-effect' relationship implies i) that the strategic action (X) precedes profitability (Y) in time and ii) that the observation of the strategic action (X) necessarily implies the subsequent observation of the incident of profitability (Y). A cause-and-effect relationship suggests that there are some general management actions that lead to financial success. Such strong assertions can only be proven by empirical observation or statistical tests of structures of the business world. Hence, the two events strategic action (X) and profitability (Y) are logically independent, which means that we cannot deduce from strategic action to profitability by logical reasoning.

First, the identification of generic relationships is interesting as it solves the problem of historically oriented accounting for decision-making. Second – given that the assumptions of the generic strategies hold – simplistic measurements can be used to anticipate future financial performance. If such a generic concept works, its indicators 'become the drivers of future performance' (Kaplan and Norton, 1996: 8). The crucial assumption of the generic strategies leading to successful financial performance gives rise to the question whether these prescriptions for obtaining results are financially sound. The question is important because companies following financially problematic generic strategies will eventually face financial difficulties. One may argue that the strategic actions in the generic models are formulated in a rather abstract way and require that the particular company *adapts* them to its business model. However, even the most abstract prescriptions are meant to *guide* practice in a generic way. This implies that these prescriptions of PMSs and hence their way of understanding can create false assumptions about conducting a financially successful business.

This chapter signals that the underlying causality between the immediate control of such qualitative PMS indicators and financial performance is merely implied, based on an unsound interpretation of complex studies such as the Performance Impact of Market Strategy (PIMS)

(Buzzell and Gale, 1987). We provide both analytical and empirical evidence on how such misinterpretation of the role of non-financial measures may ignore, or even cause deterioration in, financial performance.

The outline of the chapter is as follows: the next two sections describe some of the dominant generic strategic postulates and explain how these are embedded in the performance measurement package of the Balanced Scorecard (BSC). The penultimate section discusses the financial validity of the generic strategic actions. In the concluding section, we explain why assumptions of strategic generic relationships ignore or even deteriorate financial performance.

Generic strategic actions driving profitability

Some of the pioneers in empirically testing how strategic actions lead to profitability are the studies on profit impact of organizational structure and managerial behaviour (Likert and Bowers, 1969) and the study on the profit impact of market strategy (PIMS) (Buzzell and Gale, 1987; Buzzell, Gale, and Sultan, 1975). Based on empirical data and statistical analysis, these studies investigate which generic strategic actions lead to financial success. With great attention to detail, PMSs such as the performance pyramid and the BSC have embedded the postulates of generic strategic actions advocated by these studies. We will now briefly introduce the ideas and reasoning of these studies.

Managerial behaviour – employee behaviour – profitability

Likert and Bowers (1969) argue that organizational and managerial factors provide indications of future performance. They suggest that managerial behaviour and organizational structure affect performance through various transmission mechanisms. Figure 20.1 depicts the relationship between causal variables, intervening variables and end results. The structure of the organization and management policies, decisions, business and leadership strategies, skills and behaviour are assumed to be causal variables that determine organizational development and organizational performance. Intervening variables are the performance capabilities of the employees such as 'the loyalties, attitudes, motivations, performance goals, and perceptions of all members and their collective capacity for effective action, interaction, communication, and decision-making' (Likert and Bowers, 1969: 586). The end result is represented in performance variables such as sales volume, growth, market share, efficiency, quality and personnel costs. It follows that the observation and measurements of the causal and intervening variables create the basis for a feed-forward performance measurement system.

Likert and Bowers' (1969) study confirms their proposed model. However, they highlight that the relationships involve high complexity; e.g., the direction of causality is problematic as variables seem to be mutually enforcing. The capacity of an engineer to influence her/his own work situation may cause her/him to become a high performer. Likewise, excellent performance may increase the likelihood that he/she obtains increased influence on the work situation (Likert and Bowers, 1969: 590–591).

Likert and Bowers' (1969) thoughts bear witness to early ideas of empowerment and a learning organization. This reasoning has roots in Maslow's (1954) theory of motivation, conceptualizing the individual as constantly developing. While the initial movements, as represented by Maslow (1954), may have been driven by humanistic ideals, recent decades' new human resource management movement argues that the empowered employee is a necessity for a contemporary company competing in the global environment (Gandz, 1990). Empowerment requires

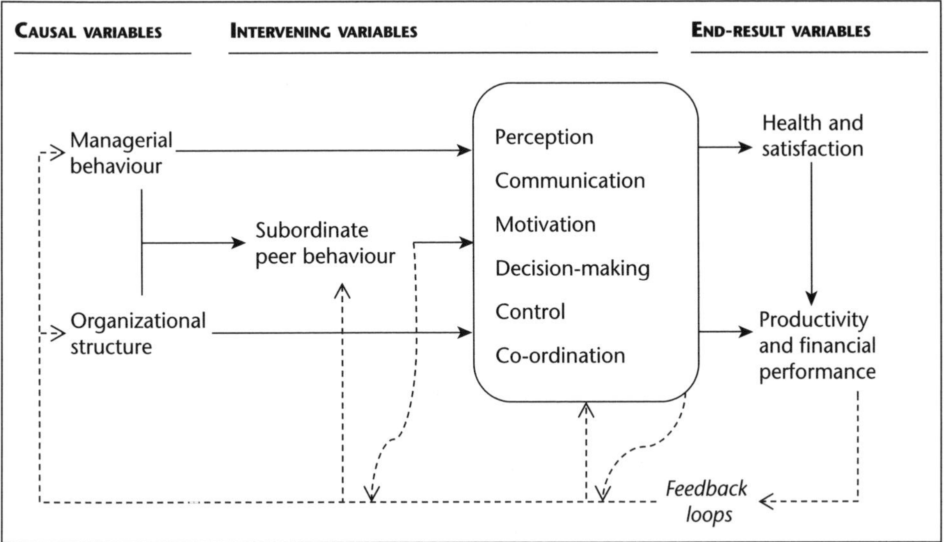

Figure 20.1 Schematic relationships between causal, intervening and end-result variables

Source: Likert and Bowers, 1969: 587.

not only skilled employees but also the employees' capability to improve these skills further (Gandz, 1990).

Superior quality – economies of scale – profitability

Drawing on a database of more than 450 business units from different industries, products and markets, the PIMS study explored generic strategic factors and their effect on financial performance. First, the PIMS study found – not very surprisingly – that the choice of the 'right' markets with the 'right' products was decisive for profitability. On average, an attractive market more than tripled ROI compared to a non-attractive market (Buzzell and Gale, 1987: 69). Second, the PIMS study found that the profitability (ROI) of a business unit was strongly linked with market share relative to the leading competitors (Buzzell and Gale, 1987; Buzzell et al., 1975). Two interacting forces explain this phenomenon: as the first force, growth facilitates the achievement of cost advantages due to economies of scale (EOS). Following the ideas of microeconomics, EOS describe the joint effect of decreasing average unit costs due to learning effects and fixed-cost digression. EOS can affect all functions within a company, e.g., purchasing, manufacturing, marketing, administration or finance, and are a widespread justification for growth. Since low cost is an important dimension of competitive advantage, companies should take this into account when developing their strategy. However, Buzzell and Gale (1987) argue that EOS do not drive high share/high profitability as an isolated force, but together with a second set of forces involving the design, production and marketing of products/services that are superior in quality relative to those of the competitor in the market. Producing superior quality involves the achievement of both perceived quality and conformance quality:

> One is to achieve superior perceived quality by developing a set of product specifications and service standards that more closely meet customer needs than competitors. The other is

> to achieve superior conformance quality by being more effective than your competitors in conforming to the appropriate product specifications and service standards. These ways of winning are not mutually exclusive so you should try to outperform your competitors on both perceived quality and conformance quality.
>
> *(Buzzell and Gale, 1987: 104).*

Buzzell and Gale (1987: 104) explain the impact of quality and growth by identifying the causal mechanisms by which superior quality – in the short term – justifies a premium price contributing to higher profitability, and by which – in the long term – superior quality drives market share. Hence, growth through higher market share drives competitive cost advantages and higher profitability.

Figure 20.2 gives an overview of how quality drives profitability. Overall, better quality is created by relatively higher performance on product attributes. The left side of the exhibit illustrates the generic assumption that delivering superior customer-perceived quality affects the relative value and price. The model also stresses that relative perceived quality gains relative market share through relative value, which drives relative market share and hence higher profitability. Together, relative quality and market share drive profitability. This applies in the case of both a low and a high level of market differentiation. The right side shows that effectiveness in the production of superior conformance quality specifications reduces quality costs and hence relative costs, which increases profit. Additionally, superior conformance quality has a positive impact on customer-perceived quality:

> The net effect seems to be that as we move from inferior to superior quality positions, the reduction in costs associated with scrap and reprocessing are offset by the increased costs of improving product or service performance on key attributes that count in the purchase decision.
>
> *(Buzzell and Gale, 1987: 108)*

Drawing on the ideas of quality management in the successful Japanese automobile industry, the view reflected in the PIMS model is that investment in conformance quality improvement is free. This view is also taken by Deming (1982), who advocates that doing things right the first time reduces costs – hence he sees little reason to bother estimating quality cost. In contrast, Juran (1985) argues for the importance of analysing the cost of quality in order to identify the optimal internal and external failure costs, or prevention and appraisal costs. One should find the quality level with the minimum total cost of quality (Shank, 1989: 59). However – given the embedded assumption of the PIMS model that customers are sensitive to relative experienced quality and hence to the delivered conformance quality – the external failure costs become high and the achievement of conformance quality becomes a generic action to increase profitability.

Additionally, Buzzell and Gale (1987) find a negative relationship between capital-intensive business and profitability. They explain this result by unfortunate fixed-asset investments causing surplus capacity and obsolete specialized technology. High levels of working capital are related to high inventories due to inaccurate sales estimates or unexpected competition. However,

> [...] this does not mean that companies should not make capital investments. It means that most companies should try to allocate capital more effectively so that they have a better chance of beating the cost of capital.
>
> *(Buzzell and Gale, 1987: 161)*

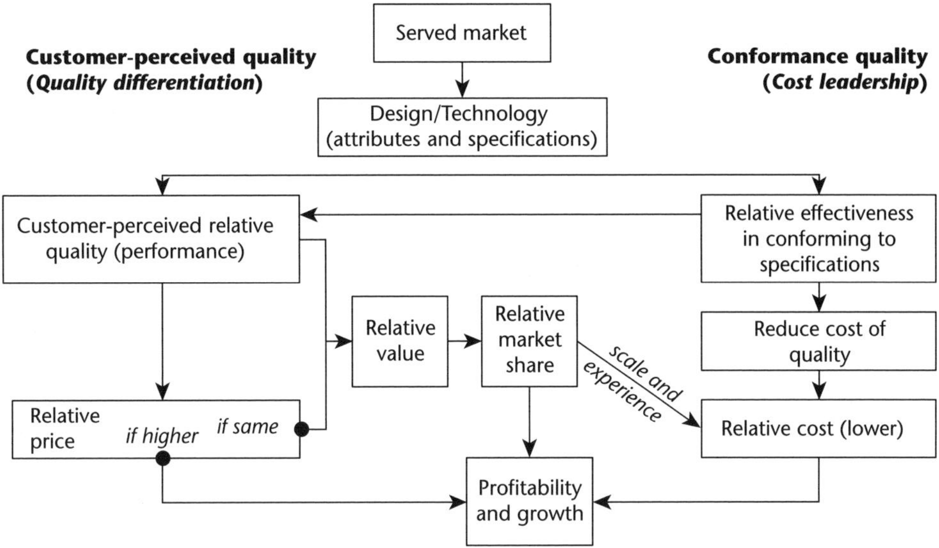

Figure 20.2 How quality drives profitability and growth

Source: Buzzell and Gale, 1985, p. 106.

As a solution to these problems, the authors advocate investment in flexible rather than specialized equipment. They also suggest greater awareness of increased labour productivity due to investments in technology. Flexible manufacturing technology and JIT processes are considered a matter of high importance – not only because fixed-asset investments become less intensive and more agile, but also because they affect working capital. In this context, especially work-in-progress, inventories are a liability that should be minimized. In addition to lower inventory levels, the advantages of a flexible manufacturing process include reduction in throughput time and space, as well as better quality and better service to customers. Overall, capital investment should facilitate superior product/service quality, customer loyalty and conformance quality.

In sum, Buzzell and Gale (1987) advocate the generic strategy formula stating that the delivery of ever-improving value to customers, together with organizational effectiveness and capabilities, drives profitability. They argue that the following causal mechanism governs:

> [...] higher profitability follows as a result of premium price, costs equal to or lower than those of competitors, and advantages in procurement and utilization of invested capital.
>
> *(Buzzell and Gale, 1987: 92)*

On top of that, high profitability makes a company capable of spending more on R&D, supporting ongoing innovation and hence providing the right product for the right market. Their study shows that high performers exhibit high levels of innovation.

The PIMS model's (Buzzell and Gale, 1987: 18) approach was a break with the classical wisdom of management accounting and micro-economics, which also governed in the beginning of the quality movement. In this vein, Feigenbaum (1956) highlights that companies would not succeed by maximizing quality, but by determining the 'optimal quality costs' (Feigenbaum, 1956: 94). The effect on both the bottom line and on customer satisfaction is optimal when the desired quality and the pertinent costs are in equilibrium. Feigenbaum (1956: 94) argues that the optimal level of quality represents a matter of both revenue maximization and cost accounting, stating that 'Marketing evaluates the level of quality which customers want and for which they are willing to pay.' Similarly, Kamen (1977) addresses the necessity of accounting information for decision-making on quality levels.

Finally, it should be noted that Buzzell and Gale (1987: 18) point out that the PIMS model does not include all factors leading to success. This implies that not all efforts in increasing quality, expanding growth and market share and decreases in capital investment translate into higher profitability. They explicitly highlight that this particular implication – as well as a balance between short-term and long-term costs and benefits – should be taken into consideration (Buzzell et al., 1975: 106).

Generic strategic actions in PMSs

Despite the authors of the PIMS model explicitly emphasizing that their study cannot lead to a general formula for strategic choices, many PMSs more or less explicitly accept the PIMS model as a generic formula describing strategic actions for financial success. As one of the first PMSs, the performance pyramid (Lynch and Cross, 1991) included measurements that support the implementation of some of the major generic assumptions embedded in the PIMS model. The performance pyramid has as an underlying strategic vision that both market share and financial success can be obtained through improvement of customer-satisfaction, asset flexibility and efficiency. It includes the measurement areas of customer satisfaction, service flexibility and productivity, which equals the key dimensions of the PIMS model, i.e. customer-perceived quality, investment intensity and quality conformance, respectively. Quality, delivery, cycle time and waste express the specific measurements of the three measurement areas. Improvement in the level of quality, delivery, cycle time and waste are assumed to be feed-forward measures of financial success.

The BSC (see Kaplan and Norton, 1996, 2000, 2001, 2004, 2008) is another PMS including a more comprehensive set of generic strategies. The aim of the BSC is not to evaluate the generic strategy a priori, but to verify that the planned strategies are implemented, and to monitor the results of the strategies applied ex post facto. The model uses both financial and non-financial metrics which aim to observe the development in the underlying strategic action. The BSC assumes that a generic set of strategies drive the following causal relationships between the variables (Kaplan and Norton, 1996: 31): *organizational learning and growth* ➔ *efficient internal business processes* ➔ *customer satisfaction and loyalty* ➔ *financial success*. The perspective of organizational learning and growth involves how the company should change and empower its employees in order to realize its visions. The next perspective defines the processes in which the company must excel in order to satisfy shareholders and customers. It concerns the development of effectiveness in conforming to specifications and innovating new products. These internal processes are in turn drivers of the next perspective – customer satisfaction and loyalty – and the last perspective – market growth and financial results. This causal relationship is expressed in the following:

> For example, Return on Capital Employed (ROCE) may be a measure in the financial perspective. The driver of this measure could be repeated and expanded sales from existing customers, the result of a high degree of loyalty among those customers. So, customer loyalty is included on the scorecard (in the customer perspective) because it is expected to have a strong influence on ROCE. But how will the organization achieve customer loyalty? Analysis of customer preferences may reveal that on-time delivery of orders is highly valued by customers. Thus, improved OTD is expected to lead to higher customer loyalty, which, in turn, is expected to lead to higher financial performance. So both customer loyalty and OTD are incorporated into the customer perspective of the scorecard.

> This process continues by asking what internal processes must the company excel at to achieve exceptional on-time delivery. To achieve improved OTD, the business may need short cycle times in operating processes and high quality internal processes. And how do organizations improve the quality and reduce the cycle times of their internal processes? By training and improving the skills of their operating employees, an objective that would be a candidate for the learning and growth perspective. We can now see how an entire chain of cause-and-effect relationships can be established as a vertical vector through the four BSC perspectives.
>
> *(Kaplan and Norton, 1996: 31)*

Although there are nuances, the BSC outlines generic strategies for becoming financially successful. Its story is rather similar to the assumptions of the PIMS model. The BSC argues that the driver of financial performance is growth through customer satisfaction, which is identical with the PIMS assumption of profitability driven by customer-perceived relative quality. Superior quality and high customer satisfaction are both expressions of high consumer surplus. Equally, the approaches agree that a high level of customer satisfaction yields a high return and hence that consumer surplus should be maximized. However, Kaplan and Norton (1996) do not base their point on Buzzell and Gale (1987) but on a later study by Jones and Sasser (1995: 90) who state that:

> This high level of satisfaction will lead to greatly increased customer loyalty. And increased customer loyalty is the single most important driver of long term financial performance. Separate research has validated these beliefs.
>
> *(Jones and Sasser, 1995: 90)*

The BSC has a dimension labelled customer value proposition, which describes the required product and service attributes that the internal processes must fulfil to satisfy customers. This appears to be similar to the PIMS model's notion of product attributes and specifications, defining the required level of compliance quality. In the PIMS model, effective and flexible manufacturing processes drive compliance quality, while in the BSC operations and services drive the fulfilment of the customer value proposition. In the PIMS model, compliance quality drives customer-perceived quality; in the BSC, efficient processes drive customer satisfaction. In both models, innovation is considered a driver of consumer surplus. However, the BSC emphasizes the importance of efficient innovation processes. More specifically, the time-to-market for product and service innovations is considered a driver of long-term customer satisfaction. The learning and growth perspective includes the empowerment aspects, which are the key dimensions in the model by Likert and Bowers (1969), but not included in the PIMS study.

The validity of generic relations – empirical findings

The aforementioned studies have advocated a generic relation between profitability and customer satisfaction, relative quality and internal processes. The causal conclusions of these studies have an intuitive appeal, especially since they do not only refer to top-line growth but also highlight the importance of the complexity of cost management necessary to achieve bottom-line growth. When the findings from strategic management transgressed management control, they surprisingly lost their link to costing.

Contemporary strategic management accounting (SMA) in the 1980s emphasized quality as a value per se, e.g., as a renunciation of traditional accounting. Kaplan (1984: 97) postulates that '[d]irect quality indicators should be reported frequently at all levels of a manufacturing organization', without linking these directly to cost measures, as is done at the beginning of the quality movement (Feigenbaum, 1956). The objective to outperform the competition by maximizing instead of optimizing quality has dissolved the link to cost accounting. This kind of interpretation of the aforementioned studies has some pitfalls. Below, we illustrate empirical findings on the generic assumptions that internal process quality causes customer satisfaction, and eventually profitability.

Do customers notice superior quality?

Turning higher quality into customer satisfaction and hence increased market share proves to be challenging. Investigating 30,000 consumers of 241 products over 12 years, Mitra and Golder (2007) find that customers need five to seven years to adjust their shopping behaviour to changes in quality. While declines are noted faster, improvements pass unnoticed for even longer periods. In addition, a focus on customer satisfaction may create opportunistic behaviour, with customers taking advantage of companies' compensation policies. Wirtz (2011) finds this to be true in particular for bigger companies.

Does customer satisfaction pay off?

Some studies on the relationships between customer satisfaction and profitability show mixed results. Ittner and Larcker (1998: 218–220) find that fewer than 55 per cent of the vice presidents in charge of quality in major US companies could relate their quality measures directly to operational, productivity or revenue improvements, only 29 per cent could relate them to accounting returns, and no more than 12 per cent could relate them to stock returns. Malina, Nørreklit and Selto (2007) find no predictive ability of a model assuming that customer satisfaction drives sales growth, which in turn drives profitability.

The British utility sector is an example of how companies can improve service quality over time. Yet, without changing the customers' willingness to pay (WTP), this may damage profitability. Before the UK utility reform in 1990/1, strategic PMSs and management rewards were mostly aimed at controlling cost efficiency, leading to maintenance reductions and insufficient network investments. Additional regulation resulted in the implementation of a new strategy emphasizing service quality improvement maximization. The British regulator defined 'quality' as the minimization of energy losses and customer minutes lost at a given cost level. This definition of 'quality' as technical efficiency – i.e. the marginal cost of improvement – disregards the customers' marginal WTP. Since managers were measured and rewarded to exceed the targeted quality at the costs given by the regulator (through caps on retail prices and revenues on the power sales), their managers' goals were to maximize technical quality instead of optimizing it from the customers' point of view. Over a 14-year time frame from 1990 to 2004, Yu, Jamasb and Pollitt (2009) documented constant improvements in the service quality of energy provision. Yet, the customers' marginal WTP for efficient service remained almost constant. This combination led to the result that the customers' WTP was on average only 86 per cent of the technical efficiency. This indicates a sub-optimal resource allocation of expenditures for quality since the utility sector is publicly regulated and should hence maximize social welfare. From an economist's point of view, the social welfare optimum is achieved when the marginal resources spent on improving the quality level ('technical efficiency') equal the marginal WTP for this quality by the consumers ('allocative efficiency'). However – as the managers had only to balance total expenditures with the quality of service and network energy losses – it is perfectly understandable that they traded potential cost reductions (i.e. allocative efficiency) for improvements in quality (i.e.

technical efficiency). Since they had no reference to the customers' WTP, the efficiency improvements had no constraint.

Alternatively, and in order to maximize social welfare, the managers of many of the utility companies could have cut prices well below the regulator's given caps instead of investing in quality that consumers did not want. Yet, the incentive contracts of the utility managers were not aligned with the customers' view of quality, leading to sub-optimal investment decision-making, according to Yu, Jamasb and Pollitt (2009). Due to a PMS that rewarded quality improvements instead of the maximization of the consumer surplus, resources were allocated inefficiently to high-quality services for which consumers had no desire to pay.

Does quality pay off?

Improvements in compliance quality may not always pay off. Although many of the winners of the US Baldrige Quality Award prize had high financial performance, research documents show that programmes on quality improvement do not necessarily lead to profitability, i.e. it is not 'a panacea guaranteed to result in economic health' (Wisner and Eakins, 1994). Wallace Co. Inc. is an example of an award winner who later struggled with financial problems due to over-investments in quality improvement:

> As a distributor of pipe fittings to Gulf Coast refineries, quality at Wallace is measured primarily in terms of delivery performance. Since 1987 when the company decided to formalize its quality improvement efforts, Wallace's on-time delivery performance has increased from 75 per cent to 92 per cent by concentrating improvement efforts on the delivery process. In 1989, Wallace associates used the Baldrige Quality Award application to grade their quality progress and to plan their short-term improvement efforts. As a result, Wallace has invested over $700,000 and 19,000 hours into training, created Point Teams to oversee quality objectives, developed a new performance evaluation process, created a worker handbook, and started a new employee assistance programme. Wallace insists on high quality from its suppliers and has developed a Vendor Certification Task Force to communicate quality requirements to vendors. Wallace was forced to enter chapter 11, reorganization, in early 1992, due in part to spending too much time helping other firms improve quality, after winning the Baldrige Award. Still, Wallace's CEO attributes their survival to their quality improvement program.
>
> *(Wisner and Eakins, 1994: 15)*

The Baldrige Quality programme may be strong in predicting customer satisfaction, but it appears substantially weaker in predicting financial results (Wilson and Collier, 2000). Indeed some winners have proven to be superior financial performers before the award, but without showing improvement in company value in the periods after. Jacob, Madu and Tang (2004) state:

> Since one of the purposes of the award is to stimulate quality awareness among US firms, the Baldrige recipients may be construed as a conspicuous centrepiece of the US quality management movement.
>
> *(Jacob et al., 2004: 897)*

As another example, a European producer of drive systems became the quality leader in its industry at the expense of production cycle time, which was three times that of its relevant competitors (Kaiser and Young, 2009). Despite marketing efforts, top managers had to admit that customers were neither able to understand nor willing to pay for the superb quality. They decided to cut on quality, with no expense on customer satisfaction. This freed up working capital at a level of 5 per cent of their annual revenue. Similarly, an Italian food manufacturer established a premium segment of food that was aged for 12–14 months, comprising 25 per cent of sales (Kaiser and Young, 2009). Internal benchmarking of segments revealed that these premium brands were significantly hurting the profitability of the business since work-in-progress was so high. The company decided to cut quality, i.e. the aging process, until it reached the average profitability of the other segments and met the customers' WTP.

On top of that, Robertson, Swan and Newell (1996) show that managers often do not have sufficient information on the profit impact of quality improvements. As a consequence, they implement technology innovations and quality improvements for their own sake. Hence, one cannot assume that quality will automatically lead to high financial gains.

In particular, when quality becomes a key performance indicator and decisions on quality levels are shifted from top management, and from the overall profit function, to the shop floor, middle management has incentives to meet or exceed quality standards (or even to add new features) irrespective of costs (Kaiser and Young, 2009). Some companies may use multiple performance measurements at the shop level, such as quality, maintenance and cost. However, multi-performance measurements are ambiguous, as they do not say anything about the relative importance of different measurements and how a change in one criterion can outweigh a change in another. Also, some of the objectives may be contradictory to each other. The problem may be solved through a composite score. However, the appropriate weights in such a score are difficult to estimate and hence rather subjective (Jensen, 2010; Ridgway, 1956).

Does efficient innovation drive customer satisfaction and profitability?

Efficient innovation and operational processes may not lead to customer satisfaction. The following story from a pharmaceutical company documents how focus on time-to-market can have fatal implications for long-term relative costumer-perceived quality and profitability (Nørreklit and Nørreklit, 2011). The company had a highly innovative drug in clinical development which was about to be launched on the market. According to clinical testing, the drug was very good; unfortunately there was uncertainty about the consequences of derived cardiovascular side-effects. As the company was approaching the commercial launch of the drug, management decided to call in a leading, international business consulting company in order to perform a thorough analysis of the company's launch preparations. After a few months of very intensive analysis involving large parts of the organization, the consultants' conclusion was that it was imperative that the drug was launched on the US market before or, at the very latest, at the same time as a major competitor launched its product. The company negotiated a solution with an American development partner which allowed the company to market the product half a year earlier at a rather high price. However, the company failed.

The company failed because through the agreement it had advanced its regulatory filing and market approval timing so much that it was not able to address the regulatory concerns from authorities with convincing arguments and robust data. And secondly, the company was left unprotected when their competitors found out about the lack of scientific documentation and started attacking the company in any way they could. The company was hit by the negative attention. As soon as it was known in the healthcare system that doctors should be careful and observe the negative side-effects of the new substance, negative over-reporting took place, effectively killing the product. The company was eventually forced to take the product off the market. However, a comprehensive and costly clinical safety study, involving thousands of patients, demonstrated that the product was not associated with a higher mortality rate than one of the most prescribed drugs within the indication area – in fact, quite to the contrary. In value terms, however, the company lost everything because commercially it did not make sense to relaunch the drug on a large scale. And it was large sums of money the company lost, not only when considering consultant fees and the high amount paid to the American partner, but in particular when considering that the competing drug which they were trying to surpass in development speed reached peak sales of 5–6 billion USD per year.

Based on the above experience, one of the executive directors of the pharmaceutical company concluded the following:

> It may well be that we initially won half a year, because the consultant could point to the fact that if you win the first-to-market battle, then you are very likely to win the battle for market shares. But the world is not so simple. It is incredibly complex. In reality, the world is so unbelievably complex that one must respond with a sort of humility and be very cautious of any straight-forward rational business model. And the lesson learned is that one must never automatically believe that people from the outside with overall industry knowledge can go in and be better to diagnose the situation of the company than we are.
>
> *(Nørreklit and Nørreklit, 2011: 128)*

Does empowerment pay off?

More recent research on the impact of TQM on financial performance has confirmed Likert and Bowers' (1969) results that management behaviour drives quality and profitability. In particular, Samson and Terziovski (1999) show that the leadership and management of people aspects of the TQM framework are highly significant predictors of operational performance. While the empowerment of employees appears to be a panacea in practice, this claim is not uncontested in academic research. Baum and Wally (2003) conducted a longitudinal study on the direct influence of empowerment on decision speed and company performance involving 318 CEOs. They also tested the indirect effect of empowerment on decision-making, and then on performance. Decision speed proves to be a predictor of company performance in their model. In summary, Baum and Wally (2003) find that the decentralization of operative decisions (empowerment) enhances both decision speed and performance. In contrast, their results suggest positive effects on decision speed and performance when keeping strategic decisions centralized (no empowerment). We have already made this argument and warned against shifting strategic decisions – e.g., on quality – to the operative shop floor level where the link to the cost of quality is lost. Similar to these first findings, Baum and Wally (2003) report that decision speed and performance increase when non-routine tasks are not formalized for employees (empowerment). Again, in distinct contrast, they show that decision speed is significantly higher when routine tasks are strictly formalized for employees (no empowerment). This last finding is also intuitive: complex, standardized processes that may occur in manufacturing, service or financial companies – or even more specifically, occurrences in nuclear power plants or military operations – require high reaction speed. Non-formalization or empowerment decreases decision speed in these contexts and can significantly endanger the success of such operations.

What happens when customer satisfaction and quality are not maximized?

As an aftermath to this evidence, we would like to show that a company can be successful when optimizing rather than maximising customer surplus. Singapore Airlines (SIA) is an example of a company balancing quality levels and profitability. It is prominent for being a quality leader in some of its operations while opting to rigorously minimize quality in other areas. Heracleous and Wirtz (2010) followed the airline industry from 2001 to 2009 and identified SIA as an industry leader in cost, quality and profitability: SIA held the cost per critical available seat kilometre (ASK) down to 4.58 US cents, setting itself far above other full-service airlines, from Europe or the US, that incurred between 8–16 cents per ASK. Hence, SIA could even compete with no-frills carriers that incur between 4–8 cents per ASK. At the same time, SIA has won several prizes for outstanding quality services. This has enabled SIA to charge premium prices at low costs and to achieve above-average industry profitability. In 2009, SIA reported a net profit margin of almost 10 per cent while the industry profitability was slightly negative on average. The recipe allowing SIA to hold this position has been high quality in some processes while rigorously neglecting quality in other processes. Financial performance measurements were always in focus.

On the one hand, the examples where SIA has opted for high quality – and has even saved money – read like many other success stories from the quality literature that a consultant may tell: in 2009, the aeroplane fleet was less than half the age of those of its competitors (74 vs. 160 months), and it depreciated faster (15 vs. 25 years). This fact has attracted customers both for reasons of comfort and safety. As a side-effect, SIA's maintenance costs were only four per cent of total costs, and thereby lower than those of the competition: e.g. United Airlines with 5.9 per cent. The 14,500 SIA employees were initially trained for 16 weeks – twice the industry average – plus 110 annual hours of retraining. This has helped SIA to establish a service culture at low cost, for instance a CRM system where cabin members memorize the names of VIP passengers as well as their preferences, e.g., in magazines. This culture also has a spontaneous side to it that may include being attentive to, e.g., passengers who are in need of a charger cable for a laptop, or who have special meal requests. Also, customers have appreciated the on-demand entertainment systems with Dolby sound in all classes, the widest business-class seats in the industry as well as the 'book-the-cook' service that allows passengers in business and first class to order their favourite meals in advance.

On the other hand, many of SIA's actions seem to contradict the quality-enthusiastic mainstream of the literature: SIA has secured its outstanding profitability by *not* differentiating itself in standard processes that do not impress customers (e.g. hygiene factors). Instead, these are quite standardized and cost-efficient. SIA has also consistently refused other quality aspects considered 'best practice' in the airline industry: SIA has eliminated marmalade from the regular menu since too few customers consumed it. Similarly, SIA has not been afraid to take only sufficient food for two-thirds of its passengers on night flights, since the historic consumption rate is lower. As another example, SIA developed an industry-leading biometric system allowing passengers to clear immigration and check-in and get their boarding passes in about 60 seconds. Once implemented, this high-quality system exhibited acceptance problems with customers. Instead of patronizing their clients with their high-quality check-in, SIA reacted quickly and abandoned the system in favour of the no-frills conventional method.

SIA's conviction that quality should not be so costly that it interferes with bottom-line profits is most apparent in back-office processes that customers do not get in touch with. SIA's revenue management system is a simplistic off-the-shelf solution well below the industry's 'best practice', e.g., the customized systems of Lufthansa and American Airlines. Other processes like ticketing, IT and payroll are outsourced to a low-cost Indian provider. The company's headquarters is – unlike that of its competitors – not a classy skyscraper but an old hangar at Changi Airport, with spartan equipment and only a few employees working on a tight schedule. The extensive training programmes are all held in-house, avoiding the cost of external facilities, catering or independent coaches. As a result, SIA has been able to hold its 'other costs' (total costs less fuel, labour, depreciation and aircraft rentals) at 29 per cent, well below the 38 per cent of relevant competitors.

To run such a system, the employees must have an incentive scheme that is consistent with the stipulated objective of ensuring quality only if customers are willing to pay for it. SIA has not linked its incentives to non-financial value drivers, like quality, but to the overall profit: while SIA's fixed salaries are well below industry average, employees can earn a bonus of up to 50 per cent depending on overall profitability. Impeccable customer satisfaction, the highest relative quality in the industry, state-of-the-art processes or innovation are not intrinsic values for SIA. They must always be commensurate with the pertinent cost and the customers' WTP.

While SIA is an interesting illustration of a solution to the quality-cost trade-off, managers faced with such a decision problem must be able to acquire the necessary information for making informed decisions. Several authors offer solutions for trade-offs between the different costs of quality when the total cost of quality is predetermined (e.g., Khang and Myint, 1999; Omurgonulsen, 2009; San Cristóbal, 2009; Su, Shi, and Lai, 2009).

Conclusions and discussion

We conclude that some of the currently dominant PMSs are influenced by the strategic issues of non-financial indicators such as quality. Consequently, they impinge directly on the use of resources and thus on costs. Also, the analysis above shows that the underlying assumption of specific generic strategic actions is not financially sound. The delivery of relative superior quality to the customers does not necessarily create high profitability. Similarly, cost-efficient internal business processes in the form of efficiency in compliance quality and innovation do not automatically lead to customer satisfaction and loyalty. In addition, organizational learning and growth do not guarantee efficient internal processes. As a result, these indicators cannot be used to anticipate future financial performance. Therefore, they do not solve the problem of historically oriented accounting data in decision-making. The assumptions of generic strategic actions do not hold because the financial results of achieving greater customer satisfaction and compliance quality of course depend on costs and customers' willingness to pay, i.e. matching of costs and revenues.

The basic problem is that the assumption of a generic relationship does not match the complexity of the individual business. Since many company actions are of a social and idiosyncratic kind, they do not follow laws like the natural sciences that retain validity over time. Many of the actions may be better described by the concept of 'finality' than a cause-and-effect relationship. Finality implies that a person believes that a given action is a means to an end. It may take several means to reach the end and any means may have numerous other effects. There is no single, stable general law. Ways of competing and becoming a successful business change over time along with changes in technological, economic and social structures.

In relation to the reliability of a finality relationship, we have to keep in mind that the generic actions depict the structure of the business world between the 1970s and the 1990s. The 'best practices' of successful peers and bold success stories of all kinds of management concepts have spread among companies – even without proving to improve profitability (Strang and Macy, 2001: 171). The danger of this is the use of the model in an unsuitable context where basic assumptions are not met. In particular, 25 years after the take-off of the quality movement, it might be time to discuss new types of strategic actions for possible inclusion in a PMS. Although the management control of quality is still important, we are not in the same context as in the period when Japanese companies were out-competing their Western competitors through far better quality. At the same time, many Western companies experienced a business context where the opportunity costs of low quality were very high. We now have to respond to new types of challenges with contemporary strategic actions and PMSs. Conceptual frameworks – updated to our current environment(!) – are needed to deepen our contemporary understanding of how business performance is created. For this reason, management accountants have to be critical as to whether the chosen strategic actions are financially sound.

Thus, a more crucial problem of the assumed generic relationships in PMSs is the mismatch of costs and revenues. Since the institutional formula of accounting has a collectively recognized status in the evaluation of companies and their actions (Nørreklit, Nørreklit, and Mitchell, 2010), the logic of the accounting formula is always at stake in the financial evaluation of an action. A logical relationship is very different from a cause-and-effect relationship. Logic is a rational element inherent in our ability to calculate and reason in a stringent logical manner (Edwards, 1972; Nørreklit, 2000; Nørreklit et al., 2010). It concerns not only maths and formal logic, but also reasoning through the building of concepts that are essential for organizing social structures, including conceptual accounting models. Accordingly, the double-entry accounting system is a logical conceptual system that has been developed to observe the financial situation of a company. For example, the profitability of a business unit or managerial action cannot be directly observed empirically but only indirectly by the logic of the accounting formula (Malina et al., 2007; Nørreklit, Nørreklit, and Mitchell, 2007). ROI, EVA and NPV are accounting concepts serving the purpose of calculating financial performance measures for performance evaluation and decision-making.

Also, it follows that profitability depends on the revenues and costs attributable to customer satisfaction. It may be that profits are conditioned by a certain level of customer satisfaction, but customer satisfaction is not the cause of profitability. Following the thoughts of micro-economics, it is reasonable to assume that any transaction with customers is conditioned by i) the customers' satisfaction, i.e. that the value to the customer is higher than the price, and ii) the company's marginal costs being lower than its marginal revenue. Similarly, gaining higher profits and quality simultaneously implies that any increase in revenue must not be exceeded by the marginal cost for achieving this quality. If customers' willingness to pay is lower than the cost incurred, producing higher quality will decrease profitability. Accordingly, in order to measure the effect of a company's strategic action on profitability, individual accounting models are used, not pooled statistical observations across industries. The distinction between a logical and a causal relationship is crucial. For decision-making and performance evaluation, it implies that companies should not solely rely on statistically proven generic strategies (causal relationship) but should rather draw on the financial calculus of accounting (logic relationship), although imperfect (Nørreklit, 2000).

Statistical analysis is often used to derive insights on companies on average, but often the uniqueness of the individual company is not taken into account. Covariance or correlation between (non-)financial value drivers is not synonymous with causality. Hence, drawing conclusions on such a basis must be done with caution. However, the PIMS model and the BSC take a dubious intellectual short-cut when deriving generic strategic actions from statistical relationships between generic actions and profitability. Specifically, Buzzell and Gale (1987) and Kaplan and Norton (1996) stress that the profitability of a company improves significantly with increasing customer satisfaction. This forms the basis for the assertion that superior customer-perceived quality leads to high profitability. However, one cannot derive from covariance or correlation between customer satisfaction and profitability that customer satisfaction leads to financial success. Taking the opposite view, one could, for example, argue that financially successful companies only sell to customers that are profitable; otherwise, the companies would not be deemed successful. Buzzell and Gale (1987) and Kaplan and Norton (1996) also omit to mention the possible importance of mediating or moderating variables. For example, it could be the accountant calculating the profitability of products and customers who prevents the company from selling to groups of satisfied or loyal customers that are not profitable. This disregard of accounting is also found in that the PIMS model only analyses companies that are profitable. Hence, the analysis does not include companies that went bankrupt by producing highly satisfied and loyal customers.[1]

In a similar vein, Buzzell and Gale (1987) argue that the choice of the 'right' markets with the 'right' products is decisive for profitability. Indirectly, they advocate that companies should target the group of customers that involves low costs and gives high prices, i.e. companies should target highly profitable customers to become highly profitable. However, that a profitable turnover produces a financially profitable result is a logical relationship inherent in the institutional formula of accounting. Seeing this as a causal relationship is therefore misleading. Similarly, when Kaplan and Norton (1996) point out that a large market share with highly profitable customers is the driver of a good financial result, the relationship to which they point is a logical one (Nørreklit, 2000). Overall, the PIMS study and the BSC disregard the constitutive role of the institutional formula of accounting.

Finally, applying conclusions from knowledge about one phenomenon to knowledge about another may pose problems. More specifically, the costs of poor quality may be high, but this does not allow for the *argumentum e contrario* that high quality is free. Likewise, non-satisfied customers may be expensive, but again this does not allow for the converse argument that satisfied customers are inexpensive. Such conclusions would be a logical fallacy, which statistical analyses are not able to detect.

In sum, applying financial measurement to decision-making, performance evaluation and managerial decisions is crucial, although the measurement instruments are imperfect. However, one may argue that by emphasizing accounting calculus, we are back to the early period of quality management when the link between quality and cost accounting was especially apparent. However, as mentioned in the introduction, these measurements have been heavily criticized for their lack of ability to estimate both future-oriented and business-relevant information. In many cases, information on future performance is a highly complex issue involving numerous aspects. We need to deal with the problems related to the estimation of the necessary information for accounting calculations. Both past results and the impact of future opportunities should form part of the provided information. However, the future being uncertain, estimation and valuation will always be partly subjective. It follows that the profoundness of the analysis of the situation, and thus of the meaning of the data, depends not only on the available techniques but also on the soundness of the way in which management perceives the information in a particular context. We need sound observation of historical accounting facts and profound estimation and judgement about the future. The dynamics of the world will always tend to make information from the past insufficient as a basis for deciding and evaluating future action. However, an important issue is to develop abilities to make future judgements. Therefore, the learning perspective becomes important when producing and judging information (Jakobsen, Mitchell, and Nørreklit, 2010; Nørreklit et al., 2007).

Note

1 Moreover, results are based on statements made by the companies themselves, only occasionally tested on customers, and corrected only if this seemed appropriate (Buzzell and Gale, 1987: 105). Of course, it is a reasonable assumption that a company with good earnings believes that its customers consider

its products better than those of the competition. It is highly probable that good results will cause company employees to make positive statements when presenting their customers' views. Thus, the direction of the causality is also questionable: it may point the other way. Or it may be a matter of greater complexity.

Bibliography

Baum, J. R. and Wally, S. 2003. Strategic Decision Speed and Firm Performance. *Strategic Management Journal*, 24(11): 1107–1129.

Biddle, G., Bowen, R. and Wallace, J. 1997. Does EVA Beat Earnings? Evidence on Associations with Stock Returns and Firm Values. *Journal of Accounting and Economics*, 24: 301–336.

Buzzell, R. D. and Gale, B.T. 1987. *The PIMS Principles: Linking Strategy to Performance*. New York, NY: The Free Press.

Buzzell, R. D., Gale, B.T. and Sultan, R. G. M. 1975. Market Share: A Key to Profitability. *Harvard Business Review*, 53(1): 97–106.

Copeland, T. E., Koller, T. and Murrin, J. 2000. *Valuation: Measuring and Managing the Value of Companies* (3rd edn). New York, NY: John Wiley and Sons.

Dearden, J. 1969. The Case against ROI Control. *Harvard Business Review*, 47(3): 124–135.

Deming, E. 1982. *Quality, Productivity and Comptetitive Position*. Boston, MA: MIT Center for Advanced Engineering Study.

Edwards, P. 1972. *The Encyclopaedia of Philosophy*. New York, NY: Macmillian Publishing Co., Inc. and The Free Press.

Feigenbaum, A.V. 1956. Total Quality Control. *Harvard Business Review*, 34(6): 93–101.

Gandz, J. 1990. The Employee Empowerment Era. *Business Quarterly*, 55(2): 74.

Heracleous, L. and Wirtz, J. 2010. Singapore Airlines' Balancing Act. *Harvard Business Review*, 88(7/8): 145–149.

Ittner, C. D. and Larcker, D. F. 1998. Innovations in Performance Measurement: Trends and Research Implications. *Journal of Management Accounting Research*, 10: 205–238.

Jacob, R., Madu, C. N. and Tang, C. 2004. An Empirical Assessment of the Financial Performance of Malcolm Baldrige Award Winners. *International Journal of Quality and Reliability Management*, 21(8): 897–914.

Jakobsen, M., Mitchell, F. and Nørreklit, H. 2010. Internal Performance Measurement Systems: Problems and Solutions. *Journal of Asian-Pacific Business*, 11(4): 258–277.

Jensen, M. C. 2010. Value Maximization, Stakeholder Theory, and the Corporate Objective Function. *Journal of Applied Corporate Finance*, 22(1): 32–42.

Jones, T. O. and Sasser Jr, W. E. 1995. Why Satisfied Customers Defect. *Harvard Business Review*, 73(6): 88–91.

Juran, J. 1985. The Quality Edge: A Management Tool. *PIMA* (May).

Kaiser, K. and Young, S. D. 2009. Need Cash? Look Inside Your Company. *Harvard Business Review*, 87(5): 64–71.

Kamen, J. M. 1977. Controlling 'Just Noticeable Differences' in Quality. *Harvard Business Review*, 55(6): 12–164.

Kaplan, R. S. 1984. Yesterday's Accounting Undermines Production. *Harvard Business Review*, 62(4): 95–101.

Kaplan, R. S. and Atkinson, A. A. 1989. *Advanced Management Accounting*. New Jersey, NY: Prentice Hall.

Kaplan, R. S. and Norton, D. P. 1996. *The Balanced Scorecard: Translating Strategy into Action*. Boston, MA: Harvard Business School Press.

Kaplan, R. S. and Norton, D. P. 2000. *The Strategy-Focussed Organization: How Balanced Scorecard Companies Thrive in the New Business Environment*. Boston, MA: Harvard Business School Press.

Kaplan, R. S. and Norton, D. P. 2001. Transforming the Balanced Scorecard from Performance Measurement to Strategic Management. *Accounting Horizons*, 15(1): 87–104.

Kaplan, R. S. and Norton, D. P. 2004. How Strategy Maps Frame an Organization's Objectives. *Financial Executive*, 20(2): 40–45.

Kaplan, R. S. and Norton, D. P. 2008. Mastering the Management System. *Harvard Business Review*, 86(1): 62–77.

Khang, D. B. and Myint, Y. M. 1999. Time, Cost and Quality Trade-Off in Project Management: A Case Study. *International Journal of Project Management*, 17(4): 249–256.

Likert, R. and Bowers, D. G. 1969. Organisational Theory and Human Resource Accounting. *The American Psychologist* (September), 585–592.

Lynch, R. I. and Cross, K. F. 1991. *Measure Up: The Essential Guide to Measuring Business Performance*. London: Mandarin.

Malina, M. A., Nørreklit, H. and Selto, F. H. 2007. Relations among Measures, Climate of Control, and Performance Measurement Models. *Contemporary Accounting Research*, 24(3): 935–982.

Maslow, A. 1954. *Motivation and Personality*. New York, NY: Harper.

Mitra, D. and Golder, P. N. 2007. Quality Is in the Eye of the Beholder. *Harvard Business Review*, 85(4): 26–28.

Nobel, J. L. 1990. A New Approach for Justifying Computer-Integrated Manufacturing. In B. J. Brinker (ed.), *Emerging Practices in Cost Mangement*. Massachusetts, MA: Warren, Gorham, Lamont.

Nørreklit, H. 2000. The Balance on the Balanced Scorecard: A Critical Analysis of Some of Its Assumptions. *Management Accounting Research*, 11(1): 65–88.

Nørreklit, H. and Nørreklit, L. 2011. Managerial Knowledge in a Research-Based Company. In M. Jakobsen, I.-L. Johanson and H. Nørreklit (eds), *An Actor's Approach to Management: Conceptual Framework and Company Practices*. Copenhagen: DJOEF.

Nørreklit, H., Nørreklit, L. and Mitchell, F. 2007. Theoretical Conditions for Validity in Accounting Performance Measurement. In A. Neely (ed.), *Business Performance Measurement*. Cambridge: Cambridge University Press.

Nørreklit, H., Nørreklit, L. and Mitchell, F. 2010. Towards a Paradigmatic Foundation for Accounting Practice. *Accounting, Auditing and Accountability Journal*, 23(6): 733–758.

Omurgonulsen, M. 2009. A Research on the Measurement of Quality Costs in the Turkish Food Manufacturing Industry. *Total Quality Management and Business Excellence*, 20(5): 547–562.

Porter, M. E. 1980. *Competitive Strategy*. New York, NY: Free Press.

Ridgway, V. F. 1956. Dysfunctional Consequences of Performance Measurements. *Administrative Science Quarterly*, 1(2): 240–247.

Robertson, M., Swan, J. and Newell, S. 1996. The Role of Networks in the Diffusion of Technological Innovation. *Journal of Management Studies*, 33(3): 333–359.

Samson, D. and Terziovski, M. 1999. The Relationship Between Total Quality Management Practices and Operational Performance. *Journal of Operations Management*, 17(4): 393–409.

San Cristóbal, J. R. 2009. Time, Cost, and Quality in a Road-Building Project. *Journal of Construction Engineering and Management*, 135(11): 1271–1274.

Shank, J. K. 1989. Strategic Cost Management: New Wine, or Just New Bottles? *Journal of Management Accounting Research*, 1: 47–65.

Stewart, G. B. 1991. *The Quest for Value: A Guide for Senior Managers*. New York, NY: Harper Business.

Strang, D. and Macy, M. W. 2001. In Search of Excellence: Fads, Success Stories, and Adaptive Emulation. *American Journal of Sociology*, 107(1): 147–182.

Su, Q., Shi, J.-H. and Lai, S.-J. 2009. Research on the Trade-Off Relationship within Quality Costs: A Case Study. *Total Quality Management and Business Excellence*, 20(12): 1395–1405.

Wilson, D. D. and Collier, D. A. 2000. An Empirical Investigation of the Malcolm Baldrige National Quality Award Causal Model. *Decision Sciences*, 31(2): 361–390.

Wirtz, J. 2011. How to Deal with Customer Shakedowns. *Harvard Business Review*, 89(4): 24–24.

Wisner, J. D. and Eakins, S. G. 1994. A Performance Assessment of the US Baldrige Quality Award Winners. *International Journal of Quality and Reliability Management*, 11(2): 8–25.

Yu, W., Jamasb, T. and Pollitt, M. 2009. Willingness-to-Pay for Quality of Service: An Application to Efficiency Analysis of the UK Electricity Distribution Utilities. *The Energy Journal*, 30(4): 1–48.

21

Methodologies for managing performance measurement

Lino Cinquini, Falconer Mitchell,
Hanne Nørreklit and Andrea Tenucci

Introduction

Over the past two decades much attention has been given to the development of performance measurement packages. Different packages have been suggested such as the SMART pyramid (Lynch and Cross, 1991), the Tableau de Bord (Chiapello and Lebas, 1996), the Performance Prism (Neely and Adams, 2001) and the Balanced Scorecard (Kaplan and Norton, 1992; 1996). From a technical point of view these proposals differ mainly in the way they classify the measurements on which they are based and the way the measurements are interrelated (Neely, 2007). However, a common characteristic is that they aim to promote operations that will allow the entity to survive and produce good financial performance. To do this in a corporate context the revenues, costs, investment and funding must all be monitored through the performance system. Thus, performance measurement has a close relationship to cost control. Without the cost consciousness that measurement brings, the cost dimension of performance can be neglected and financial performance can deteriorate.

Most research has focused on the adoption (Chenhall and Langfield-Smith, 1998), the diffusion (Ax and Bjørnenak, 2005) and the success (Ittner, Larcker, and Randall, 2003) of these models with the predominant focus on the Balanced Scorecard. Also some attention has been given to the linking of the levels of responsibilities (Haas and Kleingeld, 1999; Kolehmainen, 2010). However, little attention has been paid to the management methodology by which such performance measurement models are to be designed and used in practice and their implications for the adopting organization. This is the focal point of this paper.

In order to pursue this focus, we adopt the concept of practical methodology as our conceptual framework. Thus, we distinguish between scientific and practical methodology (Nørreklit et al., 2010). A methodology includes ideas of what reality is about (ontology) and what knowledge is and how it is acquired (epistemology) (Arbnor and Bjerke, 1994). It guides the methods and techniques for knowledge creation and use. Alternative methodologies for engaging in research are widely discussed in the literature (see e.g. Chua, 1986; Ryan, Scapens, and Theobald, 2002). However, alternative methodologies can also be applied to the practice of measuring organizational performance (Norreklit and Schoenfeld, 2000; Nørreklit, H., Nørreklit, L., and Mitchell, 2010). Nonetheless, research literature has neglected the issue of methodologies for using performance management techniques in practice. The failure to address this issue may have fatal implications for company practices as that methodology provides the framework for the knowledge creation process and employee action. Some methodologies may even destroy good company practices: 'I have so far developed the proposition that bad management theories are, at present, destroying good management practices' (Ghoshal, 2005: p. 86). Expanding Taylorism from the factory shop floor to the managerial doctrine is considered as particularly problematic. Taylorism takes a mechanical view of a company: 'As Frederick Taylor had made complex assembly repeatable by breaking it down to its simplest component tasks, so the new doctrine (. . .) aimed to make the management of complex corporations systematic and predictable' (Mintzberg, Lampel, Quinn, and Ghoshal, 1996: p. 305). One of the most significant results of this approach has been ability to model machine-like, homogeneous structures and systems even in very large, diversified companies. The methodology still exists and is used in many organizations. When striving for competitive advantage through producing standardized products at low cost, there is a risk of losing the unique resources of the firm which create supra-normal profit returns and sustained competitive advantage (Barney, 1991). Although destroying may be too strong a word, the dichotomy of competitive advantage vs. sustained competitive advantage merits the investigation of the implications of management methodologies for company practice and hence the strategic development of the company.

The purpose of this paper is to describe two contrasting methodologies of managing performance measurement and explore their implications for employee practices and hence the emerging strategy of the company. More specifically, when analysing the performance measurement system at the interface between two different parent companies and one of their respective subsidiaries, we witness two companies that use similar accounting measures as the basis of their performance system, but apply two very different methodologies for designing and using performance management. The two different methodological approaches are identified as coming close to a systems approach and a more actor-based approach (Arbnor and Bjerke, 1997). Initially, both subsidiaries were strong enterprises with high value and quality of market offering, market share, staying power and experience. Additionally, both operated within highly attractive industrial sectors. As will be further explained below, the study revealed that the two methodologies for performance measurement for controlling the subsidiaries were not only distinctly different, but they also had significant implications for human motivation and action. The observation of the profound differences in the behavioural implication of PMS methodology led to a reflection on the relationship between methodologies of performance measurement and emerging strategic positioning. Consequently the paper explores the following research questions: i) What implications do a systems approach and an actor-based approach, respectively, to performance management have on employee action? ii) What are the strategic rationales of the two types of performance measurement methodology?

Before addressing the research questions we describe our research methodology. Second, we describe our conceptual framework with respect to methodologies for design and use of performance measurement. We then explore two case companies that follow different strategies and apply the two different methodologies for design and use of PMS. We finally discuss and provide conclusions on the two different strategic rationalities behind the two methodologies of using performance measurements. Thus the study emphasizes that it is not simply the nature or design of a PMS but also the way it is used that will determine its impact on an organization, and ultimately its practical success.

Research methods and methodology

We apply an interpretive perspective in our research. Our research is not based on the establishment of a priori hypotheses. It is based on the researchers' observations grounded in their contact with the interviewees and the triangulation of this evidence with secondary sources (like internal reports and minutes) (Ryan, Scapens, and Theobald, 2002). As the paper seeks to explore aspects of human behaviour that are not objectively observable but are instead created through the interaction with the actors' perceptions and understanding (Ahrens and Chapman, 2007), the research problem requires a qualitative approach. We preferred the richness and depth of data collectable with case studies through interviews over the narrowness of quantitative methodologies.

Two multinational US companies with subsidiaries located in Italy were selected. The two companies, hereafter called Company A and Company B for anonymity, have similarities and differences in terms of organizational variables. Firstly, both are US subsidiaries located in Italy. Secondly, they are both market leaders although they belong to different sectors: Company A is in manufacturing and Company B in software.

The study is based on semi-structured interviews. The interview introduction covers the interviewee's role within the company. Then we investigate the company's approach to the design and use of performance measurement and management together with perceptions on the factors affecting the system. Three interviews were conducted in Company A with people in different roles: the Chief Administrative Office (CAO), the Finance Manager and the Commercial Operations Manager. In Company B two interviews were conducted, the first one with the Finance and Administration Manager and the second with the Business Developer. Each interview took about 90 minutes on average. They were tape-recorded and then transcribed in order to facilitate the analysis of the data.

Methodologies of performance measurement

With respect to methodology we explore two rather different methodological approaches: the systems approach and an actor's approach. The systems approach dominates within mainstream performance management while the actor's approach is an emerging framework grounded in pragmatic constructivism (Arbnor and Bjerke, 1994; Nørreklit et al., 2007; Nørreklit, 2011).

Systems approach to performance measurement

Influential scholarly research (Churchman, 1968; Anthony, 1965) has advocated the construction of management accounting systems from the point of view of systems theory. The systems approach (Arbnor and Bjerke, 1997: pp. 109–155) is rooted in a paradigm of realism that perceives the world as objective. Physical and social phenomena are approached in the same way. Accordingly, the systems approach does not include the subjective perspective of the individual. It excludes subjective phenomena and therefore does not take the individualistic intentions, perceptions and understandings of the employees into account, but considers the employees as a system component with the role of serving the interests of the whole organization that must constantly adapt to the changing environment. The individual employee does not have personal objectives. Only the organizational system has objectives, which the individual employee has to subscribe to. Within the systems approach, the objective of the management control system is to describe the organizational system in order to control and monitor the system, including its components and its relations to the environment.

The textbooks on management control systems by Anthony and Govindarajan (2007) and the Balanced Scorecard by Kaplan and Norton (1996) take the systems approach to performance management. Their frameworks for performance measurement are among the most advocated among business practitioners. Below we sketch their systems approach to the design and use of performance measurements.

When designing a performance measurement system, the point of departure of the mainstream performance management models of a business unit is the strategy formulated by the top management. Starting from an observation of the environment, the top management engages in formulating the company's overall vision, strategies, objectives and targets. The strategy relies on an inside-outside approach to strategy based on the idea that the strategy of a firm should be driven by the factual forces in the competitive environment (Porter, 1980 and 1985). Thus Porter (1980, 1985) argues that the essence of formulating a competitive strategy lies in matching a company to the competitive forces in the industry in which it competes. Its strategy has to be based on the market segments to be served. At this point the identification and optimization of the internal business processes should follow in order to excel in the specific targeted market segment. From this perspective, belonging to a sector is considered a crucial driver of performance; strategic options are limited to cost leadership, differentiation and focusing, and their sustainability is determined by the 'five forces' of competition (rivalry, the threat of substitutes, buyer power, supplier power, and barriers to entry). The strategic framework is characterized by the central role of *rationality*, which manifests itself in the adequacy of internal strengths and weaknesses with respect to the environmental context and in the sequential phases of thought before action.

The performance measurements are used in order to decide on, implement and control the strategy as formulated by the top management. During the strategy formulation process, performance measurements are needed to estimate the implications of different strategic alternatives. Also, they are proposed for use in a benchmarking process to observe the competitive position of the company and to detect non-value-adding activities and hence give feedback to the company about how to improve competitive advantages (Kaplan and Norton, 1996: p. 19), i.e. increase the fit with the environment. Resources are to be allocated to the activities and units that give the highest added value. Non-value-adding activities are to be eliminated and thereby show how the system promotes cost control and reduction.

Furthermore, the performance measurements communicate strategic objectives to the management and operational level and subsequently monitor the performance of people and activities (Anthony and Govindarajan, 2007; Kaplan and Norton, 1996). To implement the strategy of a business unit the strategic objectives and targets are to be formulated at the top level and subsequently deployed to objectives and targets at lower levels. Through a hierarchical top-down decomposition process, objectives and targets are deployed and hence transformed into lower-level goals (Anthony and Govindarajan, 2007; Kaplan and Norton, 1996). Norms and objectives are described in financial and non-financial terms. The top-down decomposition process is a sort of analytical method 'that *cascades* high level measures to lower organizational measures' (Kaplan and Norton, 1996: p. 213). The vision is communicated through executive announcements, videos and town meetings (Kaplan and Norton, 1996: p. 202) with no personal involvement of senior management.

The subsequent evaluations of individual managers and employees are based on their ability to fulfil the norms for the activities for which they are responsible. Feedback is given by comparing the actual performance with the norm. A reward system ensures that the employee is paid accordingly. The model assumes a stimulus-response pattern of action. When the individual employee's performance is compared with the norm, and the employee is paid accordingly, he will find ways of adjusting his or her behaviour to attain the required results. In accordance with systems theory, employees follow a behaviouristic reaction pattern as a mechanical component in a system with the role of serving the interests of the whole system, i.e. the company. The individuals find the motivation for their actions in rules and in the demands made by others, i.e. they are extrinsically motivated (Argyris and Kaplan, 1994).

The method assumes that top management know the right strategy and the right norm. The local conditions are supposed to be as defined by the top management. The method places little emphasis on any implementation problems and special local conditions. Also, the issue of winning support for the system is considered unproblematic.

Actor's approach to performance measurement

As we see it, an actor's approach (Arbnor and Bjerke, 1997) is rooted in the paradigm of pragmatic constructivism (Nørreklit, 2011). Pragmatic constructivism (Nørreklit et al., 2007) defines a company by virtue of the thoughts, values and actions of the individual employees, and the interaction of all employees together with available resources creates the reality of the company. A firm is a social construction created by individual human beings. The individual is an actor who constructs himself in interaction with the environment. In order to be successful, he has to integrate the following four dimensions of reality: facts, possibilities, values and communication. First, an actor's business decision has to be grounded in available possibilities as well as facts about the particular activity. In order to be real and not merely wishfully fantasize, the possibilities have to be integrated with facts. However, the integration of facts and possibilities has no meaning or any value in itself. In order to make the actor act the organization has to take into account the actor's motivating energy. There must be some values that motivate the individual actor – otherwise he will not act. Finally, in order to be social and cooperate with others the actor has to communicate with others. Accordingly, the actors' perceptions, understanding and values have to be taken into account when managing a company.

As its point of departure the actor's approach uses the phenomenological grounding of the strategy in the local practices and mind-sets of the employees as well as the overall vision and business situation of the company as it is presented by the top management (Nørreklit et al., 2007). Accordingly, the strategy is to be formulated with a phenomenological grounding in the resources and possibilities of the organization and in its employees interacting with the environment. Consequently, the strategy is developed using both a resource approach and a market-driven approach. This inside-out view argues that strategy should be driven by the firm's resources and capabilities in a dynamic learning process (Amit and Schoemaker, 1993; Wernerfelt, 1984; Prahalad and Hamel, 1990). *Resources* are the stocks of available factors owned and controlled by firms that are converted into final products or services by using a range of other firm assets and mechanisms (technology, management information systems, performance measurement systems and rewards, trust between management and labour, and more). *Capabilities* refer to a firm's capacity to deploy resources using information-based tangible or intangible organizational processes; capabilities are based on developing, carrying and exchanging information through the human capital of the firm (Amit and Schoemaker, 1993; Itami, 1987). In order to attain and sustain a competitive advantage, it is crucial to create and develop resources that will strengthen the firm's ability to obtain superior performance. Any industry or market reflects high uncertainty and in order to survive and stay ahead of competition, the company must necessarily develop new resources.

Our society is organized according to the institutional formula of accounting logic, and the business manager therefore has to take into account the issues of financial profitability and sustainability. Accordingly, the performance measurement system of accounting is to be used in a company to understand, structure and evaluate the economic aspects of decisions and to develop, co-ordinate and evaluate acts in an economically and reasonable manner. The purpose is to secure the profitability of the company. A company's use of the performance measurements and accounting methods adds an economic dimension to its decisions and actions and assures that these actions are not just based on criteria such as ideals, ambitions, power, etc.

Following an actor's approach, the goal system of the activities must be constructed on the basis of the perspectives of the top management and of the personnel. In addition, the goal system should be constructed to ensure mutual support of interdependent activities. Coherence is an important feature of the performance measurement system. It is concerned with facilitating groups of employees who, when acting in the system, 'contribute to the performance of other interdependent groups' of employees (Haas and Kleingeld, 1999: pp. 240–241) and hence contribute to the overall performance of the company. The design process is initiated from the top. However, the interaction between the various (groups of) employees involved takes place as dialogues. A dialogue is a dynamic and reflective process of conversation between two or more persons during which both parties pose questions and receive answers. Both are creative and logical in the process. Their understanding and concepts of reality get reflected in the dialogue. Information flows on several levels; concepts are developed. The dialogue is important in connection with the formulation of the performance measures linked to the point of view of the various (groups of) employees. It makes it possible to ensure that the actors in individual activities have the resources, competences and motivation to reach the end by the given means. If problems or opportunities are uncovered during performance measurement, this may contribute to strategy formulation and to bridging differences of perception and understanding so that goal congruence increases.

Not only the design of performance measurements, but also the use of the measurements has to be phenomenologically grounded. Pragmatic constructivism (Nørreklit et al., 2007) implies that performance measurements cannot be used without an understanding of the context in which they exist. An appropriate use of performance measurements means that one has to obtain knowledge about the specific situation, not only as presented by the measurement system, but also from a phenomenological perspective (Nørreklit et al., 2007). Accordingly, to get in-depth insight in a performance situation one has to uncover the reality of the business situation. This is a condition for adequately understanding the relationship between business reality and the measurement system. Thus validity, in relation to the use of performance measurements, is a quality derived from direct contact with the phenomena that are being measured. Using performance measurement may prove dangerous if one does not carefully study the actual situation at hand and instead just assume unjustifiably that the given measurements provide a true and adequate representation of the situation. Again, the dialogue can be used by the management to understand the work situation. Interaction through dialogue plays an important role in increasing both the managers' and the employees' awareness and understanding of the situation. Furthermore, it also has the advantage that the top managers can gather information relevant to the strategic development of the company and influence the employees in the direction intended. In-depth insight into the real business world is necessary for a valid interpretation of the performance measurement (Nørreklit et al., 2007).

Overall, the actor's approach assumes that people are intrinsically motivated. Intrinsic motivation means that individuals primarily find motivation within themselves while extrinsic motivation implies that they primarily find it in rules and the demands made by others (Argyris and Kaplan, 1994). Intrinsically motivated employees are vital if the organization wishes to have active and creative problem-solvers. Innovation and creative problem-solving require individuals with intrinsic drive, i.e., employees who see themselves as responsible and acting individuals. However, the extrinsic drivers of performance measurements are also important for the establishment of learning processes and for communication of rules and the kind of behaviour that is desirable and will be rewarded.

Cases of using performance measurement

In this section, we analyse the relationship between the methodology of designing and using performance measurement with a view to exploring their implications for business practice at a strategic level. For this purpose we analyse the performance measurement system of the two multinational case-study companies.

Case study 1: Company A

Company background

Company A was founded in 1956 and became a subsidiary of a large listed American company in 2002. The group turnover is about 300 million dollars of which 20 million are realized by the Italian business unit. The US parent company serves utility, industrial, and governmental customers worldwide, supplying products such as compressors, turbines, generators, and nuclear reactors. It has positioned itself as a first-class supplier of low voltage products, including wiring devices, residential and industrial electrical components, general purpose control products, enclosures and switchboards, as well as engineering solutions for industrial process automation. It also provides equipment that supports oil and gas distribution and services ranging from consulting and field engineering to environmental monitoring and product life-cycle management. The strategy of the parent company is dominated by 'mergers and acquisitions' and by outsourcing. To pursue financial success, it focuses on acquiring leading companies that have a strong business offering and operate in attractive industries.

The European division of the parent company is headquartered in Spain. Since its establishment in 1989, the division has grown rapidly through acquisitions and partnerships with ten businesses in different European countries. In 2007, it had 25 manufacturing facilities across Europe and some 6,000 employees. Company A is an Italian legal entity.

Company strategy

Ever since its foundation, Company A has been R&D-oriented. This was emphasized in 1981 when it established a Research Division with the aim of furthering the knowledge of relevant machines, techniques and methodologies. In this sense the strategy was driven by the firm's core competencies and resources with the aim of developing more and more such competencies and of investing in research in order to further develop the company resources. The company was also profit-oriented, but this orientation was seen more as a necessary condition for operation than as an objective in itself.

Following the acquisition by the multinational company in 2002 the strategy of Company A changed fundamentally. The acquired company had to move from its R&D-oriented strategy to a financially-oriented strategy. The key objective of the group was expressed in the financial result. Accounting profitability, efficiency and cost control were now of paramount importance. The strategic objectives for the acquired operation are to increase sales volume and cost efficiency and hence profitability. Operations are placed at the most efficient location. The parent company pursued standardization as a tool to obtain efficiency in its worldwide operations. The group works with Six Sigma procedures and the divisions and subsidiaries therefore operate in a highly rule-based and constrained conceptual framework. Also, the investment in R&D has been reduced. After a process of growth and efficiency improvement the intention is to resell the acquired company.

The strategic change is formulated in the following quote by the Finance Manager of Company A:

> I believe that doing business now is completely different from when we were privately owned, because the former owner spent, for example, 25% of the revenues per year on investments for new products. Thereby, you got the perception of great business continuity. The present parent company is not a product-driven company, but more a finance-driven company. The company buys companies in the market, merges them and maybe the following year they are sold to another company.
>
> *(Finance Manager)*

Performance measurement

The subsidiary is evaluated based on accounting profitability metrics and some non-financial metrics. Every four or five weeks, financial statements and reports on other performance measurements are prepared by the Financial Manager. The reports are sent to the headquarters in the US with observations on the main accounting figures (sales, profitability, credits, banks, suppliers). Each month an audit control activity is performed to establish how the subsidiary is operating. In addition, each item of the financial statement is further scrutinized every quarter and justifications are required for each balance sheet and income statement item. Within the Finance Division there is a 'special task force' that operates as a kind of internal auditor group and randomly chooses subsidiaries for in-depth control exercises. An intermediate control is scheduled by the European chief administrative officer over the alignment of all the documentation produced as well.

The performance measurement system of Company A has been constructed as a hierarchically top-down system with strict control. It has been designed and defined by headquarters. The annual target is determined by the parent company and divided into quarterly, monthly and weekly targets. Every target is then shared with each team member. For example, if the annual target is to achieve a sales level of 40 million dollars, this target is divided into a quarterly sales target of 10 million dollars. If there are five sales managers, each has an annual target of 2 million dollars, i.e. a quarterly sales target of 500,000 dollars each; this is also translated into a weekly target. Every department of the Italian subsidiary (Finance, Commercial Operations, Foreign sales and Service) has a set of metrics that are reviewed weekly. Performance metrics typically used in the Sales Office are 'the number of quotations sent out', 'the quality of quotations' or other parameters mainly based on customer survey or quality measurements.

The performance measurements are used for performance evaluation and reward. Every employee is evaluated on the basis of some metrics, established on a factual basis and considered at the end of the year. Based on the performance measurement system people are categorized into the following groups: top ten, high performers, average, and bottom ten. Thus, at the end of the year a ranking of the employee performances is issued: top 10 per cent are the 'top talent' and they get higher salary rates, 20 per cent are 'high performers', 60 per cent are average and the worst 10 per cent are the 'least effective'. The managers of the low-ranking 10 per cent need to take action to bring the 10 per cent up on the list and this process is monitored as well. A similar system exists for the Commercial Department, for Finance and for Sales. If the employee is included in the top decile, there are benefits; if in the bottom decile (the last percentage) the relevant managers need to help in developing the job with training and more focus on what the employee is doing. The manager presents a training list that the employee is expected to follow. If they remain 'least effective' for three years they seriously risk losing their jobs and careers.

Communication about performance takes place mechanically and the performance level is announced publicly, creating a 'shaming effect':

> If I prepare the reconciliation and my reconciliation is wrong or if I missed the deadline I receive an electronic letter asking for explanation, I have to justify the action to headquarters. If you reach all the milestones you can gain a bonus. On top of that your level of performance is put on the wall together with those of your colleagues – it is a race.
>
> *(Finance Manager)*

However, there are really no excuses for not living up to the standard. Thus, we witness the mechanical use of the performance system in that the standards overrule not only the individual's workflow but also life conditions such as illness:

> There is a lot of work to do. Every day is a race because every four weeks you need to create a report but you spend one week to do this report, two weeks to do the reconciliation and so when you have finished you have to start again. For example, this Sunday I completed the reconciliation for September but this is also the week for the report of October and there is no exemption, you have to do this. Also, there is no excuse; if you are sick it doesn't matter! So it is difficult because resources are so limited; I am alone, which is a problem since my boss just calls me from Ireland and says 'have this ready for tomorrow!'.
>
> *(Finance Manager)*

Company rules and standards are required to be applied in manufacturing, logistics and in making deals and managing the customers. No exceptions from the rules are allowed by the US parent company. It very much constrains the actions of the subsidiary. The managers of Company A perceive this as the parent company's way of ensuring a reliable reputation and thus overcoming possible incongruity with local habits and local culture.

> (. . .) You pursue profit, but you have to follow all the rules that headquarters decide, this is a matter of reputation. Their main reason for investing the money is to maintain the reputation of the company. So we have internal rules for compliance, for integrity, 'iron' rules – there are no exceptions, you need to comply with these rules. It is considered as the most important asset of the company. It is something more than branding . . . It is a matter of reliable reputation: 'Do the right thing always!'.
>
> *(Finance Manager)*

The performance measurements are also used in order to monitor and improve the quality. The continuous focus on the measurements implies that performance is considered and taken into account each and every day, all year round.

Implications of the performance measurement system

The mechanical application of rules and standards has behavioural implications. First the rigid standards cause problems when the standard norm does not fit the requirement for doing the job properly.

This creates frustration and disappointment in Company A. The employees feel caught between the performance norm as defined by headquarters and the norm to deliver the usual services as required by customers. The following quote illustrates that the performance system induces the employees not to do a better job, but to attain the minimum acceptable standard:

> If the work is standard, the metric is only a matter of how fast you do it, but if the work is not standard, there are a lot of other things that the metric cannot catch. So if you are to work as a standard man, you are like a 'monkey' . . . We Europeans say, 'OK, you have to do this and this but if you also make two other things that are not in the metrics, you do a better job', but for the people in the US you are just doing the job of another 'monkey'. . . .
>
> *(Finance Manager)*

The focus on achieving only the minimum standard implies that the employees feel perceived as monkeys. Also, the standard leads to non-flexibility in fulfilling customer demands. This is perceived as a problem in the Italian subsidiary because more flexibility with customers would benefit sales. Some customers do not want a monkey to serve them and hence may go to the competitor:

> (. . .) This is US policy, but this is a problem for us because our subsidiary is a small company. So when you have to apply the same terms and conditions for every product, even for one that costs only $200, it becomes very complicated. When you talk with the customer you have the proposal of one page, but the terms and conditions are thorny and the customer says 'okay, thank you but we go to your competitor'.
>
> *(Commercial Operations Manager)*

However, the performance measurement system appears efficient in controlling and improving operational quality according to the described requirement. It makes the employees focus on meeting the required quality features and commercializing the product:

> I think not everything is bad, there is also a good part, attending the quality compliance. Also I'm learning a lot about for example commercial operations. The system puts focus on the limitations and liabilities that are never taken into account in a traditional deal.
>
> *(Commercial Operations Manager)*

Secondly, the rigid, individualized and tight use of performance metrics creates some commonly recognized dysfunctional effects. Thus, it is part of conventional wisdom that what gets measured gets done, and this may create functional silos. The following quotes illustrate that the individual focus on one's own performance metrics has implications for costs incurred by others:

> (. . .) now we don't work together. Each department works alone. If my colleague needs some help for commercial operations it is his problem, not my problem. My problem is to do account reconciliation and not to create good relationships with the customers. He cannot get the metrics that can help him in his commercial operations. But in this way you create functional silos. The system does not encourage you to feel responsible for the entire process: the functions are completely separated. (. . .) you have colleagues but you don't feel you are in a team.
>
> *(Finance Manager)*

> In Hungary, the sales people are evaluated by the number of the orders entered into the SAP system. If you have a problem and you ask them to find contact information on a person you need to speak to, you can forget it. There will be no answer from them because they are not evaluated by helping you.
>
> *(Commercial Operations Manager)*

The system is not only ineffective in stimulating teamwork, but also in observing management performance and making people accountable. Since the achievement of many single objectives involves several cross-functional activities, the actions that lead to the achievement of the results are not controllable by an individual employee or a team. The following quotes illustrate that the individual feels frustrated because succeeding with a project, and hence performing, involves joint responsibilities:

> (. . .) For example my target is to send out as many proposals as possible and the metric is 'paid sales'. So if I make a high quality order proposal and then the order arrives with some documentation missing, then we will get problems in collecting the money as my proposal is not fulfilled. We cannot collect the money and so my performance metric is not good due to the inefficiency of someone else.
>
> *(Commercial Operations Manager)*

The individual employees have to deal with the pressures applied by the performance system. However, there are different ways of acting on the system. One way is a coping strategy that involves a self-defence mechanism of adapting to the middle performer:

> Here all of us are numbers . . . You learn how to survive, how to work with this mechanism. Then you can adapt and it is not a big deal at the end of the story. (. . .) At the beginning I was concerned about the metrics. But now I realize that you are okay in the metrics if you work normally and not avoid work and if someone tells you that he needs something from you then you just do it. If you are a guy that arrives late in morning, always at the coffee machine and you go home because you need to play football, for sure you will find yourself at the bottom; but if you are a normal person and you arrive at the office at 8.30 and start to work, and you take only one coffee break, it is normal and you are doing what you are expected to do.
>
> *(Finance Manager)*

Another strategy is to be among the top performers. To be a high performer one has to set the stage oneself. More specifically, it is more important to be seen as pro-active by suggesting solutions to a problem than to actually solve the problem:

> ['Top ten'] people are considered pro-active, always say 'yes, yes, yes', they bring the problem with the solution, but often the solution is worse than the problem. But they highlight the solutions and it is like marketing. Most of them are good people but sometimes you see people and you are wondering and asking yourself 'how can they be the top talent'?
>
> *(Commercial Operations Manager)*

The quote suggests a rather superficial approach to problem-solving. The system neither values the professional type of employee who is driven by an intrinsic motivation to his work or the person driven by a lifelong commitment to his profession. The values embedded in the performance mechanism are those linked to short-term results, buoyancy, and mobility. Ambitious people stay in their positions for a couple of years and then move to another field, and then they move again to another job. They always require expectations to do new things, to face new challenges. The implications are that some high-performance people are pushed beyond their personal limits and hence have to choose between the job and a life:

> The parent company pushes the employees hard, if an employee works hard and he/she has the capacities to stimulate the team, the company repetitively asks the employee to work harder. For this reason there is a high rate of employee turnover. Mobility in the parent company is very high; there is a sort of liaison officer which manages the group's job opportunities. (. . .) Well, the salary is good and there are a lot of benefits, but the company asks the employees to work so much that, at a certain point, a person must choose between their job and their life. Not all the people are willing to sacrifice their life for the job. (. . .) but in a European culture, or in my personal culture, I like to do what I do and I like to stay here!
>
> *(Commercial Operations Manager)*

Overall, the strain of being a high performer has enormous implications for the individual's life. Given its wish to further the mobile personality type, the performance measurement system hampers the possibility of developing good and sound human relations because human values such as trust evolve slowly and cannot be forced into existence:

> I have a normal human relationship with my old superior, because he has worked in the company for a long period. There is a little bit more humanity compared to the superior in the parent company headquarters. With him there is a lack of trust towards me and there isn't any human relationship either. I think if I work in a company for a long period and with the same people a reciprocal trust relation would have to be established between us, but this has not been my experience in the company.
>
> *(Commercial Operations Manager)*

Conclusion: case study A

Before the turnaround in 2002, the strategy followed by Company A was growth through the development of its internal resources including R&D activities. Accordingly, it can be defined as a resource-based strategy. After the acquisition the strategy changed markedly. The main target of the company was to maximize the short-term financial result at the expense of the sustainability of its internal resources and their long-term development. The strategy formulated by the group involves growth and innovation being achieved through 'mergers and acquisitions'. The increase in financial performance is attained by acquiring companies with attractive products and market opportunities.

The methodology of performance measurement seems to facilitate the negation of the acquired company's resource. The pressure of aggressive sales growth together with the process of standardization and efficiency does not leave space for the development of resources and capabilities of the employees. Using the systems approach to performance management, the role of the individual is neglected and the employee is seen as a monkey silently serving and subscribing to the norm of the whole corporate system. The employees feel strongly constrained by the measurements and have no control of the performance measurements that are heavily influenced by the actions of other parties, including headquarters. As pointed out by Miller and O'Leary (1987), the number of performance measurements are a powerful way to make the individual adapt and subordinate himself to the social norms and rules by comparing, ranking and making public the individual's performance.

Case study 2: Company B

Company background

Company B is an Italian subsidiary of a US parent company that is considered a leader in business analytics software and services and one of the largest vendors in the business intelligence market. It has achieved a steady revenue growth and profitability since its establishment in 1976. While many competitors have merged, changed ownership or vanished, the multinational company has remained privately held and has focused on its primary mission: to offer superior software and to develop powerful customer relationships. The group has about 11,000 employees and attains a level of revenues in excess of 2 billion USD with more than 400 offices globally.

Company B was founded in 1987 in Milan. Today it has offices in different Italian cities. Its role is to sell the software and to provide technical support. In many cases the company also offers a package of consulting activities. The technical research and development activity is not a competence of the local subsidiary, but is performed by the parent company in the US.

Company strategy

Company B and its parent company are strongly R&D-oriented. Business intelligence software is a sector that requires heavy investments in R&D activities. Such an orientation is confirmed by the fact that in 2008 and 2009, from a global perspective, 23 per cent of the revenues were invested in R&D activities. Certainly short-term financial results are important, but since the parent company of B is privately held the pressure on management for short-term profitability is more mitigated. However, products have to be cost-effective to be competitive. Focus is on long-term profitability rather than short-term profitability:

> We are not a publicly quoted company so we do not have a propensity to focus only on short-term profitability. We agree on a set of overall financial goals and targets at the strategic level, but we can decide to make investment in research and development, in resources, in what we want without having the pressure of the financial analyst. From a long-term point of view this is a very big advantage.
>
> *(Finance and Administration Manager)*

The employees are perceived as a resource. Accordingly, attention is given to the value provided by people, the growth of this value and its retention within the organization:

> . . . we try to do our best to maintain talent, in order to give people opportunities to grow in terms of operational skills . . .
>
> *(Finance and Administration Manager)*

This view seems to be general for the employees within the whole company. The parent company has recently been rated number one on *Fortune* Magazine's annual '100 Best Companies to Work For' list.

It was listed as one of the best in terms of healthcare, child-care and work–life balance. The view of the group is that happy and healthy employees are more productive.

The customer represents another important key resource in Company B's strategy. The target of the company is to build a long-term and stable relationship with its customers. This is important as they sell a software licence on a one-year contract, so the customers have to decide annually either to renew or to cancel. The following quote illustrates that customers are not resources 'to be squeezed', but resources 'to be made to grow':

> . . . We are not interested in forcing the customer to buy something that is not suitable for what they want or what they are planning to use, because this is very bad for us and very dangerous. As our sales policy is mainly to get new sales (first-year fees) plus renewals, we are interested in building a long-term relationship with the customer. One of the most important issues is to maintain a good customer relationship with a focus on long-term value. This is vital for all the companies of the group and the policy is the same worldwide.
>
> *(Finance and Administration Manager)*

In sum, Company B advocates long-term profitability rather than short-term profitability. It has its focus on R&D, the development of employee competences, and long-term customer relations. As the aim of the firm is to develop and build up unique competencies, it takes a resource-based view of strategy.

Performance measurement

The Italian subsidiary is evaluated based on accounting profitability. Within the subsidiary there are profit, revenue and cost centres. Consultancies and education are profit centres while finance, marketing etc. are only cost centres. Based on this structure, the subsidiary reports on a monthly basis to headquarters. The annual plan is created in October/November and is then divided into a monthly base. Follow-up is made on the forecast against the actual at the end of each month. The plan is based on the key items in the profit and loss statement. The revenues come from two main sources: software and services. Total software revenues are approximately 70 per cent, while the remaining 30 per cent are *services* including consultancy revenues, project and developing. As indicated above, the software revenues comprise the 'new sales', which means that new software licences have been sold and the 'renewal sales' – which means software licences – have to be renewed. The services revenues refer to consultancy and education. The consultancy activity is performed in order to enrich the goals of the customer whereas the education activity, very limited in entity, is about teaching specific courses for learning to use the software. In terms of costs the main part is represented by the royalties that the company pays on the software sales because the research and development activity is centralized in the US; in one sense this is the cost of the product. Another major cost category is the cost of the personnel.

Company B is characterized by a relatively free contextual framework in which managers show respect for the necessary constraints. Policies, rules and standards are set by the parent company, but what makes the difference in Company B is that the employees are allowed not only to look beyond merely understanding the rules but also to suggest a better way of doing things:

> . . . we have sales policy, we have rules that we can't avoid in any case, but we have some level of freedom in the way we approach some markets and some customers . . .
>
> *(Finance and Administration Manager)*

Accordingly, the performance measurement system of the Italian subsidiary is designed by the local management. The target in terms of total sales, consulting turnover and consulting margin is more or less the same all over the world. In the past, however, the Italian subsidiary has added some KPIs related to specific activities. Some other countries have imitated these. Most of the metrics are becoming standardized through an organic learning process:

> Another country will adopt our KPIs or we adopt some KPIs that come from other countries (. . .) The idea is to make things as comparable as possible.
>
> *(Finance and Administration Manager)*

To some extent the salary of the individual employee depends on key performance indicators. These metrics are specific, established on a functional basis and calculated at the end of the year. Depending on the kind of activity, a salary bonus is scheduled. For sales people, for example, the salary is approximately 60 per cent fixed and 40 per cent variable (depending on the attainment of targets). As the sales people's long-term salary in the company very much depends on the customers' licence renewals, they have incentives to be concerned about the long-term customer relationship. However, the Net New Sales, which is the amount of money for new software licenses sold, is an important metric that forms the basis for long-term sales renewals and hence long-term bonuses:

> My main target is sales in terms of new software revenues . . . some measures are related to the quality of the work.
>
> *(Business Developer)*

Also, there are metrics concerning service quality and customer satisfaction:

> . . . for example we have a department that provides technical support, that is telephone support to the customer, so we have measures about speed and response time between question and answer. These measures give us some indications about customer satisfaction . . . Also to have an idea about customer satisfaction we get comments from people coming to our training courses.
>
> *(Finance and Administration Manager)*

Reflecting the overall strategy of caring about the employees, the performance measurement system gives attention to employee satisfaction:

> Periodically, we make surveys on employee satisfaction and we have very good results. Apart from the questions related to salaries where the rating is low, they are very good in terms of environment, in terms of operations and so on.
>
> *(Finance and Administration Manager)*

Many policies and rules are made in face-to-face relationships involving interaction between the employees and the middle managers. For example, the performance system has not been designed hierarchically top-down, but in interaction with the lower management:

> Usually, we get indications and suggestions from the middle management and then we make our suggestions in the management team. Obviously, we must understand whether the middle managers are reporting something important, are manipulating the data or ar just trying to make people happier, for instance. This is something we have to discuss – in this kind of company our

> people require a lot of time to discuss, to understand, to talk because we have a very high percentage of graduates. In some subjects we have specialists and sometimes they are very good people, very intelligent, and we have to give them the opportunity to say what they have to say, you have to hear them. This makes things a little more complicated, you cannot just say these are the rules and please follow them, but we have to discuss, we have to convince them, sometimes we have to agree about what is the most suitable way, but we cannot just enforce. It simply requires time, energy and so on but it works.
>
> *(Finance and Administration Manager)*

This quote illustrates how the discussions and interactions develop the various participants' understanding and perception of reality. The idea is to create acceptance of the policies and measurements rather than to enforce them. The managers use dialogue as a vital tool not only to communicate the targets and tasks, but also to define the priorities. The interactive approach is confirmed by the Business Developer:

> The allocation of my time is usually decided in agreement with the top management. We have a planning meeting at the beginning of the year where I present my plan for the year and that must be approved by the general management . . . I need to spend a lot of time in meetings and communications with my vertical resources.
>
> *(Business Developer)*

The rules and the performance measurement system are not used mechanically but are always reflected and discussed in relation to the particular context. In particular, one has to handle the conflict of interests that the system can create between various employees when servicing the customers:

> In some cases some people have goals or targets that are not perfectly in line with those of their colleagues. For example if I am a consultant, I have to push my consultancy revenue, but next to me a sales person has to push software sales. The customer may have a problem that can be solved both within existing software by pushing software sales and with new software pushing consultancy sales. In such a case it is very important to understand exactly what the customer's problem is. The proposal should include both solutions: we can do that or that and meet the customer's wishes, what do you prefer to do? The most important thing is always to understand the needs of the customer despite the measurement that we have accepted.
>
> *(Finance and Administration Manager)*

Usually the managers have to agree with the final targets and requirements of the projects that are defining customers' needs. The subsidiary management interact with middle managers and employees in order to find suitable solutions to conflicts of interests. This may lead to a revision of the measurements:

> We can adjust the performance measurement to find the proper solutions for the customer. In general we are able to resolve after a lot of discussion, fighting and so . . . anyway, we try to give all our employees the message that customer need satisfaction is the vehicle for us.
>
> *(Finance and Administration Manager)*

This does not mean the employees are not under pressure. It means they have to develop the ability to manage their time, clearly keeping in mind both the financial results and the long-term goal of the organization:

> My boss gives me the possibilities to decide where and how to invest my time but he wants results . . . For my boss the most important thing is to get results, he doesn't care where I invest my time, he wants results, quarterly results.
>
> *(Business Developer)*

> . . . we have performance pressure but always keeping in mind that we have to create long-term relationships with our customer.
>
> *(Finance and Administration Manager)*

The performance measurement system is used from a learning perspective. As the organization gains more and more experience with the way the system influences the individual in the practical context, the system gradually changes and improves:

> It is, let me say, an ongoing process because we are not used to changing everything every year. Every year we try to adjust what we think was not appropriate from the year before. The base is always the same but with some adjustments depending on people's reactions and, in part, on our understanding of the previous year about this kind of things.
>
> *(Finance and Administration Manager)*

Implications of the system

The partly performance-based salary system has some appeal to the extrinsic motivation of the employees, as seen in the following quote:

> We introduced the first version of the bonus plan in 1996 and when we started with the sales people the reaction was very good because people felt the opportunity to get paid if their results were good. In general, they are more motivated to reach the goals, obviously it is important to set the goals and the target in a convenient way because it can have a very bad impact if targets are unreasonable or too high. Every year it is a very difficult exercise.
>
> *(Finance and Administration Manager)*

The quote also shows that the management aim to balance the intrinsic and extrinsic motivation. They seem to be quite successful in achieving this aim. Thus, as previously stated, the performance measurement system of Company B confirms the main strategic orientation: build up and retain resources. In this sense the main resources of the company are the people, and the employees know that they are investments for the company:

> . . . we are not paying people over the market, but, in general, we try to give people the opportunity to expand their professional abilities. We do not always succeed; often, for example, it happens that our customer wants our people . . .
>
> *(Finance and Administration Manager)*

A core point that differentiates the performance measurement in Company B from that of Company A is the perception of the employees as important for the organization. Interviewees of Company A felt themselves be perceived as 'numbers' and 'monkeys'. The feeling of Company B's employees is quite the opposite – they are important:

> The most important thing is that people don't feel they are just numbers. They need to think that they are important inside the organization – for me it is the best way to motivate.
>
> *(Business Developer)*

Conclusion: case study B

The strategy pursued by Company B falls into the resource-based view of a strategy. The company aims to build up unique competencies and it has a strong focus on research and development, advances in employee talents and skills, and long-term customer relationship. These focal points are pursued at the expense of short-term profitability to obtain long-term profitability.

The employees are to be treated well and are considered as 'intelligent actors' and not 'numbers'. This is reflected in the performance measurement methodology that involves a close relationship between the employees' view and the top management's view. The methodology of performance management is collaborative and involves intensive dialogue with the employees to make the measurements become contextually grounded, accepted and shared. In contrast to Company A, the people in Company B perceive the measures used for their evaluation system as sensible and fair. A performance measurement methodology that recognizes the employees as intelligent actors to be treated with fairness and respect facilitates their commitment and motivation. Even when under performance pressure the employees remain conscious that their main target is to establish long-term, cost-effective relationships with their customers. One may argue that the performance measurement methodology supports a sort of professionally-driven governance system. Professional governance means that the members of a specialized occupation make decisions on objectives, terms and methodologies for their work and hence they set the criteria for their own evaluation. The employees are expected not only to be skilled but also to have good character and an ethical set of values. The ideals of the profession should govern before profit (Laursen, 2003: p. 14). Overall, they are driven by intrinsic rather than extrinsic motivation.

Conclusion and discussion of strategic implications

Above, we demonstrated that there are different methodologies of managing performance measurements. Analysing two subsidiaries located in Europe but owned by two American multinational companies, we found similar accounting metrics, but two different methodologies applied for the design and use of performance measurements. The two methodologies were identified as a systems approach and an actor's approach, respectively. Table 21.1 summarizes the features of Company A and Company B's performance measurement methodologies and their radically different implications for human motivation and action, and hence for their strategic development.

The first subsidiary was acquired as a unit in a financially driven business portfolio strategy. This subsidiary (Company A) was tightly controlled by a systems approach that had a rather authoritative (hierarchically top-down) and mechanical pattern to performance management. The focus of the performance measurement was short-term profitability through sales growth and cost efficiency of the entire value chain of the companies including R&D. In a rigid way, a systems approach to performance management detects non-value-adding activities and activities for standardization and efficiency improvements regardless of their uniqueness and the potential long-term value of the company. The focus on result measurements and the assumptions of an optimal work procedure cause the individual's opportunities for actions to become deterministic and mechanical and hence this approach destroys the possibilities of a sustainable resource-based strategy. By this we mean a resource-based strategy that depends on the particular knowledge, creativity and expertise of the employees. In its orientation towards a competitive advantage in the market, the company negates some of the subsidiary's original strengths with respect to innovative experience, and high value and quality of offerings. Overall, we see that the outcome of the systems approach to performance measurement was resources and capabilities set to a minimum level, and hence that resources were 'broken down'. The prosperity perspective of the company appears to be a low-cost strategy in a growing market. The strategy works from a business portfolio point of view, as sustainable innovation of the whole group is driven through 'mergers and acquisitions' of companies with strong resource profiles and product offerings within highly attractive industries. Subsequently, each unit is managed with an emphasis on aggressive growth, cost efficiency and short-term profit maximizing. Through the systems approach to performance measurement, the company value passes through different life-cycle stages into a favourable position for sale to another group.

The other subsidiary (Company B) drew on an actor's approach to performance measurement. It included a phenomenological grounding and a learning perspective when designing and using performance measurement. In Company B the actor's approach to the performance measurement system gives space for resource development and innovation. Cost effectiveness is considered to be a long-term achievement. The performance measurement methodology facilitates the employees' talent development and intrinsic motivation by making decisions and evaluations based on phenomenologically grounded business knowledge. The outcome was a company that 'built up' and developed its resources and capabilities. Thus the actor-based approach to performance measurement supports B's resource-based strategy. The financial results are indeed important, but this is not the only target. Therefore Company B's methodology of performance measurement can be considered as oriented towards maintaining a position of sustainable competitive advantage. Here the concept of 'value creation' is not only a stockholder's financial requirement, but involves the deeper meaning of a 'sustained' competitive

Table 21.1 Summary of the performance measurement of Company A and Company B

	Company A	*Company B*
Background and strategy	• Business portfolio • Market growth and efficiency • Innovation through acquisition	• Single business • Resources and capabilities • Organic innovation
Performance measurements	• Financial and non-financial measurements	• Financial and non-financial measurements
Performance measurement methodology	• Systems approach • Authoritative • Standard norm • Monitoring of deviations from norms • Rewards and punishment • Direct	• Actor's approach • Interactive • Phenomenological grounding • Understanding of results in relation to context • Rewards and learning • Dialogue
Implications of performance measurement system	• Mechanical reaction • Standardization and adaptation to norm • Extrinsic motivation • Breaks down resources and capabilities	• Reflective action • Innovation and problem-solving • Intrinsic motivation • Builds up resources and capabilities

advantage that requires the design and implementation of mechanisms to enforce innovation, learning and cooperation among people (Ghoshal and Moran, 1996). In order to attain and 'sustain' the competitive advantage, the company aims to create and develop key resources (especially human) that will strengthen the firm's ability to obtain superior performance.

In sum, this paper has explored the different strategic implications of two different methodologies of managing performance measurement. It shows how the specific methodology of designing and using performance measurement facilitates the specific business philosophy of the company. Drawing on alternative methodologies of using performance measurement the two company cases show how performance measurements can be managed differently with different implications for human actions and hence strategy. In particular, the two cases of performance management suggest that a systems approach and an actor's approach, respectively, support two different types of strategic development: a competitive advantage development versus a sustained competitive advantage development. The result also suggests that, although the performance measurement system of a company shows that the targets are achieved, its resources can be destroyed and hence it may be moving in an unintended and unfruitful strategic direction. The findings stress the need of more in-depth research in the direction of understanding the methodology of performance measurement and the long-term strategic position it facilitates. This way, the implications of the different methodologies for the adopting organization can be highlighted, and their relation to the degree of success of the implemented performance measurement system can be explained in more detail.

Bibliography

Amit, R. and Schoemaker, P.J.H. (1993). Strategic assets and organizational rent. *Strategic Management Journal*, 14(1), 33–46.

Anthony, R. (1965). *Planning and Control systems*. Cambridge, MA, Harvard University Press.

Anthony, R.N., and Govindarajan V. (2007). *Management Control Systems*. Singapore, McGraw-Hill.

Arbnor, I., and Bjerke, B. (1994). *Företagsekonomisk metodlära*. Studenterlitteratur, Lund, Sweden.

Ahrens, T., and Chapman, C. S. (2007). Doing Qualitative Field Research in Management Accounting: Positioning Data to Contribute to Theory, in *Handbook of Management Accounting Research*, Vol. I, Chapman, C.S., Hopwood, A.G., Shields, M.D. (eds), Elsevier, Amsterdam.

Argyris, C. and Kaplan, R.S. (1994). Implementing new knowledge: the case of activity-based costing. *Accounting Horizons*, 8(3), 83–105.

Ax, C., and Bjornenak, T. (2005). Bundling and diffusion of management accounting innovations: the case of the Balanced Scorecard in Sweden. *Management Accounting Research*, 16(1), 1–20.

Barney, J.B. (1991). Firm resources and sustained competitive advantage. *Journal of Management*, 17(1): 97–98:

Chenhall, R.H., and Langfield-Smith, K. (1998). Adoption and benefits of management accounting practices: an Australian study. *Management Accounting Research*, 9(1), 1–19.

Chiapello, E., and Lebas, M. (1996). The Tableau de Bord, a French Approach to Management Information, paper presented at the 19th Annual Meeting of the European Accounting Association, Bergen (Norway), 2–4 May.

Chua, W.F. (1986). Radical Developments in Accounting Thought. *The Accounting Review*, 61(4), 601–632.

Churchman, C.W. (1968). *The Systems Approach*. New York, Delacorte Press.

Ghoshal, S., (2005). Bad management theories are destroying good management practices. *Academy of Management Learning and Education*, 4, 75–91.

Ghoshal, S. and Moran, P. (1996). Bad for practice: a critique of the transaction cost theory. *Academy of Management Review*. 21, 13–47.

Haas, M. de, and A. Kleingeld (1999). Multilevel design of performance measurement systems: enhancing strategic dialogue throughout the organization. *Management Accounting Research*, vol. 10, 233–261.

Itami, H. (1987). *Mobilizing Invisible Assets*. Cambridge, MA, Harvard University Press.

Ittner, C., Larcker, D. and Randall, T. (2003). Performance implications of strategic performance measurement in financial services firms. *Accounting, Organizations and Society*, vol. 28, 715–741.

Kaplan, R.S. and Norton, D.P. (1992). The Balanced Scorecard as a strategic management system. *Harvard Business Review*, Jan.–Feb., 61–66.

Kaplan, R.S. and Norton, D.P. (1996). *The Balanced Scorecard – Translating Strategy into Action*. Boston, Harvard Business School Press.

Kolehmainen, K. (2010) Dynamic strategic performance measurement systems: balancing empowerment and alignment. *Long Range Planning*, 43.

Laursen, P.F. (2003). Personlighed på dagsordene. In: Weicher, Inge and Per Fibæk Laursen (ed.) *Person og profession en udfordring for socialrådgivere, sygeplejerske, lærere og pædagoer*, Værløse: Billesøe & Baltzer Forlagene.

Lynch, R.L. and Cross, K.F. (1991). *Measure Up!: Yardsticks for Continuous Improvement*. Cambridge, Blackwell.

Mintzberg, H., Lampel, J., Quinn, J.B., and Ghoshal S. (1996). *The Strategy Process*. Essex, Pearson.

Miller, P. and O'Leary, T. (1987). Accounting and the construction of the governable person. *Accounting, Organizations and Society*, 12(3), 235–265.

Neely, A.D., and Adams, C. (2001). The performance prism perspective. *Journal of Cost Management*, 15(1), 7–15.

Neely, A.D. (ed.) (2007). *Business Performance Measurement*. Cambridge University Press, 2007.

Nørreklit, L. (2011), Actors and reality: a conceptual framework for creative governance. In Jakobsen, M., Johanson, I-L. and Nørreklit, H. (eds.), *An Actor's Approach to Management – Conceptual Framework and Company Practices*. DJOEF, Copenhagen.

Norreklit, H. and Schoenfeld, H.-M. (2000). Controlling multinational companies – an attempt to analyze some unresolved issues. *The International Journal of Accounting*, 3.

Nørreklit H., Nørreklit L., and Mitchell F. (2007) Theoretical Conditions for Validity in Accounting Performance Measurement. In Andy Neely (ed.), *Business Performance Measurement*. Cambridge University Press.

Nørreklit, H., Nørreklit, L., and Mitchell, F. (2010). Towards a paradigmatic foundation of accounting practice. *Accounting, Auditing and Accountability Journal*, 23(6), 733–758.

Porter, M.E. (1980). *Competitive Strategy: Techniques for Analyzing Industries and Competitors*. New York, Free Press.

Porter, M.E. (1985). *Competitive Advantage: Creating and Sustaining Superior Performance*. New York, Free Press.

Ryan B., Scapens, R.W., and Theobald, M. (2002). *Research Method and Methodology in Finance and Accounting*. Thomson, UK.

Prahalad, C.K. and Hamel, G. (1990). The core competence of the corporation. *Harvard Business Review*, May-June, 79–91.

Silverman, D. (1993). *Interpreting Qualitative Data: Methods for Analyzing Talk, Text and Interaction*. Sage, London.

Simons, R. (1995). *Levers of Control*. Harvard Business School Press, Boston.

Wernerfelt, B. (1984). A resource-based view of the firm. *Strategic Management Journal*, 5(2), 171–180.

22

Cost management in the digital age

Alnoor Bhimani

Introduction

Cost management is on the brink of immense change. This is not the first time the field has faced upheaval. During the 1980s, management commentators, accounting scholars and prominent accounting practitioners called for radical changes in cost management practices (see Bromwich and Bhimani, 1989). Many finance executives heeded these calls, and large numbers of enterprises adopted new approaches to managing costs. These included activity-based management, throughput accounting, life cycle costing, target cost management and the Balanced Scorecard among others. Within many companies, understandings of the role, impact and dimensions of cost management was transformed following the implementation of new accounting applications (see Bromwich and Bhimani, 1994). Today, enterprises are again facing significant challenges that will prove very disruptive. There are three main developments which will lead companies to rethink their cost management practices: the spread of internet technologies, the rise of novel organizational forms and the advent of new approaches to using, accessing and analysing information. This essay considers their impact. First, some background on how and why these forces of change have emerged.

Current forces reshaping cost management

Significant events and developments in the recent past have triggered changes in cost management thinking and practices and have started to alter the finance function in some firms. One key factor which has driven this alteration is the dotcom crash at the turn of the millennium and the subsequent transformative impact of the internet on organizational activities. The rapid pace of digitization is forcing deep changes in the modus operandi of management structures, decisions and strategies. It is giving birth to novel business models with concomitant accounting repercussions. Since 2008, enterprises have also been affected by the deepest worldwide recession since the Great Depression, accompanied by the most extensive government bailout initiatives of modern times. The now tighter corporate governance regulatory requirements facing firms in developed and emerging economies has altered their management controls and management practices. This is tied to the global financial crisis and attendant economic measures put into place by governments, oversight bodies and financial institutions which directly impact cost management and financial control systems across many enterprises. For instance, readily available finance and the achievability of high leverage for very many business organizations until early 2007 enabled specific cost structures as intentional strategies to be pursued. Such leverage was at times achieved because of the utilization of legitimate financial innovations. But also, it was often the result of undesirably lax financial practices and poor controls.

The ready access of funding which produced high cost infrastructures is no longer today easy to attain for most firms, let alone to sustain. The sourcing of fixed costs within enterprises is likely to continue to be subjected to much more demanding assessments of their rationales and sustainability. Investors and stakeholders are now more prone to the close monitoring of investment activities and of enterprise performance to ensure the achievement of expected yields and desired return on equity. It is certain that the regulatory demands on organizations will further expand going forward in most economies. Requirements for more transparency, accountability, watchful governance and greater levels of disclosure will make further demands on enterprise information systems. More regulatory hurdles and firmer monitoring of operational achievement and effectiveness will continue to affect financial controls.

Aside from technological advances and the rise of regulatory constraints on firms, industries are being reshaped by emergent organizational forms. Rather than being temporary these new entities are gaining permanence as creators of corporate value. Examples of new organizational forms are global strategic alliances, virtual companies and joint ventures, discussed below. It is unsurprising that managers regard the swift pace of change they face in their organizations as the only constant. What used to be seen as 'normal' is now rapidly being transformed. A 'new normal' is emerging (Davis, 2009). As novel disruptions, challenges and deep financial alterations at the macroeconomic level make their presence felt, there will in the near term be sustained and ongoing impact from these economic forces of change on the structuring, strategies and managerial control mechanisms deployed by enterprises. Certainly, modes of information access, analysis and reporting by cost management professionals will alter. These changes are considered below.

The digital economy and costing concerns

Computers have shaped business activities for over four decades. But it was only during the mid-1990s that a profound second-wave digital revolution took place. At that time, three effects became interlinked: the spread of user-friendly operating systems and interfaces; the rapid diffusion of the internet and the worldwide web; and the convergence of four formerly distinct industries – computers, software, communications, and media and entertainment. These factors led to the creation of a huge worldwide value network, with new business models and novel ways for enterprise architectures to form and enable the generation of wealth and the creation of value. Coinciding with this was the crowding out of established sources and channels of information by innovations in business information-gathering. When consumers act, their actions result in economic transactions which have driven the nature and type of accounting information processed by firms. Given this, enterprises have in the past designed information systems to produce formal information which system users purposefully deploy based on economic transactions reflecting consumer purchases or resources mobilized by managers.

But a shift in information design structures is currently taking place. There is now a realization that the information which information systems have traditionally discarded can be of immense relevance and usefulness as a source of business intelligence for companies. A customer buying online will often leave a trail of information disclosures prior to making the purchase, just like an internet user who does not make any purchases online. This 'data exhaust', if effectively captured and analysed, can help organizations determine how and what individuals rationalize and the path they take before making a purchase or a decision. Google.com, for instance, learns from every search process carried out. Amazon.com gathers information from online customer behaviour irrespective of whether a purchase is made. EBay monitors buyer and seller activities even where no purchase transactions take place. These companies analyse data exhaustively in the provision of important financial intelligence which can shape cost management, pricing decisions and operational controls.

Drawing business intelligence from information produced in the absence of economic flows – by searching behaviour, website visits and browsing sequences, for example – has, for many companies, become essential in the configuration and internal reporting of information for internal executive purposes. The significance of this is growing apace. As 'transaction-agnostic' information grows, data volume and information management will expand and place important challenges on financial systems.

Globally produced data grows more than ten-fold every five years. The pace is partly reflective of the increase of media, entertainment and social networking possibilities online. And while much of the information is unstructured, a significant proportion is amenable to structuring in an economically purposeful sense. This growth of information, along with the possibilities presented by data exhaust, enable useful analyses and managerial assessments by businesses. For instance, purchases made via Amazon are often tied to purchases made previously. Probabilities can be established about the likelihood of particular subsequent purchases being made based on data collected about macro-level buying behaviour, non-purchases and prior online interactive searches. EBay likewise continuously alters its listings based on prior listing activity, bidding behaviour, pricing trends, search terms used and purchase frequency. Google searches become more and more relevant because search results are based on what users with prior similar searches eventually stayed with. In this sense, data trails left by surfers invite scientific data analysis and mining whose results can point to altered pricing policy, cost containment prioritization, and cash and working capital management strategies.

Traditionally the finance function has been structured around information collection about products by information systems overseeing production processes and value creation which can be economically traced. Today data mining of activities which are not reliant on economic transactions increasingly shapes financial control and management decisions relating to revenue generation, cost containment and operational issues in enterprises. Such information is ordinarily collected by information capture devices which track activities. But the collection of information can also take place from within products and processes themselves. For instance, real-time data collection can be achieved without separate information systems being in place through the use of, for instance, pill-shaped micro-cameras, precision agricultural and industrial sensors, and radio frequency identification tags.

Continuous information collection, tied to product purchase pathways and cost incursions in the value chain, as well as dynamic pricing strategies and working capital management choices, can be achieved with products and processes themselves acting as collectors and transformers of information. This presents novel possibilities for cost management whereby the finance function becomes a receptor and assessor of information for real-time analysis and decisions.

The next part of this essay discusses altered organizational structures that are reshaping economic markets and value creation. In particular, collaborative firm linkages and pure trading relationships are considered followed by a discussion of how pure trading links between firms can be reshaped by virtual enterprise structures resting on information technology innovations. The implications of this shift for cost management are drawn out.

Novel firm structures and cost management

For management accountants, incremental cost analysis has long been regarded as a useful approach to help assess certain economic decisions executives have to make. For instance managers may need to determine the financial consequences of whether to 'make-or-buy' a subcomponent used in production, or develop or outsource a service which adds or supports a product offering. Conceptually, the costs and benefits accruing to a firm producing required parts, services or subcomponents internally are weighed against the financial and managerial consequences of outsourcing via competitive bidding to subcomponent suppliers or service providers (Callioni, Montgros, Slagmulder, Wassenhowe, and Wright, 2005; Dekker, 2004; Groot and Merchant, 2000; Meer-Kooistra, 1994; Quinn and Hilmer, 1994; Speklé, 2001).

Collaborative relationship (CR) firms exhibit a 'quasi-vertical' form of integration (Das and Teng, 2000; Tomkins, 2001) which play an increasingly prevalent role in defining relationships between enterprises today (Handfield, Krause, Scannel, and Monczka, 2000; Lambert and Cooper, 2000; Leiblein and Miller, 2003; Liker and Choi, 2004; Sako, 2008). Sheth and Sharma (1997, p. 91) remarked long ago that 'organizational buying is dramatically shifting from the transaction oriented to the relational oriented philosophy and will shift from a buying process to a supplier relationship process'. This shift is now deeply ingrained within many firms. Management accounting scholars have extensively assessed the control implications of this shift (Anderson and Sedatole, 2003; Dekker, 2004; Hakansson and Lind, 2007; Kamminga and Van der Meer-Kooistra, 2007; Kraus and Lind, 2007). Many commentators recognize that strategic and contractual issues between buyers and sellers are gaining relevance, particularly in new product development contexts (Gadde and Snehota, 2000; Narayanan and Raman, 2004). The implications for cost management are extensive in terms of product development input, price rebates, after-sales warranties, supplier inspection policies and information systems integration.

Collaborative subcontracting relationships are founded on trust and transactional dependence with specific supply undertakings (often made orally) extending over only part of the overall trading relationship. The obligations of such long-term relationships are diffuse and guide the resolution of specific transaction problems on a case-by-case basis, usually through informal channels. The collaborative link exhibits mutual indebtedness that can extend over long periods of time with a loose principle of give and take. CRs tend to have extensive and multiple channels of communication between a variety of functional managers and departments within linked-up companies. They establish non-specific terms of trade as to supply quantity, timing of supply, product specifications and product price at the time of setting up the trading relationship.

Given that there is an absence of contractual predetermination of quantity, price and timing of supply, the assessment of the financial consequences of transacting via a CR trading link is very difficult. The buyer's ability to alter quantities purchased from the supplier and to change product specifications provides operational flexibility. There will also be product life-cycle considerations that affect the viability of close relationships and it will be likely that both parties learn from producing, transacting and cooperating with one another, which will have cost advantages aside from interdependencies. A close alliance will create the possibility of rapid expansion and growth in ways not anticipated at the outset (Child, 2005).

The initial subcomponent or service offering cost of a supplier able to engage in a CR may exceed that of a pure trade with a supplier, but this higher cost could be evaluated in terms of forgoing the payoffs from a CR. In particular, the transfer of knowledge and the availability of flexibilities, say between a supplier and assembler, may over time contribute to value advantages exceeding those of pure initial subcomponent price differentials between a purchase and CR.

This is because under competitive purchasing, the assessment of certain economic transactions is based on terms that are made explicit prior to the commencement of trading without any necessary arrangement to pass on learning-derived benefits whose magnitude cannot be known at the time of contractualization. Agreements are put into place to cover recourse options for faltering on the terms of the contract and the buyer-supplier link is designed within attempts to minimize each party's dependence on the other. Thus little learning is passed on between the parties.

If there are learning effects, costs will possibly decrease with output. Process improvement, product standardization, economies of scale and other elements can all offer learning-based payoffs. The extent to which economies emerge out of learning processes will vary across and within industries, and be conditioned by differences in R&D expenditure and capital intensity as well as team effects.

Many firms opt for total outsourcing to producers, service providers and assemblers. Their only function is the co-ordination of activities, the connecting of inputs and outputs and the orchestration of movements between entities in a resource-efficient manner. Effectively such a firm need not be capitalized along traditional lines of engagement with factors of production such as land, labour and capital. It need not be concerned with investments in the means of creating flows, but only in their co-ordination. A firm can remain virtual, retaining control only over the direction, magnitude and nature of electronic interfaces. A virtual firm can be regarded as an agglomeration of multiple 'buy' transactions woven together by extensive co-ordination and structuring of flows. Virtuality has been taken to suggest transient connections between otherwise independent entities via appropriate information technology structures. It can bring together organizational resources from different companies and synthesize them into a single electronic business entity. Thus, cost management for a virtual firm will entail the consideration of many factors tied to co-ordination rather than actual production. The verification of outputs by suppliers and the extent to which they meet specifications and required standards, rather than the monitoring of ongoing operational efficiencies during production, will form the primary focus of virtual firm control systems.

Virtual firms create extremely high levels of interconnectedness between a large number of entities involved in the production of value. This influences virtual firm controls such that they are forced to implement very rigorous risk management strategies. This is because high degrees of interconnectedness between producers, service providers and assemblers bring about high levels of systemic risk. The correct response to this is to develop an extensive set of standards for suppliers to observe, and the standardization of specifications across enterprises and their information systems. What is essential for information professionals to grasp is that cost management is not simply a matter of assessing individual costs but also of developing a strong awareness of interconnections between firms which interface, and it is essential to understand the threats and risks this poses and their possible impact on costs.

A virtual enterprise is likely to have overhead costs which are largely tied to running its information systems infrastructure and carrying out co-ordination processes electronically. Additionally, overhead costs will reflect personnel costs, with employees likely being rewarded on some measure of co-ordination effectiveness. Virtual corporations may find the achievement of scale and scope economies difficult and will have to seek value creation through co-ordination structures and flow mechanisms rather than by reducing the costs of material input, such as processing or packaging for physical products.

In broad terms, the decision to enter into a collaborative relationship with a supplier – as opposed to engaging in a transaction-focused pure purchase situation for required products – entails a variety of organizational consequences with cost-benefit implications that stem from the various options affordable by the alliance. For instance, a CR can offer the possibility to alter product specifications mid-stream, depending on the volatility of market demands or competitive actions. To a degree this is also possible in virtual organizational set-ups if quantities for processing are contractually kept very low and continuously redefined. Unplanned purchase volume changes, including temporary suspension of purchases, can be made throughout the term of the buying relationship. Creating an alliance can be time-consuming, with resources being required to set up a workable trading infrastructure. There has to be an infrastructure and a willingness to share operational information, including accounting information, between the trading entities.

Learning affects the economic viability of engaging in a supplier alliance. Cost reductions can flow from a subcomponent supplier to the partner firm as part of a CR. It may be possible for the firm to earn superior returns through learning-rate differentials between CR which may not accrue via virtually structured firms. Whilst accounting systems may pick up on learning-related cost effects, the implications and consequences of having both collaborative and virtual relationships are complex; however, they will be assessed by firms seeking the most cost- and managerially-effective structuring of operations.

Information consumption and analysis changes

Cross-national comparisons of management styles and organizational practices are indicative of differences which suggest country-based specificities. But, just as some characteristics seem to be more prevalent among organizations in particular countries, so there is evidence that clusters with cultural commonalities exist which overarch country-specific characteristics (Bhimani and Bromwich, 2009b). Cultures which make high use of information communication technologies tend to exhibit polychronic work styles – whereby multiple activities are performed in parallel – as opposed to monochronic patterns of information use. There is increasing evidence that the availability of constant access to computers, networks and technologies is associated with greater polychronic behaviour. Often senior managers operating in high-tech contexts and overseeing the activities of more junior tech-savvy managers resist the extensive polychronic preferences of those they lead. Internationally, the outsourcing of work to places like Eastern Europe, the Far East, and locations in between has produced more individuals in these nations who have become habituated to the use of mobile technologies and web-based information exchange platforms. As a consequence polychronicity is fast growing as a preferred work style in these places. Cost management professionals will need to react to the information needs and preferred modes of usage to match preferred styles that are emerging, including continuously streamed information from different sources that can be fed across a multitude of information windows simultaneously.

Aside from preferring increased diversity in information communication platforms, managers operating in a highly digitized environment tend to be more receptive to collaborative working approaches rather than command-and-control work styles. Trust and visibility are given a high degree of significance, aside from a predilection for multi-platform interaction and interfacing. Consequently managers are increasingly revealing a need for constant real-time feedback about their activities. Performance evaluation systems, including accounting and financial metrics-based indicators, are emerging to reflect this (Bhimani and Bromwich, 2009a). Information systems that produce output which is qualitative, quantitative, graphical, interactive, text-based, and which shows varying degrees of structure, will increasingly be invested in. The impact on both the work content and work style of finance specialists is likely to be extensive.

Conclusion

The finance function is today confronted with novel ways of capturing, communicating and integrating sources of information. It is responding to altered platforms, sources and architectures of information output, channels, structures and modes of assessment. The sources of change are as multifaceted as the effects. Macro-level institutional changes are influencing the manner in which enterprises access finance, make use of it, report on it and monitor it. As the risks of their economic activity grow, so their information systems change. Individual information users are themselves also changing the types of information they assess and access, and are adopting novel ways of using and acting on this information.

The body of cost management expertise which, over the past two decades, has undergone significant change, is again on the brink of immense shifts in content, structure, delivery approach and mode of usage. Cost management is becoming today what was only yesterday a distant murmur of things to come.

Bibliography

Anderson, S. and Sedatole, K. 2003. Management Accounting for the Extended Enterprise. In A. Bhimani (ed.), *Management Accounting in the Digital Economy*, Oxford University Press, Oxford.

Bhimani, A. and Bromwich, M. 2009a. Management Accounting in a Digital and Global Economy. In C. Chapman, D. Cooper and P. Miller (eds.) *Accounting, Organizations and Institutions: Essays in Honour of Anthony Hopwood,* Oxford University Press, Oxford, 85–111.

Bhimani, A. and Bromwich, M. 2009b. *Management Accounting: Retrospect and Prospect*, Elsevier/CIMA, London.

Bromwich, M. and Bhimani, A. 1989. *Management Accounting: Evolution Not Revolution*, CIMA, London.

Bromwich, M. and Bhimani, A. 1994. *Management Accounting: Pathways to Progress*, CIMA, London.

Callioni, G., Montgros, X., Slagmulder, R., Wassenhowe, L. and Wright, L. 2005. Inventory-driven costs. *Harvard Business Review,* March, 271–282.

Child, J. 2005. *Cooperative Strategy*, Oxford University Press, Oxford.

Das, T.K and Teng, B. 2000. Instabilities of strategic alliances: an internal tensions perspective. *Organization Science,* 11(1), 77–101.

Dekker, H.C. 2004. Control of inter-organizational relationships: evidence on appropriate concerns and coordination requirements. *Accounting, Organizations and Society*, 29(1), 27–49.

Dunk, A. 2004. Product cost life-cycle analysis: the impact of customer profiling, competitive advantage and quality of IS information. *Management Accounting Research,* 15(4), 379–410.

Dyer, J.H. 1997. Effective interfirm collaboration: how firms minimize transaction costs and maximize transaction value. *Strategic Management Journal*, 18(7), 535–556.

Dyer, J.H. and Singh, J.H. 1998. The relational view: cooperative stategy and sources of inter-organizational competitive advantage. *The Academy of Management Review,* 23(4), 660–679.

Gadde, L. and Snehota, I. 2000. Making the most of supplier relationships. *Industrial Marketing Management,* 29, 305–316.

Groot, T.L.C.M. and Merchant, K.A. 2000. Control of international joint ventures. *Accounting, Organizations and Society*, 25(6), 579–607.

Hakansson, H. and Lind, J. 2007. Accounting in an Interorganizational Setting. In C. Chapman, A. Hopwood and M. Shileds (eds), *Handbook of Management Accounting Research*, Elsevier, 885–902.

Handfield, R.B., Krause, D.R., Scannel, T.V. and Monczka, R.M. 2000. Avoid the pitfalls in supplier development. *Sloan Management Review*, 42(2), 37–49.

Helper, S.R. and Sako, M. 1995. Supplier relations in Japan and the United States: are they converging? *Sloan Management Review*, Spring, 77–84.

Kamminga, P.E. and Van der Meer-Kooistra, J. 2007. Management control patterns in joint venture relationships: a model and an exploratory study. *Accounting, Organzations and Society,* 32, 131–154.

Krapfel, R.E. Jr., Salmond, D. and Spekman, R. 1991. A strategic approach to managing buyer–seller relationships. *European Journal of Marketing*, 25(9), 22–37.

Kraus, K and Lind, J. 2007. Management Control in Interorganizational Relationships. In T. Hopper, D. Northcott and R. Scapens (eds), *Issues in Management Accounting.* London: FT Prentice Hall, 269–296.

Kulmala, H. I. 2004. Developing cost management in customer supplier relationships: three case studies. *Journal of Purchasing and Supply Management*, 10, 65–77.

Lambert, D.M. and Cooper, M.C. 2000. Issues in supply chain management. *Industrial Marketing Management*, 29(1), 65–83.

Leiblein, M.J. and Miller, D.J. 2003. An empirical examination of transation and firm level influences on the vertical boundaries of the firm. *Strategic Management Journal*, 24, 839.

Liker, J.K. and Choi, T.Y. 2004. Building deep supplier relationships. *Harvard Business Review* (Dec.), 29–38.

Meer-Kooistra, J. van der. 1994. The coordination of internal transactions: the functioning of transfer pricing systems in the organizational context. *Management Accounting Research*, 5, 123–152.

Narayanan, V.G. and Raman, A. 2004. Aligning incentives in supply chains. *Harvard Business Review*, 82(11), 94–103.

Quinn, J.B. and Hilmer, F.G. 1994. Strategic outsourcing. *Sloan Management Review*, (Summer), 43–55.

Sako, M. 2008. *Shifting Boundaries of the Firm*. Oxford, UK: Oxford University Press.

Sheth, J.N. and Sharma A. 1997. Supplier relationships – emerging issues and challenges. *Industrial Marketing and Management*, 26(2), 91–100.

Speklé, R.F. 2001. Explaining management control structure variety: a transaction cost economics perspective. *Accounting, Organizations and Society* 3(4), 141–167.

Tomkins, C. 2001. Interdependencies, trust and information in relationships, alliances and networks. *Accounting, Organizations and Society*, 26, 161–191.

Van Weele, A.J. 2000. *Purchasing and Supply Management: Analysis, Planning and Practice*. Business Press, London.

Vining, A. and Globerman, S. 1999. A conceptual framework for understanding the outsourcing decision. *European Management Journal*, 17, 645–654.

Index

Page numbers in **bold** indicate figures and tables